The New Testament

+

Psalms & Proverbs

of the

World English Bible

The New Testament

+

Psalms & Proverbs

of the

World English Bible

http://WorldEnglishBible.org

Rainbow Missions, Inc., PO Box 275, Mesa CO 81643-0275, USA

editors@eBible.org

22 August 2003
24 Av 5763

ISBN 0-9703344-2-7 (paperback)
ISBN 0-9703344-5-1 (hardback)
Library of Congress Control Number: 2003093737

New Testament

+

Psalms & Proverbs

of the

World English Bible

PRESENTED TO

_____

ON

_____

BY

_____

Notes

Table of Contents

Notes

Preface to the World English Bible

What is the Holy Bible?

The Holy Bible is a collection of 66 books and letters written by many people who were inspired by the Holy Spirit of God. These books tell us how we can be saved from the evil of this world and gain eternal life that is truly worth living. Although the Holy Bible contains rules of conduct, it is not just a rule book. It reveals God's heart– a Father's heart, full of love and compassion. The Holy Bible tells you what you need to know and believe to be saved from sin and evil and how to live a life that is truly worth living, no matter what your current circumstances may be.

The Holy Bible consists of two main sections: the Old Testament (including Psalms and Proverbs) and the New Testament (Matthew through Revelation). The Old Testament records God's interaction with mankind before He sent His son to redeem us, while recording prophesy predicting that coming. The New Testament tells us of God's Son and Annointed One, Jesus, and the wonderful salvation that He purchased for us.

The same Holy Spirit who inspired the Holy Bible is living among us today, and He is happy to help you understand what He intended as you study His Word. Just ask Him, and He is more than happy to help you apply His message to your life.

The Old Testament was originally written mostly in Hebrew. The New Testament was originally written mostly in the common street Greek (not the formal Greek used for official legal matters). The Holy Bible is being translated into every living language in the World, so that everyone may have an opportunity to hear the Good News about Jesus Christ.

Why was the World English Bible translated?

There are already many good translations of the Holy Bible into contemporary English. Unfortunately, almost all of them are restricted by copyright and copyright holder policy. This restricts publication of God's Word in many ways, such as in downloadable files on the Internet. The World English Bible was commissioned by God in response to prayer about this subject.

Because the World English Bible is in the Public Domain (not copyrighted), it can be freely copied, distributed, and redistributed without any payment of royalties. You don't even have to ask permission to do so. You may publish the whole World English Bible in book form, bind it in leather and sell it. You may incorporate it into your Bible study software. You may make and distribute audio recordings of it. You may broadcast it. All you have to do is maintain the integrity of God's Word before God, and reserve the name "World English Bible" for faithful (unmodified except for British/American spelling issues) copies of this translation.

How was the World English Bible translated?

The World English Bible is an update of the American Standard Version (ASV) of the Holy Bible, published in 1901. A custom computer program updated the archaic words and word forms to contemporary equivalents, and then a team of volunteers proofread and updated the grammar. The New Testament was updated to conform to the Majority Text reconstruction of the original Greek manuscripts, thus taking advantage of the superior access to manuscripts that we have now compared to when the original ASV was translated.

What is different about the World English Bible?

The style of the World English Bible, while fairly literally translated, is in informal, spoken English. The World English Bible is designed to sound good and be accurate when read aloud. It is not formal in its language, just as the original Greek of the New Testament was not formal. The WEB uses contractions rather freely.

The World English Bible doesn't capitalize pronouns pertaining to God. The original manuscripts made no such distinction. Hebrew has no such thing as upper and lower case, and the original Greek manuscripts were written in all upper case letters. Attempting to add in such a distinction raises some difficulties in translating dual-meaning Scriptures such as the coronation psalms.

The World English Bible uses "Yahweh" for God's proper name in the Old Testament. This is our best reconstruction of how this most holy name was originally pronounced.

Although different publishers are free to alter the typography, this particular edition is typeset in such a way as to de-emphasize the chapter and verse markers, and encourage reading the Bible as the poetry and prose it was written in. The chapter and verse markers are still there, of course, to allow you to find references in your Bible study.

Because World English Bible (WEB) uses the Majority Text as the basis for the New Testament, you may notice the following differences in comparing the WEB to other translations:

- The order of Matthew 23:13 and 14 is reversed in some translations.

- Luke 17:36 and Acts 15:34, which are not found in the majority of the Greek Manuscripts (and are relegated to footnotes in the WEB) may be included in some other translations.

- Romans 14:24-26 in the WEB may appear as Romans 16:25-27 in other translations.

- 1 John 5:7-8 contains an addition ("in heaven: the Father, the Word, and the Holy Spirit; and these three are one. And there are three that testify on earth") in some translations, including the KJV. Erasmus admitted adding this text to his published Greek New Testament, even though he could at first find no Greek manuscript support for it, because he was being pressured by men to do so, and because he didn't see any doctrinal harm in it. Lots of things not written by John in this letter are true, but we decline to add them to what the Holy Spirit inspired through John.

With all of the above and some other places where lack of clarity in the original manuscripts has led to multiple possible readings, significant variants are listed in footnotes. The reading that in our prayerful judgement is best is in the main text. Overall, the World English Bible isn't very much different than several other good contemporary English translations of the Holy Bible. The message of Salvation through Jesus Christ is still the same. The point of this translation was not to be very different (except for legal status), but to update the ASV for readability while retaining or improving the accuracy of that well-respected translation and retaining the public domain status of the ASV.

Capitalization

Some translations capitalize pronouns pertaining to God. Some do not. Hebrew has no such thing as upper and lower case, and the original Greek manuscripts were written all in one case, anyway. This is purely a matter of English style. The KJV capitalized these pronouns because English usage at the time demanded capitalization of pronouns referring to a king, and God is certainly the greatest King. In modern English, we don't capitalize pronouns pertaining to kings and presidents. The ASV, upon which this translation was originally based, didn't capitalize these pronouns, so changing that would have potentially introduced errors. One particularly difficult place to decide on capitalization is in the coronation psalms, which were written originally for an earthly king, but later sung in praise to the King of Kings. Although there are good arguments both ways, we left the capitalization as the ASV did it.

Footnotes

In this edition, the only footnotes are the translators' footnotes, which offer clarification of shades of meanings of words and give equivalent weights, measures, and monetary values. Sometimes alternate readings are given where there is more than one way to legitimately translate a passage or where significant groups of manuscripts differ. In particular, the abbreviation "NU" is used to denote alternate readings from the critical text due primarily to the work of Nestle and Aland and published by the United Bible Societies. "TR" is used to denote alternate readings from the *Textus Receptus*, which is the basis of the *King James Version New Testament*. This translation is based on the Greek Majority Text as the most authoritative reading of the New Testament we could find. Significant alternate readings from the other two widely respected critical texts are given in the footnotes.

More Information

For answers to frequently asked questions about the World English Bible, please visit http://eBible.org/web/webfaq.htm on the Internet.

A Note to Publishers

Like the King James Version, this translation of the Holy Bible is in the Public Domain. You are free to publish editions of the World English Bible without even having to ask anyone for permission. You may do so for free or for profit. You may download the text of the World English Bible in various formats from http://eBible.org/web/ and typeset them to taste. Like the KJV, you may publish a study Bible with your own additional helps, and copyright those helps. The translators' footnotes, preface, and glossary that come with the World English Bible are also in the Public Domain, and may be published by anyone. Although U. S. law allows creation of derivative works from a Public Domain document (but see Revelation 22:18-19), we ask that you not use the name "World English Bible" to describe any revision or change to the text. This is to avoid confusion, and not to restrict your freedom to Publish God's Word in whatever way He leads you to. "World English Bible" is a trademark of Rainbow Missions, Inc., and you have permission to use it to describe the text of the World English Bible as published by Rainbow Missions, Inc.

Please check http://eBible.org/web/ for the completion status of the Old Testament before committing it to print. As of this date (22 August 2003), the World English Bible Old Testament is still being actively edited for clarity and accuracy, although the drafts are posted on the Internet. In addition, any well-justified edits are still being made to the New Testament, Psalms, and Proverbs.

If you have any questions about the World English Bible and publication issues, please see http://eBible.org/web/webfaq.htm, and if your questions are not answered there, please email your questions to editors@ebible.org.

Acknowledgements

First and foremost, we thank God Almighty, who through the Holy Spirit inspired the Holy Bible and has caused it to be preserved and published widely through his people. In addition, we acknowledge the original writers of the books of the Bible, the scribes, and the translators who diligently labored over the centuries to bring the Holy Bible to you in a language you understand. We also thank all of the many people who contributed to this volunteer translation effort. May God bless you and reward you greatly for your faithfulness and obedience to Him.

Notes

The Good News According to Matthew

[1:1] The book of the genealogy of Jesus Christ[a], the son of David, the son of Abraham. [1:2] Abraham became the father of Isaac. Isaac became the father of Jacob. Jacob became the father of Judah and his brothers. [1:3] Judah became the father of Perez and Zerah by Tamar. Perez became the father of Hezron. Hezron became the father of Ram. [1:4] Ram became the father of Amminadab. Amminadab became the father of Nahshon. Nahshon became the father of Salmon. [1:5] Salmon became the father of Boaz by Rahab. Boaz became the father of Obed by Ruth. Obed became the father of Jesse. [1:6] Jesse became the father of David the king. David became the father of Solomon by her who had been the wife of Uriah. [1:7] Solomon became the father of Rehoboam. Rehoboam became the father of Abijah. Abijah became the father of Asa. [1:8] Asa became the father of Jehoshaphat. Jehoshaphat became the father of Joram. Joram became the father of Uzziah. [1:9] Uzziah became the father of Jotham. Jotham became the father of Ahaz. Ahaz became the father of Hezekiah. [1:10] Hezekiah became the father of Manasseh. Manasseh became the father of Amon. Amon became the father of Josiah. [1:11] Josiah became the father of Jechoniah and his brothers, at the time of the exile to Babylon. [1:12] After the exile to Babylon, Jechoniah became the father of Shealtiel. Shealtiel became the father of Zerubbabel. [1:13] Zerubbabel became the father of Abiud. Abiud became the father of Eliakim. Eliakim became the father of Azor. [1:14] Azor became the father of Sadoc. Sadoc became the father of Achim. Achim became the father of Eliud. [1:15] Eliud became the father of Eleazar. Eleazar became the father of Matthan. Matthan became the father of Jacob. [1:16] Jacob became the father of Joseph, the husband of Mary, from whom was born Jesus[b], who is called Christ. [1:17] So all the generations from Abraham to David are fourteen generations; from David to the exile to Babylon fourteen generations; and from the carrying away to Babylon to the Christ, fourteen generations.

[1:18] Now the birth of Jesus Christ was like this; for after his mother, Mary, was engaged to Joseph, before they came together, she was found pregnant by the Holy Spirit. [1:19] Joseph, her husband, being a righteous man, and not willing to make her a public example, intended to put her away secretly. [1:20] But when he thought about these things, behold, an angel of the Lord appeared to him in a dream, saying, "Joseph, son of David, don't be afraid to take to yourself Mary, your wife, for that which is conceived in her is of the Holy Spirit. [1:21] She shall bring forth a son. You shall call his name Jesus, for it is he who shall save his people from their sins."

[1:22] Now all this has happened, that it might be fulfilled which was spoken by the Lord through the prophet, saying,

[1:23] "Behold, the virgin shall be with child,

and shall bring forth a son.

They shall call his name Immanuel;"

which is, being interpreted, "God with us."[c]

[1:24] Joseph arose from his sleep, and did as the angel of the Lord commanded him, and took his wife to himself; [1:25] and didn't know her sexually until she had brought forth her firstborn son. He named him Jesus.

[2:1] Now when Jesus was born in Bethlehem of Judea in the days of Herod the king, behold, wise men[d] from the east came to Jerusalem, saying, [2:2] "Where is he who is born King of the Jews? For we saw his star in the east, and have come to worship him." [2:3] When Herod the king heard it, he was troubled, and all Jerusalem with him. [2:4] Gathering together all the chief priests and scribes of the people, he asked them

---

[a] 1:1 Messiah (Hebrew) and Christ (Greek) both mean "Anointed One"

[b] 1:16 "Jesus" means "Salvation."

[c] 1:23 Isaiah 7:14

[d] 2:1 The word for "wise men" (magoi) can also mean teachers, scientists, physicians, astrologers, seers, interpreters of dreams, or sorcerers.

where the Christ would be born. ^{2:5}They said to him, "In Bethlehem of Judea, for thus it is written through the prophet,

^{2:6}'You Bethlehem, land of Judah,
 are in no way least among the princes of Judah:
for out of you shall come forth a governor,
 who shall shepherd my people, Israel.'"^e

^{2:7}Then Herod secretly called the wise men, and learned from them exactly what time the star appeared. ^{2:8}He sent them to Bethlehem, and said, "Go and search diligently for the young child. When you have found him, bring me word, so that I also may come and worship him."

^{2:9}They, having heard the king, went their way; and behold, the star, which they saw in the east, went before them, until it came and stood over where the young child was. ^{2:10}When they saw the star, they rejoiced with exceedingly great joy. ^{2:11}They came into the house and saw the young child with Mary, his mother, and they fell down and worshiped him. Opening their treasures, they offered to him gifts: gold, frankincense, and myrrh. ^{2:12}Being warned in a dream that they shouldn't return to Herod, they went back to their own country another way.

^{2:13}Now when they had departed, behold, an angel of the Lord appeared to Joseph in a dream, saying, "Arise and take the young child and his mother, and flee into Egypt, and stay there until I tell you, for Herod will seek the young child to destroy him."

^{2:14}He arose and took the young child and his mother by night, and departed into Egypt, ^{2:15}and was there until the death of Herod; that it might be fulfilled which was spoken by the Lord through the prophet, saying, "Out of Egypt I called my son."^f

^{2:16}Then Herod, when he saw that he was mocked by the wise men, was exceedingly angry, and sent out, and killed all the male children who were in Bethlehem and in all the surrounding countryside, from two years old and under, according to the exact time which he had learned from the wise men. ^{2:17}Then that which was spoken by Jeremiah the prophet was fulfilled, saying,

^{2:18}"A voice was heard in Ramah,
 lamentation, weeping and great mourning,
Rachel weeping for her children;
 she wouldn't be comforted,
 because they are no more."^g

^{2:19}But when Herod was dead, behold, an angel of the Lord appeared in a dream to Joseph in Egypt, saying, ^{2:20}"Arise and take the young child and his mother, and go into the land of Israel, for those who sought the young child's life are dead."

^{2:21}He arose and took the young child and his mother, and came into the land of Israel. ^{2:22}But when he heard that Archelaus was reigning over Judea in the place of his father, Herod, he was afraid to go there. Being warned in a dream, he withdrew into the region of Galilee, ^{2:23}and came and lived in a city called Nazareth; that it might be fulfilled which was spoken through the prophets: "He will be called a Nazarene."

^{3:1}In those days, John the Baptizer came, preaching in the wilderness of Judea, saying, ^{3:2}"Repent, for the Kingdom of Heaven is at hand!" ^{3:3}For this is he who was spoken of by Isaiah the prophet, saying,

"The voice of one crying in the wilderness,
 make ready the way of the Lord.
 Make his paths straight."^h

^{3:4}Now John himself wore clothing made of camel's hair, with a leather belt around his waist. His food was locusts and wild honey. ^{3:5}Then people from Jerusalem, all of Judea, and all the region around the Jordan went out to him. ^{3:6}They were baptizedⁱ by him in the Jordan, confessing their sins. ^{3:7}But when he saw many of the Pharisees and Sadducees coming for his

---

^e2:6 Micah 5:2
^f2:15 Hosea 11:1
^g2:18 Jeremiah 31:15
^h3:3 Isaiah 40:3
ⁱ3:6 or, immersed

baptism,[j] he said to them, "You offspring of vipers, who warned you to flee from the wrath to come? [3:8]Therefore bring forth fruit worthy of repentance! [3:9]Don't think to yourselves, 'We have Abraham for our father,' for I tell you that God is able to raise up children to Abraham from these stones. [3:10]"Even now the axe lies at the root of the trees. Therefore, every tree that doesn't bring forth good fruit is cut down, and cast into the fire. [3:11]I indeed baptize[k] you in water for repentance, but he who comes after me is mightier than I, whose shoes I am not worthy to carry. He will baptize you in the Holy Spirit.[l] [3:12]His winnowing fork is in his hand, and he will thoroughly cleanse his threshing floor. He will gather his wheat into the barn, but the chaff he will burn up with unquenchable fire."

[3:13]Then Jesus came from Galilee to the Jordan to John, to be baptized by him. [3:14]But John would have hindered him, saying, "I need to be baptized by you, and you come to me?" [3:15]But Jesus, answering, said to him, **"Allow it now, for this is the fitting way for us to fulfill all righteousness."** Then he allowed him. [3:16]Jesus, when he was baptized, went up directly from the water: and behold, the heavens were opened to him. He saw the Spirit of God descending as a dove, and coming on him. [3:17]Behold, a voice out of the heavens said, "This is my beloved Son, with whom I am well pleased."

[4:1]Then Jesus was led up by the Spirit into the wilderness to be tempted by the devil. [4:2]When he had fasted forty days and forty nights, he was hungry afterward. [4:3]The tempter came and said to him, "If you are the Son of God, command that these stones become bread." [4:4]But he answered, **"It is written, 'Man shall not live by bread alone, but by every word that proceeds out of the mouth of God.'"**[m]

[4:5]Then the devil took him into the holy city. He set him on the pinnacle of the temple, [4:6]and said to him, "If you are the Son of God, throw yourself down, for it is written, 'He will put his angels in charge of you.' and,

'On their hands they will bear you up,

so that you don't dash your foot against a stone.'"[n]

[4:7]Jesus said to him, **"Again, it is written, 'You shall not test the Lord, your God.'"**[o]

[4:8]Again, the devil took him to an exceedingly high mountain, and showed him all the kingdoms of the world, and their glory. [4:9]He said to him, "I will give you all of these things, if you will fall down and worship me."

[4:10]Then Jesus said to him, **"Get behind me,[p] Satan! For it is written, 'You shall worship the Lord your God, and you shall serve him only.'"**[q]

[4:11]Then the devil left him, and behold, angels came and served him. [4:12]Now when Jesus heard that John was delivered up, he withdrew into Galilee. [4:13]Leaving Nazareth, he came and lived in Capernaum, which is by the sea, in the region of Zebulun and Naphtali, [4:14]that it might be fulfilled which was spoken through Isaiah the prophet, saying,

[4:15]"The land of Zebulun and the land of Naphtali,

toward the sea, beyond the Jordan,

Galilee of the Gentiles,

[4:16]the people who sat in darkness saw a great light,

to those who sat in the region and shadow of death,

to them light has dawned."[r]

---

[j]3:7 or, immersion
[k]3:11 or, immerse
[l]3:11 TR and NU add "and with fire"
[m]4:4 Deuteronomy 8:3
[n]4:6 Psalm 91:11-12
[o]4:7 Deuteronomy 6:16
[p]4:10 TR and NU read "Go away" instead of "Get behind me"
[q]4:10 Deuteronomy 6:13
[r]4:16 Isaiah 9:1-2

^{4:17}From that time, Jesus began to preach, and to say, **"Repent! For the Kingdom of Heaven is at hand."**

^{4:18}Walking by the sea of Galilee, he^s saw two brothers: Simon, who is called Peter, and Andrew, his brother, casting a net into the sea; for they were fishermen. ^{4:19}He said to them, **"Come after me, and I will make you fishers for men."**

^{4:20}They immediately left their nets and followed him. ^{4:21}Going on from there, he saw two other brothers, James the son of Zebedee, and John his brother, in the boat with Zebedee their father, mending their nets. He called them. ^{4:22}They immediately left the boat and their father, and followed him.

^{4:23}Jesus went about in all Galilee, teaching in their synagogues, preaching the Good News of the Kingdom, and healing every disease and every sickness among the people. ^{4:24}The report about him went out into all Syria. They brought to him all who were sick, afflicted with various diseases and torments, possessed with demons, epileptics, and paralytics; and he healed them. ^{4:25}Great multitudes from Galilee, Decapolis, Jerusalem, Judea and from beyond the Jordan followed him.

^{5:1}Seeing the multitudes, he went up onto the mountain. When he had sat down, his disciples came to him. ^{5:2}He opened his mouth and taught them, saying,

^{5:3}**"Blessed are the poor in spirit,**
  for theirs is the Kingdom of Heaven.^t
^{5:4}**Blessed are those who mourn,**
  for they shall be comforted.^u
^{5:5}**Blessed are the gentle,**
  for they shall inherit the earth.^v
^{5:6}**Blessed are those who hunger and thirst**
    after righteousness,
  for they shall be filled.
^{5:7}**Blessed are the merciful,**
  for they shall obtain mercy.
^{5:8}**Blessed are the pure in heart,**
  for they shall see God.

^{5:9}**Blessed are the peacemakers,**
  for they shall be called children of God.

^{5:10}**Blessed are those who have been persecuted for righteousness' sake,**
  for theirs is the Kingdom of Heaven.

^{5:11}**"Blessed are you when people reproach you, persecute you, and say all kinds of evil against you falsely, for my sake. ^{5:12}Rejoice, and be exceedingly glad, for great is your reward in heaven. For that is how they persecuted the prophets who were before you.**

^{5:13}**"You are the salt of the earth, but if the salt has lost its flavor, with what will it be salted? It is then good for nothing, but to be cast out and trodden under the feet of men. ^{5:14}You are the light of the world. A city located on a hill can't be hidden. ^{5:15}Neither do you light a lamp, and put it under a measuring basket, but on a stand; and it shines to all who are in the house. ^{5:16}Even so, let your light shine before men; that they may see your good works, and glorify your Father who is in heaven.**

^{5:17}**"Don't think that I came to destroy the law or the prophets. I didn't come to destroy, but to fulfill. ^{5:18}For most certainly, I tell you, until heaven and earth pass away, not even one smallest letter^w or one tiny pen stroke^x shall in any way pass away from the law, until all things are accomplished. ^{5:19}Whoever, therefore, shall break one of these least commandments, and teach others to do so, shall be called least in the Kingdom of Heaven; but whoever shall do and teach them shall be called great in the Kingdom of Heaven. ^{5:20}For I tell you that unless your righteousness exceeds that of the scribes and Pharisees, there is no way you will enter into the Kingdom of Heaven.**

^s4:18 TR reads "Jesus" instead of "he"
^t5:3 Isaiah 57:15; 66:2
^u5:4 Isaiah 61:2; 66:10,13
^v5:5 or, land. Psalm 37:11
^w5:18 literally, iota
^x5:18 or, serif

[5:21]"You have heard that it was said to the ancient ones, 'You shall not murder;'[y] and 'Whoever shall murder shall be in danger of the judgment.' [5:22]But I tell you, that everyone who is angry with his brother without a cause[z] shall be in danger of the judgment; and whoever shall say to his brother, 'Raca[a]!' shall be in danger of the council; and whoever shall say, 'You fool!' shall be in danger of the fire of Gehenna.[b]

[5:23]"If therefore you are offering your gift at the altar, and there remember that your brother has anything against you, [5:24]leave your gift there before the altar, and go your way. First be reconciled to your brother, and then come and offer your gift. [5:25]Agree with your adversary quickly, while you are with him in the way; lest perhaps the prosecutor deliver you to the judge, and the judge deliver you to the officer, and you be cast into prison. [5:26]Most certainly I tell you, you shall by no means get out of there, until you have paid the last penny.[c]

[5:27]"You have heard that it was said, [d] 'You shall not commit adultery;'[e] [5:28]but I tell you that everyone who gazes at a woman to lust after her has committed adultery with her already in his heart. [5:29]If your right eye causes you to stumble, pluck it out and throw it away from you. For it is more profitable for you that one of your members should perish, than for your whole body to be cast into Gehenna.[f] [5:30]If your right hand causes you to stumble, cut it off, and throw it away from you. For it is more profitable for you that one of your members should perish, than for your whole body to be cast into Gehenna.[g]

[5:31]"It was also said, 'Whoever shall put away his wife, let him give her a writing of divorce,'[h] [5:32]but I tell you that whoever puts away his wife, except for the cause of sexual immorality, makes her an adulteress; and whoever marries her when she is put away commits adultery.

[5:33]"Again you have heard that it was said to them of old time, 'You shall not make false vows, but shall perform to the Lord your vows,' [5:34]but I tell you, don't swear at all: neither by heaven, for it is the throne of God; [5:35]nor by the earth, for it is the footstool of his feet; nor by Jerusalem, for it is the city of the great King. [5:36]Neither shall you swear by your head, for you can't make one hair white or black. [5:37]But let your 'Yes' be 'Yes' and your 'No' be 'No.' Whatever is more than these is of the evil one.

[5:38]"You have heard that it was said, 'An eye for an eye, and a tooth for a tooth.'[i] [5:39]But I tell you, don't resist him who is evil; but whoever strikes you on your right cheek, turn to him the other also. [5:40]If anyone sues you to take away your coat, let him have your cloak also. [5:41]Whoever compels you to go one mile, go with him two. [5:42]Give to him who asks you, and don't turn away him who desires to borrow from you.

[5:43]"You have heard that it was said, 'You shall love your neighbor,[j] and hate your enemy.[k] [5:44]But I tell you, love your enemies, bless those who curse you, do good to those who hate you, and pray

---

[y]5:21 Exodus 20:13

[z]5:22 NU omits "without a cause".

[a]5:22 "Raca" is an Aramaic insult, related to the word for "empty" and conveying the idea of empty-headedness.

[b]5:22 or, Hell

[c]5:26 literally, kodrantes. A kodrantes was a small copper coin worth about 2 lepta (widow's mites)—not enough to buy very much of anything.

[d]5:27 TR adds "to the ancients,"

[e]5:27 Exodus 20:14

[f]5:29 or, Hell

[g]5:30 or, Hell

[h]5:31 Deuteronomy 24:1

[i]5:38 Exodus 21:24; Leviticus 24:20; Deuteronomy 19:21

[j]5:43 Leviticus 19:18

[k]5:43 not in the Bible, but see Qumran Manual of Discipline Ix, 21-26

for those who mistreat you and persecute you, [5:45]that you may be children of your Father who is in heaven. For he makes his sun to rise on the evil and the good, and sends rain on the just and the unjust. [5:46]For if you love those who love you, what reward do you have? Don't even the tax collectors do the same? [5:47]If you only greet your friends, what more do you do than others? Don't even the tax collectors do the same? [5:48]Therefore you shall be perfect, just as your Father in heaven is perfect.

[6:1]"Be careful that you don't do your charitable giving before men, to be seen by them, or else you have no reward from your Father who is in heaven. [6:2]Therefore when you do merciful deeds, don't sound a trumpet before yourself, as the hypocrites do in the synagogues and in the streets, that they may get glory from men. Most certainly I tell you, they have received their reward. [6:3]But when you do merciful deeds, don't let your left hand know what your right hand does, [6:4]so that your merciful deeds may be in secret, then your Father who sees in secret will reward you openly.

[6:5]"When you pray, you shall not be as the hypocrites, for they love to stand and pray in the synagogues and in the corners of the streets, that they may be seen by men. Most certainly, I tell you, they have received their reward. [6:6]But you, when you pray, enter into your inner chamber, and having shut your door, pray to your Father who is in secret, and your Father who sees in secret will reward you openly. [6:7]In praying, don't use vain repetitions, as the Gentiles do; for they think that they will be heard for their much speaking. [6:8]Therefore don't be like them, for your Father knows what things you need, before you ask him. [6:9]Pray like this: 'Our Father in heaven, may your name be kept holy. [6:10]Let your Kingdom come. Let your will be done, as in heaven, so on earth. [6:11]Give us today our daily bread. [6:12]Forgive us our debts, as we also forgive our debtors. [6:13]Bring us not into temptation, but deliver us from the evil

one. For yours is the Kingdom, the power, and the glory forever. Amen.[l]'

[6:14]"For if you forgive men their trespasses, your heavenly Father will also forgive you. [6:15]But if you don't forgive men their trespasses, neither will your Father forgive your trespasses.

[6:16]"Moreover when you fast, don't be like the hypocrites, with sad faces. For they disfigure their faces, that they may be seen by men to be fasting. Most certainly I tell you, they have received their reward. [6:17]But you, when you fast, anoint your head, and wash your face; [6:18]so that you are not seen by men to be fasting, but by your Father who is in secret, and your Father, who sees in secret, will reward you.

[6:19]"Don't lay up treasures for yourselves on the earth, where moth and rust consume, and where thieves break through and steal; [6:20]but lay up for yourselves treasures in heaven, where neither moth nor rust consume, and where thieves don't break through and steal; [6:21]for where your treasure is, there your heart will be also.

[6:22]"The lamp of the body is the eye. If therefore your eye is sound, your whole body will be full of light. [6:23]But if your eye is evil, your whole body will be full of darkness. If therefore the light that is in you is darkness, how great is the darkness!

[6:24]"No one can serve two masters, for either he will hate the one and love the other; or else he will be devoted to one and despise the other. You can't serve both God and Mammon. [6:25]Therefore, I tell you, don't be anxious for your life: what you will eat, or what you will drink; nor yet for your body, what you will wear. Isn't life more than food, and the body more than clothing? [6:26]See the birds of the sky, that they don't sow, neither do they reap, nor gather into barns. Your heavenly Father feeds them. Aren't you of much more value than they?

[6:27]"Which of you, by being anxious,

---

[l]6:13 NU omits "For yours is the Kingdom, the power, and the glory forever. Amen."

can add one moment[m] to his lifespan? [6:28]Why are you anxious about clothing? Consider the lilies of the field, how they grow. They don't toil, neither do they spin, [6:29]yet I tell you that even Solomon in all his glory was not dressed like one of these. [6:30]But if God so clothes the grass of the field, which today exists, and tomorrow is thrown into the oven, won't he much more clothe you, you of little faith?

[6:31]"Therefore don't be anxious, saying, 'What will we eat?', 'What will we drink?' or, 'With what will we be clothed?' [6:32]For the Gentiles seek after all these things, for your heavenly Father knows that you need all these things. [6:33]But seek first God's Kingdom, and his righteousness; and all these things will be given to you as well. [6:34]Therefore don't be anxious for tomorrow, for tomorrow will be anxious for itself. Each day's own evil is sufficient.

[7:1]"Don't judge, so that you won't be judged. [7:2]For with whatever judgment you judge, you will be judged; and with whatever measure you measure, it will be measured to you. [7:3]Why do you see the speck that is in your brother's eye, but don't consider the beam that is in your own eye? [7:4]Or how will you tell your brother, 'Let me remove the speck from your eye;' and behold, the beam is in your own eye? [7:5]You hypocrite! First remove the beam out of your own eye, and then you can see clearly to remove the speck out of your brother's eye.

[7:6]"Don't give that which is holy to the dogs, neither throw your pearls before the pigs, lest perhaps they trample them under their feet, and turn and tear you to pieces.

[7:7]"Ask, and it will be given you. Seek, and you will find. Knock, and it will be opened for you. [7:8]For everyone who asks receives. He who seeks finds. To him who knocks it will be opened. [7:9]Or who is there among you, who, if his son asks him for bread, will give him a stone? [7:10]Or if he asks for a fish, who will give him a serpent? [7:11]If you then, being evil, know

how to give good gifts to your children, how much more will your Father who is in heaven give good things to those who ask him! [7:12]Therefore whatever you desire for men to do to you, you shall also do to them; for this is the law and the prophets.

[7:13]"Enter in by the narrow gate; for wide is the gate and broad is the way that leads to destruction, and many are those who enter in by it. [7:14]How[n] narrow is the gate, and restricted is the way that leads to life! Few are those who find it.

[7:15]"Beware of false prophets, who come to you in sheep's clothing, but inwardly are ravening wolves. [7:16]By their fruits you will know them. Do you gather grapes from thorns, or figs from thistles? [7:17]Even so, every good tree produces good fruit; but the corrupt tree produces evil fruit. [7:18]A good tree can't produce evil fruit, neither can a corrupt tree produce good fruit. [7:19]Every tree that doesn't grow good fruit is cut down, and thrown into the fire. [7:20]Therefore, by their fruits you will know them. [7:21]Not everyone who says to me, 'Lord, Lord,' will enter into the Kingdom of Heaven; but he who does the will of my Father who is in heaven. [7:22]Many will tell me in that day, 'Lord, Lord, didn't we prophesy in your name, in your name cast out demons, and in your name do many mighty works?' [7:23]Then I will tell them, 'I never knew you. Depart from me, you who work iniquity.'

[7:24]"Everyone therefore who hears these words of mine, and does them, I will liken him to a wise man, who built his house on a rock. [7:25]The rain came down, the floods came, and the winds blew, and beat on that house; and it didn't fall, for it was founded on the rock. [7:26]Everyone who hears these words of mine, and doesn't do them will be like a foolish man, who built his house on the sand. [7:27]The rain came down, the floods came, and the winds blew, and beat on that house; and it fell— and great was its fall."

[m]6:27 literally, cubit
[n]7:14 TR reads "Because" instead of "How"

^{7:28}It happened, when Jesus had finished saying these things, that the multitudes were astonished at his teaching, ^{7:29}for he taught them with authority, and not like the scribes.

^{8:1}When he came down from the mountain, great multitudes followed him. ^{8:2}Behold, a leper came to him and worshiped him, saying, "Lord, if you want to, you can make me clean."

^{8:3}Jesus stretched out his hand, and touched him, saying, **"I want to.   Be made clean."** Immediately his leprosy was cleansed. ^{8:4}Jesus said to him, **"See that you tell nobody, but go, show yourself to the priest, and offer the gift that Moses commanded, as a testimony to them."**

^{8:5}When he came into Capernaum, a centurion came to him, asking him, ^{8:6}and saying, "Lord, my servant lies in the house paralyzed, grievously tormented."

^{8:7}Jesus said to him, **"I will come and heal him."**

^{8:8}The centurion answered, "Lord, I'm not worthy for you to come under my roof. Just say the word, and my servant will be healed. ^{8:9}For I am also a man under authority, having under myself soldiers. I tell this one, 'Go,' and he goes; and tell another, 'Come,' and he comes; and tell my servant, 'Do this,' and he does it."

^{8:10}When Jesus heard it, he marveled, and said to those who followed, **"Most certainly I tell you, I haven't found so great a faith, not even in Israel.** ^{8:11}**I tell you that many will come from the east and the west, and will sit down with Abraham, Isaac, and Jacob in the Kingdom of Heaven,** ^{8:12}**but the children of the Kingdom will be thrown out into the outer darkness. There will be weeping and gnashing of teeth."** ^{8:13}Jesus said to the centurion, **"Go your way. Let it be done for you as you have believed."** His servant was healed in that hour.

^{8:14}When Jesus came into Peter's house, he saw his wife's mother lying sick with a fever. ^{8:15}He touched her hand, and the fever left her. She got up and served him.^o

^{8:16}When evening came, they brought to him many possessed with demons. He cast out the spirits with a word, and healed all who were sick; ^{8:17}that it might be fulfilled which was spoken through Isaiah the prophet, saying: "He took our infirmities, and bore our diseases."^p ^{8:18}Now when Jesus saw great multitudes around him, he gave the order to depart to the other side.

^{8:19}A scribe came, and said to him, "Teacher, I will follow you wherever you go."

^{8:20}Jesus said to him, **"The foxes have holes, and the birds of the sky have nests, but the Son of Man has nowhere to lay his head."**

^{8:21}Another of his disciples said to him, "Lord, allow me first to go and bury my father."

^{8:22}But Jesus said to him, **"Follow me, and leave the dead to bury their own dead."**

^{8:23}When he got into a boat, his disciples followed him. ^{8:24}Behold, a violent storm came up on the sea, so much that the boat was covered with the waves, but he was asleep. ^{8:25}They came to him, and woke him up, saying, "Save us, Lord! We are dying!"

^{8:26}He said to them, **"Why are you fearful, O you of little faith?"** Then he got up, rebuked the wind and the sea, and there was a great calm.

^{8:27}The men marveled, saying, "What kind of man is this, that even the wind and the sea obey him?"

^{8:28}When he came to the other side, into the country of the Gergesenes,^q two people possessed by demons met him there, coming out of the tombs, exceedingly fierce, so that nobody could pass that way. ^{8:29}Behold, they cried out, saying, "What do we have to do with you, Jesus, Son of God? Have you come here to torment us before the time?" ^{8:30}Now there was a herd of many pigs feeding far away from them. ^{8:31}The demons begged him, saying,

---

^o8:15 TR reads "them" instead of "him"
^p8:17 Isaiah 53:4
^q8:28 NU reads "Gadarenes"

"If you cast us out, permit us to go away into the herd of pigs."

^{8:32}He said to them, **"Go!"**

They came out, and went into the herd of pigs: and behold, the whole herd of pigs rushed down the cliff into the sea, and died in the water. ^{8:33}Those who fed them fled, and went away into the city, and told everything, including what happened to those who were possessed with demons. ^{8:34}Behold, all the city came out to meet Jesus. When they saw him, they begged that he would depart from their borders.

^{9:1}He entered into a boat, and crossed over, and came into his own city. ^{9:2}Behold, they brought to him a man who was paralyzed, lying on a bed. Jesus, seeing their faith, said to the paralytic, **"Son, cheer up! Your sins are forgiven you."**

^{9:3}Behold, some of the scribes said to themselves, "This man blasphemes."

^{9:4}Jesus, knowing their thoughts, said, **"Why do you think evil in your hearts?** ^{9:5}**For which is easier, to say, 'Your sins are forgiven;' or to say, 'Get up, and walk?'** ^{9:6}**But that you may know that the Son of Man has authority on earth to forgive sins..."** (then he said to the paralytic), **"Get up, and take up your mat, and go up to your house."**

^{9:7}He arose and departed to his house. ^{9:8}But when the multitudes saw it, they marveled and glorified God, who had given such authority to men.

^{9:9}As Jesus passed by from there, he saw a man called Matthew sitting at the tax collection office. He said to him, **"Follow me."** He got up and followed him. ^{9:10}It happened as he sat in the house, behold, many tax collectors and sinners came and sat down with Jesus and his disciples. ^{9:11}When the Pharisees saw it, they said to his disciples, "Why does your teacher eat with tax collectors and sinners?"

^{9:12}When Jesus heard it, he said to them, **"Those who are healthy have no need for a physician, but those who are sick do.** ^{9:13}**But you go and learn what this means: 'I desire mercy, and not sacrifice,'^r for I** came not to call the righteous, but sinners to repentance.^s**"**

^{9:14}Then John's disciples came to him, saying, "Why do we and the Pharisees fast often, but your disciples don't fast?"

^{9:15}Jesus said to them, **"Can the friends of the bridegroom mourn, as long as the bridegroom is with them? But the days will come when the bridegroom will be taken away from them, and then they will fast.** ^{9:16}**No one puts a piece of unshrunk cloth on an old garment; for the patch would tear away from the garment, and a worse hole is made.** ^{9:17}**Neither do people put new wine into old wineskins, or else the skins would burst, and the wine be spilled, and the skins ruined. No, they put new wine into fresh wineskins, and both are preserved."**

^{9:18}While he told these things to them, behold, a ruler came and worshiped him, saying, "My daughter has just died, but come and lay your hand on her, and she will live."

^{9:19}Jesus got up and followed him, as did his disciples. ^{9:20}Behold, a woman who had an issue of blood for twelve years came behind him, and touched the fringe^t of his garment; ^{9:21}for she said within herself, "If I just touch his garment, I will be made well."

^{9:22}But Jesus, turning around and seeing her, said, **"Daughter, cheer up! Your faith has made you well."** And the woman was made well from that hour.

^{9:23}When Jesus came into the ruler's house, and saw the flute players, and the crowd in noisy disorder, ^{9:24}he said to them, **"Make room, because the girl isn't dead, but sleeping."**

They were ridiculing him. ^{9:25}But when the crowd was put out, he entered in, took her by the hand, and the girl arose. ^{9:26}The report of this went out into all that land. ^{9:27}As Jesus passed by from there, two blind men followed him, calling out and saying, "Have mercy on us, son of David!"

^{9:28}When he had come into the house, the blind men came to him. Jesus said to them,

---

^r9:13 Hosea 6:6
^s9:13 NU omits "to repentance".
^t9:20 or, tassel

"Do you believe that I am able to do this?"

They told him, "Yes, Lord."

9:29 Then he touched their eyes, saying, **"According to your faith be it done to you."** 9:30 Their eyes were opened. Jesus strictly commanded them, saying, **"See that no one knows about this."** 9:31 But they went out and spread abroad his fame in all that land.

9:32 As they went out, behold, a mute man who was demon possessed was brought to him. 9:33 When the demon was cast out, the mute man spoke. The multitudes marveled, saying, "Nothing like this has ever been seen in Israel!"

9:34 But the Pharisees said, "By the prince of the demons, he casts out demons."

9:35 Jesus went about all the cities and the villages, teaching in their synagogues, and preaching the Good News of the Kingdom, and healing every disease and every sickness among the people. 9:36 But when he saw the multitudes, he was moved with compassion for them, because they were harassed[u] and scattered, like sheep without a shepherd. 9:37 Then he said to his disciples, **"The harvest indeed is plentiful, but the laborers are few.** 9:38 **Pray therefore that the Lord of the harvest will send out laborers into his harvest."**

10:1 He called to himself his twelve disciples, and gave them authority over unclean spirits, to cast them out, and to heal every disease and every sickness. 10:2 Now the names of the twelve apostles are these. The first, Simon, who is called Peter; Andrew, his brother; James the son of Zebedee; John, his brother; 10:3 Philip; Bartholomew; Thomas; Matthew the tax collector; James the son of Alphaeus; Lebbaeus, whose surname was[v] Thaddaeus; 10:4 Simon the Canaanite; and Judas Iscariot, who also betrayed him.

10:5 Jesus sent these twelve out, and commanded them, saying, **"Don't go among the Gentiles, and don't enter into any city of the Samaritans.** 10:6 **Rather, go to the lost sheep of the house of Israel.** 10:7 **As you go, preach, saying, 'The Kingdom of Heaven is at hand!'** 10:8 **Heal the sick, cleanse the lepers[w], and cast out demons. Freely you received, so freely give.** 10:9 **Don't take any gold, nor silver, nor brass in your money belts.** 10:10 **Take no bag for your journey, neither two coats, nor shoes, nor staff: for the laborer is worthy of his food.** 10:11 **Into whatever city or village you enter, find out who in it is worthy; and stay there until you go on.** 10:12 **As you enter into the household, greet it.** 10:13 **If the household is worthy, let your peace come on it, but if it isn't worthy, let your peace return to you.** 10:14 **Whoever doesn't receive you, nor hear your words, as you go out of that house or that city, shake off the dust from your feet.** 10:15 **Most certainly I tell you, it will be more tolerable for the land of Sodom and Gomorrah in the day of judgment than for that city.**

10:16 **"Behold, I send you out as sheep in the midst of wolves. Therefore be wise as serpents, and harmless as doves.** 10:17 **But beware of men: for they will deliver you up to councils, and in their synagogues they will scourge you.** 10:18 **Yes, and you will be brought before governors and kings for my sake, for a testimony to them and to the nations.** 10:19 **But when they deliver you up, don't be anxious how or what you will say, for it will be given you in that hour what you will say.** 10:20 **For it is not you who speak, but the Spirit of your Father who speaks in you.**

10:21 **"Brother will deliver up brother to death, and the father his child. Children will rise up against parents, and cause them to be put to death.** 10:22 **You will be hated by all men for my name's sake, but he who endures to the end will be saved.** 10:23 **But when they persecute you in this city, flee into the next, for most certainly I tell you, you will not have gone through the cities of Israel, until the Son of Man has come.**

10:24 **"A disciple is not above his teacher, nor a servant above his lord.** 10:25 **It is enough for the disciple that he be like his**

---

u 9:36 TR reads "weary" instead of "harassed"

v 10:3 NU omits "Lebbaeus, whose surname was"

w 10:8 TR adds ", raise the dead"

teacher, and the servant like his lord. If they have called the master of the house Beelzebul, how much more those of his household! [10:26]Therefore don't be afraid of them, for there is nothing covered that will not be revealed; and hidden that will not be known. [10:27]What I tell you in the darkness, speak in the light; and what you hear whispered in the ear, proclaim on the housetops. [10:28]Don't be afraid of those who kill the body, but are not able to kill the soul. Rather, fear him who is able to destroy both soul and body in Gehenna.[x]

[10:29]"Aren't two sparrows sold for an assarion coin[y]? Not one of them falls on the ground apart from your Father's will, [10:30]but the very hairs of your head are all numbered. [10:31]Therefore don't be afraid. You are of more value than many sparrows. [10:32]Everyone therefore who confesses me before men, him I will also confess before my Father who is in heaven. [10:33]But whoever denies me before men, him I will also deny before my Father who is in heaven.

[10:34]"Don't think that I came to send peace on the earth. I didn't come to send peace, but a sword. [10:35]For I came to set a man at odds against his father, and a daughter against her mother, and a daughter-in-law against her mother-in-law. [10:36]A man's foes will be those of his own household.[z] [10:37]He who loves father or mother more than me is not worthy of me; and he who loves son or daughter more than me isn't worthy of me. [10:38]He who doesn't take his cross and follow after me, isn't worthy of me. [10:39]He who seeks his life will lose it; and he who loses his life for my sake will find it. [10:40]He who receives you receives me, and he who receives me receives him who sent me. [10:41]He who receives a prophet in the name of a prophet will receive a prophet's reward: and he who receives a righteous man in the name of a righteous man will receive a righteous man's reward. [10:42]Whoever gives one of these little ones just a cup of cold water to drink in the name of a disciple, most certainly I tell you he will in no way lose his reward."

[11:1]It happened that when Jesus had finished directing his twelve disciples, he departed from there to teach and preach in their cities. [11:2]Now when John heard in the prison the works of Christ, he sent two of his disciples [11:3]and said to him, "Are you he who comes, or should we look for another?"

[11:4]Jesus answered them, **"Go and tell John the things which you hear and see: [11:5]the blind receive their sight, the lame walk, the lepers are cleansed, the deaf hear,[a] the dead are raised up, and the poor have good news preached to them.[b] [11:6]Blessed is he who finds no occasion for stumbling in me."**

[11:7]As these went their way, Jesus began to say to the multitudes concerning John, **"What did you go out into the wilderness to see? A reed shaken by the wind? [11:8]But what did you go out to see? A man in soft clothing? Behold, those who wear soft clothing are in king's houses. [11:9]But why did you go out? To see a prophet? Yes, I tell you, and much more than a prophet. [11:10]For this is he, of whom it is written, 'Behold, I send my messenger before your face, who will prepare your way before you.'[c] [11:11]Most certainly I tell you, among those who are born of women there has not arisen anyone greater than John the Baptizer; yet he who is least in the Kingdom of Heaven is greater than he. [11:12]From the days of John the Baptizer until now, the Kingdom of Heaven suffers violence, and the violent take it by force.[d] [11:13]For all the prophets and the**

---

[x]10:28 or, Hell.

[y]10:29 An assarion is a small coin worth one tenth of a drachma or a sixteenth of a denarius (approximately the wages of one half hour of agricultural labor).

[z]10:36 Micah 7:6

[a]11:5 Isaiah 35:5

[b]11:5 Isaiah 61:1-4

[c]11:10 Malachi 3:1

[d]11:12 or, plunder it.

law prophesied until John. [11:14]If you are willing to receive it, this is Elijah, who is to come. [11:15]He who has ears to hear, let him hear.

[11:16]"But to what shall I compare this generation? It is like children sitting in the marketplaces, who call to their companions [11:17]and say, 'We played the flute for you, and you didn't dance. We mourned for you, and you didn't lament.' [11:18]For John came neither eating nor drinking, and they say, 'He has a demon.' [11:19]The Son of Man came eating and drinking, and they say, 'Behold, a gluttonous man and a drunkard, a friend of tax collectors and sinners!' But wisdom is justified by her children.[e]"

[11:20]Then he began to denounce the cities in which most of his mighty works had been done, because they didn't repent. [11:21]"Woe to you, Chorazin! Woe to you, Bethsaida! For if the mighty works had been done in Tyre and Sidon which were done in you, they would have repented long ago in sackcloth and ashes. [11:22]But I tell you, it will be more tolerable for Tyre and Sidon on the day of judgment than for you. [11:23]You, Capernaum, who are exalted to heaven, you will go down to Hades.[f] For if the mighty works had been done in Sodom which were done in you, it would have remained until this day. [11:24]But I tell you that it will be more tolerable for the land of Sodom, on the day of judgment, than for you."

[11:25]At that time, Jesus answered, "I thank you, Father, Lord of heaven and earth, that you hid these things from the wise and understanding, and revealed them to infants. [11:26]Yes, Father, for so it was well-pleasing in your sight. [11:27]All things have been delivered to me by my Father. No one knows the Son, except the Father; neither does anyone know the Father, except the Son, and he to whom the Son desires to reveal him.

[11:28]"Come to me, all you who labor and are heavily burdened, and I will give you rest. [11:29]Take my yoke upon you, and learn from me, for I am gentle and lowly in heart; and you will find rest for your souls. [11:30]For my yoke is easy, and my burden is light."

[12:1]At that time, Jesus went on the Sabbath day through the grain fields. His disciples were hungry and began to pluck heads of grain and to eat. [12:2]But the Pharisees, when they saw it, said to him, "Behold, your disciples do what is not lawful to do on the Sabbath."

[12:3]But he said to them, "Haven't you read what David did, when he was hungry, and those who were with him; [12:4]how he entered into the house of God, and ate the show bread, which was not lawful for him to eat, neither for those who were with him, but only for the priests?[g] [12:5]Or have you not read in the law, that on the Sabbath day, the priests in the temple profane the Sabbath, and are guiltless? [12:6]But I tell you that one greater than the temple is here. [12:7]But if you had known what this means, 'I desire mercy, and not sacrifice,'[h] you would not have condemned the guiltless. [12:8]For the Son of Man is Lord of the Sabbath."

[12:9]He departed there, and went into their synagogue. [12:10]And behold there was a man with a withered hand. They asked him, "Is it lawful to heal on the Sabbath day?" that they might accuse him.

[12:11]He said to them, "What man is there among you, who has one sheep, and if this one falls into a pit on the Sabbath day, won't he grab on to it, and lift it out? [12:12]Of how much more value then is a man than a sheep! Therefore it is lawful to do good on the Sabbath day." [12:13]Then he told the man, "Stretch out your hand." He stretched it out; and it was restored whole, just like the other. [12:14]But the Pharisees went out, and conspired against him, how they might destroy him. [12:15]Jesus, perceiving that, withdrew from there. Great multitudes followed him; and he healed

---

[e]11:19 NU reads "actions" instead of "children"
[f]11:23 or, Hell
[g]12:4 1 Samuel 21:3-6
[h]12:7 Hosea 6:6

them all, [12:16]and commanded them that they should not make him known: [12:17]that it might be fulfilled which was spoken through Isaiah the prophet, saying,

[12:18]"Behold, my servant whom I have chosen;

my beloved in whom my soul is well pleased:

I will put my Spirit on him.

He will proclaim justice to the nations.

[12:19]He will not strive, nor shout;

neither will anyone hear his voice in the streets.

[12:20]He won't break a bruised reed.

He won't quench a smoking flax,

until he leads justice to victory.

[12:21]In his name, the nations will hope."[i]

[12:22]Then one possessed by a demon, blind and mute, was brought to him and he healed him, so that the blind and mute man both spoke and saw. [12:23]All the multitudes were amazed, and said, "Can this be the son of David?" [12:24]But when the Pharisees heard it, they said, "This man does not cast out demons, except by Beelzebul, the prince of the demons."

[12:25]Knowing their thoughts, Jesus said to them, **"Every kingdom divided against itself is brought to desolation, and every city or house divided against itself will not stand. [12:26]If Satan casts out Satan, he is divided against himself. How then will his kingdom stand? [12:27]If I by Beelzebul cast out demons, by whom do your children cast them out? Therefore they will be your judges. [12:28]But if I by the Spirit of God cast out demons, then the Kingdom of God has come upon you. [12:29]Or how can one enter into the house of the strong man, and plunder his goods, unless he first bind the strong man? Then he will plunder his house.**

[12:30]**"He who is not with me is against me, and he who doesn't gather with me, scatters. [12:31]Therefore I tell you, every sin and blasphemy will be forgiven men, but the blasphemy against the Spirit will not be forgiven men. [12:32]Whoever speaks a word against the Son of Man, it will be** forgiven him; but whoever speaks against the Holy Spirit, it will not be forgiven him, neither in this age, nor in that which is to come.

[12:33]**"Either make the tree good, and its fruit good, or make the tree corrupt, and its fruit corrupt; for the tree is known by its fruit. [12:34]You offspring of vipers, how can you, being evil, speak good things? For out of the abundance of the heart, the mouth speaks. [12:35]The good man out of his good treasure brings out good things, and the evil man out of his evil treasure[j] brings out evil things. [12:36]I tell you that every idle word that men speak, they will give account of it in the day of judgment. [12:37]For by your words you will be justified, and by your words you will be condemned."**

[12:38]Then certain of the scribes and Pharisees answered, "Teacher, we want to see a sign from you."

[12:39]But he answered them, **"An evil and adulterous generation seeks after a sign, but no sign will be given it but the sign of Jonah the prophet. [12:40]For as Jonah was three days and three nights in the belly of the whale, so will the Son of Man be three days and three nights in the heart of the earth. [12:41]The men of Nineveh will stand up in the judgment with this generation, and will condemn it, for they repented at the preaching of Jonah; and behold, someone greater than Jonah is here. [12:42]The queen of the south will rise up in the judgment with this generation, and will condemn it, for she came from the ends of the earth to hear the wisdom of Solomon; and behold, someone greater than Solomon is here. [12:43]But the unclean spirit, when he is gone out of the man, passes through waterless places, seeking rest, and doesn't find it. [12:44]Then he says, 'I will return into my house from which I came out,' and when he has come back, he finds it empty, swept, and put in order. [12:45]Then he goes, and takes with himself seven other spirits more evil than he is, and they enter in and dwell there. The**

[i]12:21 Isaiah 42:1-4
[j]12:35 TR adds "of the heart"

last state of that man becomes worse than the first. Even so will it be also to this evil generation."

¹²:⁴⁶While he was yet speaking to the multitudes, behold, his mother and his brothers stood outside, seeking to speak to him. ¹²:⁴⁷One said to him, "Behold, your mother and your brothers stand outside, seeking to speak to you."

¹²:⁴⁸But he answered him who spoke to him, **"Who is my mother? Who are my brothers?"** ¹²:⁴⁹He stretched out his hand towards his disciples, and said, **"Behold, my mother and my brothers!** ¹²:⁵⁰**For whoever does the will of my Father who is in heaven, he is my brother, and sister, and mother."**

¹³:¹On that day Jesus went out of the house, and sat by the seaside. ¹³:²Great multitudes gathered to him, so that he entered into a boat, and sat, and all the multitude stood on the beach. ¹³:³He spoke to them many things in parables, saying, **"Behold, a farmer went out to sow.** ¹³:⁴**As he sowed, some seeds fell by the roadside, and the birds came and devoured them.** ¹³:⁵**Others fell on rocky ground, where they didn't have much soil, and immediately they sprang up, because they had no depth of earth.** ¹³:⁶**When the sun had risen, they were scorched. Because they had no root, they withered away.** ¹³:⁷**Others fell among thorns. The thorns grew up and choked them:** ¹³:⁸**and others fell on good soil, and yielded fruit: some one hundred times as much, some sixty, and some thirty.** ¹³:⁹**He who has ears to hear, let him hear."**

¹³:¹⁰The disciples came, and said to him, "Why do you speak to them in parables?"

¹³:¹¹He answered them, **"To you it is given to know the mysteries of the Kingdom of Heaven, but it is not given to them.** ¹³:¹²**For whoever has, to him will be given, and he will have abundance, but whoever doesn't have, from him will be taken away even that which he has.** ¹³:¹³**Therefore I speak to them in parables, because seeing they don't see, and hearing, they don't hear, neither do they understand.** ¹³:¹⁴**In them the prophecy of Isaiah is fulfilled,**

which says,

'By hearing you will hear,
    and will in no way understand;
Seeing you will see,
    and will in no way perceive:
¹³:¹⁵for this people's heart has grown callous,
    their ears are dull of hearing,
    they have closed their eyes;
or else perhaps they might perceive with their eyes,
    hear with their ears,
    understand with their heart,
and should turn again;
    and I would heal them.'ᵏ

¹³:¹⁶**"But blessed are your eyes, for they see; and your ears, for they hear.** ¹³:¹⁷**For most certainly I tell you that many prophets and righteous men desired to see the things which you see, and didn't see them; and to hear the things which you hear, and didn't hear them.**

¹³:¹⁸**"Hear, then, the parable of the farmer.** ¹³:¹⁹**When anyone hears the word of the Kingdom, and doesn't understand it, the evil one comes, and snatches away that which has been sown in his heart. This is what was sown by the roadside.** ¹³:²⁰**What was sown on the rocky places, this is he who hears the word, and immediately with joy receives it;** ¹³:²¹**yet he has no root in himself, but endures for a while. When oppression or persecution arises because of the word, immediately he stumbles.** ¹³:²²**What was sown among the thorns, this is he who hears the word, but the cares of this age and the deceitfulness of riches choke the word, and he becomes unfruitful.** ¹³:²³**What was sown on the good ground, this is he who hears the word, and understands it, who most certainly bears fruit, and brings forth, some one hundred times as much, some sixty, and some thirty."**

¹³:²⁴He set another parable before them, saying, **"The Kingdom of Heaven is like a man who sowed good seed in his field,** ¹³:²⁵**but while people slept, his**

ᵏ13:15 Isaiah 6:9-10

enemy came and sowed darnel weeds[l] also among the wheat, and went away. [13:26] But when the blade sprang up and brought forth fruit, then the darnel weeds appeared also. [13:27] The servants of the householder came and said to him, 'Sir, didn't you sow good seed in your field? Where did this darnel come from?'

[13:28] "He said to them, 'An enemy has done this.'

"The servants asked him, 'Do you want us to go and gather them up?'

[13:29] "But he said, 'No, lest perhaps while you gather up the darnel weeds, you root up the wheat with them. [13:30] Let both grow together until the harvest, and in the harvest time I will tell the reapers, "First, gather up the darnel weeds, and bind them in bundles to burn them; but gather the wheat into my barn."'"

[13:31] He set another parable before them, saying, "The Kingdom of Heaven is like a grain of mustard seed, which a man took, and sowed in his field; [13:32] which indeed is smaller than all seeds. But when it is grown, it is greater than the herbs, and becomes a tree, so that the birds of the air come and lodge in its branches."

[13:33] He spoke another parable to them. "The Kingdom of Heaven is like yeast, which a woman took, and hid in three measures[m] of meal, until it was all leavened."

[13:34] Jesus spoke all these things in parables to the multitudes; and without a parable, he didn't speak to them, [13:35] that it might be fulfilled which was spoken through the prophet, saying,

"I will open my mouth in parables;
   I will utter things hidden from the
   foundation of the world."[n]

[13:36] Then Jesus sent the multitudes away, and went into the house. His disciples came to him, saying, "Explain to us the parable of the darnel weeds of the field."

[13:37] He answered them, "He who sows the good seed is the Son of Man, [13:38] the field is the world; and the good seed, these are the children of the Kingdom; and the darnel weeds are the children of the evil one. [13:39] The enemy who sowed them is the devil. The harvest is the end of the age, and the reapers are angels. [13:40] As therefore the darnel weeds are gathered up and burned with fire; so will it be at the end of this age. [13:41] The Son of Man will send out his angels, and they will gather out of his Kingdom all things that cause stumbling, and those who do iniquity, [13:42] and will cast them into the furnace of fire. There will be weeping and the gnashing of teeth. [13:43] Then the righteous will shine forth like the sun in the Kingdom of their Father. He who has ears to hear, let him hear.

[13:44] "Again, the Kingdom of Heaven is like a treasure hidden in the field, which a man found, and hid. In his joy, he goes and sells all that he has, and buys that field.

[13:45] "Again, the Kingdom of Heaven is like a man who is a merchant seeking fine pearls, [13:46] who having found one pearl of great price, he went and sold all that he had, and bought it.

[13:47] "Again, the Kingdom of Heaven is like a dragnet, that was cast into the sea, and gathered some fish of every kind, [13:48] which, when it was filled, they drew up on the beach. They sat down, and gathered the good into containers, but the bad they threw away. [13:49] So will it be in the end of the world. The angels will come forth, and separate the wicked from among the righteous, [13:50] and will cast them into the furnace of fire. There will be the weeping and the gnashing of teeth." [13:51] Jesus said to them, "Have you understood all these things?"

They answered him, "Yes, Lord."

[13:52] He said to them, "Therefore, every scribe who has been made a disciple in the Kingdom of Heaven is like a man who is a householder, who brings out of his treasure new and old things."

---

[l]13:25 darnel is a weed grass (probably bearded darnel or lolium temulentum) that looks very much like wheat until it is mature, when the difference becomes very apparent.

[m]13:33 literally, three sata. 3 sata is about 39 litres or a bit more than a bushel

[n]13:35 Psalm 78:2

[13:53]It happened that when Jesus had finished these parables, he departed from there. [13:54]Coming into his own country, he taught them in their synagogue, so that they were astonished, and said, "Where did this man get this wisdom, and these mighty works? [13:55]Isn't this the carpenter's son? Isn't his mother called Mary, and his brothers, James, Joses, Simon, and Judas[o]? [13:56]Aren't all of his sisters with us? Where then did this man get all of these things?" [13:57]They were offended by him.

But Jesus said to them, **"A prophet is not without honor, except in his own country, and in his own house."** [13:58]He didn't do many mighty works there because of their unbelief.

[14:1]At that time, Herod the tetrarch heard the report concerning Jesus, [14:2]and said to his servants, "This is John the Baptizer. He is risen from the dead. That is why these powers work in him." [14:3]For Herod had laid hold of John, and bound him, and put him in prison for the sake of Herodias, his brother Philip's wife. [14:4]For John said to him, "It is not lawful for you to have her." [14:5]When he would have put him to death, he feared the multitude, because they counted him as a prophet. [14:6]But when Herod's birthday came, the daughter of Herodias danced among them and pleased Herod. [14:7]Whereupon he promised with an oath to give her whatever she should ask. [14:8]She, being prompted by her mother, said, "Give me here on a platter the head of John the Baptizer."

[14:9]The king was grieved, but for the sake of his oaths, and of those who sat at the table with him, he commanded it to be given, [14:10]and he sent and beheaded John in the prison. [14:11]His head was brought on a platter, and given to the young lady: and she brought it to her mother. [14:12]His disciples came, and took the body, and buried it; and they went and told Jesus. [14:13]Now when Jesus heard this, he withdrew from there in a boat, to a deserted place apart. When the multitudes heard it, they followed him on foot from the cities.

[14:14]Jesus went out, and he saw a great multitude. He had compassion on them, and healed their sick. [14:15]When evening had come, his disciples came to him, saying, "This place is deserted, and the hour is already late. Send the multitudes away, that they may go into the villages, and buy themselves food."

[14:16]But Jesus said to them, **"They don't need to go away. You give them something to eat."**

[14:17]They told him, "We only have here five loaves and two fish."

[14:18]He said, **"Bring them here to me."** [14:19]He commanded the multitudes to sit down on the grass; and he took the five loaves and the two fish, and looking up to heaven, he blessed, broke and gave the loaves to the disciples, and the disciples gave to the multitudes. [14:20]They all ate, and were filled. They took up twelve baskets full of that which remained left over from the broken pieces. [14:21]Those who ate were about five thousand men, besides women and children.

[14:22]Immediately Jesus made the disciples get into the boat, and to go ahead of him to the other side, while he sent the multitudes away. [14:23]After he had sent the multitudes away, he went up into the mountain by himself to pray. When evening had come, he was there alone. [14:24]But the boat was now in the middle of the sea, distressed by the waves, for the wind was contrary. [14:25]In the fourth watch of the night,[p] Jesus came to them, walking on the sea.[q] [14:26]When the disciples saw him walking on the sea, they were troubled, saying, "It's a ghost!" and they cried out for fear. [14:27]But immediately Jesus spoke to them, saying **"Cheer up! It is I![r] Don't be afraid."**

[14:28]Peter answered him and said, "Lord, if it is you, command me to come to you on the waters."

---

[o]13:55 or, Judah

[p]14:25 The night was equally divided into four watches, so the fourth watch is approximately 3:00 A. M. to sunrise.

[q]14:25 see Job 9:8

[r]14:27 or, I AM!

¹⁴:²⁹He said, **"Come!"**

Peter stepped down from the boat, and walked on the waters to come to Jesus. ¹⁴:³⁰But when he saw that the wind was strong, he was afraid, and beginning to sink, he cried out, saying, "Lord, save me!" ¹⁴:³¹Immediately Jesus stretched out his hand, took hold of him, and said to him, **"You of little faith, why did you doubt?"** ¹⁴:³²When they got up into the boat, the wind ceased. ¹⁴:³³Those who were in the boat came and worshiped him, saying, "You are truly the Son of God!"

¹⁴:³⁴When they had crossed over, they came to the land of Gennesaret. ¹⁴:³⁵When the people of that place recognized him, they sent into all that surrounding region, and brought to him all who were sick, ¹⁴:³⁶and they begged him that they might just touch the fringeˢ of his garment. As many as touched it were made whole.

¹⁵:¹Then Pharisees and scribes came to Jesus from Jerusalem, saying, ¹⁵:²"Why do your disciples disobey the tradition of the elders? For they don't wash their hands when they eat bread."

¹⁵:³He answered them, **"Why do you also disobey the commandment of God because of your tradition?** ¹⁵:⁴**For God commanded, 'Honor your father and your mother,'ᵗ and, 'He who speaks evil of father or mother, let him be put to death.'ᵘ** ¹⁵:⁵**But you say, 'Whoever may tell his father or his mother, "Whatever help you might otherwise have gotten from me is a gift devoted to God,"** ¹⁵:⁶**he shall not honor his father or mother.' You have made the commandment of God void because of your tradition.** ¹⁵:⁷**You hypocrites! Well did Isaiah prophesy of you, saying,**

¹⁵:⁸**'These people draw near to me with their mouth,**
    and honor me with their lips;
    but their heart is far from me.
¹⁵:⁹**And in vain do they worship me,**
    teaching as doctrine rules made by men.'"ᵛ

¹⁵:¹⁰He summoned the multitude, and said to them, **"Hear, and understand.** ¹⁵:¹¹**That which enters into the mouth doesn't defile the man; but that which proceeds out of the mouth, this defiles the man."**

¹⁵:¹²Then the disciples came, and said to him, "Do you know that the Pharisees were offended, when they heard this saying?"

¹⁵:¹³But he answered, **"Every plant which my heavenly Father didn't plant will be uprooted.** ¹⁵:¹⁴**Leave them alone. They are blind guides of the blind. If the blind guide the blind, both will fall into a pit."**

¹⁵:¹⁵Peter answered him, "Explain the parable to us."

¹⁵:¹⁶So Jesus said, **"Do you also still not understand?** ¹⁵:¹⁷**Don't you understand that whatever goes into the mouth passes into the belly, and then out of the body?** ¹⁵:¹⁸**But the things which proceed out of the mouth come out of the heart, and they defile the man.** ¹⁵:¹⁹**For out of the heart come forth evil thoughts, murders, adulteries, sexual sins, thefts, false testimony, and blasphemies.** ¹⁵:²⁰**These are the things which defile the man; but to eat with unwashed hands doesn't defile the man."**

¹⁵:²¹Jesus went out from there, and withdrew into the region of Tyre and Sidon. ¹⁵:²²Behold, a Canaanite woman came out from those borders, and cried, saying, "Have mercy on me, Lord, you son of David! My daughter is severely demonized!"

¹⁵:²³But he answered her not a word.

His disciples came and begged him, saying, "Send her away; for she cries after us."

¹⁵:²⁴But he answered, **"I wasn't sent to anyone but the lost sheep of the house of Israel."**

¹⁵:²⁵But she came and worshiped him, saying, "Lord, help me."

¹⁵:²⁶But he answered, **"It is not appropriate to take the children's bread and throw it to the dogs."**

ˢ14:36 or, tassel
ᵗ15:4 Exodus 20:12; Deuteronomy 5:16
ᵘ15:4 Exodus 21:17; Leviticus 20:9
ᵛ15:9 Isaiah 29:13

^{15:27}But she said, "Yes, Lord, but even the dogs eat the crumbs which fall from their masters' table."

^{15:28}Then Jesus answered her, **"Woman, great is your faith! Be it done to you even as you desire."** And her daughter was healed from that hour.

^{15:29}Jesus departed there, and came near to the sea of Galilee; and he went up into the mountain, and sat there. ^{15:30}Great multitudes came to him, having with them the lame, blind, mute, maimed, and many others, and they put them down at his feet. He healed them, ^{15:31}so that the multitude wondered when they saw the mute speaking, injured whole, lame walking, and blind seeing—and they glorified the God of Israel.

^{15:32}Jesus summoned his disciples and said, **"I have compassion on the multitude, because they continue with me now three days and have nothing to eat. I don't want to send them away fasting, or they might faint on the way."**

^{15:33}The disciples said to him, "Where should we get so many loaves in a deserted place as to satisfy so great a multitude?"

^{15:34}Jesus said to them, **"How many loaves do you have?"**

They said, "Seven, and a few small fish."

^{15:35}He commanded the multitude to sit down on the ground; ^{15:36}and he took the seven loaves and the fish. He gave thanks and broke them, and gave to the disciples, and the disciples to the multitudes. ^{15:37}They all ate, and were filled. They took up seven baskets full of the broken pieces that were left over. ^{15:38}Those who ate were four thousand men, besides women and children. ^{15:39}Then he sent away the multitudes, got into the boat, and came into the borders of Magdala.

^{16:1}The Pharisees and Sadducees came, and testing him, asked him to show them a sign from heaven. ^{16:2}But he answered them, **"When it is evening, you say, 'It will be fair weather, for the sky is red.'** ^{16:3}**In the morning, 'It will be foul weather today, for the sky is red and threatening.'**

Hypocrites! You know how to discern the appearance of the sky, but you can't discern the signs of the times!** ^{16:4}**An evil and adulterous generation seeks after a sign, and there will be no sign given to it, except the sign of the prophet Jonah."**

He left them, and departed. ^{16:5}The disciples came to the other side and had forgotten to take bread. ^{16:6}Jesus said to them, **"Take heed and beware of the yeast of the Pharisees and Sadducees."**

^{16:7}They reasoned among themselves, saying, "We brought no bread."

^{16:8}Jesus, perceiving it, said, **"Why do you reason among yourselves, you of little faith, 'because you have brought no bread?'** ^{16:9}**Don't you yet perceive, neither remember the five loaves for the five thousand, and how many baskets you took up?** ^{16:10}**Nor the seven loaves for the four thousand, and how many baskets you took up?** ^{16:11}**How is it that you don't perceive that I didn't speak to you concerning bread? But beware of the yeast of the Pharisees and Sadducees."**

^{16:12}Then they understood that he didn't tell them to beware of the yeast of bread, but of the teaching of the Pharisees and Sadducees. ^{16:13}Now when Jesus came into the parts of Caesarea Philippi, he asked his disciples, saying, **"Who do men say that I, the Son of Man, am?"**

^{16:14}They said, "Some say John the Baptizer, some, Elijah, and others, Jeremiah, or one of the prophets."

^{16:15}He said to them, **"But who do you say that I am?"**

^{16:16}Simon Peter answered, "You are the Christ, the Son of the living God."

^{16:17}Jesus answered him, **"Blessed are you, Simon Bar Jonah, for flesh and blood has not revealed this to you, but my Father who is in heaven.** ^{16:18}**I also tell you that you are Peter,^w and on this rock^x I will build my assembly, and the gates of Hades^y will not prevail against it.** ^{16:19}**I will give to you the keys of the Kingdom of Heaven, and whatever you bind on**

---

^w16:18 Peter's name, Petros in Greek, is the word for a specific rock or stone.

^x16:18 Greek, petra, a rock mass or bedrock.

^y16:18 or, Hell

earth will have been bound in heaven; and whatever you release on earth will have been released in heaven." ^{16:20}Then he commanded the disciples that they should tell no one that he is Jesus the Christ. ^{16:21}From that time, Jesus began to show his disciples that he must go to Jerusalem and suffer many things from the elders, chief priests, and scribes, and be killed, and the third day be raised up.

^{16:22}Peter took him aside, and began to rebuke him, saying, "Far be it from you, Lord! This will never be done to you."

^{16:23}But he turned, and said to Peter, **"Get behind me, Satan! You are a stumbling block to me, for you are not setting your mind on the things of God, but on the things of men."** ^{16:24}Then Jesus said to his disciples, **"If anyone desires to come after me, let him deny himself, and take up his cross, and follow me. ^{16:25}For whoever desires to save his life will lose it, and whoever will lose his life for my sake will find it. ^{16:26}For what will it profit a man, if he gains the whole world, and forfeits his life? Or what will a man give in exchange for his life? ^{16:27}For the Son of Man will come in the glory of his Father with his angels, and then he will render to everyone according to his deeds. ^{16:28}Most certainly I tell you, there are some standing here who will in no way taste of death, until they see the Son of Man coming in his Kingdom."**

^{17:1}After six days, Jesus took with him Peter, James, and John his brother, and brought them up into a high mountain by themselves. ^{17:2}He was transfigured before them. His face shone like the sun, and his garments became as white as the light. ^{17:3}Behold, Moses and Elijah appeared to them talking with him.

^{17:4}Peter answered, and said to Jesus, "Lord, it is good for us to be here. If you want, let's make three tents here: one for you, one for Moses, and one for Elijah."

^{17:5}While he was still speaking, behold, a bright cloud overshadowed them. Behold, a voice came out of the cloud, saying, "This is my beloved Son, in whom I am well pleased. Listen to him."

^{17:6}When the disciples heard it, they fell on their faces, and were very afraid. ^{17:7}Jesus came and touched them and said, **"Get up, and don't be afraid."** ^{17:8}Lifting up their eyes, they saw no one, except Jesus alone. ^{17:9}As they were coming down from the mountain, Jesus commanded them, saying, **"Don't tell anyone what you saw, until the Son of Man has risen from the dead."**

^{17:10}His disciples asked him, saying, "Then why do the scribes say that Elijah must come first?"

^{17:11}Jesus answered them, **"Elijah indeed comes first, and will restore all things, ^{17:12}but I tell you that Elijah has come already, and they didn't recognize him, but did to him whatever they wanted to. Even so the Son of Man will also suffer by them."** ^{17:13}Then the disciples understood that he spoke to them of John the Baptizer.

^{17:14}When they came to the multitude, a man came to him, kneeling down to him, saying, ^{17:15}"Lord, have mercy on my son, for he is epileptic, and suffers grievously; for he often falls into the fire, and often into the water. ^{17:16}So I brought him to your disciples, and they could not cure him."

^{17:17}Jesus answered, **"Faithless and perverse generation! How long will I be with you? How long will I bear with you? Bring him here to me."** ^{17:18}Jesus rebuked him, the demon went out of him, and the boy was cured from that hour.

^{17:19}Then the disciples came to Jesus privately, and said, "Why weren't we able to cast it out?"

^{17:20}He said to them, **"Because of your unbelief. For most certainly I tell you, if you have faith as a grain of mustard seed, you will tell this mountain, 'Move from here to there,' and it will move; and nothing will be impossible for you. ^{17:21}But this kind doesn't go out except by prayer and fasting."**

^{17:22}While they were staying in Galilee, Jesus said to them, **"The Son of Man is about to be delivered up into the hands of men, ^{17:23}and they will kill him, and the third day he will be raised up."**

They were exceedingly sorry. ^{17:24}When they had come to Capernaum, those who collected the didrachma coins[z] came to Peter, and said, "Doesn't your teacher pay the didrachma?" [17:25]He said, "Yes."

When he came into the house, Jesus anticipated him, saying, **"What do you think, Simon? From whom do the kings of the earth receive toll or tribute? From their children, or from strangers?"**

[17:26]Peter said to him, "From strangers."

Jesus said to him, **"Therefore the children are exempt. [17:27]But, lest we cause them to stumble, go to the sea, cast a hook, and take up the first fish that comes up. When you have opened its mouth, you will find a stater coin.[a] Take that, and give it to them for me and you."**

[18:1]In that hour the disciples came to Jesus, saying, "Who then is greatest in the Kingdom of Heaven?"

[18:2]Jesus called a little child to himself, and set him in the midst of them, [18:3]and said, **"Most certainly I tell you, unless you turn, and become as little children, you will in no way enter into the Kingdom of Heaven. [18:4]Whoever therefore humbles himself as this little child, the same is the greatest in the Kingdom of Heaven. [18:5]Whoever receives one such little child in my name receives me, [18:6]but whoever causes one of these little ones who believe in me to stumble, it would be better for him that a huge millstone should be hung around his neck, and that he should be sunk in the depths of the sea. [18:7]"Woe to the world because of occasions of stumbling! For it must be that the occasions come, but woe to that person through whom the occasion comes! [18:8]If your hand or your foot causes you to stumble, cut it off, and cast it from you. It is better for you to enter into life maimed or crippled, rather than having two hands or two feet to be cast into the eternal fire. [18:9]If your eye causes you to stumble, pluck it out, and cast it from you.**

It is better for you to enter into life with one eye, rather than having two eyes to be cast into the Gehenna[b] of fire. [18:10]See that you don't despise one of these little ones, for I tell you that in heaven their angels always see the face of my Father who is in heaven. [18:11]For the Son of Man came to save that which was lost.

[18:12]**"What do you think? If a man has one hundred sheep, and one of them goes astray, doesn't he leave the ninety-nine, go to the mountains, and seek that which has gone astray? [18:13]If he finds it, most certainly I tell you, he rejoices over it more than over the ninety-nine which have not gone astray. [18:14]Even so it is not the will of your Father who is in heaven that one of these little ones should perish.**

[18:15]**"If your brother sins against you, go, show him his fault between you and him alone. If he listens to you, you have gained back your brother. [18:16]But if he doesn't listen, take one or two more with you, that at the mouth of two or three witnesses every word may be established.[c] [18:17]If he refuses to listen to them, tell it to the assembly. If he refuses to hear the assembly also, let him be to you as a Gentile or a tax collector. [18:18]Most certainly I tell you, whatever things you bind on earth will have been bound in heaven, and whatever things you release on earth will have been released in heaven. [18:19]Again, assuredly I tell you, that if two of you will agree on earth concerning anything that they will ask, it will be done for them by my Father who is in heaven. [18:20]For where two or three are gathered together in my name, there I am in the midst of them."**

[18:21]Then Peter came and said to him, "Lord, how often shall my brother sin against me, and I forgive him? Until seven times?"

---

[z]17:24 A didrachma is a Greek silver coin worth 2 drachmas, about as much as 2 Roman denarii, or about 2 days' wages. It was commonly used to pay the half-shekel temple tax, because 2 drachmas were worth one half shekel of silver.

[a]17:27 A stater is a silver coin equivalent to four Attic or two Alexandrian drachmas, or a Jewish shekel: just exactly enough to cover the half-shekel temple tax for two people.

[b]18:9 or, Hell

[c]18:16 Deuteronomy 19:15

18:22Jesus said to him, **"I don't tell you until seven times, but, until seventy times seven.** 18:23**Therefore the Kingdom of Heaven is like a certain king, who wanted to reconcile accounts with his servants.** 18:24**When he had begun to reconcile, one was brought to him who owed him ten thousand talents.**d 18:25**But because he couldn't pay, his lord commanded him to be sold, with his wife, his children, and all that he had, and payment to be made.** 18:26**The servant therefore fell down and kneeled before him, saying, 'Lord, have patience with me, and I will repay you all!'** 18:27**The lord of that servant, being moved with compassion, released him, and forgave him the debt.**

18:28**"But that servant went out, and found one of his fellow servants, who owed him one hundred denarii,**e **and he grabbed him, and took him by the throat, saying, 'Pay me what you owe!'** 18:29**"So his fellow servant fell down at his feet and begged him, saying, 'Have patience with me, and I will repay you!'** 18:30**He would not, but went and cast him into prison, until he should pay back that which was due.** 18:31**So when his fellow servants saw what was done, they were exceedingly sorry, and came and told to their lord all that was done.** 18:32**Then his lord called him in, and said to him, 'You wicked servant! I forgave you all that debt, because you begged me.** 18:33**Shouldn't you also have had mercy on your fellow servant, even as I had mercy on you?'** 18:34**His lord was angry, and delivered him to the tormentors, until he should pay all that was due to him.** 18:35**So my heavenly Father will also do to you, if you don't each forgive your brother from your hearts for his misdeeds."**

19:1It happened when Jesus had finished these words, he departed from Galilee, and came into the borders of Judea beyond the Jordan. 19:2Great multitudes followed him, and he healed them there. 19:3Pharisees came to him, testing him, and saying, "Is it lawful for a man to divorce his wife for any reason?"

19:4He answered, **"Haven't you read that he who made them from the beginning made them male and female,**f 19:5**and said, 'For this cause a man shall leave his father and mother, and shall join to his wife; and the two shall become one flesh?'**g 19:6**So that they are no more two, but one flesh. What therefore God has joined together, don't let man tear apart."**

19:7They asked him, "Why then did Moses command us to give her a bill of divorce, and divorce her?"

19:8He said to them, **"Moses, because of the hardness of your hearts, allowed you to divorce your wives, but from the beginning it has not been so.** 19:9**I tell you that whoever divorces his wife, except for sexual immorality, and marries another, commits adultery; and he who marries her when she is divorced commits adultery."**

19:10His disciples said to him, "If this is the case of the man with his wife, it is not expedient to marry."

19:11But he said to them, **"Not all men can receive this saying, but those to whom it is given.** 19:12**For there are eunuchs who were born that way from their mother's womb, and there are eunuchs who were made eunuchs by men; and there are eunuchs who made themselves eunuchs for the Kingdom of Heaven's sake. He who is able to receive it, let him receive it."**

19:13Then little children were brought to him, that he should lay his hands on them and pray; and the disciples rebuked them. 19:14But Jesus said, **"Allow the little children, and don't forbid them to come to me; for the Kingdom of Heaven belongs to ones like these."** 19:15He laid his hands on them, and departed from there.

19:16Behold, one came to him and said, "Good teacher, what good thing shall I do, that I may have eternal life?"

---

d18:24 Ten thousand talents represents an extremely large sum of money, equivalent to about 60,000,000 denarii, where one denarius was typical of one day's wages for agricultural labor.

e18:28 100 denarii was about one sixtieth of a talent.

f19:4 Genesis 1:27

g19:5 Genesis 2:24

[19:17]He said to him, "Why do you call me good? No one is good but one, that is, God. But if you want to enter into life, keep the commandments."

[19:18]He said to him, "Which ones?"

Jesus said, "'You shall not murder.' 'You shall not commit adultery.' 'You shall not steal.' 'You shall not offer false testimony.' [19:19]'Honor your father and mother.'[h] And, 'You shall love your neighbor as yourself.'"[i]

[19:20]The young man said to him, "All these things I have observed from my youth. What do I still lack?"

[19:21]Jesus said to him, "If you want to be perfect, go, sell what you have, and give to the poor, and you will have treasure in heaven; and come, follow me." [19:22]But when the young man heard the saying, he went away sad, for he was one who had great possessions. [19:23]Jesus said to his disciples, "Most certainly I say to you, a rich man will enter into the Kingdom of Heaven with difficulty. [19:24]Again I tell you, it is easier for a camel to go through a needle's eye, than for a rich man to enter into the Kingdom of God."

[19:25]When the disciples heard it, they were exceedingly astonished, saying, "Who then can be saved?"

[19:26]Looking at them, Jesus said, "With men this is impossible, but with God all things are possible."

[19:27]Then Peter answered, "Behold, we have left everything, and followed you. What then will we have?"

[19:28]Jesus said to them, "Most certainly I tell you that you who have followed me, in the regeneration when the Son of Man will sit on the throne of his glory, you also will sit on twelve thrones, judging the twelve tribes of Israel. [19:29]Everyone who has left houses, or brothers, or sisters, or father, or mother, or wife, or children, or lands, for my name's sake, will receive one hundred times, and will inherit eternal life. [19:30]But many will be last who are first; and first who are last.

[20:1]"For the Kingdom of Heaven is like a man who was the master of a household, who went out early in the morning to hire laborers for his vineyard. [20:2]When he had agreed with the laborers for a denarius[j] a day, he sent them into his vineyard. [20:3]He went out about the third hour,[k] and saw others standing idle in the marketplace. [20:4]To them he said, 'You also go into the vineyard, and whatever is right I will give you.' So they went their way. [20:5]Again he went out about the sixth and the ninth hour,[l] and did likewise. [20:6]About the eleventh hour[m] he went out, and found others standing idle. He said to them, 'Why do you stand here all day idle?'

[20:7]"They said to him, 'Because no one has hired us.'

"He said to them, 'You also go into the vineyard, and you will receive whatever is right.' [20:8]When evening had come, the lord of the vineyard said to his manager, 'Call the laborers and pay them their wages, beginning from the last to the first.'

[20:9]"When those who were hired at about the eleventh hour came, they each received a denarius. [20:10]When the first came, they supposed that they would receive more; and they likewise each received a denarius. [20:11]When they received it, they murmured against the master of the household, [20:12]saying, 'These last have spent one hour, and you have made them equal to us, who have borne the burden of the day and the scorching heat!'

[20:13]"But he answered one of them, 'Friend, I am doing you no wrong. Didn't you agree with me for a denarius? [20:14]Take that which is yours, and go your way. It is my desire to give to this last just as much as to you. [20:15]Isn't it lawful

---

[h]19:19 Exodus 20:12-16; Deuteronomy 5:16-20

[i]19:19 Leviticus 19:18

[j]20:2 A denarius is a silver Roman coin worth 1/25th of a Roman aureus. This was a common wage for a day of farm labor.

[k]20:3 Time was measured from sunrise to sunset, so the third hour would be about 9:00 AM.

[l]20:5 noon and 3:00 P. M.

[m]20:6 5:00 PM

for me to do what I want to with what I own? Or is your eye evil, because I am good?' ²⁰:¹⁶So the last will be first, and the first last. For many are called, but few are chosen."

²⁰:¹⁷As Jesus was going up to Jerusalem, he took the twelve disciples aside, and on the way he said to them, ²⁰:¹⁸"Behold, we are going up to Jerusalem, and the Son of Man will be delivered to the chief priests and scribes, and they will condemn him to death, ²⁰:¹⁹and will hand him over to the Gentiles to mock, to scourge, and to crucify; and the third day he will be raised up."

²⁰:²⁰Then the mother of the sons of Zebedee came to him with her sons, kneeling and asking a certain thing of him. ²⁰:²¹He said to her, "What do you want?"

She said to him, "Command that these, my two sons, may sit, one on your right hand, and one on your left hand, in your Kingdom."

²⁰:²²But Jesus answered, "You don't know what you are asking. Are you able to drink the cup that I am about to drink, and be baptized with the baptism that I am baptized with?"

They said to him, "We are able."

²⁰:²³He said to them, "You will indeed drink my cup, and be baptized with the baptism that I am baptized with, but to sit on my right hand and on my left hand is not mine to give; but it is for whom it has been prepared by my Father."

²⁰:²⁴When the ten heard it, they were indignant with the two brothers. ²⁰:²⁵But Jesus summoned them, and said, "You know that the rulers of the nations lord it over them, and their great ones exercise authority over them. ²⁰:²⁶It shall not be so among you, but whoever desires to become great among you shall be[n] your servant. ²⁰:²⁷Whoever desires to be first among you shall be your bondservant, ²⁰:²⁸even as the Son of Man came not to be served, but to serve, and to give his life as a ransom for many."

²⁰:²⁹As they went out from Jericho, a great multitude followed him. ²⁰:³⁰Behold, two blind men sitting by the road, when they heard that Jesus was passing by, cried out, "Lord, have mercy on us, you son of David!" ²⁰:³¹The multitude rebuked them, telling them that they should be quiet, but they cried out even more, "Lord, have mercy on us, you son of David!"

²⁰:³²Jesus stood still, and called them, and asked, "What do you want me to do for you?"

²⁰:³³They told him, "Lord, that our eyes may be opened."

²⁰:³⁴Jesus, being moved with compassion, touched their eyes; and immediately their eyes received their sight, and they followed him.

²¹:¹When they drew near to Jerusalem, and came to Bethsphage,[o] to the Mount of Olives, then Jesus sent two disciples, ²¹:²saying to them, "Go into the village that is opposite you, and immediately you will find a donkey tied, and a colt with her. Untie them, and bring them to me. ²¹:³If anyone says anything to you, you shall say, 'The Lord needs them,' and immediately he will send them."

²¹:⁴All this was done, that it might be fulfilled which was spoken through the prophet, saying,

²¹:⁵"Tell the daughter of Zion,

behold, your King comes to you,

humble, and riding on a donkey,

on a colt, the foal of a donkey."[p]

²¹:⁶The disciples went, and did just as Jesus commanded them, ²¹:⁷and brought the donkey and the colt, and laid their clothes on them; and he sat on them. ²¹:⁸A very great multitude spread their clothes on the road. Others cut branches from the trees, and spread them on the road. ²¹:⁹The multitudes who went before him, and who followed kept shouting, "Hosanna[q] to the son of David! Blessed is he who comes

---

[n]20:26 TR reads "let him be" instead of "shall be"
[o]21:1 TR & NU read "Bethphage" instead of "Bethsphage"
[p]21:5 Zechariah 9:9
[q]21:9 "Hosanna" means "save us" or "help us, we pray."

in the name of the Lord! Hosanna in the highest!"[r]

21:10When he had come into Jerusalem, all the city was stirred up, saying, "Who is this?" 21:11The multitudes said, "This is the prophet, Jesus, from Nazareth of Galilee."

21:12Jesus entered into the temple of God, and drove out all of those who sold and bought in the temple, and overthrew the money changers' tables and the seats of those who sold the doves. 21:13He said to them, **"It is written, 'My house shall be called a house of prayer,'[s] but you have made it a den of robbers!"[t]**

21:14The blind and the lame came to him in the temple, and he healed them. 21:15But when the chief priests and the scribes saw the wonderful things that he did, and the children who were crying in the temple and saying, "Hosanna to the son of David!" they were indignant, 21:16and said to him, "Do you hear what these are saying?"

Jesus said to them, **"Yes. Did you never read, 'Out of the mouth of babes and nursing babies you have perfected praise?'"[u]**

21:17He left them, and went out of the city to Bethany, and lodged there. 21:18Now in the morning, as he returned to the city, he was hungry. 21:19Seeing a fig tree by the road, he came to it, and found nothing on it but leaves. He said to it, **"Let there be no fruit from you forever!"**

Immediately the fig tree withered away. 21:20When the disciples saw it, they marveled, saying, "How did the fig tree immediately wither away?"

21:21Jesus answered them, **"Most certainly I tell you, if you have faith, and don't doubt, you will not only do what was done to the fig tree, but even if you told this mountain, 'Be taken up and cast into the sea,' it would be done. 21:22All things, whatever you ask in prayer, believing, you will receive."**

21:23When he had come into the temple, the chief priests and the elders of the people came to him as he was teaching, and said, "By what authority do you do these things? Who gave you this authority?"

21:24Jesus answered them, **"I also will ask you one question, which if you tell me, I likewise will tell you by what authority I do these things. 21:25The baptism of John, where was it from? From heaven or from men?"**

They reasoned with themselves, saying, "If we say, 'From heaven,' he will ask us, 'Why then did you not believe him?' 21:26But if we say, 'From men,' we fear the multitude, for all hold John as a prophet." 21:27They answered Jesus, and said, "We don't know."

He also said to them, **"Neither will I tell you by what authority I do these things. 21:28But what do you think? A man had two sons, and he came to the first, and said, 'Son, go work today in my vineyard.' 21:29He answered, 'I will not,' but afterward he changed his mind, and went. 21:30He came to the second, and said the same thing. He answered, 'I go, sir,' but he didn't go. 21:31Which of the two did the will of his father?"**

They said to him, "The first."

Jesus said to them, **"Most certainly I tell you that the tax collectors and the prostitutes are entering into the Kingdom of God before you. 21:32For John came to you in the way of righteousness, and you didn't believe him, but the tax collectors and the prostitutes believed him. When you saw it, you didn't even repent afterward, that you might believe him.**

21:33**"Hear another parable. There was a man who was a master of a household, who planted a vineyard, set a hedge about it, dug a winepress in it, built a tower, leased it out to farmers, and went into another country. 21:34When the season for the fruit drew near, he sent his servants to the farmers, to receive his fruit. 21:35The farmers took his servants, beat one, killed another, and stoned another. 21:36Again, he sent other servants more than the first: and they treated them the**

---

r 21:9 Psalm 118:26
s 21:13 Isaiah 56:7
t 21:13 Jeremiah 7:11
u 21:16 Psalm 8:2

same way. [21:37]But afterward he sent to them his son, saying, 'They will respect my son.' [21:38]But the farmers, when they saw the son, said among themselves, 'This is the heir. Come, let's kill him, and seize his inheritance.' [21:39]So they took him, and threw him out of the vineyard, and killed him. [21:40]When therefore the lord of the vineyard comes, what will he do to those farmers?"

[21:41]They told him, "He will miserably destroy those miserable men, and will lease out the vineyard to other farmers, who will give him the fruit in its season."

[21:42]Jesus said to them, **"Did you never read in the Scriptures,**

'The stone which the builders rejected,
   the same was made the head of the corner.

This was from the Lord.

   It is marvelous in our eyes?"[v]

[21:43]**"Therefore I tell you, the Kingdom of God will be taken away from you, and will be given to a nation bringing forth its fruit.** [21:44]**He who falls on this stone will be broken to pieces, but on whoever it will fall, it will scatter him as dust."**

[21:45]When the chief priests and the Pharisees heard his parables, they perceived that he spoke about them. [21:46]When they sought to seize him, they feared the multitudes, because they considered him to be a prophet.

[22:1]Jesus answered and spoke again in parables to them, saying, [22:2]**"The Kingdom of Heaven is like a certain king, who made a marriage feast for his son,** [22:3]**and sent out his servants to call those who were invited to the marriage feast, but they would not come.** [22:4]**Again he sent out other servants, saying, 'Tell those who are invited, "Behold, I have made ready my dinner. My cattle and my fatlings are killed, and all things are ready. Come to the marriage feast!"'** [22:5]**But they made light of it, and went their ways, one to his own farm, another to his merchandise,** [22:6]**and the rest grabbed his servants, and treated them shamefully, and killed them.** [22:7]**When the king heard that, he was angry, and sent his armies, destroyed those**

murderers, and burned their city.

[22:8]**"Then he said to his servants, 'The wedding is ready, but those who were invited weren't worthy.** [22:9]**Go therefore to the intersections of the highways, and as many as you may find, invite to the marriage feast.'** [22:10]**Those servants went out into the highways, and gathered together as many as they found, both bad and good. The wedding was filled with guests.** [22:11]**But when the king came in to see the guests, he saw there a man who didn't have on wedding clothing,** [22:12]**and he said to him, 'Friend, how did you come in here not wearing wedding clothing?' He was speechless.** [22:13]**Then the king said to the servants, 'Bind him hand and foot, take him away, and throw him into the outer darkness; there is where the weeping and grinding of teeth will be.'** [22:14]**For many are called, but few chosen."**

[22:15]Then the Pharisees went and took counsel how they might entrap him in his talk. [22:16]They sent their disciples to him, along with the Herodians, saying, "Teacher, we know that you are honest, and teach the way of God in truth, no matter who you teach, for you aren't partial to anyone. [22:17]Tell us therefore, what do you think? Is it lawful to pay taxes to Caesar, or not?"

[22:18]But Jesus perceived their wickedness, and said, **"Why do you test me, you hypocrites?** [22:19]**Show me the tax money."**

They brought to him a denarius.

[22:20]He asked them, **"Whose is this image and inscription?"**

[22:21]They said to him, "Caesar's."

Then he said to them, **"Give therefore to Caesar the things that are Caesar's, and to God the things that are God's."**

[22:22]When they heard it, they marveled, and left him, and went away.

[22:23]On that day Sadducees (those who say that there is no resurrection) came to him. They asked him, [22:24]saying, "Teacher, Moses said, 'If a man dies, having no children, his brother shall marry his wife, and raise up seed for his brother.' [22:25]Now there were with us seven brothers. The first married and died, and having no seed

---

[v]21:42 Psalm 118:22-23

left his wife to his brother. [22:26] In like manner the second also, and the third, to the seventh. [22:27] After them all, the woman died. [22:28] In the resurrection therefore, whose wife will she be of the seven? For they all had her."

[22:29] But Jesus answered them, **"You are mistaken, not knowing the Scriptures, nor the power of God.** [22:30] **For in the resurrection they neither marry, nor are given in marriage, but are like God's angels in heaven.** [22:31] **But concerning the resurrection of the dead, haven't you read that which was spoken to you by God, saying,** [22:32] **'I am the God of Abraham, and the God of Isaac, and the God of Jacob?'[w] God is not the God of the dead, but of the living."**

[22:33] When the multitudes heard it, they were astonished at his teaching. [22:34] But the Pharisees, when they heard that he had silenced the Sadducees, gathered themselves together. [22:35] One of them, a lawyer, asked him a question, testing him. [22:36] "Teacher, which is the greatest commandment in the law?"

[22:37] Jesus said to him, **"'You shall love the Lord your God with all your heart, with all your soul, and with all your mind.'[x]** [22:38] **This is the first and great commandment.** [22:39] **A second likewise is this, 'You shall love your neighbor as yourself.'[y]** [22:40] **The whole law and the prophets depend on these two commandments."**

[22:41] Now while the Pharisees were gathered together, Jesus asked them a question, [22:42] saying, **"What do you think of the Christ? Whose son is he?"**

They said to him, "Of David."

[22:43] He said to them, **"How then does David in the Spirit call him Lord, saying,** [22:44] **'The Lord said to my Lord,**

    sit on my right hand,

    until I make your enemies a footstool

for your feet?'[z]

[22:45] **"If then David calls him Lord, how is he his son?"**

[22:46] No one was able to answer him a word, neither did any man dare ask him any more questions from that day forth.

[23:1] Then Jesus spoke to the multitudes and to his disciples, [23:2] saying, **"The scribes and the Pharisees sat on Moses' seat.** [23:3] **All things therefore whatever they tell you to observe, observe and do, but don't do their works; for they say, and don't do.** [23:4] **For they bind heavy burdens that are grievous to be borne, and lay them on men's shoulders; but they themselves will not lift a finger to help them.** [23:5] **But all their works they do to be seen by men. They make their phylacteries[a] broad, enlarge the fringes[b] of their garments,** [23:6] **and love the place of honor at feasts, the best seats in the synagogues,** [23:7] **the salutations in the marketplaces, and to be called 'Rabbi, Rabbi' by men.** [23:8] **But don't you be called 'Rabbi,' for one is your teacher, the Christ, and all of you are brothers.** [23:9] **Call no man on the earth your father, for one is your Father, he who is in heaven.** [23:10] **Neither be called masters, for one is your master, the Christ.** [23:11] **But he who is greatest among you will be your servant.** [23:12] **Whoever exalts himself will be humbled, and whoever humbles himself will be exalted.**

[23:13] **"Woe to you, scribes and Pharisees, hypocrites! For you devour widows' houses, and as a pretense you make long prayers. Therefore you will receive greater condemnation.**

[23:14] **"But woe to you, scribes and Pharisees, hypocrites! Because you shut up the Kingdom of Heaven against men; for you don't enter in yourselves, neither do you**

---

[w] 22:32 Exodus 3:6
[x] 22:37 Deuteronomy 6:5
[y] 22:39 Leviticus 19:18
[z] 22:44 Psalm 110:1
[a] 23:5 phylacteries (tefillin in Hebrew) are small leather pouches that some Jewish men wear on their forehead and arm in prayer. They are used to carry a small scroll with some Scripture in it. See Deuteronomy 6:8.
[b] 23:5 or, tassels

allow those who are entering in to enter.[c]
23:15 Woe to you, scribes and Pharisees, hypocrites! For you travel around by sea and land to make one proselyte; and when he becomes one, you make him twice as much of a son of Gehenna[d] as yourselves.

23:16 "Woe to you, you blind guides, who say, 'Whoever swears by the temple, it is nothing; but whoever swears by the gold of the temple, he is obligated.' 23:17 You blind fools! For which is greater, the gold, or the temple that sanctifies the gold? 23:18 'Whoever swears by the altar, it is nothing; but whoever swears by the gift that is on it, he is obligated?' 23:19 You blind fools! For which is greater, the gift, or the altar that sanctifies the gift? 23:20 He therefore who swears by the altar, swears by it, and by everything on it. 23:21 He who swears by the temple, swears by it, and by him who was living in it. 23:22 He who swears by heaven, swears by the throne of God, and by him who sits on it.

23:23 "Woe to you, scribes and Pharisees, hypocrites! For you tithe mint, dill, and cumin,[e] and have left undone the weightier matters of the law: justice, mercy, and faith. But you ought to have done these, and not to have left the other undone. 23:24 You blind guides, who strain out a gnat, and swallow a camel!

23:25 "Woe to you, scribes and Pharisees, hypocrites! For you clean the outside of the cup and of the platter, but within they are full of extortion and unrighteousness.[f] 23:26 You blind Pharisee, first clean the inside of the cup and of the platter, that its outside may become clean also.

23:27 "Woe to you, scribes and Pharisees, hypocrites! For you are like whitened tombs, which outwardly appear beautiful, but inwardly are full of dead men's bones, and of all uncleanness. 23:28 Even so you also outwardly appear righteous to men, but inwardly you are full of hypocrisy and iniquity.

23:29 "Woe to you, scribes and Pharisees, hypocrites! For you build the tombs of the prophets, and decorate the tombs of the righteous, 23:30 and say, 'If we had lived in the days of our fathers, we wouldn't have been partakers with them in the blood of the prophets.' 23:31 Therefore you testify to yourselves that you are children of those who killed the prophets. 23:32 Fill up, then, the measure of your fathers. 23:33 You serpents, you offspring of vipers, how will you escape the judgment of Gehenna[g]? 23:34 Therefore, behold, I send to you prophets, wise men, and scribes. Some of them you will kill and crucify; and some of them you will scourge in your synagogues, and persecute from city to city; 23:35 that on you may come all the righteous blood shed on the earth, from the blood of righteous Abel to the blood of Zachariah son of Barachiah, whom you killed between the sanctuary and the altar. 23:36 Most certainly I tell you, all these things will come upon this generation.

23:37 "Jerusalem, Jerusalem, who kills the prophets, and stones those who are sent to her! How often I would have gathered your children together, even as a hen gathers her chicks under her wings, and you would not! 23:38 Behold, your house is left to you desolate. 23:39 For I tell you, you will not see me from now on, until you say, 'Blessed is he who comes in the name of the Lord!'"[h]

24:1 Jesus went out from the temple, and was going on his way. His disciples came to him to show him the buildings of the temple. 24:2 But he answered them, "Don't you see all of these things? Most certainly I tell you, there will not be left here one stone on another, that will not be thrown down."

---

[c]23:14 Some Greek manuscripts reverse the order of verses 13 and 14, and some omit verse 13, numbering verse 14 as 13.

[d]23:15 or, Hell

[e]23:23 cumin is an aromatic seed from Cuminum cyminum, resembling caraway in flavor and appearance. It is used as a spice.

[f]23:25 TR reads "self-indulgence" instead of "unrighteousness"

[g]23:33 or, Hell

[h]23:39 Psalm 118:26

24:3 As he sat on the Mount of Olives, the disciples came to him privately, saying, "Tell us, when will these things be? What is the sign of your coming, and of the end of the age?"

24:4 Jesus answered them, **"Be careful that no one leads you astray.** 24:5 **For many will come in my name, saying, 'I am the Christ,' and will lead many astray.** 24:6 **You will hear of wars and rumors of wars. See that you aren't troubled, for all this must happen, but the end is not yet.** 24:7 **For nation will rise against nation, and kingdom against kingdom; and there will be famines, plagues, and earthquakes in various places.** 24:8 **But all these things are the beginning of birth pains.** 24:9 **Then they will deliver you up to oppression, and will kill you. You will be hated by all of the nations for my name's sake.** 24:10 **Then many will stumble, and will deliver up one another, and will hate one another.** 24:11 **Many false prophets will arise, and will lead many astray.** 24:12 **Because iniquity will be multiplied, the love of many will grow cold.** 24:13 **But he who endures to the end, the same will be saved.** 24:14 **This Good News of the Kingdom will be preached in the whole world for a testimony to all the nations, and then the end will come.**

24:15 **"When, therefore, you see the abomination of desolation,**[i] **which was spoken of through Daniel the prophet, standing in the holy place (let the reader understand),** 24:16 **then let those who are in Judea flee to the mountains.** 24:17 **Let him who is on the housetop not go down to take out things that are in his house.** 24:18 **Let him who is in the field not return back to get his clothes.** 24:19 **But woe to those who are with child and to nursing mothers in those days!** 24:20 **Pray that your flight will not be in the winter, nor on a Sabbath,** 24:21 **for then there will be great oppression, such as has not been from the beginning of the world until now, no, nor ever will be.** 24:22 **Unless those days had been shortened, no flesh would have been saved. But for the sake of the chosen ones, those days will be shortened.**

24:23 **"Then if any man tells you, 'Behold, here is the Christ,' or, 'There,' don't believe it.** 24:24 **For there will arise false christs, and false prophets, and they will show great signs and wonders, so as to lead astray, if possible, even the chosen ones.**

24:25 **"Behold, I have told you beforehand.** 24:26 **If therefore they tell you, 'Behold, he is in the wilderness,' don't go out; 'Behold, he is in the inner chambers,' don't believe it.** 24:27 **For as the lightning flashes from the east, and is seen even to the west, so will be the coming of the Son of Man.** 24:28 **For wherever the carcass is, there is where the vultures**[j] **gather together.** 24:29 **But immediately after the oppression of those days, the sun will be darkened, the moon will not give its light, the stars will fall from the sky, and the powers of the heavens will be shaken;**[k] 24:30 **and then the sign of the Son of Man will appear in the sky. Then all the tribes of the earth will mourn, and they will see the Son of Man coming on the clouds of the sky with power and great glory.** 24:31 **He will send out his angels with a great sound of a trumpet, and they will gather together his chosen ones from the four winds, from one end of the sky to the other.**

24:32 **"Now from the fig tree learn this parable. When its branch has now become tender, and puts forth its leaves, you know that the summer is near.** 24:33 **Even so you also, when you see all these things, know that it is near, even at the doors.** 24:34 **Most certainly I tell you, this generation**[l] **will not pass away, until all these things are accomplished.** 24:35 **Heaven and earth will pass away, but my words will not pass away.** 24:36 **But no one knows of that day and hour, not even the angels of heaven, but my Father only.**

---

i 24:15 Daniel 9:27; 11:31; 12:11

j 24:28 or, eagles

k 24:29 Isaiah 13:10; 34:4

l 24:34 The word for "generation" (genea) can also be translated as "race."

[24:37] "As the days of Noah were, so will be the coming of the Son of Man. [24:38] For as in those days which were before the flood they were eating and drinking, marrying and giving in marriage, until the day that Noah entered into the ship, [24:39] and they didn't know until the flood came, and took them all away, so will be the coming of the Son of Man. [24:40] Then two men will be in the field: one will be taken and one will be left; [24:41] two women grinding at the mill, one will be taken and one will be left. [24:42] Watch therefore, for you don't know in what hour your Lord comes. [24:43] But know this, that if the master of the house had known in what watch of the night the thief was coming, he would have watched, and would not have allowed his house to be broken into. [24:44] Therefore also be ready, for in an hour that you don't expect, the Son of Man will come.

[24:45] "Who then is the faithful and wise servant, whom his lord has set over his household, to give them their food in due season? [24:46] Blessed is that servant whom his lord finds doing so when he comes. [24:47] Most certainly I tell you that he will set him over all that he has. [24:48] But if that evil servant should say in his heart, 'My lord is delaying his coming,' [24:49] and begins to beat his fellow servants, and eat and drink with the drunkards, [24:50] the lord of that servant will come in a day when he doesn't expect it, and in an hour when he doesn't know it, [24:51] and will cut him in pieces, and appoint his portion with the hypocrites. There is where the weeping and grinding of teeth will be.

[25:1] "Then the Kingdom of Heaven will be like ten virgins, who took their lamps, and went out to meet the bridegroom. [25:2] Five of them were foolish, and five were wise. [25:3] Those who were foolish, when they took their lamps, took no oil with them, [25:4] but the wise took oil in their vessels with their lamps. [25:5] Now while the bridegroom delayed, they all slumbered and slept. [25:6] But at midnight there was a cry, 'Behold! The bridegroom is coming! Come out to meet him!' [25:7] Then all those virgins arose, and trimmed their lamps.[m] [25:8] The foolish said to the wise, 'Give us some of your oil, for our lamps are going out.' [25:9] But the wise answered, saying, 'What if there isn't enough for us and you? You go rather to those who sell, and buy for yourselves.' [25:10] While they went away to buy, the bridegroom came, and those who were ready went in with him to the marriage feast, and the door was shut. [25:11] Afterward the other virgins also came, saying, 'Lord, Lord, open to us.' [25:12] But he answered, 'Most certainly I tell you, I don't know you.' [25:13] Watch therefore, for you don't know the day nor the hour in which the Son of Man is coming.

[25:14] "For it is like a man, going into another country, who called his own servants, and entrusted his goods to them. [25:15] To one he gave five talents, to another two, to another one; to each according to his own ability. Then he went on his journey. [25:16] Immediately he who received the five talents went and traded with them, and made another five talents. [25:17] In like manner he also who got the two gained another two. [25:18] But he who received the one went away and dug in the earth, and hid his lord's money.

[25:19] "Now after a long time the lord of those servants came, and reconciled accounts with them. [25:20] He who received the five talents came and brought another five talents, saying, 'Lord, you delivered to me five talents. Behold, I have gained another five talents besides them.'

[25:21] "His lord said to him, 'Well done, good and faithful servant. You have been faithful over a few things, I will set you over many things. Enter into the joy of your lord.'

[25:22] "He also who got the two talents came and said, 'Lord, you delivered to me two talents. Behold, I have gained another two talents besides them.'

[25:23] "His lord said to him, 'Well done,

---

[m] 25:7 The end of the wick of an oil lamp needs to be cut off periodically to avoid having it become clogged with carbon deposits. The wick height is also adjusted so that the flame burns evenly and gives good light without producing a lot of smoke.

good and faithful servant. You have been faithful over a few things, I will set you over many things. Enter into the joy of your lord.'

25:24 "He also who had received the one talent came and said, 'Lord, I knew you that you are a hard man, reaping where you did not sow, and gathering where you did not scatter. 25:25 I was afraid, and went away and hid your talent in the earth. Behold, you have what is yours.'

25:26 "But his lord answered him, 'You wicked and slothful servant. You knew that I reap where I didn't sow, and gather where I didn't scatter. 25:27 You ought therefore to have deposited my money with the bankers, and at my coming I should have received back my own with interest. 25:28 Take away therefore the talent from him, and give it to him who has the ten talents. 25:29 For to everyone who has will be given, and he will have abundance, but from him who doesn't have, even that which he has will be taken away. 25:30 Throw out the unprofitable servant into the outer darkness, where there will be weeping and gnashing of teeth.'

25:31 "But when the Son of Man comes in his glory, and all the holy angels with him, then he will sit on the throne of his glory. 25:32 Before him all the nations will be gathered, and he will separate them one from another, as a shepherd separates the sheep from the goats. 25:33 He will set the sheep on his right hand, but the goats on the left. 25:34 Then the King will tell those on his right hand, 'Come, blessed of my Father, inherit the Kingdom prepared for you from the foundation of the world; 25:35 for I was hungry, and you gave me food to eat; I was thirsty, and you gave me drink; I was a stranger, and you took me in; 25:36 naked, and you clothed me; I was sick, and you visited me; I was in prison, and you came to me.'

25:37 "Then the righteous will answer him, saying, 'Lord, when did we see you hungry, and feed you; or thirsty, and give you a drink? 25:38 When did we see you

as a stranger, and take you in; or naked, and clothe you? 25:39 When did we see you sick, or in prison, and come to you?'

25:40 "The King will answer them, 'Most certainly I tell you, inasmuch as you did it to one of the least of these my brothers[n], you did it to me.' 25:41 Then he will say also to those on the left hand, 'Depart from me, you cursed, into the eternal fire which is prepared for the devil and his angels; 25:42 for I was hungry, and you didn't give me food to eat; I was thirsty, and you gave me no drink; 25:43 I was a stranger, and you didn't take me in; naked, and you didn't clothe me; sick, and in prison, and you didn't visit me.'

25:44 "Then they will also answer, saying, 'Lord, when did we see you hungry, or thirsty, or a stranger, or naked, or sick, or in prison, and didn't help you?'

25:45 "Then he will answer them, saying, 'Most certainly I tell you, inasmuch as you didn't do it to one of the least of these, you didn't do it to me.' 25:46 These will go away into eternal punishment, but the righteous into eternal life."

26:1 It happened, when Jesus had finished all these words, that he said to his disciples, 26:2 "You know that after two days the Passover is coming, and the Son of Man will be delivered up to be crucified."

26:3 Then the chief priests, the scribes, and the elders of the people were gathered together in the court of the high priest, who was called Caiaphas. 26:4 They took counsel together that they might take Jesus by deceit, and kill him. 26:5 But they said, "Not during the feast, lest a riot occur among the people."

26:6 Now when Jesus was in Bethany, in the house of Simon the leper, 26:7 a woman came to him having an alabaster jar of very expensive ointment, and she poured it on his head as he sat at the table. 26:8 But when his disciples saw this, they were indignant, saying, "Why this waste? 26:9 For this ointment might have been sold for much, and given to the poor."

---

[n]25:40 The word for "brothers" here may be also correctly translated "brothers and sisters" or "siblings."

26:10However, knowing this, Jesus said to them, **"Why do you trouble the woman? Because she has done a good work for me.** 26:11**For you always have the poor with you; but you don't always have me.** 26:12**For in pouring this ointment on my body, she did it to prepare me for burial.** 26:13**Most certainly I tell you, wherever this Good News is preached in the whole world, what this woman has done will also be spoken of as a memorial of her."**

26:14Then one of the twelve, who was called Judas Iscariot, went to the chief priests, 26:15and said, "What are you willing to give me, that I should deliver him to you?" They weighed out for him thirty pieces of silver. 26:16From that time he sought opportunity to betray him.

26:17Now on the first day of unleavened bread, the disciples came to Jesus, saying to him, "Where do you want us to prepare for you to eat the Passover?"

26:18He said, **"Go into the city to a certain person, and tell him, 'The Teacher says, "My time is at hand. I will keep the Passover at your house with my disciples."'"**

26:19The disciples did as Jesus commanded them, and they prepared the Passover. 26:20Now when evening had come, he was reclining at the table with the twelve disciples. 26:21As they were eating, he said, **"Most certainly I tell you that one of you will betray me."**

26:22They were exceedingly sorrowful, and each began to ask him, "It isn't me, is it, Lord?"

26:23He answered, **"He who dipped his hand with me in the dish, the same will betray me.** 26:24**The Son of Man goes, even as it is written of him, but woe to that man through whom the Son of Man is betrayed! It would be better for that man if he had not been born."**

26:25Judas, who betrayed him, answered, "It isn't me, is it, Rabbi?"

He said to him, **"You said it."**

26:26As they were eating, Jesus took bread, gave thanks for° it, and broke it. He gave to the disciples, and said, **"Take, eat; this is my body."** 26:27He took the cup, gave thanks, and gave to them, saying, **"All of you drink it,** 26:28**for this is my blood of the new covenant, which is poured out for many for the remission of sins.** 26:29**But I tell you that I will not drink of this fruit of the vine from now on, until that day when I drink it anew with you in my Father's Kingdom."** 26:30When they had sung a hymn, they went out to the Mount of Olives.

26:31Then Jesus said to them, **"All of you will be made to stumble because of me tonight, for it is written, 'I will strike the shepherd, and the sheep of the flock will be scattered.'ᴾ** 26:32**But after I am raised up, I will go before you into Galilee."**

26:33But Peter answered him, "Even if all will be made to stumble because of you, I will never be made to stumble."

26:34Jesus said to him, **"Most certainly I tell you that tonight, before the rooster crows, you will deny me three times."**

26:35Peter said to him, "Even if I must die with you, I will not deny you." All of the disciples also said likewise.

26:36Then Jesus came with them to a place called Gethsemane, and said to his disciples, **"Sit here, while I go there and pray."** 26:37He took with him Peter and the two sons of Zebedee, and began to be sorrowful and severely troubled. 26:38Then he said to them, **"My soul is exceedingly sorrowful, even to death. Stay here, and watch with me."**

26:39He went forward a little, fell on his face, and prayed, saying, **"My Father, if it is possible, let this cup pass away from me; nevertheless, not what I desire, but what you desire."**

26:40He came to the disciples, and found them sleeping, and said to Peter, **"What, couldn't you watch with me for one hour?** 26:41**Watch and pray, that you don't enter into temptation. The spirit indeed is willing, but the flesh is weak."**

26:42Again, a second time he went away, and prayed, saying, **"My Father, if this cup can't pass away from me unless I drink**

°26:26 TR reads "blessed" instead of "gave thanks for"
ᴾ26:31 Zechariah 13:7

it, **your desire be done."** ²⁶:⁴³He came again and found them sleeping, for their eyes were heavy. ²⁶:⁴⁴He left them again, went away, and prayed a third time, saying the same words. ²⁶:⁴⁵Then he came to his disciples, and said to them, **"Sleep on now, and take your rest. Behold, the hour is at hand, and the Son of Man is betrayed into the hands of sinners. ²⁶:⁴⁶Arise, let's be going. Behold, he who betrays me is at hand."**

²⁶:⁴⁷While he was still speaking, behold, Judas, one of the twelve, came, and with him a great multitude with swords and clubs, from the chief priest and elders of the people. ²⁶:⁴⁸Now he who betrayed him gave them a sign, saying, "Whoever I kiss, he is the one. Seize him." ²⁶:⁴⁹Immediately he came to Jesus, and said, "Hail, Rabbi!" and kissed him.

²⁶:⁵⁰Jesus said to him, **"Friend, why are you here?"** Then they came and laid hands on Jesus, and took him. ²⁶:⁵¹Behold, one of those who were with Jesus stretched out his hand, and drew his sword, and struck the servant of the high priest, and struck off his ear. ²⁶:⁵²Then Jesus said to him, **"Put your sword back into its place, for all those who take the sword will die by the sword. ²⁶:⁵³Or do you think that I couldn't ask my Father, and he would even now send me more than twelve legions of angels? ²⁶:⁵⁴How then would the Scriptures be fulfilled that it must be so?"**

²⁶:⁵⁵In that hour Jesus said to the multitudes, **"Have you come out as against a robber with swords and clubs to seize me? I sat daily in the temple teaching, and you didn't arrest me. ²⁶:⁵⁶But all this has happened, that the Scriptures of the prophets might be fulfilled."**

Then all the disciples left him, and fled. ²⁶:⁵⁷Those who had taken Jesus led him away to Caiaphas the high priest, where the scribes and the elders were gathered together. ²⁶:⁵⁸But Peter followed him from a distance, to the court of the high priest, and entered in and sat with the officers, to see the end. ²⁶:⁵⁹Now the chief priests, the elders, and the whole council sought false testimony against Jesus, that they might put him to death; ²⁶:⁶⁰and they found none.

Even though many false witnesses came forward, they found none. But at last two false witnesses came forward, ²⁶:⁶¹and said, "This man said, 'I am able to destroy the temple of God, and to build it in three days.'"

²⁶:⁶²The high priest stood up, and said to him, "Have you no answer? What is this that these testify against you?" ²⁶:⁶³But Jesus held his peace. The high priest answered him, "I adjure you by the living God, that you tell us whether you are the Christ, the Son of God."

²⁶:⁶⁴Jesus said to him, **"You have said it. Nevertheless, I tell you, after this you will see the Son of Man sitting at the right hand of Power, and coming on the clouds of the sky."**

²⁶:⁶⁵Then the high priest tore his clothing, saying, "He has spoken blasphemy! Why do we need any more witnesses? Behold, now you have heard his blasphemy. ²⁶:⁶⁶What do you think?"

They answered, "He is worthy of death!" ²⁶:⁶⁷Then they spit in his face and beat him with their fists, and some slapped him, ²⁶:⁶⁸saying, "Prophesy to us, you Christ! Who hit you?"

²⁶:⁶⁹Now Peter was sitting outside in the court, and a maid came to him, saying, "You were also with Jesus, the Galilean!" ²⁶:⁷⁰But he denied it before them all, saying, "I don't know what you are talking about."

²⁶:⁷¹When he had gone out onto the porch, someone else saw him, and said to those who were there, "This man also was with Jesus of Nazareth."

²⁶:⁷²Again he denied it with an oath, "I don't know the man."

²⁶:⁷³After a little while those who stood by came and said to Peter, "Surely you are also one of them, for your speech makes you known."

²⁶:⁷⁴Then he began to curse and to swear, "I don't know the man!"

Immediately the rooster crowed. ²⁶:⁷⁵Peter remembered the word which Jesus had said to him, "Before the rooster crows, you will deny me three times." He went out and wept bitterly.

[27:1] Now when morning had come, all the chief priests and the elders of the people took counsel against Jesus to put him to death: [27:2] and they bound him, and led him away, and delivered him up to Pontius Pilate, the governor. [27:3] Then Judas, who betrayed him, when he saw that Jesus was condemned, felt remorse, and brought back the thirty pieces of silver to the chief priests and elders, [27:4] saying, "I have sinned in that I betrayed innocent blood."

But they said, "What is that to us? You see to it."

[27:5] He threw down the pieces of silver in the sanctuary, and departed. He went away and hanged himself. [27:6] The chief priests took the pieces of silver, and said, "It's not lawful to put them into the treasury, since it is the price of blood." [27:7] They took counsel, and bought the potter's field with them, to bury strangers in. [27:8] Therefore that field was called "The Field of Blood" to this day. [27:9] Then that which was spoken through Jeremiah[q] the prophet was fulfilled, saying, "They took the thirty pieces of silver,

the price of him upon whom a price had been set,

whom some of the children of Israel priced,

[27:10] and they gave them for the potter's field,

as the Lord commanded me."[r]

[27:11] Now Jesus stood before the governor: and the governor asked him, saying, "Are you the King of the Jews?"

Jesus said to him, **"So you say."**

[27:12] When he was accused by the chief priests and elders, he answered nothing. [27:13] Then Pilate said to him, "Don't you hear how many things they testify against you?"

[27:14] He gave him no answer, not even one word, so that the governor marveled greatly. [27:15] Now at the feast the governor was accustomed to release to the multitude one prisoner, whom they desired. [27:16] They had then a notable prisoner, called Barabbas. [27:17] When therefore they were gathered together, Pilate said to them, "Whom do you want me to release to you? Barabbas, or Jesus, who is called Christ?" [27:18] For he knew that because of envy they had delivered him up.

[27:19] While he was sitting on the judgment seat, his wife sent to him, saying, "Have nothing to do with that righteous man, for I have suffered many things this day in a dream because of him." [27:20] Now the chief priests and the elders persuaded the multitudes to ask for Barabbas, and destroy Jesus. [27:21] But the governor answered them, "Which of the two do you want me to release to you?"

They said, "Barabbas!"

[27:22] Pilate said to them, "What then shall I do to Jesus, who is called Christ?"

They all said to him, "Let him be crucified!"

[27:23] But the governor said, "Why? What evil has he done?"

But they cried out exceedingly, saying, "Let him be crucified!"

[27:24] So when Pilate saw that nothing was being gained, but rather that a disturbance was starting, he took water, and washed his hands before the multitude, saying, "I am innocent of the blood of this righteous person. You see to it."

[27:25] All the people answered, "May his blood be on us, and on our children!"

[27:26] Then he released to them Barabbas, but Jesus he flogged and delivered to be crucified. [27:27] Then the governor's soldiers took Jesus into the Praetorium, and gathered the whole garrison together against him. [27:28] They stripped him, and put a scarlet robe on him. [27:29] They braided a crown of thorns and put it on his head, and a reed in his right hand; and they kneeled down before him, and mocked him, saying, "Hail, King of the Jews!" [27:30] They spat on him, and took the reed and struck him on the head. [27:31] When they had mocked him, they took the robe off of him, and put his clothes on him, and led him away to crucify him.

[27:32] As they came out, they found a man of Cyrene, Simon by name, and they compelled him to go with them, that he might

---

[q] 27:9 some manuscripts omit "Jeremiah"
[r] 27:10 Zechariah 11:12-13; Jeremiah 19:1-13; 32:6-9

carry his cross. [27:33] They came to a place called "Golgotha," that is to say, "The place of a skull." [27:34] They gave him sour wine to drink mixed with gall. When he had tasted it, he would not drink. [27:35] When they had crucified him, they divided his clothing among them, casting lots,[s] [27:36] and they sat and watched him there. [27:37] They set up over his head the accusation against him written, "THIS IS JESUS, THE KING OF THE JEWS."

[27:38] Then there were two robbers crucified with him, one on his right hand and one on the left. [27:39] Those who passed by blasphemed him, wagging their heads, [27:40] and saying, "You who destroy the temple, and build it in three days, save yourself! If you are the Son of God, come down from the cross!"

[27:41] Likewise the chief priests also mocking, with the scribes, the Pharisees,[t] and the elders, said, [27:42] "He saved others, but he can't save himself. If he is the King of Israel, let him come down from the cross now, and we will believe in him. [27:43] He trusts in God. Let God deliver him now, if he wants him; for he said, 'I am the Son of God.'" [27:44] The robbers also who were crucified with him cast on him the same reproach.

[27:45] Now from the sixth hour[u] there was darkness over all the land until the ninth hour.[v] [27:46] About the ninth hour Jesus cried with a loud voice, saying, **"Eli, Eli, lima[w] sabachthani?"** That is, **"My God, my God, why have you forsaken me?"**[x]

[27:47] Some of them who stood there, when they heard it, said, "This man is calling Elijah." [27:48] Immediately one of them ran, and took a sponge, and filled it with vinegar, and put it on a reed, and gave him a drink. [27:49] The rest said, "Let him be. Let's see whether Elijah comes to save him."

[27:50] Jesus cried again with a loud voice, and yielded up his spirit. [27:51] Behold, the veil of the temple was torn in two from the top to the bottom. The earth quaked and the rocks were split. [27:52] The tombs were opened, and many bodies of the saints who had fallen asleep were raised; [27:53] and coming out of the tombs after his resurrection, they entered into the holy city and appeared to many. [27:54] Now the centurion, and those who were with him watching Jesus, when they saw the earthquake, and the things that were done, feared exceedingly, saying, "Truly this was the Son of God."

[27:55] Many women were there watching from afar, who had followed Jesus from Galilee, serving him. [27:56] Among them were Mary Magdalene, Mary the mother of James and Joses, and the mother of the sons of Zebedee. [27:57] When evening had come, a rich man from Arimathaea, named Joseph, who himself was also Jesus' disciple came. [27:58] This man went to Pilate, and asked for Jesus' body. Then Pilate commanded the body to be given up. [27:59] Joseph took the body, and wrapped it in a clean linen cloth, [27:60] and laid it in his own new tomb, which he had cut out in the rock, and he rolled a great stone to the door of the tomb, and departed. [27:61] Mary Magdalene was there, and the other Mary, sitting opposite the tomb. [27:62] Now on the next day, which was the day after the Preparation Day, the chief priests and the Pharisees were gathered together to Pilate, [27:63] saying, "Sir, we remember what that deceiver said while he was still alive: 'After three days I will rise again.' [27:64] Command therefore that the tomb be made secure until the third day, lest perhaps his disciples come at night and steal him away, and tell the people, 'He is risen from the dead;' and the last deception will be worse than the first."

[27:65] Pilate said to them, "You have a guard. Go, make it as secure as you can."

---

[s] 27:35 TR adds "that it might be fulfilled which was spoken by the prophet: 'They divided my garments among them, and for my clothing they cast lots;'" [see Psalm 22:18 and John 19:24]

[t] 27:41 TR omits "the Pharisees"

[u] 27:45 noon

[v] 27:45 3:00 P. M.

[w] 27:46 TR reads "lama" instead of "lima"

[x] 27:46 Psalm 22:1

$^{27:66}$So they went with the guard and made the tomb secure, sealing the stone.

$^{28:1}$Now after the Sabbath, as it began to dawn on the first day of the week, Mary Magdalene and the other Mary came to see the tomb. $^{28:2}$Behold, there was a great earthquake, for an angel of the Lord descended from the sky, and came and rolled away the stone from the door, and sat on it. $^{28:3}$His appearance was like lightning, and his clothing white as snow. $^{28:4}$For fear of him, the guards shook, and became like dead men. $^{28:5}$The angel answered the women, "Don't be afraid, for I know that you seek Jesus, who has been crucified. $^{28:6}$He is not here, for he has risen, just like he said. Come, see the place where the Lord was lying. $^{28:7}$Go quickly and tell his disciples, 'He has risen from the dead, and behold, he goes before you into Galilee; there you will see him.' Behold, I have told you."

$^{28:8}$They departed quickly from the tomb with fear and great joy, and ran to bring his disciples word. $^{28:9}$As they went to tell his disciples, behold, Jesus met them, saying, **"Rejoice!"**

They came and took hold of his feet, and worshiped him.

$^{28:10}$Then Jesus said to them, **"Don't be afraid. Go tell my brothers^y that they should go into Galilee, and there they will see me."**

$^{28:11}$Now while they were going, behold, some of the guards came into the city, and told the chief priests all the things that had happened. $^{28:12}$When they were assembled with the elders, and had taken counsel, they gave a large amount of silver to the soldiers, $^{28:13}$saying, "Say that his disciples came by night, and stole him away while we slept. $^{28:14}$If this comes to the governor's ears, we will persuade him and make you free of worry." $^{28:15}$So they took the money and did as they were told. This saying was spread abroad among the Jews, and continues until this day.

$^{28:16}$But the eleven disciples went into Galilee, to the mountain where Jesus had sent them. $^{28:17}$When they saw him, they bowed down to him, but some doubted. $^{28:18}$Jesus came to them and spoke to them, saying, **"All authority has been given to me in heaven and on earth. $^{28:19}$Therefore go, and make disciples of all nations, baptizing them in the name of the Father and of the Son and of the Holy Spirit, $^{28:20}$teaching them to observe all things that I commanded you. Behold, I am with you always, even to the end of the age."** Amen.

The Good News According to Mark

$^{1:1}$The beginning of the Good News of Jesus Christ, the Son of God. $^{1:2}$As it is written in the prophets,

"Behold, I send my messenger before your face,
who will prepare your way before you.^{a}
$^{1:3}$The voice of one crying in the wilderness,
'Make ready the way of the Lord!
Make his paths straight!'"^{b}

$^{1:4}$John came baptizing^c in the wilderness and preaching the baptism of repentance for forgiveness of sins. $^{1:5}$All the country of Judea and all those of Jerusalem went out to him. They were baptized by him in the Jordan river, confessing their sins. $^{1:6}$John was clothed with camel's hair and a leather belt around his waist. He ate locusts and wild honey. $^{1:7}$He preached, saying, "After me comes he who is mightier than I, the thong of whose sandals I am not worthy to stoop down and loosen. $^{1:8}$I baptized you in^d water, but he will baptize you in the Holy Spirit."

---

^{y}28:10 The word for "brothers" here may be also correctly translated "brothers and sisters" or "siblings."

^{a}1:2 Malachi 3:1

^{b}1:3 Isaiah 40:3

^{c}1:4 or, immersing

^{d}1:8 The Greek word (en) translated here as "in" could also be translated as "with" in some contexts.

^{1:9}It happened in those days, that Jesus came from Nazareth of Galilee, and was baptized by John in the Jordan. ^{1:10}Immediately coming up from the water, he saw the heavens parting, and the Spirit descending on him like a dove. ^{1:11}A voice came out of the sky, "You are my beloved Son, in whom I am well pleased."

^{1:12}Immediately the Spirit drove him out into the wilderness. ^{1:13}He was there in the wilderness forty days tempted by Satan. He was with the wild animals; and the angels were serving him.

^{1:14}Now after John was taken into custody, Jesus came into Galilee, preaching the Good News of the Kingdom of God, ^{1:15}and saying, **"The time is fulfilled, and the Kingdom of God is at hand! Repent, and believe in the Good News."**

^{1:16}Passing along by the sea of Galilee, he saw Simon and Andrew the brother of Simon casting a net into the sea, for they were fishermen. ^{1:17}Jesus said to them, **"Come after me, and I will make you into fishers for men."**

^{1:18}Immediately they left their nets, and followed him. ^{1:19}Going on a little further from there, he saw James the son of Zebedee, and John, his brother, who were also in the boat mending the nets. ^{1:20}Immediately he called them, and they left their father, Zebedee, in the boat with the hired servants, and went after him. ^{1:21}They went into Capernaum, and immediately on the Sabbath day he entered into the synagogue and taught. ^{1:22}They were astonished at his teaching, for he taught them as having authority, and not as the scribes. ^{1:23}Immediately there was in their synagogue a man with an unclean spirit, and he cried out, ^{1:24}saying, "Ha! What do we have to do with you, Jesus, you Nazarene? Have you come to destroy us? I know you who you are: the Holy One of God!"

^{1:25}Jesus rebuked him, saying, **"Be quiet, and come out of him!"**

^{1:26}The unclean spirit, convulsing him and crying with a loud voice, came out of him. ^{1:27}They were all amazed, so that they questioned among themselves, saying, "What is this? A new teaching? For with authority he commands even the unclean spirits, and they obey him!" ^{1:28}The report of him went out immediately everywhere into all the region of Galilee and its surrounding area.

^{1:29}Immediately, when they had come out of the synagogue, they came into the house of Simon and Andrew, with James and John. ^{1:30}Now Simon's wife's mother lay sick with a fever, and immediately they told him about her. ^{1:31}He came and took her by the hand, and raised her up. The fever left her, and she served them. ^{1:32}At evening, when the sun had set, they brought to him all who were sick, and those who were possessed by demons. ^{1:33}All the city was gathered together at the door. ^{1:34}He healed many who were sick with various diseases, and cast out many demons. He didn't allow the demons to speak, because they knew him.

^{1:35}Early in the morning, while it was still dark, he rose up and went out, and departed into a deserted place, and prayed there. ^{1:36}Simon and those who were with him followed after him; ^{1:37}and they found him, and told him, "Everyone is looking for you."

^{1:38}He said to them, **"Let's go elsewhere into the next towns, that I may preach there also, because I came out for this reason."** ^{1:39}He went into their synagogues throughout all Galilee, preaching and casting out demons.

^{1:40}A leper came to him, begging him, kneeling down to him, and saying to him, "If you want to, you can make me clean."

^{1:41}Being moved with compassion, he stretched out his hand, and touched him, and said to him, **"I want to. Be made clean."** ^{1:42}When he had said this, immediately the leprosy departed from him, and he was made clean. ^{1:43}He strictly warned him, and immediately sent him out, ^{1:44}and said to him, **"See you say nothing to anybody, but go show yourself to the priest, and offer for your cleansing the things which Moses commanded, for a testimony to them."**

^{1:45}But he went out, and began to proclaim it much, and to spread about the matter, so that Jesus could no more openly enter

into a city, but was outside in desert places: and they came to him from everywhere.

2:1When he entered again into Capernaum after some days, it was heard that he was in the house. 2:2Immediately many were gathered together, so that there was no more room, not even around the door; and he spoke the word to them. 2:3Four people came, carrying a paralytic to him. 2:4When they could not come near to him for the crowd, they removed the roof where he was. When they had broken it up, they let down the mat that the paralytic was lying on. 2:5Jesus, seeing their faith, said to the paralytic, **"Son, your sins are forgiven you."**

2:6But there were some of the scribes sitting there, and reasoning in their hearts, 2:7"Why does this man speak blasphemies like that? Who can forgive sins but God alone?"

2:8Immediately Jesus, perceiving in his spirit that they so reasoned within themselves, said to them, **"Why do you reason these things in your hearts?** 2:9**Which is easier, to tell the paralytic, 'Your sins are forgiven;' or to say, 'Arise, and take up your bed, and walk?'** 2:10**But that you may know that the Son of Man has authority on earth to forgive sins"**—he said to the paralytic—2:11**"I tell you, arise, take up your mat, and go to your house."**

2:12He arose, and immediately took up the mat, and went out in front of them all; so that they were all amazed, and glorified God, saying, "We never saw anything like this!"

2:13He went out again by the seaside. All the multitude came to him, and he taught them. 2:14As he passed by, he saw Levi, the son of Alphaeus, sitting at the tax office, and he said to him, **"Follow me."** And he arose and followed him.

2:15It happened, that he was reclining at the table in his house, and many tax collectors and sinners sat down with Jesus and his disciples, for there were many, and they followed him. 2:16The scribes and the Pharisees, when they saw that he was eating with the sinners and tax collectors, said to his disciples, "Why is it that he eats and drinks with tax collectors and sinners?"

2:17When Jesus heard it, he said to them, **"Those who are healthy have no need for a physician, but those who are sick. I came not to call the righteous, but sinners to repentance."**

2:18John's disciples and the Pharisees were fasting, and they came and asked him, "Why do John's disciples and the disciples of the Pharisees fast, but your disciples don't fast?"

2:19Jesus said to them, **"Can the groomsmen fast while the bridegroom is with them? As long as they have the bridegroom with them, they can't fast.** 2:20**But the days will come when the bridegroom will be taken away from them, and then will they fast in that day.** 2:21**No one sews a piece of unshrunk cloth on an old garment, or else the patch shrinks and the new tears away from the old, and a worse hole is made.** 2:22**No one puts new wine into old wineskins, or else the new wine will burst the skins, and the wine pours out, and the skins will be destroyed; but they put new wine into fresh wineskins."**

2:23It happened that he was going on the Sabbath day through the grain fields, and his disciples began, as they went, to pluck the ears of grain. 2:24The Pharisees said to him, "Behold, why do they do that which is not lawful on the Sabbath day?"

2:25He said to them, **"Did you never read what David did, when he had need, and was hungry—he, and those who were with him?** 2:26**How he entered into the house of God when Abiathar was high priest, and ate the show bread, which is not lawful to eat except for the priests, and gave also to those who were with him?"** 2:27He said to them, **"The Sabbath was made for man, not man for the Sabbath.** 2:28**Therefore the Son of Man is lord even of the Sabbath."**

3:1He entered again into the synagogue, and there was a man there who had his hand withered. 3:2They watched him, whether he would heal him on the Sabbath day, that they might accuse him. 3:3He said to the man who had his hand withered, **"Stand up."** 3:4He said to them, **"Is it lawful on the Sabbath day to do good, or to do harm? To save a life, or to kill?"** But they were silent. ^{3:5}When he had looked around at them with anger, being grieved at the hardening of their hearts, he said to the man, **"Stretch out your hand."** He stretched it out, and his hand was restored as healthy as the other. ^{3:6}The Pharisees went out, and immediately conspired with the Herodians against him, how they might destroy him.

^{3:7}Jesus withdrew to the sea with his disciples, and a great multitude followed him from Galilee, from Judea, ^{3:8}from Jerusalem, from Idumaea, beyond the Jordan, and those from around Tyre and Sidon. A great multitude, hearing what great things he did, came to him. ^{3:9}He spoke to his disciples that a little boat should stay near him because of the crowd, so that they wouldn't press on him. ^{3:10}For he had healed many, so that as many as had diseases pressed on him that they might touch him. ^{3:11}The unclean spirits, whenever they saw him, fell down before him, and cried, "You are the Son of God!" ^{3:12}He sternly warned them that they should not make him known.

^{3:13}He went up into the mountain, and called to himself those whom he wanted, and they went to him. ^{3:14}He appointed twelve, that they might be with him, and that he might send them out to preach, ^{3:15}and to have authority to heal sicknesses and to cast out demons: ^{3:16}Simon, to whom he gave the name Peter; ^{3:17}James the son of Zebedee; John, the brother of James, and he surnamed them Boanerges, which means, Sons of Thunder; ^{3:18}Andrew; Philip; Bartholomew; Matthew; Thomas; James, the son of Alphaeus; Thaddaeus; Simon the Zealot; ^{3:19}and Judas Iscariot, who also betrayed him.

He came into a house. ^{3:20}The multitude came together again, so that they could not so much as eat bread. ^{3:21}When his friends heard it, they went out to seize him: for they said, "He is insane." ^{3:22}The scribes who came down from Jerusalem said, "He has Beelzebul," and, "By the prince of the demons he casts out the demons."

^{3:23}He summoned them, and said to them in parables, **"How can Satan cast out Satan?** ^{3:24}**If a kingdom is divided against itself, that kingdom cannot stand.** ^{3:25}**If a house is divided against itself, that house cannot stand.** ^{3:26}**If Satan has risen up against himself, and is divided, he can't stand, but has an end.** ^{3:27}**But no one can enter into the house of the strong man to plunder, unless he first binds the strong man; and then he will plunder his house.** ^{3:28}**Most certainly I tell you, all sins of the descendants of man will be forgiven, including their blasphemies with which they may blaspheme;** ^{3:29}**but whoever may blaspheme against the Holy Spirit never has forgiveness, but is guilty of an eternal sin"**^{3:30}—because they said, "He has an unclean spirit."

^{3:31}His mother and his brothers came, and standing outside, they sent to him, calling him. ^{3:32}A multitude was sitting around him, and they told him, "Behold, your mother, your brothers, and your sisters^e are outside looking for you."

^{3:33}He answered them, **"Who are my mother and my brothers?"** ^{3:34}Looking around at those who sat around him, he said, **"Behold, my mother and my brothers!** ^{3:35}**For whoever does the will of God, the same is my brother, and my sister, and mother."**

^{4:1}Again he began to teach by the seaside. A great multitude was gathered to him, so that he entered into a boat in the sea, and sat down. All the multitude were on the land by the sea. ^{4:2}He taught them many things in parables, and told them in his teaching, ^{4:3}**"Listen! Behold, the farmer went out to sow,** ^{4:4}**and it happened, as he sowed, some seed fell by the road, and the birds**^f **came and devoured it.** ^{4:5}**Others fell on the rocky ground, where it had little soil, and immediately it sprang up, because it had no depth of soil.** ^{4:6}**When the sun had risen, it was scorched; and because it had no root, it withered away.** ^{4:7}**Others fell among the thorns, and the thorns grew up, and choked it, and it yielded no fruit.**

---

^e3:32 TR omits "your sisters"
^f4:4 TR adds "of the air"

4:8 Others fell into the good ground, and yielded fruit, growing up and increasing. Some brought forth thirty times, some sixty times, and some one hundred times as much." 4:9 He said, "Whoever has ears to hear, let him hear."

4:10 When he was alone, those who were around him with the twelve asked him about the parables. 4:11 He said to them, "To you is given the mystery of the Kingdom of God, but to those who are outside, all things are done in parables, 4:12 that 'seeing they may see, and not perceive; and hearing they may hear, and not understand; lest perhaps they should turn again, and their sins should be forgiven them.'"[g]

4:13 He said to them, "Don't you understand this parable? How will you understand all of the parables? 4:14 The farmer sows the word. 4:15 The ones by the road are the ones where the word is sown; and when they have heard, immediately Satan comes, and takes away the word which has been sown in them. 4:16 These in like manner are those who are sown on the rocky places, who, when they have heard the word, immediately receive it with joy. 4:17 They have no root in themselves, but are short-lived. When oppression or persecution arises because of the word, immediately they stumble. 4:18 Others are those who are sown among the thorns. These are those who have heard the word, 4:19 and the cares of this age, and the deceitfulness of riches, and the lusts of other things entering in choke the word, and it becomes unfruitful. 4:20 Those which were sown on the good ground are those who hear the word, and accept it, and bear fruit, some thirty times, some sixty times, and some one hundred times."

4:21 He said to them, "Is the lamp brought to be put under a basket[h] or under a bed? Isn't it put on a stand? 4:22 For there is nothing hidden, except that it should be made known; neither was anything made secret, but that it should come to light. 4:23 If any man has ears to hear, let him hear."

4:24 He said to them, "Take heed what you hear. With whatever measure you measure, it will be measured to you, and more will be given to you who hear. 4:25 For whoever has, to him will more be given, and he who doesn't have, even that which he has will be taken away from him."

4:26 He said, "The Kingdom of God is as if a man should cast seed on the earth, 4:27 and should sleep and rise night and day, and the seed should spring up and grow, he doesn't know how. 4:28 For the earth bears fruit: first the blade, then the ear, then the full grain in the ear. 4:29 But when the fruit is ripe, immediately he puts forth the sickle, because the harvest has come."

4:30 He said, "How will we liken the Kingdom of God? Or with what parable will we illustrate it? 4:31 It's like a grain of mustard seed, which, when it is sown in the earth, though it is less than all the seeds that are on the earth, 4:32 yet when it is sown, grows up, and becomes greater than all the herbs, and puts out great branches, so that the birds of the sky can lodge under its shadow."

4:33 With many such parables he spoke the word to them, as they were able to hear it. 4:34 Without a parable he didn't speak to them; but privately to his own disciples he explained everything.

4:35 On that day, when evening had come, he said to them, "Let's go over to the other side." 4:36 Leaving the multitude, they took him with them, even as he was, in the boat. Other small boats were also with him. 4:37 A big wind storm arose, and the waves beat into the boat, so much that the boat was already filled. 4:38 He himself was in the stern, asleep on the cushion, and they woke him up, and told him, "Teacher, don't you care that we are dying?"

4:39 He awoke, and rebuked the wind, and said to the sea, "Peace! Be still!" The wind ceased, and there was a great calm. 4:40 He said to them, "Why are you so afraid? How is it that you have no faith?"

---

g 4:12 Isaiah 6:9-10
h 4:21 literally, a modion, a dry measuring basket containing about a peck (about 9 litres)

⁴:⁴¹They were greatly afraid, and said to one another, "Who then is this, that even the wind and the sea obey him?"

⁵:¹They came to the other side of the sea, into the country of the Gadarenes. ⁵:²When he had come out of the boat, immediately a man with an unclean spirit met him out of the tombs. ⁵:³He lived in the tombs. Nobody could bind him any more, not even with chains, ⁵:⁴because he had been often bound with fetters and chains, and the chains had been torn apart by him, and the fetters broken in pieces. Nobody had the strength to tame him. ⁵:⁵Always, night and day, in the tombs and in the mountains, he was crying out, and cutting himself with stones. ⁵:⁶When he saw Jesus from afar, he ran and bowed down to him, ⁵:⁷and crying out with a loud voice, he said, "What have I to do with you, Jesus, you Son of the Most High God? I adjure you by God, don't torment me." ⁵:⁸For he said to him, **"Come out of the man, you unclean spirit!"**

⁵:⁹He asked him, **"What is your name?"**

He said to him, "My name is Legion, for we are many." ⁵:¹⁰He begged him much that he would not send them away out of the country. ⁵:¹¹Now on the mountainside there was a great herd of pigs feeding. ⁵:¹²All the demons begged him, saying, "Send us into the pigs, that we may enter into them."

⁵:¹³At once Jesus gave them permission. The unclean spirits came out and entered into the pigs. The herd of about two thousand rushed down the steep bank into the sea, and they were drowned in the sea. ⁵:¹⁴Those who fed them fled, and told it in the city and in the country.

The people came to see what it was that had happened. ⁵:¹⁵They came to Jesus, and saw him who had been possessed by demons sitting, clothed, and in his right mind, even him who had the legion; and they were afraid. ⁵:¹⁶Those who saw it declared to them how it happened to him who was possessed by demons, and about the pigs. ⁵:¹⁷They began to beg him to depart from their region.

⁵:¹⁸As he was entering into the boat, he who had been possessed by demons begged him that he might be with him.

⁵:¹⁹He didn't allow him, but said to him, **"Go to your house, to your friends, and tell them what great things the Lord has done for you, and how he had mercy on you."**

⁵:²⁰He went his way, and began to proclaim in Decapolis how Jesus had done great things for him, and everyone marveled.

⁵:²¹When Jesus had crossed back over in the boat to the other side, a great multitude was gathered to him; and he was by the sea. ⁵:²²Behold, one of the rulers of the synagogue, Jairus by name, came; and seeing him, he fell at his feet, ⁵:²³and begged him much, saying, "My little daughter is at the point of death. Please come and lay your hands on her, that she may be made healthy, and live."

⁵:²⁴He went with him, and a great multitude followed him, and they pressed upon him on all sides. ⁵:²⁵A certain woman, who had an issue of blood for twelve years, ⁵:²⁶and had suffered many things by many physicians, and had spent all that she had, and was no better, but rather grew worse, ⁵:²⁷having heard the things concerning Jesus, came up behind him in the crowd, and touched his clothes. ⁵:²⁸For she said, "If I just touch his clothes, I will be made well." ⁵:²⁹Immediately the flow of her blood was dried up, and she felt in her body that she was healed of her affliction.

⁵:³⁰Immediately Jesus, perceiving in himself that the power had gone out from him, turned around in the crowd, and asked, **"Who touched my clothes?"**

⁵:³¹His disciples said to him, "You see the multitude pressing against you, and you say, 'Who touched me?'"

⁵:³²He looked around to see her who had done this thing. ⁵:³³But the woman, fearing and trembling, knowing what had been done to her, came and fell down before him, and told him all the truth. ⁵:³⁴He said to her, **"Daughter, your faith has made you well. Go in peace, and be cured of your disease."**

⁵:³⁵While he was still speaking, people came from the synagogue ruler's house saying, "Your daughter is dead. Why bother the Teacher any more?"

^{5:36}But Jesus, when he heard the message spoken, immediately said to the ruler of the synagogue, **"Don't be afraid, only believe."** ^{5:37}He allowed no one to follow him, except Peter, James, and John the brother of James. ^{5:38}He came to the synagogue ruler's house, and he saw an uproar, weeping, and great wailing. ^{5:39}When he had entered in, he said to them, **"Why do you make an uproar and weep? The child is not dead, but is asleep."**

^{5:40}They ridiculed him. But he, having put them all out, took the father of the child, her mother, and those who were with him, and went in where the child was lying. ^{5:41}Taking the child by the hand, he said to her, **"Talitha cumi!"** which means, being interpreted, **"Girl, I tell you, get up!"** ^{5:42}Immediately the girl rose up and walked, for she was twelve years old. They were amazed with great amazement. ^{5:43}He strictly ordered them that no one should know this, and commanded that something should be given to her to eat.

^{6:1}He went out from there. He came into his own country, and his disciples followed him. ^{6:2}When the Sabbath had come, he began to teach in the synagogue, and many hearing him were astonished, saying, "Where did this man get these things?" and, "What is the wisdom that is given to this man, that such mighty works come about by his hands? ^{6:3}Isn't this the carpenter, the son of Mary, and brother of James, Joses, Judah, and Simon? Aren't his sisters here with us?" They were offended at him.

^{6:4}Jesus said to them, **"A prophet is not without honor, except in his own country, and among his own relatives, and in his own house."** ^{6:5}He could do no mighty work there, except that he laid his hands on a few sick people, and healed them. ^{6:6}He marveled because of their unbelief.

He went around the villages teaching. ^{6:7}He called to himself the twelve, and began to send them out two by two; and he gave them authority over the unclean spirits. ^{6:8}He commanded them that they should take nothing for their journey, except a staff only: no bread, no wallet, no money in their purse, ^{6:9}but to wear sandals, and not put on two tunics. ^{6:10}He said to them, **"Wherever you enter into a house, stay there until you depart from there. ^{6:11}Whoever will not receive you nor hear you, as you depart from there, shake off the dust that is under your feet for a testimony against them. Assuredly, I tell you, it will be more tolerable for Sodom and Gomorrah in the day of judgment than for that city!"**

^{6:12}They went out and preached that people should repent. ^{6:13}They cast out many demons, and anointed many with oil who were sick, and healed them. ^{6:14}King Herod heard this, for his name had become known, and he said, "John the Baptizer has risen from the dead, and therefore these powers are at work in him." ^{6:15}But others said, "He is Elijah." Others said, "He is a prophet, or like one of the prophets." ^{6:16}But Herod, when he heard this, said, "This is John, whom I beheaded. He has risen from the dead." ^{6:17}For Herod himself had sent out and arrested John, and bound him in prison for the sake of Herodias, his brother Philip's wife, for he had married her. ^{6:18}For John said to Herod, "It is not lawful for you to have your brother's wife." ^{6:19}Herodias set herself against him, and desired to kill him, but she couldn't, ^{6:20}for Herod feared John, knowing that he was a righteous and holy man, and kept him safe. When he heard him, he did many things, and he heard him gladly.

^{6:21}Then a convenient day came, that Herod on his birthday made a supper for his nobles, the high officers, and the chief men of Galilee. ^{6:22}When the daughter of Herodias herself came in and danced, she pleased Herod and those sitting with him. The king said to the young lady, "Ask me whatever you want, and I will give it to you." ^{6:23}He swore to her, "Whatever you shall ask of me, I will give you, up to half of my kingdom."

^{6:24}She went out, and said to her mother, "What shall I ask?"

She said, "The head of John the Baptizer."

^{6:25}She came in immediately with haste to the king, and asked, "I want you to give me right now the head of John the Baptizer on a platter."

6:26The king was exceedingly sorry, but for the sake of his oaths, and of his dinner guests, he didn't wish to refuse her. 6:27Immediately the king sent out a soldier of his guard, and commanded to bring John's head, and he went and beheaded him in the prison, 6:28and brought his head on a platter, and gave it to the young lady; and the young lady gave it to her mother.

6:29When his disciples heard this, they came and took up his corpse, and laid it in a tomb.

6:30The apostles gathered themselves together to Jesus, and they told him all things, whatever they had done, and whatever they had taught. 6:31He said to them, **"You come apart into a deserted place, and rest awhile."** For there were many coming and going, and they had no leisure so much as to eat. 6:32They went away in the boat to a deserted place by themselves. 6:33They[i] saw them going, and many recognized him and ran there on foot from all the cities. They arrived before them and came together to him. 6:34Jesus came out, saw a great multitude, and he had compassion on them, because they were like sheep without a shepherd, and he began to teach them many things. 6:35When it was late in the day, his disciples came to him, and said, "This place is deserted, and it is late in the day. 6:36Send them away, that they may go into the surrounding country and villages, and buy themselves bread, for they have nothing to eat."

6:37But he answered them, **"You give them something to eat."**

They asked him, "Shall we go and buy two hundred denarii[j] worth of bread, and give them something to eat?"

6:38He said to them, **"How many loaves do you have? Go see."**

When they knew, they said, "Five, and two fish."

6:39He commanded them that everyone should sit down in groups on the green grass. 6:40They sat down in ranks, by hundreds and by fifties. 6:41He took the five loaves and the two fish, and looking up to heaven, he blessed and broke the loaves, and he gave to his disciples to set before them, and he divided the two fish among them all. 6:42They all ate, and were filled. 6:43They took up twelve baskets full of broken pieces and also of the fish. 6:44Those who ate the loaves were[k] five thousand men.

6:45Immediately he made his disciples get into the boat, and to go ahead to the other side, to Bethsaida, while he himself sent the multitude away. 6:46After he had taken leave of them, he went up the mountain to pray.

6:47When evening had come, the boat was in the midst of the sea, and he was alone on the land. 6:48Seeing them distressed in rowing, for the wind was contrary to them, about the fourth watch of the night he came to them, walking on the sea,[l] and he would have passed by them, 6:49but they, when they saw him walking on the sea, supposed that it was a ghost, and cried out; 6:50for they all saw him, and were troubled. But he immediately spoke with them, and said to them, **"Cheer up! It is I![m] Don't be afraid."** 6:51He got into the boat with them; and the wind ceased, and they were very amazed among themselves, and marveled; 6:52for they hadn't understood about the loaves, but their hearts were hardened.

6:53When they had crossed over, they came to land at Gennesaret, and moored to the shore. 6:54When they had come out of the boat, immediately the people recognized him, 6:55and ran around that whole region, and began to bring those who were sick, on their mats, to where they heard he was. 6:56Wherever he entered, into villages, or into cities, or into the country, they laid the sick in the marketplaces, and begged him that they might touch just the fringe[n]

---

[i]6:33 TR reads "The multitudes" instead of "They"

[j]6:37 200 denarii was about 7 or 8 months wages for an agricultural laborer.

[k]6:44 TR adds "about"

[l]6:48 see Job 9:8

[m]6:50 or, "I AM!"

[n]6:56 or, tassel

of his garment; and as many as touched him were made well.

[7:1] Then the Pharisees, and some of the scribes gathered together to him, having come from Jerusalem. [7:2] Now when they saw some of his disciples eating bread with defiled, that is, unwashed, hands, they found fault. [7:3] (For the Pharisees, and all the Jews, don't eat unless they wash their hands and forearms, holding to the tradition of the elders. [7:4] They don't eat when they come from the marketplace, unless they bathe themselves, and there are many other things, which they have received to hold to: washings of cups, pitchers, bronze vessels, and couches.) [7:5] The Pharisees and the scribes asked him, "Why don't your disciples walk according to the tradition of the elders, but eat their bread with unwashed hands?"

[7:6] He answered them, **"Well did Isaiah prophesy of you hypocrites, as it is written,**

'This people honors me with their lips,
      but their heart is far from me.
[7:7] But in vain do they worship me,
      teaching as doctrines the commandments of men.'**[o]**

[7:8] **"For you set aside the commandment of God, and hold tightly to the tradition of men—the washing of pitchers and cups, and you do many other such things."** [7:9] He said to them, **"Full well do you reject the commandment of God, that you may keep your tradition.** [7:10] **For Moses said,** 'Honor your father and your mother;'**[p]** and, 'He who speaks evil of father or mother, let him be put to death.'**[q]** [7:11] **But you say, 'If a man tells his father or his mother, "Whatever profit you might have received from me is Corban**[r]**, that is to say, given to God;"'** [7:12] **then you no longer allow him to do anything for his father or his mother,** [7:13] **making void the word of God by your tradition, which you have handed down. You do many things like this."**

[7:14] He called all the multitude to himself, and said to them, **"Hear me, all of you, and understand.** [7:15] **There is nothing from outside of the man, that going into him can defile him; but the things which proceed out of the man are those that defile the man.** [7:16] **If anyone has ears to hear, let him hear!"**

[7:17] When he had entered into a house away from the multitude, his disciples asked him about the parable. [7:18] He said to them, **"Are you thus without understanding also? Don't you perceive that whatever goes into the man from outside can't defile him,** [7:19] **because it doesn't go into his heart, but into his stomach, then into the latrine, thus making all foods clean?"** [7:20] He said, **"That which proceeds out of the man, that defiles the man.** [7:21] **For from within, out of the hearts of men, proceed evil thoughts, adulteries, sexual sins, murders, thefts,** [7:22] **covetings, wickedness, deceit, lustful desires, an evil eye, blasphemy, pride, and foolishness.** [7:23] **All these evil things come from within, and defile the man."**

[7:24] From there he arose, and went away into the borders of Tyre and Sidon. He entered into a house, and didn't want anyone to know it, but he couldn't escape notice. [7:25] For a woman, whose little daughter had an unclean spirit, having heard of him, came and fell down at his feet. [7:26] Now the woman was a Greek, a Syrophoenician by race. She begged him that he would cast the demon out of her daughter. [7:27] But Jesus said to her, **"Let the children be filled first, for it is not appropriate to take the children's bread and throw it to the dogs."**

[7:28] But she answered him, "Yes, Lord. Yet even the dogs under the table eat the children's crumbs."

[7:29] He said to her, **"For this saying, go your way. The demon has gone out of your daughter."**

[7:30] She went away to her house, and found the child having been laid on the bed, with the demon gone out.

---

[o] 7:7 Isaiah 29:13
[p] 7:10 Exodus 20:12; Deuteronomy 5:16
[q] 7:10 Exodus 21:17; Leviticus 20:9
[r] 7:11 Corban is a Hebrew word for an offering devoted to God.

^{7:31}Again he departed from the borders of Tyre and Sidon, and came to the sea of Galilee, through the midst of the region of Decapolis. ^{7:32}They brought to him one who was deaf and had an impediment in his speech. They begged him to lay his hand on him. ^{7:33}He took him aside from the multitude, privately, and put his fingers into his ears, and he spat, and touched his tongue. ^{7:34}Looking up to heaven, he sighed, and said to him, **"Ephphatha!"** that is, **"Be opened!"** ^{7:35}Immediately his ears were opened, and the impediment of his tongue was released, and he spoke clearly. ^{7:36}He commanded them that they should tell no one, but the more he commanded them, so much the more widely they proclaimed it. ^{7:37}They were astonished beyond measure, saying, "He has done all things well. He makes even the deaf hear, and the mute speak!"

^{8:1}In those days, when there was a very great multitude, and they had nothing to eat, Jesus called his disciples to himself, and said to them, ^{8:2}**"I have compassion on the multitude, because they have stayed with me now three days, and have nothing to eat. ^{8:3}If I send them away fasting to their home, they will faint on the way, for some of them have come a long way."**

^{8:4}His disciples answered him, "From where could one satisfy these people with bread here in a deserted place?"

^{8:5}He asked them, **"How many loaves do you have?"**

They said, "Seven."

^{8:6}He commanded the multitude to sit down on the ground, and he took the seven loaves. Having given thanks, he broke them, and gave them to his disciples to serve, and they served the multitude. ^{8:7}They had a few small fish. Having blessed them, he said to serve these also. ^{8:8}They ate, and were filled. They took up seven baskets of broken pieces that were left over. ^{8:9}Those who had eaten were about four thousand. Then he sent them away.

^{8:10}Immediately he entered into the boat with his disciples, and came into the region of Dalmanutha. ^{8:11}The Pharisees came out and began to question him, seeking from him a sign from heaven, and testing him. ^{8:12}He sighed deeply in his spirit, and said, **"Why does this generation**^s **seek a sign? Most certainly I tell you, no sign will be given to this generation."**

^{8:13}He left them, and again entering into the boat, departed to the other side. ^{8:14}They forgot to take bread; and they didn't have more than one loaf in the boat with them. ^{8:15}He warned them, saying, **"Take heed: beware of the yeast of the Pharisees and the yeast of Herod."**

^{8:16}They reasoned with one another, saying, "It's because we have no bread."

^{8:17}Jesus, perceiving it, said to them, **"Why do you reason that it's because you have no bread? Don't you perceive yet, neither understand? Is your heart still hardened? ^{8:18}Having eyes, don't you see? Having ears, don't you hear? Don't you remember? ^{8:19}When I broke the five loaves among the five thousand, how many baskets full of broken pieces did you take up?"**

They told him, "Twelve."

^{8:20}**"When the seven loaves fed the four thousand, how many baskets full of broken pieces did you take up?"**

They told him, "Seven."

^{8:21}He asked them, **"Don't you understand, yet?"**

^{8:22}He came to Bethsaida. They brought a blind man to him, and begged him to touch him. ^{8:23}He took hold of the blind man by the hand, and brought him out of the village. When he had spit on his eyes, and laid his hands on him, he asked him if he saw anything.

^{8:24}He looked up, and said, "I see men; for I see them like trees walking."

^{8:25}Then again he laid his hands on his eyes. He looked intently, and was restored, and saw everyone clearly. ^{8:26}He sent him away to his house, saying, **"Don't enter into the village, nor tell anyone in the village."**

---

^s8:12 The word translated "generation" here (genea) could also be translated "people," "race," or "family."

^{8:27}Jesus went out, with his disciples, into the villages of Caesarea Philippi. On the way he asked his disciples, **"Who do men say that I am?"**

^{8:28}They told him, "John the Baptizer, and others say Elijah, but others: one of the prophets."

^{8:29}He said to them, **"But who do you say that I am?"**

Peter answered, "You are the Christ."

^{8:30}He commanded them that they should tell no one about him. ^{8:31}He began to teach them that the Son of Man must suffer many things, and be rejected by the elders, the chief priests, and the scribes, and be killed, and after three days rise again. ^{8:32}He spoke to them openly. Peter took him, and began to rebuke him. ^{8:33}But he, turning around, and seeing his disciples, rebuked Peter, and said, **"Get behind me, Satan! For you have in mind not the things of God, but the things of men."**

^{8:34}He called the multitude to himself with his disciples, and said to them, **"Whoever wants to come after me, let him deny himself, and take up his cross, and follow me. ^{8:35}For whoever wants to save his life will lose it; and whoever will lose his life for my sake and the sake of the Good News will save it. ^{8:36}For what does it profit a man, to gain the whole world, and forfeit his life? ^{8:37}For what will a man give in exchange for his life? ^{8:38}For whoever will be ashamed of me and of my words in this adulterous and sinful generation, the Son of Man also will be ashamed of him, when he comes in the glory of his Father with the holy angels."**

^{9:1}He said to them, **"Most certainly I tell you, there are some standing here who will in no way taste death until they see the Kingdom of God come with power."**

^{9:2}After six days Jesus took with him Peter, James, and John, and brought them up onto a high mountain privately by themselves, and he was changed into another form in front of them. ^{9:3}His clothing became glistening, exceedingly white, like snow, such as no launderer on earth can whiten them. ^{9:4}Elijah and Moses appeared to them, and they were talking with Jesus. ^{9:5}Peter answered Jesus, "Rabbi, it is good for us to be here. Let's make three tents: one for you, one for Moses, and one for Elijah." ^{9:6}For he didn't know what to say, for they were very afraid.

^{9:7}A cloud came, overshadowing them, and a voice came out of the cloud, "This is my beloved Son. Listen to him."

^{9:8}Suddenly looking around, they saw no one with them any more, except Jesus only.

^{9:9}As they were coming down from the mountain, he commanded them that they should tell no one what things they had seen, until after the Son of Man had risen from the dead. ^{9:10}They kept this saying to themselves, questioning what the "rising from the dead" meant.

^{9:11}They asked him, saying, "Why do the scribes say that Elijah must come first?"

^{9:12}He said to them, **"Elijah indeed comes first, and restores all things. How is it written about the Son of Man, that he should suffer many things and be despised? ^{9:13}But I tell you that Elijah has come, and they have also done to him whatever they wanted to, even as it is written about him."**

^{9:14}Coming to the disciples, he saw a great multitude around them, and scribes questioning them. ^{9:15}Immediately all the multitude, when they saw him, were greatly amazed, and running to him greeted him. ^{9:16}He asked the scribes, **"What are you asking them?"**

^{9:17}One of the multitude answered, "Teacher, I brought to you my son, who has a mute spirit; ^{9:18}and wherever it seizes him, it throws him down, and he foams at the mouth, and grinds his teeth, and wastes away. I asked your disciples to cast it out, and they weren't able."

^{9:19}He answered him, **"Unbelieving generation, how long shall I be with you? How long shall I bear with you? Bring him to me."**

^{9:20}They brought him to him, and when he saw him, immediately the spirit convulsed him, and he fell on the ground, wallowing and foaming at the mouth.

^{9:21}He asked his father, **"How long has it been since this has come to him?"**

He said, "From childhood. ^{9:22}Often it has cast him both into the fire and into the water, to destroy him. But if you can do anything, have compassion on us, and help us."

9:23 Jesus said to him, **"If you can believe, all things are possible to him who believes."**

9:24 Immediately the father of the child cried out with tears, "I believe. Help my unbelief!"

9:25 When Jesus saw that a multitude came running together, he rebuked the unclean spirit, saying to him, **"You mute and deaf spirit, I command you, come out of him, and never enter him again!"**

9:26 Having cried out, and convulsed greatly, it came out of him. The boy became like one dead; so much that most of them said, "He is dead." 9:27 But Jesus took him by the hand, and raised him up; and he arose.

9:28 When he had come into the house, his disciples asked him privately, "Why couldn't we cast it out?" 9:29 He said to them, **"This kind can come out by nothing, except by prayer and fasting."**

9:30 They went out from there, and passed through Galilee. He didn't want anyone to know it. 9:31 For he was teaching his disciples, and said to them, **"The Son of Man is being handed over to the hands of men, and they will kill him; and when he is killed, on the third day he will rise again."**

9:32 But they didn't understand the saying, and were afraid to ask him.

9:33 He came to Capernaum, and when he was in the house he asked them, **"What were you arguing among yourselves on the way?"**

9:34 But they were silent, for they had disputed one with another on the way about who was the greatest.

9:35 He sat down, and called the twelve; and he said to them, **"If any man wants to be first, he shall be last of all, and servant of all."** 9:36 He took a little child, and set him in the midst of them. Taking him in his arms, he said to them, 9:37 **"Whoever receives one such little child in my name, receives me, and whoever receives me, doesn't receive me, but him who sent me."**

9:38 John said to him, "Teacher, we saw someone who doesn't follow us casting out demons in your name; and we forbade him, because he doesn't follow us."

9:39 But Jesus said, **"Don't forbid him, for there is no one who will do a mighty work in my name, and be able quickly to speak evil of me. 9:40 For whoever is not against us is on our side. 9:41 For whoever will give you a cup of water to drink in my name, because you are Christ's, most certainly I tell you, he will in no way lose his reward. 9:42 Whoever will cause one of these little ones who believe in me to stumble, it would be better for him if he was thrown into the sea with a millstone hung around his neck. 9:43 If your hand causes you to stumble, cut it off. It is better for you to enter into life maimed, rather than having your two hands to go into Gehenna,[t] into the unquenchable fire, 9:44 'where their worm doesn't die, and the fire is not quenched.' 9:45 If your foot causes you to stumble, cut it off. It is better for you to enter into life lame, rather than having your two feet to be cast into Gehenna,[u] into the fire that will never be quenched— 9:46 'where their worm doesn't die, and the fire is not quenched.' 9:47 If your eye causes you to stumble, cast it out. It is better for you to enter into the Kingdom of God with one eye, rather than having two eyes to be cast into the Gehenna[v] of fire, 9:48 'where their worm doesn't die, and the fire is not quenched.'[w] 9:49 For everyone will be salted with fire, and every sacrifice will be seasoned with salt. 9:50 Salt is good, but if the salt has lost its saltiness, with what will you season it? Have salt in yourselves, and be at peace with one another."**

10:1 He arose from there and came into the borders of Judea and beyond the Jordan. Multitudes came together to him again. As

---

[t]9:43 or, Hell
[u]9:45 or, Hell
[v]9:47 or, Hell
[w]9:48 Isaiah 66:24

he usually did, he was again teaching them. ¹⁰:²Pharisees came to him testing him, and asked him, "Is it lawful for a man to divorce his wife?"

¹⁰:³He answered, **"What did Moses command you?"**

¹⁰:⁴They said, "Moses allowed a certificate of divorce to be written, and to divorce her."

¹⁰:⁵But Jesus said to them, **"For your hardness of heart, he wrote you this commandment.** ¹⁰:⁶**But from the beginning of the creation, God made them male and female.**ˣ ¹⁰:⁷**For this cause a man will leave his father and mother, and will join to his wife,** ¹⁰:⁸**and the two will become one flesh,**ʸ **so that they are no longer two, but one flesh.** ¹⁰:⁹**What therefore God has joined together, let no man separate."**

¹⁰:¹⁰In the house, his disciples asked him again about the same matter. ¹⁰:¹¹He said to them, **"Whoever divorces his wife, and marries another, commits adultery against her.** ¹⁰:¹²**If a woman herself divorces her husband, and marries another, she commits adultery."**

¹⁰:¹³They were bringing to him little children, that he should touch them, but the disciples rebuked those who were bringing them. ¹⁰:¹⁴But when Jesus saw it, he was moved with indignation, and said to them, **"Allow the little children to come to me! Don't forbid them, for the Kingdom of God belongs to such as these.** ¹⁰:¹⁵**Most certainly I tell you, whoever will not receive the Kingdom of God like a little child, he will in no way enter into it."** ¹⁰:¹⁶He took them in his arms, and blessed them, laying his hands on them.

¹⁰:¹⁷As he was going out into the way, one ran to him, knelt before him, and asked him, "Good Teacher, what shall I do that I may inherit eternal life?"

¹⁰:¹⁸Jesus said to him, **"Why do you call me good? No one is good except one— God.** ¹⁰:¹⁹**You know the commandments: 'Do not murder,' 'Do not commit adultery,' 'Do not steal,' 'Do not give false testimony,' 'Do not defraud,' 'Honor your father and mother.'"**ᶻ

¹⁰:²⁰He said to him, "Teacher, I have observed all these things from my youth."

¹⁰:²¹Jesus looking at him loved him, and said to him, **"One thing you lack. Go, sell whatever you have, and give to the poor, and you will have treasure in heaven; and come, follow me, taking up the cross."**

¹⁰:²²But his face fell at that saying, and he went away sorrowful, for he was one who had great possessions. ¹⁰:²³Jesus looked around, and said to his disciples, **"How difficult it is for those who have riches to enter into the Kingdom of God!"**

¹⁰:²⁴The disciples were amazed at his words. But Jesus answered again, **"Children, how hard is it for those who trust in riches to enter into the Kingdom of God!** ¹⁰:²⁵**It is easier for a camel to go through a needle's eye than for a rich man to enter into the Kingdom of God."**

¹⁰:²⁶They were exceedingly astonished, saying to him, "Then who can be saved?"

¹⁰:²⁷Jesus, looking at them, said, **"With men it is impossible, but not with God, for all things are possible with God."**

¹⁰:²⁸Peter began to tell him, "Behold, we have left all, and have followed you."

¹⁰:²⁹Jesus said, **"Most certainly I tell you, there is no one who has left house, or brothers, or sisters, or father, or mother, or wife, or children, or land, for my sake, and for the sake of the Good News,** ¹⁰:³⁰**but he will receive one hundred times more now in this time, houses, brothers, sisters, mothers, children, and land, with persecutions; and in the age to come eternal life.** ¹⁰:³¹**But many who are first will be last; and the last first."**

¹⁰:³²They were on the way, going up to Jerusalem; and Jesus was going in front of them, and they were amazed; and those who followed were afraid. He again took the twelve, and began to tell them the things that were going to happen to him. ¹⁰:³³**"Behold, we are going up to Jerusalem. The Son of Man will be delivered to the chief priests and the scribes.**

ˣ10:6 Genesis 1:27
ʸ10:8 Genesis 2:24
ᶻ10:19 Exodus 20:12-16; Deuteronomy 5:16-20

They will condemn him to death, and will deliver him to the Gentiles. [10:34]**They will mock him, spit on him, scourge him, and kill him. On the third day he will rise again."**

[10:35]James and John, the sons of Zebedee, came near to him, saying, "Teacher, we want you to do for us whatever we will ask."

[10:36]He said to them, **"What do you want me to do for you?"**

[10:37]They said to him, "Grant to us that we may sit, one at your right hand, and one at your left hand, in your glory."

[10:38]But Jesus said to them, **"You don't know what you are asking. Are you able to drink the cup that I drink, and to be baptized with the baptism that I am baptized with?"**

[10:39]They said to him, "We are able."

Jesus said to them, **"You shall indeed drink the cup that I drink, and you shall be baptized with the baptism that I am baptized with;** [10:40]**but to sit at my right hand and at my left hand is not mine to give, but for whom it has been prepared."**

[10:41]When the ten heard it, they began to be indignant towards James and John.

[10:42]Jesus summoned them, and said to them, **"You know that they who are recognized as rulers over the nations lord it over them, and their great ones exercise authority over them.** [10:43]**But it shall not be so among you, but whoever wants to become great among you shall be your servant.** [10:44]**Whoever of you wants to become first among you, shall be bondservant of all.** [10:45]**For the Son of Man also came not to be served, but to serve, and to give his life as a ransom for many."**

[10:46]They came to Jericho. As he went out from Jericho, with his disciples and a great multitude, the son of Timaeus, Bartimaeus, a blind beggar, was sitting by the road. [10:47]When he heard that it was Jesus the Nazarene, he began to cry out, and say, "Jesus, you son of David, have mercy on me!" [10:48]Many rebuked him, that he should be quiet, but he cried out much more, "You son of David, have mercy on me!"

[10:49]Jesus stood still, and said, **"Call him."**

They called the blind man, saying to him, "Cheer up! Get up. He is calling you!"

[10:50]He, casting away his cloak, sprang up, and came to Jesus.

[10:51]Jesus asked him, **"What do you want me to do for you?"**

The blind man said to him, "Rhabboni,[a] that I may see again."

[10:52]Jesus said to him, **"Go your way. Your faith has made you well."** Immediately he received his sight, and followed Jesus in the way.

[11:1]When they drew near to Jerusalem, to Bethsphage[b] and Bethany, at the Mount of Olives, he sent two of his disciples, [11:2]and said to them, **"Go your way into the village that is opposite you. Immediately as you enter into it, you will find a young donkey tied, on which no one has sat. Untie him, and bring him.** [11:3]**If anyone asks you, 'Why are you doing this?' say, 'The Lord needs him;' and immediately he will send him back here."**

[11:4]They went away, and found a young donkey tied at the door outside in the open street, and they untied him. [11:5]Some of those who stood there asked them, "What are you doing, untying the young donkey?" [11:6]They said to them just as Jesus had said, and they let them go.

[11:7]They brought the young donkey to Jesus, and threw their garments on it, and Jesus sat on it. [11:8]Many spread their garments on the way, and others were cutting down branches from the trees, and spreading them on the road. [11:9]Those who went in front, and those who followed, cried out, "Hosanna[c]! Blessed is he who comes in the name of the Lord![d] [11:10]Blessed is the kingdom of our father David that is coming in the name of the Lord! Hosanna in the highest!"

---

[a]10:51 Rhabboni is a transliteration of the Hebrew word for "great teacher."
[b]11:1 TR & NU read "Bethphage" instead of "Bethsphage"
[c]11:9 "Hosanna" means "save us" or "help us, we pray."
[d]11:9 Psalm 118:25-26

¹¹:¹¹Jesus entered into the temple in Jerusalem. When he had looked around at everything, it being now evening, he went out to Bethany with the twelve.

¹¹:¹²The next day, when they had come out from Bethany, he was hungry. ¹¹:¹³Seeing a fig tree afar off having leaves, he came to see if perhaps he might find anything on it. When he came to it, he found nothing but leaves, for it was not the season for figs. ¹¹:¹⁴Jesus told it, **"May no one ever eat fruit from you again!"** and his disciples heard it.

¹¹:¹⁵They came to Jerusalem, and Jesus entered into the temple, and began to throw out those who sold and those who bought in the temple, and overthrew the tables of the money changers, and the seats of those who sold the doves. ¹¹:¹⁶He would not allow anyone to carry a container through the temple. ¹¹:¹⁷He taught, saying to them, **"Isn't it written, 'My house will be called a house of prayer for all the nations?'ᵉ But you have made it a den of robbers!"ᶠ**

¹¹:¹⁸The chief priests and the scribes heard it, and sought how they might destroy him. For they feared him, because all the multitude was astonished at his teaching.

¹¹:¹⁹When evening came, he went out of the city. ¹¹:²⁰As they passed by in the morning, they saw the fig tree withered away from the roots. ¹¹:²¹Peter, remembering, said to him, "Rabbi, look! The fig tree which you cursed has withered away."

¹¹:²²Jesus answered them, **"Have faith in God. ¹¹:²³For most certainly I tell you, whoever may tell this mountain, 'Be taken up and cast into the sea,' and doesn't doubt in his heart, but believes that what he says is happening; he shall have whatever he says. ¹¹:²⁴Therefore I tell you, all things whatever you pray and ask for, believe that you have received them, and you shall have them. ¹¹:²⁵Whenever you stand praying, forgive, if you have anything against anyone; so that your Father, who is in heaven, may also forgive you your transgressions. ¹¹:²⁶But if you do not forgive, neither will your Father in heaven forgive your transgressions."**

¹¹:²⁷They came again to Jerusalem, and as he was walking in the temple, the chief priests, and the scribes, and the elders came to him, ¹¹:²⁸and they began saying to him, "By what authority do you do these things? Or who gave you this authority to do these things?"

¹¹:²⁹Jesus said to them, **"I will ask you one question. Answer me, and I will tell you by what authority I do these things. ¹¹:³⁰The baptism of John—was it from heaven, or from men? Answer me."**

¹¹:³¹They reasoned with themselves, saying, "If we should say, 'From heaven;' he will say, 'Why then did you not believe him?' ¹¹:³²If we should say, 'From men'"— they feared the people, for all held John to really be a prophet. ¹¹:³³They answered Jesus, "We don't know."

Jesus said to them, **"Neither do I tell you by what authority I do these things."**

¹²:¹He began to speak to them in parables. **"A man planted a vineyard, put a hedge around it, dug a pit for the winepress, built a tower, rented it out to a farmer, and went into another country. ¹²:²When it was time, he sent a servant to the farmer to get from the farmer his share of the fruit of the vineyard. ¹²:³They took him, beat him, and sent him away empty. ¹²:⁴Again, he sent another servant to them; and they threw stones at him, wounded him in the head, and sent him away shamefully treated. ¹²:⁵Again he sent another; and they killed him; and many others, beating some, and killing some. ¹²:⁶Therefore still having one, his beloved son, he sent him last to them, saying, 'They will respect my son.' ¹²:⁷But those farmers said among themselves, 'This is the heir. Come, let's kill him, and the inheritance will be ours.' ¹²:⁸They took him, killed him, and cast him out of the vineyard. ¹²:⁹What therefore will the lord of the vineyard do? He will come and destroy the farmers, and will give the vineyard to others. ¹²:¹⁰Haven't you even read this Scripture:**

ᵉ11:17 Isaiah 56:7
ᶠ11:17 Jeremiah 7:11

'The stone which the builders rejected,
    the same was made the head of the
    corner.
[12:11] This was from the Lord,
    it is marvelous in our eyes'?"[g]
[12:12] They tried to seize him, but they feared the multitude; for they perceived that he spoke the parable against them. They left him, and went away. [12:13] They sent some of the Pharisees and of the Herodians to him, that they might trap him with words. [12:14] When they had come, they asked him, "Teacher, we know that you are honest, and don't defer to anyone; for you aren't partial to anyone, but truly teach the way of God. Is it lawful to pay taxes to Caesar, or not? [12:15] Shall we give, or shall we not give?"

But he, knowing their hypocrisy, said to them, **"Why do you test me? Bring me a denarius, that I may see it."**

[12:16] They brought it.

He said to them, **"Whose is this image and inscription?"**

They said to him, "Caesar's."

[12:17] Jesus answered them, **"Render to Caesar the things that are Caesar's, and to God the things that are God's."**

They marveled greatly at him.

[12:18] There came to him Sadducees, who say that there is no resurrection. They asked him, saying, [12:19] "Teacher, Moses wrote to us, 'If a man's brother dies, and leaves a wife behind him, and leaves no children, that his brother should take his wife, and raise up offspring for his brother.' [12:20] There were seven brothers. The first took a wife, and dying left no offspring. [12:21] The second took her, and died, leaving no children behind him. The third likewise; [12:22] and the seven took her and left no children. Last of all the woman also died. [12:23] In the resurrection, when they rise, whose wife will she be of them? For the seven had her as a wife."

[12:24] Jesus answered them, **"Isn't this because you are mistaken, not knowing the Scriptures, nor the power of God?** [12:25] **For when they will rise from the dead, they neither marry, nor are given in marriage, but are like angels in heaven.** [12:26] **But about the dead, that they are raised; haven't you read in the book of Moses, about the Bush, how God spoke to him, saying, 'I am the God of Abraham, the God of Isaac, and the God of Jacob'[h]?** [12:27] **He is not the God of the dead, but of the living. You are therefore badly mistaken."**

[12:28] One of the scribes came, and heard them questioning together. Knowing that he had answered them well, asked him, "Which commandment is the greatest of all?"

[12:29] Jesus answered, **"The greatest is, 'Hear, Israel, the Lord our God, the Lord is one:** [12:30] **you shall love the Lord your God with all your heart, and with all your soul, and with all your mind, and with all your strength.'[i] This is the first commandment.** [12:31] **The second is like this, 'You shall love your neighbor as yourself.'[j] There is no other commandment greater than these."**

[12:32] The scribe said to him, "Truly, teacher, you have said well that he is one, and there is none other but he, [12:33] and to love him with all the heart, and with all the understanding, with all the soul, and with all the strength, and to love his neighbor as himself, is more important than all whole burnt offerings and sacrifices."

[12:34] When Jesus saw that he answered wisely, he said to him, **"You are not far from the Kingdom of God."**

No one dared ask him any question after that. [12:35] Jesus responded, as he taught in the temple, **"How is it that the scribes say that the Christ is the son of David?** [12:36] **For David himself said in the Holy Spirit,**

'The Lord said to my Lord,
    "Sit at my right hand,
        until I make your enemies the footstool of your feet."'[k]

---

[g] 12:11 Psalm 118:22-23
[h] 12:26 Exodus 3:6
[i] 12:30 Deuteronomy 6:4-5
[j] 12:31 Leviticus 19:18
[k] 12:36 Psalm 110:1

[12:37]Therefore David himself calls him Lord, so how can he be his son?"

The common people heard him gladly. [12:38]In his teaching he said to them, "Beware of the scribes, who like to walk in long robes, and to get greetings in the marketplaces, [12:39]and the best seats in the synagogues, and the best places at feasts: [12:40]those who devour widows' houses, and for a pretense make long prayers. These will receive greater condemnation."

[12:41]Jesus sat down opposite the treasury, and saw how the multitude cast money into the treasury. Many who were rich cast in much. [12:42]A poor widow came, and she cast in two small brass coins,[l] which equal a quadrans coin.[m] [12:43]He called his disciples to himself, and said to them, "Most certainly I tell you, this poor widow gave more than all those who are giving into the treasury, [12:44]for they all gave out of their abundance, but she, out of her poverty, gave all that she had to live on."

[13:1]As he went out of the temple, one of his disciples said to him, "Teacher, see what kind of stones and what kind of buildings!"

[13:2]Jesus said to him, "Do you see these great buildings? There will not be left here one stone on another, which will not be thrown down."

[13:3]As he sat on the Mount of Olives opposite the temple, Peter, James, John, and Andrew asked him privately, [13:4]"Tell us, when will these things be? What is the sign that these things are all about to be fulfilled?"

[13:5]Jesus, answering, began to tell them, "Be careful that no one leads you astray. [13:6]For many will come in my name, saying, 'I am he!'[n] and will lead many astray.

[13:7]"When you hear of wars and rumors of wars, don't be troubled. For those must happen, but the end is not yet. [13:8]For nation will rise against nation, and kingdom against kingdom. There will be earthquakes in various places. There will be famines and troubles. These things are the beginning of birth pains. [13:9]But watch yourselves, for they will deliver you up to councils. You will be beaten in synagogues. You will stand before rulers and kings for my sake, for a testimony to them. [13:10]The Good News must first be preached to all the nations. [13:11]When they lead you away and deliver you up, don't be anxious beforehand, or premeditate what you will say, but say whatever will be given you in that hour. For it is not you who speak, but the Holy Spirit.

[13:12]"Brother will deliver up brother to death, and the father his child. Children will rise up against parents, and cause them to be put to death. [13:13]You will be hated by all men for my name's sake, but he who endures to the end, the same will be saved. [13:14]But when you see the abomination of desolation,[o] spoken of by Daniel the prophet, standing where it ought not (let the reader understand), then let those who are in Judea flee to the mountains, [13:15]and let him who is on the housetop not go down, nor enter in, to take anything out of his house. [13:16]Let him who is in the field not return back to take his cloak. [13:17]But woe to those who are with child and to those who nurse babies in those days! [13:18]Pray that your flight won't be in the winter. [13:19]For in those days there will be oppression, such as there has not been the like from the beginning of the creation which God created until now, and never will be. [13:20]Unless the Lord had shortened the days, no flesh would have been saved; but for the sake of the chosen ones, whom he picked out, he shortened the days. [13:21]Then if anyone tells you, 'Look, here is the Christ!' or, 'Look, there!' don't believe it. [13:22]For there will arise false christs and false prophets, and will show

---

[l]12:42 literally, lepta (or widow's mites). Lepta are very small brass coins worth half a quadrans each, which is a quarter of the copper assarion. Lepta are worth less than 1% of an agricultural worker's daily wages.
[m]12:42 A quadrans is a coin worth about 1/64 of a denarius. A denarius is about one day's wages for an agricultural laborer.
[n]13:6 or, "I AM!"
[o]13:14 Daniel 9:17; 11:31; 12:11

signs and wonders, that they may lead astray, if possible, even the chosen ones. [13:23]But you watch.

"Behold, I have told you all things beforehand. [13:24]But in those days, after that oppression, the sun will be darkened, the moon will not give its light, [13:25]the stars will be falling from the sky, and the powers that are in the heavens will be shaken.[p] [13:26]Then they will see the Son of Man coming in clouds with great power and glory. [13:27]Then he will send out his angels, and will gather together his chosen ones from the four winds, from the ends of the earth to the ends of the sky.

[13:28]"Now from the fig tree, learn this parable. When the branch has now become tender, and puts forth its leaves, you know that the summer is near; [13:29]even so you also, when you see these things coming to pass, know that it is near, at the doors. [13:30]Most certainly I say to you, this generation[q] will not pass away until all these things happen. [13:31]Heaven and earth will pass away, but my words will not pass away. [13:32]But of that day or that hour no one knows, not even the angels in heaven, nor the Son, but only the Father. [13:33]Watch, keep alert, and pray; for you don't know when the time is.

[13:34]"It is like a man, traveling to another country, having left his house, and given authority to his servants, and to each one his work, and also commanded the doorkeeper to keep watch. [13:35]Watch therefore, for you don't know when the lord of the house is coming, whether at evening, or at midnight, or when the rooster crows, or in the morning; [13:36]lest coming suddenly he might find you sleeping. [13:37]What I tell you, I tell all: Watch."

[14:1]It was now two days before the feast of the Passover and the unleavened bread, and the chief priests and the scribes sought how they might seize him by deception, and kill him. [14:2]For they said, "Not during the feast, because there might be a riot of the people."

[14:3]While he was at Bethany, in the house of Simon the leper, as he sat at the table, a woman came having an alabaster jar of ointment of pure nard—very costly. She broke the jar, and poured it over his head. [14:4]But there were some who were indignant among themselves, saying, "Why has this ointment been wasted? [14:5]For this might have been sold for more than three hundred denarii,[r] and given to the poor." They grumbled against her.

[14:6]But Jesus said, **"Leave her alone. Why do you trouble her? She has done a good work for me. [14:7]For you always have the poor with you, and whenever you want to, you can do them good; but you will not always have me. [14:8]She has done what she could. She has anointed my body beforehand for the burying. [14:9]Most certainly I tell you, wherever this Good News may be preached throughout the whole world, that which this woman has done will also be spoken of for a memorial of her."**

[14:10]Judas Iscariot, who was one of the twelve, went away to the chief priests, that he might deliver him to them. [14:11]They, when they heard it, were glad, and promised to give him money. He sought how he might conveniently deliver him. [14:12]On the first day of unleavened bread, when they sacrificed the Passover, his disciples asked him, "Where do you want us to go and make ready that you may eat the Passover?"

[14:13]He sent two of his disciples, and said to them, **"Go into the city, and there you will meet a man carrying a pitcher of water. Follow him, [14:14]and wherever he enters in, tell the master of the house, 'The Teacher says, "Where is the guest room, where I may eat the Passover with my disciples?"' [14:15]He will himself show you a large upper room furnished and ready. Make ready for us there."**

[14:16]His disciples went out, and came into the city, and found things as he had said to them, and they prepared the Passover.

---

[p]13:25 Isaiah 13:10; 34:4

[q]13:30 The word translated "generation" (genea) could also be translated "race," "family," or "people."

[r]14:5 300 denarii was about a years wages for an agricultural laborer.

¹⁴:¹⁷When it was evening he came with the twelve. ¹⁴:¹⁸As they sat and were eating, Jesus said, **"Most certainly I tell you, one of you will betray me—he who eats with me."**

¹⁴:¹⁹They began to be sorrowful, and to ask him one by one, "Surely not I?" And another said, "Surely not I?"

¹⁴:²⁰He answered them, **"It is one of the twelve, he who dips with me in the dish.** ¹⁴:²¹**For the Son of Man goes, even as it is written about him, but woe to that man by whom the Son of Man is betrayed! It would be better for that man if he had not been born."**

¹⁴:²²As they were eating, Jesus took bread, and when he had blessed, he broke it, and gave to them, and said, **"Take, eat. This is my body."**

¹⁴:²³He took the cup, and when he had given thanks, he gave to them. They all drank of it. ¹⁴:²⁴He said to them, **"This is my blood of the new covenant, which is poured out for many.** ¹⁴:²⁵**Most certainly I tell you, I will no more drink of the fruit of the vine, until that day when I drink it anew in the Kingdom of God."** ¹⁴:²⁶When they had sung a hymn, they went out to the Mount of Olives.

¹⁴:²⁷Jesus said to them, **"All of you will be made to stumble because of me tonight, for it is written, 'I will strike the shepherd, and the sheep will be scattered.'ˢ** ¹⁴:²⁸**However, after I am raised up, I will go before you into Galilee."**

¹⁴:²⁹But Peter said to him, "Although all will be offended, yet I will not."

¹⁴:³⁰Jesus said to him, **"Most certainly I tell you, that you today, even this night, before the rooster crows twice, you will deny me three times."**

¹⁴:³¹But he spoke all the more, "If I must die with you, I will not deny you." They all said the same thing.

¹⁴:³²They came to a place which was named Gethsemane. He said to his disciples, **"Sit here, while I pray."** ¹⁴:³³He took with him Peter, James, and John, and began to be greatly troubled and distressed. ¹⁴:³⁴He said to them, **"My soul is exceedingly sorrowful, even to death. Stay here, and watch."**

¹⁴:³⁵He went forward a little, and fell on the ground, and prayed that, if it were possible, the hour might pass away from him. ¹⁴:³⁶He said, **"Abba, Father, all things are possible to you. Please remove this cup from me. However, not what I desire, but what you desire."**

¹⁴:³⁷He came and found them sleeping, and said to Peter, **"Simon, are you sleeping? Couldn't you watch one hour?** ¹⁴:³⁸**Watch and pray, that you may not enter into temptation. The spirit indeed is willing, but the flesh is weak."**

¹⁴:³⁹Again he went away, and prayed, saying the same words. ¹⁴:⁴⁰Again he returned, and found them sleeping, for their eyes were very heavy, and they didn't know what to answer him. ¹⁴:⁴¹He came the third time, and said to them, **"Sleep on now, and take your rest. It is enough. The hour has come. Behold, the Son of Man is betrayed into the hands of sinners.** ¹⁴:⁴²**Arise, let us be going. Behold, he who betrays me is at hand."**

¹⁴:⁴³Immediately, while he was still speaking, Judas, one of the twelve, came—and with him a multitude with swords and clubs, from the chief priests, the scribes, and the elders. ¹⁴:⁴⁴Now he who betrayed him had given them a sign, saying, "Whoever I will kiss, that is he. Seize him, and lead him away safely." ¹⁴:⁴⁵When he had come, immediately he came to him, and said, "Rabbi! Rabbi!" and kissed him. ¹⁴:⁴⁶They laid their hands on him, and seized him. ¹⁴:⁴⁷But a certain one of those who stood by drew his sword, and struck the servant of the high priest, and cut off his ear.

¹⁴:⁴⁸Jesus answered them, **"Have you come out, as against a robber, with swords and clubs to seize me?** ¹⁴:⁴⁹**I was daily with you in the temple teaching, and you didn't arrest me. But this is so that the Scriptures might be fulfilled."**

¹⁴:⁵⁰They all left him, and fled. ¹⁴:⁵¹A certain young man followed him, having a linen cloth thrown around himself, over his naked body. The young men grabbed him, ¹⁴:⁵²but he left the linen cloth, and fled

ˢ14:27 Zechariah 13:7

from them naked. [14:53] They led Jesus away to the high priest. All the chief priests, the elders, and the scribes came together with him.

[14:54] Peter had followed him from a distance, until he came into the court of the high priest. He was sitting with the officers, and warming himself in the light of the fire. [14:55] Now the chief priests and the whole council sought witnesses against Jesus to put him to death, and found none. [14:56] For many gave false testimony against him, and their testimony didn't agree with each other. [14:57] Some stood up, and gave false testimony against him, saying, [14:58] "We heard him say, 'I will destroy this temple that is made with hands, and in three days I will build another made without hands.'" [14:59] Even so, their testimony did not agree.

[14:60] The high priest stood up in the midst, and asked Jesus, "Have you no answer? What is it which these testify against you?" [14:61] But he stayed quiet, and answered nothing.   Again the high priest asked him, "Are you the Christ, the Son of the Blessed?"

[14:62] Jesus said, **"I am. You will see the Son of Man sitting at the right hand of Power, and coming with the clouds of the sky."**

[14:63] The high priest tore his clothes, and said, "What further need have we of witnesses?   [14:64] You have heard the blasphemy! What do you think?" They all condemned him to be worthy of death. [14:65] Some began to spit on him, and to cover his face, and to beat him with fists, and to tell him, "Prophesy!" The officers struck him with the palms of their hands.

[14:66] As Peter was in the courtyard below, one of the maids of the high priest came, [14:67] and seeing Peter warming himself, she looked at him, and said, "You were also with the Nazarene, Jesus!"

[14:68] But he denied it, saying, "I neither know, nor understand what you are saying." He went out on the porch, and the rooster crowed.

[14:69] The maid saw him, and began again to tell those who stood by, "This is one of them." [14:70] But he again denied it. After a little while again those who stood by said

to Peter, "You truly are one of them, for you are a Galilean, and your speech shows it."   [14:71] But he began to curse, and to swear, "I don't know this man of whom you speak!"   [14:72] The rooster crowed the second time. Peter remembered the word, how that Jesus said to him, **"Before the rooster crows twice, you will deny me three times."** When he thought about that, he wept.

[15:1] Immediately in the morning the chief priests, with the elders and scribes, and the whole council, held a consultation, and bound Jesus, and carried him away, and delivered him up to Pilate. [15:2] Pilate asked him, "Are you the King of the Jews?"

He answered, **"So you say."**

[15:3] The chief priests accused him of many things. [15:4] Pilate again asked him, "Have you no answer? See how many things they testify against you!"

[15:5] But Jesus made no further answer, so that Pilate marveled.

[15:6] Now at the feast he used to release to them one prisoner, whom they asked of him.   [15:7] There was one called Barabbas, bound with those who had made insurrection, men who in the insurrection had committed murder.   [15:8] The multitude, crying aloud, began to ask him to do as he always did for them.   [15:9] Pilate answered them, saying, "Do you want me to release to you the King of the Jews?" [15:10] For he perceived that for envy the chief priests had delivered him up.   [15:11] But the chief priests stirred up the multitude, that he should release Barabbas to them instead. [15:12] Pilate again asked them, "What then should I do to him whom you call the King of the Jews?"

[15:13] They cried out again, "Crucify him!"

[15:14] Pilate said to them, "Why, what evil has he done?"

But they cried out exceedingly, "Crucify him!"

[15:15] Pilate, wishing to please the multitude, released Barabbas to them, and handed over Jesus, when he had flogged him, to be crucified.   [15:16] The soldiers led him away within the court, which is the Praetorium; and they called together the whole cohort.   [15:17] They clothed him with purple, and weaving a crown of thorns, they put it on him. ^{15:18}They began to salute him, "Hail, King of the Jews!" ^{15:19}They struck his head with a reed, and spat on him, and bowing their knees, did homage to him. ^{15:20}When they had mocked him, they took the purple off of him, and put his own garments on him. They led him out to crucify him. ^{15:21}They compelled one passing by, coming from the country, Simon of Cyrene, the father of Alexander and Rufus, to go with them, that he might bear his cross. ^{15:22}They brought him to the place called Golgotha, which is, being interpreted, "The place of a skull." ^{15:23}They offered him wine mixed with myrrh to drink, but he didn't take it.

^{15:24}Crucifying him, they parted his garments among them, casting lots on them, what each should take. ^{15:25}It was the third hour,^t and they crucified him. ^{15:26}The superscription of his accusation was written over him, "THE KING OF THE JEWS." ^{15:27}With him they crucified two robbers; one on his right hand, and one on his left. ^{15:28}The Scripture was fulfilled, which says, "He was numbered with transgressors."

^{15:29}Those who passed by blasphemed him, wagging their heads, and saying, "Ha! You who destroy the temple, and build it in three days, ^{15:30}save yourself, and come down from the cross!"

^{15:31}Likewise, also the chief priests mocking among themselves with the scribes said, "He saved others. He can't save himself. ^{15:32}Let the Christ, the King of Israel, now come down from the cross, that we may see and believe him.^u" Those who were crucified with him insulted him.

^{15:33}When the sixth hour^v had come, there was darkness over the whole land until the ninth hour.^w ^{15:34}At the ninth hour Jesus cried with a loud voice, saying, **"Eloi, Eloi, lama sabachthani?"** which is, being interpreted, **"My God, my God, why have you forsaken me?"**^x

^{15:35}Some of those who stood by, when they heard it, said, "Behold, he is calling Elijah."

^{15:36}One ran, and filling a sponge full of vinegar, put it on a reed, and gave it to him to drink, saying, "Let him be. Let's see whether Elijah comes to take him down."

^{15:37}Jesus cried out with a loud voice, and gave up the spirit. ^{15:38}The veil of the temple was torn in two from the top to the bottom. ^{15:39}When the centurion, who stood by opposite him, saw that he cried out like this and breathed his last, he said, "Truly this man was the Son of God!"

^{15:40}There were also women watching from afar, among whom were both Mary Magdalene, and Mary the mother of James the less and of Joses, and Salome; ^{15:41}who, when he was in Galilee, followed him, and served him; and many other women who came up with him to Jerusalem.

^{15:42}When evening had now come, because it was the Preparation Day, that is, the day before the Sabbath, ^{15:43}Joseph of Arimathaea, a prominent council member who also himself was looking for the Kingdom of God, came. He boldly went in to Pilate, and asked for Jesus' body. ^{15:44}Pilate marveled if he were already dead; and summoning the centurion, he asked him whether he had been dead long. ^{15:45}When he found out from the centurion, he granted the body to Joseph. ^{15:46}He bought a linen cloth, and taking him down, wound him in the linen cloth, and laid him in a tomb which had been cut out of a rock. He rolled a stone against the door of the tomb. ^{15:47}Mary Magdalene and Mary, the mother of Joses, saw where he was laid.

^{16:1}When the Sabbath was past, Mary Magdalene, and Mary the mother of James, and Salome, bought spices, that they might come and anoint him. ^{16:2}Very early on the first day of the week, they came to the tomb when the sun had risen. ^{16:3}They were saying among themselves, "Who will roll away the stone from the door of the tomb for us?" ^{16:4}for it was very big. Looking up, they saw that the stone was rolled back.

---

^t15:25 9:00 A. M.
^u15:32 TR omits "him"
^v15:33 or, noon
^w15:33 3:00 PM
^x15:34 Psalm 22:1

16:5Entering into the tomb, they saw a young man sitting on the right side, dressed in a white robe, and they were amazed. 16:6He said to them, "Don't be amazed. You seek Jesus, the Nazarene, who has been crucified. He has risen. He is not here. Behold, the place where they laid him! 16:7But go, tell his disciples and Peter, 'He goes before you into Galilee. There you will see him, as he said to you.'"

16:8They went out,ʸ and fled from the tomb, for trembling and astonishment had come on them. They said nothing to anyone; for they were afraid. 16:9Now when he had risen early on the first day of the week, he appeared first to Mary Magdalene, from whom he had cast out seven demons. 16:10She went and told those who had been with him, as they mourned and wept. 16:11When they heard that he was alive, and had been seen by her, they disbelieved. 16:12After these things he was revealed in another form to two of them, as they walked, on their way into the country. 16:13They went away and told it to the rest. They didn't believe them, either.

16:14Afterward he was revealed to the eleven themselves as they sat at the table, and he rebuked them for their unbelief and hardness of heart, because they didn't believe those who had seen him after he had risen. 16:15He said to them, **"Go into all the world, and preach the Good News to the whole creation. 16:16He who believes and is baptized will be saved; but he who disbelieves will be condemned. 16:17These signs will accompany those who believe: in my name they will cast out demons; they will speak with new languages; 16:18they will take up serpents; and if they drink any deadly thing, it will in no way hurt them; they will lay hands on the sick, and they will recover."**

16:19So then the Lord Jesus, after he had spoken to them, was received up into heaven, and sat down at the right hand of God. 16:20They went out, and preached everywhere, the Lord working with them, and confirming the word by the signs that followed. Amen.

_____
ʸ16:8 TR adds "quickly"

The Good News According to Luke

1:1Since many have undertaken to set in order a narrative concerning those matters which have been fulfilled among us, 1:2even as those who from the beginning were eyewitnesses and servants of the word delivered them to us, 1:3it seemed good to me also, having traced the course of all things accurately from the first, to write to you in order, most excellent Theophilus; 1:4that you might know the certainty concerning the things in which you were instructed.

1:5There was in the days of Herod, the king of Judea, a certain priest named Zacharias, of the priestly division of Abijah. He had a wife of the daughters of Aaron, and her name was Elizabeth. 1:6They were both righteous before God, walking blamelessly in all the commandments and ordinances of the Lord. 1:7But they had no child, because Elizabeth was barren, and they both were well advanced in years. 1:8Now it happened, while he executed the priest's office before God in the order of his division, 1:9according to the custom of the priest's office, his lot was to enter into the temple of the Lord and burn incense. 1:10The whole multitude of the people were praying outside at the hour of incense.

1:11An angel of the Lord appeared to him, standing on the right side of the altar of incense. 1:12Zacharias was troubled when he saw him, and fear fell upon him. 1:13But the angel said to him, "Don't be afraid, Zacharias, because your request has been heard, and your wife, Elizabeth, will bear you a son, and you shall call his name John. 1:14You will have joy and gladness; and many will rejoice at his birth. 1:15For he will be great in the sight of the Lord, and he will drink no wine nor strong drink. He will be filled with the Holy Spirit, even from his mother's womb. 1:16He will turn many of the children of Israel to the Lord, their God.

1:17He will go before him in the spirit and power of Elijah, 'to turn the hearts of the fathers to the children,' and the disobedient to the wisdom of the just; to make ready a people prepared for the Lord."

1:18Zacharias said to the angel, "How can I be sure of this? For I am an old man, and my wife is well advanced in years."

1:19The angel answered him, "I am Gabriel, who stands in the presence of God. I was sent to speak to you, and to bring you this good news. 1:20Behold, you will be silent and not able to speak, until the day that these things will happen, because you didn't believe my words, which will be fulfilled in their proper time."

1:21The people were waiting for Zacharias, and they marveled that he delayed in the temple. 1:22When he came out, he could not speak to them, and they perceived that he had seen a vision in the temple. He continued making signs to them, and remained mute. 1:23It happened, when the days of his service were fulfilled, he departed to his house. 1:24After these days Elizabeth, his wife, conceived, and she hid herself five months, saying, 1:25"Thus has the Lord done to me in the days in which he looked at me, to take away my reproach among men."

1:26Now in the sixth month, the angel Gabriel was sent from God to a city of Galilee, named Nazareth, 1:27to a virgin pledged to be married to a man whose name was Joseph, of the house of David. The virgin's name was Mary. 1:28Having come in, the angel said to her, "Rejoice, you highly favored one! The Lord is with you. Blessed are you among women!"

1:29But when she saw him, she was greatly troubled at the saying, and considered what kind of salutation this might be. 1:30The angel said to her, "Don't be afraid, Mary, for you have found favor with God. 1:31Behold, you will conceive in your womb, and bring forth a son, and will call his name 'Jesus.' 1:32He will be great, and will be called the Son of the Most High. The Lord God will give him the throne of his father, David, 1:33and he will reign over the house of Jacob forever. There will be no end to his Kingdom."

1:34Mary said to the angel, "How can this be, seeing I am a virgin?"

1:35The angel answered her, "The Holy Spirit will come on you, and the power of the Most High will overshadow you. Therefore also the holy one who is born from you will be called the Son of God. 1:36Behold, Elizabeth, your relative, also has conceived a son in her old age; and this is the sixth month with her who was called barren. 1:37For everything spoken by God is possible."

1:38Mary said, "Behold, the handmaid of the Lord; be it to me according to your word."

The angel departed from her. 1:39Mary arose in those days and went into the hill country with haste, into a city of Judah, 1:40and entered into the house of Zacharias and greeted Elizabeth. 1:41It happened, when Elizabeth heard Mary's greeting, that the baby leaped in her womb, and Elizabeth was filled with the Holy Spirit. 1:42She called out with a loud voice, and said, "Blessed are you among women, and blessed is the fruit of your womb! 1:43Why am I so favored, that the mother of my Lord should come to me? 1:44For behold, when the voice of your greeting came into my ears, the baby leaped in my womb for joy! 1:45Blessed is she who believed, for there will be a fulfillment of the things which have been spoken to her from the Lord!"

1:46Mary said,

"My soul magnifies the Lord.
1:47My spirit has rejoiced in God my Savior,
1:48for he has looked at the humble state of his handmaid.

For behold, from now on, all generations will call me blessed.
1:49For he who is mighty has done great things for me.

Holy is his name.
1:50His mercy is for generations of generations on those who fear him.
1:51He has shown strength with his arm.

He has scattered the proud in the imagination of their heart.
1:52He has put down princes from their thrones.

And has exalted the lowly.

^{1:53}He has filled the hungry with good things.

He has sent the rich away empty.
^{1:54}He has given help to Israel, his servant, that he might remember mercy,
^{1:55}As he spoke to our fathers, to Abraham and his seed forever."

^{1:56}Mary stayed with her about three months, and then returned to her house. ^{1:57}Now the time that Elizabeth should give birth was fulfilled, and she brought forth a son. ^{1:58}Her neighbors and her relatives heard that the Lord had magnified his mercy towards her, and they rejoiced with her. ^{1:59}It happened on the eighth day, that they came to circumcise the child; and they would have called him Zacharias, after the name of the father. ^{1:60}His mother answered, "Not so; but he will be called John."

^{1:61}They said to her, "There is no one among your relatives who is called by this name." ^{1:62}They made signs to his father, what he would have him called.

^{1:63}He asked for a writing tablet, and wrote, "His name is John."

They all marveled. ^{1:64}His mouth was opened immediately, and his tongue freed, and he spoke, blessing God. ^{1:65}Fear came on all who lived around them, and all these sayings were talked about throughout all the hill country of Judea. ^{1:66}All who heard them laid them up in their heart, saying, "What then will this child be?" The hand of the Lord was with him. ^{1:67}His father, Zacharias, was filled with the Holy Spirit, and prophesied, saying,

^{1:68}"Blessed be the Lord, the God of Israel, for he has visited and worked redemption for his people;
^{1:69}and has raised up a horn of salvation for us in the house of his servant David
^{1:70}(as he spoke by the mouth of his holy prophets who have been from of old),
^{1:71}salvation from our enemies, and from the hand of all who hate us;
^{1:72}to show mercy towards our fathers, to remember his holy covenant,
^{1:73}the oath which he spoke to Abraham, our father,

^{1:74}to grant to us that we, being delivered out of the hand of our enemies, should serve him without fear,
^{1:75}In holiness and righteousness before him all the days of our life.
^{1:76}And you, child, will be called a prophet of the Most High,
for you will go before the face of the Lord to make ready his ways,
^{1:77}to give knowledge of salvation to his people by the remission of their sins,
^{1:78}because of the tender mercy of our God, whereby the dawn from on high will visit us,
^{1:79}to shine on those who sit in darkness and the shadow of death;
to guide our feet into the way of peace."

^{1:80}The child was growing, and becoming strong in spirit, and was in the desert until the day of his public appearance to Israel.

^{2:1}Now it happened in those days, that a decree went out from Caesar Augustus that all the world should be enrolled. ^{2:2}This was the first enrollment made when Quirinius was governor of Syria. ^{2:3}All went to enroll themselves, everyone to his own city. ^{2:4}Joseph also went up from Galilee, out of the city of Nazareth, into Judea, to the city of David, which is called Bethlehem, because he was of the house and family of David; ^{2:5}to enroll himself with Mary, who was pledged to be married to him as wife, being pregnant.

^{2:6}It happened, while they were there, that the day had come that she should give birth. ^{2:7}She brought forth her firstborn son, and she wrapped him in bands of cloth, and laid him in a feeding trough, because there was no room for them in the inn. ^{2:8}There were shepherds in the same country staying in the field, and keeping watch by night over their flock. ^{2:9}Behold, an angel of the Lord stood by them, and the glory of the Lord shone around them, and they were terrified. ^{2:10}The angel said to them, "Don't be afraid, for behold, I bring you good news of great joy which will be to all the people. ^{2:11}For there is born to you, this day, in the city of David, a Savior, who is Christ the Lord. ^{2:12}This is the sign

to you: you will find a baby wrapped in strips of cloth, lying in a feeding trough." 2:13Suddenly, there was with the angel a multitude of the heavenly army praising God, and saying,
2:14"Glory to God in the highest,
    on earth peace, good will toward men."
2:15It happened, when the angels went away from them into the sky, that the shepherds said one to another, "Let's go to Bethlehem, now, and see this thing that has happened, which the Lord has made known to us." 2:16They came with haste, and found both Mary and Joseph, and the baby was lying in the feeding trough. 2:17When they saw it, they publicized widely the saying which was spoken to them about this child. 2:18All who heard it wondered at the things which were spoken to them by the shepherds. 2:19But Mary kept all these sayings, pondering them in her heart. 2:20The shepherds returned, glorifying and praising God for all the things that they had heard and seen, just as it was told them.
2:21When eight days were fulfilled for the circumcision of the child, his name was called Jesus, which was given by the angel before he was conceived in the womb.
2:22When the days of their purification according to the law of Moses were fulfilled, they brought him up to Jerusalem, to present him to the Lord 2:23(as it is written in the law of the Lord, "Every male who opens the womb shall be called holy to the Lord"),a 2:24and to offer a sacrifice according to that which is said in the law of the Lord, "A pair of turtledoves, or two young pigeons."b
2:25Behold, there was a man in Jerusalem whose name was Simeon. This man was righteous and devout, looking for the consolation of Israel, and the Holy Spirit was on him. 2:26It had been revealed to him by the Holy Spirit that he should not see death before he had seen the Lord's Christ.c 2:27He came in the Spirit into the temple. When the parents brought in the child, Jesus, that they might do concerning him according to the custom of the law, 2:28then

he received him into his arms, and blessed God, and said,
2:29"Now you are releasing your servant, Master,
    according to your word, in peace;
2:30for my eyes have seen your salvation,
    2:31which you have prepared before the face of all peoples;
2:32a light for revelation to the nations,
    and the glory of your people Israel."
2:33Joseph and his mother were marveling at the things which were spoken concerning him, 2:34and Simeon blessed them, and said to Mary, his mother, "Behold, this child is set for the falling and the rising of many in Israel, and for a sign which is spoken against. 2:35Yes, a sword will pierce through your own soul, that the thoughts of many hearts may be revealed."
2:36There was one Anna, a prophetess, the daughter of Phanuel, of the tribe of Asher (she was of a great age, having lived with a husband seven years from her virginity, 2:37and she had been a widow for about eighty-four years), who didn't depart from the temple, worshipping with fastings and petitions night and day. 2:38Coming up at that very hour, she gave thanks to the Lord, and spoke of him to all those who were looking for redemption in Jerusalem.
2:39When they had accomplished all things that were according to the law of the Lord, they returned into Galilee, to their own city, Nazareth. 2:40The child was growing, and was becoming strong in spirit, being filled with wisdom, and the grace of God was upon him. 2:41His parents went every year to Jerusalem at the feast of the Passover.
2:42When he was twelve years old, they went up to Jerusalem according to the custom of the feast, 2:43and when they had fulfilled the days, as they were returning, the boy Jesus stayed behind in Jerusalem. Joseph and his mother didn't know it, 2:44but supposing him to be in the company, they went a day's journey, and they looked for him among their relatives and

a2:23 Exodus 13:2,12
b2:24 Leviticus 12:8
c2:26 "Christ" (Greek) and "Messiah" (Hebrew) both mean "Anointed One"

acquaintances. [2:45]When they didn't find him, they returned to Jerusalem, looking for him. [2:46]It happened after three days they found him in the temple, sitting in the midst of the teachers, both listening to them, and asking them questions. [2:47]All who heard him were amazed at his understanding and his answers. [2:48]When they saw him, they were astonished, and his mother said to him, "Son, why have you treated us this way? Behold, your father and I were anxiously looking for you."

[2:49]He said to them, **"Why were you looking for me? Didn't you know that I must be in my Father's house?"** [2:50]They didn't understand the saying which he spoke to them. [2:51]And he went down with them, and came to Nazareth. He was subject to them, and his mother kept all these sayings in her heart. [2:52]And Jesus increased in wisdom and stature, and in favor with God and men.

[3:1]Now in the fifteenth year of the reign of Tiberius Caesar, Pontius Pilate being governor of Judea, and Herod being tetrarch of Galilee, and his brother Philip tetrarch of the region of Ituraea and Trachonitis, and Lysanias tetrarch of Abilene, [3:2]in the high priesthood of Annas and Caiaphas, the word of God came to John, the son of Zacharias, in the wilderness. [3:3]He came into all the region around the Jordan, preaching the baptism of repentance for remission of sins. [3:4]As it is written in the book of the words of Isaiah the prophet,
"The voice of one crying in the wilderness,
  'Make ready the way of the Lord.
Make his paths straight.
[3:5]Every valley will be filled.
Every mountain and hill will be brought
    low.
  The crooked will become straight,
    and the rough ways smooth.
[3:6]All flesh will see God's salvation.'"[d]

[3:7]He said therefore to the multitudes who went out to be baptized by him, "You offspring of vipers, who warned you to flee from the wrath to come? [3:8]Bring forth therefore fruits worthy of repentance, and don't begin to say among yourselves, 'We have Abraham for our father;' for I tell you that God is able to raise up children to Abraham from these stones! [3:9]Even now the axe also lies at the root of the trees. Every tree therefore that doesn't bring forth good fruit is cut down, and thrown into the fire."

[3:10]The multitudes asked him, "What then must we do?"

[3:11]He answered them, "He who has two coats, let him give to him who has none. He who has food, let him do likewise."

[3:12]Tax collectors also came to be baptized, and they said to him, "Teacher, what must we do?"

[3:13]He said to them, "Collect no more than that which is appointed to you."

[3:14]Soldiers also asked him, saying, "What about us? What must we do?"

He said to them, "Extort from no one by violence, neither accuse anyone wrongfully. Be content with your wages."

[3:15]As the people were in expectation, and all men reasoned in their hearts concerning John, whether perhaps he was the Christ, [3:16]John answered them all, "I indeed baptize you with water, but he comes who is mightier than I, the latchet of whose sandals I am not worthy to loosen. He will baptize you in the Holy Spirit and fire, [3:17]whose fan is in his hand, and he will thoroughly cleanse his threshing floor, and will gather the wheat into his barn; but he will burn up the chaff with unquenchable fire."

[3:18]Then with many other exhortations he preached good news to the people, [3:19]but Herod the tetrarch, being reproved by him for Herodias, his brother's[e] wife, and for all the evil things which Herod had done, [3:20]added this also to them all, that he shut up John in prison. [3:21]Now it happened, when all the people were baptized, Jesus also had been baptized, and was praying. The sky was opened, [3:22]and the Holy Spirit descended in a bodily form as a dove on him; and a voice came out of the sky, saying "You are my beloved Son. In you I am well pleased."

---

[d]3:6 Isaiah 40:3-5
[e]3:19 TR reads "brother Philip's" instead of "brother's"

^{3:23}Jesus himself, when he began to teach, was about thirty years old, being the son (as was supposed) of Joseph, the son of Heli, ^{3:24}the son of Matthat, the son of Levi, the son of Melchi, the son of Jannai, the son of Joseph, ^{3:25}the son of Mattathias, the son of Amos, the son of Nahum, the son of Esli, the son of Naggai, ^{3:26}the son of Maath, the son of Mattathias, the son of Semein, the son of Joseph, the son of Judah, ^{3:27}the son of Joanan, the son of Rhesa, the son of Zerubbabel, the son of Shealtiel, the son of Neri, ^{3:28}the son of Melchi, the son of Addi, the son of Cosam, the son of Elmodam, the son of Er, ^{3:29}the son of Jose, the son of Eliezer, the son of Jorim, the son of Matthat, the son of Levi, ^{3:30}the son of Simeon, the son of Judah, the son of Joseph, the son of Jonan, the son of Eliakim, ^{3:31}the son of Melea, the son of Menan, the son of Mattatha, the son of Nathan, the son of David, ^{3:32}the son of Jesse, the son of Obed, the son of Boaz, the son of Salmon, the son of Nahshon, ^{3:33}the son of Amminadab, the son of Aram,^f the son of Hezron, the son of Perez, the son of Judah, ^{3:34}the son of Jacob, the son of Isaac, the son of Abraham, the son of Terah, the son of Nahor, ^{3:35}the son of Serug, the son of Reu, the son of Peleg, the son of Eber, the son of Shelah, ^{3:36}the son of Cainan, the son of Arphaxad, the son of Shem, the son of Noah, the son of Lamech, ^{3:37}the son of Methuselah, the son of Enoch, the son of Jared, the son of Mahalaleel, the son of Cainan, ^{3:38}the son of Enos, the son of Seth, the son of Adam, the son of God.

^{4:1}Jesus, full of the Holy Spirit, returned from the Jordan, and was led by the Spirit into the wilderness ^{4:2}for forty days, being tempted by the devil. He ate nothing in those days. Afterward, when they were completed, he was hungry. ^{4:3}The devil said to him, "If you are the Son of God, command this stone to become bread."

^{4:4}Jesus answered him, saying, **"It is written, 'Man shall not live by bread alone, but by every word of God.'"^g**

^{4:5}The devil, leading him up on a high mountain, showed him all the kingdoms of the world in a moment of time. ^{4:6}The devil said to him, "I will give you all this authority, and their glory, for it has been delivered to me; and I give it to whomever I want. ^{4:7}If you therefore will worship before me, it will all be yours."

^{4:8}Jesus answered him, **"Get behind me Satan! For it is written, 'You shall worship the Lord your God, and you shall serve him only.'"^h**

^{4:9}He led him to Jerusalem, and set him on the pinnacle of the temple, and said to him, "If you are the Son of God, cast yourself down from here, ^{4:10}for it is written,

'He will put his angels in charge of you, to
> guard you;'

^{4:11}and,

'On their hands they will bear you up,
> lest perhaps you dash your foot against
> a stone.'"ⁱ

^{4:12}Jesus answering, said to him, **"It has been said, 'You shall not tempt the Lord your God.'"^j**

^{4:13}When the devil had completed every temptation, he departed from him until another time.

^{4:14}Jesus returned in the power of the Spirit into Galilee, and news about him spread through all the surrounding area. ^{4:15}He taught in their synagogues, being glorified by all.

^{4:16}He came to Nazareth, where he had been brought up. He entered, as was his custom, into the synagogue on the Sabbath day, and stood up to read. ^{4:17}The book of the prophet Isaiah was handed to him. He opened the book, and found the place where it was written,

^{4:18}**"The Spirit of the Lord is on me,
> because he has anointed me to preach
> good news to the poor.
He has sent me to heal the broken-
> hearted,^k**

---

^f3:33 NU reads "Admin, the son of Arni" instead of "Aram"
^g4:4 Deuteronomy 8:3
^h4:8 Deuteronomy 6:13
ⁱ4:11 Psalm 91:11-12
^j4:12 Deuteronomy 6:16
^k4:18 NU omits "to heal the brokenhearted"

to proclaim release to the captives,
recovering of sight to the blind,
to deliver those who are crushed,
[4:19]and to proclaim the acceptable
year of the Lord."[l]
[4:20]He closed the book, gave it back to
the attendant, and sat down. The eyes
of all in the synagogue were fastened on
him. [4:21]He began to tell them, **"Today,
this Scripture has been fulfilled in your
hearing."**
[4:22]All testified about him, and wondered
at the gracious words which proceeded out
of his mouth, and they said, "Isn't this
Joseph's son?"
[4:23]He said to them, **"Doubtless you
will tell me this parable, 'Physician, heal
yourself! Whatever we have heard done
at Capernaum, do also here in your hometown.'"** [4:24]He said, **"Most certainly I
tell you, no prophet is acceptable in his
hometown. [4:25]But truly I tell you, there
were many widows in Israel in the days
of Elijah, when the sky was shut up three
years and six months, when a great famine
came over all the land. [4:26]Elijah was sent
to none of them, except to Zarephath, in
the land of Sidon, to a woman who was
a widow. [4:27]There were many lepers in
Israel in the time of Elisha the prophet,
yet not one of them was cleansed, except
Naaman, the Syrian."**
[4:28]They were all filled with wrath in
the synagogue, as they heard these things.
[4:29]They rose up, threw him out of the city,
and led him to the brow of the hill that their
city was built on, that they might throw him
off the cliff. [4:30]But he, passing through the
midst of them, went his way.
[4:31]He came down to Capernaum, a city
of Galilee. He was teaching them on the
Sabbath day, [4:32]and they were astonished
at his teaching, for his word was with
authority. [4:33]In the synagogue there was
a man who had a spirit of an unclean
demon, and he cried out with a loud voice,
[4:34]saying, "Ah! what have we to do with
you, Jesus of Nazareth? Have you come to
destroy us? I know you who you are: the
Holy One of God!"
[4:35]Jesus rebuked him, saying, **"Be silent,**

and come out of him!"** When the demon
had thrown him down in their midst, he
came out of him, having done him no harm.
[4:36]Amazement came on all, and they
spoke together, one with another, saying,
"What is this word? For with authority and
power he commands the unclean spirits,
and they come out!" [4:37]News about him
went out into every place of the surrounding region.
[4:38]He rose up from the synagogue,
and entered into Simon's house. Simon's
mother-in-law was afflicted with a great
fever, and they begged him for her. [4:39]He
stood over her, and rebuked the fever; and
it left her. Immediately she rose up and
served them. [4:40]When the sun was setting,
all those who had any sick with various
diseases brought them to him; and he laid
his hands on every one of them, and healed
them. [4:41]Demons also came out from
many, crying out, and saying, "You are the
Christ, the Son of God!" Rebuking them,
he didn't allow them to speak, because they
knew that he was the Christ.
[4:42]When it was day, he departed and
went into an uninhabited place, and the
multitudes looked for him, and came to
him, and held on to him, so that he
wouldn't go away from them. [4:43]But he
said to them, **"I must preach the good news
of the Kingdom of God to the other cities
also. For this reason I have been sent."**
[4:44]He was preaching in the synagogues of
Galilee.
[5:1]Now it happened, while the multitude
pressed on him and heard the word of
God, that he was standing by the lake of
Gennesaret. [5:2]He saw two boats standing
by the lake, but the fishermen had gone out
of them, and were washing their nets. [5:3]He
entered into one of the boats, which was
Simon's, and asked him to put out a little
from the land. He sat down and taught the
multitudes from the boat. [5:4]When he had
finished speaking, he said to Simon, **"Put
out into the deep, and let down your nets
for a catch."**
[5:5]Simon answered him, "Master, we
worked all night, and took nothing; but

[l]4:19 Isaiah 61:1-2

at your word I will let down the net." ⁵:⁶When they had done this, they caught a great multitude of fish, and their net was breaking. ⁵:⁷They beckoned to their partners in the other boat, that they should come and help them. They came, and filled both boats, so that they began to sink. ⁵:⁸But Simon Peter, when he saw it, fell down at Jesus' knees, saying, "Depart from me, for I am a sinful man, Lord." ⁵:⁹For he was amazed, and all who were with him, at the catch of fish which they had caught; ⁵:¹⁰and so also were James and John, sons of Zebedee, who were partners with Simon.

Jesus said to Simon, **"Don't be afraid. From now on you will be catching people alive."**

⁵:¹¹When they had brought their boats to land, they left everything, and followed him. ⁵:¹²It happened, while he was in one of the cities, behold, there was a man full of leprosy. When he saw Jesus, he fell on his face, and begged him, saying, "Lord, if you want to, you can make me clean."

⁵:¹³He stretched out his hand, and touched him, saying, **"I want to. Be made clean."**

Immediately the leprosy left him. ⁵:¹⁴He commanded him to tell no one, **"But go your way, and show yourself to the priest, and offer for your cleansing according to what Moses commanded, for a testimony to them."** ⁵:¹⁵But the report concerning him spread much more, and great multitudes came together to hear, and to be healed by him of their infirmities. ⁵:¹⁶But he withdrew himself into the desert, and prayed.

⁵:¹⁷It happened on one of those days, that he was teaching; and there were Pharisees and teachers of the law sitting by, who had come out of every village of Galilee, Judea, and Jerusalem. The power of the Lord was with him to heal them. ⁵:¹⁸Behold, men brought a paralyzed man on a cot, and they sought to bring him in to lay before Jesus. ⁵:¹⁹Not finding a way to bring him in because of the multitude, they went up to the housetop, and let him down through the tiles with his cot into the midst before Jesus. ⁵:²⁰Seeing their faith, he said to him, **"Man, your sins are forgiven you."**

⁵:²¹The scribes and the Pharisees began to reason, saying, "Who is this that speaks blasphemies? Who can forgive sins, but God alone?"

⁵:²²But Jesus, perceiving their thoughts, answered them, **"Why are you reasoning so in your hearts? ⁵:²³Which is easier to say, 'Your sins are forgiven you;' or to say, 'Arise and walk?' ⁵:²⁴But that you may know that the Son of Man has authority on earth to forgive sins"** (he said to the paralyzed man), **"I tell you, arise, and take up your cot, and go to your house."**

⁵:²⁵Immediately he rose up before them, and took up that which he was laying on, and departed to his house, glorifying God. ⁵:²⁶Amazement took hold on all, and they glorified God. They were filled with fear, saying, "We have seen strange things today."

⁵:²⁷After these things he went out, and saw a tax collector named Levi sitting at the tax office, and said to him, **"Follow me!"**

⁵:²⁸He left everything, and rose up and followed him. ⁵:²⁹Levi made a great feast for him in his house. There was a great crowd of tax collectors and others who were reclining with them. ⁵:³⁰Their scribes and the Pharisees murmured against his disciples, saying, "Why do you eat and drink with the tax collectors and sinners?" ⁵:³¹Jesus answered them, **"Those who are healthy have no need for a physician, but those who are sick do. ⁵:³²I have not come to call the righteous, but sinners to repentance."**

⁵:³³They said to him, "Why do John's disciples often fast and pray, likewise also the disciples of the Pharisees, but yours eat and drink?"

⁵:³⁴He said to them, **"Can you make the friends of the bridegroom fast, while the bridegroom is with them? ⁵:³⁵But the days will come when the bridegroom will be taken away from them. Then they will fast in those days."** ⁵:³⁶He also told a parable to them. **"No one puts a piece from a new garment on an old garment, or else he will tear the new, and also the piece from the new will not match the old. ⁵:³⁷No one puts new wine into old wineskins, or else the new wine will burst the skins, and it will be spilled, and the**

skins will be destroyed. ⁵:³⁸But new wine must be put into fresh wineskins, and both are preserved. ⁵:³⁹No man having drunk old wine immediately desires new, for he says, 'The old is better.'"

⁶:¹Now it happened on the second Sabbath after the first, that he was going through the grain fields. His disciples plucked the heads of grain, and ate, rubbing them in their hands. ⁶:²But some of the Pharisees said to them, "Why do you do that which is not lawful to do on the Sabbath day?"

⁶:³Jesus, answering them, said, **"Haven't you read what David did when he was hungry, he, and those who were with him;** ⁶:⁴**how he entered into the house of God, and took and ate the show bread, and gave also to those who were with him, which is not lawful to eat except for the priests alone?"** ⁶:⁵He said to them, **"The Son of Man is lord of the Sabbath."**

⁶:⁶It also happened on another Sabbath that he entered into the synagogue and taught. There was a man there, and his right hand was withered. ⁶:⁷The scribes and the Pharisees watched him, to see whether he would heal on the Sabbath, that they might find an accusation against him. ⁶:⁸But he knew their thoughts; and he said to the man who had the withered hand, **"Rise up, and stand in the middle."** He arose and stood. ⁶:⁹Then Jesus said to them, **"I will ask you something: Is it lawful on the Sabbath to do good, or to do harm? To save a life, or to kill?"** ⁶:¹⁰He looked around at them all, and said to the man, **"Stretch out your hand."** He did, and his hand was restored as sound as the other. ⁶:¹¹But they were filled with rage, and talked with one another about what they might do to Jesus.

⁶:¹²It happened in these days, that he went out to the mountain to pray, and he continued all night in prayer to God. ⁶:¹³When it was day, he called his disciples, and from them he chose twelve, whom he also named apostles: ⁶:¹⁴Simon, whom he also named Peter; Andrew, his brother; James; John; Philip; Bartholomew;

⁶:¹⁵Matthew; Thomas; James, the son of Alphaeus; Simon, who was called the Zealot; ⁶:¹⁶Judas the son of James; and Judas Iscariot, who also became a traitor. ⁶:¹⁷He came down with them, and stood on a level place, with a crowd of his disciples, and a great number of the people from all Judea and Jerusalem, and the sea coast of Tyre and Sidon, who came to hear him and to be healed of their diseases; ⁶:¹⁸as well as those who were troubled by unclean spirits, and they were being healed. ⁶:¹⁹All the multitude sought to touch him, for power came out from him and healed them all.

⁶:²⁰He lifted up his eyes to his disciples, and said,

"Blessed are you who are poor,
    for yours is the Kingdom of God.
⁶:²¹**Blessed are you who hunger now,**
    for you will be filled.
Blessed are you who weep now,
    for you will laugh.
⁶:²²**Blessed are you when men shall hate you, and when they shall exclude and mock you, and throw out your name as evil, for the Son of Man's sake.**
    ⁶:²³**Rejoice in that day, and leap for joy, for behold, your reward is great in heaven, for their fathers did the same thing to the prophets.**
⁶:²⁴**"But woe to you who are rich!**
    For you have received your consolation.
⁶:²⁵**Woe to you, you who are full now,**
    for you will be hungry.
Woe to you who laugh now,
    for you will mourn and weep.
⁶:²⁶**Woe,ᵐ whenⁿ men speak well of you,**
    for their fathers did the same thing to the false prophets.
⁶:²⁷**"But I tell you who hear: love your enemies, do good to those who hate you,** ⁶:²⁸**bless those who curse you, and pray for those who mistreat you.** ⁶:²⁹**To him who strikes you on the cheek, offer also the other; and from him who takes away your cloak, don't withhold your coat also.** ⁶:³⁰**Give to everyone who asks you, and**

ᵐ6:26 TR adds "to you"
ⁿ6:26 TR adds "all"

don't ask him who takes away your goods to give them back again.

⁶:³¹"As you would like people to do to you, do exactly so to them. ⁶:³²If you love those who love you, what credit is that to you? For even sinners love those who love them. ⁶:³³If you do good to those who do good to you, what credit is that to you? For even sinners do the same. ⁶:³⁴If you lend to those from whom you hope to receive, what credit is that to you? Even sinners lend to sinners, to receive back as much. ⁶:³⁵But love your enemies, and do good, and lend, expecting nothing back; and your reward will be great, and you will be children of the Most High; for he is kind toward the unthankful and evil. ⁶:³⁶Therefore be merciful,

even as your Father is also merciful. ⁶:³⁷Don't judge,

and you won't be judged.

Don't condemn,

and you won't be condemned.

Set free,

and you will be set free.

⁶:³⁸"Give, and it will be given to you: good measure, pressed down, shaken together, and running over, will be given to you.° For with the same measure you measure it will be measured back to you."

⁶:³⁹He spoke a parable to them. "Can the blind guide the blind? Won't they both fall into a pit? ⁶:⁴⁰A disciple is not above his teacher, but everyone when he is fully trained will be like his teacher. ⁶:⁴¹Why do you see the speck of chaff that is in your brother's eye, but don't consider the beam that is in your own eye? ⁶:⁴²Or how can you tell your brother, 'Brother, let me remove the speck of chaff that is in your eye,' when you yourself don't see the beam that is in your own eye? You hypocrite! First remove the beam from your own eye, and then you can see clearly to remove the speck of chaff that is in your brother's eye. ⁶:⁴³For there is no good tree that brings forth rotten fruit; nor again a rotten tree that brings forth good fruit. ⁶:⁴⁴For each tree is known by its own fruit. For people don't gather figs from thorns, nor do they gather grapes from a bramble

bush. ⁶:⁴⁵The good man out of the good treasure of his heart brings out that which is good, and the evil man out of the evil treasure of his heart brings out that which is evil, for out of the abundance of the heart, his mouth speaks.

⁶:⁴⁶"Why do you call me, 'Lord, Lord,' and don't do the things which I say? ⁶:⁴⁷Everyone who comes to me, and hears my words, and does them, I will show you who he is like. ⁶:⁴⁸He is like a man building a house, who dug and went deep, and laid a foundation on the rock. When a flood arose, the stream broke against that house, and could not shake it, because it was founded on the rock. ⁶:⁴⁹But he who hears, and doesn't do, is like a man who built a house on the earth without a foundation, against which the stream broke, and immediately it fell, and the ruin of that house was great."

⁷:¹After he had finished speaking in the hearing of the people, he entered into Capernaum. ⁷:²A certain centurion's servant, who was dear to him, was sick and at the point of death. ⁷:³When he heard about Jesus, he sent to him elders of the Jews, asking him to come and save his servant. ⁷:⁴When they came to Jesus, they begged him earnestly, saying, "He is worthy for you to do this for him, ⁷:⁵for he loves our nation, and he built our synagogue for us." ⁷:⁶Jesus went with them. When he was now not far from the house, the centurion sent friends to him, saying to him, "Lord, don't trouble yourself, for I am not worthy for you to come under my roof. ⁷:⁷Therefore I didn't even think myself worthy to come to you; but say the word, and my servant will be healed. ⁷:⁸For I also am a man placed under authority, having under myself soldiers. I tell this one, 'Go!' and he goes; and to another, 'Come!' and he comes; and to my servant, 'Do this,' and he does it."

⁷:⁹When Jesus heard these things, he marveled at him, and turned and said to the multitude who followed him, **"I tell you, I have not found such great faith, no, not in Israel."** ⁷:¹⁰Those who were sent, returning

---

°6:38 literally, into your bosom.

to the house, found that the servant who had been sick was well.

[7:11]It happened soon afterwards, that he went to a city called Nain. Many of his disciples, along with a great multitude, went with him. [7:12]Now when he drew near to the gate of the city, behold, one who was dead was carried out, the only son of his mother, and she was a widow. Many people of the city were with her. [7:13]When the Lord saw her, he had compassion on her, and said to her, **"Don't cry."** [7:14]He came near and touched the coffin, and the bearers stood still. He said, **"Young man, I tell you, arise!"** [7:15]He who was dead sat up, and began to speak. And he gave him to his mother.

[7:16]Fear took hold of all, and they glorified God, saying, "A great prophet has arisen among us!" and, "God has visited his people!" [7:17]This report went out concerning him in the whole of Judea, and in all the surrounding region.

[7:18]The disciples of John told him about all these things. [7:19]John, calling to himself two of his disciples, sent them to Jesus, saying, "Are you the one who is coming, or should we look for another?" [7:20]When the men had come to him, they said, "John the Baptizer has sent us to you, saying, 'Are you he who comes, or should we look for another?'"

[7:21]In that hour he cured many of diseases and plagues and evil spirits; and to many who were blind he gave sight. [7:22]Jesus answered them, **"Go and tell John the things which you have seen and heard: that the blind receive their sight, the lame walk, the lepers are cleansed, the deaf hear, the dead are raised up, and the poor have good news preached to them.** [7:23]**Blessed is he who is not offended by me."**

[7:24]When John's messengers had departed, he began to tell the multitudes about John, **"What did you go out into the wilderness to see? A reed shaken by the wind?** [7:25]**But what did you go out to see? A man clothed in soft clothing? Behold, those who are gorgeously dressed, and**

live delicately, are in kings' courts. [7:26]**But what did you go out to see? A prophet? Yes, I tell you, and much more than a prophet.** [7:27]**This is he of whom it is written,**

'Behold, I send my messenger before your face,

who will prepare your way before you.'[p]

[7:28]**"For I tell you, among those who are born of women there is not a greater prophet than John the Baptizer, yet he who is least in the Kingdom of God is greater than he."**

[7:29]When all the people and the tax collectors heard this, they declared God to be just, having been baptized with John's baptism. [7:30]But the Pharisees and the lawyers rejected the counsel of God, not being baptized by him themselves.

[7:31][q]**"To what then will I liken the people of this generation? What are they like?** [7:32]**They are like children who sit in the marketplace, and call one to another, saying, 'We piped to you, and you didn't dance. We mourned, and you didn't weep.'** [7:33]**For John the Baptizer came neither eating bread nor drinking wine, and you say, 'He has a demon.'** [7:34]**The Son of Man has come eating and drinking, and you say, 'Behold, a gluttonous man, and a drunkard; a friend of tax collectors and sinners!'** [7:35]**Wisdom is justified by all her children."**

[7:36]One of the Pharisees invited him to eat with him. He entered into the Pharisee's house, and sat at the table. [7:37]Behold, a woman in the city who was a sinner, when she knew that he was reclining in the Pharisee's house, she brought an alabaster jar of ointment. [7:38]Standing behind at his feet weeping, she began to wet his feet with her tears, and she wiped them with the hair of her head, kissed his feet, and anointed them with the ointment. [7:39]Now when the Pharisee who had invited him saw it, he said to himself, "This man, if he were a prophet, would have perceived who and

---

[p]7:27 Malachi 3:1
[q]7:31 TR adds "But the Lord said,"

what kind of woman this is who touches him, that she is a sinner."

⁷:⁴⁰Jesus answered him, **"Simon, I have something to tell you."**

He said, "Teacher, say on."

⁷:⁴¹**"A certain lender had two debtors. The one owed five hundred denarii, and the other fifty. ⁷:⁴²When they couldn't pay, he forgave them both. Which of them therefore will love him most?"**

⁷:⁴³Simon answered, "He, I suppose, to whom he forgave the most."

He said to him, **"You have judged correctly." ⁷:⁴⁴**Turning to the woman, he said to Simon, **"Do you see this woman? I entered into your house, and you gave me no water for my feet, but she has wet my feet with her tears, and wiped them with the hair of her head. ⁷:⁴⁵You gave me no kiss, but she, since the time I came in, has not ceased to kiss my feet. ⁷:⁴⁶You didn't anoint my head with oil, but she has anointed my feet with ointment. ⁷:⁴⁷Therefore I tell you, her sins, which are many, are forgiven, for she loved much. But to whom little is forgiven, the same loves little." ⁷:⁴⁸**He said to her, **"Your sins are forgiven."**

⁷:⁴⁹Those who sat at the table with him began to say to themselves, "Who is this who even forgives sins?"

⁷:⁵⁰He said to the woman, **"Your faith has saved you. Go in peace."**

⁸:¹It happened soon afterwards, that he went about through cities and villages, preaching and bringing the good news of the Kingdom of God. With him were the twelve, ⁸:²and certain women who had been healed of evil spirits and infirmities: Mary who was called Magdalene, from whom seven demons had gone out; ⁸:³and Joanna, the wife of Chuzas, Herod's steward; Susanna; and many others; who served them^r from their possessions. ⁸:⁴When a great multitude came together, and people from every city were coming to him, he spoke by a parable. ⁸:⁵**"The farmer went out to sow his seed. As he sowed, some fell along the road, and it was trampled under foot, and the birds of the sky de-**voured it. ⁸:⁶Other seed fell on the rock, and as soon as it grew, it withered away, because it had no moisture. ⁸:⁷Other fell amid the thorns, and the thorns grew with it, and choked it. ⁸:⁸Other fell into the good ground, and grew, and brought forth fruit one hundred times."** As he said these things, he called out, **"He who has ears to hear, let him hear!"**

⁸:⁹Then his disciples asked him, "What does this parable mean?"

⁸:¹⁰He said, **"To you it is given to know the mysteries of the Kingdom of God, but to the rest in parables; that 'seeing they may not see, and hearing they may not understand.'ˢ ⁸:¹¹**Now the parable is this: The seed is the word of God. ⁸:¹²Those along the road are those who hear, then the devil comes, and takes away the word from their heart, that they may not believe and be saved. ⁸:¹³Those on the rock are they who, when they hear, receive the word with joy; but these have no root, who believe for a while, then fall away in time of temptation. ⁸:¹⁴That which fell among the thorns, these are those who have heard, and as they go on their way they are choked with cares, riches, and pleasures of life, and bring no fruit to maturity. ⁸:¹⁵That in the good ground, these are such as in an honest and good heart, having heard the word, hold it tightly, and bring forth fruit with patience.**

⁸:¹⁶**"No one, when he has lit a lamp, covers it with a container, or puts it under a bed; but puts it on a stand, that those who enter in may see the light. ⁸:¹⁷For nothing is hidden, that will not be revealed; nor anything secret, that will not be known and come to light. ⁸:¹⁸Be careful therefore how you hear. For whoever has, to him will be given; and whoever doesn't have, from him will be taken away even that which he thinks he has."**

⁸:¹⁹His mother and brothers came to him, and they could not come near him for the crowd. ⁸:²⁰It was told him by some saying, "Your mother and your brothers stand outside, desiring to see you."

---

^r8:3 TR reads "him" instead of "them"
ˢ8:10 Isaiah 6:9

8:21 But he answered them, **"My mother and my brothers are these who hear the word of God, and do it."**

8:22 Now it happened on one of those days, that he entered into a boat, himself and his disciples, and he said to them, **"Let's go over to the other side of the lake."** So they launched out. 8:23 But as they sailed, he fell asleep. A wind storm came down on the lake, and they were taking on dangerous amounts of water. 8:24 They came to him, and awoke him, saying, "Master, master, we are dying!" He awoke, and rebuked the wind and the raging of the water, and they ceased, and it was calm. 8:25 He said to them, **"Where is your faith?"** Being afraid they marveled, saying one to another, "Who is this, then, that he commands even the winds and the water, and they obey him?" 8:26 They arrived at the country of the Gadarenes, which is opposite Galilee.

8:27 When Jesus stepped ashore, a certain man out of the city who had demons for a long time met him. He wore no clothes, and didn't live in a house, but in the tombs. 8:28 When he saw Jesus, he cried out, and fell down before him, and with a loud voice said, "What do I have to do with you, Jesus, you Son of the Most High God? I beg you, don't torment me!" 8:29 For Jesus was commanding the unclean spirit to come out of the man. For the unclean spirit had often seized the man. He was kept under guard, and bound with chains and fetters. Breaking the bands apart, he was driven by the demon into the desert.

8:30 Jesus asked him, **"What is your name?"**

He said, "Legion," for many demons had entered into him. 8:31 They begged him that he would not command them to go into the abyss. 8:32 Now there was there a herd of many pigs feeding on the mountain, and they begged him that he would allow them to enter into those. He allowed them. 8:33 The demons came out from the man, and entered into the pigs, and the herd rushed down the steep bank into the lake, and were drowned. 8:34 When those who fed them saw what had happened, they

fled, and told it in the city and in the country.

8:35 People went out to see what had happened. They came to Jesus, and found the man from whom the demons had gone out, sitting at Jesus' feet, clothed and in his right mind; and they were afraid. 8:36 Those who saw it told them how he who had been possessed by demons was healed. 8:37 All the people of the surrounding country of the Gadarenes asked him to depart from them, for they were very much afraid. He entered into the boat, and returned. 8:38 But the man from whom the demons had gone out begged him that he might go with him, but Jesus sent him away, saying, 8:39 **"Return to your house, and declare what great things God has done for you."** He went his way, proclaiming throughout the whole city what great things Jesus had done for him.

8:40 It happened, when Jesus returned, that the multitude welcomed him, for they were all waiting for him. 8:41 Behold, there came a man named Jairus, and he was a ruler of the synagogue. He fell down at Jesus' feet, and begged him to come into his house, 8:42 for he had an only daughter, about twelve years of age, and she was dying. But as he went, the multitudes pressed against him. 8:43 A woman who had a flow of blood for twelve years, who had spent all her living on physicians, and could not be healed by any, 8:44 came behind him, and touched the fringe[t] of his cloak, and immediately the flow of her blood stopped. 8:45 Jesus said, **"Who touched me?"**

When all denied it, Peter and those with him said, "Master, the multitudes press and jostle you, and you say, **'Who touched me?'"**

8:46 But Jesus said, **"Someone did touch me, for I perceived that power has gone out of me."** 8:47 When the woman saw that she was not hidden, she came trembling, and falling down before him declared to him in the presence of all the people the reason why she had touched him, and how she was healed immediately. 8:48 He said to

---

[t]8:44 or, tassel

her, **"Daughter, cheer up. Your faith has made you well. Go in peace."**

⁸:⁴⁹While he still spoke, one from the ruler of the synagogue's house came, saying to him, "Your daughter is dead. Don't trouble the Teacher."

⁸:⁵⁰But Jesus hearing it, answered him, **"Don't be afraid. Only believe, and she will be healed."**

⁸:⁵¹When he came to the house, he didn't allow anyone to enter in, except Peter, John, James, the father of the child, and her mother. ⁸:⁵²All were weeping and mourning her, but he said, **"Don't weep. She isn't dead, but sleeping."**

⁸:⁵³They were ridiculing him, knowing that she was dead. ⁸:⁵⁴But he put them all outside, and taking her by the hand, he called, saying, **"Child, arise!"** ⁸:⁵⁵Her spirit returned, and she rose up immediately. He commanded that something be given to her to eat. ⁸:⁵⁶Her parents were amazed, but he commanded them to tell no one what had been done.

⁹:¹He called the twelve[u] together, and gave them power and authority over all demons, and to cure diseases. ⁹:²He sent them forth to preach the Kingdom of God, and to heal the sick. ⁹:³He said to them, **"Take nothing for your journey—neither staffs, nor wallet, nor bread, nor money; neither have two coats apiece.** ⁹:⁴**Into whatever house you enter, stay there, and depart from there.** ⁹:⁵**As many as don't receive you, when you depart from that city, shake off even the dust from your feet for a testimony against them."**

⁹:⁶They departed, and went throughout the villages, preaching the Good News, and healing everywhere. ⁹:⁷Now Herod the tetrarch heard of all that was done by him; and he was very perplexed, because it was said by some that John had risen from the dead, ⁹:⁸and by some that Elijah had appeared, and by others that one of the old prophets had risen again. ⁹:⁹Herod said, "John I beheaded, but who is this, about whom I hear such things?" He sought to see him. ⁹:¹⁰The apostles, when they had returned, told him what things they had done.

He took them, and withdrew apart to a deserted place of a city called Bethsaida. ⁹:¹¹But the multitudes, perceiving it, followed him. He welcomed them, and spoke to them of the Kingdom of God, and he cured those who needed healing. ⁹:¹²The day began to wear away; and the twelve came, and said to him, "Send the multitude away, that they may go into the surrounding villages and farms, and lodge, and get food, for we are here in a deserted place."

⁹:¹³But he said to them, **"You give them something to eat."**

They said, "We have no more than five loaves and two fish, unless we should go and buy food for all these people." ⁹:¹⁴For they were about five thousand men.

He said to his disciples, **"Make them sit down in groups of about fifty each."** ⁹:¹⁵They did so, and made them all sit down. ⁹:¹⁶He took the five loaves and the two fish, and looking up to the sky, he blessed them, and broke them, and gave them to the disciples to set before the multitude. ⁹:¹⁷They ate, and were all filled. They gathered up twelve baskets of broken pieces that were left over.

⁹:¹⁸It happened, as he was praying alone, that the disciples were with him, and he asked them, **"Who do the multitudes say that I am?"**

⁹:¹⁹They answered, "'John the Baptizer,' but others say, 'Elijah,' and others, that one of the old prophets is risen again."

⁹:²⁰He said to them, **"But who do you say that I am?"**

Peter answered, "The Christ of God."

⁹:²¹But he warned them, and commanded them to tell this to no one, ⁹:²²saying, **"The Son of Man must suffer many things, and be rejected by the elders, chief priests, and scribes, and be killed, and the third day be raised up."**

⁹:²³He said to all, **"If anyone desires to come after me, let him deny himself, take up his cross,[v] and follow me.** ⁹:²⁴**For whoever desires to save his life will lose it, but whoever will lose his life for my**

---

[u]9:1 TR reads "his twelve disciples" instead of "the twelve"
[v]9:23 TR, NU add "daily"

sake, the same will save it. ^{9:25}For what does it profit a man if he gains the whole world, and loses or forfeits his own self? ^{9:26}For whoever will be ashamed of me and of my words, of him will the Son of Man be ashamed, when he comes in his glory, and the glory of the Father, and of the holy angels. ^{9:27}But I tell you the truth: There are some of those who stand here, who will in no way taste of death, until they see the Kingdom of God."

^{9:28}It happened about eight days after these sayings, that he took with him Peter, John, and James, and went up onto the mountain to pray. ^{9:29}As he was praying, the appearance of his face was altered, and his clothing became white and dazzling. ^{9:30}Behold, two men were talking with him, who were Moses and Elijah, ^{9:31}who appeared in glory, and spoke of his departure,^w which he was about to accomplish at Jerusalem.

^{9:32}Now Peter and those who were with him were heavy with sleep, but when they were fully awake, they saw his glory, and the two men who stood with him. ^{9:33}It happened, as they were parting from him, that Peter said to Jesus, "Master, it is good for us to be here. Let's make three tents: one for you, and one for Moses, and one for Elijah," not knowing what he said. ^{9:34}While he said these things, a cloud came and overshadowed them, and they were afraid as they entered into the cloud. ^{9:35}A voice came out of the cloud, saying, "This is my beloved Son. Listen to him!" ^{9:36}When the voice came, Jesus was found alone. They were silent, and told no one in those days any of the things which they had seen.

^{9:37}It happened on the next day, when they had come down from the mountain, that a great multitude met him. ^{9:38}Behold, a man from the crowd called out, saying, "Teacher, I beg you to look at my son, for he is my only child. ^{9:39}Behold, a spirit takes him, he suddenly cries out, and it convulses him so that he foams, and it hardly departs from him, bruising him severely. ^{9:40}I begged your disciples to cast it out, and they couldn't."

^{9:41}Jesus answered, **"Faithless and perverse generation, how long shall I be with you and bear with you? Bring your son here."**

^{9:42}While he was still coming, the demon threw him down and convulsed him violently. But Jesus rebuked the unclean spirit, and healed the boy, and gave him back to his father. ^{9:43}They were all astonished at the majesty of God.

But while all were marveling at all the things which Jesus did, he said to his disciples, ^{9:44}**"Let these words sink into your ears, for the Son of Man will be delivered up into the hands of men."** ^{9:45}But they didn't understand this saying. It was concealed from them, that they should not perceive it, and they were afraid to ask him about this saying.

^{9:46}There arose an argument among them about which of them was the greatest. ^{9:47}Jesus, perceiving the reasoning of their hearts, took a little child, and set him by his side, ^{9:48}and said to them, **"Whoever receives this little child in my name receives me. Whoever receives me receives him who sent me. For whoever is least among you all, this one will be great."**

^{9:49}John answered, "Master, we saw someone casting out demons in your name, and we forbade him, because he doesn't follow with us."

^{9:50}Jesus said to him, **"Don't forbid him, for he who is not against us is for us."**

^{9:51}It came to pass, when the days were near that he should be taken up, he intently set his face to go to Jerusalem, ^{9:52}and sent messengers before his face. They went, and entered into a village of the Samaritans, so as to prepare for him. ^{9:53}They didn't receive him, because he was traveling with his face set towards Jerusalem. ^{9:54}When his disciples, James and John, saw this, they said, "Lord, do you want us to command fire to come down from the sky, and destroy them, just as Elijah did?"

^{9:55}But he turned and rebuked them, **"You don't know of what kind of spirit you are. ^{9:56}For the Son of Man didn't**

---

^w9:31 literally, "exodus"

come to destroy men's lives, but to save them."

They went to another village. ^{9:57}As they went on the way, a certain man said to him, "I want to follow you wherever you go, Lord."

^{9:58}Jesus said to him, "The foxes have holes, and the birds of the sky have nests, but the Son of Man has no place to lay his head."

^{9:59}He said to another, "Follow me!"

But he said, "Lord, allow me first to go and bury my father."

^{9:60}But Jesus said to him, "Leave the dead to bury their own dead, but you go and announce the Kingdom of God."

^{9:61}Another also said, "I want to follow you, Lord, but first allow me to bid farewell to those who are at my house."

^{9:62}But Jesus said to him, "No one, having put his hand to the plow, and looking back, is fit for the Kingdom of God."

^{10:1}Now after these things, the Lord also appointed seventy others, and sent them two by two ahead of him^x into every city and place, where he was about to come. ^{10:2}Then he said to them, "The harvest is indeed plentiful, but the laborers are few. Pray therefore to the Lord of the harvest, that he may send out laborers into his harvest. ^{10:3}Go your ways. Behold, I send you out as lambs among wolves. ^{10:4}Carry no purse, nor wallet, nor sandals. Greet no one on the way. ^{10:5}Into whatever house you enter, first say, 'Peace be to this house.' ^{10:6}If a son of peace is there, your peace will rest on him; but if not, it will return to you. ^{10:7}Remain in that same house, eating and drinking the things they give, for the laborer is worthy of his wages. Don't go from house to house. ^{10:8}Into whatever city you enter, and they receive you, eat the things that are set before you. ^{10:9}Heal the sick who are therein, and tell them, 'The Kingdom of God has come near to you.' ^{10:10}But into whatever city you enter, and they don't receive you, go out into its streets and say, ^{10:11}'Even the dust from your city that clings to us, we wipe off against you. Nevertheless know

this, that the Kingdom of God has come near to you.' ^{10:12}I tell you, it will be more tolerable in that day for Sodom than for that city.

^{10:13}"Woe to you, Chorazin! Woe to you, Bethsaida! For if the mighty works had been done in Tyre and Sidon which were done in you, they would have repented long ago, sitting in sackcloth and ashes. ^{10:14}But it will be more tolerable for Tyre and Sidon in the judgment than for you. ^{10:15}You, Capernaum, who are exalted to heaven, will be brought down to Hades.^y ^{10:16}Whoever listens to you listens to me, and whoever rejects you rejects me. Whoever rejects me rejects him who sent me."

^{10:17}The seventy returned with joy, saying, "Lord, even the demons are subject to us in your name!"

^{10:18}He said to them, "I saw Satan having fallen like lightning from heaven. ^{10:19}Behold, I give you authority to tread on serpents and scorpions, and over all the power of the enemy. Nothing will in any way hurt you. ^{10:20}Nevertheless, don't rejoice in this, that the spirits are subject to you, but rejoice that your names are written in heaven."

^{10:21}In that same hour Jesus rejoiced in the Holy Spirit, and said, "I thank you, O Father, Lord of heaven and earth, that you have hidden these things from the wise and understanding, and revealed them to little children. Yes, Father, for so it was well-pleasing in your sight."

^{10:22}Turning to the disciples, he said, "All things have been delivered to me by my Father. No one knows who the Son is, except the Father, and who the Father is, except the Son, and he to whomever the Son desires to reveal him."

^{10:23}Turning to the disciples, he said privately, "Blessed are the eyes which see the things that you see, ^{10:24}for I tell you that many prophets and kings desired to see the things which you see, and didn't see them, and to hear the things which you hear, and didn't hear them."

^x10:1 literally, "before his face"
^y10:15 Hades is the lower realm of the dead, or Hell.

10:25Behold, a certain lawyer stood up and tested him, saying, "Teacher, what shall I do to inherit eternal life?"

10:26He said to him, **"What is written in the law? How do you read it?"**

10:27He answered, "You shall love the Lord your God with all your heart, with all your soul, with all your strength, and with all your mind;[z] and your neighbor as yourself."[a]

10:28He said to him, **"You have answered correctly. Do this, and you will live."**

10:29But he, desiring to justify himself, asked Jesus, "Who is my neighbor?"

10:30Jesus answered, **"A certain man was going down from Jerusalem to Jericho, and he fell among robbers, who both stripped him and beat him, and departed, leaving him half dead.** 10:31**By chance a certain priest was going down that way. When he saw him, he passed by on the other side.** 10:32**In the same way a Levite also, when he came to the place, and saw him, passed by on the other side.** 10:33**But a certain Samaritan, as he traveled, came where he was. When he saw him, he was moved with compassion,** 10:34**came to him, and bound up his wounds, pouring on oil and wine. He set him on his own animal, and brought him to an inn, and took care of him.** 10:35**On the next day, when he departed, he took out two denarii, and gave them to the host, and said to him, 'Take care of him. Whatever you spend beyond that, I will repay you when I return.'** 10:36**Now which of these three do you think seemed to be a neighbor to him who fell among the robbers?"**

10:37He said, "He who showed mercy on him."

Then Jesus said to him, **"Go and do likewise."**

10:38It happened as they went on their way, he entered into a certain village, and a certain woman named Martha received him into her house. 10:39She had a sister called Mary, who also sat at Jesus' feet, and heard his word. 10:40But Martha was distracted with much serving, and she came up to him, and said, "Lord, don't you care that my sister left me to serve alone? Ask her therefore to help me."

10:41Jesus answered her, **"Martha, Martha, you are anxious and troubled about many things,** 10:42**but one thing is needed. Mary has chosen the good part, which will not be taken away from her."**

11:1It happened, that when he finished praying in a certain place, one of his disciples said to him, "Lord, teach us to pray, just as John also taught his disciples."

11:2He said to them, **"When you pray, say,**

'Our Father in heaven,
    may your name be kept holy.
May your Kingdom come.
    May your will be done on Earth, as it is in heaven.
11:3**Give us day by day our daily bread.**
11:4**Forgive us our sins,**
    for we ourselves also forgive everyone who is indebted to us.
Bring us not into temptation,
    but deliver us from the evil one.'"

11:5He said to them, "Which of you, if you go to a friend at midnight, and tell him, 'Friend, lend me three loaves of bread, 11:6for a friend of mine has come to me from a journey, and I have nothing to set before him,' 11:7and he from within will answer and say, 'Don't bother me. The door is now shut, and my children are with me in bed. I can't get up and give it to you'? 11:8I tell you, although he will not rise and give it to him because he is his friend, yet because of his persistence, he will get up and give him as many as he needs.

11:9"I tell you, keep asking, and it will be given you. Keep seeking, and you will find. Keep knocking, and it will be opened to you. 11:10For everyone who asks receives. He who seeks finds. To him who knocks it will be opened.

11:11**"Which of you fathers, if your son asks for bread, will give him a stone? Or if he asks for a fish, he won't give him a snake instead of a fish, will he?** 11:12**Or if he asks for an egg, he won't give**

---

z10:27 Deuteronomy 6:5
a10:27 Leviticus 19:18

him a scorpion, will he? [11:13]If you then, being evil, know how to give good gifts to your children, how much more will your heavenly Father give the Holy Spirit to those who ask him?"

[11:14]He was casting out a demon, and it was mute. It happened, when the demon had gone out, the mute man spoke; and the multitudes marveled. [11:15]But some of them said, "He casts out demons by Beelzebul, the prince of the demons." [11:16]Others, testing him, sought from him a sign from heaven. [11:17]But he, knowing their thoughts, said to them, "Every kingdom divided against itself is brought to desolation. A house divided against itself falls. [11:18]If Satan also is divided against himself, how will his kingdom stand? For you say that I cast out demons by Beelzebul. [11:19]But if I cast out demons by Beelzebul, by whom do your children cast them out? Therefore will they be your judges. [11:20]But if I by the finger of God cast out demons, then the Kingdom of God has come to you.

[11:21]"When the strong man, fully armed, guards his own dwelling, his goods are safe. [11:22]But when someone stronger attacks him and overcomes him, he takes from him his whole armor in which he trusted, and divides his spoils.

[11:23]"He that is not with me is against me. He who doesn't gather with me scatters. [11:24]The unclean spirit, when he has gone out of the man, passes through dry places, seeking rest, and finding none, he says, 'I will turn back to my house from which I came out.' [11:25]When he returns, he finds it swept and put in order. [11:26]Then he goes, and takes seven other spirits more evil than himself, and they enter in and dwell there. The last state of that man becomes worse than the first."

[11:27]It came to pass, as he said these things, a certain woman out of the multitude lifted up her voice, and said to him, "Blessed is the womb that bore you, and the breasts which nursed you!"

[11:28]But he said, "On the contrary, blessed are those who hear the word of God, and keep it."

[11:29]When the multitudes were gathering together to him, he began to say, "This is an evil generation. It seeks after a sign. No sign will be given to it but the sign of Jonah, the prophet. [11:30]For even as Jonah became a sign to the Ninevites, so will also the Son of Man be to this generation. [11:31]The Queen of the South will rise up in the judgment with the men of this generation, and will condemn them: for she came from the ends of the earth to hear the wisdom of Solomon; and behold, one greater than Solomon is here. [11:32]The men of Nineveh will stand up in the judgment with this generation, and will condemn it: for they repented at the preaching of Jonah, and behold, one greater than Jonah is here.

[11:33]"No one, when he has lit a lamp, puts it in a cellar or under a basket, but on a stand, that those who come in may see the light. [11:34]The lamp of the body is the eye. Therefore when your eye is good, your whole body is also full of light; but when it is evil, your body also is full of darkness. [11:35]Therefore see whether the light that is in you isn't darkness. [11:36]If therefore your whole body is full of light, having no part dark, it will be wholly full of light, as when the lamp with its bright shining gives you light."

[11:37]Now as he spoke, a certain Pharisee asked him to dine with him. He went in, and sat at the table. [11:38]When the Pharisee saw it, he marveled that he had not first washed himself before dinner. [11:39]The Lord said to him, "Now you Pharisees cleanse the outside of the cup and of the platter, but your inward part is full of extortion and wickedness. [11:40]You foolish ones, didn't he who made the outside make the inside also? [11:41]But give for gifts to the needy those things which are within, and behold, all things will be clean to you. [11:42]But woe to you Pharisees! For you tithe mint and rue and every herb, but you bypass justice and the love of God. You ought to have done these, and not to have left the other undone. [11:43]Woe to you Pharisees! For you love the best seats in the synagogues, and the greetings in the marketplaces. [11:44]Woe to you, scribes and Pharisees, hypocrites! For you are like hidden graves, and the men who walk over them don't know it."

[11:45] One of the lawyers answered him, "Teacher, in saying this you insult us also."

[11:46] He said, **"Woe to you lawyers also! For you load men with burdens that are difficult to carry, and you yourselves won't even lift one finger to help carry those burdens.** [11:47] **Woe to you! For you build the tombs of the prophets, and your fathers killed them.** [11:48] **So you testify and consent to the works of your fathers. For they killed them, and you build their tombs.** [11:49] **Therefore also the wisdom of God said, 'I will send to them prophets and apostles; and some of them they will kill and persecute,** [11:50] **that the blood of all the prophets, which was shed from the foundation of the world, may be required of this generation;** [11:51] **from the blood of Abel to the blood of Zachariah, who perished between the altar and the sanctuary.' Yes, I tell you, it will be required of this generation.** [11:52] **Woe to you lawyers! For you took away the key of knowledge. You didn't enter in yourselves, and those who were entering in, you hindered."**

[11:53] As he said these things to them, the scribes and the Pharisees began to be terribly angry, and to draw many things out of him; [11:54] lying in wait for him, and seeking to catch him in something he might say, that they might accuse him.

[12:1] Meanwhile, when a multitude of many thousands had gathered together, so much so that they trampled on each other, he began to tell his disciples first of all, **"Beware of the yeast of the Pharisees, which is hypocrisy.** [12:2] **But there is nothing covered up, that will not be revealed, nor hidden, that will not be known.** [12:3] **Therefore whatever you have said in the darkness will be heard in the light. What you have spoken in the ear in the inner chambers will be proclaimed on the housetops.** [12:4] **I tell you, my friends, don't be afraid of those who kill the body, and after that have no more that they can do.** [12:5] **But I will warn you whom you should fear. Fear him, who after he has killed, has** power to cast into Gehenna.**[b]** Yes, I tell you, fear him.**

[12:6] **"Aren't five sparrows sold for two assaria coins[c]? Not one of them is forgotten by God.** [12:7] **But the very hairs of your head are all numbered. Therefore don't be afraid. You are of more value than many sparrows.**

[12:8] **"I tell you, everyone who confesses me before men, him will the Son of Man also confess before the angels of God;** [12:9] **but he who denies me in the presence of men will be denied in the presence of the angels of God.** [12:10] **Everyone who speaks a word against the Son of Man will be forgiven, but those who blaspheme against the Holy Spirit will not be forgiven.** [12:11] **When they bring you before the synagogues, the rulers, and the authorities, don't be anxious how or what you will answer, or what you will say;** [12:12] **for the Holy Spirit will teach you in that same hour what you must say."**

[12:13] One of the multitude said to him, "Teacher, tell my brother to divide the inheritance with me."

[12:14] But he said to him, **"Man, who made me a judge or an arbitrator over you?"** [12:15] He said to them, **"Beware! Keep yourselves from covetousness, for a man's life doesn't consist of the abundance of the things which he possesses."**

[12:16] He spoke a parable to them, saying, **"The ground of a certain rich man brought forth abundantly.** [12:17] **He reasoned within himself, saying, 'What will I do, because I don't have room to store my crops?'** [12:18] **He said, 'This is what I will do. I will pull down my barns, and build bigger ones, and there I will store all my grain and my goods.** [12:19] **I will tell my soul, "Soul, you have many goods laid up for many years. Take your ease, eat, drink, be merry."'**

[12:20] **"But God said to him, 'You foolish one, tonight your soul is required of you. The things which you have prepared— whose will they be?'** [12:21] **So is he who**

---

[b]12:5 or, Hell
[c]12:6 An assarion was a small copper coin worth about an hour's wages for an agricultural laborer.

lays up treasure for himself, and is not rich toward God."

[12:22]He said to his disciples, "Therefore I tell you, don't be anxious for your life, what you will eat, nor yet for your body, what you will wear. [12:23]Life is more than food, and the body is more than clothing. [12:24]Consider the ravens: they don't sow, they don't reap, they have no warehouse or barn, and God feeds them. How much more valuable are you than birds! [12:25]Which of you by being anxious can add a cubit to his height? [12:26]If then you aren't able to do even the least things, why are you anxious about the rest? [12:27]Consider the lilies, how they grow. They don't toil, neither do they spin; yet I tell you, even Solomon in all his glory was not arrayed like one of these. [12:28]But if this is how God clothes the grass in the field, which today exists, and tomorrow is cast into the oven, how much more will he clothe you, O you of little faith? [12:29]Don't seek what you will eat or what you will drink; neither be anxious. [12:30]For the nations of the world seek after all of these things, but your Father knows that you need these things. [12:31]But seek God's Kingdom, and all these things will be added to you. [12:32]Don't be afraid, little flock, for it is your Father's good pleasure to give you the Kingdom. [12:33]Sell that which you have, and give gifts to the needy. Make for yourselves purses which don't grow old, a treasure in the heavens that doesn't fail, where no thief approaches, neither moth destroys. [12:34]For where your treasure is, there will your heart be also.

[12:35]"Let your waist be girded and your lamps burning. [12:36]Be like men watching for their lord, when he returns from the marriage feast; that, when he comes and knocks, they may immediately open to him. [12:37]Blessed are those servants, whom the lord will find watching when he comes. Most certainly I tell you, that he will dress himself, and make them recline, and will come and serve them. [12:38]They will be blessed if he comes in the second or third watch, and finds them so. [12:39]But know this, that if the master of the house had known in what hour the thief was coming, he would have watched, and not allowed his house to be broken into. [12:40]Therefore be ready also, for the Son of Man is coming in an hour that you don't expect him."

[12:41]Peter said to him, "Lord, are you telling this parable to us, or to everybody?"

[12:42]The Lord said, "Who then is the faithful and wise steward, whom his lord will set over his household, to give them their portion of food at the right times? [12:43]Blessed is that servant whom his lord will find doing so when he comes. [12:44]Truly I tell you, that he will set him over all that he has. [12:45]But if that servant says in his heart, 'My lord delays his coming,' and begins to beat the menservants and the maidservants, and to eat and drink, and to be drunken, [12:46]then the lord of that servant will come in a day when he isn't expecting him, and in an hour that he doesn't know, and will cut him in two, and place his portion with the unfaithful. [12:47]That servant, who knew his lord's will, and didn't prepare, nor do what he wanted, will be beaten with many stripes, [12:48]but he who didn't know, and did things worthy of stripes, will be beaten with few stripes. To whoever much is given, of him will much be required; and to whom much was entrusted, of him more will be asked.

[12:49]"I came to throw fire on the earth. I wish it were already kindled. [12:50]But I have a baptism to be baptized with, and how distressed I am until it is accomplished! [12:51]Do you think that I have come to give peace in the earth? I tell you, no, but rather division. [12:52]For from now on, there will be five in one house divided, three against two, and two against three. [12:53]They will be divided, father against son, and son against father; mother against daughter, and daughter against her mother; mother-in-law against her daughter-in-law, and daughter-in-law against her mother-in-law."

[12:54]He said to the multitudes also, "When you see a cloud rising from the west, immediately you say, 'A shower is coming,' and so it happens. [12:55]When a south wind blows, you say, 'There will be a scorching heat,' and it happens. ^{12:56}You hypocrites! You know how to interpret the appearance of the earth and the sky, but how is it that you don't interpret this time? ^{12:57}Why don't you judge for yourselves what is right? ^{12:58}For when you are going with your adversary before the magistrate, try diligently on the way to be released from him, lest perhaps he drag you to the judge, and the judge deliver you to the officer, and the officer throw you into prison. ^{12:59}I tell you, you will by no means get out of there, until you have paid the very last penny.^d"

^{13:1}Now there were some present at the same time who told him about the Galileans, whose blood Pilate had mixed with their sacrifices. ^{13:2}Jesus answered them, **"Do you think that these Galileans were worse sinners than all the other Galileans, because they suffered such things? ^{13:3}I tell you, no, but, unless you repent, you will all perish in the same way. ^{13:4}Or those eighteen, on whom the tower in Siloam fell, and killed them; do you think that they were worse offenders than all the men who dwell in Jerusalem? ^{13:5}I tell you, no, but, unless you repent, you will all perish in the same way."**

^{13:6}He spoke this parable. **"A certain man had a fig tree planted in his vineyard, and he came seeking fruit on it, and found none. ^{13:7}He said to the vine dresser, 'Behold, these three years I have come looking for fruit on this fig tree, and found none. Cut it down. Why does it waste the soil?' ^{13:8}He answered, 'Lord, leave it alone this year also, until I dig around it, and fertilize it. ^{13:9}If it bears fruit, fine; but if not, after that, you can cut it down.'"**

^{13:10}He was teaching in one of the synagogues on the Sabbath day. ^{13:11}Behold, there was a woman who had a spirit of infirmity eighteen years, and she was bent over, and could in no way straighten herself up. ^{13:12}When Jesus saw her, he called her, and said to her, **"Woman, you are freed from your infirmity."** ^{13:13}He laid his hands on her, and immediately she stood up straight, and glorified God.

^{13:14}The ruler of the synagogue, being indignant because Jesus had healed on the Sabbath, said to the multitude, "There are six days in which men ought to work. Therefore come on those days and be healed, and not on the Sabbath day!"

^{13:15}Therefore the Lord answered him, **"You hypocrites! Doesn't each one of you free his ox or his donkey from the stall on the Sabbath, and lead him away to water? ^{13:16}Ought not this woman, being a daughter of Abraham, whom Satan had bound eighteen long years, be freed from this bondage on the Sabbath day?"**

^{13:17}As he said these things, all his adversaries were disappointed, and all the multitude rejoiced for all the glorious things that were done by him.

^{13:18}He said, **"What is the Kingdom of God like? To what shall I compare it? ^{13:19}It is like a grain of mustard seed, which a man took, and put in his own garden. It grew, and became a large tree, and the birds of the sky lodged in its branches."**

^{13:20}Again he said, **"To what shall I compare the Kingdom of God? ^{13:21}It is like yeast, which a woman took and hid in three measures^e of flour, until it was all leavened."**

^{13:22}He went on his way through cities and villages, teaching, and traveling on to Jerusalem. ^{13:23}One said to him, "Lord, are they few who are saved?"

He said to them, ^{13:24}**"Strive to enter in by the narrow door, for many, I tell you, will seek to enter in, and will not be able. ^{13:25}When once the master of the house has risen up, and has shut the door, and you begin to stand outside, and to knock at the door, saying, 'Lord, Lord, open to us!' then he will answer and tell you, 'I don't know you or where you come from.' ^{13:26}Then you will begin to say,**

---

^d12:59 literally, lepton. A lepton is a very small brass Jewish coin worth half a Roman quadrans each, which is worth a quarter of the copper assarion. Lepta are worth less than 1% of an agricultural worker's daily wages.

^e13:21 literally, three sata. 3 sata is about 39 litres or a bit more than a bushel

'We ate and drank in your presence, and you taught in our streets.' ^{13:27}He will say, 'I tell you, I don't know where you come from. Depart from me, all you workers of iniquity.' ^{13:28}There will be weeping and gnashing of teeth, when you see Abraham, Isaac, Jacob, and all the prophets, in the Kingdom of God, and yourselves being thrown outside. ^{13:29}They will come from the east, west, north, and south, and will sit down in the Kingdom of God. ^{13:30}Behold, there are some who are last who will be first, and there are some who are first who will be last."

^{13:31}On that same day, some Pharisees came, saying to him, "Get out of here, and go away, for Herod wants to kill you."

^{13:32}He said to them, "Go and tell that fox, 'Behold, I cast out demons and perform cures today and tomorrow, and the third day I complete my mission. ^{13:33}Nevertheless I must go on my way today and tomorrow and the next day, for it can't be that a prophet perish outside of Jerusalem.'

^{13:34}"Jerusalem, Jerusalem, that kills the prophets, and stones those who are sent to her! How often I wanted to gather your children together, like a hen gathers her own brood under her wings, and you refused! ^{13:35}Behold, your house is left to you desolate. I tell you, you will not see me, until you say, 'Blessed is he who comes in the name of the Lord!'"^f

^{14:1}It happened, when he went into the house of one of the rulers of the Pharisees on a Sabbath to eat bread, that they were watching him. ^{14:2}Behold, a certain man who had dropsy was in front of him. ^{14:3}Jesus, answering, spoke to the lawyers and Pharisees, saying, "Is it lawful to heal on the Sabbath?"

^{14:4}But they were silent.

He took him, and healed him, and let him go. ^{14:5}He answered them, "Which of you, if your son^g or an ox fell into a well, wouldn't immediately pull him out on a Sabbath day?"

^{14:6}They couldn't answer him regarding these things.

^{14:7}He spoke a parable to those who were invited, when he noticed how they chose the best seats, and said to them, ^{14:8}"When you are invited by anyone to a marriage feast, don't sit in the best seat, since perhaps someone more honorable than you might be invited by him, ^{14:9}and he who invited both of you would come and tell you, 'Make room for this person.' Then you would begin, with shame, to take the lowest place. ^{14:10}But when you are invited, go and sit in the lowest place, so that when he who invited you comes, he may tell you, 'Friend, move up higher.' Then you will be honored in the presence of all who sit at the table with you. ^{14:11}For everyone who exalts himself will be humbled, and whoever humbles himself will be exalted."

^{14:12}He also said to the one who had invited him, "When you make a dinner or a supper, don't call your friends, nor your brothers, nor your kinsmen, nor rich neighbors, or perhaps they might also return the favor, and pay you back. ^{14:13}But when you make a feast, ask the poor, the maimed, the lame, or the blind; ^{14:14}and you will be blessed, because they don't have the resources to repay you. For you will be repaid in the resurrection of the righteous."

^{14:15}When one of those who sat at the table with him heard these things, he said to him, "Blessed is he who will feast in the Kingdom of God!"

^{14:16}But he said to him, "A certain man made a great supper, and he invited many people. ^{14:17}He sent out his servant at supper time to tell those who were invited, 'Come, for everything is ready now.' ^{14:18}They all as one began to make excuses.

"The first said to him, 'I have bought a field, and I must go and see it. Please have me excused.'

^{14:19}"Another said, 'I have bought five yoke of oxen, and I must go try them out. Please have me excused.'

---

^f13:35 Psalm 118:26
^g14:5 TR reads "donkey" instead of "son"

^{14:20}"Another said, 'I have married a wife, and therefore I can't come.'

^{14:21}"That servant came, and told his lord these things. Then the master of the house, being angry, said to his servant, 'Go out quickly into the streets and lanes of the city, and bring in the poor, maimed, blind, and lame.'

^{14:22}"The servant said, 'Lord, it is done as you commanded, and there is still room.'

^{14:23}"The lord said to the servant, 'Go out into the highways and hedges, and compel them to come in, that my house may be filled. ^{14:24}For I tell you that none of those men who were invited will taste of my supper.'"

^{14:25}Now great multitudes were going with him. He turned and said to them, ^{14:26}"If anyone comes to me, and doesn't hate his own father, mother, wife, children, brothers, and sisters, yes, and his own life also, he can't be my disciple. ^{14:27}Whoever doesn't bear his own cross, and come after me, can't be my disciple. ^{14:28}For which of you, desiring to build a tower, doesn't first sit down and count the cost, to see if he has enough to complete it? ^{14:29}Or perhaps, when he has laid a foundation, and is not able to finish, everyone who sees begins to mock him, ^{14:30}saying, 'This man began to build, and wasn't able to finish.' ^{14:31}Or what king, as he goes to encounter another king in war, will not sit down first and consider whether he is able with ten thousand to meet him who comes against him with twenty thousand? ^{14:32}Or else, while the other is yet a great way off, he sends an envoy, and asks for conditions of peace. ^{14:33}So therefore whoever of you who doesn't renounce all that he has, he can't be my disciple. ^{14:34}Salt is good, but if the salt becomes flat and tasteless, with what do you season it? ^{14:35}It is fit neither for the soil nor for the manure pile. It is thrown out. He who has ears to hear, let him hear."

^{15:1}Now all the tax collectors and sinners were coming close to him to hear him. ^{15:2}The Pharisees and the scribes murmured, saying, "This man welcomes sinners, and eats with them."

^{15:3}He told them this parable. ^{15:4}"Which of you men, if you had one hundred sheep, and lost one of them, wouldn't leave the ninety-nine in the wilderness, and go after the one that was lost, until he found it? ^{15:5}When he has found it, he carries it on his shoulders, rejoicing. ^{15:6}When he comes home, he calls together his friends and his neighbors, saying to them, 'Rejoice with me, for I have found my sheep which was lost!' ^{15:7}I tell you that even so there will be more joy in heaven over one sinner who repents, than over ninety-nine righteous people who need no repentance. ^{15:8}Or what woman, if she had ten drachma[h] coins, if she lost one drachma coin, wouldn't light a lamp, sweep the house, and seek diligently until she found it? ^{15:9}When she has found it, she calls together her friends and neighbors, saying, 'Rejoice with me, for I have found the drachma which I had lost.' ^{15:10}Even so, I tell you, there is joy in the presence of the angels of God over one sinner repenting."

^{15:11}He said, "A certain man had two sons. ^{15:12}The younger of them said to his father, 'Father, give me my share of your property.' He divided his livelihood between them. ^{15:13}Not many days after, the younger son gathered all of this together and traveled into a far country. There he wasted his property with riotous living. ^{15:14}When he had spent all of it, there arose a severe famine in that country, and he began to be in need. ^{15:15}He went and joined himself to one of the citizens of that country, and he sent him into his fields to feed pigs. ^{15:16}He wanted to fill his belly with the husks that the pigs ate, but no one gave him any. ^{15:17}But when he came to himself he said, 'How many hired servants of my father's have bread enough to spare, and I'm dying with hunger! ^{15:18}I will get up and go to my father, and will tell him, "Father, I have sinned against heaven, and in your sight. ^{15:19}I am no

---

[h]15:8 A drachma coin was worth about 2 days wages for an agricultural laborer.

more worthy to be called your son. Make me as one of your hired servants."'

¹⁵:²⁰"He arose, and came to his father. But while he was still far off, his father saw him, and was moved with compassion, and ran, and fell on his neck, and kissed him. ¹⁵:²¹The son said to him, 'Father, I have sinned against heaven, and in your sight. I am no longer worthy to be called your son.'

¹⁵:²²"But the father said to his servants, 'Bring out the best robe, and put it on him. Put a ring on his hand, and shoes on his feet. ¹⁵:²³Bring the fattened calf, kill it, and let us eat, and celebrate; ¹⁵:²⁴for this, my son, was dead, and is alive again. He was lost, and is found.' They began to celebrate.

¹⁵:²⁵"Now his elder son was in the field. As he came near to the house, he heard music and dancing. ¹⁵:²⁶He called one of the servants to him, and asked what was going on. ¹⁵:²⁷He said to him, 'Your brother has come, and your father has killed the fattened calf, because he has received him back safe and healthy.' ¹⁵:²⁸But he was angry, and would not go in. Therefore his father came out, and begged him. ¹⁵:²⁹But he answered his father, 'Behold, these many years I have served you, and I never disobeyed a commandment of yours, but you never gave me a goat, that I might celebrate with my friends. ¹⁵:³⁰But when this, your son, came, who has devoured your living with prostitutes, you killed the fattened calf for him.'

¹⁵:³¹"He said to him, 'Son, you are always with me, and all that is mine is yours. ¹⁵:³²But it was appropriate to celebrate and be glad, for this, your brother, was dead, and is alive again. He was lost, and is found.'"

¹⁶:¹He also said to his disciples, "There was a certain rich man who had a manager. An accusation was made to him that this man was wasting his possessions. ¹⁶:²He called him, and said to him, 'What is this that I hear about you? Give an accounting of your management, for you can no longer be manager.'

¹⁶:³"The manager said within himself, 'What will I do, seeing that my lord is taking away the management position from me? I don't have strength to dig. I am ashamed to beg. ¹⁶:⁴I know what I will do, so that when I am removed from management, they may receive me into their houses.' ¹⁶:⁵Calling each one of his lord's debtors to him, he said to the first, 'How much do you owe to my lord?' ¹⁶:⁶He said, 'A hundred batosⁱ of oil.' He said to him, 'Take your bill, and sit down quickly and write fifty.' ¹⁶:⁷Then said he to another, 'How much do you owe?' He said, 'A hundred corsʲ of wheat.' He said to him, 'Take your bill, and write eighty.'

¹⁶:⁸"His lord commended the dishonest manager because he had done wisely, for the children of this world are, in their own generation, wiser than the children of the light. ¹⁶:⁹I tell you, make for yourselves friends by means of unrighteous mammon, so that when you fail, they may receive you into the eternal tents. ¹⁶:¹⁰He who is faithful in a very little is faithful also in much. He who is dishonest in a very little is also dishonest in much. ¹⁶:¹¹If therefore you have not been faithful in the unrighteous mammon, who will commit to your trust the true riches? ¹⁶:¹²If you have not been faithful in that which is another's, who will give you that which is your own? ¹⁶:¹³No servant can serve two masters, for either he will hate the one, and love the other; or else he will hold to one, and despise the other. You aren't able to serve God and mammonᵏ."

¹⁶:¹⁴The Pharisees, who were lovers of money, also heard all these things, and they scoffed at him. ¹⁶:¹⁵He said to them, "You are those who justify yourselves in the sight of men, but God knows your hearts. For that which is exalted among men is an abomination in the sight of God. ¹⁶:¹⁶The law and the prophets were until John. From that time the Good

---

ⁱ16:6 100 batos is about 395 litres, 104 U. S. gallons, or 87 imperial gallons.

ʲ16:7 100 cors = about 3,910 litres or 600 bushels.

ᵏ16:13 "Mammon" refers to riches or a false god of wealth.

News of the Kingdom of God is preached, and everyone is forcing his way into it. [16:17]But it is easier for heaven and earth to pass away, than for one tiny stroke of a pen in the law to fall. [16:18]Everyone who divorces his wife, and marries another, commits adultery. He who marries one who is divorced from a husband commits adultery.

[16:19]"Now there was a certain rich man, and he was clothed in purple and fine linen, living in luxury every day. [16:20]A certain beggar, named Lazarus, was laid at his gate, full of sores, [16:21]and desiring to be fed with the crumbs that fell from the rich man's table. Yes, even the dogs came and licked his sores. [16:22]It happened that the beggar died, and that he was carried away by the angels to Abraham's bosom. The rich man also died, and was buried. [16:23]In Hades[1], he lifted up his eyes, being in torment, and saw Abraham far off, and Lazarus at his bosom. [16:24]He cried and said, 'Father Abraham, have mercy on me, and send Lazarus, that he may dip the tip of his finger in water, and cool my tongue! For I am in anguish in this flame.'

[16:25]"But Abraham said, 'Son, remember that you, in your lifetime, received your good things, and Lazarus, in like manner, bad things. But now here he is comforted and you are in anguish. [16:26]Besides all this, between us and you there is a great gulf fixed, that those who want to pass from here to you are not able, and that none may cross over from there to us.'

[16:27]"He said, 'I ask you therefore, father, that you would send him to my father's house; [16:28]for I have five brothers, that he may testify to them, so they won't also come into this place of torment.'

[16:29]"But Abraham said to him, 'They have Moses and the prophets. Let them listen to them.'

[16:30]"He said, 'No, father Abraham, but if one goes to them from the dead, they will repent.'

[16:31]"He said to him, 'If they don't listen to Moses and the prophets, neither will they be persuaded if one rises from the dead.'"

[17:1]He said to the disciples, "It is impossible that no occasions of stumbling should come, but woe to him through whom they come! [17:2]It would be better for him if a millstone were hung around his neck, and he were thrown into the sea, rather than that he should cause one of these little ones to stumble. [17:3]Be careful. If your brother sins against you, rebuke him. If he repents, forgive him. [17:4]If he sins against you seven times in the day, and seven times returns, saying, 'I repent,' you shall forgive him."

[17:5]The apostles said to the Lord, "Increase our faith."

[17:6]The Lord said, "If you had faith like a grain of mustard seed, you would tell this sycamore tree, 'Be uprooted, and be planted in the sea,' and it would obey you. [17:7]But who is there among you, having a servant plowing or keeping sheep, that will say, when he comes in from the field, 'Come immediately and sit down at the table,' [17:8]and will not rather tell him, 'Prepare my supper, clothe yourself properly, and serve me, while I eat and drink. Afterward you shall eat and drink'? [17:9]Does he thank that servant because he did the things that were commanded? I think not. [17:10]Even so you also, when you have done all the things that are commanded you, say, 'We are unworthy servants. We have done our duty.'"

[17:11]It happened as he was on his way to Jerusalem, that he was passing along the borders of Samaria and Galilee. [17:12]As he entered into a certain village, ten men who were lepers met him, who stood at a distance. [17:13]They lifted up their voices, saying, "Jesus, Master, have mercy on us!"

[17:14]When he saw them, he said to them, "Go and show yourselves to the priests." It happened that as they went, they were cleansed. [17:15]One of them, when he saw that he was healed, turned back, glorifying God with a loud voice. [17:16]He fell on his face at Jesus' feet, giving him thanks; and he was a Samaritan. [17:17]Jesus answered, "Weren't the ten cleansed? But where are

---

[1]16:23 or, Hell

the nine? [17:18]Were there none found who returned to give glory to God, except this stranger?" [17:19]Then he said to him, "Get up, and go your way. Your faith has healed you."

[17:20]Being asked by the Pharisees when the Kingdom of God would come, he answered them, "The Kingdom of God doesn't come with observation; [17:21]neither will they say, 'Look, here!' or, 'Look, there!' for behold, the Kingdom of God is within you."

[17:22]He said to the disciples, "The days will come, when you will desire to see one of the days of the Son of Man, and you will not see it. [17:23]They will tell you, 'Look, here!' or 'Look, there!' Don't go away, nor follow after them, [17:24]for as the lightning, when it flashes out of the one part under the sky, shines to the other part under the sky; so will the Son of Man be in his day. [17:25]But first, he must suffer many things and be rejected by this generation. [17:26]As it happened in the days of Noah, even so will it be also in the days of the Son of Man. [17:27]They ate, they drank, they married, they were given in marriage, until the day that Noah entered into the ship, and the flood came, and destroyed them all. [17:28]Likewise, even as it happened in the days of Lot: they ate, they drank, they bought, they sold, they planted, they built; [17:29]but in the day that Lot went out from Sodom, it rained fire and sulfur from the sky, and destroyed them all. [17:30]It will be the same way in the day that the Son of Man is revealed. [17:31]In that day, he who will be on the housetop, and his goods in the house, let him not go down to take them away. Let him who is in the field likewise not turn back. [17:32]Remember Lot's wife! [17:33]Whoever seeks to save his life loses it, but whoever loses his life preserves it. [17:34]I tell you, in that night there will be two people in one bed. The one will be taken, and the other will be left. [17:35]There will be two grinding grain together. One will be taken, and the other will be left." [17:36m]

[17:37]They, answering, asked him,

"Where, Lord?"

He said to them, "Where the body is, there will the vultures also be gathered together."

[18:1]He also spoke a parable to them that they must always pray, and not give up, [18:2]saying, "There was a judge in a certain city who didn't fear God, and didn't respect man. [18:3]A widow was in that city, and she often came to him, saying, 'Defend me from my adversary!' [18:4]He wouldn't for a while, but afterward he said to himself, 'Though I neither fear God, nor respect man, [18:5]yet because this widow bothers me, I will defend her, or else she will wear me out by her continual coming.'"

[18:6]The Lord said, "Listen to what the unrighteous judge says. [18:7]Won't God avenge his chosen ones, who are crying out to him day and night, and yet he exercises patience with them? [18:8]I tell you that he will avenge them quickly. Nevertheless, when the Son of Man comes, will he find faith on the earth?"

[18:9]He spoke also this parable to certain people who were convinced of their own righteousness, and who despised all others. [18:10]"Two men went up into the temple to pray; one was a Pharisee, and the other was a tax collector. [18:11]The Pharisee stood and prayed to himself like this: 'God, I thank you, that I am not like the rest of men, extortioners, unrighteous, adulterers, or even like this tax collector. [18:12]I fast twice a week. I give tithes of all that I get.' [18:13]But the tax collector, standing far away, wouldn't even lift up his eyes to heaven, but beat his breast, saying, 'God, be merciful to me, a sinner!' [18:14]I tell you, this man went down to his house justified rather than the other; for everyone who exalts himself will be humbled, but he who humbles himself will be exalted."

[18:15]They were also bringing their babies to him, that he might touch them. But when the disciples saw it, they rebuked them. [18:16]Jesus summoned them, saying, "Allow the little children to come to me, and don't

m17:36 Some Greek manuscripts add: "Two will be in the field: the one taken, and the other left."

hinder them, for the Kingdom of God belongs to such as these. [18:17]Most certainly, I tell you, whoever doesn't receive the Kingdom of God like a little child, he will in no way enter into it."

[18:18]A certain ruler asked him, saying, "Good Teacher, what shall I do to inherit eternal life?"

[18:19]Jesus asked him, **"Why do you call me good? No one is good, except one—God. [18:20]You know the commandments: 'Don't commit adultery,' 'Don't murder,' 'Don't steal,' 'Don't give false testimony,' 'Honor your father and your mother.'"**[n]

[18:21]He said, "I have observed all these things from my youth up."

[18:22]When Jesus heard these things, he said to him, **"You still lack one thing. Sell all that you have, and distribute it to the poor. You will have treasure in heaven. Come, follow me."**

[18:23]But when he heard these things, he became very sad, for he was very rich.

[18:24]Jesus, seeing that he became very sad, said, **"How hard it is for those who have riches to enter into the Kingdom of God! [18:25]For it is easier for a camel to enter in through a needle's eye, than for a rich man to enter into the Kingdom of God."**

[18:26]Those who heard it said, "Then who can be saved?"

[18:27]But he said, **"The things which are impossible with men are possible with God."**

[18:28]Peter said, "Look, we have left everything, and followed you."

[18:29]He said to them, **"Most certainly I tell you, there is no one who has left house, or wife, or brothers, or parents, or children, for the Kingdom of God's sake, [18:30]who will not receive many times more in this time, and in the world to come, eternal life."**

[18:31]He took the twelve aside, and said to them, **"Behold, we are going up to Jerusalem, and all the things that are written through the prophets concerning the Son of Man will be completed. [18:32]For he will be delivered up to the Gentiles, will be mocked, treated shamefully, and**

spit on. [18:33]**They will scourge and kill him. On the third day, he will rise again."**

[18:34]They understood none of these things. This saying was hidden from them, and they didn't understand the things that were said. [18:35]It happened, as he came near Jericho, a certain blind man sat by the road, begging. [18:36]Hearing a multitude going by, he asked what this meant. [18:37]They told him that Jesus of Nazareth was passing by. [18:38]He cried out, "Jesus, you son of David, have mercy on me!" [18:39]Those who led the way rebuked him, that he should be quiet; but he cried out all the more, "You son of David, have mercy on me!"

[18:40]Standing still, Jesus commanded him to be brought to him. When he had come near, he asked him, [18:41]**"What do you want me to do?"**

He said, "Lord, that I may see again."

[18:42]Jesus said to him, **"Receive your sight. Your faith has healed you."**

[18:43]Immediately he received his sight, and followed him, glorifying God. All the people, when they saw it, praised God.

[19:1]He entered and was passing through Jericho. [19:2]There was a man named Zacchaeus. He was a chief tax collector, and he was rich. [19:3]He was trying to see who Jesus was, and couldn't because of the crowd, because he was short. [19:4]He ran on ahead, and climbed up into a sycamore tree to see him, for he was to pass that way. [19:5]When Jesus came to the place, he looked up and saw him, and said to him, **"Zacchaeus, hurry and come down, for today I must stay at your house."** [19:6]He hurried, came down, and received him joyfully. [19:7]When they saw it, they all murmured, saying, "He has gone in to lodge with a man who is a sinner."

[19:8]Zacchaeus stood and said to the Lord, "Behold, Lord, half of my goods I give to the poor. If I have wrongfully exacted anything of anyone, I restore four times as much."

[19:9]Jesus said to him, "Today, salvation has come to this house, because he also is a son of Abraham. [19:10]For the Son of Man

[n]18:20 Exodus 20:12-16; Deuteronomy 5:16-20

came to seek and to save that which was lost."

[19:11] As they heard these things, he went on and told a parable, because he was near Jerusalem, and they supposed that the Kingdom of God would be revealed immediately. [19:12] He said therefore, **"A certain nobleman went into a far country to receive for himself a kingdom, and to return. [19:13] He called ten servants of his, and gave them ten mina coins,[o] and told them, 'Conduct business until I come.' [19:14] But his citizens hated him, and sent an envoy after him, saying, 'We don't want this man to reign over us.'**

[19:15] **"It happened when he had come back again, having received the kingdom, that he commanded these servants, to whom he had given the money, to be called to him, that he might know what they had gained by conducting business. [19:16] The first came before him, saying, 'Lord, your mina has made ten more minas.'**

[19:17] **"He said to him, 'Well done, you good servant! Because you were found faithful with very little, you shall have authority over ten cities.'**

[19:18] **"The second came, saying, 'Your mina, Lord, has made five minas.'**

[19:19] **"So he said to him, 'And you are to be over five cities.' [19:20] Another came, saying, 'Lord, behold, your mina, which I kept laid away in a handkerchief, [19:21] for I feared you, because you are an exacting man. You take up that which you didn't lay down, and reap that which you didn't sow.'**

[19:22] **"He said to him, 'Out of your own mouth will I judge you, you wicked servant! You knew that I am an exacting man, taking up that which I didn't lay down, and reaping that which I didn't sow. [19:23] Then why didn't you deposit my money in the bank, and at my coming, I might have earned interest on it?' [19:24] He said to those who stood by, 'Take the mina away from him, and give it to him who has the ten minas.'**

[19:25] **"They said to him, 'Lord, he has ten minas!' [19:26] 'For I tell you that to everyone who has, will more be given; but from him who doesn't have, even that which he has will be taken away from him. [19:27] But bring those enemies of mine who didn't want me to reign over them here, and kill them before me.'"** [19:28] Having said these things, he went on ahead, going up to Jerusalem.

[19:29] It happened, when he drew near to Bethsphage[p] and Bethany, at the mountain that is called Olivet, he sent two of his disciples, [19:30] saying, **"Go your way into the village on the other side, in which, as you enter, you will find a colt tied, whereon no man ever yet sat. Untie it, and bring it. [19:31] If anyone asks you, 'Why are you untying it?' say to him: 'The Lord needs it.'"**

[19:32] Those who were sent went away, and found things just as he had told them. [19:33] As they were untying the colt, its owners said to them, "Why are you untying the colt?" [19:34] They said, "The Lord needs it." [19:35] They brought it to Jesus. They threw their cloaks on the colt, and set Jesus on them. [19:36] As he went, they spread their cloaks in the way. [19:37] As he was now getting near, at the descent of the Mount of Olives, the whole multitude of the disciples began to rejoice and praise God with a loud voice for all the mighty works which they had seen, [19:38] saying, "Blessed is the King who comes in the name of the Lord![q] Peace in heaven, and glory in the highest!"

[19:39] Some of the Pharisees from the multitude said to him, "Teacher, rebuke your disciples!"

[19:40] He answered them, **"I tell you that if these were silent, the stones would cry out."**

[19:41] When he drew near, he saw the city and wept over it, [19:42] saying, **"If you, even you, had known today the things which belong to your peace! But now, they are hidden from your eyes. [19:43] For the days will come on you, when your enemies**

[o]19:13 10 minas was more than 3 years' wages for an agricultural laborer.
[p]19:29 TR, NU read "Bethpage" instead of "Bethsphage"
[q]19:38 Psalm 118:26

will throw up a barricade against you, surround you, hem you in on every side, [19:44] and will dash you and your children within you to the ground. They will not leave in you one stone on another, because you didn't know the time of your visitation."

[19:45] He entered into the temple, and began to drive out those who bought and sold in it, [19:46] saying to them, **"It is written, 'My house is a house of prayer,'[r] but you have made it a 'den of robbers'!"[s]**

[19:47] He was teaching daily in the temple, but the chief priests and the scribes and the leading men among the people sought to destroy him. [19:48] They couldn't find what they might do, for all the people hung on to every word that he said.

[20:1] It happened on one of those days, as he was teaching the people in the temple and preaching the Good News, that the [t] priests and scribes came to him with the elders. [20:2] They asked him, "Tell us: by what authority do you do these things? Or who is giving you this authority?"

[20:3] He answered them, **"I also will ask you one question. Tell me: [20:4] the baptism of John, was it from heaven, or from men?"**

[20:5] They reasoned with themselves, saying, "If we say, 'From heaven,' he will say, 'Why didn't you believe him?' [20:6] But if we say, 'From men,' all the people will stone us, for they are persuaded that John was a prophet." [20:7] They answered that they didn't know where it was from.

[20:8] Jesus said to them, **"Neither will I tell you by what authority I do these things."**

[20:9] He began to tell the people this parable. **"A [u] man planted a vineyard, and rented it out to some farmers, and went into another country for a long time. [20:10] At the proper season, he sent a servant to the farmers to collect his share of the fruit of the vineyard. But the farmers beat him, and sent him away empty. [20:11] He sent yet another servant, and they also** beat him, and treated him shamefully, and sent him away empty. [20:12] He sent yet a third, and they also wounded him, and threw him out. [20:13] The lord of the vineyard said, 'What shall I do? I will send my beloved son. It may be that seeing him, they will respect him.'

[20:14] **"But when the farmers saw him, they reasoned among themselves, saying, 'This is the heir. Come, let's kill him, that the inheritance may be ours.' [20:15] They threw him out of the vineyard, and killed him. What therefore will the lord of the vineyard do to them? [20:16] He will come and destroy these farmers, and will give the vineyard to others."**

When they heard it, they said, "May it never be!"

[20:17] But he looked at them, and said, **"Then what is this that is written,**

'The stone which the builders rejected,
>   **the same was made the chief cornerstone?'[v]**
[20:18] **Everyone who falls on that stone will be broken to pieces,**
>   **but it will crush whomever it falls on to dust."**

[20:19] The chief priests and the scribes sought to lay hands on him that very hour, but they feared the people—for they knew he had spoken this parable against them. [20:20] They watched him, and sent out spies, who pretended to be righteous, that they might trap him in something he said, so as to deliver him up to the power and authority of the governor. [20:21] They asked him, "Teacher, we know that you say and teach what is right, and aren't partial to anyone, but truly teach the way of God. [20:22] Is it lawful for us to pay taxes to Caesar, or not?"

[20:23] But he perceived their craftiness, and said to them, **"Why do you test me? [20:24] Show me a denarius. Whose image and inscription are on it?"**

They answered, "Caesar's."

---

[r] 19:46 Isaiah 56:7
[s] 19:46 Jeremiah 7:11
[t] 20:1 TR adds "chief"
[u] 20:9 NU (in brackets) and TR add "certain"
[v] 20:17 Psalm 118:22

^{20:25}He said to them, **"Then give to Caesar the things that are Caesar's, and to God the things that are God's."**

^{20:26}They weren't able to trap him in his words before the people. They marveled at his answer, and were silent. ^{20:27}Some of the Sadducees came to him, those who deny that there is a resurrection. ^{20:28}They asked him, "Teacher, Moses wrote to us that if a man's brother dies having a wife, and he is childless, his brother should take the wife, and raise up children for his brother. ^{20:29}There were therefore seven brothers. The first took a wife, and died childless. ^{20:30}The second took her as wife, and he died childless. ^{20:31}The third took her, and likewise the seven all left no children, and died. ^{20:32}Afterward the woman also died. ^{20:33}Therefore in the resurrection whose wife of them will she be? For the seven had her as a wife."

^{20:34}Jesus said to them, **"The children of this age marry, and are given in marriage. ^{20:35}But those who are considered worthy to attain to that age and the resurrection from the dead, neither marry, nor are given in marriage. ^{20:36}For they can't die any more, for they are like the angels, and are children of God, being children of the resurrection. ^{20:37}But that the dead are raised, even Moses showed at the bush, when he called the Lord 'The God of Abraham, the God of Isaac, and the God of Jacob.'**^w ^{20:38}**Now he is not the God of the dead, but of the living, for all are alive to him."**

^{20:39}Some of the scribes answered, "Teacher, you speak well." ^{20:40}They didn't dare to ask him any more questions.

^{20:41}He said to them, **"Why do they say that the Christ is David's son? ^{20:42}David himself says in the book of Psalms,**
'The Lord said to my Lord,
  "Sit at my right hand,
    ^{20:43}**until I make your enemies the footstool of your feet."'**^x
^{20:44}**"David therefore calls him Lord, so how is he his son?"**

^{20:45}In the hearing of all the people, he said to his disciples, ^{20:46}**"Beware of the scribes, who like to walk in long robes, and love greetings in the marketplaces, the best seats in the synagogues, and the best places at feasts; ^{20:47}who devour widows' houses, and for a pretense make long prayers: these will receive greater condemnation."**

^{21:1}He looked up, and saw the rich people who were putting their gifts into the treasury. ^{21:2}He saw a certain poor widow casting in two small brass coins.^y ^{21:3}He said, **"Truly I tell you, this poor widow put in more than all of them, ^{21:4}for all these put in gifts for God from their abundance, but she, out of her poverty, put in all that she had to live on."**

^{21:5}As some were talking about the temple and how it was decorated with beautiful stones and gifts, he said, ^{21:6}**"As for these things which you see, the days will come, in which there will not be left here one stone on another that will not be thrown down."**

^{21:7}They asked him, "Teacher, so when will these things be? What is the sign that these things are about to happen?"

^{21:8}He said, **"Watch out that you don't get led astray, for many will come in my name, saying, 'I am he^z,' and, 'The time is at hand.' Therefore don't follow them. ^{21:9}When you hear of wars and disturbances, don't be terrified, for these things must happen first, but the end won't come immediately."**

^{21:10}Then he said to them, **"Nation will rise against nation, and kingdom against kingdom. ^{21:11}There will be great earthquakes, famines, and plagues in various places. There will be terrors and great signs from heaven. ^{21:12}But before all these things, they will lay their hands on you and will persecute you, delivering you up to synagogues and prisons, bringing you before kings and governors for my name's sake. ^{21:13}It will turn out as a**

---

^w20:37 Exodus 3:6
^x20:43 Psalm 110:1
^y21:2 literally, "two lepta." 2 lepta was about 1% of a day's wages for an agricultural laborer.
^z21:8 or, I AM

testimony for you. ²¹:¹⁴Settle it therefore in your hearts not to meditate beforehand how to answer, ²¹:¹⁵for I will give you a mouth and wisdom which all your adversaries will not be able to withstand or to contradict. ²¹:¹⁶You will be handed over even by parents, brothers, relatives, and friends. They will cause some of you to be put to death. ²¹:¹⁷You will be hated by all men for my name's sake. ²¹:¹⁸And not a hair of your head will perish.

²¹:¹⁹"By your endurance you will win your lives.

²¹:²⁰"But when you see Jerusalem surrounded by armies, then know that its desolation is at hand. ²¹:²¹Then let those who are in Judea flee to the mountains. Let those who are in the midst of her depart. Let those who are in the country not enter therein. ²¹:²²For these are days of vengeance, that all things which are written may be fulfilled. ²¹:²³Woe to those who are pregnant and to those who nurse infants in those days! For there will be great distress in the land, and wrath to this people. ²¹:²⁴They will fall by the edge of the sword, and will be led captive into all the nations. Jerusalem will be trampled down by the Gentiles, until the times of the Gentiles are fulfilled. ²¹:²⁵There will be signs in the sun, moon, and stars; and on the earth anxiety of nations, in perplexity for the roaring of the sea and the waves; ²¹:²⁶men fainting for fear, and for expectation of the things which are coming on the world: for the powers of the heavens will be shaken. ²¹:²⁷Then they will see the Son of Man coming in a cloud with power and great glory. ²¹:²⁸But when these things begin to happen, look up, and lift up your heads, because your redemption is near."

²¹:²⁹He told them a parable. "See the fig tree, and all the trees. ²¹:³⁰When they are already budding, you see it and know by your own selves that the summer is already near. ²¹:³¹Even so you also, when you see these things happening, know that the Kingdom of God is near. ²¹:³²Most certainly I tell you, this generation will not pass away until all things are accomplished. ²¹:³³Heaven and earth will pass away, but my words will by no means pass away.

²¹:³⁴"So be careful, or your hearts will be loaded down with carousing, drunkenness, and cares of this life, and that day will come on you suddenly. ²¹:³⁵For it will come like a snare on all those who dwell on the surface of all the earth. ²¹:³⁶Therefore be watchful all the time, praying that you may be counted worthy to escape all these things that will happen, and to stand before the Son of Man."

²¹:³⁷Every day Jesus was teaching in the temple, and every night he would go out and spend the night on the mountain that is called Olivet. ²¹:³⁸All the people came early in the morning to him in the temple to hear him.

²²:¹Now the feast of unleavened bread, which is called the Passover, drew near. ²²:²The chief priests and the scribes sought how they might put him to death, for they feared the people. ²²:³Satan entered into Judas, who was surnamed Iscariot, who was numbered with the twelve. ²²:⁴He went away, and talked with the chief priests and captains about how he might deliver him to them. ²²:⁵They were glad, and agreed to give him money. ²²:⁶He consented, and sought an opportunity to deliver him to them in the absence of the multitude. ²²:⁷The day of unleavened bread came, on which the Passover must be sacrificed. ²²:⁸He sent Peter and John, saying, **"Go and prepare the Passover for us, that we may eat."**

²²:⁹They said to him, "Where do you want us to prepare?"

²²:¹⁰He said to them, **"Behold, when you have entered into the city, a man carrying a pitcher of water will meet you. Follow him into the house which he enters. ²²:¹¹Tell the master of the house, 'The Teacher says to you, "Where is the guest room, where I may eat the Passover with my disciples?"' ²²:¹²He will show you a large, furnished upper room. Make preparations there."**

²²:¹³They went, found things as he had told them, and they prepared the Passover. ²²:¹⁴When the hour had come, he sat down with the twelve apostles. ²²:¹⁵He said to

them, "I have earnestly desired to eat this Passover with you before I suffer, ^{22:16}for I tell you, I will no longer by any means eat of it until it is fulfilled in the Kingdom of God." ^{22:17}He received a cup, and when he had given thanks, he said, "Take this, and share it among yourselves, ^{22:18}for I tell you, I will not drink at all again from the fruit of the vine, until the Kingdom of God comes."

^{22:19}He took bread, and when he had given thanks, he broke it, and gave to them, saying, "This is my body which is given for you.　Do this in memory of me." ^{22:20}Likewise, he took the cup after supper, saying, "This cup is the new covenant in my blood, which is poured out for you. ^{22:21}But behold, the hand of him who betrays me is with me on the table. ^{22:22}The Son of Man indeed goes, as it has been determined, but woe to that man through whom he is betrayed!"

^{22:23}They began to question among themselves, which of them it was who would do this thing. ^{22:24}There arose also a contention among them, which of them was considered to be greatest. ^{22:25}He said to them, "The kings of the nations lord it over them, and those who have authority over them are called 'benefactors.' ^{22:26}But not so with you.　But one who is the greater among you, let him become as the younger, and one who is governing, as one who serves. ^{22:27}For who is greater, one who sits at the table, or one who serves? Isn't it he who sits at the table?　But I am in the midst of you as one who serves. ^{22:28}But you are those who have continued with me in my trials. ^{22:29}I confer on you a kingdom, even as my Father conferred on me, ^{22:30}that you may eat and drink at my table in my Kingdom.　You will sit on thrones, judging the twelve tribes of Israel."

^{22:31}The Lord said, "Simon, Simon, behold, Satan asked to have you, that he might sift you as wheat, ^{22:32}but I prayed for you, that your faith wouldn't fail. You, when once you have turned again,

establish your brothers[a]."

^{22:33}He said to him, "Lord, I am ready to go with you both to prison and to death!"

^{22:34}He said, "I tell you, Peter, the rooster will by no means crow today until you deny that you know me three times."

^{22:35}He said to them, "When I sent you out without purse, and wallet, and shoes, did you lack anything?"

They said, "Nothing."

^{22:36}Then he said to them, "But now, whoever has a purse, let him take it, and likewise a wallet.　Whoever has none, let him sell his cloak, and buy a sword. ^{22:37}For I tell you that this which is written must still be fulfilled in me: 'He was counted with the lawless.'[b] For that which concerns me has an end."

^{22:38}They said, "Lord, behold, here are two swords."

He said to them, "That is enough."

^{22:39}He came out, and went, as his custom was, to the Mount of Olives.　His disciples also followed him. ^{22:40}When he was at the place, he said to them, "Pray that you don't enter into temptation."

^{22:41}He was withdrawn from them about a stone's throw, and he knelt down and prayed, ^{22:42}saying, "Father, if you are willing, remove this cup from me. Nevertheless, not my will, but yours, be done."

^{22:43}An angel from heaven appeared to him, strengthening him. ^{22:44}Being in agony he prayed more earnestly. His sweat became like great drops of blood falling down on the ground.

^{22:45}When he rose up from his prayer, he came to the disciples, and found them sleeping because of grief, ^{22:46}and said to them, "Why do you sleep? Rise and pray that you may not enter into temptation."

^{22:47}While he was still speaking, behold, a multitude, and he who was called Judas, one of the twelve, was leading them.　He came near to Jesus to kiss him. ^{22:48}But Jesus said to him, "Judas, do you betray the Son of Man with a kiss?"

---

[a]22:32 The word for "brothers" here may be also correctly translated "brothers and sisters" or "siblings."
[b]22:37 Isaiah 53:12

²²:⁴⁹When those who were around him saw what was about to happen, they said to him, "Lord, shall we strike with the sword?" ²²:⁵⁰A certain one of them struck the servant of the high priest, and cut off his right ear.

²²:⁵¹But Jesus answered, **"Let me at least do this"**—and he touched his ear, and healed him. ²²:⁵²Jesus said to the chief priests, captains of the temple, and elders, who had come against him, **"Have you come out as against a robber, with swords and clubs? ²²:⁵³When I was with you in the temple daily, you didn't stretch out your hands against me. But this is your hour, and the power of darkness."**

²²:⁵⁴They seized him, and led him away, and brought him into the high priest's house. But Peter followed from a distance. ²²:⁵⁵When they had kindled a fire in the middle of the courtyard, and had sat down together, Peter sat among them. ²²:⁵⁶A certain servant girl saw him as he sat in the light, and looking intently at him, said, "This man also was with him."

²²:⁵⁷He denied Jesus, saying, "Woman, I don't know him."

²²:⁵⁸After a little while someone else saw him, and said, "You also are one of them!"

But Peter answered, "Man, I am not!"

²²:⁵⁹After about one hour passed, another confidently affirmed, saying, "Truly this man also was with him, for he is a Galilean!"

²²:⁶⁰But Peter said, "Man, I don't know what you are talking about!" Immediately, while he was still speaking, a rooster crowed. ²²:⁶¹The Lord turned, and looked at Peter. Then Peter remembered the Lord's word, how he said to him, **"Before the rooster crows you will deny me three times."** ²²:⁶²He went out, and wept bitterly.

²²:⁶³The men who held Jesus mocked him and beat him. ²²:⁶⁴Having blindfolded him, they struck him on the face and asked him, "Prophesy! Who is the one who struck you?" ²²:⁶⁵They spoke many other things against him, insulting him.

²²:⁶⁶As soon as it was day, the assembly of the elders of the people was gathered together, both chief priests and scribes, and they led him away into their council,

saying, ²²:⁶⁷"If you are the Christ, tell us."

But he said to them, **"If I tell you, you won't believe, ²²:⁶⁸and if I ask, you will in no way answer me or let me go. ²²:⁶⁹From now on, the Son of Man will be seated at the right hand of the power of God."**

²²:⁷⁰They all said, "Are you then the Son of God?"

He said to them, **"You say it, because I am."**

²²:⁷¹They said, "Why do we need any more witness? For we ourselves have heard from his own mouth!"

²³:¹The whole company of them rose up and brought him before Pilate. ²³:²They began to accuse him, saying, "We found this man perverting the nation, forbidding paying taxes to Caesar, and saying that he himself is Christ, a king."

²³:³Pilate asked him, "Are you the King of the Jews?"

He answered him, **"So you say."**

²³:⁴Pilate said to the chief priests and the multitudes, "I find no basis for a charge against this man."

²³:⁵But they insisted, saying, "He stirs up the people, teaching throughout all Judea, beginning from Galilee even to this place." ²³:⁶But when Pilate heard Galilee mentioned, he asked if the man was a Galilean. ²³:⁷When he found out that he was in Herod's jurisdiction, he sent him to Herod, who was also in Jerusalem during those days.

²³:⁸Now when Herod saw Jesus, he was exceedingly glad, for he had wanted to see him for a long time, because he had heard many things about him. He hoped to see some miracle done by him. ²³:⁹He questioned him with many words, but he gave no answers. ²³:¹⁰The chief priests and the scribes stood, vehemently accusing him. ²³:¹¹Herod with his soldiers humiliated him and mocked him. Dressing him in luxurious clothing, they sent him back to Pilate. ²³:¹²Herod and Pilate became friends with each other that very day, for before that they were enemies with each other.

²³:¹³Pilate called together the chief priests and the rulers and the people, ²³:¹⁴and said to them, "You brought this man to

me as one that perverts the people, and see, I have examined him before you, and found no basis for a charge against this man concerning those things of which you accuse him. ²³:¹⁵Neither has Herod, for I sent you to him, and see, nothing worthy of death has been done by him. ²³:¹⁶I will therefore chastise him and release him."

²³:¹⁷Now he had to release one prisoner to them at the feast. ²³:¹⁸But they all cried out together, saying, "Away with this man! Release to us Barabbas!"—²³:¹⁹one who was thrown into prison for a certain revolt in the city, and for murder.

²³:²⁰Then Pilate spoke to them again, wanting to release Jesus, ²³:²¹but they shouted, saying, "Crucify! Crucify him!"

²³:²²He said to them the third time, "Why? What evil has this man done? I have found no capital crime in him. I will therefore chastise him and release him." ²³:²³But they were urgent with loud voices, asking that he might be crucified. Their voices and the voices of the chief priests prevailed. ²³:²⁴Pilate decreed that what they asked for should be done. ²³:²⁵He released him who had been thrown into prison for insurrection and murder, for whom they asked, but he delivered Jesus up to their will.

²³:²⁶When they led him away, they grabbed one Simon of Cyrene, coming from the country, and laid on him the cross, to carry it after Jesus. ²³:²⁷A great multitude of the people followed him, including women who also mourned and lamented him. ²³:²⁸But Jesus, turning to them, said, **"Daughters of Jerusalem, don't weep for me, but weep for yourselves and for your children.** ²³:²⁹**For behold, the days are coming in which they will say, 'Blessed are the barren, the wombs that never bore, and the breasts that never nursed.'** ²³:³⁰**Then they will begin to tell the mountains, 'Fall on us!' and tell the hills, 'Cover us.'ᶜ** ²³:³¹**For if they do these things in the green tree, what will be done in the dry?"**

²³:³²There were also others, two criminals, led with him to be put to death.

²³:³³When they came to the place that is called The Skull, they crucified him there with the criminals, one on the right and the other on the left.

²³:³⁴Jesus said, **"Father, forgive them, for they don't know what they are doing."**

Dividing his garments among them, they cast lots. ²³:³⁵The people stood watching. The rulers with them also scoffed at him, saying, "He saved others. Let him save himself, if this is the Christ of God, his chosen one!"

²³:³⁶The soldiers also mocked him, coming to him and offering him vinegar, ²³:³⁷and saying, "If you are the King of the Jews, save yourself!"

²³:³⁸An inscription was also written over him in letters of Greek, Latin, and Hebrew: "THIS IS THE KING OF THE JEWS."

²³:³⁹One of the criminals who was hanged insulted him, saying, "If you are the Christ, save yourself and us!"

²³:⁴⁰But the other answered, and rebuking him said, "Don't you even fear God, seeing you are under the same condemnation? ²³:⁴¹And we indeed justly, for we receive the due reward for our deeds, but this man has done nothing wrong." ²³:⁴²He said to Jesus, "Lord, remember me when you come into your Kingdom."

²³:⁴³Jesus said to him, **"Assuredly I tell you, today you will be with me in Paradise."**

²³:⁴⁴It was now about the sixth hourᵈ, and darkness came over the whole land until the ninth hour.ᵉ ²³:⁴⁵The sun was darkened, and the veil of the temple was torn in two. ²³:⁴⁶Jesus, crying with a loud voice, said, **"Father, into your hands I commit my spirit!"** Having said this, he breathed his last.

²³:⁴⁷When the centurion saw what was done, he glorified God, saying, "Certainly this was a righteous man." ²³:⁴⁸All the multitudes that came together to see this, when they saw the things that were done, returned home beating their breasts. ²³:⁴⁹All his acquaintances, and the women who

---

ᶜ23:30 Hosea 10:8
ᵈ23:44 Time was counted from sunrise, so the sixth hour was about noon.
ᵉ23:44 3:00 PM

followed with him from Galilee, stood at a distance, watching these things.

²³:⁵⁰Behold, a man named Joseph, who was a member of the council, a good and righteous man ²³:⁵¹(he had not consented to their counsel and deed), from Arimathaea, a city of the Jews, who was also waiting for the Kingdom of God: ²³:⁵²this man went to Pilate, and asked for Jesus' body. ²³:⁵³He took it down, and wrapped it in a linen cloth, and laid him in a tomb that was cut in stone, where no one had ever been laid. ²³:⁵⁴It was the day of the Preparation, and the Sabbath was drawing near. ²³:⁵⁵The women, who had come with him out of Galilee, followed after, and saw the tomb, and how his body was laid. ²³:⁵⁶They returned, and prepared spices and ointments. On the Sabbath they rested according to the commandment.

²⁴:¹But on the first day of the week, at early dawn, they and some others came to the tomb, bringing the spices which they had prepared. ²⁴:²They found the stone rolled away from the tomb. ²⁴:³They entered in, and didn't find the Lord Jesus' body. ²⁴:⁴It happened, while they were greatly perplexed about this, behold, two men stood by them in dazzling clothing. ²⁴:⁵Becoming terrified, they bowed their faces down to the earth.

They said to them, "Why do you seek the living among the dead? ²⁴:⁶He isn't here, but is risen. Remember what he told you when he was still in Galilee, ²⁴:⁷saying that the Son of Man must be delivered up into the hands of sinful men, and be crucified, and the third day rise again?"

²⁴:⁸They remembered his words, ²⁴:⁹returned from the tomb, and told all these things to the eleven, and to all the rest. ²⁴:¹⁰Now they were Mary Magdalene, Joanna, and Mary the mother of James. The other women with them told these things to the apostles. ²⁴:¹¹These words seemed to them to be nonsense, and they didn't believe them. ²⁴:¹²But Peter got up and ran to the tomb. Stooping and looking in, he saw the strips of linen lying by themselves, and he departed to his home, wondering what had happened.

²⁴:¹³Behold, two of them were going that very day to a village named Emmaus, which was sixty stadia^f from Jerusalem. ²⁴:¹⁴They talked with each other about all of these things which had happened. ²⁴:¹⁵It happened, while they talked and questioned together, that Jesus himself came near, and went with them. ²⁴:¹⁶But their eyes were kept from recognizing him. ²⁴:¹⁷He said to them, **"What are you talking about as you walk, and are sad?"**

²⁴:¹⁸One of them, named Cleopas, answered him, "Are you the only stranger in Jerusalem who doesn't know the things which have happened there in these days?"

²⁴:¹⁹He said to them, **"What things?"**

They said to him, "The things concerning Jesus, the Nazarene, who was a prophet mighty in deed and word before God and all the people; ²⁴:²⁰and how the chief priests and our rulers delivered him up to be condemned to death, and crucified him. ²⁴:²¹But we were hoping that it was he who would redeem Israel. Yes, and besides all this, it is now the third day since these things happened. ²⁴:²²Also, certain women of our company amazed us, having arrived early at the tomb; ²⁴:²³and when they didn't find his body, they came saying that they had also seen a vision of angels, who said that he was alive. ²⁴:²⁴Some of us went to the tomb, and found it just like the women had said, but they didn't see him."

²⁴:²⁵He said to them, **"Foolish men, and slow of heart to believe in all that the prophets have spoken!** ²⁴:²⁶**Didn't the Christ have to suffer these things and to enter into his glory?"** ²⁴:²⁷Beginning from Moses and from all the prophets, he explained to them in all the Scriptures the things concerning himself. ²⁴:²⁸They drew near to the village, where they were going, and he acted like he would go further.

²⁴:²⁹They urged him, saying, "Stay with us, for it is almost evening, and the day is almost over."

He went in to stay with them. ²⁴:³⁰It happened, that when he had sat down at the table with them, he took the bread and gave thanks. Breaking it, he gave

---

^f24:13 60 stadia = about 11 kilometers or about 7 miles.

to them. ²⁴:³¹Their eyes were opened, and they recognized him, and he vanished out of their sight. ²⁴:³²They said one to another, "Weren't our hearts burning within us, while he spoke to us along the way, and while he opened the Scriptures to us?" ²⁴:³³They rose up that very hour, returned to Jerusalem, and found the eleven gathered together, and those who were with them, ²⁴:³⁴saying, "The Lord is risen indeed, and has appeared to Simon!" ²⁴:³⁵They related the things that happened along the way, and how he was recognized by them in the breaking of the bread.

²⁴:³⁶As they said these things, Jesus himself stood among them, and said to them, **"Peace be to you."**

²⁴:³⁷But they were terrified and filled with fear, and supposed that they had seen a spirit.

²⁴:³⁸He said to them, **"Why are you troubled? Why do doubts arise in your hearts? ²⁴:³⁹See my hands and my feet, that it is truly me. Touch me and see, for a spirit doesn't have flesh and bones, as you see that I have."** ²⁴:⁴⁰When he had said this, he showed them his hands and his feet. ²⁴:⁴¹While they still didn't believe for joy, and wondered, he said to them, **"Do you have anything here to eat?"**

²⁴:⁴²They gave him a piece of a broiled fish and some honeycomb. ²⁴:⁴³He took them, and ate in front of them. ²⁴:⁴⁴He said to them, **"This is what I told you, while I was still with you, that all things which are written in the law of Moses, the prophets, and the psalms, concerning me must be fulfilled."**

²⁴:⁴⁵Then he opened their minds, that they might understand the Scriptures. ²⁴:⁴⁶He said to them, **"Thus it is written, and thus it was necessary for the Christ to suffer and to rise from the dead the third day, ²⁴:⁴⁷and that repentance and remission of sins should be preached in his name to all the nations, beginning at Jerusalem. ²⁴:⁴⁸You are witnesses of these things. ²⁴:⁴⁹Behold, I send forth the promise of my Father on you. But wait in the city of Jerusalem until you are clothed with power from on high."**

²⁴:⁵⁰He led them out as far as Bethany, and he lifted up his hands, and blessed them. ²⁴:⁵¹It happened, while he blessed them, that he withdrew from them, and was carried up into heaven. ²⁴:⁵²They worshiped him, and returned to Jerusalem with great joy, ²⁴:⁵³and were continually in the temple, praising and blessing God. Amen.

The Good News According to John

¹:¹In the beginning was the Word, and the Word was with God, and the Word was God. ¹:²The same was in the beginning with God. ¹:³All things were made through him. Without him was not anything made that has been made. ¹:⁴In him was life, and the life was the light of men. ¹:⁵The light shines in the darkness, and the darkness hasn't overcomeᵃ it. ¹:⁶There came a man, sent from God, whose name was John. ¹:⁷The same came as a witness, that he might testify about the light, that all might believe through him. ¹:⁸He was not the light, but was sent that he might testify about the light. ¹:⁹The true light that enlightens everyone was coming into the world.

¹:¹⁰He was in the world, and the world was made through him, and the world didn't recognize him. ¹:¹¹He came to his own, and those who were his own didn't receive him. ¹:¹²But as many as received him, to them he gave the right to become God's children, to those who believe in his name: ¹:¹³who were born not of blood, nor of the will of the flesh, nor of the will of man, but of God. ¹:¹⁴The Word became flesh, and lived among us. We saw his glory, such glory as of the one and only Son of the Father, full of grace and truth. ¹:¹⁵John testified about him. He cried out, saying, "This was he of whom I said, 'He who comes after me has surpassed

---

ᵃ1:5 The word translated "overcome" (katelaben) can also be translated "comprehended." It refers to getting a grip on an enemy to defeat him.

me, for he was before me.'" [1:16]From his fullness we all received grace upon grace. [1:17]For the law was given through Moses. Grace and truth came through Jesus Christ. [1:18]No one has seen God at any time. The one and only Son,[b] who is in the bosom of the Father, he has declared him.

[1:19]This is John's testimony, when the Jews sent priests and Levites from Jerusalem to ask him, "Who are you?"

[1:20]He confessed, and didn't deny, but he confessed, "I am not the Christ."

[1:21]They asked him, "What then? Are you Elijah?"

He said, "I am not."

"Are you the prophet?"

He answered, "No."

[1:22]They said therefore to him, "Who are you? Give us an answer to take back to those who sent us. What do you say about yourself?"

[1:23]He said, "I am the voice of one crying in the wilderness, 'Make straight the way of the Lord,'[c] as Isaiah the prophet said."

[1:24]The ones who had been sent were from the Pharisees. [1:25]They asked him, "Why then do you baptize, if you are not the Christ, nor Elijah, nor the prophet?"

[1:26]John answered them, "I baptize in water, but among you stands one whom you don't know. [1:27]He is the one who comes after me, who is preferred before me, whose sandal strap I'm not worthy to loosen." [1:28]These things were done in Bethany beyond the Jordan, where John was baptizing.

[1:29]The next day, he saw Jesus coming to him, and said, "Behold, the Lamb of God, who takes away the sin of the world! [1:30]This is he of whom I said, 'After me comes a man who is preferred before me, for he was before me.' [1:31]I didn't know him, but for this reason I came baptizing in water: that he would be revealed to Israel." [1:32]John testified, saying, "I have seen the Spirit descending like a dove out of heaven, and it remained on him. [1:33]I didn't recognize him, but he who sent me

to baptize in water, he said to me, 'On whomever you will see the Spirit descending, and remaining on him, the same is he who baptizes in the Holy Spirit.' [1:34]I have seen, and have testified that this is the Son of God."

[1:35]Again, the next day, John was standing with two of his disciples, [1:36]and he looked at Jesus as he walked, and said, "Behold, the Lamb of God!" [1:37]The two disciples heard him speak, and they followed Jesus. [1:38]Jesus turned, and saw them following, and said to them, **"What are you looking for?"**

They said to him, "Rabbi" (which is to say, being interpreted, Teacher), "where are you staying?"

[1:39]He said to them, **"Come, and see."**

They came and saw where he was staying, and they stayed with him that day. It was about the tenth hour.[d] [1:40]One of the two who heard John, and followed him, was Andrew, Simon Peter's brother. [1:41]He first found his own brother, Simon, and said to him, "We have found the Messiah!" (which is, being interpreted, Christ[e]). [1:42]He brought him to Jesus. Jesus looked at him, and said, **"You are Simon the son of Jonah. You shall be called Cephas"** (which is by interpretation, Peter). [1:43]On the next day, he was determined to go out into Galilee, and he found Philip. Jesus said to him, **"Follow me."** [1:44]Now Philip was from Bethsaida, of the city of Andrew and Peter. [1:45]Philip found Nathanael, and said to him, "We have found him, of whom Moses in the law, and the prophets, wrote: Jesus of Nazareth, the son of Joseph."

[1:46]Nathanael said to him, "Can any good thing come out of Nazareth?"

Philip said to him, "Come and see."

[1:47]Jesus saw Nathanael coming to him, and said about him, **"Behold, an Israelite indeed, in whom is no deceit!"**

[1:48]Nathanael said to him, "How do you know me?"

---

[b]1:18 NU reads "God"
[c]1:23 Isaiah 40:3
[d]1:39 4:00 PM.
[e]1:41 "Messiah" (Hebrew) and "Christ" (Greek) both mean "Anointed One".

Jesus answered him, **"Before Philip called you, when you were under the fig tree, I saw you."**

[1:49]Nathanael answered him, "Rabbi, you are the Son of God! You are King of Israel!"

[1:50]Jesus answered him, **"Because I told you, 'I saw you underneath the fig tree,' do you believe? You will see greater things than these!"** [1:51]He said to him, **"Most certainly, I tell you, hereafter you will see heaven opened, and the angels of God ascending and descending on the Son of Man."**

[2:1]The third day, there was a marriage in Cana of Galilee. Jesus' mother was there. [2:2]Jesus also was invited, with his disciples, to the marriage. [2:3]When the wine ran out, Jesus' mother said to him, "They have no wine."

[2:4]Jesus said to her, **"Woman, what does that have to do with you and me? My hour has not yet come."**

[2:5]His mother said to the servants, "Whatever he says to you, do it." [2:6]Now there were six water pots of stone set there after the Jews' manner of purifying, containing two or three metretes[f] apiece. [2:7]Jesus said to them, **"Fill the water pots with water."** They filled them up to the brim. [2:8]He said to them, **"Now draw some out, and take it to the ruler of the feast."** So they took it. [2:9]When the ruler of the feast tasted the water now become wine, and didn't know where it came from (but the servants who had drawn the water knew), the ruler of the feast called the bridegroom, [2:10]and said to him, "Everyone serves the good wine first, and when the guests have drunk freely, then that which is worse. You have kept the good wine until now!" [2:11]This beginning of his signs Jesus did in Cana of Galilee, and revealed his glory; and his disciples believed in him.

[2:12]After this, he went down to Capernaum, he, and his mother, his brothers, and his disciples; and they stayed there a few days. [2:13]The Passover of the Jews was at hand, and Jesus went up to Jerusalem. [2:14]He found in the temple those who sold oxen, sheep, and doves, and the changers of money sitting. [2:15]He made a whip of cords, and threw all out of the temple, both the sheep and the oxen; and he poured out the changers' money, and overthrew their tables. [2:16]To those who sold the doves, he said, **"Take these things out of here! Don't make my Father's house a marketplace!"** [2:17]His disciples remembered that it was written, "Zeal for your house will eat me up."[g]

[2:18]The Jews therefore answered him, "What sign do you show us, seeing that you do these things?"

[2:19]Jesus answered them, **"Destroy this temple, and in three days I will raise it up."**

[2:20]The Jews therefore said, "Forty-six years was this temple in building, and will you raise it up in three days?" [2:21]But he spoke of the temple of his body. [2:22]When therefore he was raised from the dead, his disciples remembered that he said this, and they believed the Scripture, and the word which Jesus had said.

[2:23]Now when he was in Jerusalem at the Passover, during the feast, many believed in his name, observing his signs which he did. [2:24]But Jesus didn't trust himself to them, because he knew everyone, [2:25]and because he didn't need for anyone to testify concerning man; for he himself knew what was in man.

[3:1]Now there was a man of the Pharisees named Nicodemus, a ruler of the Jews. [3:2]The same came to him by night, and said to him, "Rabbi, we know that you are a teacher come from God, for no one can do these signs that you do, unless God is with him."

[3:3]Jesus answered him, **"Most certainly, I tell you, unless one is born anew,[h] he can't see the Kingdom of God."**

[3:4]Nicodemus said to him, "How can a man be born when he is old? Can he enter

---

[f]2:6 2 to 3 metretes is about 20 to 30 U. S. Gallons, 16 to 25 imperial gallons, or 75 to 115 litres.
[g]2:17 Psalm 69:9
[h]3:3 The word translated "anew" here and in John 3:7 (anothen) also means "again" and "from above".

a second time into his mother's womb, and be born?"

3:5 Jesus answered, **"Most certainly I tell you, unless one is born of water and spirit, he can't enter into the Kingdom of God!** 3:6 **That which is born of the flesh is flesh. That which is born of the Spirit is spirit.** 3:7 **Don't marvel that I said to you, 'You must be born anew.'** 3:8 **The wind**[i] **blows where it wants to, and you hear its sound, but don't know where it comes from and where it is going. So is everyone who is born of the Spirit."**

3:9 Nicodemus answered him, "How can these things be?"

3:10 Jesus answered him, **"Are you the teacher of Israel, and don't understand these things?** 3:11 **Most certainly I tell you, we speak that which we know, and testify of that which we have seen, and you don't receive our witness.** 3:12 **If I told you earthly things and you don't believe, how will you believe if I tell you heavenly things?** 3:13 **No one has ascended into heaven, but he who descended out of heaven, the Son of Man, who is in heaven.** 3:14 **As Moses lifted up the serpent in the wilderness, even so must the Son of Man be lifted up,** 3:15 **that whoever believes in him should not perish, but have eternal life.** 3:16 **For God so loved the world, that he gave his one and only Son, that whoever believes in him should not perish, but have eternal life.** 3:17 **For God didn't send his Son into the world to judge the world, but that the world should be saved through him.** 3:18 **He who believes in him is not judged. He who doesn't believe has been judged already, because he has not believed in the name of the one and only Son of God.** 3:19 **This is the judgment, that the light has come into the world, and men loved the darkness rather than the light; for their works were evil.** 3:20 **For everyone who does evil hates the light, and doesn't come to the light, lest his works would be exposed.** 3:21 **But he who does the truth comes to the light, that his works may be revealed, that they have been done in God."**

3:22 After these things, Jesus came with his disciples into the land of Judea. He stayed there with them, and baptized. 3:23 John also was baptizing in Enon near Salim, because there was much water there. They came, and were baptized. 3:24 For John was not yet thrown into prison. 3:25 There arose therefore a questioning on the part of John's disciples with some Jews about purification. 3:26 They came to John, and said to him, "Rabbi, he who was with you beyond the Jordan, to whom you have testified, behold, the same baptizes, and everyone is coming to him."

3:27 John answered, "A man can receive nothing, unless it has been given him from heaven. 3:28 You yourselves testify that I said, 'I am not the Christ,' but, 'I have been sent before him.' 3:29 He who has the bride is the bridegroom; but the friend of the bridegroom, who stands and hears him, rejoices greatly because of the bridegroom's voice. This, my joy, therefore is made full. 3:30 He must increase, but I must decrease. 3:31 He who comes from above is above all. He who is from the Earth belongs to the Earth, and speaks of the Earth. He who comes from heaven is above all. 3:32 What he has seen and heard, of that he testifies; and no one receives his witness. 3:33 He who has received his witness has set his seal to this, that God is true. 3:34 For he whom God has sent speaks the words of God; for God gives the Spirit without measure. 3:35 The Father loves the Son, and has given all things into his hand. 3:36 One who believes in the Son has eternal life, but one who disobeys[j] the Son won't see life, but the wrath of God remains on him."

4:1 Therefore when the Lord knew that the Pharisees had heard that Jesus was making and baptizing more disciples than John 4:2 (although Jesus himself didn't baptize, but his disciples), 4:3 he left Judea, and departed into Galilee. 4:4 He needed to pass through Samaria. 4:5 So he came to a city of Samaria, called Sychar, near the parcel of ground that Jacob gave to his son, Joseph. 4:6 Jacob's well was there. Jesus therefore,

---

i 3:8 The same Greek word (pneuma) means wind, breath, and spirit.
j 3:36 The same word can be translated "disobeys" or "disbelieves" in this context.

being tired from his journey, sat down by the well. It was about the sixth hour[k]. ⁴:⁷A woman of Samaria came to draw water. Jesus said to her, **"Give me a drink."** ⁴:⁸For his disciples had gone away into the city to buy food.

⁴:⁹The Samaritan woman therefore said to him, "How is it that you, being a Jew, ask for a drink from me, a Samaritan woman?" (For Jews have no dealings with Samaritans.)

⁴:¹⁰Jesus answered her, **"If you knew the gift of God, and who it is who says to you, 'Give me a drink,' you would have asked him, and he would have given you living water."**

⁴:¹¹The woman said to him, "Sir, you have nothing to draw with, and the well is deep. From where then have you that living water? ⁴:¹²Are you greater than our father, Jacob, who gave us the well, and drank of it himself, as did his children, and his livestock?"

⁴:¹³Jesus answered her, **"Everyone who drinks of this water will thirst again, ⁴:¹⁴but whoever drinks of the water that I will give him will never thirst again; but the water that I will give him will become in him a well of water springing up to eternal life."**

⁴:¹⁵The woman said to him, "Sir, give me this water, so that I don't get thirsty, neither come all the way here to draw."

⁴:¹⁶Jesus said to her, **"Go, call your husband, and come here."**

⁴:¹⁷The woman answered, "I have no husband."

Jesus said to her, **"You said well, 'I have no husband,' ⁴:¹⁸for you have had five husbands; and he whom you now have is not your husband. This you have said truly."**

⁴:¹⁹The woman said to him, "Sir, I perceive that you are a prophet. ⁴:²⁰Our fathers worshiped in this mountain, and you Jews say that in Jerusalem is the place where people ought to worship."

⁴:²¹Jesus said to her, **"Woman, believe me, the hour comes, when neither in this mountain, nor in Jerusalem, will you worship the Father. ⁴:²²You worship that** which you don't know. We worship that which we know; for salvation is from the Jews. ⁴:²³But the hour comes, and now is, when the true worshippers will worship the Father in spirit and truth, for the Father seeks such to be his worshippers. ⁴:²⁴God is spirit, and those who worship him must worship in spirit and truth."**

⁴:²⁵The woman said to him, "I know that Messiah comes," (he who is called Christ). "When he has come, he will declare to us all things."

⁴:²⁶Jesus said to her, **"I am he, the one who speaks to you."** ⁴:²⁷At this, his disciples came. They marveled that he was speaking with a woman; yet no one said, "What are you looking for?" or, "Why do you speak with her?" ⁴:²⁸So the woman left her water pot, and went away into the city, and said to the people, ⁴:²⁹"Come, see a man who told me everything that I did. Can this be the Christ?"

⁴:³⁰They went out of the city, and were coming to him. ⁴:³¹In the meanwhile, the disciples urged him, saying, "Rabbi, eat."

⁴:³²But he said to them, **"I have food to eat that you don't know about."**

⁴:³³The disciples therefore said one to another, "Has anyone brought him something to eat?"

⁴:³⁴Jesus said to them, **"My food is to do the will of him who sent me, and to accomplish his work. ⁴:³⁵Don't you say, 'There are yet four months until the harvest?' Behold, I tell you, lift up your eyes, and look at the fields, that they are white for harvest already. ⁴:³⁶He who reaps receives wages, and gathers fruit to eternal life; that both he who sows and he who reaps may rejoice together. ⁴:³⁷For in this the saying is true, 'One sows, and another reaps.' ⁴:³⁸I sent you to reap that for which you haven't labored. Others have labored, and you have entered into their labor."**

⁴:³⁹From that city many of the Samaritans believed in him because of the word of the woman, who testified, "He told me everything that I did." ⁴:⁴⁰So when the

---

[k]4:6 noon

Samaritans came to him, they begged him to stay with them. He stayed there two days. [4:41]Many more believed because of his word. [4:42]They said to the woman, "Now we believe, not because of your speaking; for we have heard for ourselves, and know that this is indeed the Christ, the Savior of the world."

[4:43]After the two days he went out from there and went into Galilee. [4:44]For Jesus himself testified that a prophet has no honor in his own country. [4:45]So when he came into Galilee, the Galileans received him, having seen all the things that he did in Jerusalem at the feast, for they also went to the feast. [4:46]Jesus came therefore again to Cana of Galilee, where he made the water into wine. There was a certain nobleman whose son was sick at Capernaum. [4:47]When he heard that Jesus had come out of Judea into Galilee, he went to him, and begged him that he would come down and heal his son, for he was at the point of death. [4:48]Jesus therefore said to him, **"Unless you see signs and wonders, you will in no way believe."**

[4:49]The nobleman said to him, "Sir, come down before my child dies." [4:50]Jesus said to him, **"Go your way. Your son lives."** The man believed the word that Jesus spoke to him, and he went his way. [4:51]As he was now going down, his servants met him and reported, saying "Your child lives!" [4:52]So he inquired of them the hour when he began to get better. They said therefore to him, "Yesterday at the seventh hour,[1] the fever left him." [4:53]So the father knew that it was at that hour in which Jesus said to him, **"Your son lives."** He believed, as did his whole house. [4:54]This is again the second sign that Jesus did, having come out of Judea into Galilee.

[5:1]After these things, there was a feast of the Jews, and Jesus went up to Jerusalem. [5:2]Now in Jerusalem by the sheep gate, there is a pool, which is called in Hebrew, "Bethesda," having five porches. [5:3]In these lay a great multitude of those who were sick, blind, lame, or paralyzed, waiting for the moving of the water; [5:4]for an angel of the Lord went down at certain times into the pool, and stirred up the water. Whoever stepped in first after the stirring of the water was made whole of whatever disease he had. [5:5]A certain man was there, who had been sick for thirty-eight years. [5:6]When Jesus saw him lying there, and knew that he had been sick for a long time, he asked him, **"Do you want to be made well?"**

[5:7]The sick man answered him, "Sir, I have no one to put me into the pool when the water is stirred up, but while I'm coming, another steps down before me."

[5:8]Jesus said to him, **"Arise, take up your mat, and walk."**

[5:9]Immediately, the man was made well, and took up his mat and walked.

Now it was the Sabbath on that day. [5:10]So the Jews said to him who was cured, "It is the Sabbath. It is not lawful for you to carry the mat."

[5:11]He answered them, "He who made me well, the same said to me, 'Take up your mat, and walk.'"

[5:12]Then they asked him, "Who is the man who said to you, 'Take up your mat, and walk'?"

[5:13]But he who was healed didn't know who it was, for Jesus had withdrawn, a crowd being in the place.

[5:14]Afterward Jesus found him in the temple, and said to him, **"Behold, you are made well. Sin no more, so that nothing worse happens to you."**

[5:15]The man went away, and told the Jews that it was Jesus who had made him well. [5:16]For this cause the Jews persecuted Jesus, and sought to kill him, because he did these things on the Sabbath. [5:17]But Jesus answered them, **"My Father is still working, so I am working, too."** [5:18]For this cause therefore the Jews sought all the more to kill him, because he not only broke the Sabbath, but also called God his own Father, making himself equal with God. [5:19]Jesus therefore answered them, **"Most certainly, I tell you, the Son can do nothing of himself, but what he sees the Father doing. For whatever things he does, these the Son also does likewise.**

---
[1]4:52 1:00 P. M.

⁵:²⁰For the Father has affection for the Son, and shows him all things that he himself does. He will show him greater works than these, that you may marvel. ⁵:²¹For as the Father raises the dead and gives them life, even so the Son also gives life to whom he desires. ⁵:²²For the Father judges no one, but he has given all judgment to the Son, ⁵:²³that all may honor the Son, even as they honor the Father. He who doesn't honor the Son doesn't honor the Father who sent him.

⁵:²⁴"Most certainly I tell you, he who hears my word, and believes him who sent me, has eternal life, and doesn't come into judgment, but has passed out of death into life. ⁵:²⁵Most certainly, I tell you, the hour comes, and now is, when the dead will hear the Son of God's voice; and those who hear will live. ⁵:²⁶For as the Father has life in himself, even so he gave to the Son also to have life in himself. ⁵:²⁷He also gave him authority to execute judgment, because he is a son of man. ⁵:²⁸Don't marvel at this, for the hour comes, in which all that are in the tombs will hear his voice, ⁵:²⁹and will come out; those who have done good, to the resurrection of life; and those who have done evil, to the resurrection of judgment. ⁵:³⁰I can of myself do nothing. As I hear, I judge, and my judgment is righteous; because I don't seek my own will, but the will of my Father who sent me.

⁵:³¹"If I testify about myself, my witness is not valid. ⁵:³²It is another who testifies about me. I know that the testimony which he testifies about me is true. ⁵:³³You have sent to John, and he has testified to the truth. ⁵:³⁴But the testimony which I receive is not from man. However, I say these things that you may be saved. ⁵:³⁵He was the burning and shining lamp, and you were willing to rejoice for a while in his light. ⁵:³⁶But the testimony which I have is greater than that of John, for the works which the Father gave me to accomplish, the very works that I do, testify about me, that the Father has sent me. ⁵:³⁷The Father himself, who sent me, has testified about me. You have neither heard his voice at any time, nor seen his form. ⁵:³⁸You don't have his word living in you; because you don't believe him whom he sent.

⁵:³⁹"You search the Scriptures, because you think that in them you have eternal life; and these are they which testify about me. ⁵:⁴⁰Yet you will not come to me, that you may have life. ⁵:⁴¹I don't receive glory from men. ⁵:⁴²But I know you, that you don't have God's love in yourselves. ⁵:⁴³I have come in my Father's name, and you don't receive me. If another comes in his own name, you will receive him. ⁵:⁴⁴How can you believe, who receive glory from one another, and you don't seek the glory that comes from the only God?

⁵:⁴⁵"Don't think that I will accuse you to the Father. There is one who accuses you, even Moses, on whom you have set your hope. ⁵:⁴⁶For if you believed Moses, you would believe me; for he wrote about me. ⁵:⁴⁷But if you don't believe his writings, how will you believe my words?"

⁶:¹After these things, Jesus went away to the other side of the sea of Galilee, which is also called the Sea of Tiberias. ⁶:²A great multitude followed him, because they saw his signs which he did on those who were sick. ⁶:³Jesus went up into the mountain, and he sat there with his disciples. ⁶:⁴Now the Passover, the feast of the Jews, was at hand. ⁶:⁵Jesus therefore lifting up his eyes, and seeing that a great multitude was coming to him, said to Philip, **"Where are we to buy bread, that these may eat?"** ⁶:⁶This he said to test him, for he himself knew what he would do.

⁶:⁷Philip answered him, "Two hundred denarii worth of bread is not sufficient for them, that everyone of them may receive a little."

⁶:⁸One of his disciples, Andrew, Simon Peter's brother, said to him, ⁶:⁹"There is a boy here who has five barley loaves and two fish, but what are these among so many?"

⁶:¹⁰Jesus said, **"Have the people sit down."** Now there was much grass in that place. So the men sat down, in number about five thousand. ⁶:¹¹Jesus took the loaves; and having given thanks, he distributed to the disciples, and the disciples

to those who were sitting down; likewise also of the fish as much as they desired. [6:12]When they were filled, he said to his disciples, **"Gather up the broken pieces which are left over, that nothing be lost."** [6:13]So they gathered them up, and filled twelve baskets with broken pieces from the five barley loaves, which were left over by those who had eaten. [6:14]When therefore the people saw the sign which Jesus did, they said, "This is truly the prophet who comes into the world." [6:15]Jesus therefore, perceiving that they were about to come and take him by force, to make him king, withdrew again to the mountain by himself.

[6:16]When evening came, his disciples went down to the sea, [6:17]and they entered into the boat, and were going over the sea to Capernaum. It was now dark, and Jesus had not come to them. [6:18]The sea was tossed by a great wind blowing. [6:19]When therefore they had rowed about twenty-five or thirty stadia,[m] they saw Jesus walking on the sea,[n] and drawing near to the boat; and they were afraid. [6:20]But he said to them, **"It is I[o]. Don't be afraid."** [6:21]They were willing therefore to receive him into the boat. Immediately the boat was at the land where they were going.

[6:22]On the next day, the multitude that stood on the other side of the sea saw that there was no other boat there, except the one in which his disciples had embarked, and that Jesus hadn't entered with his disciples into the boat, but his disciples had gone away alone. [6:23]However boats from Tiberias came near to the place where they ate the bread after the Lord had given thanks. [6:24]When the multitude therefore saw that Jesus wasn't there, nor his disciples, they themselves got into the boats, and came to Capernaum, seeking Jesus. [6:25]When they found him on the other side of the sea, they asked him, "Rabbi, when did you come here?"

[6:26]Jesus answered them, **"Most certainly I tell you, you seek me, not because you saw signs, but because you ate of the loaves, and were filled.** [6:27]**Don't work for the food which perishes, but for the food which remains to eternal life, which the Son of Man will give to you. For God the Father has sealed him."**

[6:28]They said therefore to him, "What must we do, that we may work the works of God?"

[6:29]Jesus answered them, **"This is the work of God, that you believe in him whom he has sent."**

[6:30]They said therefore to him, "What then do you do for a sign, that we may see, and believe you? What work do you do? [6:31]Our fathers ate the manna in the wilderness. As it is written, 'He gave them bread out of heaven[p] to eat.'"[q]

[6:32]Jesus therefore said to them, **"Most certainly, I tell you, it wasn't Moses who gave you the bread out of heaven, but my Father gives you the true bread out of heaven.** [6:33]**For the bread of God is that which comes down out of heaven, and gives life to the world."**

[6:34]They said therefore to him, "Lord, always give us this bread."

[6:35]Jesus said to them, **"I am the bread of life. He who comes to me will not be hungry, and he who believes in me will never be thirsty.** [6:36]**But I told you that you have seen me, and yet you don't believe.** [6:37]**All those who the Father gives me will come to me. Him who comes to me I will in no way throw out.** [6:38]**For I have come down from heaven, not to do my own will, but the will of him who sent me.** [6:39]**This is the will of my Father who sent me, that of all he has given to me I should lose nothing, but should raise him up at the last day.** [6:40]**This is the will of the one who sent me, that everyone who sees the Son, and believes in him, should have eternal life; and I will raise him up at the last day."**

[6:41]The Jews therefore murmured concerning him, because he said, **"I am the bread which came down out of heaven."**

---

[m]6:19 25 to 30 stadia is about 5 to 6 kilometers or about 3 to 4 miles
[n]6:19 see Job 9:8
[o]6:20 or, I AM
[p]6:31 Greek and Hebrew use the same word for "heaven", "the heavens", "the sky", and "the air".
[q]6:31 Exodus 16:4; Nehemiah 9:15; Psalm 78:24-25

6:42They said, "Isn't this Jesus, the son of Joseph, whose father and mother we know? How then does he say, 'I have come down out of heaven?'"

6:43Therefore Jesus answered them, "Don't murmur among yourselves. 6:44No one can come to me unless the Father who sent me draws him, and I will raise him up in the last day. 6:45It is written in the prophets, 'They will all be taught by God.'ʳ Therefore everyone who hears from the Father, and has learned, comes to me. 6:46Not that anyone has seen the Father, except he who is from God. He has seen the Father. 6:47Most certainly, I tell you, he who believes in me has eternal life. 6:48I am the bread of life. 6:49Your fathers ate the manna in the wilderness, and they died. 6:50This is the bread which comes down out of heaven, that anyone may eat of it and not die. 6:51I am the living bread which came down out of heaven. If anyone eats of this bread, he will live forever. Yes, the bread which I will give for the life of the world is my flesh."

6:52The Jews therefore contended with one another, saying, "How can this man give us his flesh to eat?"

6:53Jesus therefore said to them, "Most certainly I tell you, unless you eat the flesh of the Son of Man and drink his blood, you don't have life in yourselves. 6:54He who eats my flesh and drinks my blood has eternal life, and I will raise him up at the last day. 6:55For my flesh is food indeed, and my blood is drink indeed. 6:56He who eats my flesh and drinks my blood lives in me, and I in him. 6:57As the living Father sent me, and I live because of the Father; so he who feeds on me, he will also live because of me. 6:58This is the bread which came down out of heaven—not as our fathers ate the manna, and died. He who eats this bread will live forever."

6:59He said these things in the synagogue, as he taught in Capernaum.

6:60Therefore many of his disciples, when they heard this, said, "This is a hard saying! Who can listen to it?"

6:61But Jesus knowing in himself that his disciples murmured at this, said to them, "Does this cause you to stumble? 6:62Then what if you would see the Son of Man ascending to where he was before? 6:63It is the spirit who gives life. The flesh profits nothing. The words that I speak to you are spirit, and are life. 6:64But there are some of you who don't believe." For Jesus knew from the beginning who they were who didn't believe, and who it was who would betray him. 6:65He said, "For this cause have I said to you that no one can come to me, unless it is given to him by my Father."

6:66At this, many of his disciples went back, and walked no more with him. 6:67Jesus said therefore to the twelve, "You don't also want to go away, do you?"

6:68Simon Peter answered him, "Lord, to whom would we go? You have the words of eternal life. 6:69We have come to believe and know that you are the Christ, the Son of the living God."

6:70Jesus answered them, "Didn't I choose you, the twelve, and one of you is a devil?" 6:71Now he spoke of Judas, the son of Simon Iscariot, for it was he who would betray him, being one of the twelve.

7:1After these things, Jesus was walking in Galilee, for he wouldn't walk in Judea, because the Jews sought to kill him. 7:2Now the feast of the Jews, the Feast of Booths, was at hand. 7:3His brothers therefore said to him, "Depart from here, and go into Judea, that your disciples also may see your works which you do. 7:4For no one does anything in secret, and himself seeks to be known openly. If you do these things, reveal yourself to the world." 7:5For even his brothers didn't believe in him.

7:6Jesus therefore said to them, "My time has not yet come, but your time is always ready. 7:7The world can't hate you, but it hates me, because I testify about it, that its works are evil. 7:8You go up to the feast. I am not yet going up to this feast, because my time is not yet fulfilled."

7:9Having said these things to them, he stayed in Galilee. 7:10But when his brothers had gone up to the feast, then he also went

ʳ6:45 Isaiah 54:13

up, not publicly, but as it were in secret. [7:11] The Jews therefore sought him at the feast, and said, "Where is he?" [7:12] There was much murmuring among the multitudes concerning him. Some said, "He is a good man." Others said, "Not so, but he leads the multitude astray." [7:13] Yet no one spoke openly of him for fear of the Jews. [7:14] But when it was now the midst of the feast, Jesus went up into the temple and taught. [7:15] The Jews therefore marveled, saying, "How does this man know letters, having never been educated?"

[7:16] Jesus therefore answered them, **"My teaching is not mine, but his who sent me. [7:17] If anyone desires to do his will, he will know about the teaching, whether it is from God, or if I am speaking from myself. [7:18] He who speaks from himself seeks his own glory, but he who seeks the glory of him who sent him is true, and no unrighteousness is in him. [7:19] Didn't Moses give you the law, and yet none of you keeps the law? Why do you seek to kill me?"**

[7:20] The multitude answered, "You have a demon! Who seeks to kill you?"

[7:21] Jesus answered them, **"I did one work, and you all marvel because of it. [7:22] Moses has given you circumcision (not that it is of Moses, but of the fathers), and on the Sabbath you circumcise a boy. [7:23] If a boy receives circumcision on the Sabbath, that the law of Moses may not be broken, are you angry with me, because I made a man completely healthy on the Sabbath? [7:24] Don't judge according to appearance, but judge righteous judgment."**

[7:25] Therefore some of them of Jerusalem said, "Isn't this he whom they seek to kill? [7:26] Behold, he speaks openly, and they say nothing to him. Can it be that the rulers indeed know that this is truly the Christ? [7:27] However we know where this man comes from, but when the Christ comes, no one will know where he comes from."

[7:28] Jesus therefore cried out in the temple, teaching and saying, **"You both know me, and know where I am from. I have not come of myself, but he who sent me is true, whom you don't know. [7:29] I know him, because I am from him, and he sent me."**

[7:30] They sought therefore to take him; but no one laid a hand on him, because his hour had not yet come. [7:31] But of the multitude, many believed in him. They said, "When the Christ comes, he won't do more signs than those which this man has done, will he?" [7:32] The Pharisees heard the multitude murmuring these things concerning him, and the chief priests and the Pharisees sent officers to arrest him.

[7:33] Then Jesus said, **"I will be with you a little while longer, then I go to him who sent me. [7:34] You will seek me, and won't find me; and where I am, you can't come."**

[7:35] The Jews therefore said among themselves, "Where will this man go that we won't find him? Will he go to the Dispersion among the Greeks, and teach the Greeks? [7:36] What is this word that he said, 'You will seek me, and won't find me; and where I am, you can't come'?"

[7:37] Now on the last and greatest day of the feast, Jesus stood and cried out, **"If anyone is thirsty, let him come to me and drink! [7:38] He who believes in me, as the Scripture has said, from within him will flow rivers of living water."** [7:39] But he said this about the Spirit, which those believing in him were to receive. For the Holy Spirit was not yet given, because Jesus wasn't yet glorified.

[7:40] Many of the multitude therefore, when they heard these words, said, "This is truly the prophet." [7:41] Others said, "This is the Christ." But some said, "What, does the Christ come out of Galilee? [7:42] Hasn't the Scripture said that the Christ comes of the seed of David,[s] and from Bethlehem,[t] the village where David was?" [7:43] So there arose a division in the multitude because of him. [7:44] Some of them would have arrested him, but no one laid hands on him. [7:45] The officers therefore came to the chief priests and Pharisees, and they said to them, "Why didn't you bring him?"

[s]7:42 2 Samuel 7:12
[t]7:42 Micah 5:2

[7:46]The officers answered, "No man ever spoke like this man!"

[7:47]The Pharisees therefore answered them, "You aren't also led astray, are you? [7:48]Have any of the rulers believed in him, or of the Pharisees? [7:49]But this multitude that doesn't know the law is accursed."

[7:50]Nicodemus (he who came to him by night, being one of them) said to them, [7:51]"Does our law judge a man, unless it first hears from him personally and knows what he does?"

[7:52]They answered him, "Are you also from Galilee? Search, and see that no prophet has arisen out of Galilee.[u]"

[7:53]Everyone went to his own house, [8:1]but Jesus went to the Mount of Olives. [8:2]Now very early in the morning, he came again into the temple, and all the people came to him. He sat down, and taught them. [8:3]The scribes and the Pharisees brought a woman taken in adultery. Having set her in the midst, [8:4]they told him, "Teacher, we found this woman in adultery, in the very act. [8:5]Now in our law, Moses commanded us to stone such.[v] What then do you say about her?" [8:6]They said this testing him, that they might have something to accuse him of.

But Jesus stooped down, and wrote on the ground with his finger. [8:7]But when they continued asking him, he looked up and said to them, **"He who is without sin among you, let him throw the first stone at her."** [8:8]Again he stooped down, and with his finger wrote on the ground.

[8:9]They, when they heard it, being convicted by their conscience, went out one by one, beginning from the oldest, even to the last. Jesus was left alone with the woman where she was, in the middle. [8:10]Jesus, standing up, saw her and said, **"Woman, where are your accusers? Did no one condemn you?"**

[8:11]She said, "No one, Lord."

Jesus said, **"Neither do I condemn you. Go your way. From now on, sin no more."**

[8:12]Again, therefore, Jesus spoke to them, saying, **"I am the light of the world.[w] He who follows me will not walk in the darkness, but will have the light of life."**

[8:13]The Pharisees therefore said to him, "You testify about yourself. Your testimony is not valid."

[8:14]Jesus answered them, **"Even if I testify about myself, my testimony is true, for I know where I came from, and where I am going; but you don't know where I came from, or where I am going. [8:15]You judge according to the flesh. I judge no one. [8:16]Even if I do judge, my judgment is true, for I am not alone, but I am with the Father who sent me. [8:17]It's also written in your law that the testimony of two people is valid.[x] [8:18]I am one who testifies about myself, and the Father who sent me testifies about me."**

[8:19]They said therefore to him, "Where is your Father?"

Jesus answered, **"You know neither me, nor my Father. If you knew me, you would know my Father also."** [8:20]Jesus spoke these words in the treasury, as he taught in the temple. Yet no one arrested him, because his hour had not yet come. [8:21]Jesus said therefore again to them, **"I am going away, and you will seek me, and you will die in your sins. Where I go, you can't come."**

[8:22]The Jews therefore said, "Will he kill himself, that he says, 'Where I am going, you can't come?'"

[8:23]He said to them, **"You are from beneath. I am from above. You are of this world. I am not of this world. [8:24]I said therefore to you that you will die in your sins; for unless you believe that I am[y] he, you will die in your sins."**

[8:25]They said therefore to him, "Who are you?"

Jesus said to them, **"Just what I have been saying to you from the beginning. [8:26]I have many things to speak and to judge concerning you. However he who**

---

[u]7:52 See Isaiah 9:1 and Matthew 4:13-16.

[v]8:5 Leviticus 20:10; Deuteronomy 22:22

[w]8:12 Isaiah 60:1

[x]8:17 Deuteronomy 17:6; 19:15

[y]8:24 or, I AM

sent me is true; and the things which I heard from him, these I say to the world."

8:27 They didn't understand that he spoke to them about the Father. 8:28 Jesus therefore said to them, **"When you have lifted up the Son of Man, then you will know that I am he, and I do nothing of myself, but as my Father taught me, I say these things.** 8:29 **He who sent me is with me. The Father hasn't left me alone, for I always do the things that are pleasing to him."**

8:30 As he spoke these things, many believed in him. 8:31 Jesus therefore said to those Jews who had believed him, **"If you remain in my word, then you are truly my disciples.** 8:32 **You will know the truth, and the truth will make you free."**ᶻ

8:33 They answered him, "We are Abraham's seed, and have never been in bondage to anyone. How do you say, 'You will be made free?'"

8:34 Jesus answered them, **"Most certainly I tell you, everyone who commits sin is the bondservant of sin.** 8:35 **A bondservant doesn't live in the house forever. A son remains forever.** 8:36 **If therefore the Son makes you free, you will be free indeed.** 8:37 **I know that you are Abraham's seed, yet you seek to kill me, because my word finds no place in you.** 8:38 **I say the things which I have seen with my Father; and you also do the things which you have seen with your father."**

8:39 They answered him, "Our father is Abraham."

Jesus said to them, **"If you were Abraham's children, you would do the works of Abraham.** 8:40 **But now you seek to kill me, a man who has told you the truth, which I heard from God. Abraham didn't do this.** 8:41 **You do the works of your father."**

They said to him, "We were not born of sexual immorality. We have one Father, God."

8:42 Therefore Jesus said to them, **"If God were your father, you would love me, for I came out and have come from God. For I haven't come of myself, but he sent me.** 8:43 **Why don't you understand my speech?**

Because you can't hear my word. 8:44 **You are of your father, the devil, and you want to do the desires of your father. He was a murderer from the beginning, and doesn't stand in the truth, because there is no truth in him. When he speaks a lie, he speaks on his own; for he is a liar, and its father.** 8:45 **But because I tell the truth, you don't believe me.** 8:46 **Which of you convicts me of sin? If I tell the truth, why do you not believe me?** 8:47 **He who is of God hears the words of God. For this cause you don't hear, because you are not of God."**

8:48 Then the Jews answered him, "Don't we say well that you are a Samaritan, and have a demon?"

8:49 Jesus answered, **"I don't have a demon, but I honor my Father, and you dishonor me.** 8:50 **But I don't seek my own glory. There is one who seeks and judges.** 8:51 **Most certainly, I tell you, if a person keeps my word, he will never see death."**

8:52 Then the Jews said to him, "Now we know that you have a demon. Abraham died, and the prophets; and you say, 'If a man keeps my word, he will never taste of death.' 8:53 Are you greater than our father, Abraham, who died? The prophets died. Who do you make yourself out to be?"

8:54 Jesus answered, **"If I glorify myself, my glory is nothing. It is my Father who glorifies me, of whom you say that he is our God.** 8:55 **You have not known him, but I know him. If I said, 'I don't know him,' I would be like you, a liar. But I know him, and keep his word.** 8:56 **Your father Abraham rejoiced to see my day. He saw it, and was glad."**

8:57 The Jews therefore said to him, "You are not yet fifty years old, and have you seen Abraham?"

8:58 Jesus said to them, **"Most certainly, I tell you, before Abraham came into existence, I AM."**ᵃ

8:59 Therefore they took up stones to throw at him, but Jesus was hidden, and went out of the temple, having gone through the midst of them, and so passed by.

ᶻ8:32 Psalm 119:45
ᵃ8:58 or, I am

[9:1]As he passed by, he saw a man blind from birth. [9:2]His disciples asked him, "Rabbi, who sinned, this man or his parents, that he was born blind?"

[9:3]Jesus answered, **"Neither did this man sin, nor his parents; but, that the works of God might be revealed in him. [9:4]I must work the works of him who sent me, while it is day. The night is coming, when no one can work. [9:5]While I am in the world, I am the light of the world."** [9:6]When he had said this, he spat on the ground, made mud with the saliva, anointed the blind man's eyes with the mud, [9:7]and said to him, **"Go, wash in the pool of Siloam"** (which means "Sent"). So he went away, washed, and came back seeing. [9:8]The neighbors therefore, and those who saw that he was blind before, said, "Isn't this he who sat and begged?" [9:9]Others were saying, "It is he." Still others were saying, "He looks like him."

He said, "I am he." [9:10]They therefore were asking him, "How were your eyes opened?"

[9:11]He answered, "A man called Jesus made mud, anointed my eyes, and said to me, **'Go to the pool of Siloam, and wash.'** So I went away and washed, and I received sight."

[9:12]Then they asked him, "Where is he?"

He said, "I don't know."

[9:13]They brought him who had been blind to the Pharisees. [9:14]It was a Sabbath when Jesus made the mud and opened his eyes. [9:15]Again therefore the Pharisees also asked him how he received his sight. He said to them, "He put mud on my eyes, I washed, and I see."

[9:16]Some therefore of the Pharisees said, "This man is not from God, because he doesn't keep the Sabbath." Others said, "How can a man who is a sinner do such signs?" There was division among them. [9:17]Therefore they asked the blind man again, "What do you say about him, because he opened your eyes?"

He said, "He is a prophet."

[9:18]The Jews therefore did not believe concerning him, that he had been blind, and had received his sight, until they called the parents of him who had received his sight, [9:19]and asked them, "Is this your son, who you say was born blind? How then does he now see?"

[9:20]His parents answered them, "We know that this is our son, and that he was born blind; [9:21]but how he now sees, we don't know; or who opened his eyes, we don't know. He is of age. Ask him. He will speak for himself." [9:22]His parents said these things because they feared the Jews; for the Jews had already agreed that if any man would confess him as Christ, he would be put out of the synagogue. [9:23]Therefore his parents said, "He is of age. Ask him."

[9:24]So they called the man who was blind a second time, and said to him, "Give glory to God. We know that this man is a sinner."

[9:25]He therefore answered, "I don't know if he is a sinner. One thing I do know: that though I was blind, now I see."

[9:26]They said to him again, "What did he do to you? How did he open your eyes?"

[9:27]He answered them, "I told you already, and you didn't listen. Why do you want to hear it again? You don't also want to become his disciples, do you?"

[9:28]They insulted him and said, "You are his disciple, but we are disciples of Moses. [9:29]We know that God has spoken to Moses. But as for this man, we don't know where he comes from."

[9:30]The man answered them, "How amazing! You don't know where he comes from, yet he opened my eyes. [9:31]We know that God doesn't listen to sinners, but if anyone is a worshipper of God, and does his will, he listens to him.[b] [9:32]Since the world began it has never been heard of that anyone opened the eyes of someone born blind. [9:33]If this man were not from God, he could do nothing."

[9:34]They answered him, "You were altogether born in sins, and do you teach us?" They threw him out.

[9:35]Jesus heard that they had thrown him out, and finding him, he said, **"Do you believe in the Son of God?"**

[9:36]He answered, "Who is he, Lord, that I may believe in him?"

---

[b]9:31 Psalm 66:18, Proverbs 15:29; 28:9

9:37Jesus said to him, **"You have both seen him, and it is he who speaks with you."**

9:38He said, "Lord, I believe!" and he worshiped him.

9:39Jesus said, **"I came into this world for judgment, that those who don't see may see; and that those who see may become blind."**

9:40Those of the Pharisees who were with him heard these things, and said to him, "Are we also blind?"

9:41Jesus said to them, **"If you were blind, you would have no sin; but now you say, 'We see.' Therefore your sin remains.**

10:1**"Most certainly, I tell you, one who doesn't enter by the door into the sheep fold, but climbs up some other way, the same is a thief and a robber.** 10:2**But one who enters in by the door is the shepherd of the sheep.** 10:3**The gatekeeper opens the gate for him, and the sheep listen to his voice. He calls his own sheep by name, and leads them out.** 10:4**Whenever he brings out his own sheep, he goes before them, and the sheep follow him, for they know his voice.** 10:5**They will by no means follow a stranger, but will flee from him; for they don't know the voice of strangers."** 10:6Jesus spoke this parable to them, but they didn't understand what he was telling them.

10:7Jesus therefore said to them again, **"Most certainly, I tell you, I am the sheep's door.** 10:8**All who came before me are thieves and robbers, but the sheep didn't listen to them.** 10:9**I am the door. If anyone enters in by me, he will be saved, and will go in and go out, and will find pasture.** 10:10**The thief only comes to steal, kill, and destroy. I came that they may have life, and may have it abundantly.** 10:11**I am the good shepherd.**c **The good shepherd lays down his life for the sheep.** 10:12**He who is a hired hand, and not a**

shepherd, who doesn't own the sheep, sees the wolf coming, leaves the sheep, and flees. The wolf snatches the sheep, and scatters them. 10:13**The hired hand flees because he is a hired hand, and doesn't care for the sheep.** 10:14**I am the good shepherd. I know my own, and I'm known by my own;** 10:15**even as the Father knows me, and I know the Father. I lay down my life for the sheep.** 10:16**I have other sheep, which are not of this fold.**d **I must bring them also, and they will hear my voice. They will become one flock with one shepherd.** 10:17**Therefore the Father loves me, because I lay down my life,**e **that I may take it again.** 10:18**No one takes it away from me, but I lay it down by myself. I have power to lay it down, and I have power to take it again. I received this commandment from my Father."**

10:19Therefore a division arose again among the Jews because of these words. 10:20Many of them said, "He has a demon, and is insane! Why do you listen to him?" 10:21Others said, "These are not the sayings of one possessed by a demon. It isn't possible for a demon to open the eyes of the blind, is it?"f

10:22It was the Feast of the Dedicationg at Jerusalem. 10:23It was winter, and Jesus was walking in the temple, in Solomon's porch. 10:24The Jews therefore came around him and said to him, "How long will you hold us in suspense? If you are the Christ, tell us plainly."

10:25Jesus answered them, **"I told you, and you don't believe. The works that I do in my Father's name, these testify about me.** 10:26**But you don't believe, because you are not of my sheep, as I told you.** 10:27**My sheep hear my voice, and I know them, and they follow me.** 10:28**I give eternal life to them. They will never perish, and no one will snatch them out of my hand.** 10:29**My Father, who has given them to me, is greater than all. No one**

---

c10:11 Isaiah 40:11; Ezekiel 34:11-12,15,22

d10:16 Isaiah 56:8

e10:17 Isaiah 53:7-8

f10:21 Exodus 4:11

g10:22 The "Feast of the Dedication" is the Greek name for "Hanukkah," a celebration of the rededication of the Temple.

is able to snatch them out of my Father's hand. **10:30 I and the Father are one."**

10:31 Therefore Jews took up stones again to stone him. 10:32 Jesus answered them, **"I have shown you many good works from my Father. For which of those works do you stone me?"**

10:33 The Jews answered him, "We don't stone you for a good work, but for blasphemy: because you, being a man, make yourself God."

10:34 Jesus answered them, **"Isn't it written in your law, 'I said, you are gods?'**[h] **10:35 If he called them gods, to whom the word of God came (and the Scripture can't be broken), 10:36 do you say of him whom the Father sanctified and sent into the world, 'You blaspheme,' because I said, 'I am the Son of God?' 10:37 If I don't do the works of my Father, don't believe me. 10:38 But if I do them, though you don't believe me, believe the works; that you may know and believe that the Father is in me, and I in the Father."**

10:39 They sought again to seize him, and he went out of their hand. 10:40 He went away again beyond the Jordan into the place where John was baptizing at first, and there he stayed. 10:41 Many came to him. They said, "John indeed did no sign, but everything that John said about this man is true." 10:42 Many believed in him there.

11:1 Now a certain man was sick, Lazarus from Bethany, of the village of Mary and her sister, Martha. 11:2 It was that Mary who had anointed the Lord with ointment, and wiped his feet with her hair, whose brother, Lazarus, was sick. 11:3 The sisters therefore sent to him, saying, "Lord, behold, he for whom you have great affection is sick." 11:4 But when Jesus heard it, he said, **"This sickness is not to death, but for the glory of God, that God's Son may be glorified by it."** 11:5 Now Jesus loved Martha, and her sister, and Lazarus. 11:6 When therefore he heard that he was sick, he stayed two days in the place where he was. 11:7 Then after this he said to the disciples, **"Let's go into Judea again."**

11:8 The disciples told him, "Rabbi, the Jews were just trying to stone you, and are you going there again?"

11:9 Jesus answered, **"Aren't there twelve hours of daylight? If a man walks in the day, he doesn't stumble, because he sees the light of this world. 11:10 But if a man walks in the night, he stumbles, because the light isn't in him."** 11:11 He said these things, and after that, he said to them, **"Our friend, Lazarus, has fallen asleep, but I am going so that I may awake him out of sleep."**

11:12 The disciples therefore said, "Lord, if he has fallen asleep, he will recover."

11:13 Now Jesus had spoken of his death, but they thought that he spoke of taking rest in sleep. 11:14 So Jesus said to them plainly then, **"Lazarus is dead. 11:15 I am glad for your sakes that I was not there, so that you may believe. Nevertheless, let's go to him."**

11:16 Thomas therefore, who is called Didymus,[i] said to his fellow disciples, "Let's go also, that we may die with him."

11:17 So when Jesus came, he found that he had been in the tomb four days already. 11:18 Now Bethany was near Jerusalem, about fifteen stadia[j] away. 11:19 Many of the Jews had joined the women around Martha and Mary, to console them concerning their brother. 11:20 Then when Martha heard that Jesus was coming, she went and met him, but Mary stayed in the house. 11:21 Therefore Martha said to Jesus, "Lord, if you would have been here, my brother wouldn't have died. 11:22 Even now I know that, whatever you ask of God, God will give you." 11:23 Jesus said to her, **"Your brother will rise again."**

11:24 Martha said to him, "I know that he will rise again in the resurrection at the last day."

11:25 Jesus said to her, **"I am the resurrection and the life. He who believes in me will still live, even if he dies. 11:26 Whoever lives and believes in me will never die. Do you believe this?"**

---

[h]10:34 Psalm 82:6
[i]11:16 "Didymus" means "Twin"
[j]11:18 15 stadia is about 2.8 kilometers or 1.7 miles

^{11:27}She said to him, "Yes, Lord. I have come to believe that you are the Christ, God's Son, he who comes into the world."

^{11:28}When she had said this, she went away, and called Mary, her sister, secretly, saying, "The Teacher is here, and is calling you."

^{11:29}When she heard this, she arose quickly, and went to him. ^{11:30}Now Jesus had not yet come into the village, but was in the place where Martha met him. ^{11:31}Then the Jews who were with her in the house, and were consoling her, when they saw Mary, that she rose up quickly and went out, followed her, saying, "She is going to the tomb to weep there." ^{11:32}Therefore when Mary came to where Jesus was, and saw him, she fell down at his feet, saying to him, "Lord, if you would have been here, my brother wouldn't have died."

^{11:33}When Jesus therefore saw her weeping, and the Jews weeping who came with her, he groaned in the spirit, and was troubled, ^{11:34}and said, **"Where have you laid him?"**

They told him, "Lord, come and see."

^{11:35}Jesus wept.

^{11:36}The Jews therefore said, "See how much affection he had for him!" ^{11:37}Some of them said, "Couldn't this man, who opened the eyes of him who was blind, have also kept this man from dying?"

^{11:38}Jesus therefore, again groaning in himself, came to the tomb. Now it was a cave, and a stone lay against it. ^{11:39}Jesus said, **"Take away the stone."**

Martha, the sister of him who was dead, said to him, "Lord, by this time there is a stench, for he has been dead four days."

^{11:40}Jesus said to her, **"Didn't I tell you that if you believed, you would see God's glory?"**

^{11:41}So they took away the stone from the place where the dead man was lying.^k Jesus lifted up his eyes, and said, **"Father, I thank you that you listened to me. ^{11:42}I know that you always listen to me, but because of the multitude that stands around I said this, that they may believe that you sent me."** ^{11:43}When he had said this, he cried with a loud voice, **"Lazarus, come out!"**

^{11:44}He who was dead came out, bound hand and foot with wrappings, and his face was wrapped around with a cloth.

Jesus said to them, **"Free him, and let him go."**

^{11:45}Therefore many of the Jews, who came to Mary and saw what Jesus did, believed in him. ^{11:46}But some of them went away to the Pharisees, and told them the things which Jesus had done. ^{11:47}The chief priests therefore and the Pharisees gathered a council, and said, "What are we doing? For this man does many signs. ^{11:48}If we leave him alone like this, everyone will believe in him, and the Romans will come and take away both our place and our nation."

^{11:49}But a certain one of them, Caiaphas, being high priest that year, said to them, "You know nothing at all, ^{11:50}nor do you consider that it is advantageous for us that one man should die for the people, and that the whole nation not perish." ^{11:51}Now he didn't say this of himself, but being high priest that year, he prophesied that Jesus would die for the nation, ^{11:52}and not for the nation only, but that he might also gather together into one the children of God who are scattered abroad. ^{11:53}So from that day forward they took counsel that they might put him to death. ^{11:54}Jesus therefore walked no more openly among the Jews, but departed from there into the country near the wilderness, to a city called Ephraim. He stayed there with his disciples.

^{11:55}Now the Passover of the Jews was at hand. Many went up from the country to Jerusalem before the Passover, to purify themselves. ^{11:56}Then they sought for Jesus and spoke one with another, as they stood in the temple, "What do you think—that he isn't coming to the feast at all?" ^{11:57}Now the chief priests and the Pharisees had commanded that if anyone knew where he was, he should report it, that they might seize him.

^{12:1}Then six days before the Passover, Jesus came to Bethany, where Lazarus was,

---

^k11:41 NU omits "from the place where the dead man was lying."

who had been dead, whom he raised from the dead. [12:2]So they made him a supper there. Martha served, but Lazarus was one of those who sat at the table with him. [12:3]Mary, therefore, took a pound[l] of ointment of pure nard, very precious, and anointed the feet of Jesus, and wiped his feet with her hair. The house was filled with the fragrance of the ointment. [12:4]Then Judas Iscariot, Simon's son, one of his disciples, who would betray him, said, [12:5]"Why wasn't this ointment sold for three hundred denarii,[m] and given to the poor?" [12:6]Now he said this, not because he cared for the poor, but because he was a thief, and having the money box, used to steal what was put into it. [12:7]But Jesus said, **"Leave her alone. She has kept this for the day of my burial. [12:8]For you always have the poor with you, but you don't always have me."**

[12:9]A large crowd therefore of the Jews learned that he was there, and they came, not for Jesus' sake only, but that they might see Lazarus also, whom he had raised from the dead. [12:10]But the chief priests conspired to put Lazarus to death also, [12:11]because on account of him many of the Jews went away and believed in Jesus.

[12:12]On the next day a great multitude had come to the feast. When they heard that Jesus was coming to Jerusalem, [12:13]they took the branches of the palm trees, and went out to meet him, and cried out, "Hosanna[n]! Blessed is he who comes in the name of the Lord,[o] the King of Israel!"

[12:14]Jesus, having found a young donkey, sat on it. As it is written, [12:15]"Don't be afraid, daughter of Zion. Behold, your King comes, sitting on a donkey's colt."[p] [12:16]His disciples didn't understand these things at first, but when Jesus was glorified, then they remembered that these things were written about him, and that they had done these things to him. [12:17]The multitude therefore that was with him when he called Lazarus out of the tomb, and raised him

from the dead, was testifying about it. [12:18]For this cause also the multitude went and met him, because they heard that he had done this sign. [12:19]The Pharisees therefore said among themselves, "See how you accomplish nothing. Behold, the world has gone after him."

[12:20]Now there were certain Greeks among those that went up to worship at the feast. [12:21]These, therefore, came to Philip, who was from Bethsaida of Galilee, and asked him, saying, "Sir, we want to see Jesus." [12:22]Philip came and told Andrew, and in turn, Andrew came with Philip, and they told Jesus. [12:23]Jesus answered them, **"The time has come for the Son of Man to be glorified. [12:24]Most certainly I tell you, unless a grain of wheat falls into the earth and dies, it remains by itself alone. But if it dies, it bears much fruit. [12:25]He who loves his life will lose it. He who hates his life in this world will keep it to eternal life. [12:26]If anyone serves me, let him follow me. Where I am, there will my servant also be. If anyone serves me, the Father will honor him.**

[12:27]**"Now my soul is troubled. What shall I say? 'Father, save me from this time?' But for this cause I came to this time. [12:28]Father, glorify your name!"**

Then there came a voice out of the sky, saying, "I have both glorified it, and will glorify it again."

[12:29]The multitude therefore, who stood by and heard it, said that it had thundered. Others said, "An angel has spoken to him."

[12:30]Jesus answered, **"This voice hasn't come for my sake, but for your sakes. [12:31]Now is the judgment of this world. Now the prince of this world will be cast out. [12:32]And I, if I am lifted up from the earth, will draw all people to myself."** [12:33]But he said this, signifying by what kind of death he should die. [12:34]The multitude answered him, "We have heard out

---

[l]12:3 a Roman pound of 12 ounces, or about 340 grams
[m]12:5 300 denarii was about a year's wages for an agricultural laborer.
[n]12:13 "Hosanna" means "save us" or "help us, we pray."
[o]12:13 Psalm 118:25-26
[p]12:15 Zechariah 9:9

of the law that the Christ remains forever.[q] How do you say, **'The Son of Man must be lifted up?'** Who is this Son of Man?"

[12:35] Jesus therefore said to them, **"Yet a little while the light is with you. Walk while you have the light, that darkness doesn't overtake you. He who walks in the darkness doesn't know where he is going.** [12:36] **While you have the light, believe in the light, that you may become children of light."** Jesus said these things, and he departed and hid himself from them. [12:37] But though he had done so many signs before them, yet they didn't believe in him, [12:38] that the word of Isaiah the prophet might be fulfilled, which he spoke,

"Lord, who has believed our report?

To whom has the arm of the Lord been revealed?"[r]

[12:39] For this cause they couldn't believe, for Isaiah said again,

[12:40] "He has blinded their eyes and he hardened their heart,

lest they should see with their eyes,

and perceive with their heart,

and would turn,

and I would heal them."[s]

[12:41] Isaiah said these things when he saw his glory, and spoke of him.[t] [12:42] Nevertheless even of the rulers many believed in him, but because of the Pharisees they didn't confess it, so that they wouldn't be put out of the synagogue, [12:43] for they loved men's praise more than God's praise.

[12:44] Jesus cried out and said, **"Whoever believes in me, believes not in me, but in him who sent me.** [12:45] **He who sees me sees him who sent me.** [12:46] **I have come as a light into the world, that whoever believes in me may not remain in the darkness.** [12:47] **If anyone listens to my sayings, and doesn't believe, I don't judge him. For I came not to judge the world, but to save the world.** [12:48] **He who rejects me, and doesn't receive my sayings, has one who judges him. The word that I spoke, the same will judge him in the last day.** [12:49] **For I spoke not from myself, but the Father who sent me, he gave me a commandment, what I should say, and what I should speak.** [12:50] **I know that his commandment is eternal life. The things therefore which I speak, even as the Father has said to me, so I speak."**

[13:1] Now before the feast of the Passover, Jesus, knowing that his time had come that he would depart from this world to the Father, having loved his own who were in the world, he loved them to the end. [13:2] After supper, the devil having already put into the heart of Judas Iscariot, Simon's son, to betray him, [13:3] Jesus, knowing that the Father had given all things into his hands, and that he came forth from God, and was going to God, [13:4] arose from supper, and laid aside his outer garments. He took a towel, and wrapped a towel around his waist. [13:5] Then he poured water into the basin, and began to wash the disciples' feet, and to wipe them with the towel that was wrapped around him. [13:6] Then he came to Simon Peter. He said to him, "Lord, do you wash my feet?"

[13:7] Jesus answered him, **"You don't know what I am doing now, but you will understand later."**

[13:8] Peter said to him, "You will never wash my feet!"

Jesus answered him, **"If I don't wash you, you have no part with me."**

[13:9] Simon Peter said to him, "Lord, not my feet only, but also my hands and my head!"

[13:10] Jesus said to him, **"Someone who has bathed only needs to have his feet washed, but is completely clean. You are clean, but not all of you."** [13:11] For he knew him who would betray him, therefore he said, **"You are not all clean."** [13:12] So when he had washed their feet, put his outer garment back on, and sat down again, he said to them, **"Do you know what I have done to you?** [13:13] **You call me, 'Teacher' and 'Lord.' You say so correctly, for so**

---

[q]12:34 Isaiah 9:7; Daniel 2:44 (but see also Isaiah 53:8)

[r]12:38 Isaiah 53:1

[s]12:40 Isaiah 6:10

[t]12:41 Isaiah 6:1

I am. ¹³:¹⁴If I then, the Lord and the Teacher, have washed your feet, you also ought to wash one another's feet. ¹³:¹⁵For I have given you an example, that you also should do as I have done to you. ¹³:¹⁶Most certainly I tell you, a servant is not greater than his lord, neither one who is sent greater than he who sent him. ¹³:¹⁷If you know these things, blessed are you if you do them. ¹³:¹⁸I don't speak concerning all of you. I know whom I have chosen. But that the Scripture may be fulfilled, 'He who eats bread with me has lifted up his heel against me.'ᵘ ¹³:¹⁹From now on, I tell you before it happens, that when it happens, you may believe that I am he. ¹³:²⁰Most certainly I tell you, he who receives whomever I send, receives me; and he who receives me, receives him who sent me."

¹³:²¹When Jesus had said this, he was troubled in spirit, and testified, **"Most certainly I tell you that one of you will betray me."**

¹³:²²The disciples looked at one another, perplexed about whom he spoke. ¹³:²³One of his disciples, whom Jesus loved, was at the table, leaning against Jesus' breast. ¹³:²⁴Simon Peter therefore beckoned to him, and said to him, "Tell us who it is of whom he speaks."

¹³:²⁵He, leaning back, as he was, on Jesus' breast, asked him, "Lord, who is it?"

¹³:²⁶Jesus therefore answered, **"It is he to whom I will give this piece of bread when I have dipped it."** So when he had dipped the piece of bread, he gave it to Judas, the son of Simon Iscariot. ¹³:²⁷After the piece of bread, then Satan entered into him.

Then Jesus said to him, **"What you do, do quickly."**

¹³:²⁸Now no man at the table knew why he said this to him. ¹³:²⁹For some thought, because Judas had the money box, that Jesus said to him, "Buy what things we need for the feast," or that he should give something to the poor. ¹³:³⁰Therefore, having received that morsel, he went out immediately. It was night.

¹³:³¹When he had gone out, Jesus said, "Now the Son of Man has been glorified, and God has been glorified in him. ¹³:³²If God has been glorified in him, God will also glorify him in himself, and he will glorify him immediately. ¹³:³³Little children, I will be with you a little while longer. You will seek me, and as I said to the Jews, 'Where I am going, you can't come,' so now I tell you. ¹³:³⁴A new commandment I give to you, that you love one another, just like I have loved you; that you also love one another. ¹³:³⁵By this everyone will know that you are my disciples, if you have love for one another."

¹³:³⁶Simon Peter said to him, "Lord, where are you going?"

Jesus answered, **"Where I am going, you can't follow now, but you will follow afterwards."**

¹³:³⁷Peter said to him, "Lord, why can't I follow you now? I will lay down my life for you."

¹³:³⁸Jesus answered him, **"Will you lay down your life for me? Most certainly I tell you, the rooster won't crow until you have denied me three times.**

¹⁴:¹**"Don't let your heart be troubled. Believe in God. Believe also in me.** ¹⁴:²In my Father's house are many homes. If it weren't so, I would have told you. I am going to prepare a place for you. ¹⁴:³If I go and prepare a place for you, I will come again, and will receive you to myself; that where I am, you may be there also. ¹⁴:⁴Where I go, you know, and you know the way."

¹⁴:⁵Thomas said to him, "Lord, we don't know where you are going. How can we know the way?"

¹⁴:⁶Jesus said to him, **"I am the way, the truth, and the life. No one comes to the Father, except through me.** ¹⁴:⁷If you had known me, you would have known my Father also. From now on, you know him, and have seen him."

¹⁴:⁸Philip said to him, "Lord, show us the Father, and that will be enough for us."

¹⁴:⁹Jesus said to him, **"Have I been with you such a long time, and do you not know me, Philip? He who has seen me has seen the Father. How do you say, 'Show**

ᵘ13:18 Psalm 41:9

us the Father?' [14:10]Don't you believe that I am in the Father, and the Father in me? The words that I tell you, I speak not from myself; but the Father who lives in me does his works. [14:11]Believe me that I am in the Father, and the Father in me; or else believe me for the very works' sake. [14:12]Most certainly I tell you, he who believes in me, the works that I do, he will do also; and he will do greater works than these, because I am going to my Father. [14:13]Whatever you will ask in my name, that will I do, that the Father may be glorified in the Son. [14:14]If you will ask anything in my name, I will do it. [14:15]If you love me, keep my commandments. [14:16]I will pray to the Father, and he will give you another Counselor,[v] that he may be with you forever,—[14:17]the Spirit of truth, whom the world can't receive; for it doesn't see him, neither knows him. You know him, for he lives with you, and will be in you. [14:18]I will not leave you orphans. I will come to you. [14:19]Yet a little while, and the world will see me no more; but you will see me. Because I live, you will live also. [14:20]In that day you will know that I am in my Father, and you in me, and I in you. [14:21]One who has my commandments, and keeps them, that person is one who loves me. One who loves me will be loved by my Father, and I will love him, and will reveal myself to him."

[14:22]Judas (not Iscariot) said to him, "Lord, what has happened that you are about to reveal yourself to us, and not to the world?"

[14:23]Jesus answered him, "If a man loves me, he will keep my word. My Father will love him, and we will come to him, and make our home with him. [14:24]He who doesn't love me doesn't keep my words. The word which you hear isn't mine, but the Father's who sent me. [14:25]I have said these things to you, while still living with you. [14:26]But the Counselor, the Holy Spirit, whom the Father will send in my name, he will teach you all things, and will remind you of all that I said to you. [14:27]Peace I leave with you. My peace I give to you; not as the world gives, give I to you. Don't let your heart be troubled, neither let it be fearful. [14:28]You heard how I told you, 'I go away, and I come to you.' If you loved me, you would have rejoiced, because I said 'I am going to my Father;' for the Father is greater than I. [14:29]Now I have told you before it happens so that, when it happens, you may believe. [14:30]I will no more speak much with you, for the prince of the world comes, and he has nothing in me. [14:31]But that the world may know that I love the Father, and as the Father commanded me, even so I do. Arise, let us go from here.

[15:1]"I am the true vine, and my Father is the farmer. [15:2]Every branch in me that doesn't bear fruit, he takes away. Every branch that bears fruit, he prunes, that it may bear more fruit. [15:3]You are already pruned clean because of the word which I have spoken to you. [15:4]Remain in me, and I in you. As the branch can't bear fruit by itself, unless it remains in the vine, so neither can you, unless you remain in me. [15:5]I am the vine. You are the branches. He who remains in me, and I in him, the same bears much fruit, for apart from me you can do nothing. [15:6]If a man doesn't remain in me, he is thrown out as a branch, and is withered; and they gather them, throw them into the fire, and they are burned. [15:7]If you remain in me, and my words remain in you, you will ask whatever you desire, and it will be done for you.

[15:8]"In this is my Father glorified, that you bear much fruit; and so you will be my disciples. [15:9]Even as the Father has loved me, I also have loved you. Remain in my love. [15:10]If you keep my commandments, you will remain in my love; even as I have kept my Father's commandments, and remain in his love. [15:11]I have spoken these things to you, that my joy may remain in you, and that your joy may be made full.

[15:12]"This is my commandment, that you love one another, even as I have loved you. [15:13]Greater love has no one than

---

[v]14:16 Greek Parakleton: Counselor, Helper, Intercessor, Advocate, and Comfortor.

this, that someone lay down his life for his friends. [15:14]You are my friends, if you do whatever I command you. [15:15]No longer do I call you servants, for the servant doesn't know what his lord does. But I have called you friends, for everything that I heard from my Father, I have made known to you. [15:16]You didn't choose me, but I chose you, and appointed you, that you should go and bear fruit, and that your fruit should remain; that whatever you will ask of the Father in my name, he may give it to you.

[15:17]"I command these things to you, that you may love one another. [15:18]If the world hates you, you know that it has hated me before it hated you. [15:19]If you were of the world, the world would love its own. But because you are not of the world, since I chose you out of the world, therefore the world hates you. [15:20]Remember the word that I said to you: 'A servant is not greater than his lord.'[w] If they persecuted me, they will also persecute you. If they kept my word, they will keep yours also. [15:21]But all these things will they do to you for my name's sake, because they don't know him who sent me. [15:22]If I had not come and spoken to them, they would not have had sin; but now they have no excuse for their sin. [15:23]He who hates me, hates my Father also. [15:24]If I hadn't done among them the works which no one else did, they wouldn't have had sin. But now have they seen and also hated both me and my Father. [15:25]But this happened so that the word may be fulfilled which was written in their law, 'They hated me without a cause.'[x]

[15:26]"When the Counselor[y] has come, whom I will send to you from the Father, the Spirit of truth, who proceeds from the Father, he will testify about me. [15:27]You will also testify, because you have been with me from the beginning.

[16:1]"These things have I spoken to you, so that you wouldn't be caused to stumble. [16:2]They will put you out of the synagogues. Yes, the time comes that whoever kills you will think that he offers service to God. [16:3]They will do these things[z] because they have not known the Father, nor me. [16:4]But I have told you these things, so that when the time comes, you may remember that I told you about them. I didn't tell you these things from the beginning, because I was with you. [16:5]But now I am going to him who sent me, and none of you asks me, 'Where are you going?' [16:6]But because I have told you these things, sorrow has filled your heart. [16:7]Nevertheless I tell you the truth: It is to your advantage that I go away, for if I don't go away, the Counselor won't come to you. But if I go, I will send him to you. [16:8]When he has come, he will convict the world about sin, about righteousness, and about judgment; [16:9]about sin, because they don't believe in me; [16:10]about righteousness, because I am going to my Father, and you won't see me any more; [16:11]about judgment, because the prince of this world has been judged.

[16:12]"I have yet many things to tell you, but you can't bear them now. [16:13]However when he, the Spirit of truth, has come, he will guide you into all truth, for he will not speak from himself; but whatever he hears, he will speak. He will declare to you things that are coming. [16:14]He will glorify me, for he will take from what is mine, and will declare it to you. [16:15]All things whatever the Father has are mine; therefore I said that he takes[a] of mine, and will declare it to you. [16:16]A little while, and you will not see me. Again a little while, and you will see me."

[16:17]Some of his disciples therefore said to one another, "What is this that he says to us, 'A little while, and you won't see me, and again a little while, and you will see me;' and, 'Because I go to the Father?'"

w 15:20 John 13:16
x 15:25 Psalms 35:19; 69:4
y 15:26 Greek Parakletos: Counselor, Helper, Advocate, Intercessor, and Comforter.
z 16:3 TR adds "to you"
a 16:15 TR reads "will take" instead of "takes"

16:18They said therefore, "What is this that he says, 'A little while?' We don't know what he is saying."

16:19Therefore Jesus perceived that they wanted to ask him, and he said to them, "Do you inquire among yourselves concerning this, that I said, 'A little while, and you won't see me, and again a little while, and you will see me?' 16:20Most certainly I tell you, that you will weep and lament, but the world will rejoice. You will be sorrowful, but your sorrow will be turned into joy. 16:21A woman, when she gives birth, has sorrow, because her time has come. But when she has delivered the child, she doesn't remember the anguish any more, for the joy that a human being is born into the world. 16:22Therefore you now have sorrow, but I will see you again, and your heart will rejoice, and no one will take your joy away from you.

16:23"In that day you will ask me no questions. Most certainly I tell you, whatever you may ask of the Father in my name, he will give it to you. 16:24Until now, you have asked nothing in my name. Ask, and you will receive, that your joy may be made full. 16:25I have spoken these things to you in figures of speech. But the time is coming when I will no more speak to you in figures of speech, but will tell you plainly about the Father. 16:26In that day you will ask in my name; and I don't say to you, that I will pray to the Father for you, 16:27for the Father himself loves you, because you have loved me, and have believed that I came forth from God. 16:28I came out from the Father, and have come into the world. Again, I leave the world, and go to the Father."

16:29His disciples said to him, "Behold, now you speak plainly, and speak no figures of speech. 16:30Now we know that you know all things, and don't need for anyone to question you. By this we believe that you came forth from God."

16:31Jesus answered them, "Do you now believe? 16:32Behold, the time is coming, yes, and has now come, that you will be scattered, everyone to his own place, and you will leave me alone. Yet I am not alone, because the Father is with me. 16:33I

have told you these things, that in me you may have peace. In the world you have oppression; but cheer up! I have overcome the world."

17:1Jesus said these things, and lifting up his eyes to heaven, he said, "Father, the time has come. Glorify your Son, that your Son may also glorify you; 17:2even as you gave him authority over all flesh, he will give eternal life to all whom you have given him. 17:3This is eternal life, that they should know you, the only true God, and him whom you sent, Jesus Christ. 17:4I glorified you on the earth. I have accomplished the work which you have given me to do. 17:5Now, Father, glorify me with your own self with the glory which I had with you before the world existed. 17:6I revealed your name to the people whom you have given me out of the world. They were yours, and you have given them to me. They have kept your word. 17:7Now they have known that all things whatever you have given me are from you, 17:8for the words which you have given me I have given to them, and they received them, and knew for sure that I came forth from you, and they have believed that you sent me. 17:9I pray for them. I don't pray for the world, but for those whom you have given me, for they are yours. 17:10All things that are mine are yours, and yours are mine, and I am glorified in them. 17:11I am no more in the world, but these are in the world, and I am coming to you. Holy Father, keep them through your name which you have given me, that they may be one, even as we are. 17:12While I was with them in the world, I kept them in your name. Those whom you have given me I have kept. None of them is lost, except the son of destruction, that the Scripture might be fulfilled. 17:13But now I come to you, and I say these things in the world, that they may have my joy made full in themselves. 17:14I have given them your word. The world hated them, because they are not of the world, even as I am not of the world. 17:15I pray not that you would take them from the world, but that you would keep them from the evil one. 17:16They are not of the world even as I am not of the world. ¹⁷:¹⁷Sanctify them in your truth. Your word is truth.ᵇ ¹⁷:¹⁸As you sent me into the world, even so I have sent them into the world. ¹⁷:¹⁹For their sakes I sanctify myself, that they themselves also may be sanctified in truth. ¹⁷:²⁰Not for these only do I pray, but for those also who believe in me through their word, ¹⁷:²¹that they may all be one; even as you, Father, are in me, and I in you, that they also may be one in us; that the world may believe that you sent me. ¹⁷:²²The glory which you have given me, I have given to them; that they may be one, even as we are one; ¹⁷:²³I in them, and you in me, that they may be perfected into one; that the world may know that you sent me, and loved them, even as you loved me. ¹⁷:²⁴Father, I desire that they also whom you have given me be with me where I am, that they may see my glory, which you have given me, for you loved me before the foundation of the world. ¹⁷:²⁵Righteous Father, the world hasn't known you, but I knew you; and these knew that you sent me. ¹⁷:²⁶I made known to them your name, and will make it known; that the love with which you loved me may be in them, and I in them."

¹⁸:¹When Jesus had spoken these words, he went out with his disciples over the brook Kidron, where there was a garden, into which he and his disciples entered. ¹⁸:²Now Judas, who betrayed him, also knew the place, for Jesus often met there with his disciples. ¹⁸:³Judas then, having taken a detachment of soldiers and officers from the chief priests and the Pharisees, came there with lanterns, torches, and weapons. ¹⁸:⁴Jesus therefore, knowing all the things that were happening to him, went forth, and said to them, "Who are you looking for?"

¹⁸:⁵They answered him, "Jesus of Nazareth."

Jesus said to them, "I am he."

Judas also, who betrayed him, was standing with them. ¹⁸:⁶When therefore he said to them, "I am he," they went backward, and fell to the ground.

¹⁸:⁷Again therefore he asked them, "Who are you looking for?"

They said, "Jesus of Nazareth."

¹⁸:⁸Jesus answered, "I told you that I am he. If therefore you seek me, let these go their way," ¹⁸:⁹that the word might be fulfilled which he spoke, "Of those whom you have given me, I have lost none."ᶜ

¹⁸:¹⁰Simon Peter therefore, having a sword, drew it, and struck the high priest's servant, and cut off his right ear. The servant's name was Malchus. ¹⁸:¹¹Jesus therefore said to Peter, "Put the sword into its sheath. The cup which the Father has given me, shall I not surely drink it?"

¹⁸:¹²So the detachment, the commanding officer, and the officers of the Jews, seized Jesus and bound him, ¹⁸:¹³and led him to Annas first, for he was father-in-law to Caiaphas, who was high priest that year. ¹⁸:¹⁴Now it was Caiaphas who advised the Jews that it was expedient that one man should perish for the people. ¹⁸:¹⁵Simon Peter followed Jesus, as did another disciple. Now that disciple was known to the high priest, and entered in with Jesus into the court of the high priest; ¹⁸:¹⁶but Peter was standing at the door outside. So the other disciple, who was known to the high priest, went out and spoke to her who kept the door, and brought in Peter. ¹⁸:¹⁷Then the maid who kept the door said to Peter, "Are you also one of this man's disciples?"

He said, "I am not."

¹⁸:¹⁸Now the servants and the officers were standing there, having made a fire of coals, for it was cold. They were warming themselves. Peter was with them, standing and warming himself. ¹⁸:¹⁹The high priest therefore asked Jesus about his disciples, and about his teaching. ¹⁸:²⁰Jesus answered him, "I spoke openly to the world. I always taught in synagogues, and in the temple, where the Jews always meet. I said nothing in secret. ¹⁸:²¹Why do you ask me? Ask those who have heard me what I said to them. Behold, these know the things which I said."

ᵇ17:17 Psalm 119:142
ᶜ18:9 John 6:39

18:22When he had said this, one of the officers standing by slapped Jesus with his hand, saying, "Do you answer the high priest like that?"

18:23Jesus answered him, **"If I have spoken evil, testify of the evil; but if well, why do you beat me?"**

18:24Annas sent him bound to Caiaphas, the high priest. 18:25Now Simon Peter was standing and warming himself. They said therefore to him, "You aren't also one of his disciples, are you?"

He denied it, and said, "I am not."

18:26One of the servants of the high priest, being a relative of him whose ear Peter had cut off, said, "Didn't I see you in the garden with him?"

18:27Peter therefore denied it again, and immediately the rooster crowed.

18:28They led Jesus therefore from Caiaphas into the Praetorium. It was early, and they themselves didn't enter into the Praetorium, that they might not be defiled, but might eat the Passover. 18:29Pilate therefore went out to them, and said, "What accusation do you bring against this man?"

18:30They answered him, "If this man weren't an evildoer, we wouldn't have delivered him up to you."

18:31Pilate therefore said to them, "Take him yourselves, and judge him according to your law."

Therefore the Jews said to him, "It is not lawful for us to put anyone to death," 18:32that the word of Jesus might be fulfilled, which he spoke, signifying by what kind of death he should die.

18:33Pilate therefore entered again into the Praetorium, called Jesus, and said to him, "Are you the King of the Jews?"

18:34Jesus answered him, **"Do you say this by yourself, or did others tell you about me?"**

18:35Pilate answered, "I'm not a Jew, am I? Your own nation and the chief priests delivered you to me. What have you done?"

18:36Jesus answered, **"My Kingdom is not of this world. If my Kingdom were of this world, then my servants would fight, that I wouldn't be delivered to the Jews. But now my Kingdom is not from here."**

18:37Pilate therefore said to him, "Are you a king then?"

Jesus answered, **"You say that I am a king. For this reason I have been born, and for this reason I have come into the world, that I should testify to the truth. Everyone who is of the truth listens to my voice."**

18:38Pilate said to him, "What is truth?"

When he had said this, he went out again to the Jews, and said to them, "I find no basis for a charge against him. 18:39But you have a custom, that I should release someone to you at the Passover. Therefore do you want me to release to you the King of the Jews?"

18:40Then they all shouted again, saying, "Not this man, but Barabbas!" Now Barabbas was a robber.

19:1So Pilate then took Jesus, and flogged him. 19:2The soldiers twisted thorns into a crown, and put it on his head, and dressed him in a purple garment. 19:3They kept saying, "Hail, King of the Jews!" and they kept slapping him.

19:4Then Pilate went out again, and said to them, "Behold, I bring him out to you, that you may know that I find no basis for a charge against him."

19:5Jesus therefore came out, wearing the crown of thorns and the purple garment. Pilate said to them, "Behold, the man!"

19:6When therefore the chief priests and the officers saw him, they shouted, saying, "Crucify! Crucify!"

Pilate said to them, "Take him yourselves, and crucify him, for I find no basis for a charge against him."

19:7The Jews answered him, "We have a law, and by our law he ought to die, because he made himself the Son of God."

19:8When therefore Pilate heard this saying, he was more afraid. 19:9He entered into the Praetorium again, and said to Jesus, "Where are you from?" But Jesus gave him no answer. 19:10Pilate therefore said to him, "Aren't you speaking to me? Don't you know that I have power to release you, and have power to crucify you?"

19:11Jesus answered, **"You would have no power at all against me, unless it were** given to you from above. **Therefore he who delivered me to you has greater sin."**

^{19:12} At this, Pilate was seeking to release him, but the Jews cried out, saying, "If you release this man, you aren't Caesar's friend! Everyone who makes himself a king speaks against Caesar!"

^{19:13} When Pilate therefore heard these words, he brought Jesus out, and sat down on the judgment seat at a place called "The Pavement," but in Hebrew, "Gabbatha." ^{19:14} Now it was the Preparation Day of the Passover, at about the sixth hour.^d He said to the Jews, "Behold, your King!"

^{19:15} They cried out, "Away with him! Away with him! Crucify him!"

Pilate said to them, "Shall I crucify your King?"

The chief priests answered, "We have no king but Caesar!"

^{19:16} So then he delivered him to them to be crucified. So they took Jesus and led him away. ^{19:17} He went out, bearing his cross, to the place called "The Place of a Skull," which is called in Hebrew, "Golgotha," ^{19:18} where they crucified him, and with him two others, on either side one, and Jesus in the middle. ^{19:19} Pilate wrote a title also, and put it on the cross. There was written, "JESUS OF NAZARETH, THE KING OF THE JEWS." ^{19:20} Therefore many of the Jews read this title, for the place where Jesus was crucified was near the city; and it was written in Hebrew, in Latin, and in Greek. ^{19:21} The chief priests of the Jews therefore said to Pilate, "Don't write, 'The King of the Jews,' but, 'he said, I am King of the Jews.'"

^{19:22} Pilate answered, "What I have written, I have written."

^{19:23} Then the soldiers, when they had crucified Jesus, took his garments and made four parts, to every soldier a part; and also the coat. Now the coat was without seam, woven from the top throughout. ^{19:24} Then they said to one another, "Let's not tear it, but cast lots for it to decide whose it will

be," that the Scripture might be fulfilled, which says,

"They parted my garments among them.

For my cloak they cast lots."^e

Therefore the soldiers did these things. ^{19:25} But there were standing by the cross of Jesus his mother, and his mother's sister, Mary the wife of Clopas, and Mary Magdalene. ^{19:26} Therefore when Jesus saw his mother, and the disciple whom he loved standing there, he said to his mother, **"Woman, behold your son!"** ^{19:27} Then he said to the disciple, **"Behold, your mother!"** From that hour, the disciple took her to his own home.

^{19:28} After this, Jesus, seeing^f that all things were now finished, that the Scripture might be fulfilled, said, **"I am thirsty."** ^{19:29} Now a vessel full of vinegar was set there; so they put a sponge full of the vinegar on hyssop, and held it at his mouth. ^{19:30} When Jesus therefore had received the vinegar, he said, **"It is finished."** He bowed his head, and gave up his spirit.

^{19:31} Therefore the Jews, because it was the Preparation Day, so that the bodies wouldn't remain on the cross on the Sabbath (for that Sabbath was a special one), asked of Pilate that their legs might be broken, and that they might be taken away. ^{19:32} Therefore the soldiers came, and broke the legs of the first, and of the other who was crucified with him; ^{19:33} but when they came to Jesus, and saw that he was already dead, they didn't break his legs. ^{19:34} However one of the soldiers pierced his side with a spear, and immediately blood and water came out. ^{19:35} He who has seen has testified, and his testimony is true. He knows that he tells the truth, that you may believe. ^{19:36} For these things happened, that the Scripture might be fulfilled, "A bone of him will not be broken."^g ^{19:37} Again another Scripture says, "They will look on him whom they pierced."^h

^{19:38} After these things, Joseph of Arimathaea, being a disciple of Jesus, but

---

^d 19:14 noon
^e 19:24 Psalm 22:18
^f 19:28 NU, TR read "knowing" instead of "seeing"
^g 19:36 Exodus 12:46; Numbers 9:12; Psalm 34:20
^h 19:37 Zechariah 12:10

secretly for fear of the Jews, asked of Pilate that he might take away Jesus' body. Pilate gave him permission. He came therefore and took away his body. [19:39] Nicodemus, who at first came to Jesus by night, also came bringing a mixture of myrrh and aloes, about a hundred pounds.[i] [19:40] So they took Jesus' body, and bound it in linen cloths with the spices, as the custom of the Jews is to bury. [19:41] Now in the place where he was crucified there was a garden. In the garden was a new tomb in which no man had ever yet been laid. [19:42] Then because of the Jews' Preparation Day (for the tomb was near at hand) they laid Jesus there. [20:1] Now on the first day of the week, Mary Magdalene went early, while it was still dark, to the tomb, and saw the stone taken away from the tomb. [20:2] Therefore she ran and came to Simon Peter, and to the other disciple whom Jesus loved, and said to them, "They have taken away the Lord out of the tomb, and we don't know where they have laid him!"

[20:3] Therefore Peter and the other disciple went out, and they went toward the tomb. [20:4] They both ran together. The other disciple outran Peter, and came to the tomb first. [20:5] Stooping and looking in, he saw the linen cloths lying, yet he didn't enter in. [20:6] Then Simon Peter came, following him, and entered into the tomb. He saw the linen cloths lying, [20:7] and the cloth that had been on his head, not lying with the linen cloths, but rolled up in a place by itself. [20:8] So then the other disciple who came first to the tomb also entered in, and he saw and believed. [20:9] For as yet they didn't know the Scripture, that he must rise from the dead. [20:10] So the disciples went away again to their own homes.

[20:11] But Mary was standing outside at the tomb weeping. So, as she wept, she stooped and looked into the tomb, [20:12] and she saw two angels in white sitting, one at the head, and one at the feet, where the body of Jesus had lain. [20:13] They told her, "Woman, why are you weeping?"

She said to them, "Because they have taken away my Lord, and I don't know where they have laid him." [20:14] When she had said this, she turned around and saw Jesus standing, and didn't know that it was Jesus.

[20:15] Jesus said to her, **"Woman, why are you weeping? Who are you looking for?"**

She, supposing him to be the gardener, said to him, "Sir, if you have carried him away, tell me where you have laid him, and I will take him away."

[20:16] Jesus said to her, **"Mary."**

She turned and said to him, "Rhabbouni!" which is to say, "Teacher!"

[20:17] Jesus said to her, **"Don't touch me, for I haven't yet ascended to my Father; but go to my brothers, and tell them, 'I am ascending to my Father and your Father, to my God and your God.'"**

[20:18] Mary Magdalene came and told the disciples that she had seen the Lord, and that he had said these things to her. [20:19] When therefore it was evening, on that day, the first day of the week, and when the doors were locked where the disciples were assembled, for fear of the Jews, Jesus came and stood in the midst, and said to them, **"Peace be to you."**

[20:20] When he had said this, he showed them his hands and his side. The disciples therefore were glad when they saw the Lord. [20:21] Jesus therefore said to them again, **"Peace be to you. As the Father has sent me, even so I send you."** [20:22] When he had said this, he breathed on them, and said to them, **"Receive the Holy Spirit!** [20:23] Whoever's sins you forgive, they are forgiven them. Whoever's sins you retain, they have been retained."**

[20:24] But Thomas, one of the twelve, called Didymus, wasn't with them when Jesus came. [20:25] The other disciples therefore said to him, "We have seen the Lord!"

But he said to them, "Unless I see in his hands the print of the nails, and put my hand into his side, I will not believe."

[20:26] After eight days again his disciples were inside, and Thomas was with them. Jesus came, the doors being locked, and stood in the midst, and said, **"Peace be to you."** [20:27] Then he said to Thomas, **"Reach here your finger, and see my hands. Reach**

---

[i] 19:39 100 Roman pounds of 12 ounces each, or about 72 pounds, or 33 Kilograms.

here your hand, and put it into my side. Don't be unbelieving, but believing."

20:28 Thomas answered him, "My Lord and my God!"

20:29 Jesus said to him, **"Because you have seen me,ʲ you have believed. Blessed are those who have not seen, and have believed."**

20:30 Therefore Jesus did many other signs in the presence of his disciples, which are not written in this book; 20:31 but these are written, that you may believe that Jesus is the Christ, the Son of God, and that believing you may have life in his name.

21:1 After these things, Jesus revealed himself again to the disciples at the sea of Tiberias. He revealed himself this way. 21:2 Simon Peter, Thomas called Didymus, Nathanael of Cana in Galilee, and the sons of Zebedee, and two others of his disciples were together. 21:3 Simon Peter said to them, "I'm going fishing."

They told him, "We are also coming with you." They immediately went out, and entered into the boat. That night, they caught nothing. 21:4 But when day had already come, Jesus stood on the beach, yet the disciples didn't know that it was Jesus. 21:5 Jesus therefore said to them, **"Children, have you anything to eat?"**

They answered him, "No."

21:6 He said to them, **"Cast the net on the right side of the boat, and you will find some."**

They cast it therefore, and now they weren't able to draw it in for the multitude of fish. 21:7 That disciple therefore whom Jesus loved said to Peter, "It's the Lord!"

So when Simon Peter heard that it was the Lord, he wrapped his coat around him (for he was naked), and threw himself into the sea. 21:8 But the other disciples came in the little boat (for they were not far from the land, but about two hundred cubitsᵏ away), dragging the net full of fish. 21:9 So when they got out on the land, they saw a fire of coals there, and fish laid on it, and bread. 21:10 Jesus said to them, **"Bring some of the fish which you have just caught."**

21:11 Simon Peter went up, and drew the net to land, full of great fish, one hundred fifty-three; and even though there were so many, the net wasn't torn.

21:12 Jesus said to them, **"Come and eat breakfast."**

None of the disciples dared inquire of him, "Who are you?" knowing that it was the Lord.

21:13 Then Jesus came and took the bread, gave it to them, and the fish likewise. 21:14 This is now the third time that Jesus was revealed to his disciples, after he had risen from the dead. 21:15 So when they had eaten their breakfast, Jesus said to Simon Peter, **"Simon, son of Jonah, do you love me more than these?"**

He said to him, "Yes, Lord; you know that I have affection for you."

He said to him, **"Feed my lambs."** 21:16 He said to him again a second time, **"Simon, son of Jonah, do you love me?"**

He said to him, "Yes, Lord; you know that I have affection for you."

He said to him, **"Tend my sheep."** 21:17 He said to him the third time, **"Simon, son of Jonah, do you have affection for me?"**

Peter was grieved because he asked him the third time, **"Do you have affection for me?"** He said to him, "Lord, you know everything. You know that I have affection for you."

Jesus said to him, **"Feed my sheep. 21:18 Most certainly I tell you, when you were young, you dressed yourself, and walked where you wanted to. But when you are old, you will stretch out your hands, and another will dress you, and carry you where you don't want to go."**

21:19 Now he said this, signifying by what kind of death he would glorify God. When he had said this, he said to him, **"Follow me."**

21:20 Then Peter, turning around, saw a disciple following. This was the disciple whom Jesus sincerely loved, the one who had also leaned on Jesus' breast at the supper and asked, "Lord, who is going to

---

ʲ20:29 TR adds " Thomas,"
ᵏ21:8 200 cubits is about 100 yards or about 91 meters

betray You?" [21:21] Peter seeing him, said to Jesus, "Lord, what about this man?"

[21:22] Jesus said to him, **"If I desire that he stay until I come, what is that to you? You follow me."** [21:23] This saying therefore went out among the brothers[1], that this disciple wouldn't die. Yet Jesus didn't say to him that he wouldn't die, but, **"If I desire that he stay until I come, what is that to you?"** [21:24] This is the disciple who testifies about these things, and wrote these things. We know that his witness is true. [21:25] There are also many other things which Jesus did, which if they would all be written, I suppose that even the world itself wouldn't have room for the books that would be written.

---

[1] 21:23 The word for "brothers" here may be also correctly translated "brothers and sisters" or "siblings."

The Acts of the Apostles

[1:1]The first book I wrote, Theophilus, concerned all that Jesus began both to do and to teach, [1:2]until the day in which he was received up, after he had given commandment through the Holy Spirit to the apostles whom he had chosen. [1:3]To these he also showed himself alive after he suffered, by many proofs, appearing to them over a period of forty days, and speaking about God's Kingdom. [1:4]Being assembled together with them, he commanded them, **"Don't depart from Jerusalem, but wait for the promise of the Father, which you heard from me. [1:5]For John indeed baptized in water, but you will be baptized in the Holy Spirit not many days from now."** [1:6]Therefore, when they had come together, they asked him, "Lord, are you now restoring the kingdom to Israel?"

[1:7]He said to them, **"It isn't for you to know times or seasons which the Father has set within his own authority. [1:8]But you will receive power when the Holy Spirit has come upon you. You will be witnesses to me in Jerusalem, in all Judea and Samaria, and to the uttermost parts of the earth."** [1:9]When he had said these things, as they were looking, he was taken up, and a cloud received him out of their sight. [1:10]While they were looking steadfastly into the sky as he went, behold, two men stood by them in white clothing, [1:11]who also said, "You men of Galilee, why do you stand looking into the sky? This Jesus, who was received up from you into the sky will come back in the same way as you saw him going into the sky."

[1:12]Then they returned to Jerusalem from the mountain called Olivet, which is near Jerusalem, a Sabbath day's journey away. [1:13]When they had come in, they went up into the upper room, where they were staying; that is Peter, John, James, Andrew, Philip, Thomas, Bartholomew, Matthew, James the son of Alphaeus, Simon the Zealot, and Judas the son of James. [1:14]All these with one accord continued steadfastly in prayer and supplication, along with the women, and Mary the mother of Jesus, and with his brothers.

[1:15]In these days, Peter stood up in the midst of the disciples (and the number of names was about one hundred twenty), and said, [1:16]"Brothers, it was necessary that this Scripture should be fulfilled, which the Holy Spirit spoke before by the mouth of David concerning Judas, who was guide to those who took Jesus. [1:17]For he was numbered with us, and received his portion in this ministry. [1:18]Now this man obtained a field with the reward for his wickedness, and falling headlong, his body burst open, and all his intestines gushed out. [1:19]It became known to everyone who lived in Jerusalem that in their language that field was called 'Akeldama,' that is, 'The field of blood.' [1:20]For it is written in the book of Psalms,

'Let his habitation be made desolate.

Let no one dwell therein;'[a]

and,

'Let another take his office.'[b]

[1:21]"Of the men therefore who have accompanied us all the time that the Lord Jesus went in and out among us, [1:22]beginning from the baptism of John, to the day that he was received up from us, of these one must become a witness with us of his resurrection."

[1:23]They put forward two, Joseph called Barsabbas, who was surnamed Justus, and Matthias. [1:24]They prayed, and said, "You, Lord, who know the hearts of all men, show which one of these two you have chosen [1:25]to take part in this ministry and apostleship from which Judas fell away, that he might go to his own place." [1:26]They drew lots for them, and the lot fell on Matthias, and he was numbered with the eleven apostles.

[2:1]Now when the day of Pentecost had come, they were all with one accord in one place. [2:2]Suddenly there came from the sky a sound like the rushing of a

---

[a]1:20 Psalm 69:25
[b]1:20 Psalm 109:8

mighty wind, and it filled all the house where they were sitting. 2:3Tongues like fire appeared and were distributed to them, and one sat on each of them. 2:4They were all filled with the Holy Spirit, and began to speak with other languages, as the Spirit gave them the ability to speak. 2:5Now there were dwelling in Jerusalem Jews, devout men, from every nation under the sky. 2:6When this sound was heard, the multitude came together, and were bewildered, because everyone heard them speaking in his own language. 2:7They were all amazed and marveled, saying to one another, "Behold, aren't all these who speak Galileans? 2:8How do we hear, everyone in our own native language? 2:9Parthians, Medes, Elamites, and people from Mesopotamia, Judea, Cappadocia, Pontus, Asia, 2:10Phrygia, Pamphylia, Egypt, the parts of Libya around Cyrene, visitors from Rome, both Jews and proselytes, 2:11Cretans and Arabians: we hear them speaking in our languages the mighty works of God!" 2:12They were all amazed, and were perplexed, saying one to another, "What does this mean?" 2:13Others, mocking, said, "They are filled with new wine."

2:14But Peter, standing up with the eleven, lifted up his voice, and spoke out to them, "You men of Judea, and all you who dwell at Jerusalem, let this be known to you, and listen to my words. 2:15For these aren't drunken, as you suppose, seeing it is only the third hour of the dayc. 2:16But this is what has been spoken through the prophet Joel:

2:17'It will be in the last days, says God,
that I will pour out my Spirit on all flesh.
Your sons and your daughters will prophesy.
Your young men will see visions.
Your old men will dream dreams.
2:18Yes, and on my servants and on my handmaidens in those days,
I will pour out my Spirit, and they will prophesy.

2:19I will show wonders in the sky above,
and signs on the earth beneath;
blood, and fire, and billows of smoke.
2:20The sun will be turned into darkness,
and the moon into blood,
before the great and glorious day of the Lord comes.
2:21It will be, that whoever will call on the name of the Lord will be saved.'d

2:22"Men of Israel, hear these words! Jesus of Nazareth, a man approved by God to you by mighty works and wonders and signs which God did by him in the midst of you, even as you yourselves know, 2:23him, being delivered up by the determined counsel and foreknowledge of God, you have taken by the hand of lawless men, crucified and killed; 2:24whom God raised up, having freed him from the agony of death, because it was not possible that he should be held by it. 2:25For David says concerning him,

'I saw the Lord always before my face,
For he is on my right hand, that I should not be moved.
2:26Therefore my heart was glad, and my tongue rejoiced.
Moreover my flesh also will dwell in hope;
2:27because you will not leave my soul in Hadese,
neither will you allow your Holy One to see decay.
2:28You made known to me the ways of life.
You will make me full of gladness with your presence.'f

2:29"Brothers, I may tell you freely of the patriarch David, that he both died and was buried, and his tomb is with us to this day. 2:30Therefore, being a prophet, and knowing that God had sworn with an oath to him that of the fruit of his body, according to the flesh, he would raise up the Christ to sit on his throne, 2:31he foreseeing this spoke about the resurrection of the Christ, that neither was his soul left in

---

c2:15 about 9:00 AM
d2:21 Joel 2:28-32
e2:27 or, Hell
f2:28 Psalm 16:8-11

Hades[g], nor did his flesh see decay. [2:32]This Jesus God raised up, to which we all are witnesses. [2:33]Being therefore exalted by the right hand of God, and having received from the Father the promise of the Holy Spirit, he has poured out this, which you now see and hear. [2:34]For David didn't ascend into the heavens, but he says himself, 'The Lord said to my Lord, "Sit by my right hand,

[2:35]until I make your enemies a footstool for your feet."'[h]

[2:36]"Let all the house of Israel therefore know certainly that God has made him both Lord and Christ, this Jesus whom you crucified."

[2:37]Now when they heard this, they were cut to the heart, and said to Peter and the rest of the apostles, "Brothers, what shall we do?"

[2:38]Peter said to them, "Repent, and be baptized, every one of you, in the name of Jesus Christ for the forgiveness of sins, and you will receive the gift of the Holy Spirit. [2:39]For to you is the promise, and to your children, and to all who are far off, even as many as the Lord our God will call to himself." [2:40]With many other words he testified, and exhorted them, saying, "Save yourselves from this crooked generation!"

[2:41]Then those who gladly received his word were baptized. There were added that day about three thousand souls. [2:42]They continued steadfastly in the apostles' teaching and fellowship, in the breaking of bread, and prayer. [2:43]Fear came on every soul, and many wonders and signs were done through the apostles. [2:44]All who believed were together, and had all things in common. [2:45]They sold their possessions and goods, and distributed them to all, according as anyone had need. [2:46]Day by day, continuing steadfastly with one accord in the temple, and breaking bread at home, they took their food with gladness and singleness of heart, [2:47]praising God, and having favor with all the people. The Lord added to the assembly day by day those who were being saved.

[3:1]Peter and John were going up into the temple at the hour of prayer, the ninth hour[i]. [3:2]A certain man who was lame from his mother's womb was being carried, whom they laid daily at the door of the temple which is called Beautiful, to ask gifts for the needy of those who entered into the temple. [3:3]Seeing Peter and John about to go into the temple, he asked to receive gifts for the needy. [3:4]Peter, fastening his eyes on him, with John, said, "Look at us." [3:5]He listened to them, expecting to receive something from them. [3:6]But Peter said, "Silver and gold have I none, but what I have, that I give you. In the name of Jesus Christ of Nazareth, get up and walk!" [3:7]He took him by the right hand, and raised him up. Immediately his feet and his ankle bones received strength. [3:8]Leaping up, he stood, and began to walk. He entered with them into the temple, walking, leaping, and praising God. [3:9]All the people saw him walking and praising God. [3:10]They recognized him, that it was he who used to sit begging for gifts for the needy at the Beautiful Gate of the temple. They were filled with wonder and amazement at what had happened to him. [3:11]As the lame man who was healed held on to Peter and John, all the people ran together to them in the porch that is called Solomon's, greatly wondering.

[3:12]When Peter saw it, he responded to the people, "You men of Israel, why do you marvel at this man? Why do you fasten your eyes on us, as though by our own power or godliness we had made him walk? [3:13]The God of Abraham, Isaac, and Jacob, the God of our fathers, has glorified his Servant Jesus, whom you delivered up, and denied in the presence of Pilate, when he had determined to release him. [3:14]But you denied the Holy and Righteous One, and asked for a murderer to be granted to you, [3:15]and killed the Prince of life, whom God raised from the dead, to which we are witnesses. [3:16]By faith in his name, his name has made this man strong, whom

---

[g]2:31 or, Hell
[h]2:35 Psalm 110:1
[i]3:1 3:00 PM

you see and know. Yes, the faith which is through him has given him this perfect soundness in the presence of you all.

³:¹⁷"Now, brothersʲ, I know that you did this in ignorance, as did also your rulers. ³:¹⁸But the things which God announced by the mouth of all his prophets, that Christ should suffer, he thus fulfilled.

³:¹⁹"Repent therefore, and turn again, that your sins may be blotted out, so that there may come times of refreshing from the presence of the Lord, ³:²⁰and that he may send Christ Jesus, who was ordained for you before, ³:²¹whom heaven must receive until the times of restoration of all things, which God spoke long ago by the mouth of his holy prophets. ³:²²For Moses indeed said to the fathers, 'The Lord God will raise up a prophet for you from among your brothers, like me. You shall listen to him in all things whatever he says to you. ³:²³It will be, that every soul that will not listen to that prophet will be utterly destroyed from among the people.'ᵏ ³:²⁴Yes, and all the prophets from Samuel and those who followed after, as many as have spoken, they also told of these days. ³:²⁵You are the children of the prophets, and of the covenant which God made with our fathers, saying to Abraham, 'In your seed will all the families of the earth be blessed.'ˡ ³:²⁶God, having raised up his servant, Jesus, sent him to you first, to bless you, in turning away everyone of you from your wickedness."

⁴:¹As they spoke to the people, the priests and the captain of the temple and the Sadducees came to them, ⁴:²being upset because they taught the people and proclaimed in Jesus the resurrection from the dead. ⁴:³They laid hands on them, and put them in custody until the next day, for it was now evening. ⁴:⁴But many of those who heard the word believed, and the number of the men came to be about five thousand.

⁴:⁵It happened in the morning, that their rulers, elders, and scribes were gathered together in Jerusalem. ⁴:⁶Annas the high priest was there, with Caiaphas, John, Alexander, and as many as were relatives of the high priest. ⁴:⁷When they had stood them in the middle of them, they inquired, "By what power, or in what name, have you done this?"

⁴:⁸Then Peter, filled with the Holy Spirit, said to them, "You rulers of the people, and elders of Israel, ⁴:⁹if we are examined today concerning a good deed done to a crippled man, by what means this man has been healed, ⁴:¹⁰be it known to you all, and to all the people of Israel, that in the name of Jesus Christ of Nazareth, whom you crucified, whom God raised from the dead, in him does this man stand here before you whole. ⁴:¹¹He is 'the stone which was regarded as worthless by you, the builders, which has become the head of the corner.'ᵐ ⁴:¹²There is salvation in none other, for neither is there any other name under heaven, that is given among men, by which we must be saved!"

⁴:¹³Now when they saw the boldness of Peter and John, and had perceived that they were unlearned and ignorant men, they marveled. They recognized that they had been with Jesus. ⁴:¹⁴Seeing the man who was healed standing with them, they could say nothing against it. ⁴:¹⁵But when they had commanded them to go aside out of the council, they conferred among themselves, ⁴:¹⁶saying, "What shall we do to these men? Because indeed a notable miracle has been done through them, as can be plainly seen by all who dwell in Jerusalem, and we can't deny it. ⁴:¹⁷But so that this spreads no further among the people, let's threaten them, that from now on they don't speak to anyone in this name." ⁴:¹⁸They called them, and commanded them not to speak at all nor teach in the name of Jesus.

⁴:¹⁹But Peter and John answered them, "Whether it is right in the sight of God to

---

ʲ3:17 The word for "brothers" here may be also correctly translated "brothers and sisters" or "siblings."
ᵏ3:23 Deuteronomy 18:15,18-19
ˡ3:25 Genesis 22:18; 26:4
ᵐ4:11 Psalm 118:22

listen to you rather than to God, judge for yourselves, [4:20] for we can't help telling the things which we saw and heard."

[4:21] When they had further threatened them, they let them go, finding no way to punish them, because of the people; for everyone glorified God for that which was done. [4:22] For the man on whom this miracle of healing was performed was more than forty years old.

[4:23] Being let go, they came to their own company, and reported all that the chief priests and the elders had said to them. [4:24] When they heard it, they lifted up their voice to God with one accord, and said, "O Lord, you are God, who made the heaven, the earth, the sea, and all that is in them; [4:25] who by the mouth of your servant, David, said,

'Why do the nations rage,
     and the peoples plot a vain thing?
[4:26] The kings of the earth take a stand,
     and the rulers take council together,
     against the Lord, and against his
         Christ[n].'[o]

[4:27] "For truly, in this city against your holy servant, Jesus, whom you anointed, both Herod and Pontius Pilate, with the Gentiles and the people of Israel, were gathered together [4:28] to do whatever your hand and your council foreordained to happen. [4:29] Now, Lord, look at their threats, and grant to your servants to speak your word with all boldness, [4:30] while you stretch out your hand to heal; and that signs and wonders may be done through the name of your holy Servant Jesus."

[4:31] When they had prayed, the place was shaken where they were gathered together. They were all filled with the Holy Spirit, and they spoke the word of God with boldness. [4:32] The multitude of those who believed were of one heart and soul. Not one of them claimed that anything of the things which he possessed was his own, but they had all things in common. [4:33] With great power, the apostles gave their testimony of the resurrection of the Lord Jesus. Great grace was on them all. [4:34] For neither was there among them any who lacked, for

as many as were owners of lands or houses sold them, and brought the proceeds of the things that were sold, [4:35] and laid them at the apostles' feet, and distribution was made to each, according as anyone had need. [4:36] Joses, who by the apostles was surnamed Barnabas (which is, being interpreted, Son of Encouragement), a Levite, a man of Cyprus by race, [4:37] having a field, sold it, and brought the money and laid it at the apostles' feet.

[5:1] But a certain man named Ananias, with Sapphira, his wife, sold a possession, [5:2] and kept back part of the price, his wife also being aware of it, and brought a certain part, and laid it at the apostles' feet. [5:3] But Peter said, "Ananias, why has Satan filled your heart to lie to the Holy Spirit, and to keep back part of the price of the land? [5:4] While you kept it, didn't it remain your own? After it was sold, wasn't it in your power? How is it that you have conceived this thing in your heart? You haven't lied to men, but to God."

[5:5] Ananias, hearing these words, fell down and died. Great fear came on all who heard these things. [5:6] The young men arose and wrapped him up, and they carried him out and buried him. [5:7] About three hours later, his wife, not knowing what had happened, came in. [5:8] Peter answered her, "Tell me whether you sold the land for so much."

She said, "Yes, for so much."

[5:9] But Peter asked her, "How is it that you have agreed together to tempt the Spirit of the Lord? Behold, the feet of those who have buried your husband are at the door, and they will carry you out."

[5:10] She fell down immediately at his feet, and died. The young men came in and found her dead, and they carried her out and buried her by her husband. [5:11] Great fear came on the whole assembly, and on all who heard these things. [5:12] By the hands of the apostles many signs and wonders were done among the people. They were all with one accord in Solomon's porch. [5:13] None of the rest dared to join them, however the

[n]4:26 Christ (Greek) and Messiah (Hebrew) both mean Anointed One.
[o]4:26 Psalm 2:1-2

people honored them. [5:14]More believers were added to the Lord, multitudes of both men and women. [5:15]They even carried out the sick into the streets, and laid them on cots and mattresses, so that as Peter came by, at the least his shadow might overshadow some of them. [5:16]Multitudes also came together from the cities around Jerusalem, bringing sick people, and those who were tormented by unclean spirits: and they were all healed.

[5:17]But the high priest rose up, and all those who were with him (which is the sect of the Sadducees), and they were filled with jealousy, [5:18]and laid hands on the apostles, and put them in public custody. [5:19]But an angel of the Lord opened the prison doors by night, and brought them out, and said, [5:20]"Go stand and speak in the temple to the people all the words of this life."

[5:21]When they heard this, they entered into the temple about daybreak, and taught. But the high priest came, and those who were with him, and called the council together, and all the senate of the children of Israel, and sent to the prison to have them brought. [5:22]But the officers who came didn't find them in the prison. They returned and reported, [5:23]"We found the prison shut and locked, and the guards standing before the doors, but when we opened them, we found no one inside!"

[5:24]Now when the high priest, the captain of the temple, and the chief priests heard these words, they were very perplexed about them and what might become of this. [5:25]One came and told them, "Behold, the men whom you put in prison are in the temple, standing and teaching the people." [5:26]Then the captain went with the officers, and brought them without violence, for they were afraid that the people might stone them.

[5:27]When they had brought them, they set them before the council. The high priest questioned them, [5:28]saying, "Didn't we strictly command you not to teach in this name? Behold, you have filled Jerusalem with your teaching, and intend to bring this man's blood on us."

[5:29]But Peter and the apostles answered, "We must obey God rather than men. [5:30]The God of our fathers raised up Jesus, whom you killed, hanging him on a tree. [5:31]God exalted him with his right hand to be a Prince and a Savior, to give repentance to Israel, and remission of sins. [5:32]We are His witnesses of these things; and so also is the Holy Spirit, whom God has given to those who obey him."

[5:33]But they, when they heard this, were cut to the heart, and determined to kill them. [5:34]But one stood up in the council, a Pharisee named Gamaliel, a teacher of the law, honored by all the people, and commanded to put the apostles out for a little while. [5:35]He said to them, "You men of Israel, be careful concerning these men, what you are about to do. [5:36]For before these days Theudas rose up, making himself out to be somebody; to whom a number of men, about four hundred, joined themselves: who was slain; and all, as many as obeyed him, were dispersed, and came to nothing. [5:37]After this man, Judas of Galilee rose up in the days of the enrollment, and drew away some people after him. He also perished, and all, as many as obeyed him, were scattered abroad. [5:38]Now I tell you, withdraw from these men, and leave them alone. For if this counsel or this work is of men, it will be overthrown. [5:39]But if it is of God, you will not be able to overthrow it, and you would be found even to be fighting against God!"

[5:40]They agreed with him. Summoning the apostles, they beat them and commanded them not to speak in the name of Jesus, and let them go. [5:41]They therefore departed from the presence of the council, rejoicing that they were counted worthy to suffer dishonor for Jesus' name.

[5:42]Every day, in the temple and at home, they never stopped teaching and preaching Jesus, the Christ.

[6:1]Now in those days, when the number of the disciples was multiplying, a complaint arose from the Hellenists[P] against the Hebrews, because their widows were

---

[P]6:1 The Hellenists used Greek language and culture, even though they were also of Hebrew descent.

neglected in the daily service. ^{6:2}The twelve summoned the multitude of the disciples and said, "It is not appropriate for us to forsake the word of God and serve tables. ^{6:3}Therefore select from among you, brothers, seven men of good report, full of the Holy Spirit and of wisdom, whom we may appoint over this business. ^{6:4}But we will continue steadfastly in prayer and in the ministry of the word."

^{6:5}These words pleased the whole multitude. They chose Stephen, a man full of faith and of the Holy Spirit, Philip, Prochorus, Nicanor, Timon, Parmenas, and Nicolaus, a proselyte of Antioch; ^{6:6}whom they set before the apostles. When they had prayed, they laid their hands on them. ^{6:7}The word of God increased and the number of the disciples multiplied in Jerusalem exceedingly. A great company of the priests were obedient to the faith.

^{6:8}Stephen, full of faith and power, performed great wonders and signs among the people. ^{6:9}But some of those who were of the synagogue called "The Libertines," and of the Cyrenians, of the Alexandrians, and of those of Cilicia and Asia arose, disputing with Stephen. ^{6:10}They weren't able to withstand the wisdom and the Spirit by which he spoke. ^{6:11}Then they secretly induced men to say, "We have heard him speak blasphemous words against Moses and God." ^{6:12}They stirred up the people, the elders, and the scribes, and came against him and seized him, and brought him in to the council, ^{6:13}and set up false witnesses who said, "This man never stops speaking blasphemous words against this holy place and the law. ^{6:14}For we have heard him say that this Jesus of Nazareth will destroy this place, and will change the customs which Moses delivered to us." ^{6:15}All who sat in the council, fastening their eyes on him, saw his face like it was the face of an angel.

^{7:1}The high priest said, "Are these things so?"

^{7:2}He said, "Brothers and fathers, listen. The God of glory appeared to our father Abraham, when he was in Mesopotamia,

before he lived in Haran, ^{7:3}and said to him, 'Get out of your land, and from your relatives, and come into a land which I will show you.'^q ^{7:4}Then he came out of the land of the Chaldaeans, and lived in Haran. From there, when his father was dead, God moved him into this land, where you are now living. ^{7:5}He gave him no inheritance in it, no, not so much as to set his foot on. He promised that he would give it to him for a possession, and to his seed after him, when he still had no child. ^{7:6}God spoke in this way: that his seed would live as aliens in a strange land, and that they would be enslaved and mistreated for four hundred years. ^{7:7}'I will judge the nation to which they will be in bondage,' said God, 'and after that will they come out, and serve me in this place.'^r ^{7:8}He gave him the covenant of circumcision. So Abraham became the father of Isaac, and circumcised him the eighth day. Isaac became the father of Jacob, and Jacob became the father of the twelve patriarchs.

^{7:9}"The patriarchs, moved with jealousy against Joseph, sold him into Egypt. God was with him, ^{7:10}and delivered him out of all his afflictions, and gave him favor and wisdom before Pharaoh, king of Egypt. He made him governor over Egypt and all his house. ^{7:11}Now a famine came over all the land of Egypt and Canaan, and great affliction. Our fathers found no food. ^{7:12}But when Jacob heard that there was grain in Egypt, he sent out our fathers the first time. ^{7:13}On the second time Joseph was made known to his brothers, and Joseph's race was revealed to Pharaoh. ^{7:14}Joseph sent, and summoned Jacob, his father, and all his relatives, seventy-five souls. ^{7:15}Jacob went down into Egypt, and he died, himself and our fathers, ^{7:16}and they were brought back to Shechem, and laid in the tomb that Abraham bought for a price in silver from the children of Hamor of Shechem.

^{7:17}"But as the time of the promise came close which God had sworn to Abraham, the people grew and multiplied in Egypt, ^{7:18}until there arose a different king, who

---

^q7:3 Genesis 12:1
^r7:7 Genesis 15:13-14

didn't know Joseph. [7:19]The same took advantage of our race, and mistreated our fathers, and forced them to throw out their babies, so that they wouldn't stay alive. [7:20]At that time Moses was born, and was exceedingly handsome. He was nourished three months in his father's house. [7:21]When he was thrown out, Pharaoh's daughter took him up, and reared him as her own son. [7:22]Moses was instructed in all the wisdom of the Egyptians. He was mighty in his words and works. [7:23]But when he was forty years old, it came into his heart to visit his brothers[s], the children of Israel. [7:24]Seeing one of them suffer wrong, he defended him, and avenged him who was oppressed, striking the Egyptian. [7:25]He supposed that his brothers understood that God, by his hand, was giving them deliverance; but they didn't understand.

[7:26]"The day following, he appeared to them as they fought, and urged them to be at peace again, saying, 'Sirs, you are brothers. Why do you wrong one another?' [7:27]But he who did his neighbor wrong pushed him away, saying, 'Who made you a ruler and a judge over us? [7:28]Do you want to kill me, as you killed the Egyptian yesterday?'[t] [7:29]Moses fled at this saying, and became a stranger in the land of Midian, where he became the father of two sons.

[7:30]"When forty years were fulfilled, an angel of the Lord appeared to him in the wilderness of Mount Sinai, in a flame of fire in a bush. [7:31]When Moses saw it, he wondered at the sight. As he came close to see, a voice of the Lord came to him, [7:32]'I am the God of your fathers, the God of Abraham, the God of Isaac, and the God of Jacob.'[u] Moses trembled, and dared not look. [7:33]The Lord said to him, 'Take your sandals off of your feet, for the place where you stand is holy ground. [7:34]I have surely seen the affliction of my people that is in Egypt, and have heard their groaning. I have come down to deliver them. Now come, I will send you into Egypt.'[v]

[7:35]"This Moses, whom they refused, saying, 'Who made you a ruler and a judge?'— God has sent him as both a ruler and a deliverer by the hand of the angel who appeared to him in the bush. [7:36]This man led them out, having worked wonders and signs in Egypt, in the Red Sea, and in the wilderness for forty years. [7:37]This is that Moses, who said to the children of Israel, 'The Lord our God will raise up a prophet for you from among your brothers, like me.'[w][x] [7:38]This is he who was in the assembly in the wilderness with the angel that spoke to him on Mount Sinai, and with our fathers, who received living oracles to give to us, [7:39]to whom our fathers wouldn't be obedient, but rejected him, and turned back in their hearts to Egypt, [7:40]saying to Aaron, 'Make us gods that will go before us, for as for this Moses, who led us out of the land of Egypt, we don't know what has become of him.'[y] [7:41]They made a calf in those days, and brought a sacrifice to the idol, and rejoiced in the works of their hands. [7:42]But God turned, and gave them up to serve the army of the sky,[z] as it is written in the book of the prophets,

'Did you offer to me slain animals and
    sacrifices
      forty years in the wilderness, O house
        of Israel?
[7:43]You took up the tent of Moloch,
    the star of your god Rephan,
the figures which you made to worship.

    I will carry you away[a] beyond Babylon.'

---

[s]7:23 The word for "brothers" here and where the context allows may be also correctly translated "brothers and sisters" or "siblings."

[t]7:28 Exodus 2:14

[u]7:32 Exodus 3:6

[v]7:34 Exodus 3:5,7-8,10

[w]7:37 TR adds "You shall listen to him."

[x]7:37 Deuteronomy 18:15

[y]7:40 Exodus 32:1

[z]7:42 This idiom could also be translated "host of heaven," or "angelic beings," or "heavenly bodies."

[a]7:43 Amos 5:25-27

7:44 "Our fathers had the tent of the testimony in the wilderness, even as he who spoke to Moses commanded him to make it according to the pattern that he had seen; 7:45 which also our fathers, in their turn, brought in with Joshua when they entered into the possession of the nations, whom God drove out before the face of our fathers, to the days of David, 7:46 who found favor in the sight of God, and asked to find a habitation for the God of Jacob. 7:47 But Solomon built him a house. 7:48 However, the Most High doesn't dwell in temples made with hands, as the prophet says,
7:49 'heaven is my throne,
　　and the earth a footstool for my feet.
What kind of house will you build me?'
　　says the Lord;
　　'or what is the place of my rest?
7:50 Didn't my hand make all these things?'[b]
7:51 "You stiff-necked and uncircumcised in heart and ears, you always resist the Holy Spirit! As your fathers did, so you do. 7:52 Which of the prophets didn't your fathers persecute? They killed those who foretold the coming of the Righteous One, of whom you have now become betrayers and murderers. 7:53 You received the law as it was ordained by angels, and didn't keep it!"

7:54 Now when they heard these things, they were cut to the heart, and they gnashed at him with their teeth. 7:55 But he, being full of the Holy Spirit, looked up steadfastly into heaven, and saw the glory of God, and Jesus standing on the right hand of God, 7:56 and said, "Behold, I see the heavens opened, and the Son of Man standing at the right hand of God!"

7:57 But they cried out with a loud voice, and stopped their ears, and rushed at him with one accord. 7:58 They threw him out of the city, and stoned him. The witnesses placed their garments at the feet of a young man named Saul. 7:59 They stoned Stephen as he called out, saying, "Lord Jesus, receive my spirit!" 7:60 He kneeled down, and cried with a loud voice, "Lord, don't hold this sin against them!" When he had said this, he fell asleep.

8:1 Saul was consenting to his death. A great persecution arose against the assembly which was in Jerusalem in that day. They were all scattered abroad throughout the regions of Judea and Samaria, except for the apostles. 8:2 Devout men buried Stephen, and lamented greatly over him. 8:3 But Saul ravaged the assembly, entering into every house, and dragged both men and women off to prison. 8:4 Therefore those who were scattered abroad went around preaching the word. 8:5 Philip went down to the city of Samaria, and proclaimed to them the Christ. 8:6 The multitudes listened with one accord to the things that were spoken by Philip, when they heard and saw the signs which he did. 8:7 For unclean spirits came out of many of those who had them. They came out, crying with a loud voice. Many who had been paralyzed and lame were healed. 8:8 There was great joy in that city.

8:9 But there was a certain man, Simon by name, who used to practice sorcery in the city, and amazed the people of Samaria, making himself out to be some great one, 8:10 to whom they all listened, from the least to the greatest, saying, "This man is that great power of God." 8:11 They listened to him, because for a long time he had amazed them with his sorceries. 8:12 But when they believed Philip preaching good news concerning the Kingdom of God and the name of Jesus Christ, they were baptized, both men and women. 8:13 Simon himself also believed. Being baptized, he continued with Philip. Seeing signs and great miracles occurring, he was amazed.

8:14 Now when the apostles who were at Jerusalem heard that Samaria had received the word of God, they sent Peter and John to them, 8:15 who, when they had come down, prayed for them, that they might receive the Holy Spirit; 8:16 for as yet he had fallen on none of them. They had only been baptized in the name of Christ Jesus. 8:17 Then they laid their hands on them, and they received the Holy Spirit. 8:18 Now when Simon saw that the Holy Spirit was given through the laying on of the apostles' hands, he offered them money, 8:19 saying,

b 7:50 Isaiah 66:1-2

"Give me also this power, that whoever I lay my hands on may receive the Holy Spirit." ^{8:20}But Peter said to him, "May your silver perish with you, because you thought you could obtain the gift of God with money! ^{8:21}You have neither part nor lot in this matter, for your heart isn't right before God. ^{8:22}Repent therefore of this, your wickedness, and ask God if perhaps the thought of your heart may be forgiven you. ^{8:23}For I see that you are in the gall of bitterness and in the bondage of iniquity."

^{8:24}Simon answered, "Pray for me to the Lord, that none of the things which you have spoken happen to me."

^{8:25}They therefore, when they had testified and spoken the word of the Lord, returned to Jerusalem, and preached the Good News to many villages of the Samaritans. ^{8:26}But an angel of the Lord spoke to Philip, saying, "Arise, and go toward the south to the way that goes down from Jerusalem to Gaza. This is a desert."

^{8:27}He arose and went; and behold, there was a man of Ethiopia, a eunuch of great authority under Candace, queen of the Ethiopians, who was over all her treasure, who had come to Jerusalem to worship. ^{8:28}He was returning and sitting in his chariot, and was reading the prophet Isaiah.

^{8:29}The Spirit said to Philip, "Go near, and join yourself to this chariot."

^{8:30}Philip ran to him, and heard him reading Isaiah the prophet, and said, "Do you understand what you are reading?"

^{8:31}He said, "How can I, unless someone explains it to me?" He begged Philip to come up and sit with him. ^{8:32}Now the passage of the Scripture which he was reading was this,

"He was led as a sheep to the slaughter.
As a lamb before his shearer is silent,
so he doesn't open his mouth.
^{8:33}In his humiliation, his judgment was taken away.
Who will declare His generation?
For his life is taken from the earth."^c

^{8:34}The eunuch answered Philip, "Who is the prophet talking about? About himself, or about someone else?"

^{8:35}Philip opened his mouth, and beginning from this Scripture, preached to him Jesus. ^{8:36}As they went on the way, they came to some water, and the eunuch said, "Behold, here is water. What is keeping me from being baptized?"

^{8:37d} ^{8:38}He commanded the chariot to stand still, and they both went down into the water, both Philip and the eunuch, and he baptized him.

^{8:39}When they came up out of the water, the Spirit of the Lord caught Philip away, and the eunuch didn't see him any more, for he went on his way rejoicing. ^{8:40}But Philip was found at Azotus. Passing through, he preached the Good News to all the cities, until he came to Caesarea.

^{9:1}But Saul, still breathing threats and slaughter against the disciples of the Lord, went to the high priest, ^{9:2}and asked for letters from him to the synagogues of Damascus, that if he found any who were of the Way, whether men or women, he might bring them bound to Jerusalem. ^{9:3}As he traveled, it happened that he got close to Damascus, and suddenly a light from the sky shone around him. ^{9:4}He fell on the earth, and heard a voice saying to him, **"Saul, Saul, why do you persecute me?"**

^{9:5}He said, "Who are you, Lord?"

The Lord said, **"I am Jesus, whom you are persecuting.^e ^{9:6}But^f rise up, and enter into the city, and you will be told what you must do."**

^{9:7}The men who traveled with him stood speechless, hearing the sound, but seeing no one. ^{9:8}Saul arose from the ground, and when his eyes were opened, he saw no one. They led him by the hand, and brought him into Damascus. ^{9:9}He was without sight for three days, and neither ate nor drank.

^{9:10}Now there was a certain disciple at Damascus named Ananias. The Lord said to him in a vision, **"Ananias!"**

---

^c8:33 Isaiah 53:7,8
^d8:37 TR adds "Philip said, 'If you believe with all your heart, you may.' He answered, 'I believe that Jesus Christ is the Son of God.'"
^e9:5 TR adds "It's hard for you to kick against the goads."
^f9:6 TR omits "But"

He said, "Behold, it's me, Lord."

9:11 The Lord said to him, **"Arise, and go to the street which is called Straight, and inquire in the house of Judah**g **for one named Saul, a man of Tarsus. For behold, he is praying,** 9:12 **and in a vision he has seen a man named Ananias coming in, and laying his hands on him, that he might receive his sight."**

9:13 But Ananias answered, "Lord, I have heard from many about this man, how much evil he did to your saints at Jerusalem. 9:14 Here he has authority from the chief priests to bind all who call on your name."

9:15 But the Lord said to him, **"Go your way, for he is my chosen vessel to bear my name before the nations and kings, and the children of Israel.** 9:16 **For I will show him how many things he must suffer for my name's sake."**

9:17 Ananias departed, and entered into the house. Laying his hands on him, he said, "Brother Saul, the Lord, who appeared to you on the road by which you came, has sent me, that you may receive your sight, and be filled with the Holy Spirit." 9:18 Immediately something like scales fell from his eyes, and he received his sight. He arose and was baptized. 9:19 He took food and was strengthened. Saul stayed several days with the disciples who were at Damascus. 9:20 Immediately in the synagogues he proclaimed the Christ, that he is the Son of God. 9:21 All who heard him were amazed, and said, "Isn't this he who in Jerusalem made havoc of those who called on this name? And he had come here intending to bring them bound before the chief priests!"

9:22 But Saul increased more in strength, and confounded the Jews who lived at Damascus, proving that this is the Christ. 9:23 When many days were fulfilled, the Jews conspired together to kill him, 9:24 but their plot became known to Saul. They watched the gates both day and night that they might kill him, 9:25 but his disciples took him by night, and let him down through the wall, lowering him in a basket. 9:26 When Saul had come to Jerusalem, he tried to join himself to the disciples; but they were all afraid of him, not believing that he was a disciple. 9:27 But Barnabas took him, and brought him to the apostles, and declared to them how he had seen the Lord in the way, and that he had spoken to him, and how at Damascus he had preached boldly in the name of Jesus. 9:28 He was with them entering intoh Jerusalem, 9:29 preaching boldly in the name of the Lord. He spoke and disputed against the Hellenists,i but they were seeking to kill him. 9:30 When the brothersj knew it, they brought him down to Caesarea, and sent him off to Tarsus. 9:31 So the assemblies throughout all Judea and Galilee and Samaria had peace, and were built up. They were multiplied, walking in the fear of the Lord and in the comfort of the Holy Spirit.

9:32 It happened, as Peter went throughout all those parts, he came down also to the saints who lived at Lydda. 9:33 There he found a certain man named Aeneas, who had been bedridden for eight years, because he was paralyzed. 9:34 Peter said to him, "Aeneas, Jesus Christ heals you. Get up and make your bed!" Immediately he arose. 9:35 All who lived at Lydda and in Sharon saw him, and they turned to the Lord.

9:36 Now there was at Joppa a certain disciple named Tabitha, which when translated, means Dorcas.k This woman was full of good works and acts of mercy which she did. 9:37 It happened in those days that she fell sick, and died. When they had washed her, they laid her in an upper chamber. 9:38 As Lydda was near Joppa, the disciples, hearing that Peter was there,

g9:11 or, Judas
h9:28 TR and NU add "and going out"
i9:29 The Hellenists were Hebrews who used Greek language and culture.
j9:30 The word for "brothers" here and where the context allows may also be correctly translated "brothers and sisters" or "siblings."
k9:36 "Dorcas" is Greek for "Gazelle."

sent two men[l] to him, imploring him not to delay in coming to them. 9:39 Peter got up and went with them. When he had come, they brought him into the upper chamber. All the widows stood by him weeping, and showing the coats and garments which Dorcas had made while she was with them. 9:40 Peter put them all out, and kneeled down and prayed. Turning to the body, he said, "Tabitha, get up!" She opened her eyes, and when she saw Peter, she sat up. 9:41 He gave her his hand, and raised her up. Calling the saints and widows, he presented her alive. 9:42 And it became known throughout all Joppa, and many believed in the Lord. 9:43 It happened, that he stayed many days in Joppa with one Simon, a tanner.

10:1 Now there was a certain man in Caesarea, Cornelius by name, a centurion of what was called the Italian Regiment, 10:2 a devout man, and one who feared God with all his house, who gave gifts for the needy generously to the people, and always prayed to God. 10:3 At about the ninth hour of the day[m], he clearly saw in a vision an angel of God coming to him, and saying to him, "Cornelius!"

10:4 He, fastening his eyes on him, and being frightened, said, "What is it, Lord?"

He said to him, "Your prayers and your gifts to the needy have gone up for a memorial before God. 10:5 Now send men to Joppa, and get Simon, who is surnamed Peter. 10:6 He lodges with one Simon, a tanner, whose house is by the seaside.[n]"

10:7 When the angel who spoke to him had departed, Cornelius called two of his household servants and a devout soldier of those who waited on him continually. 10:8 Having explained everything to them, he sent them to Joppa. 10:9 Now on the next day as they were on their journey, and got close to the city, Peter went up on the housetop to pray at about noon. 10:10 He became hungry and desired to eat, but while they were preparing, he fell into a trance. 10:11 He saw heaven opened and a certain container descending to him, like a great sheet let down by four corners on the earth, 10:12 in which were all kinds of four-footed animals of the earth, wild animals, reptiles, and birds of the sky. 10:13 A voice came to him, **"Rise, Peter, kill and eat!"**

10:14 But Peter said, "Not so, Lord; for I have never eaten anything that is common or unclean."

10:15 A voice came to him again the second time, **"What God has cleansed, you must not call unclean."** 10:16 This was done three times, and immediately the vessel was received up into heaven. 10:17 Now while Peter was very perplexed in himself what the vision which he had seen might mean, behold, the men who were sent by Cornelius, having made inquiry for Simon's house, stood before the gate, 10:18 and called and asked whether Simon, who was surnamed Peter, was lodging there. 10:19 While Peter was pondering the vision, the Spirit said to him, "Behold, three[o] men seek you. 10:20 But arise, get down, and go with them, doubting nothing; for I have sent them."

10:21 Peter went down to the men, and said, "Behold, I am he whom you seek. Why have you come?"

10:22 They said, "Cornelius, a centurion, a righteous man and one who fears God, and well spoken of by all the nation of the Jews, was directed by a holy angel to invite you to his house, and to listen to what you say." 10:23 So he called them in and lodged them. On the next day Peter arose and went out with them, and some of the brothers from Joppa accompanied him. 10:24 On the next day they entered into Caesarea. Cornelius was waiting for them, having called together his relatives and his near friends. 10:25 When it happened that Peter entered, Cornelius met him, fell down at his feet, and worshiped him. 10:26 But Peter raised him up, saying, "Stand up! I myself am also a man." 10:27 As he talked with him, he went in and found many

---

[l]9:38 Reading from NU, TR; MT omits "two men"

[m]10:3 3:00 PM

[n]10:6 TR adds "This one will tell you what it is necessary for you to do."

[o]10:19 Reading from TR and NU. MT omits "three"

gathered together. ^{10:28}He said to them, "You yourselves know how it is an unlawful thing for a man who is a Jew to join himself or come to one of another nation, but God has shown me that I shouldn't call any man unholy or unclean. ^{10:29}Therefore also I came without complaint when I was sent for. I ask therefore, why did you send for me?"

^{10:30}Cornelius said, "Four days ago, I was fasting until this hour, and at the ninth hour,^P I prayed in my house, and behold, a man stood before me in bright clothing, ^{10:31}and said, 'Cornelius, your prayer is heard, and your gifts to the needy are remembered in the sight of God. ^{10:32}Send therefore to Joppa, and summon Simon, who is surnamed Peter. He lodges in the house of Simon a tanner, by the seaside. When he comes, he will speak to you.' ^{10:33}Therefore I sent to you at once, and it was good of you to come. Now therefore we are all here present in the sight of God to hear all things that have been commanded you by God."

^{10:34}Peter opened his mouth and said, "Truly I perceive that God doesn't show favoritism; ^{10:35}but in every nation he who fears him and works righteousness is acceptable to him. ^{10:36}The word which he sent to the children of Israel, preaching good news of peace by Jesus Christ— he is Lord of all—^{10:37}that spoken word you yourselves know, which was proclaimed throughout all Judea, beginning from Galilee, after the baptism which John preached; ^{10:38}even Jesus of Nazareth, how God anointed him with the Holy Spirit and with power, who went about doing good and healing all who were oppressed by the devil, for God was with him. ^{10:39}We are witnesses of everything he did both in the country of the Jews, and in Jerusalem; whom they also^q killed, hanging him on a tree. ^{10:40}God raised him up the third day, and gave him to be revealed, ^{10:41}not to all the people, but to witnesses who were chosen before by God, to us, who ate and

drank with him after he rose from the dead. ^{10:42}He commanded us to preach to the people and to testify that this is he who is appointed by God as the Judge of the living and the dead. ^{10:43}All the prophets testify about him, that through his name everyone who believes in him will receive remission of sins."

^{10:44}While Peter was still speaking these words, the Holy Spirit fell on all those who heard the word. ^{10:45}They of the circumcision who believed were amazed, as many as came with Peter, because the gift of the Holy Spirit was also poured out on the Gentiles. ^{10:46}For they heard them speaking in other languages and magnifying God.

Then Peter answered, ^{10:47}"Can any man forbid the water, that these who have received the Holy Spirit as well as we should not be baptized?" ^{10:48}He commanded them to be baptized in the name of Jesus Christ. Then they asked him to stay some days.

^{11:1}Now the apostles and the brothers^r who were in Judea heard that the Gentiles had also received the word of God. ^{11:2}When Peter had come up to Jerusalem, those who were of the circumcision contended with him, ^{11:3}saying, "You went in to uncircumcised men, and ate with them!"

^{11:4}But Peter began, and explained to them in order, saying, ^{11:5}"I was in the city of Joppa praying, and in a trance I saw a vision: a certain container descending, like it was a great sheet let down from heaven by four corners. It came as far as me. ^{11:6}When I had looked intently at it, I considered, and saw the four-footed animals of the earth, wild animals, creeping things, and birds of the sky. ^{11:7}I also heard a voice saying to me, **'Rise, Peter, kill and eat!'** ^{11:8}But I said, 'Not so, Lord, for nothing unholy or unclean has ever entered into my mouth.' ^{11:9}But a voice answered me the second time out of heaven, **'What God has cleansed, don't you call unclean.'** ^{11:10}This was done three

P10:30 3:00 P. M.

q10:39 TR omits "also"

r11:1 The word for "brothers" here and where context allows may also be correctly translated "brothers and sisters" or "siblings."

times, and all were drawn up again into heaven. [11:11]Behold, immediately three men stood before the house where I was, having been sent from Caesarea to me. [11:12]The Spirit told me to go with them, without discriminating. These six brothers also accompanied me, and we entered into the man's house. [11:13]He told us how he had seen the angel standing in his house, and saying to him, 'Send to Joppa, and get Simon, whose surname is Peter, [11:14]who will speak to you words by which you will be saved, you and all your house.' [11:15]As I began to speak, the Holy Spirit fell on them, even as on us at the beginning. [11:16]I remembered the word of the Lord, how he said, **'John indeed baptized in water, but you will be baptized in the Holy Spirit.'** [11:17]If then God gave to them the same gift as us, when we believed in the Lord Jesus Christ, who was I, that I could withstand God?"

[11:18]When they heard these things, they held their peace, and glorified God, saying, "Then God has also granted to the Gentiles repentance to life!"

[11:19]They therefore who were scattered abroad by the oppression that arose about Stephen traveled as far as Phoenicia, Cyprus, and Antioch, speaking the word to no one except to Jews only. [11:20]But there were some of them, men of Cyprus and Cyrene, who, when they had come to Antioch, spoke to the Hellenists,[s] preaching the Lord Jesus. [11:21]The hand of the Lord was with them, and a great number believed and turned to the Lord. [11:22]The report concerning them came to the ears of the assembly which was in Jerusalem. They sent out Barnabas to go as far as Antioch, [11:23]who, when he had come, and had seen the grace of God, was glad. He exhorted them all, that with purpose of heart they should remain near to the Lord. [11:24]For he was a good man, and full of the Holy Spirit and of faith, and many people were added to the Lord.

[11:25]Barnabas went out to Tarsus to look for Saul. [11:26]When he had found him, he brought him to Antioch. It happened, that for a whole year they were gathered together with the assembly, and taught many people. The disciples were first called Christians in Antioch.

[11:27]Now in these days, prophets came down from Jerusalem to Antioch. [11:28]One of them named Agabus stood up, and indicated by the Spirit that there should be a great famine all over the world, which also happened in the days of Claudius. [11:29]As any of the disciples had plenty, each determined to send relief to the brothers who lived in Judea; [11:30]which they also did, sending it to the elders by the hands of Barnabas and Saul.

[12:1]Now about that time, Herod the king stretched out his hands to oppress some of the assembly. [12:2]He killed James, the brother of John, with the sword. [12:3]When he saw that it pleased the Jews, he proceeded to seize Peter also. This was during the days of unleavened bread. [12:4]When he had arrested him, he put him in prison, and delivered him to four squads of four soldiers each to guard him, intending to bring him out to the people after the Passover. [12:5]Peter therefore was kept in the prison, but constant prayer was made by the assembly to God for him. [12:6]The same night when Herod was about to bring him out, Peter was sleeping between two soldiers, bound with two chains. Guards in front of the door kept the prison.

[12:7]And behold, an angel of the Lord stood by him, and a light shone in the cell. He struck Peter on the side, and woke him up, saying, "Stand up quickly!" His chains fell off from his hands. [12:8]The angel said to him, "Get dressed and put on your sandals." He did so. He said to him, "Put on your cloak, and follow me." [12:9]And he went out and followed him. He didn't know that what was being done by the angel was real, but thought he saw a vision. [12:10]When they were past the first and the second guard, they came to the iron gate that leads into the city, which opened to them by itself. They went out, and went down one street, and immediately the angel departed from him.

---

[s]11:20 A Hellenist is someone who keeps Greek customs and culture.

12:11 When Peter had come to himself, he said, "Now I truly know that the Lord has sent out his angel and delivered me out of the hand of Herod, and from everything the Jewish people were expecting." 12:12 Thinking about that, he came to the house of Mary, the mother of John whose surname was Mark, where many were gathered together and were praying. 12:13 When Peter knocked at the door of the gate, a maid named Rhoda came to answer. 12:14 When she recognized Peter's voice, she didn't open the gate for joy, but ran in, and reported that Peter was standing in front of the gate.

12:15 They said to her, "You are crazy!" But she insisted that it was so. They said, "It is his angel." 12:16 But Peter continued knocking. When they had opened, they saw him, and were amazed. 12:17 But he, beckoning to them with his hand to be silent, declared to them how the Lord had brought him out of the prison. He said, "Tell these things to James, and to the brothers." Then he departed, and went to another place.

12:18 Now as soon as it was day, there was no small stir among the soldiers about what had become of Peter. 12:19 When Herod had sought for him, and didn't find him, he examined the guards, and commanded that they should be put to death. He went down from Judea to Caesarea, and stayed there. 12:20 Now Herod was very angry with the people of Tyre and Sidon. They came with one accord to him, and, having made Blastus, the king's personal aide, their friend, they asked for peace, because their country depended on the king's country for food. 12:21 On an appointed day, Herod dressed himself in royal clothing, sat on the throne, and gave a speech to them. 12:22 The people shouted, "The voice of a god, and not of a man!" 12:23 Immediately an angel of the Lord struck him, because he didn't give God the glory, and he was eaten by worms and died.

12:24 But the word of God grew and multiplied. 12:25 Barnabas and Saul returned to† Jerusalem, when they had fulfilled their service, also taking with them John whose surname was Mark.

13:1 Now in the assembly that was at Antioch there were some prophets and teachers: Barnabas, Simeon who was called Niger, Lucius of Cyrene, Manaen the foster brother of Herod the tetrarch, and Saul. 13:2 As they served the Lord and fasted, the Holy Spirit said, "Separate Barnabas and Saul for me, for the work to which I have called them."

13:3 Then, when they had fasted and prayed and laid their hands on them, they sent them away. 13:4 So, being sent out by the Holy Spirit, they went down to Seleucia. From there they sailed to Cyprus. 13:5 When they were at Salamis, they proclaimed the word of God in the Jewish synagogues. They had also John as their attendant. 13:6 When they had gone through the island to Paphos, they found a certain sorcerer, a false prophet, a Jew, whose name was Bar Jesus, 13:7 who was with the proconsul, Sergius Paulus, a man of understanding. This man summoned Barnabas and Saul, and sought to hear the word of God. 13:8 But Elymas the sorcerer (for so is his name by interpretation) withstood them, seeking to turn aside the proconsul from the faith. 13:9 But Saul, who is also called Paul, filled with the Holy Spirit, fastened his eyes on him, 13:10 and said, "Full of all deceit and all cunning, you son of the devil, you enemy of all righteousness, will you not cease to pervert the right ways of the Lord? 13:11 Now, behold, the hand of the Lord is on you, and you will be blind, not seeing the sun for a season!"

Immediately a mist and darkness fell on him. He went around seeking someone to lead him by the hand. 13:12 Then the proconsul, when he saw what was done, believed, being astonished at the teaching of the Lord.

13:13 Now Paul and his company set sail from Paphos, and came to Perga in Pamphylia. John departed from them and returned to Jerusalem. 13:14 But they, passing on from Perga, came to Antioch of Pisidia. They went into the synagogue on the Sabbath day, and sat down. 13:15 After

---
†12:25 TR reads "from" instead of "to"

the reading of the law and the prophets, the rulers of the synagogue sent to them, saying, "Brothers, if you have any word of exhortation for the people, speak."

¹³:¹⁶Paul stood up, and beckoning with his hand said, "Men of Israel, and you who fear God, listen. ¹³:¹⁷The God of this people[u] chose our fathers, and exalted the people when they stayed as aliens in the land of Egypt, and with an uplifted arm, he led them out of it. ¹³:¹⁸For a period of about forty years he put up with them in the wilderness. ¹³:¹⁹When he had destroyed seven nations in the land of Canaan, he gave them their land for an inheritance, for about four hundred fifty years. ¹³:²⁰After these things he gave them judges until Samuel the prophet. ¹³:²¹Afterward they asked for a king, and God gave to them Saul the son of Kish, a man of the tribe of Benjamin, for forty years. ¹³:²²When he had removed him, he raised up David to be their king, to whom he also testified, 'I have found David the son of Jesse, a man after my heart, who will do all my will.' ¹³:²³From this man's seed, God has brought salvation[v] to Israel according to his promise, ¹³:²⁴before his coming, when John had first preached the baptism of repentance to Israel.[w] ¹³:²⁵As John was fulfilling his course, he said, 'What do you suppose that I am? I am not he. But behold, one comes after me the sandals of whose feet I am not worthy to untie.' ¹³:²⁶Brothers, children of the stock of Abraham, and those among you who fear God, the word of this salvation is sent out to you. ¹³:²⁷For those who dwell in Jerusalem, and their rulers, because they didn't know him, nor the voices of the prophets which are read every Sabbath, fulfilled them by condemning him. ¹³:²⁸Though they found no cause for death, they still asked Pilate to have him killed. ¹³:²⁹When they had fulfilled all

things that were written about him, they took him down from the tree, and laid him in a tomb. ¹³:³⁰But God raised him from the dead, ¹³:³¹and he was seen for many days by those who came up with him from Galilee to Jerusalem, who are his witnesses to the people. ¹³:³²We bring you good news of the promise made to the fathers, ¹³:³³that God has fulfilled the same to us, their children, in that he raised up Jesus. As it is also written in the second psalm,

'You are my Son.

Today I have become your father.'[x]

¹³:³⁴"Concerning that he raised him up from the dead, now no more to return to corruption, he has spoken thus: 'I will give you the holy and sure blessings of David.'[y] ¹³:³⁵Therefore he says also in another psalm, 'You will not allow your Holy One to see decay.'[z] ¹³:³⁶For David, after he had in his own generation served the counsel of God, fell asleep, and was laid with his fathers, and saw decay. ¹³:³⁷But he whom God raised up saw no decay. ¹³:³⁸Be it known to you therefore, brothers[a], that through this man is proclaimed to you remission of sins, ¹³:³⁹and by him everyone who believes is justified from all things, from which you could not be justified by the law of Moses. ¹³:⁴⁰Beware therefore, lest that come on you which is spoken in the prophets:

¹³:⁴¹'Behold, you scoffers, and wonder, and perish;

for I work a work in your days,

a work which you will in no way believe, if one declares it to you.'"[b]

¹³:⁴²So when the Jews went out of the synagogue, the Gentiles begged that these words might be preached to them the next Sabbath. ¹³:⁴³Now when the synagogue broke up, many of the Jews and of the

---

[u]13:17 TR, NU add "Israel"
[v]13:23 TR, NU read "a Savior, Jesus" instead of "salvation"
[w]13:24 TR, NU read "to all the people of Israel" instead of "to Israel"
[x]13:33 Psalm 2:7
[y]13:34 Isaiah 55:3
[z]13:35 Psalm 16:10
[a]13:38 The word for "brothers" here and where the context allows may also be correctly translated "brothers and sisters" or "siblings."
[b]13:41 Habakkuk 1:5

devout proselytes followed Paul and Barnabas; who, speaking to them, urged them to continue in the grace of God. [13:44]The next Sabbath almost the whole city was gathered together to hear the word of God. [13:45]But when the Jews saw the multitudes, they were filled with jealousy, and contradicted the things which were spoken by Paul, and blasphemed.

[13:46]Paul and Barnabas spoke out boldly, and said, "It was necessary that God's word should be spoken to you first. Since indeed you thrust it from you, and judge yourselves unworthy of eternal life, behold, we turn to the Gentiles. [13:47]For so has the Lord commanded us, saying,

'I have set you as a light for the Gentiles,

that you should bring salvation to the uttermost parts of the earth.'"[c]

[13:48]As the Gentiles heard this, they were glad, and glorified the word of God. As many as were appointed to eternal life believed. [13:49]The Lord's word was spread abroad throughout all the region. [13:50]But the Jews stirred up the devout and prominent women and the chief men of the city, and stirred up a persecution against Paul and Barnabas, and threw them out of their borders. [13:51]But they shook off the dust of their feet against them, and came to Iconium. [13:52]The disciples were filled with joy with the Holy Spirit.

[14:1]It happened in Iconium that they entered together into the synagogue of the Jews, and so spoke that a great multitude both of Jews and of Greeks believed. [14:2]But the disbelieving[d] Jews stirred up and embittered the souls of the Gentiles against the brothers. [14:3]Therefore they stayed there a long time, speaking boldly in the Lord, who testified to the word of his grace, granting signs and wonders to be done by their hands. [14:4]But the multitude of the city was divided. Part sided with the Jews, and part with the apostles. [14:5]When some of both the Gentiles and the Jews, with their rulers, made a violent attempt to mistreat and stone them, [14:6]they became aware of it, and fled to the cities of Lycaonia,

Lystra, Derbe, and the surrounding region. [14:7]There they preached the Good News.

[14:8]At Lystra a certain man sat, impotent in his feet, a cripple from his mother's womb, who never had walked. [14:9]He was listening to Paul speaking, who, fastening eyes on him, and seeing that he had faith to be made whole, [14:10]said with a loud voice, "Stand upright on your feet!" He leaped up and walked. [14:11]When the multitude saw what Paul had done, they lifted up their voice, saying in the language of Lycaonia, "The gods have come down to us in the likeness of men!" [14:12]They called Barnabas "Jupiter," and Paul "Mercury," because he was the chief speaker. [14:13]The priest of Jupiter, whose temple was in front of their city, brought oxen and garlands to the gates, and would have made a sacrifice along with the multitudes. [14:14]But when the apostles, Barnabas and Paul, heard of it, they tore their clothes, and sprang into the multitude, crying out, [14:15]"Men, why are you doing these things? We also are men of like passions with you, and bring you good news, that you should turn from these vain things to the living God, who made the sky and the earth and the sea, and all that is in them; [14:16]who in the generations gone by allowed all the nations to walk in their own ways. [14:17]Yet he didn't leave himself without witness, in that he did good and gave you[e] rains from the sky and fruitful seasons, filling our hearts with food and gladness."

[14:18]Even saying these things, they hardly stopped the multitudes from making a sacrifice to them. [14:19]But some Jews from Antioch and Iconium came there, and having persuaded the multitudes, they stoned Paul, and dragged him out of the city, supposing that he was dead.

[14:20]But as the disciples stood around him, he rose up, and entered into the city. On the next day he went out with Barnabas to Derbe. [14:21]When they had preached the Good News to that city, and had made many disciples, they returned to Lystra,

---

[c]13:47 Isaiah 49:6

[d]14:2 or, disobedient

[e]14:17 TR reads "us" instead of "you"

Iconium, and Antioch, [14:22]confirming the souls of the disciples, exhorting them to continue in the faith, and that through many afflictions we must enter into the Kingdom of God. [14:23]When they had appointed elders for them in every assembly, and had prayed with fasting, they commended them to the Lord, on whom they had believed.

[14:24]They passed through Pisidia, and came to Pamphylia. [14:25]When they had spoken the word in Perga, they went down to Attalia. [14:26]From there they sailed to Antioch, from where they had been committed to the grace of God for the work which they had fulfilled. [14:27]When they had arrived, and had gathered the assembly together, they reported all the things that God had done with them, and that he had opened a door of faith to the nations. [14:28]They stayed there with the disciples for a long time.

[15:1]Some men came down from Judea and taught the brothers, "Unless you are circumcised after the custom of Moses, you can't be saved." [15:2]Therefore when Paul and Barnabas had no small discord and discussion with them, they appointed Paul and Barnabas, and some others of them, to go up to Jerusalem to the apostles and elders about this question. [15:3]They, being sent on their way by the assembly, passed through both Phoenicia and Samaria, declaring the conversion of the Gentiles. They caused great joy to all the brothers.[f] [15:4]When they had come to Jerusalem, they were received by the assembly and the apostles and the elders, and they reported all things that God had done with them.

[15:5]But some of the sect of the Pharisees who believed rose up, saying, "It is necessary to circumcise them, and to command them to keep the law of Moses."

[15:6]The apostles and the elders were gathered together to see about this matter. [15:7]When there had been much discussion, Peter rose up and said to them, "Brothers,

you know that a good while ago God made a choice among you, that by my mouth the nations should hear the word of the Good News, and believe. [15:8]God, who knows the heart, testified about them, giving them the Holy Spirit, just like he did to us. [15:9]He made no distinction between us and them, cleansing their hearts by faith. [15:10]Now therefore why do you tempt God, that you should put a yoke on the neck of the disciples which neither our fathers nor we were able to bear? [15:11]But we believe that we are saved through the grace of the Lord Jesus,[g] just as they are."

[15:12]All the multitude kept silence, and they listened to Barnabas and Paul reporting what signs and wonders God had done among the nations through them. [15:13]After they were silent, James answered, "Brothers, listen to me. [15:14]Simeon has reported how God first visited the nations, to take out of them a people for his name. [15:15]This agrees with the words of the prophets. As it is written,

[15:16]'After these things I will return.

> I will again build the tent of David,
>   which has fallen.
> I will again build its ruins.

I will set it up,

> [15:17]That the rest of men may seek after
>   the Lord;
> All the Gentiles who are called by my
>   name,

Says the Lord, who does all these things.[h]
> [15:18]All his works are known to God
>   from eternity.'

[15:19]"Therefore my judgment is that we don't trouble those from among the Gentiles who turn to God, [15:20]but that we write to them that they abstain from the pollution of idols, from sexual immorality, from what is strangled, and from blood. [15:21]For Moses from generations of old has in every city those who preach him, being read in the synagogues every Sabbath."

[15:22]Then it seemed good to the apostles and the elders, with the whole assembly, to

---

[f]15:3 The word for "brothers" here and where the context allows may also be correctly translated "brothers and sisters" or "siblings."

[g]15:11 TR adds "Christ"

[h]15:17 Amos 9:11-12

choose men out of their company, and send them to Antioch with Paul and Barnabas: Judas called Barsabbas, and Silas, chief men among the brothers.[i] [15:23]They wrote these things by their hand:

"The apostles, the elders, and the brothers, to the brothers who are of the Gentiles in Antioch, Syria, and Cilicia: greetings. [15:24]Because we have heard that some who went out from us have troubled you with words, unsettling your souls, saying, 'You must be circumcised and keep the law,' to whom we gave no commandment; [15:25]it seemed good to us, having come to one accord, to choose out men and send them to you with our beloved Barnabas and Paul, [15:26]men who have risked their lives for the name of our Lord Jesus Christ. [15:27]We have sent therefore Judas and Silas, who themselves will also tell you the same things by word of mouth. [15:28]For it seemed good to the Holy Spirit, and to us, to lay no greater burden on you than these necessary things: [15:29]that you abstain from things sacrificed to idols, from blood, from things strangled, and from sexual immorality, from which if you keep yourselves, it will be well with you. Farewell."

[15:30]So, when they were sent off, they came to Antioch. Having gathered the multitude together, they delivered the letter. [15:31]When they had read it, they rejoiced over the encouragement. [15:32]Judas and Silas, also being prophets themselves, encouraged the brothers with many words, and strengthened them. [15:33]After they had spent some time there, they were sent back with greetings from the brothers to the apostles. [15:34j] [15:35]But Paul and Barnabas stayed in Antioch, teaching and preaching the word of the Lord, with many others also.

[15:36]After some days Paul said to Barnabas, "Let's return now and visit our brothers in every city in which we proclaimed the word of the Lord, to see how they are doing." [15:37]Barnabas planned to take John, who was called Mark, with them also. [15:38]But Paul didn't think that it was a good idea to take with them someone who had withdrawn from them in Pamphylia, and didn't go with them to do the work. [15:39]Then the contention grew so sharp that they separated from each other. Barnabas took Mark with him, and sailed away to Cyprus, [15:40]but Paul chose Silas, and went out, being commended by the brothers to the grace of God. [15:41]He went through Syria and Cilicia, strengthening the assemblies.

[16:1]He came to Derbe and Lystra: and behold, a certain disciple was there, named Timothy, the son of a Jewess who believed; but his father was a Greek. [16:2]The brothers who were at Lystra and Iconium gave a good testimony about him. [16:3]Paul wanted to have him go out with him, and he took and circumcised him because of the Jews who were in those parts; for they all knew that his father was a Greek. [16:4]As they went on their way through the cities, they delivered the decrees to them to keep which had been ordained by the apostles and elders who were at Jerusalem. [16:5]So the assemblies were strengthened in the faith, and increased in number daily.

[16:6]When they had gone through the region of Phrygia and Galatia, they were forbidden by the Holy Spirit to speak the word in Asia. [16:7]When they had come opposite Mysia, they tried to go into Bithynia, but the Spirit didn't allow them. [16:8]Passing by Mysia, they came down to Troas. [16:9]A vision appeared to Paul in the night. There was a man of Macedonia standing, begging him, and saying, "Come over into Macedonia and help us." [16:10]When he had seen the vision, immediately we sought to go out to Macedonia, concluding that the Lord had called us to preach the Good News to them. [16:11]Setting sail therefore from Troas, we made a straight course to Samothrace, and the day following to Neapolis; [16:12]and from there to Philippi, which is a city of Macedonia, the foremost of the district, a Roman colony. We were staying some days in this city.

---

[i]15:22 The word for "brothers" here and where the context allows may also be correctly translated "brothers and sisters" or "siblings."

[j]15:34 Some manuscripts add: But it seemed good to Silas to stay there.

16:13On the Sabbath day we went forth outside of the city by a riverside, where we supposed there was a place of prayer, and we sat down, and spoke to the women who had come together. 16:14A certain woman named Lydia, a seller of purple, of the city of Thyatira, one who worshiped God, heard us; whose heart the Lord opened to listen to the things which were spoken by Paul. 16:15When she and her household were baptized, she begged us, saying, "If you have judged me to be faithful to the Lord, come into my house, and stay." So she persuaded us.

16:16It happened, as we were going to prayer, that a certain girl having a spirit of divination met us, who brought her masters much gain by fortune telling. 16:17Following Paul and us, she cried out, "These men are servants of the Most High God, who proclaim to us the way of salvation!" 16:18She was doing this for many days.

But Paul, becoming greatly annoyed, turned and said to the spirit, "I command you in the name of Jesus Christ to come out of her!" It came out that very hour. 16:19But when her masters saw that the hope of their gain was gone, they seized Paul and Silas, and dragged them into the marketplace before the rulers. 16:20When they had brought them to the magistrates, they said, "These men, being Jews, are agitating our city, 16:21and set forth customs which it is not lawful for us to accept or to observe, being Romans."

16:22The multitude rose up together against them, and the magistrates tore their clothes off of them, and commanded them to be beaten with rods. 16:23When they had laid many stripes on them, they threw them into prison, charging the jailer to keep them safely, 16:24who, having received such a command, threw them into the inner prison, and secured their feet in the stocks.

16:25But about midnight Paul and Silas were praying and singing hymns to God, and the prisoners were listening to them. 16:26Suddenly there was a great earthquake, so that the foundations of the prison were shaken; and immediately all the doors were opened, and everyone's bonds were loosened. 16:27The jailer, being roused out of sleep and seeing the prison doors open, drew his sword and was about to kill himself, supposing that the prisoners had escaped. 16:28But Paul cried with a loud voice, saying, "Don't harm yourself, for we are all here!"

16:29He called for lights and sprang in, and, fell down trembling before Paul and Silas, 16:30and brought them out and said, "Sirs, what must I do to be saved?"

16:31They said, "Believe in the Lord Jesus Christ, and you will be saved, you and your household." 16:32They spoke the word of the Lord to him, and to all who were in his house.

16:33He took them the same hour of the night, and washed their stripes, and was immediately baptized, he and all his household. 16:34He brought them up into his house, and set food before them, and rejoiced greatly, with all his household, having believed in God.

16:35But when it was day, the magistrates sent the sergeants, saying, "Let those men go."

16:36The jailer reported these words to Paul, saying, "The magistrates have sent to let you go; now therefore come out, and go in peace."

16:37But Paul said to them, "They have beaten us publicly, without a trial, men who are Romans, and have cast us into prison! Do they now release us secretly? No, most certainly, but let them come themselves and bring us out!"

16:38The sergeants reported these words to the magistrates, and they were afraid when they heard that they were Romans, 16:39and they came and begged them. When they had brought them out, they asked them to depart from the city. 16:40They went out of the prison, and entered into Lydia's house. When they had seen the brothers, they encouraged them, and departed.

17:1Now when they had passed through Amphipolis and Apollonia, they came to Thessalonica, where there was a Jewish synagogue. 17:2Paul, as was his custom, went in to them, and for three Sabbath days reasoned with them from the Scriptures,

[17:3]explaining and demonstrating that the Christ had to suffer and rise again from the dead, and saying, "This Jesus, whom I proclaim to you, is the Christ."

[17:4]Some of them were persuaded, and joined Paul and Silas, of the devout Greeks a great multitude, and not a few of the chief women. [17:5]But the unpersuaded Jews took along[k] some wicked men from the marketplace, and gathering a crowd, set the city in an uproar. Assaulting the house of Jason, they sought to bring them out to the people. [17:6]When they didn't find them, they dragged Jason and certain brothers[l] before the rulers of the city, crying, "These who have turned the world upside down have come here also, [17:7]whom Jason has received. These all act contrary to the decrees of Caesar, saying that there is another king, Jesus!" [17:8]The multitude and the rulers of the city were troubled when they heard these things. [17:9]When they had taken security from Jason and the rest, they let them go. [17:10]The brothers immediately sent Paul and Silas away by night to Beroea. When they arrived, they went into the Jewish synagogue.

[17:11]Now these were more noble than those in Thessalonica, in that they received the word with all readiness of the mind, examining the Scriptures daily to see whether these things were so. [17:12]Many of them therefore believed; also of the prominent Greek women, and not a few men. [17:13]But when the Jews of Thessalonica had knowledge that the word of God was proclaimed by Paul at Beroea also, they came there likewise, agitating the multitudes. [17:14]Then the brothers immediately sent out Paul to go as far as to the sea, and Silas and Timothy still stayed there. [17:15]But those who escorted Paul brought him as far as Athens. Receiving a commandment to Silas and Timothy that they should come to him very quickly, they departed.

[17:16]Now while Paul waited for them at Athens, his spirit was provoked within him as he saw the city full of idols. [17:17]So he reasoned in the synagogue with the Jews and the devout persons, and in the marketplace every day with those who met him. [17:18]Some of the Epicurean and Stoic philosophers also[m] were conversing with him. Some said, "What does this babbler want to say?"

Others said, "He seems to be advocating foreign deities," because he preached Jesus and the resurrection.

[17:19]They took hold of him, and brought him to the Areopagus, saying, "May we know what this new teaching is, which is spoken by you? [17:20]For you bring certain strange things to our ears. We want to know therefore what these things mean." [17:21]Now all the Athenians and the strangers living there spent their time in nothing else, but either to tell or to hear some new thing.

[17:22]Paul stood in the middle of the Areopagus, and said, "You men of Athens, I perceive that you are very religious in all things. [17:23]For as I passed along, and observed the objects of your worship, I found also an altar with this inscription: 'TO AN UNKNOWN GOD.' What therefore you worship in ignorance, this I announce to you. [17:24]The God who made the world and all things in it, he, being Lord of heaven and earth, doesn't dwell in temples made with hands, [17:25]neither is he served by men's hands, as though he needed anything, seeing he himself gives to all life and breath, and all things. [17:26]He made from one blood every nation of men to dwell on all the surface of the earth, having determined appointed seasons, and the boundaries of their dwellings, [17:27]that they should seek the Lord, if perhaps they might reach out for him and find him, though he is not far from each one of us. [17:28]'For in him we live, and move, and have our being.' As some of your own poets have said, 'For we are also his offspring.' [17:29]Being then the offspring of God, we ought not to think

---

[k]17:5 TR reads "And the Jews who were unpersuaded, becoming envious and taking along" instead of "But the unpersuaded Jews took along"

[l]17:6 The word for "brothers" here and where the context allows may be also correctly translated "brothers and sisters" or "siblings."

[m]17:18 TR omits "also"

that the Divine Nature is like gold, or silver, or stone, engraved by art and design of man. [17:30]The times of ignorance therefore God overlooked. But now he commands that all people everywhere should repent, [17:31]because he has appointed a day in which he will judge the world in righteousness by the man whom he has ordained; of which he has given assurance to all men, in that he has raised him from the dead."

[17:32]Now when they heard of the resurrection of the dead, some mocked; but others said, "We want to hear you again concerning this."

[17:33]Thus Paul went out from among them. [17:34]But certain men joined with him, and believed, among whom also was Dionysius the Areopagite, and a woman named Damaris, and others with them.

[18:1]After these things Paul departed from Athens, and came to Corinth. [18:2]He found a certain Jew named Aquila, a man of Pontus by race, who had recently come from Italy, with his wife Priscilla, because Claudius had commanded all the Jews to depart from Rome. He came to them, [18:3]and because he practiced the same trade, he lived with them and worked, for by trade they were tent makers. [18:4]He reasoned in the synagogue every Sabbath, and persuaded Jews and Greeks. [18:5]But when Silas and Timothy came down from Macedonia, Paul was compelled by the Spirit, testifying to the Jews that Jesus was the Christ. [18:6]When they opposed him and blasphemed, he shook out his clothing and said to them, "Your blood be on your own heads! I am clean. From now on, I will go to the Gentiles!"

[18:7]He departed there, and went into the house of a certain man named Justus, one who worshiped God, whose house was next door to the synagogue. [18:8]Crispus, the ruler of the synagogue, believed in the Lord with all his house. Many of the Corinthians, when they heard, believed and were baptized. [18:9]The Lord said to Paul in the night by a vision, **"Don't be afraid, but speak and don't be silent; [18:10]for I am with you, and no one will attack you to harm you, for I have many people in this city."**

[18:11]He lived there a year and six months, teaching the word of God among them. [18:12]But when Gallio was proconsul of Achaia, the Jews with one accord rose up against Paul and brought him before the judgment seat, [18:13]saying, "This man persuades men to worship God contrary to the law."

[18:14]But when Paul was about to open his mouth, Gallio said to the Jews, "If indeed it were a matter of wrong or of wicked crime, you Jews, it would be reasonable that I should bear with you; [18:15]but if they are questions about words and names and your own law, look to it yourselves. For I don't want to be a judge of these matters." [18:16]He drove them from the judgment seat.

[18:17]Then all the Greeks laid hold on Sosthenes, the ruler of the synagogue, and beat him before the judgment seat. Gallio didn't care about any of these things.

[18:18]Paul, having stayed after this many more days, took his leave of the brothers,[n] and sailed from there for Syria, together with Priscilla and Aquila. He shaved his head in Cenchreae, for he had a vow. [18:19]He came to Ephesus, and he left them there; but he himself entered into the synagogue, and reasoned with the Jews. [18:20]When they asked him to stay with them a longer time, he declined; [18:21]but taking his leave of them, and saying, "I must by all means keep this coming feast in Jerusalem, but I will return again to you if God wills," he set sail from Ephesus.

[18:22]When he had landed at Caesarea, he went up and greeted the assembly, and went down to Antioch. [18:23]Having spent some time there, he departed, and went through the region of Galatia, and Phrygia, in order, establishing all the disciples. [18:24]Now a certain Jew named Apollos, an Alexandrian by race, an eloquent man, came to Ephesus. He was mighty in the Scriptures. [18:25]This man had been instructed in the way of the Lord; and being

---

[n]18:18 The word for "brothers" here and where the context allows may also be correctly translated "brothers and sisters" or "siblings."

fervent in spirit, he spoke and taught accurately the things concerning Jesus, although he knew only the baptism of John. [18:26] He began to speak boldly in the synagogue. But when Priscilla and Aquila heard him, they took him aside, and explained to him the way of God more accurately.

[18:27] When he had determined to pass over into Achaia, the brothers encouraged him, and wrote to the disciples to receive him. When he had come, he greatly helped those who had believed through grace; [18:28] for he powerfully refuted the Jews, publicly showing by the Scriptures that Jesus was the Christ.

[19:1] It happened that, while Apollos was at Corinth, Paul, having passed through the upper country, came to Ephesus, and found certain disciples. [19:2] He said to them, "Did you receive the Holy Spirit when you believed?"

They said to him, "No, we haven't even heard that there is a Holy Spirit."

[19:3] He said, "Into what then were you baptized?"

They said, "Into John's baptism."

[19:4] Paul said, "John indeed baptized with the baptism of repentance, saying to the people that they should believe in the one who would come after him, that is, in Jesus."

[19:5] When they heard this, they were baptized in the name of the Lord Jesus. [19:6] When Paul had laid his hands on them, the Holy Spirit came on them, and they spoke with other languages and prophesied. [19:7] They were about twelve men in all. [19:8] He entered into the synagogue, and spoke boldly for a period of three months, reasoning and persuading about the things concerning the Kingdom of God.

[19:9] But when some were hardened and disobedient, speaking evil of the Way before the multitude, he departed from them, and separated the disciples, reasoning daily in the school of Tyrannus. [19:10] This continued for two years, so that all those who lived in Asia heard the word of the Lord Jesus, both Jews and Greeks.

[19:11] God worked special miracles by the hands of Paul, [19:12] so that even handkerchiefs or aprons were carried away from his body to the sick, and the evil spirits went out. [19:13] But some of the itinerant Jews, exorcists, took on themselves to invoke over those who had the evil spirits the name of the Lord Jesus, saying, "We adjure you by Jesus whom Paul preaches." [19:14] There were seven sons of one Sceva, a Jewish chief priest, who did this.

[19:15] The evil spirit answered, "Jesus I know, and Paul I know, but who are you?" [19:16] The man in whom the evil spirit was leaped on them, and overpowered them, and prevailed against them, so that they fled out of that house naked and wounded. [19:17] This became known to all, both Jews and Greeks, who lived at Ephesus. Fear fell on them all, and the name of the Lord Jesus was magnified. [19:18] Many also of those who had believed came, confessing, and declaring their deeds. [19:19] Many of those who practiced magical arts brought their books together and burned them in the sight of all. They counted the price of them, and found it to be fifty thousand pieces of silver.° [19:20] So the word of the Lord was growing and becoming mighty.

[19:21] Now after these things had ended, Paul determined in the spirit, when he had passed through Macedonia and Achaia, to go to Jerusalem, saying, "After I have been there, I must also see Rome."

[19:22] Having sent into Macedonia two of those who served him, Timothy and Erastus, he himself stayed in Asia for a while. [19:23] About that time there arose no small stir concerning the Way. [19:24] For a certain man named Demetrius, a silversmith, who made silver shrines of Artemis, brought no little business to the craftsmen, [19:25] whom he gathered together, with the workmen of like occupation, and said, "Sirs, you know that by this business we have our wealth. [19:26] You see and hear, that not at Ephesus alone, but almost throughout all Asia, this Paul has persuaded and turned away many people, saying that they are no gods, that are made with hands. [19:27] Not only is

---

° 19:19 The 50,000 pieces of silver here probably referred to 50,000 drachmas. If so, the value of the burned books was equivalent to about 160 man-years of wages for agricultural laborers

there danger that this our trade come into disrepute, but also that the temple of the great goddess Artemis will be counted as nothing, and her majesty destroyed, whom all Asia and the world worships."

¹⁹:²⁸When they heard this they were filled with anger, and cried out, saying, "Great is Artemis of the Ephesians!" ¹⁹:²⁹The whole city was filled with confusion, and they rushed with one accord into the theater, having seized Gaius and Aristarchus, men of Macedonia, Paul's companions in travel. ¹⁹:³⁰When Paul wanted to enter in to the people, the disciples didn't allow him. ¹⁹:³¹Certain also of the Asiarchs, being his friends, sent to him and begged him not to venture into the theater. ¹⁹:³²Some therefore cried one thing, and some another, for the assembly was in confusion. Most of them didn't know why they had come together. ¹⁹:³³They brought Alexander out of the multitude, the Jews putting him forward. Alexander beckoned with his hand, and would have made a defense to the people. ¹⁹:³⁴But when they perceived that he was a Jew, all with one voice for a time of about two hours cried out, "Great is Artemis of the Ephesians!"

¹⁹:³⁵When the town clerk had quieted the multitude, he said, "You men of Ephesus, what man is there who doesn't know that the city of the Ephesians is temple keeper of the great goddess Artemis, and of the image which fell down from Zeus? ¹⁹:³⁶Seeing then that these things can't be denied, you ought to be quiet, and to do nothing rash. ¹⁹:³⁷For you have brought these men here, who are neither robbers of temples nor blasphemers of your goddess. ¹⁹:³⁸If therefore Demetrius and the craftsmen who are with him have a matter against anyone, the courts are open, and there are proconsuls. Let them press charges against one another. ¹⁹:³⁹But if you seek anything about other matters, it will be settled in the regular assembly. ¹⁹:⁴⁰For indeed we are in danger of being accused concerning this day's riot, there being no cause. Concerning it, we wouldn't be able to give an account of this commotion." ¹⁹:⁴¹When he had thus spoken, he dismissed the assembly.

²⁰:¹After the uproar had ceased, Paul sent for the disciples, took leave of them, and departed to go into Macedonia. ²⁰:²When he had gone through those parts, and had encouraged them with many words, he came into Greece. ²⁰:³When he had spent three months there, and a plot was made against him by Jews as he was about to set sail for Syria, he determined to return through Macedonia. ²⁰:⁴These accompanied him as far as Asia: Sopater of Beroea; Aristarchus and Secundus of the Thessalonians; Gaius of Derbe; Timothy; and Tychicus and Trophimus of Asia. ²⁰:⁵But these had gone ahead, and were waiting for us at Troas. ²⁰:⁶We sailed away from Philippi after the days of Unleavened Bread, and came to them at Troas in five days, where we stayed seven days.

²⁰:⁷On the first day of the week, when the disciples were gathered together to break bread, Paul talked with them, intending to depart on the next day, and continued his speech until midnight. ²⁰:⁸There were many lights in the upper chamber where we^p were gathered together. ²⁰:⁹A certain young man named Eutychus sat in the window, weighed down with deep sleep. As Paul spoke still longer, being weighed down by his sleep, he fell down from the third story, and was taken up dead. ²⁰:¹⁰Paul went down, and fell upon him, and embracing him said, "Don't be troubled, for his life is in him."

²⁰:¹¹When he had gone up, and had broken bread, and eaten, and had talked with them a long while, even until break of day, he departed. ²⁰:¹²They brought the boy in alive, and were greatly comforted.

²⁰:¹³But we who went ahead to the ship set sail for Assos, intending to take Paul aboard there, for he had so arranged, intending himself to go by land. ²⁰:¹⁴When he met us at Assos, we took him aboard, and came to Mitylene. ²⁰:¹⁵Sailing from there, we came the following day opposite Chios. The next day we touched at Samos and stayed at Trogyllium, and the day after we came to Miletus. ²⁰:¹⁶For Paul had determined to sail past Ephesus, that he

---

ᵖ20:8 TR reads "they" instead of "we"

might not have to spend time in Asia; for he was hastening, if it were possible for him, to be in Jerusalem on the day of Pentecost.

20:17 From Miletus he sent to Ephesus, and called to himself the elders of the assembly. 20:18 When they had come to him, he said to them, "You yourselves know, from the first day that I set foot in Asia, how I was with you all the time, 20:19 serving the Lord with all humility, with many tears, and with trials which happened to me by the plots of the Jews; 20:20 how I didn't shrink from declaring to you anything that was profitable, teaching you publicly and from house to house, 20:21 testifying both to Jews and to Greeks repentance toward God, and faith toward our Lord Jesus.q 20:22 Now, behold, I go bound by the Spirit to Jerusalem, not knowing what will happen to me there; 20:23 except that the Holy Spirit testifies in every city, saying that bonds and afflictions wait for me. 20:24 But these things don't count; nor do I hold my life dear to myself, so that I may finish my race with joy, and the ministry which I received from the Lord Jesus, to fully testify to the Good News of the grace of God.

20:25 "Now, behold, I know that you all, among whom I went about preaching the Kingdom of God, will see my face no more. 20:26 Therefore I testify to you this day that I am clean from the blood of all men, 20:27 for I didn't shrink from declaring to you the whole counsel of God. 20:28 Take heed, therefore, to yourselves, and to all the flock, in which the Holy Spirit has made you overseers, to shepherd the assembly of the Lord andr God which he purchased with his own blood. 20:29 For I know that after my departure, vicious wolves will enter in among you, not sparing the flock. 20:30 Men will arise from among your own selves, speaking perverse things, to draw away the disciples after them. 20:31 Therefore watch, remembering that for a period of three years I didn't cease to admonish everyone night and day with tears. 20:32 Now, brothers,s I entrust you to God, and to

the word of his grace, which is able to build up, and to give you the inheritance among all those who are sanctified. 20:33 I coveted no one's silver, or gold, or clothing. 20:34 You yourselves know that these hands served my necessities, and those who were with me. 20:35 In all things I gave you an example, that so laboring you ought to help the weak, and to remember the words of the Lord Jesus, that he himself said, **'It is more blessed to give than to receive.'"**

20:36 When he had spoken these things, he knelt down and prayed with them all. 20:37 They all wept a lot, and fell on Paul's neck and kissed him, 20:38 sorrowing most of all because of the word which he had spoken, that they should see his face no more. And they accompanied him to the ship.

21:1 When it happened that we had parted from them and had set sail, we came with a straight course to Cos, and the next day to Rhodes, and from there to Patara. 21:2 Having found a ship crossing over to Phoenicia, we went aboard, and set sail. 21:3 When we had come in sight of Cyprus, leaving it on the left hand, we sailed to Syria, and landed at Tyre, for there the ship was to unload her cargo. 21:4 Having found disciples, we stayed there seven days. These said to Paul through the Spirit, that he should not go up to Jerusalem. 21:5 When it happened that we had accomplished the days, we departed and went on our journey. They all, with wives and children, brought us on our way until we were out of the city. Kneeling down on the beach, we prayed. 21:6 After saying goodbye to each other, we went on board the ship, and they returned home again.

21:7 When we had finished the voyage from Tyre, we arrived at Ptolemais. We greeted the brothers, and stayed with them one day. 21:8 On the next day, we, who were Paul's companions, departed, and came to Caesarea.

---

q20:21 TR adds "Christ"

r20:28 TR, NU omit "the Lord and"

s20:32 The word for "brothers" here and where the context allows may also be correctly translated "brothers and sisters" or "siblings."

We entered into the house of Philip the evangelist, who was one of the seven, and stayed with him. ²¹:⁹Now this man had four virgin daughters who prophesied. ²¹:¹⁰As we stayed there some days, a certain prophet named Agabus came down from Judea. ²¹:¹¹Coming to us, and taking Paul's belt, he bound his own feet and hands, and said, "Thus says the Holy Spirit: 'So will the Jews at Jerusalem bind the man who owns this belt, and will deliver him into the hands of the Gentiles.'"

²¹:¹²When we heard these things, both we and they of that place begged him not to go up to Jerusalem. ²¹:¹³Then Paul answered, "What are you doing, weeping and breaking my heart? For I am ready not only to be bound, but also to die at Jerusalem for the name of the Lord Jesus."

²¹:¹⁴When he would not be persuaded, we ceased, saying, "The Lord's will be done."

²¹:¹⁵After these days we took up our baggage and went up to Jerusalem. ²¹:¹⁶Some of the disciples from Caesarea also went with us, bringing one Mnason of Cyprus, an early disciple, with whom we would stay.

²¹:¹⁷When we had come to Jerusalem, the brothers received us gladly. ²¹:¹⁸The day following, Paul went in with us to James; and all the elders were present. ²¹:¹⁹When he had greeted them, he reported one by one the things which God had worked among the Gentiles through his ministry. ²¹:²⁰They, when they heard it, glorified God. They said to him, "You see, brother, how many thousands there are among the Jews of those who have believed, and they are all zealous for the law. ²¹:²¹They have been informed about you, that you teach all the Jews who are among the Gentiles to forsake Moses, telling them not to circumcise their children neither to walk after the customs. ²¹:²²What then? The assembly must certainly meet, for they will hear that you have come. ²¹:²³Therefore do what we tell you. We have four men who have taken a vow. ²¹:²⁴Take them, and purify yourself with them, and pay their expenses for them, that they may shave their heads. Then all will know that there is no truth in the things

that they have been informed about you, but that you yourself also walk keeping the law. ²¹:²⁵But concerning the Gentiles who believe, we have written our decision that they should observe no such thing, except that they should keep themselves from food offered to idols, from blood, from strangled things, and from sexual immorality."

²¹:²⁶Then Paul took the men, and the next day, purified himself and went with them into the temple, declaring the fulfillment of the days of purification, until the offering was offered for every one of them. ²¹:²⁷When the seven days were almost completed, the Jews from Asia, when they saw him in the temple, stirred up all the multitude and laid hands on him, ²¹:²⁸crying out, "Men of Israel, help! This is the man who teaches all men everywhere against the people, and the law, and this place. Moreover, he also brought Greeks into the temple, and has defiled this holy place!" ²¹:²⁹For they had seen Trophimus, the Ephesian, with him in the city, and they supposed that Paul had brought him into the temple.

²¹:³⁰All the city was moved, and the people ran together. They seized Paul and dragged him out of the temple. Immediately the doors were shut. ²¹:³¹As they were trying to kill him, news came up to the commanding officer of the regiment that all Jerusalem was in an uproar. ²¹:³²Immediately he took soldiers and centurions, and ran down to them. They, when they saw the chief captain and the soldiers, stopped beating Paul. ²¹:³³Then the commanding officer came near, arrested him, commanded him to be bound with two chains, and inquired who he was and what he had done. ²¹:³⁴Some shouted one thing, and some another, among the crowd. When he couldn't find out the truth because of the noise, he commanded him to be brought into the barracks.

²¹:³⁵When he came to the stairs, it happened that he was carried by the soldiers because of the violence of the crowd; ²¹:³⁶for the multitude of the people followed after, crying out, "Away with him!" ²¹:³⁷As Paul was about to be brought into the barracks, he asked the commanding

officer, "May I speak to you?"

He said, "Do you know Greek? [21:38] Aren't you then the Egyptian, who before these days stirred up to sedition and led out into the wilderness the four thousand men of the Assassins?"

[21:39] But Paul said, "I am a Jew, from Tarsus in Cilicia, a citizen of no insignificant city. I beg you, allow me to speak to the people."

[21:40] When he had given him permission, Paul, standing on the stairs, beckoned with his hand to the people. When there was a great silence, he spoke to them in the Hebrew language, saying,

[22:1] "Brothers and fathers, listen to the defense which I now make to you."

[22:2] When they heard that he spoke to them in the Hebrew language, they were even more quiet. He said, [22:3] "I am indeed a Jew, born in Tarsus of Cilicia, but brought up in this city at the feet of Gamaliel, instructed according to the strict manner of the law of our fathers, being zealous for God, even as you all are this day. [22:4] I persecuted this Way to the death, binding and delivering into prisons both men and women. [22:5] As also the high priest and all the council of the elders testify, from whom also I received letters to the brothers, and traveled to Damascus to bring them also who were there to Jerusalem in bonds to be punished. [22:6] It happened that, as I made my journey, and came close to Damascus, about noon, suddenly there shone from the sky a great light around me. [22:7] I fell to the ground, and heard a voice saying to me, **'Saul, Saul, why are you persecuting me?'** [22:8] I answered, 'Who are you, Lord?' He said to me, **'I am Jesus of Nazareth, whom you persecute.'**

[22:9] "Those who were with me indeed saw the light and were afraid, but they didn't understand the voice of him who spoke to me. [22:10] I said, 'What shall I do, Lord?' The Lord said to me, **'Arise, and go into Damascus. There you will be told about all things which are appointed for you to do.'** [22:11] When I couldn't see for the glory of that light, being led by the hand of those who were with me, I came into Damascus. [22:12] One Ananias, a devout man according to the law, well reported of by all the Jews who lived in Damascus, [22:13] came to me, and standing by me said to me, 'Brother Saul, receive your sight!' In that very hour I looked up at him. [22:14] He said, 'The God of our fathers has appointed you to know his will, and to see the Righteous One, and to hear a voice from his mouth. [22:15] For you will be a witness for him to all men of what you have seen and heard. [22:16] Now why do you wait? Arise, be baptized, and wash away your sins, calling on the name of the Lord.'

[22:17] "It happened that, when I had returned to Jerusalem, and while I prayed in the temple, I fell into a trance, [22:18] and saw him saying to me, **'Hurry and get out of Jerusalem quickly, because they will not receive testimony concerning me from you.'** [22:19] I said, 'Lord, they themselves know that I imprisoned and beat in every synagogue those who believed in you. [22:20] When the blood of Stephen, your witness, was shed, I also was standing by, and consenting to his death, and guarding the cloaks of those who killed him.'

[22:21] "He said to me, **'Depart, for I will send you out far from here to the Gentiles.'**"

[22:22] They listened to him until he said that; then they lifted up their voice, and said, "Rid the earth of this fellow, for he isn't fit to live!"

[22:23] As they cried out, and threw off their cloaks, and threw dust into the air, [22:24] the commanding officer commanded him to be brought into the barracks, ordering him to be examined by scourging, that he might know for what crime they shouted against him like that. [22:25] When they had tied him up with thongs, Paul asked the centurion who stood by, "Is it lawful for you to scourge a man who is a Roman, and not found guilty?"

[22:26] When the centurion heard it, he went to the commanding officer and told him, "Watch what you are about to do, for this man is a Roman!"

[22:27] The commanding officer came and asked him, "Tell me, are you a Roman?"

He said, "Yes."

²²:²⁸The commanding officer answered, "I bought my citizenship for a great price."

Paul said, "But I was born a Roman."

²²:²⁹Immediately those who were about to examine him departed from him, and the commanding officer also was afraid when he realized that he was a Roman, because he had bound him. ²²:³⁰But on the next day, desiring to know the truth about why he was accused by the Jews, he freed him from the bonds, and commanded the chief priests and all the council to come together, and brought Paul down and set him before them.

²³:¹Paul, looking steadfastly at the council, said, "Brothers, I have lived before God in all good conscience until this day."

²³:²The high priest, Ananias, commanded those who stood by him to strike him on the mouth.

²³:³Then Paul said to him, "God will strike you, you whitewashed wall! Do you sit to judge me according to the law, and command me to be struck contrary to the law?"

²³:⁴Those who stood by said, "Do you malign God's high priest?"

²³:⁵Paul said, "I didn't know, brothers, that he was high priest. For it is written, 'You shall not speak evil of a ruler of your people.'"† ²³:⁶But when Paul perceived that the one part were Sadducees and the other Pharisees, he cried out in the council, "Men and brothers, I am a Pharisee, a son of Pharisees. Concerning the hope and resurrection of the dead I am being judged!"

²³:⁷When he had said this, an argument arose between the Pharisees and Sadducees, and the assembly was divided. ²³:⁸For the Sadducees say that there is no resurrection, nor angel, nor spirit; but the Pharisees confess all of these. ²³:⁹A great clamor arose, and some of the scribes of the Pharisees part stood up, and contended, saying, "We find no evil in this man. But if a spirit or angel has spoken to him, let's not fight against God!"

²³:¹⁰When a great argument arose, the commanding officer, fearing that Paul would be torn in pieces by them, commanded the soldiers to go down and take him by force from among them, and bring him into the barracks.

²³:¹¹The following night, the Lord stood by him, and said, **"Cheer up, Paul, for as you have testified about me at Jerusalem, so you must testify also at Rome."**

²³:¹²When it was day, some of the Jews banded together, and bound themselves under a curse, saying that they would neither eat nor drink until they had killed Paul. ²³:¹³There were more than forty people who had made this conspiracy. ²³:¹⁴They came to the chief priests and the elders, and said, "We have bound ourselves under a great curse, to taste nothing until we have killed Paul. ²³:¹⁵Now therefore, you with the council inform the commanding officer that he should bring him down to you tomorrow, as though you were going to judge his case more exactly. We are ready to kill him before he comes near."

²³:¹⁶But Paul's sister's son heard of their lying in wait, and he came and entered into the barracks and told Paul. ²³:¹⁷Paul summoned one of the centurions, and said, "Bring this young man to the commanding officer, for he has something to tell him."

²³:¹⁸So he took him, and brought him to the commanding officer, and said, "Paul, the prisoner, summoned me and asked me to bring this young man to you, who has something to tell you."

²³:¹⁹The commanding officer took him by the hand, and going aside, asked him privately, "What is it that you have to tell me?"

²³:²⁰He said, "The Jews have agreed to ask you to bring Paul down to the council tomorrow, as though intending to inquire somewhat more accurately concerning him. ²³:²¹Therefore don't yield to them, for more than forty men lie in wait for him, who have bound themselves under a curse neither to eat nor to drink until they have killed him. Now they are ready, looking for the promise from you."

²³:²²So the commanding officer let the young man go, charging him, "Tell no one that you have revealed these things

†23:5 Exodus 22:28

to me." [23:23]He called to himself two of the centurions, and said, "Prepare two hundred soldiers to go as far as Caesarea, with seventy horsemen, and two hundred men armed with spears, at the third hour of the night[u]." [23:24]He asked them to provide animals, that they might set Paul on one, and bring him safely to Felix the governor. [23:25]He wrote a letter like this:

[23:26]"Claudius Lysias to the most excellent governor Felix: Greetings.

[23:27]"This man was seized by the Jews, and was about to be killed by them, when I came with the soldiers and rescued him, having learned that he was a Roman. [23:28]Desiring to know the cause why they accused him, I brought him down to their council. [23:29]I found him to be accused about questions of their law, but not to be charged with anything worthy of death or of imprisonment. [23:30]When I was told that the Jews lay in wait for the man, I sent him to you immediately, charging his accusers also to bring their accusations against him before you. Farewell."

[23:31]So the soldiers, carrying out their orders, took Paul and brought him by night to Antipatris. [23:32]But on the next day they left the horsemen to go with him, and returned to the barracks. [23:33]When they came to Caesarea and delivered the letter to the governor, they also presented Paul to him. [23:34]When the governor had read it, he asked what province he was from. When he understood that he was from Cilicia, he said, [23:35]"I will hear you fully when your accusers also arrive." He commanded that he be kept in Herod's palace.

[24:1]After five days, the high priest, Ananias, came down with certain elders and an orator, one Tertullus. They informed the governor against Paul. [24:2]When he was called, Tertullus began to accuse him, saying, "Seeing that by you we enjoy much peace, and that excellent measures are coming to this nation, [24:3]we accept it in all ways and in all places, most excellent Felix, with all thankfulness. [24:4]But, that I don't delay you, I entreat you to bear with us and hear a few words. [24:5]For we have found this man to be a plague, an instigator of insurrections among all the Jews throughout the world, and a ringleader of the sect of the Nazarenes. [24:6]He even tried to profane the temple, and we arrested him.[v] [24:7w] [24:8x]By examining him yourself you may ascertain all these things of which we accuse him."

[24:9]The Jews also joined in the attack, affirming that these things were so. [24:10]When the governor had beckoned to him to speak, Paul answered, "Because I know that you have been a judge of this nation for many years, I cheerfully make my defense, [24:11]seeing that you can recognize that it is not more than twelve days since I went up to worship at Jerusalem. [24:12]In the temple they didn't find me disputing with anyone or stirring up a crowd, either in the synagogues, or in the city. [24:13]Nor can they prove to you the things of which they now accuse me. [24:14]But this I confess to you, that after the Way, which they call a sect, so I serve the God of our fathers, believing all things which are according to the law, and which are written in the prophets; [24:15]having hope toward God, which these also themselves look for, that there will be a resurrection of the dead, both of the just and unjust. [24:16]Herein I also practice always having a conscience void of offense toward God and men. [24:17]Now after some years, I came to bring gifts for the needy to my nation, and offerings; [24:18]amid which certain Jews from Asia found me purified in the temple, not with a mob, nor with turmoil. [24:19]They ought to have been here before you, and to make accusation, if they had anything against me. [24:20]Or else let these men themselves say what injustice they found in me when I stood before the council, [24:21]unless it is for this one thing that I cried standing among them, 'Concerning the resurrection of the dead I am being judged before you today!'"

[u]23:23 about 9:00 PM

[v]24:6 TR adds "We wanted to judge him according to our law,"

[w]24:7 TR adds "but the commanding officer, Lysias, came by and with great violence took him out of our hands,"

[x]24:8 TR adds "commanding his accusers to come to you."

[24:22]But Felix, having more exact knowledge concerning the Way, deferred them, saying, "When Lysias, the commanding officer, comes down, I will decide your case." [24:23]He ordered the centurion that Paul should be kept in custody, and should have some privileges, and not to forbid any of his friends to serve him or to visit him. [24:24]But after some days, Felix came with Drusilla, his wife, who was a Jewess, and sent for Paul, and heard him concerning the faith in Christ Jesus. [24:25]As he reasoned about righteousness, self-control, and the judgment to come, Felix was terrified, and answered, "Go your way for this time, and when it is convenient for me, I will summon you." [24:26]Meanwhile, he also hoped that money would be given to him by Paul, that he might release him. Therefore also he sent for him more often, and talked with him. [24:27]But when two years were fulfilled, Felix was succeeded by Porcius Festus, and desiring to gain favor with the Jews, Felix left Paul in bonds.

[25:1]Festus therefore, having come into the province, after three days went up to Jerusalem from Caesarea. [25:2]Then the high priest and the principal men of the Jews informed him against Paul, and they begged him, [25:3]asking a favor against him, that he would summon him to Jerusalem; plotting to kill him on the way. [25:4]However Festus answered that Paul should be kept in custody at Caesarea, and that he himself was about to depart shortly. [25:5]"Let them therefore," said he, "that are in power among you go down with me, and if there is anything wrong in the man, let them accuse him."

[25:6]When he had stayed among them more than ten days, he went down to Caesarea, and on the next day he sat on the judgment seat, and commanded Paul to be brought. [25:7]When he had come, the Jews who had come down from Jerusalem stood around him, bringing against him many and grievous charges which they could not prove, [25:8]while he said in his defense, "Neither against the law of the Jews, nor against the temple, nor against Caesar, have I sinned at all."

[25:9]But Festus, desiring to gain favor with the Jews, answered Paul and said, "Are you willing to go up to Jerusalem, and be judged by me there concerning these things?"

[25:10]But Paul said, "I am standing before Caesar's judgment seat, where I ought to be tried. I have done no wrong to the Jews, as you also know very well. [25:11]For if I have done wrong, and have committed anything worthy of death, I don't refuse to die; but if none of those things is true that they accuse me of, no one can give me up to them. I appeal to Caesar!"

[25:12]Then Festus, when he had conferred with the council, answered, "You have appealed to Caesar. To Caesar you shall go."

[25:13]Now when some days had passed, Agrippa the King and Bernice arrived at Caesarea, and greeted Festus. [25:14]As he stayed there many days, Festus laid Paul's case before the king, saying, "There is a certain man left a prisoner by Felix; [25:15]about whom, when I was at Jerusalem, the chief priests and the elders of the Jews informed me, asking for a sentence against him. [25:16]To whom I answered that it is not the custom of the Romans to give up any man to destruction, before the accused has met the accusers face to face, and has had opportunity to make his defense concerning the matter laid against him. [25:17]When therefore they had come together here, I didn't delay, but on the next day sat on the judgment seat, and commanded the man to be brought. [25:18]Concerning whom, when the accusers stood up, they brought no charge of such things as I supposed; [25:19]but had certain questions against him about their own religion, and about one Jesus, who was dead, whom Paul affirmed to be alive. [25:20]Being perplexed how to inquire concerning these things, I asked whether he was willing to go to Jerusalem and there be judged concerning these matters. [25:21]But when Paul had appealed to be kept for the decision of the emperor, I commanded him to be kept until I could send him to Caesar."

[25:22]Agrippa said to Festus, "I also would like to hear the man myself."

"Tomorrow," he said, "you shall hear

him."

²⁵:²³So on the next day, when Agrippa and Bernice had come with great pomp, and they had entered into the place of hearing with the commanding officers and principal men of the city, at the command of Festus, Paul was brought in. ²⁵:²⁴Festus said, "King Agrippa, and all men who are here present with us, you see this man, about whom all the multitude of the Jews petitioned me, both at Jerusalem and here, crying that he ought not to live any longer. ²⁵:²⁵But when I found that he had committed nothing worthy of death, and as he himself appealed to the emperor I determined to send him. ²⁵:²⁶Of whom I have no certain thing to write to my lord. Therefore I have brought him forth before you, and especially before you, King Agrippa, that, after examination, I may have something to write. ²⁵:²⁷For it seems to me unreasonable, in sending a prisoner, not to also specify the charges against him."

²⁶:¹Agrippa said to Paul, "You may speak for yourself."

Then Paul stretched out his hand, and made his defense. ²⁶:²"I think myself happy, King Agrippa, that I am to make my defense before you this day concerning all the things that I am accused by the Jews, ²⁶:³especially because you are expert in all customs and questions which are among the Jews. Therefore I beg you to hear me patiently.

²⁶:⁴"Indeed, all the Jews know my way of life from my youth up, which was from the beginning among my own nation and at Jerusalem; ²⁶:⁵having known me from the first, if they are willing to testify, that after the strictest sect of our religion I lived a Pharisee. ²⁶:⁶Now I stand here to be judged for the hope of the promise made by God to our fathers, ²⁶:⁷which our twelve tribes, earnestly serving night and day, hope to attain. Concerning this hope I am accused by the Jews, King Agrippa! ²⁶:⁸Why is it judged incredible with you, if God does raise the dead?

²⁶:⁹"I myself most certainly thought that I ought to do many things contrary to the name of Jesus of Nazareth. ²⁶:¹⁰This I also did in Jerusalem. I both shut up many of the saints in prisons, having received authority from the chief priests, and when they were put to death I gave my vote against them. ²⁶:¹¹Punishing them often in all the synagogues, I tried to make them blaspheme. Being exceedingly enraged against them, I persecuted them even to foreign cities.

²⁶:¹²"Whereupon as I traveled to Damascus with the authority and commission from the chief priests, ²⁶:¹³at noon, O King, I saw on the way a light from the sky, brighter than the sun, shining around me and those who traveled with me. ²⁶:¹⁴When we had all fallen to the earth, I heard a voice saying to me in the Hebrew language, **'Saul, Saul, why are you persecuting me? It is hard for you to kick against the goads.'**

²⁶:¹⁵"I said, 'Who are you, Lord?'

"He said, **'I am Jesus, whom you are persecuting. ²⁶:¹⁶But arise, and stand on your feet, for I have appeared to you for this purpose: to appoint you a servant and a witness both of the things which you have seen, and of the things which I will reveal to you; ²⁶:¹⁷delivering you from the people, and from the Gentiles, to whom I send you, ²⁶:¹⁸to open their eyes, that they may turn from darkness to light and from the power of Satan to God, that they may receive remission of sins and an inheritance among those who are sanctified by faith in me.'**

²⁶:¹⁹"Therefore, King Agrippa, I was not disobedient to the heavenly vision, ²⁶:²⁰but declared first to them of Damascus, at Jerusalem, and throughout all the country of Judea, and also to the Gentiles, that they should repent and turn to God, doing works worthy of repentance. ²⁶:²¹For this reason the Jews seized me in the temple, and tried to kill me. ²⁶:²²Having therefore obtained the help that is from God, I stand to this day testifying both to small and great, saying nothing but what the prophets and Moses said would happen, ²⁶:²³how the Christ must suffer, and how, by the resurrection of the dead, he would be first to proclaim light both to these people and to the Gentiles."

²⁶:²⁴As he thus made his defense, Festus

said with a loud voice, "Paul, you are crazy! Your great learning is driving you insane!" ^{26:25}But he said, "I am not crazy, most excellent Festus, but boldly declare words of truth and reasonableness. ^{26:26}For the king knows of these things, to whom also I speak freely. For I am persuaded that none of these things is hidden from him, for this has not been done in a corner. ^{26:27}King Agrippa, do you believe the prophets? I know that you believe."

^{26:28}Agrippa said to Paul, "With a little persuasion are you trying to make me a Christian?"

^{26:29}Paul said, "I pray to God, that whether with little or with much, not only you, but also all that hear me this day, might become such as I am, except for these bonds."

^{26:30}The king rose up with the governor, and Bernice, and those who sat with them. ^{26:31}When they had withdrawn, they spoke one to another, saying, "This man does nothing worthy of death or of bonds." ^{26:32}Agrippa said to Festus, "This man might have been set free if he had not appealed to Caesar."

^{27:1}When it was determined that we should sail for Italy, they delivered Paul and certain other prisoners to a centurion named Julius, of the Augustan band. ^{27:2}Embarking in a ship of Adramyttium, which was about to sail to places on the coast of Asia, we put to sea; Aristarchus, a Macedonian of Thessalonica, being with us. ^{27:3}The next day, we touched at Sidon. Julius treated Paul kindly, and gave him permission to go to his friends and refresh himself. ^{27:4}Putting to sea from there, we sailed under the lee of Cyprus, because the winds were contrary. ^{27:5}When we had sailed across the sea which is off Cilicia and Pamphylia, we came to Myra, a city of Lycia. ^{27:6}There the centurion found a ship of Alexandria sailing for Italy, and he put us on board. ^{27:7}When we had sailed slowly many days, and had come with difficulty opposite Cnidus, the wind not allowing us further, we sailed under the lee of Crete, opposite Salmone. ^{27:8}With difficulty sailing along it we came to a certain place called Fair Havens, near the city of Lasea.

^{27:9}When much time had passed and the voyage was now dangerous, because the Fast had now already gone by, Paul admonished them, ^{27:10}and said to them, "Sirs, I perceive that the voyage will be with injury and much loss, not only of the cargo and the ship, but also of our lives." ^{27:11}But the centurion gave more heed to the master and to the owner of the ship than to those things which were spoken by Paul. ^{27:12}Because the haven was not suitable to winter in, the majority advised going to sea from there, if by any means they could reach Phoenix, and winter there, which is a port of Crete, looking northeast and southeast.

^{27:13}When the south wind blew softly, supposing that they had obtained their purpose, they weighed anchor and sailed along Crete, close to shore. ^{27:14}But before long, a stormy wind beat down from shore, which is called Euroclydon.^y ^{27:15}When the ship was caught, and couldn't face the wind, we gave way to it, and were driven along. ^{27:16}Running under the lee of a small island called Clauda, we were able, with difficulty, to secure the boat. ^{27:17}After they had hoisted it up, they used cables to help reinforce the ship. Fearing that they would run aground on the Syrtis sand bars, they lowered the sea anchor, and so were driven along. ^{27:18}As we labored exceedingly with the storm, the next day they began to throw things overboard. ^{27:19}On the third day, they threw out the ship's tackle with their own hands. ^{27:20}When neither sun nor stars shone on us for many days, and no small storm pressed on us, all hope that we would be saved was now taken away.

^{27:21}When they had been long without food, Paul stood up in the middle of them, and said, "Sirs, you should have listened to me, and not have set sail from Crete, and have gotten this injury and loss. ^{27:22}Now I exhort you to cheer up, for there will be no loss of life among you, but only of the ship. ^{27:23}For there stood by me this night an angel, belonging to the God whose I am

---

^y27:14 Or, "a northeaster."

and whom I serve, [27:24]saying, 'Don't be afraid, Paul. You must stand before Caesar. Behold, God has granted you all those who sail with you.' [27:25]Therefore, sirs, cheer up! For I believe God, that it will be just as it has been spoken to me. [27:26]But we must run aground on a certain island."

[27:27]But when the fourteenth night had come, as we were driven back and forth in the Adriatic Sea, about midnight the sailors surmised that they were drawing near to some land. [27:28]They took soundings, and found twenty fathoms.[z] After a little while, they took soundings again, and found fifteen fathoms.[a] [27:29]Fearing that we would run aground on rocky ground, they let go four anchors from the stern, and wished for daylight. [27:30]As the sailors were trying to flee out of the ship, and had lowered the boat into the sea, pretending that they would lay out anchors from the bow, [27:31]Paul said to the centurion and to the soldiers, "Unless these stay in the ship, you can't be saved." [27:32]Then the soldiers cut away the ropes of the boat, and let it fall off.

[27:33]While the day was coming on, Paul begged them all to take some food, saying, "This day is the fourteenth day that you wait and continue fasting, having taken nothing. [27:34]Therefore I beg you to take some food, for this is for your safety; for not a hair will perish from any of your heads." [27:35]When he had said this, and had taken bread, he gave thanks to God in the presence of all, and he broke it, and began to eat. [27:36]Then they all cheered up, and they also took food. [27:37]In all, we were two hundred seventy-six souls on the ship. [27:38]When they had eaten enough, they lightened the ship, throwing out the wheat into the sea. [27:39]When it was day, they didn't recognize the land, but they noticed a certain bay with a beach, and they decided to try to drive the ship onto it. [27:40]Casting off the anchors, they left them in the sea, at the same time untying the rudder ropes. Hoisting up the foresail to the wind, they made for the beach. [27:41]But

coming to a place where two seas met, they ran the vessel aground. The bow struck and remained immovable, but the stern began to break up by the violence of the waves.

[27:42]The soldiers' counsel was to kill the prisoners, so that none of them would swim out and escape. [27:43]But the centurion, desiring to save Paul, stopped them from their purpose, and commanded that those who could swim should throw themselves overboard first to go toward the land; [27:44]and the rest should follow, some on planks, and some on other things from the ship. So it happened that they all escaped safely to the land.

[28:1]When we had escaped, then they[b] learned that the island was called Malta. [28:2]The natives showed us uncommon kindness; for they kindled a fire, and received us all, because of the present rain, and because of the cold. [28:3]But when Paul had gathered a bundle of sticks and laid them on the fire, a viper came out because of the heat, and fastened on his hand. [28:4]When the natives saw the creature hanging from his hand, they said one to another, "No doubt this man is a murderer, whom, though he has escaped from the sea, yet Justice has not allowed to live." [28:5]However he shook off the creature into the fire, and wasn't harmed. [28:6]But they expected that he would have swollen or fallen down dead suddenly, but when they watched for a long time and saw nothing bad happen to him, they changed their minds, and said that he was a god.

[28:7]Now in the neighborhood of that place were lands belonging to the chief man of the island, named Publius, who received us, and courteously entertained us for three days. [28:8]It happened that the father of Publius lay sick of fever and dysentery. Paul entered in to him, prayed, and laying his hands on him, healed him. [28:9]Then when this was done, the rest also who had diseases in the island came, and were cured. [28:10]They also honored us with many honors, and when we sailed, they put

---

[z]27:28 20 fathoms = 120 feet = 36.6 meters
[a]27:28 15 fathoms = 90 feet = 27.4 meters
[b]28:1 NU reads "we"

on board the things that we needed.

28:11 After three months, we set sail in a ship of Alexandria which had wintered in the island, whose sign was "The Twin Brothers." 28:12 Touching at Syracuse, we stayed there three days. 28:13 From there we circled around and arrived at Rhegium. After one day, a south wind sprang up, and on the second day we came to Puteoli, 28:14 where we found brothers,c and were entreated to stay with them for seven days. So we came to Rome. 28:15 From there the brothers, when they heard of us, came to meet us as far as The Market of Appius and The Three Taverns. When Paul saw them, he thanked God, and took courage. 28:16 When we entered into Rome, the centurion delivered the prisoners to the captain of the guard, but Paul was allowed to stay by himself with the soldier who guarded him.

28:17 It happened that after three days Paul called together those who were the leaders of the Jews. When they had come together, he said to them, "I, brothers, though I had done nothing against the people, or the customs of our fathers, still was delivered prisoner from Jerusalem into the hands of the Romans, 28:18 who, when they had examined me, desired to set me free, because there was no cause of death in me. 28:19 But when the Jews spoke against it, I was constrained to appeal to Caesar, not that I had anything about which to accuse my nation. 28:20 For this cause therefore I asked to see you and to speak with you. For because of the hope of Israel I am bound with this chain."

28:21 They said to him, "We neither received letters from Judea concerning you, nor did any of the brothers come here and report or speak any evil of you. 28:22 But we desire to hear from you what you think. For, as concerning this sect, it is known to us that everywhere it is spoken against."

28:23 When they had appointed him a day, many people came to him at his lodging. He explained to them, testifying about the Kingdom of God, and persuading them concerning Jesus, both from the law of Moses and from the prophets, from morning until evening. 28:24 Some believed the things which were spoken, and some disbelieved. 28:25 When they didn't agree among themselves, they departed after Paul had spoken one word, "The Holy Spirit spoke rightly through Isaiah, the prophet, to our fathers, 28:26 saying,

'Go to this people, and say,
in hearing, you will hear,
    but will in no way understand.
In seeing, you will see,
    but will in no way perceive.
28:27 For this people's heart has grown callous.
    Their ears are dull of hearing.
    Their eyes they have closed.
Lest they should see with their eyes,
    hear with their ears,
    understand with their heart,
    and would turn again,
    and I would heal them.'d

28:28 "Be it known therefore to you, that the salvation of God is sent to the nations. They will also listen."

28:29 When he had said these words, the Jews departed, having a great dispute among themselves.

28:30 Paul stayed two whole years in his own rented house, and received all who were coming to him, 28:31 preaching the Kingdom of God, and teaching the things concerning the Lord Jesus Christ with all boldness, without hindrance.

---

c28:14 The word for "brothers" here and where context allows may also be correctly translated "brothers and sisters" or "siblings."

d28:27 Isaiah 6:9-10

Paul's Letter to the Romans

[1:1] Paul, a servant of Jesus Christ, called to be an apostle, set apart for the Good News of God, [1:2] which he promised before through his prophets in the holy Scriptures, [1:3] concerning his Son, who was born of the seed of David according to the flesh, [1:4] who was declared to be the Son of God with power, according to the Spirit of holiness, by the resurrection from the dead, Jesus Christ our Lord, [1:5] through whom we received grace and apostleship, for obedience of faith among all the nations, for his name's sake; [1:6] among whom you are also called to belong to Jesus Christ; [1:7] to all who are in Rome, beloved of God, called to be saints: Grace to you and peace from God our Father and the Lord Jesus Christ.

[1:8] First, I thank my God through Jesus Christ for all of you, that your faith is proclaimed throughout the whole world. [1:9] For God is my witness, whom I serve in my spirit in the Good News of his Son, how unceasingly I make mention of you always in my prayers, [1:10] requesting, if by any means now at last I may be prospered by the will of God to come to you. [1:11] For I long to see you, that I may impart to you some spiritual gift, to the end that you may be established; [1:12] that is, that I with you may be encouraged in you, each of us by the other's faith, both yours and mine.

[1:13] Now I don't desire to have you unaware, brothers, that I often planned to come to you, and was hindered so far, that I might have some fruit among you also, even as among the rest of the Gentiles. [1:14] I am debtor both to Greeks and to foreigners, both to the wise and to the foolish. [1:15] So, as much as is in me, I am eager to preach the Good News to you also who are in Rome. [1:16] For I am not ashamed of the Good News of Christ, for it is the power of God for salvation for everyone who believes; for the Jew first, and also for the Greek. [1:17] For in it is revealed God's righteousness from faith to faith. As it is written, "But the righteous shall live by faith."[a] [1:18] For the wrath of God is revealed from heaven against all ungodliness and unrighteousness of men, who suppress the truth in unrighteousness, [1:19] because that which is known of God is revealed in them, for God revealed it to them. [1:20] For the invisible things of him since the creation of the world are clearly seen, being perceived through the things that are made, even his everlasting power and divinity; that they may be without excuse. [1:21] Because, knowing God, they didn't glorify him as God, neither gave thanks, but became vain in their reasoning, and their senseless heart was darkened.

[1:22] Professing themselves to be wise, they became fools, [1:23] and traded the glory of the incorruptible God for the likeness of an image of corruptible man, and of birds, and four-footed animals, and creeping things. [1:24] Therefore God also gave them up in the lusts of their hearts to uncleanness, that their bodies should be dishonored among themselves, [1:25] who exchanged the truth of God for a lie, and worshiped and served the creature rather than the Creator, who is blessed forever. Amen.

[1:26] For this reason, God gave them up to vile passions. For their women changed the natural function into that which is against nature. [1:27] Likewise also the men, leaving the natural function of the woman, burned in their lust toward one another, men doing what is inappropriate with men, and receiving in themselves the due penalty of their error. [1:28] Even as they refused to have God in their knowledge, God gave them up to a reprobate mind, to do those things which are not fitting; [1:29] being filled with all unrighteousness, sexual immorality, wickedness, covetousness, maliciousness; full of envy, murder, strife, deceit, evil habits, secret slanderers, [1:30] backbiters, hateful to God, insolent, haughty, boastful, inventors of evil things, disobedient to parents, [1:31] without understanding, covenant breakers, without natural affection, unforgiving, unmerciful; [1:32] who, knowing the ordinance of God, that those who practice such things are worthy of death, not only

---

[a] 1:17 Habakkuk 2:4

do the same, but also approve of those who practice them.

²:¹Therefore you are without excuse, O man, whoever you are who judge. For in that which you judge another, you condemn yourself. For you who judge practice the same things. ²:²We know that the judgment of God is according to truth against those who practice such things. ²:³Do you think this, O man who judges those who practice such things, and do the same, that you will escape the judgment of God? ²:⁴Or do you despise the riches of his goodness, forbearance, and patience, not knowing that the goodness of God leads you to repentance? ²:⁵But according to your hardness and unrepentant heart you are treasuring up for yourself wrath in the day of wrath, revelation, and of the righteous judgment of God; ²:⁶who "will pay back to everyone according to their works:"[b] ²:⁷to those who by patience in well-doing seek for glory, honor, and incorruptibility, eternal life; ²:⁸but to those who are self-seeking, and don't obey the truth, but obey unrighteousness, will be wrath and indignation, ²:⁹oppression and anguish, on every soul of man who works evil, to the Jew first, and also to the Greek.

²:¹⁰But glory, honor, and peace go to every man who works good, to the Jew first, and also to the Greek. ²:¹¹For there is no partiality with God. ²:¹²For as many as have sinned without law will also perish without the law. As many as have sinned under the law will be judged by the law. ²:¹³For it isn't the hearers of the law who are righteous before God, but the doers of the law will be justified ²:¹⁴(for when Gentiles who don't have the law do by nature the things of the law, these, not having the law, are a law to themselves, ²:¹⁵in that they show the work of the law written in their hearts, their conscience testifying with them, and their thoughts among themselves accusing or else excusing them) ²:¹⁶in the day when God will judge the secrets of men, according to my Good News, by Jesus Christ.

²:¹⁷Indeed you bear the name of a Jew,

and rest on the law, and glory in God, ²:¹⁸and know his will, and approve the things that are excellent, being instructed out of the law, ²:¹⁹and are confident that you yourself are a guide of the blind, a light to those who are in darkness, ²:²⁰a corrector of the foolish, a teacher of babies, having in the law the form of knowledge and of the truth. ²:²¹You therefore who teach another, don't you teach yourself? You who preach that a man shouldn't steal, do you steal? ²:²²You who say a man shouldn't commit adultery. Do you commit adultery? You who abhor idols, do you rob temples? ²:²³You who glory in the law, through your disobedience of the law do you dishonor God? ²:²⁴For "the name of God is blasphemed among the Gentiles because of you,"[c] just as it is written. ²:²⁵For circumcision indeed profits, if you are a doer of the law, but if you are a transgressor of the law, your circumcision has become uncircumcision. ²:²⁶If therefore the uncircumcised keep the ordinances of the law, won't his uncircumcision be accounted as circumcision? ²:²⁷Won't the uncircumcision which is by nature, if it fulfills the law, judge you, who with the letter and circumcision are a transgressor of the law? ²:²⁸For he is not a Jew who is one outwardly, neither is that circumcision which is outward in the flesh; ²:²⁹but he is a Jew who is one inwardly, and circumcision is that of the heart, in the spirit not in the letter; whose praise is not from men, but from God.

³:¹Then what advantage does the Jew have? Or what is the profit of circumcision? ³:²Much in every way! Because first of all, they were entrusted with the oracles of God. ³:³For what if some were without faith? Will their lack of faith nullify the faithfulness of God? ³:⁴May it never be! Yes, let God be found true, but every man a liar. As it is written,

"That you might be justified in your words,

and might prevail when you come into

---

[b]2:6 Psalm 62:12; Proverbs 24:12
[c]2:24 Isaiah 52:5; Ezekiel 36:22

judgment."[d]

[3:5] But if our unrighteousness commends the righteousness of God, what will we say? Is God unrighteous who inflicts wrath? I speak like men do. [3:6] May it never be! For then how will God judge the world? [3:7] For if the truth of God through my lie abounded to his glory, why am I also still judged as a sinner? [3:8] Why not (as we are slanderously reported, and as some affirm that we say), "Let us do evil, that good may come?" Those who say so are justly condemned. [3:9] What then? Are we better than they? No, in no way. For we previously warned both Jews and Greeks, that they are all under sin. [3:10] As it is written,

"There is no one righteous;
    no, not one.
[3:11] There is no one who understands.
    There is no one who seeks after God.
[3:12] They have all turned aside.
    They have together become unprofitable.
There is no one who does good,
    no, not, so much as one."[e]
[3:13] "Their throat is an open tomb.
    With their tongues they have used deceit."[f]
"The poison of vipers is under their lips;"[g]
    [3:14] "Whose mouth is full of cursing and bitterness."[h]
[3:15] "Their feet are swift to shed blood.
    [3:16] Destruction and misery are in their ways.
    [3:17] The way of peace, they haven't known."[i]
[3:18] "There is no fear of God before their eyes."[j]

[3:19] Now we know that whatever things the law says, it speaks to those who are under the law, that every mouth may be closed, and all the world may be brought under the judgment of God. [3:20] Because by the works of the law, no flesh will be justified in his sight. For through the law comes the knowledge of sin. [3:21] But now apart from the law, a righteousness of God has been revealed, being testified by the law and the prophets; [3:22] even the righteousness of God through faith in Jesus Christ to all and on all those who believe. For there is no distinction, [3:23] for all have sinned, and fall short of the glory of God; [3:24] being justified freely by his grace through the redemption that is in Christ Jesus; [3:25] whom God set forth to be an atoning sacrifice[k], through faith in his blood, for a demonstration of his righteousness through the passing over of prior sins, in God's forbearance; [3:26] to demonstrate his righteousness at this present time; that he might himself be just, and the justifier of him who has faith in Jesus.

[3:27] Where then is the boasting? It is excluded. By what manner of law? Of works? No, but by a law of faith. [3:28] We maintain therefore that a man is justified by faith apart from the works of the law. [3:29] Or is God the God of Jews only? Isn't he the God of Gentiles also? Yes, of Gentiles also, [3:30] since indeed there is one God who will justify the circumcised by faith, and the uncircumcised through faith. [3:31] Do we then nullify the law through faith? May it never be! No, we establish the law.

[4:1] What then will we say that Abraham, our forefather, has found according to the flesh? [4:2] For if Abraham was justified by works, he has something to boast about, but not toward God. [4:3] For what does the Scripture say? "Abraham believed God, and it was accounted to him for righteousness."[l] [4:4] Now to him who works, the reward is not counted as grace, but as debt. [4:5] But to him who doesn't work, but believes in him who justifies the ungodly,

[d]3:4 Psalm 51:4
[e]3:12 Psalms 14:1-3; 53:1-3; Ecclesiastes 7:20
[f]3:13 Psalm 5:9
[g]3:13 Psalm 140:3
[h]3:14 Psalm 10:7
[i]3:17 Isaiah 59:7-8
[j]3:18 Psalm 36:1
[k]3:25 or, a propitiation
[l]4:3 Genesis 15:6

his faith is accounted for righteousness. [4:6]Even as David also pronounces blessing on the man to whom God counts righteousness apart from works,

[4:7]"Blessed are they whose iniquities are forgiven,

whose sins are covered.

[4:8]Blessed is the man whom the Lord will by no means charge with sin."[m]

[4:9]Is this blessing then pronounced on the circumcised, or on the uncircumcised also? For we say that faith was accounted to Abraham for righteousness. [4:10]How then was it counted? When he was in circumcision, or in uncircumcision? Not in circumcision, but in uncircumcision. [4:11]He received the sign of circumcision, a seal of the righteousness of the faith which he had while he was in uncircumcision, that he might be the father of all those who believe, though they be in uncircumcision, that righteousness might also be accounted to them. [4:12]The father of circumcision to those who not only are of the circumcision, but who also walk in the steps of that faith of our father Abraham, which he had in uncircumcision. [4:13]For the promise to Abraham and to his seed that he should be heir of the world wasn't through the law, but through the righteousness of faith. [4:14]For if those who are of the law are heirs, faith is made void, and the promise is made of no effect. [4:15]For the law works wrath, for where there is no law, neither is there disobedience. [4:16]For this cause it is of faith, that it may be according to grace, to the end that the promise may be sure to all the seed, not to that only which is of the law, but to that also which is of the faith of Abraham, who is the father of us all. [4:17]As it is written, "I have made you a father of many nations."[n] This is in the presence of him whom he believed: God, who gives life to the dead, and calls the things that are not, as though they were. [4:18]Who in hope believed against hope, to the end that he might become a father of many nations, according to that

which had been spoken, "So will your seed be."[o] [4:19]Without being weakened in faith, he didn't consider his own body, already having been worn out, (he being about a hundred years old), and the deadness of Sarah's womb. [4:20]Yet, looking to the promise of God, he didn't waver through unbelief, but grew strong through faith, giving glory to God, [4:21]and being fully assured that what he had promised, he was able also to perform. [4:22]Therefore it also was "reckoned to him for righteousness."[p] [4:23]Now it was not written that it was accounted to him for his sake alone, [4:24]but for our sake also, to whom it will be accounted, who believe in him who raised Jesus, our Lord, from the dead, [4:25]who was delivered up for our trespasses, and was raised for our justification.

[5:1]Being therefore justified by faith, we have peace with God through our Lord Jesus Christ; [5:2]through whom we also have our access by faith into this grace in which we stand. We rejoice in hope of the glory of God. [5:3]Not only this, but we also rejoice in our sufferings, knowing that suffering works perseverance; [5:4]and perseverance, proven character; and proven character, hope: [5:5]and hope doesn't disappoint us, because God's love has been poured out into our hearts through the Holy Spirit who was given to us. [5:6]For while we were yet weak, at the right time Christ died for the ungodly. [5:7]For one will hardly die for a righteous man. Yet perhaps for a righteous person someone would even dare to die. [5:8]But God commends his own love toward us, in that while we were yet sinners, Christ died for us.

[5:9]Much more then, being now justified by his blood, we will be saved from God's wrath through him. [5:10]For if, while we were enemies, we were reconciled to God through the death of his Son, much more, being reconciled, we will be saved by his life.

[5:11]Not only so, but we also rejoice in God through our Lord Jesus Christ, through

---

[m]4:8 Psalm 32:1-2
[n]4:17 Genesis 17:5
[o]4:18 Genesis 15:5
[p]4:22 Genesis 15:6

whom we have now received the reconciliation. [5:12]Therefore, as sin entered into the world through one man, and death through sin; and so death passed to all men, because all sinned. [5:13]For until the law, sin was in the world; but sin is not charged when there is no law. [5:14]Nevertheless death reigned from Adam until Moses, even over those whose sins weren't like Adam's disobedience, who is a foreshadowing of him who was to come. [5:15]But the free gift isn't like the trespass. For if by the trespass of the one the many died, much more did the grace of God, and the gift by the grace of the one man, Jesus Christ, abound to the many. [5:16]The gift is not as through one who sinned: for the judgment came by one to condemnation, but the free gift came of many trespasses to justification. [5:17]For if by the trespass of the one, death reigned through the one; so much more will those who receive the abundance of grace and of the gift of righteousness reign in life through the one, Jesus Christ. [5:18]So then as through one trespass, all men were condemned; even so through one act of righteousness, all men were justified to life. [5:19]For as through the one man's disobedience many were made sinners, even so through the obedience of the one, many will be made righteous. [5:20]The law came in besides, that the trespass might abound; but where sin abounded, grace abounded more exceedingly; [5:21]that as sin reigned in death, even so grace might reign through righteousness to eternal life through Jesus Christ our Lord.

[6:1]What shall we say then? Shall we continue in sin, that grace may abound? [6:2]May it never be! We who died to sin, how could we live in it any longer? [6:3]Or don't you know that all we who were baptized into Christ Jesus were baptized into his death? [6:4]We were buried therefore with him through baptism to death, that just like Christ was raised from the dead through the glory of the Father, so we also might walk in newness of life. [6:5]For if we have become united with him in the likeness of his death, we will also be part of his resurrection; [6:6]knowing this, that our old man was crucified with him, that the body of sin might be done away with, so that we would no longer be in bondage to sin. [6:7]For he who has died has been freed from sin. [6:8]But if we died with Christ, we believe that we will also live with him; [6:9]knowing that Christ, being raised from the dead, dies no more. Death no more has dominion over him! [6:10]For the death that he died, he died to sin one time; but the life that he lives, he lives to God. [6:11]Thus consider yourselves also to be dead to sin, but alive to God in Christ Jesus our Lord.

[6:12]Therefore don't let sin reign in your mortal body, that you should obey it in its lusts. [6:13]Neither present your members to sin as instruments of unrighteousness, but present yourselves to God, as alive from the dead, and your members as instruments of righteousness to God. [6:14]For sin will not have dominion over you. For you are not under law, but under grace. [6:15]What then? Shall we sin, because we are not under law, but under grace? May it never be! [6:16]Don't you know that to whom you present yourselves as servants to obedience, his servants you are whom you obey; whether of sin to death, or of obedience to righteousness? [6:17]But thanks be to God, that, whereas you were bondservants of sin, you became obedient from the heart to that form of teaching whereunto you were delivered. [6:18]Being made free from sin, you became bondservants of righteousness.

[6:19]I speak in human terms because of the weakness of your flesh, for as you presented your members as servants to uncleanness and to wickedness upon wickedness, even so now present your members as servants to righteousness for sanctification. [6:20]For when you were servants of sin, you were free in regard to righteousness. [6:21]What fruit then did you have at that time in the things of which you are now ashamed? For the end of those things is death. [6:22]But now, being made free from sin, and having become servants of God, you have your fruit of sanctification, and the result of eternal life. [6:23]For the wages of sin is death, but the free gift of God is eternal life in Christ Jesus our Lord.

^{7:1}Or don't you know, brothers^q (for I speak to men who know the law), that the law has dominion over a man for as long as he lives? ^{7:2}For the woman that has a husband is bound by law to the husband while he lives, but if the husband dies, she is discharged from the law of the husband. ^{7:3}So then if, while the husband lives, she is joined to another man, she would be called an adulteress. But if the husband dies, she is free from the law, so that she is no adulteress, though she is joined to another man. ^{7:4}Therefore, my brothers, you also were made dead to the law through the body of Christ, that you would be joined to another, to him who was raised from the dead, that we might bring forth fruit to God. ^{7:5}For when we were in the flesh, the sinful passions which were through the law, worked in our members to bring forth fruit to death. ^{7:6}But now we have been discharged from the law, having died to that in which we were held; so that we serve in newness of the spirit, and not in oldness of the letter.

^{7:7}What shall we say then? Is the law sin? May it never be! However, I wouldn't have known sin, except through the law. For I wouldn't have known coveting, unless the law had said, "You shall not covet."^r ^{7:8}But sin, finding occasion through the commandment, produced in me all kinds of coveting. For apart from the law, sin is dead. ^{7:9}I was alive apart from the law once, but when the commandment came, sin revived, and I died. ^{7:10}The commandment, which was for life, this I found to be for death; ^{7:11}for sin, finding occasion through the commandment, deceived me, and through it killed me. ^{7:12}Therefore the law indeed is holy, and the commandment holy, and righteous, and good.

^{7:13}Did then that which is good become death to me? May it never be! But sin, that it might be shown to be sin, by working death to me through that which is good; that through the commandment sin might become exceeding sinful. ^{7:14}For we know that the law is spiritual, but I am fleshly, sold under sin. ^{7:15}For I don't know what I am doing. For I don't practice what I desire to do; but what I hate, that I do. ^{7:16}But if what I don't desire, that I do, I consent to the law that it is good. ^{7:17}So now it is no more I that do it, but sin which dwells in me. ^{7:18}For I know that in me, that is, in my flesh, dwells no good thing. For desire is present with me, but I don't find it doing that which is good. ^{7:19}For the good which I desire, I don't do; but the evil which I don't desire, that I practice. ^{7:20}But if what I don't desire, that I do, it is no more I that do it, but sin which dwells in me. ^{7:21}I find then the law, that, to me, while I desire to do good, evil is present. ^{7:22}For I delight in God's law after the inward man, ^{7:23}but I see a different law in my members, warring against the law of my mind, and bringing me into captivity under the law of sin which is in my members. ^{7:24}What a wretched man I am! Who will deliver me out of the body of this death? ^{7:25}I thank God through Jesus Christ, our Lord! So then with the mind, I myself serve God's law, but with the flesh, the sin's law.

^{8:1}There is therefore now no condemnation to those who are in Christ Jesus, who don't walk according to the flesh, but according to the Spirit.^s ^{8:2}For the law of the Spirit of life in Christ Jesus made me free from the law of sin and of death. ^{8:3}For what the law couldn't do, in that it was weak through the flesh, God did, sending his own Son in the likeness of sinful flesh and for sin, he condemned sin in the flesh; ^{8:4}that the ordinance of the law might be fulfilled in us, who walk not after the flesh, but after the Spirit. ^{8:5}For those who live according to the flesh set their minds on the things of the flesh, but those who live according to the Spirit, the things of the Spirit. ^{8:6}For the mind of the flesh is death, but the mind of the Spirit is life and peace; ^{8:7}because the mind of the flesh is hostile towards God; for it is not subject to God's law, neither indeed can it be. ^{8:8}Those who

---

^q7:1 The word for "brothers" here and where context allows may also be correctly translated "brothers and sisters" or "siblings."

^r7:7 Exodus 20:17; Deuteronomy 5:21

^s8:1 NU omits "who don't walk according to the flesh, but according to the Spirit"

are in the flesh can't please God. [8:9]But you are not in the flesh but in the Spirit, if it is so that the Spirit of God dwells in you. But if any man doesn't have the Spirit of Christ, he is not his. [8:10]If Christ is in you, the body is dead because of sin, but the spirit is alive because of righteousness. [8:11]But if the Spirit of him who raised up Jesus from the dead dwells in you, he who raised up Christ Jesus from the dead will also give life to your mortal bodies through his Spirit who dwells in you. [8:12]So then, brothers, we are debtors, not to the flesh, to live after the flesh. [8:13]For if you live after the flesh, you must die; but if by the Spirit you put to death the deeds of the body, you will live. [8:14]For as many as are led by the Spirit of God, these are children of God. [8:15]For you didn't receive the spirit of bondage again to fear, but you received the Spirit of adoption, by whom we cry, "Abba[t]! Father!"

[8:16]The Spirit himself testifies with our spirit that we are children of God; [8:17]and if children, then heirs; heirs of God, and joint heirs with Christ; if indeed we suffer with him, that we may also be glorified with him. [8:18]For I consider that the sufferings of this present time are not worthy to be compared with the glory which will be revealed toward us. [8:19]For the creation waits with eager expectation for the children of God to be revealed. [8:20]For the creation was subjected to vanity, not of its own will, but because of him who subjected it, in hope [8:21]that the creation itself also will be delivered from the bondage of decay into the liberty of the glory of the children of God. [8:22]For we know that the whole creation groans and travails in pain together until now. [8:23]Not only so, but ourselves also, who have the first fruits of the Spirit, even we ourselves groan within ourselves, waiting for adoption, the redemption of our body. [8:24]For we were saved in hope, but hope that is seen is not hope. For who hopes for that which he sees? [8:25]But if we hope for that which we don't see, we wait

for it with patience. [8:26]In the same way, the Spirit also helps our weaknesses, for we don't know how to pray as we ought. But the Spirit himself makes intercession for us with groanings which can't be uttered. [8:27]He who searches the hearts knows what is on the Spirit's mind, because he makes intercession for the saints according to God.

[8:28]We know that all things work together for good for those who love God, to those who are called according to his purpose. [8:29]For whom he foreknew, he also predestined to be conformed to the image of his Son, that he might be the firstborn among many brothers.[u] [8:30]Whom he predestined, those he also called. Whom he called, those he also justified. Whom he justified, those he also glorified.

[8:31]What then shall we say about these things? If God is for us, who can be against us? [8:32]He who didn't spare his own Son, but delivered him up for us all, how would he not also with him freely give us all things? [8:33]Who could bring a charge against God's chosen ones? It is God who justifies. [8:34]Who is he who condemns? It is Christ who died, yes rather, who was raised from the dead, who is at the right hand of God, who also makes intercession for us.

[8:35]Who shall separate us from the love of Christ? Could oppression, or anguish, or persecution, or famine, or nakedness, or peril, or sword? [8:36]Even as it is written, "For your sake we are killed all day long. We were accounted as sheep for the slaughter."[v] [8:37]No, in all these things, we are more than conquerors through him who loved us. [8:38]For I am persuaded, that neither death, nor life, nor angels, nor principalities, nor things present, nor things to come, nor powers, [8:39]nor height, nor depth, nor any other created thing, will be able to separate us from the love of God, which is in Christ Jesus our Lord.

[9:1]I tell the truth in Christ. I am not lying, my conscience testifying with me in the Holy Spirit, [9:2]that I have great sorrow

---

[t]8:15 Abba is an Aramaic word for father or daddy, often used affectionately and respectfully in prayer to our Father in heaven.

[u]8:29 The word for "brothers" here and where context allows may also be correctly translated "brothers and sisters" or "siblings."

[v]8:36 Psalm 44:22

and unceasing pain in my heart. [9:3]For I could wish that I myself were accursed from Christ for my brothers' sake, my relatives according to the flesh, [9:4]who are Israelites; whose is the adoption, the glory, the covenants, the giving of the law, the service, and the promises; [9:5]of whom are the fathers, and from whom is Christ as concerning the flesh, who is over all, God, blessed forever. Amen.

[9:6]But it is not as though the word of God has come to nothing. For they are not all Israel, that are of Israel. [9:7]Neither, because they are Abraham's seed, are they all children. But, "In Isaac will your seed be called."[w] [9:8]That is, it is not the children of the flesh who are children of God, but the children of the promise are counted as a seed. [9:9]For this is a word of promise, "At the appointed time I will come, and Sarah will have a son."[x] [9:10]Not only so, but Rebecca also conceived by one, by our father Isaac. [9:11]For being not yet born, neither having done anything good or bad, that the purpose of God according to election might stand, not of works, but of him who calls, [9:12]it was said to her, "The elder will serve the younger."[y] [9:13]Even as it is written, "Jacob I loved, but Esau I hated."[z]

[9:14]What shall we say then? Is there unrighteousness with God? May it never be! [9:15]For he said to Moses, "I will have mercy on whom I have mercy, and I will have compassion on whom I have compassion."[a] [9:16]So then it is not of him who wills, nor of him who runs, but of God who has mercy. [9:17]For the Scripture says to Pharaoh, "For this very purpose I caused you to be raised up, that I might show in you my power, and that my name might be proclaimed in all the earth."[b] [9:18]So then, he has mercy on whom he desires, and he hardens whom he desires. [9:19]You will say then to me, "Why does he still find fault? For who withstands his will?" [9:20]But indeed, O man, who are you to reply against God? Will the thing formed ask him who formed it, "Why did you make me like this?"[c] [9:21]Or hasn't the potter a right over the clay, from the same lump to make one part a vessel for honor, and another for dishonor? [9:22]What if God, willing to show his wrath, and to make his power known, endured with much patience vessels of wrath made for destruction, [9:23]and that he might make known the riches of his glory on vessels of mercy, which he prepared beforehand for glory, [9:24]us, whom he also called, not from the Jews only, but also from the Gentiles? [9:25]As he says also in Hosea,

"I will call them 'my people,' which were not my people;

and her 'beloved,' who was not beloved."[d]

[9:26]"It will be that in the place where it was said to them, 'You are not my people,'

There they will be called 'children of the living God.'"[e]

[9:27]Isaiah cries concerning Israel,

"If the number of the children of Israel are as the sand of the sea,

it is the remnant who will be saved;

[9:28]for He will finish the work and cut it short in righteousness,

because the LORD will make a short work upon the earth."[f]

[9:29]As Isaiah has said before,

"Unless the Lord of Armies[g] had left us a seed,

we would have become like Sodom,

---

[w]9:7 Genesis 21:12
[x]9:9 Genesis 18:10,14
[y]9:12 Genesis 25:23
[z]9:13 Malachi 1:2-3
[a]9:15 Exodus 33:19
[b]9:17 Exodus 9:16
[c]9:20 Isaiah 29:16; 45:9
[d]9:25 Hosea 2:23
[e]9:26 Hosea 1:10
[f]9:28 Isaiah 10:22-23
[g]9:29 Greek: Sabaoth (for Hebrew: Tze'va'ot)

and would have been made like Gomorrah."[h]

[9:30] What shall we say then? That the Gentiles, who didn't follow after righteousness, attained to righteousness, even the righteousness which is of faith; [9:31] but Israel, following after a law of righteousness, didn't arrive at the law of righteousness. [9:32] Why? Because they didn't seek it by faith, but as it were by works of the law. They stumbled over the stumbling stone; [9:33] even as it is written,

"Behold, I lay in Zion a stumbling stone and
    a rock of offense;

    and no one who believes in him will be
        disappointed."[i]

[10:1] Brothers, my heart's desire and my prayer to God is for Israel, that they may be saved. [10:2] For I testify about them that they have a zeal for God, but not according to knowledge. [10:3] For being ignorant of God's righteousness, and seeking to establish their own righteousness, they didn't subject themselves to the righteousness of God. [10:4] For Christ is the fulfillment[j] of the law for righteousness to everyone who believes. [10:5] For Moses writes about the righteousness of the law, "The one who does them will live by them."[k] [10:6] But the righteousness which is of faith says this, "Don't say in your heart, 'Who will ascend into heaven?'[l] (that is, to bring Christ down); [10:7] or, 'Who will descend into the abyss?'[m] (that is, to bring Christ up from the dead.)" [10:8] But what does it say? "The word is near you, in your mouth, and in your heart;"[n] that is, the word of faith, which we preach: [10:9] that if you will confess with your mouth that Jesus is Lord, and believe in your heart that

God raised him from the dead, you will be saved. [10:10] For with the heart, one believes unto righteousness; and with the mouth confession is made unto salvation. [10:11] For the Scripture says, "Whoever believes in him will not be disappointed."[o]

[10:12] For there is no distinction between Jew and Greek; for the same Lord is Lord of all, and is rich to all who call on him. [10:13] For, "Whoever will call on the name of the Lord will be saved."[p] [10:14] How then will they call on him in whom they have not believed? How will they believe in him whom they have not heard? How will they hear without a preacher? [10:15] And how will they preach unless they are sent? As it is written:

"How beautiful are the feet of those who
    preach the Good News of peace,

    who bring glad tidings of good
        things!"[q]

[10:16] But they didn't all listen to the glad news. For Isaiah says, "Lord, who has believed our report?"[r] [10:17] So faith comes by hearing, and hearing by the word of God. [10:18] But I say, didn't they hear? Yes, most certainly,

"Their sound went out into all the earth,

    their words to the ends of the world."[s]

[10:19] But I ask, didn't Israel know? First Moses says,

"I will provoke you to jealousy with that
    which is no nation,

    with a nation void of understanding I
        will make you angry."[t]

[10:20] Isaiah is very bold, and says,

"I was found by those who didn't seek me.

---

[h]9:29 Isaiah 1:9
[i]9:33 Isaiah 8:14; 28:16
[j]10:4 or, completion, or end
[k]10:5 Leviticus 18:5
[l]10:6 Deuteronomy 30:12
[m]10:7 Deuteronomy 30:13
[n]10:8 Deuteronomy 30:14
[o]10:11 Isaiah 28:16
[p]10:13 Joel 2:32
[q]10:15 Isaiah 52:7
[r]10:16 Isaiah 53:1
[s]10:18 Psalm 19:4
[t]10:19 Deuteronomy 32:31

I was revealed to those who didn't ask for me."[u]

[10:21]But as to Israel he says, "All day long I stretched out my hands to a disobedient and contrary people."[v]

[11:1]I ask then, did God reject his people? May it never be! For I also am an Israelite, a descendant of Abraham, of the tribe of Benjamin. [11:2]God didn't reject his people, which he foreknew. Or don't you know what the Scripture says about Elijah? How he pleads with God against Israel: [11:3]"Lord, they have killed your prophets, they have broken down your altars; and I am left alone, and they seek my life."[w] [11:4]But how does God answer him? "I have reserved for myself seven thousand men, who have not bowed the knee to Baal."[x] [11:5]Even so then at this present time also there is a remnant according to the election of grace. [11:6]And if by grace, then it is no longer of works; otherwise grace is no longer grace. But if it is of works, it is no longer grace; otherwise work is no longer work.

[11:7]What then? That which Israel seeks for, that he didn't obtain, but the chosen ones obtained it, and the rest were hardened. [11:8]According as it is written, "God gave them a spirit of stupor, eyes that they should not see, and ears that they should not hear, to this very day."[y] [11:9]David says, "Let their table be made a snare, and a trap, a stumbling block, and a retribution to them.

[11:10]Let their eyes be darkened, that they may not see.

Bow down their back always."[z]

[11:11]I ask then, did they stumble that they might fall? May it never be! But by their fall salvation has come to the Gentiles, to provoke them to jealousy. [11:12]Now if their fall is the riches of the world, and their loss the riches of the Gentiles; how much more their fullness? [11:13]For I speak to you who

are Gentiles. Since then as I am an apostle to Gentiles, I glorify my ministry; [11:14]if by any means I may provoke to jealousy those who are my flesh, and may save some of them. [11:15]For if the rejection of them is the reconciling of the world, what would their acceptance be, but life from the dead? [11:16]If the first fruit is holy, so is the lump. If the root is holy, so are the branches. [11:17]But if some of the branches were broken off, and you, being a wild olive, were grafted in among them, and became partaker with them of the root and of the richness of the olive tree; [11:18]don't boast over the branches. But if you boast, it is not you who support the root, but the root supports you. [11:19]You will say then, "Branches were broken off, that I might be grafted in." [11:20]True; by their unbelief they were broken off, and you stand by your faith. Don't be conceited, but fear; [11:21]for if God didn't spare the natural branches, neither will he spare you. [11:22]See then the goodness and severity of God. Toward those who fell, severity; but toward you, goodness, if you continue in his goodness; otherwise you also will be cut off. [11:23]They also, if they don't continue in their unbelief, will be grafted in, for God is able to graft them in again. [11:24]For if you were cut out of that which is by nature a wild olive tree, and were grafted contrary to nature into a good olive tree, how much more will these, which are the natural branches, be grafted into their own olive tree? [11:25]For I don't desire you to be ignorant, brothers,[a] of this mystery, so that you won't be wise in your own conceits, that a partial hardening has happened to Israel, until the fullness of the Gentiles has come in, [11:26]and so all Israel will be saved. Even as it is written,

"There will come out of Zion the Deliverer,

and he will turn away ungodliness from Jacob.

---

[u]10:20 Isaiah 65:1
[v]10:21 Isaiah 65:2
[w]11:3 1 Kings 19:10,14
[x]11:4 1 Kings 19:18
[y]11:8 Deuteronomy 29:4; Isaiah 29:10
[z]11:10 Psalm 69:22,23
[a]11:25 The word for "brothers" here and where context allows may also be correctly translated "brothers and sisters" or "siblings."

[11:27] This is my covenant to them,

when I will take away their sins."[b]

[11:28] Concerning the Good News, they are enemies for your sake. But concerning the election, they are beloved for the fathers' sake. [11:29] For the gifts and the calling of God are irrevocable. [11:30] For as you in time past were disobedient to God, but now have obtained mercy by their disobedience, [11:31] even so these also have now been disobedient, that by the mercy shown to you they may also obtain mercy. [11:32] For God has shut up all to disobedience, that he might have mercy on all.

[11:33] Oh the depth of the riches both of the wisdom and the knowledge of God! How unsearchable are his judgments, and his ways past tracing out!

[11:34] "For who has known the mind of the Lord?

Or who has been his counselor?"[c]

[11:35] "Or who has first given to him,

and it will be repaid to him again?"[d]

[11:36] For of him, and through him, and to him, are all things. To him be the glory for ever! Amen.

[12:1] Therefore I urge you, brothers, by the mercies of God, to present your bodies a living sacrifice, holy, acceptable to God, which is your spiritual service. [12:2] Don't be conformed to this world, but be transformed by the renewing of your mind, so that you may prove what is the good, well-pleasing, and perfect will of God. [12:3] For I say, through the grace that was given me, to every man who is among you, not to think of himself more highly than he ought to think; but to think reasonably, as God has apportioned to each person a measure of faith. [12:4] For even as we have many members in one body, and all the members don't have the same function, [12:5] so we, who are many, are one body in Christ, and individually members one of another. [12:6] Having gifts differing according to the grace that was given to us, if prophecy, let us prophesy according to the proportion

of our faith; [12:7] or service, let us give ourselves to service; or he who teaches, to his teaching; [12:8] or he who exhorts, to his exhorting: he who gives, let him do it with liberality; he who rules, with diligence; he who shows mercy, with cheerfulness.

[12:9] Let love be without hypocrisy. Abhor that which is evil. Cling to that which is good. [12:10] In love of the brothers be tenderly affectionate one to another; in honor preferring one another; [12:11] not lagging in diligence; fervent in spirit; serving the Lord; [12:12] rejoicing in hope; enduring in troubles; continuing steadfastly in prayer; [12:13] contributing to the needs of the saints; given to hospitality. [12:14] Bless those who persecute you; bless, and don't curse. [12:15] Rejoice with those who rejoice. Weep with those who weep. [12:16] Be of the same mind one toward another. Don't set your mind on high things, but associate with the humble. Don't be wise in your own conceits. [12:17] Repay no one evil for evil. Respect what is honorable in the sight of all men. [12:18] If it is possible, as much as it is up to you, be at peace with all men. [12:19] Don't seek revenge yourselves, beloved, but give place to God's wrath. For it is written, "Vengeance belongs to me; I will repay, says the Lord."[e] [12:20] Therefore

"If your enemy is hungry, feed him.

If he is thirsty, give him a drink;

for in doing so, you will heap coals of fire on his head."[f]

[12:21] Don't be overcome by evil, but overcome evil with good.

[13:1] Let every soul be in subjection to the higher authorities, for there is no authority except from God, and those who exist are ordained by God. [13:2] Therefore he who resists the authority, withstands the ordinance of God; and those who withstand will receive to themselves judgment. [13:3] For rulers are not a terror to the good work, but to the evil. Do you desire to have no fear of the authority? Do that

[b] 11:27 Isaiah 59:20-21; 27:9; Jeremiah 31:33-34

[c] 11:34 Isaiah 40:13

[d] 11:35 Job 41:11

[e] 12:19 Deuteronomy 32:35

[f] 12:20 Proverbs 25:21-22

which is good, and you will have praise from the same, [13:4]for he is a servant of God to you for good. But if you do that which is evil, be afraid, for he doesn't bear the sword in vain; for he is a servant of God, an avenger for wrath to him who does evil. [13:5]Therefore you need to be in subjection, not only because of the wrath, but also for conscience' sake. [13:6]For this reason you also pay taxes, for they are servants of God's service, attending continually on this very thing. [13:7]Give therefore to everyone what you owe: taxes to whom taxes are due; customs to whom customs; respect to whom respect; honor to whom honor. [13:8]Owe no one anything, except to love one another; for he who loves his neighbor has fulfilled the law.

[13:9]For the commandments, "You shall not commit adultery," "You shall not murder," "You shall not steal," "You shall not give false testimony," "You shall not covet,"[g][h] and whatever other commandments there are, are all summed up in this saying, namely, "You shall love your neighbor as yourself."[i] [13:10]Love doesn't harm a neighbor. Love therefore is the fulfillment of the law. [13:11]Do this, knowing the time, that it is already time for you to awaken out of sleep, for salvation is now nearer to us than when we first believed. [13:12]The night is far gone, and the day is near. Let's therefore throw off the works of darkness, and let's put on the armor of light. [13:13]Let us walk properly, as in the day; not in reveling and drunkenness, not in sexual promiscuity and lustful acts, and not in strife and jealousy. [13:14]But put on the Lord Jesus Christ, and make no provision for the flesh, for its lusts.

[14:1]Now accept one who is weak in faith, but not for disputes over opinions. [14:2]One man has faith to eat all things, but he who is weak eats only vegetables. [14:3]Don't let him who eats despise him who doesn't eat. Don't let him who doesn't eat judge him who eats, for God has accepted him. [14:4]Who are you who judge another's ser-vant? To his own lord he stands or falls. Yes, he will be made to stand, for God has power to make him stand.

[14:5]One man esteems one day as more important. Another esteems every day alike. Let each man be fully assured in his own mind. [14:6]He who observes the day, observes it to the Lord; and he who does not observe the day, to the Lord he does not observe it. He who eats, eats to the Lord, for he gives God thanks. He who doesn't eat, to the Lord he doesn't eat, and gives God thanks. [14:7]For none of us lives to himself, and none dies to himself. [14:8]For if we live, we live to the Lord. Or if we die, we die to the Lord. If therefore we live or die, we are the Lord's. [14:9]For to this end Christ died, rose, and lived again, that he might be Lord of both the dead and the living.

[14:10]But you, why do you judge your brother? Or you again, why do you despise your brother? For we will all stand before the judgment seat of Christ. [14:11]For it is written,

"'As I live,' says the Lord, 'to me every knee
    will bow.

Every tongue will confess to God.'"[j]

[14:12]So then each one of us will give account of himself to God. [14:13]Therefore let's not judge one another any more, but judge this rather, that no man put a stumbling block in his brother's way, or an occasion for falling. [14:14]I know, and am persuaded in the Lord Jesus, that nothing is unclean of itself; except that to him who considers anything to be unclean, to him it is unclean. [14:15]Yet if because of food your brother is grieved, you walk no longer in love. Don't destroy with your food him for whom Christ died. [14:16]Then don't let your good be slandered, [14:17]for the Kingdom of God is not eating and drinking, but righteousness, peace, and joy in the Holy Spirit. [14:18]For he who serves Christ in these things is acceptable to God and approved by men. [14:19]So then, let us follow after things which make for peace,

---

[g]13:9 TR adds "You shall not give false testimony,"
[h]13:9 Exodus 20:13-15,17; Deuteronomy 5:17-19,21
[i]13:9 Leviticus 19:18
[j]14:11 Isaiah 45:23

and things by which we may build one another up. [14:20]Don't overthrow God's work for food's sake. All things indeed are clean, however it is evil for that man who creates a stumbling block by eating. [14:21]It is good to not eat meat, drink wine, nor do anything by which your brother stumbles, is offended, or is made weak.

[14:22]Do you have faith? Have it to yourself before God. Happy is he who doesn't judge himself in that which he approves. [14:23]But he who doubts is condemned if he eats, because it isn't of faith; and whatever is not of faith is sin.

[14:24]Now to him who is able to establish you according to my Good News and the preaching of Jesus Christ, according to the revelation of the mystery which has been kept secret through long ages, [14:25]but now is revealed, and by the Scriptures of the prophets, according to the commandment of the eternal God, is made known for obedience of faith to all the nations; [14:26]to the only wise God, through Jesus Christ, to whom be the glory forever! Amen.[k]

[15:1]Now we who are strong ought to bear the weaknesses of the weak, and not to please ourselves. [15:2]Let each one of us please his neighbor for that which is good, to be building him up. [15:3]For even Christ didn't please himself. But, as it is written, "The reproaches of those who reproached you fell on me."[l] [15:4]For whatever things were written before were written for our learning, that through patience and through encouragement of the Scriptures we might have hope. [15:5]Now the God of patience and of encouragement grant you to be of the same mind one with another according to Christ Jesus, [15:6]that with one accord you may with one mouth glorify the God and Father of our Lord Jesus Christ.

[15:7]Therefore accept one another, even as Christ also accepted you,[m] to the glory of God. [15:8]Now I say that Christ has been made a servant of the circumcision for the truth of God, that he might confirm the promises given to the fathers, [15:9]and that the Gentiles might glorify God for his mercy. As it is written,

"Therefore will I give praise to you among
the Gentiles,
and sing to your name."[n]

[15:10]Again he says,

"Rejoice, you Gentiles, with his people."[o]

[15:11]Again,

"Praise the Lord, all you Gentiles!
Let all the peoples praise him."[p]

[15:12]Again, Isaiah says,

"There will be the root of Jesse,
he who arises to rule over the Gentiles;
in him the Gentiles will hope."[q]

[15:13]Now may the God of hope fill you with all joy and peace in believing, that you may abound in hope, in the power of the Holy Spirit. [15:14]I myself am also persuaded about you, my brothers[r], that you yourselves are full of goodness, filled with all knowledge, able also to admonish others. [15:15]But I write the more boldly to you in part, as reminding you, because of the grace that was given to me by God, [15:16]that I should be a servant of Christ Jesus to the Gentiles, serving as a priest the Good News of God, that the offering up of the Gentiles might be made acceptable, sanctified by the Holy Spirit. [15:17]I have therefore my boasting in Christ Jesus in things pertaining to God. [15:18]For I will not dare to speak of any things except those which Christ worked through me, for the obedience of the Gentiles, by word and deed, [15:19]in the power of signs and wonders, in the power of God's Spirit; so that from Jerusalem, and around as far as to Illyricum, I have fully preached the Good

---

[k]14:26 TR places verses 24-26 after Romans 16:24 as verses 25-27.

[l]15:3 Psalm 69:9

[m]15:7 TR reads "us" instead of "you"

[n]15:9 2 Samuel 22:50; Psalm 18:49

[o]15:10 Deuteronomy 32:43

[p]15:11 Psalm 117:1

[q]15:12 Isaiah 11:10

[r]15:14 The word for "brothers" here and where context allows may also be correctly translated "brothers and sisters" or "siblings."

News of Christ; [15:20]yes, making it my aim to preach the Good News, not where Christ was already named, that I might not build on another's foundation. [15:21]But, as it is written,

"They will see, to whom no news of him came.

They who haven't heard will understand."[s]

[15:22]Therefore also I was hindered these many times from coming to you, [15:23]but now, no longer having any place in these regions, and having these many years a longing to come to you, [15:24]whenever I journey to Spain, I will come to you. For I hope to see you on my journey, and to be helped on my way there by you, if first I may enjoy your company for a while. [15:25]But now, I say, I am going to Jerusalem, serving the saints. [15:26]For it has been the good pleasure of Macedonia and Achaia to make a certain contribution for the poor among the saints who are at Jerusalem. [15:27]Yes, it has been their good pleasure, and they are their debtors. For if the Gentiles have been made partakers of their spiritual things, they owe it to them also to serve them in fleshly things. [15:28]When therefore I have accomplished this, and have sealed to them this fruit, I will go on by way of you to Spain. [15:29]I know that, when I come to you, I will come in the fullness of the blessing of the Good News of Christ.

[15:30]Now I beg you, brothers, by our Lord Jesus Christ, and by the love of the Spirit, that you strive together with me in your prayers to God for me, [15:31]that I may be delivered from those who are disobedient in Judea, and that my service which I have for Jerusalem may be acceptable to the saints; [15:32]that I may come to you in joy through the will of God, and together with you, find rest. [15:33]Now the God of peace be with you all. Amen.

[16:1]I commend to you Phoebe, our sister, who is a servant[t] of the assembly that is at Cenchreae, [16:2]that you receive her in the Lord, in a way worthy of the saints, and that you assist her in whatever matter she may need from you, for she herself also has been a helper of many, and of my own self.

[16:3]Greet Prisca and Aquila, my fellow workers in Christ Jesus, [16:4]who for my life, laid down their own necks; to whom not only I give thanks, but also all the assemblies of the Gentiles. [16:5]Greet the assembly that is in their house. Greet Epaenetus, my beloved, who is the first fruits of Achaia to Christ. [16:6]Greet Mary, who labored much for us. [16:7]Greet Andronicus and Junias, my relatives and my fellow prisoners, who are notable among the apostles, who also were in Christ before me. [16:8]Greet Amplias, my beloved in the Lord. [16:9]Greet Urbanus, our fellow worker in Christ, and Stachys, my beloved. [16:10]Greet Apelles, the approved in Christ. Greet those who are of the household of Aristobulus. [16:11]Greet Herodion, my kinsman. Greet them of the household of Narcissus, who are in the Lord. [16:12]Greet Tryphaena and Tryphosa, who labor in the Lord. Greet Persis, the beloved, who labored much in the Lord. [16:13]Greet Rufus, the chosen in the Lord, and his mother and mine. [16:14]Greet Asyncritus, Phlegon, Hermes, Patrobas, Hermas, and the brothers[u] who are with them. [16:15]Greet Philologus and Julia, Nereus and his sister, and Olympas, and all the saints who are with them. [16:16]Greet one another with a holy kiss. The assemblies of Christ greet you.

[16:17]Now I beg you, brothers, look out for those who are causing the divisions and occasions of stumbling, contrary to the doctrine which you learned, and turn away from them. [16:18]For those who are such don't serve our Lord, Jesus Christ, but their own belly; and by their smooth and flattering speech, they deceive the hearts of the innocent. [16:19]For your obedience has become known to all. I rejoice therefore over you. But I desire to have you wise in that which is good, but innocent in that

[s]15:21 Isaiah 52:15
[t]16:1 or, deacon
[u]16:14 The word for "brothers" here and where context allows may also be correctly translated "brothers and sisters" or "siblings."

which is evil. [16:20]And the God of peace will quickly crush Satan under your feet. The grace of our Lord Jesus Christ be with you. [16:21]Timothy, my fellow worker, greets you, as do Lucius, Jason, and Sosipater, my relatives. [16:22]I, Tertius, who write the letter, greet you in the Lord. [16:23]Gaius, my host and host of the whole assembly, greets you. Erastus, the treasurer of the city, greets you, as does Quartus, the brother. [16:24]The grace of our Lord Jesus Christ be with you all! Amen.[16:25v]

Paul's First Letter to the Corinthians

[1:1]Paul, called to be an apostle of Jesus Christ through the will of God, and our brother Sosthenes, [1:2]to the assembly of God which is at Corinth; those who are sanctified in Christ Jesus, called to be saints, with all who call on the name of our Lord Jesus Christ in every place, both theirs and ours: [1:3]Grace to you and peace from God our Father and the Lord Jesus Christ.

[1:4]I always thank my God concerning you, for the grace of God which was given you in Christ Jesus; [1:5]that in everything you were enriched in him, in all speech and all knowledge; [1:6]even as the testimony of Christ was confirmed in you: [1:7]so that you come behind in no gift; waiting for the revelation of our Lord Jesus Christ; [1:8]who will also confirm you until the end, blameless in the day of our Lord Jesus Christ. [1:9]God is faithful, through whom you were called into the fellowship of his Son, Jesus Christ, our Lord. [1:10]Now I beg you, brothers,[a] through the name of our Lord, Jesus Christ, that you all speak the same thing and that there be no divisions among you, but that you be perfected together in the same mind and in the same judgment. [1:11]For it has been reported to me concerning you, my brothers, by those who are from Chloe's household, that there are contentions among you. [1:12]Now I mean this, that each one of you says, "I follow Paul," "I follow Apollos," "I follow Cephas," and, "I follow Christ." [1:13]Is Christ divided? Was Paul crucified for you? Or were you baptized into the name of Paul? [1:14]I thank God that I baptized none of you, except Crispus and Gaius, [1:15]so that no one should say that I had baptized you into my own name. [1:16](I also baptized the household of Stephanas; besides them, I don't know whether I baptized any other.) [1:17]For Christ sent me not to baptize, but to preach the Good News—not in wisdom of words, so that the cross of Christ wouldn't be made void. [1:18]For the word of the cross is foolishness to those who are dying, but to us who are saved it is the power of God. [1:19]For it is written,

"I will destroy the wisdom of the wise,

I will bring the discernment of the discerning to nothing."[b]

[1:20]Where is the wise? Where is the scribe? Where is the lawyer of this world? Hasn't God made foolish the wisdom of this world? [1:21]For seeing that in the wisdom of God, the world through its wisdom didn't know God, it was God's good pleasure through the foolishness of the preaching to save those who believe. [1:22]For Jews ask for signs, Greeks seek after wisdom, [1:23]but we preach Christ crucified; a stumbling block to Jews, and foolishness to Greeks, [1:24]but to those who are called, both Jews and Greeks, Christ is the power of God and the wisdom of God. [1:25]Because the foolishness of God is wiser than men, and the weakness of God is stronger than men. [1:26]For you see your calling, brothers, that not many are wise according to the flesh, not many mighty, and not many noble; [1:27]but God chose the foolish things of the world that he might put to shame those who are wise. God chose the weak

---

[v]16:25 TR places Romans 14:24-26 at the end of Romans instead of at the end of chapter 14, and numbers these verses 16:25-27.

[a]1:10 The word for "brothers" here and where context allows may also be correctly translated "brothers and sisters" or "siblings."

[b]1:19 Isaiah 29:14

things of the world, that he might put to shame the things that are strong; [1:28]and God chose the lowly things of the world, and the things that are despised, and the things that are not, that he might bring to nothing the things that are: [1:29]that no flesh should boast before God. [1:30]But of him, you are in Christ Jesus, who was made to us wisdom from God, and righteousness and sanctification, and redemption: [1:31]that, according as it is written, "He who boasts, let him boast in the Lord."[c]

[2:1]When I came to you, brothers, I didn't come with excellence of speech or of wisdom, proclaiming to you the testimony of God. [2:2]For I determined not to know anything among you, except Jesus Christ, and him crucified. [2:3]I was with you in weakness, in fear, and in much trembling. [2:4]My speech and my preaching were not in persuasive words of human wisdom, but in demonstration of the Spirit and of power, [2:5]that your faith wouldn't stand in the wisdom of men, but in the power of God. [2:6]We speak wisdom, however, among those who are full grown; yet a wisdom not of this world, nor of the rulers of this world, who are coming to nothing. [2:7]But we speak God's wisdom in a mystery, the wisdom that has been hidden, which God foreordained before the worlds for our glory, [2:8]which none of the rulers of this world has known. For had they known it, they wouldn't have crucified the Lord of glory. [2:9]But as it is written,

"Things which an eye didn't see, and an ear didn't hear,
which didn't enter into the heart of man,
these God has prepared for those who love him."[d]

[2:10]But to us, God revealed them through the Spirit. For the Spirit searches all things, yes, the deep things of God. [2:11]For who among men knows the things of a man, except the spirit of the man, which is in him? Even so, no one knows the things of God, except God's Spirit. [2:12]But we received, not the spirit of the world, but the Spirit which is from God, that we might know the things that were freely given to us by God. [2:13]Which things also we speak, not in words which man's wisdom teaches, but which the Holy Spirit teaches, comparing spiritual things with spiritual things. [2:14]Now the natural man doesn't receive the things of God's Spirit, for they are foolishness to him, and he can't know them, because they are spiritually discerned. [2:15]But he who is spiritual discerns all things, and he himself is judged by no one. [2:16]"For who has known the mind of the Lord, that he should instruct him?"[e] But we have Christ's mind.

[3:1]Brothers, I couldn't speak to you as to spiritual, but as to fleshly, as to babies in Christ. [3:2]I fed you with milk, not with meat; for you weren't yet ready. Indeed, not even now are you ready, [3:3]for you are still fleshly. For insofar as there is jealousy, strife, and factions among you, aren't you fleshly, and don't you walk in the ways of men? [3:4]For when one says, "I follow Paul," and another, "I follow Apollos," aren't you fleshly? [3:5]Who then is Apollos, and who is Paul, but servants through whom you believed; and each as the Lord gave to him? [3:6]I planted. Apollos watered. But God gave the increase. [3:7]So then neither he who plants is anything, nor he who waters, but God who gives the increase. [3:8]Now he who plants and he who waters are the same, but each will receive his own reward according to his own labor. [3:9]For we are God's fellow workers. You are God's farming, God's building. [3:10]According to the grace of God which was given to me, as a wise master builder I laid a foundation, and another builds on it. But let each man be careful how he builds on it. [3:11]For no one can lay any other foundation than that which has been laid, which is Jesus Christ. [3:12]But if anyone builds on the foundation with gold, silver, costly stones, wood, hay, or stubble; [3:13]each man's work will be revealed. For the Day will declare it, because it is revealed in fire; and the

---

[c]1:31 Jeremiah 9:24
[d]2:9 Isaiah 64:4
[e]2:16 Isaiah 40:13

fire itself will test what sort of work each man's work is. ^{3:14}If any man's work remains which he built on it, he will receive a reward. ^{3:15}If any man's work is burned, he will suffer loss, but he himself will be saved, but as through fire.

^{3:16}Don't you know that you are a temple of God, and that God's Spirit lives in you? ^{3:17}If anyone destroys the temple of God, God will destroy him; for God's temple is holy, which you are. ^{3:18}Let no one deceive himself. If anyone thinks that he is wise among you in this world, let him become a fool, that he may become wise. ^{3:19}For the wisdom of this world is foolishness with God. For it is written, "He has taken the wise in their craftiness."^f ^{3:20}And again, "The Lord knows the reasoning of the wise, that it is worthless."^g ^{3:21}Therefore let no one boast in men. For all things are yours, ^{3:22}whether Paul, or Apollos, or Cephas, or the world, or life, or death, or things present, or things to come. All are yours, ^{3:23}and you are Christ's, and Christ is God's.

^{4:1}So let a man think of us as Christ's servants, and stewards of God's mysteries. ^{4:2}Here, moreover, it is required of stewards, that they be found faithful. ^{4:3}But with me it is a very small thing that I should be judged by you, or by man's judgment. Yes, I don't judge my own self. ^{4:4}For I know nothing against myself. Yet I am not justified by this, but he who judges me is the Lord. ^{4:5}Therefore judge nothing before the time, until the Lord comes, who will both bring to light the hidden things of darkness, and reveal the counsels of the hearts. Then each man will get his praise from God.

^{4:6}Now these things, brothers, I have in a figure transferred to myself and Apollos for your sakes, that in us you might learn not to think beyond the things which are written, that none of you be puffed up against one another. ^{4:7}For who makes you different? And what do you have that you didn't receive? But if you did receive it, why do you boast as if you had not received it? ^{4:8}You are already filled. You have already become rich. You have come to reign without us. Yes, and I wish that you did reign, that we also might reign with you. ^{4:9}For, I think that God has displayed us, the apostles, last of all, like men sentenced to death. For we are made a spectacle to the world, both to angels and men. ^{4:10}We are fools for Christ's sake, but you are wise in Christ. We are weak, but you are strong. You have honor, but we have dishonor. ^{4:11}Even to this present hour we hunger, thirst, are naked, are beaten, and have no certain dwelling place. ^{4:12}We toil, working with our own hands. When people curse us, we bless. Being persecuted, we endure. ^{4:13}Being defamed, we entreat. We are made as the filth of the world, the dirt wiped off by all, even until now. ^{4:14}I don't write these things to shame you, but to admonish you as my beloved children. ^{4:15}For though you have ten thousand tutors in Christ, yet not many fathers. For in Christ Jesus, I became your father through the Good News. ^{4:16}I beg you therefore, be imitators of me. ^{4:17}Because of this I have sent Timothy to you, who is my beloved and faithful child in the Lord, who will remind you of my ways which are in Christ, even as I teach everywhere in every assembly. ^{4:18}Now some are puffed up, as though I were not coming to you. ^{4:19}But I will come to you shortly, if the Lord is willing. And I will know, not the word of those who are puffed up, but the power. ^{4:20}For the Kingdom of God is not in word, but in power. ^{4:21}What do you want? Shall I come to you with a rod, or in love and a spirit of gentleness?

^{5:1}It is actually reported that there is sexual immorality among you, and such sexual immorality as is not even named among the Gentiles, that one has his father's wife. ^{5:2}You are puffed up, and didn't rather mourn, that he who had done this deed might be removed from among you. ^{5:3}For I most certainly, as being absent in body but present in spirit, have already, as though I were present, judged him who has done

---

^f3:19 Job 5:13
^g3:20 Psalm 94:11

this thing. [5:4]In the name of our Lord Jesus Christ, you being gathered together, and my spirit, with the power of our Lord Jesus Christ, [5:5]are to deliver such a one to Satan for the destruction of the flesh, that the spirit may be saved in the day of the Lord Jesus.

[5:6]Your boasting is not good. Don't you know that a little yeast leavens the whole lump? [5:7]Purge out the old yeast, that you may be a new lump, even as you are unleavened. For indeed Christ, our Passover, has been sacrificed in our place. [5:8]Therefore let us keep the feast, not with old yeast, neither with the yeast of malice and wickedness, but with the unleavened bread of sincerity and truth. [5:9]I wrote to you in my letter to have no company with sexual sinners; [5:10]yet not at all meaning with the sexual sinners of this world, or with the covetous and extortioners, or with idolaters; for then you would have to leave the world. [5:11]But as it is, I wrote to you not to associate with anyone who is called a brother who is a sexual sinner, or covetous, or an idolater, or a slanderer, or a drunkard, or an extortioner. Don't even eat with such a person. [5:12]For what have I to do with also judging those who are outside? Don't you judge those who are within? [5:13]But those who are outside, God judges. "Put away the wicked man from among yourselves."[h]

[6:1]Dare any of you, having a matter against his neighbor, go to law before the unrighteous, and not before the saints? [6:2]Don't you know that the saints will judge the world? And if the world is judged by you, are you unworthy to judge the smallest matters? [6:3]Don't you know that we will judge angels? How much more, things that pertain to this life? [6:4]If then, you have to judge things pertaining to this life, do you set them to judge who are of no account in the assembly? [6:5]I say this to move you to shame. Isn't there even one wise man among you who would be able to decide between his brothers? [6:6]But brother goes to law with brother, and that before unbelievers! [6:7]Therefore it is

already altogether a defect in you, that you have lawsuits one with another. Why not rather be wronged? Why not rather be defrauded? [6:8]No, but you yourselves do wrong, and defraud, and that against your brothers. [6:9]Or don't you know that the unrighteous will not inherit the Kingdom of God? Don't be deceived. Neither the sexually immoral, nor idolaters, nor adulterers, nor male prostitutes, nor homosexuals, [6:10]nor thieves, nor covetous, nor drunkards, nor slanderers, nor extortioners, will inherit the Kingdom of God. [6:11]Such were some of you, but you were washed. But you were sanctified. But you were justified in the name of the Lord Jesus, and in the Spirit of our God. [6:12]"All things are lawful for me," but not all things are expedient. "All things are lawful for me," but I will not be brought under the power of anything. [6:13]"Foods for the belly, and the belly for foods," but God will bring to nothing both it and them. But the body is not for sexual immorality, but for the Lord; and the Lord for the body. [6:14]Now God raised up the Lord, and will also raise us up by his power. [6:15]Don't you know that your bodies are members of Christ? Shall I then take the members of Christ, and make them members of a prostitute? May it never be! [6:16]Or don't you know that he who is joined to a prostitute is one body? For, "The two," says he, "will become one flesh."[i] [6:17]But he who is joined to the Lord is one spirit. [6:18]Flee sexual immorality! "Every sin that a man does is outside the body," but he who commits sexual immorality sins against his own body. [6:19]Or don't you know that your body is a temple of the Holy Spirit which is in you, which you have from God? You are not your own, [6:20]for you were bought with a price. Therefore glorify God in your body and in your spirit, which are God's.

[7:1]Now concerning the things about which you wrote to me: it is good for a man not to touch a woman. [7:2]But, because of sexual immoralities, let each man have his own wife, and let each woman have her own husband. [7:3]Let the husband

[h]5:13 Deuteronomy 17:7; 19:19; 21:21; 22:21; 24:7
[i]6:16 Genesis 2:24

render to his wife the affection owed her, and likewise also the wife to her husband. 7:4The wife doesn't have authority over her own body, but the husband. Likewise also the husband doesn't have authority over his own body, but the wife. 7:5Don't deprive one another, unless it is by consent for a season, that you may give yourselves to fasting and prayer, and may be together again, that Satan doesn't tempt you because of your lack of self-control.

7:6But this I say by way of concession, not of commandment. 7:7Yet I wish that all men were like me. However each man has his own gift from God, one of this kind, and another of that kind. 7:8But I say to the unmarried and to widows, it is good for them if they remain even as I am. 7:9But if they don't have self-control, let them marry. For it's better to marry than to burn. 7:10But to the married I command—not I, but the Lord—that the wife not leave her husband 7:11(but if she departs, let her remain unmarried, or else be reconciled to her husband), and that the husband not leave his wife.

7:12But to the rest I—not the Lord—say, if any brother has an unbelieving wife, and she is content to live with him, let him not leave her. 7:13The woman who has an unbelieving husband, and he is content to live with her, let her not leave her husband. 7:14For the unbelieving husband is sanctified in the wife, and the unbelieving wife is sanctified in the husband. Otherwise your children would be unclean, but now they are holy. 7:15Yet if the unbeliever departs, let there be separation. The brother or the sister is not under bondage in such cases, but God has called us in peace. 7:16For how do you know, wife, whether you will save your husband? Or how do you know, husband, whether you will save your wife? 7:17Only, as the Lord has distributed to each man, as God has called each, so let him walk. So I command in all the assemblies.

7:18Was anyone called having been circumcised? Let him not become uncircumcised. Has anyone been called in uncircumcision? Let him not be circumcised. 7:19Circumcision is nothing, and uncircumcision is nothing, but the keeping of the commandments of God. 7:20Let each man stay in that calling in which he was called. 7:21Were you called being a bondservant? Don't let that bother you, but if you get an opportunity to become free, use it. 7:22For he who was called in the Lord being a bondservant is the Lord's free man. Likewise he who was called being free is Christ's bondservant. 7:23You were bought with a price. Don't become bondservants of men. 7:24Brothers, let each man, in whatever condition he was called, stay in that condition with God.

7:25Now concerning virgins, I have no commandment from the Lord, but I give my judgment as one who has obtained mercy from the Lord to be trustworthy. 7:26I think that it is good therefore, because of the distress that is on us, that it is good for a man to be as he is. 7:27Are you bound to a wife? Don't seek to be freed. Are you free from a wife? Don't seek a wife. 7:28But if you marry, you have not sinned. If a virgin marries, she has not sinned. Yet such will have oppression in the flesh, and I want to spare you. 7:29But I say this, brothers: the time is short, that from now on, both those who have wives may be as though they had none; 7:30and those who weep, as though they didn't weep; and those who rejoice, as though they didn't rejoice; and those who buy, as though they didn't possess; 7:31and those who use the world, as not using it to the fullest. For the mode of this world passes away. 7:32But I desire to have you to be free from cares. He who is unmarried is concerned for the things of the Lord, how he may please the Lord; 7:33but he who is married is concerned about the things of the world, how he may please his wife. 7:34There is also a difference between a wife and a virgin. The unmarried woman cares about the things of the Lord, that she may be holy both in body and in spirit. But she who is married cares about the things of the world—how she may please her husband. 7:35This I say for your own profit; not that I may ensnare you, but for that which is appropriate, and that you may attend to the Lord without distraction. 7:36But if any man thinks that he is behaving inappropriately toward his virgin, if she is past the flower of her age, and if need so requires, let him do what he desires. He doesn't sin. Let them marry. [7:37]But he who stands steadfast in his heart, having no necessity, but has power over his own heart, to keep his own virgin, does well. [7:38]So then both he who gives his own virgin in marriage does well, and he who doesn't give her in marriage does better. [7:39]A wife is bound by law for as long as her husband lives; but if the husband is dead, she is free to be married to whoever she desires, only in the Lord. [7:40]But she is happier if she stays as she is, in my judgment, and I think that I also have God's Spirit.

[8:1]Now concerning things sacrificed to idols: We know that we all have knowledge. Knowledge puffs up, but love builds up. [8:2]But if anyone thinks that he knows anything, he doesn't yet know as he ought to know. [8:3]But if anyone loves God, the same is known by him. [8:4]Therefore concerning the eating of things sacrificed to idols, we know that no idol is anything in the world, and that there is no other God but one. [8:5]For though there are things that are called "gods," whether in the heavens or on earth; as there are many "gods" and many "lords;" [8:6]yet to us there is one God, the Father, of whom are all things, and we for him; and one Lord, Jesus Christ, through whom are all things, and we live through him. [8:7]However, that knowledge isn't in all men. But some, with consciousness of the idol until now, eat as of a thing sacrificed to an idol, and their conscience, being weak, is defiled. [8:8]But food will not commend us to God. For neither, if we don't eat, are we the worse; nor, if we eat, are we the better. [8:9]But be careful that by no means does this liberty of yours become a stumbling block to the weak. [8:10]For if a man sees you who have knowledge sitting in an idol's temple, won't his conscience, if he is weak, be emboldened to eat things sacrificed to idols? [8:11]And through your knowledge, he who is weak perishes, the brother for whose sake Christ died. [8:12]Thus, sinning against the brothers, and wounding their

conscience when it is weak, you sin against Christ. [8:13]Therefore, if food causes my brother to stumble, I will eat no meat forevermore, that I don't cause my brother to stumble.

[9:1]Am I not free? Am I not an apostle? Haven't I seen Jesus Christ, our Lord? Aren't you my work in the Lord? [9:2]If to others I am not an apostle, yet at least I am to you; for you are the seal of my apostleship in the Lord. [9:3]My defense to those who examine me is this. [9:4]Have we no right to eat and to drink? [9:5]Have we no right to take along a wife who is a believer, even as the rest of the apostles, and the brothers of the Lord, and Cephas? [9:6]Or have only Barnabas and I no right to not work? [9:7]What soldier ever serves at his own expense? Who plants a vineyard, and doesn't eat of its fruit? Or who feeds a flock, and doesn't drink from the flock's milk? [9:8]Do I speak these things according to the ways of men? Or doesn't the law also say the same thing? [9:9]For it is written in the law of Moses, "You shall not muzzle an ox while it treads out the grain."[j] Is it for the oxen that God cares, [9:10]or does he say it assuredly for our sake? Yes, it was written for our sake, because he who plows ought to plow in hope, and he who threshes in hope should partake of his hope. [9:11]If we sowed to you spiritual things, is it a great thing if we reap your fleshly things? [9:12]If others partake of this right over you, don't we yet more? Nevertheless we did not use this right, but we bear all things, that we may cause no hindrance to the Good News of Christ. [9:13]Don't you know that those who serve around sacred things eat from the things of the temple, and those who wait on the altar have their portion with the altar? [9:14]Even so the Lord ordained that those who proclaim the Good News should live from the Good News. [9:15]But I have used none of these things, and I don't write these things that it may be done so in my case; for I would rather die, than that anyone should make my boasting void. [9:16]For if I preach the Good News, I have nothing to boast about; for necessity is laid

[j]9:9 Deuteronomy 25:4

on me; but woe is to me, if I don't preach the Good News. ⁹:¹⁷For if I do this of my own will, I have a reward. But if not of my own will, I have a stewardship entrusted to me. ⁹:¹⁸What then is my reward? That, when I preach the Good News, I may present the Good News of Christ without charge, so as not to abuse my authority in the Good News. ⁹:¹⁹For though I was free from all, I brought myself under bondage to all, that I might gain the more. ⁹:²⁰To the Jews I became as a Jew, that I might gain Jews; to those who are under the law, as under the law, that I might gain those who are under the law; ⁹:²¹to those who are without law, as without law (not being without law toward God, but under law toward Christ), that I might win those who are without law. ⁹:²²To the weak I became as weak, that I might gain the weak. I have become all things to all men, that I may by all means save some. ⁹:²³Now I do this for the sake of the Good News, that I may be a joint partaker of it. ⁹:²⁴Don't you know that those who run in a race all run, but one receives the prize? Run like that, that you may win. ⁹:²⁵Every man who strives in the games exercises self-control in all things. Now they do it to receive a corruptible crown, but we an incorruptible. ⁹:²⁶I therefore run like that, as not uncertainly. I fight like that, as not beating the air, ⁹:²⁷but I beat my body and bring it into submission, lest by any means, after I have preached to others, I myself should be rejected.

¹⁰:¹Now I would not have you ignorant, brothers, that our fathers were all under the cloud, and all passed through the sea; ¹⁰:²and were all baptized into Moses in the cloud and in the sea; ¹⁰:³and all ate the same spiritual food; ¹⁰:⁴and all drank the same spiritual drink. For they drank of a spiritual rock that followed them, and the rock was Christ. ¹⁰:⁵However with most of them, God was not well pleased, for they were overthrown in the wilderness. ¹⁰:⁶Now these things were our examples, to the intent we should not lust after evil things, as they also lusted. ¹⁰:⁷Neither be idolaters, as some of them were. As it is written,

"The people sat down to eat and drink, and rose up to play."ᵏ ¹⁰:⁸Neither let us commit sexual immorality, as some of them committed, and in one day twenty-three thousand fell. ¹⁰:⁹Neither let us test the Lord, as some of them tested, and perished by the serpents. ¹⁰:¹⁰Neither grumble, as some of them also grumbled, and perished by the destroyer. ¹⁰:¹¹Now all these things happened to them by way of example, and they were written for our admonition, on whom the ends of the ages have come. ¹⁰:¹²Therefore let him who thinks he stands be careful that he doesn't fall.

¹⁰:¹³No temptation has taken you except what is common to man. God is faithful, who will not allow you to be tempted above what you are able, but will with the temptation also make the way of escape, that you may be able to endure it. ¹⁰:¹⁴Therefore, my beloved, flee from idolatry. ¹⁰:¹⁵I speak as to wise men. Judge what I say. ¹⁰:¹⁶The cup of blessing which we bless, isn't it a sharing of the blood of Christ? The bread which we break, isn't it a sharing of the body of Christ? ¹⁰:¹⁷Because there is one loaf of bread, we, who are many, are one body; for we all partake of the one loaf of bread. ¹⁰:¹⁸Consider Israel according to the flesh. Don't those who eat the sacrifices participate in the altar?

¹⁰:¹⁹What am I saying then? That a thing sacrificed to idols is anything, or that an idol is anything? ¹⁰:²⁰But I say that the things which the Gentiles sacrifice, they sacrifice to demons, and not to God, and I don't desire that you would have fellowship with demons. ¹⁰:²¹You can't both drink the cup of the Lord and the cup of demons. You can't both partake of the table of the Lord, and of the table of demons. ¹⁰:²²Or do we provoke the Lord to jealousy? Are we stronger than he? ¹⁰:²³"All things are lawful for me," but not all things are profitable. "All things are lawful for me," but not all things build up. ¹⁰:²⁴Let no one seek his own, but each one his neighbor's good. ¹⁰:²⁵Whatever is sold in the butcher shop, eat, asking no question for the sake of conscience, ¹⁰:²⁶for "the earth is the Lord's,

---

ᵏ10:7 Exodus 32:6

and its fullness."[l] [10:27]But if one of those who don't believe invites you to a meal, and you are inclined to go, eat whatever is set before you, asking no questions for the sake of conscience. [10:28]But if anyone says to you, "This was offered to idols," don't eat it for the sake of the one who told you, and for the sake of conscience. For "the earth is the Lord's, and all its fullness." [10:29]Conscience, I say, not your own, but the other's conscience. For why is my liberty judged by another conscience? [10:30]If I partake with thankfulness, why am I denounced for that for which I give thanks? [10:31]Whether therefore you eat, or drink, or whatever you do, do all to the glory of God. [10:32]Give no occasions for stumbling, either to Jews, or to Greeks, or to the assembly of God; [10:33]even as I also please all men in all things, not seeking my own profit, but the profit of the many, that they may be saved.

[11:1]Be imitators of me, even as I also am of Christ. [11:2]Now I praise you, brothers, that you remember me in all things, and hold firm the traditions, even as I delivered them to you. [11:3]But I would have you know that the head of every man is Christ, and the head of the woman is the man, and the head of Christ is God. [11:4]Every man praying or prophesying, having his head covered, dishonors his head. [11:5]But every woman praying or prophesying with her head unveiled dishonors her head. For it is one and the same thing as if she were shaved. [11:6]For if a woman is not covered, let her also be shorn. But if it is shameful for a woman to be shorn or shaved, let her be covered. [11:7]For a man indeed ought not to have his head covered, because he is the image and glory of God, but the woman is the glory of the man. [11:8]For man is not from woman, but woman from man; [11:9]for neither was man created for the woman, but woman for the man. [11:10]For this cause the woman ought to have authority on her head, because of the angels.

[11:11]Nevertheless, neither is the woman independent of the man, nor the man independent of the woman, in the Lord. [11:12]For as woman came from man, so a man also comes through a woman; but all things are from God. [11:13]Judge for yourselves. Is it appropriate that a woman pray to God unveiled? [11:14]Doesn't even nature itself teach you that if a man has long hair, it is a dishonor to him? [11:15]But if a woman has long hair, it is a glory to her, for her hair is given to her for a covering. [11:16]But if any man seems to be contentious, we have no such custom, neither do God's assemblies.

[11:17]But in giving you this command, I don't praise you, that you come together not for the better but for the worse. [11:18]For first of all, when you come together in the assembly, I hear that divisions exist among you, and I partly believe it. [11:19]For there also must be factions among you, that those who are approved may be revealed among you. [11:20]When therefore you assemble yourselves together, it is not the Lord's supper that you eat. [11:21]For in your eating each one takes his own supper first. One is hungry, and another is drunken. [11:22]What, don't you have houses to eat and to drink in? Or do you despise God's assembly, and put them to shame who don't have? What shall I tell you? Shall I praise you? In this I don't praise you.

[11:23]For I received from the Lord that which also I delivered to you, that the Lord Jesus on the night in which he was betrayed took bread. [11:24]When he had given thanks, he broke it, and said, **"Take, eat. This is my body, which is broken for you. Do this in memory of me."** [11:25]In the same way he also took the cup, after supper, saying, **"This cup is the new covenant in my blood. Do this, as often as you drink, in memory of me."** [11:26]For as often as you eat this bread and drink this cup, you proclaim the Lord's death until he comes. [11:27]Therefore whoever eats this bread or drinks the Lord's cup in a manner unworthy of the Lord will be guilty of the body and the blood of the Lord. [11:28]But let a man examine himself, and so let him eat of the bread, and drink of the cup. [11:29]For he who eats and drinks in an unworthy manner eats and drinks judgment to himself, if he doesn't discern the Lord's

---

[l]10:26 Psalm 24:1

body. [11:30] For this cause many among you are weak and sickly, and not a few sleep. [11:31] For if we discerned ourselves, we wouldn't be judged. [11:32] But when we are judged, we are punished by the Lord, that we may not be condemned with the world. [11:33] Therefore, my brothers, when you come together to eat, wait one for another. [11:34] But if anyone is hungry, let him eat at home, lest your coming together be for judgment. The rest I will set in order whenever I come.

[12:1] Now concerning spiritual things, brothers, I don't want you to be ignorant. [12:2] You know that when you were heathen[m], you were led away to those mute idols, however you might be led. [12:3] Therefore I make known to you that no man speaking by God's Spirit says, "Jesus is accursed." No one can say, "Jesus is Lord," but by the Holy Spirit. [12:4] Now there are various kinds of gifts, but the same Spirit. [12:5] There are various kinds of service, and the same Lord. [12:6] There are various kinds of workings, but the same God, who works all things in all. [12:7] But to each one is given the manifestation of the Spirit for the profit of all. [12:8] For to one is given through the Spirit the word of wisdom, and to another the word of knowledge, according to the same Spirit; [12:9] to another faith, by the same Spirit; and to another gifts of healings, by the same Spirit; [12:10] and to another workings of miracles; and to another prophecy; and to another discerning of spirits; to another different kinds of languages; and to another the interpretation of languages. [12:11] But the one and the same Spirit works all of these, distributing to each one separately as he desires.

[12:12] For as the body is one, and has many members, and all the members of the body, being many, are one body; so also is Christ. [12:13] For in one Spirit we were all baptized into one body, whether Jews or Greeks, whether bond or free; and were all given to drink into one Spirit. [12:14] For the body is not one member, but many. [12:15] If the foot would say, "Because I'm not the hand, I'm not part of the body," it is

not therefore not part of the body. [12:16] If the ear would say, "Because I'm not the eye, I'm not part of the body," it's not therefore not part of the body. [12:17] If the whole body were an eye, where would the hearing be? If the whole were hearing, where would the smelling be? [12:18] But now God has set the members, each one of them, in the body, just as he desired. [12:19] If they were all one member, where would the body be? [12:20] But now they are many members, but one body. [12:21] The eye can't tell the hand, "I have no need for you," or again the head to the feet, "I have no need for you." [12:22] No, much rather, those members of the body which seem to be weaker are necessary. [12:23] Those parts of the body which we think to be less honorable, on those we bestow more abundant honor; and our unpresentable parts have more abundant propriety; [12:24] whereas our presentable parts have no such need. But God composed the body together, giving more abundant honor to the inferior part, [12:25] that there should be no division in the body, but that the members should have the same care for one another. [12:26] When one member suffers, all the members suffer with it. Or when one member is honored, all the members rejoice with it.

[12:27] Now you are the body of Christ, and members individually. [12:28] God has set some in the assembly: first apostles, second prophets, third teachers, then miracle workers, then gifts of healings, helps, governments, and various kinds of languages. [12:29] Are all apostles? Are all prophets? Are all teachers? Are all miracle workers? [12:30] Do all have gifts of healings? Do all speak with various languages? Do all interpret? [12:31] But earnestly desire the best gifts. Moreover, I show a most excellent way to you.

[13:1] If I speak with the languages of men and of angels, but don't have love, I have become sounding brass, or a clanging cymbal. [13:2] If I have the gift of prophecy, and know all mysteries and all knowledge; and if I have all faith, so as to remove mountains, but don't have love, I am nothing.

---

[m] 12:2 or Gentiles

[13:3]If I dole out all my goods to feed the poor, and if I give my body to be burned, but don't have love, it profits me nothing.

[13:4]Love is patient and is kind; love doesn't envy. Love doesn't brag, is not proud, [13:5]doesn't behave itself inappropriately, doesn't seek its own way, is not provoked, takes no account of evil; [13:6]doesn't rejoice in unrighteousness, but rejoices with the truth; [13:7]bears all things, believes all things, hopes all things, endures all things. [13:8]Love never fails. But where there are prophecies, they will be done away with. Where there are various languages, they will cease. Where there is knowledge, it will be done away with. [13:9]For we know in part, and we prophesy in part; [13:10]but when that which is complete has come, then that which is partial will be done away with. [13:11]When I was a child, I spoke as a child, I felt as a child, I thought as a child. Now that I have become a man, I have put away childish things. [13:12]For now we see in a mirror, dimly, but then face to face. Now I know in part, but then I will know fully, even as I was also fully known. [13:13]But now faith, hope, and love remain— these three. The greatest of these is love.

[14:1]Follow after love, and earnestly desire spiritual gifts, but especially that you may prophesy. [14:2]For he who speaks in another language speaks not to men, but to God; for no one understands; but in the Spirit he speaks mysteries. [14:3]But he who prophesies speaks to men for their edification, exhortation, and consolation. [14:4]He who speaks in another language edifies himself, but he who prophesies edifies the assembly. [14:5]Now I desire to have you all speak with other languages, but rather that you would prophesy. For he is greater who prophesies than he who speaks with other languages, unless he interprets, that the assembly may be built up. [14:6]But now, brothers,[n] if I come to you speaking with other languages, what would I profit you, unless I speak to you either by way of revelation, or of knowledge, or of prophesying, or of teaching?

[14:7]Even things without life, giving a voice, whether pipe or harp, if they didn't give a distinction in the sounds, how would it be known what is piped or harped? [14:8]For if the trumpet gave an uncertain sound, who would prepare himself for war? [14:9]So also you, unless you uttered by the tongue words easy to understand, how would it be known what is spoken? For you would be speaking into the air. [14:10]There are, it may be, so many kinds of sounds in the world, and none of them is without meaning. [14:11]If then I don't know the meaning of the sound, I would be to him who speaks a foreigner, and he who speaks would be a foreigner to me. [14:12]So also you, since you are zealous for spiritual gifts, seek that you may abound to the building up of the assembly. [14:13]Therefore let him who speaks in another language pray that he may interpret. [14:14]For if I pray in another language, my spirit prays, but my understanding is unfruitful.

[14:15]What is it then? I will pray with the spirit, and I will pray with the understanding also. I will sing with the spirit, and I will sing with the understanding also. [14:16]Otherwise if you bless with the spirit, how will he who fills the place of the unlearned say the "Amen" at your giving of thanks, seeing he doesn't know what you say? [14:17]For you most certainly give thanks well, but the other person is not built up. [14:18]I thank my God, I speak with other languages more than you all. [14:19]However in the assembly I would rather speak five words with my understanding, that I might instruct others also, than ten thousand words in another language.

[14:20]Brothers, don't be children in thoughts, yet in malice be babies, but in thoughts be mature. [14:21]In the law it is written, "By men of strange languages and by the lips of strangers I will speak to this people. Not even thus will they hear me, says the Lord."[o] [14:22]Therefore other languages are for a sign, not to those who believe, but to

---

[n]14:6 The word for "brothers" here and where context allows may also be correctly translated "brothers and sisters" or "siblings."
[o]14:21 Isaiah 28:11-12

the unbelieving; but prophesying is for a sign, not to the unbelieving, but to those who believe. ¹⁴:²³If therefore the whole assembly is assembled together and all speak with other languages, and unlearned or unbelieving people come in, won't they say that you are crazy? ¹⁴:²⁴But if all prophesy, and someone unbelieving or unlearned comes in, he is reproved by all, and he is judged by all. ¹⁴:²⁵And thus the secrets of his heart are revealed. So he will fall down on his face and worship God, declaring that God is among you indeed.

¹⁴:²⁶What is it then, brothers? When you come together, each one of you has a psalm, has a teaching, has a revelation, has another language, has an interpretation. Let all things be done to build each other up. ¹⁴:²⁷If any man speaks in another language, let it be two, or at the most three, and in turn; and let one interpret. ¹⁴:²⁸But if there is no interpreter, let him keep silent in the assembly, and let him speak to himself, and to God. ¹⁴:²⁹Let the prophets speak, two or three, and let the others discern. ¹⁴:³⁰But if a revelation is made to another sitting by, let the first keep silent. ¹⁴:³¹For you all can prophesy one by one, that all may learn, and all may be exhorted. ¹⁴:³²The spirits of the prophets are subject to the prophets, ¹⁴:³³for God is not a God of confusion, but of peace.

As in all the assemblies of the saints, ¹⁴:³⁴let your wives keep silent in the assemblies, for it has not been permitted for them to speak; but let them be in subjection, as the law also says. ¹⁴:³⁵If they desire to learn anything, let them ask their own husbands at home, for it is shameful for a woman to chatter in the assembly. ¹⁴:³⁶What? Was it from you that the word of God went out? Or did it come to you alone? ¹⁴:³⁷If any man thinks himself to be a prophet, or spiritual, let him recognize the things which I write to you, that they are the commandment of the Lord. ¹⁴:³⁸But if anyone is ignorant, let him be ignorant. ¹⁴:³⁹Therefore, brothers, desire earnestly to prophesy, and don't forbid speaking with other languages. ¹⁴:⁴⁰Let all things be done decently and in order.

¹⁵:¹Now I declare to you, brothers, the Good News which I preached to you, which also you received, in which you also stand, ¹⁵:²by which also you are saved, if you hold firmly the word which I preached to you—unless you believed in vain. ¹⁵:³For I delivered to you first of all that which I also received: that Christ died for our sins according to the Scriptures, ¹⁵:⁴that he was buried, that he was raised on the third day according to the Scriptures, ¹⁵:⁵and that he appeared to Cephas, then to the twelve. ¹⁵:⁶Then he appeared to over five hundred brothers at once, most of whom remain until now, but some have also fallen asleep. ¹⁵:⁷Then he appeared to James, then to all the apostles, ¹⁵:⁸and last of all, as to the child born at the wrong time, he appeared to me also. ¹⁵:⁹For I am the least of the apostles, who is not worthy to be called an apostle, because I persecuted the assembly of God. ¹⁵:¹⁰But by the grace of God I am what I am. His grace which was bestowed on me was not futile, but I worked more than all of them; yet not I, but the grace of God which was with me. ¹⁵:¹¹Whether then it is I or they, so we preach, and so you believed.

¹⁵:¹²Now if Christ is preached, that he has been raised from the dead, how do some among you say that there is no resurrection of the dead? ¹⁵:¹³But if there is no resurrection of the dead, neither has Christ been raised. ¹⁵:¹⁴If Christ has not been raised, then our preaching is in vain, and your faith also is in vain. ¹⁵:¹⁵Yes, we are found false witnesses of God, because we testified about God that he raised up Christ, whom he didn't raise up, if it is so that the dead are not raised. ¹⁵:¹⁶For if the dead aren't raised, neither has Christ been raised. ¹⁵:¹⁷If Christ has not been raised, your faith is vain; you are still in your sins. ¹⁵:¹⁸Then they also who are fallen asleep in Christ have perished. ¹⁵:¹⁹If we have only hoped in Christ in this life, we are of all men most pitiable.

¹⁵:²⁰But now Christ has been raised from the dead. He became the first fruits of those who are asleep. ¹⁵:²¹For since death came by man, the resurrection of the dead also came by man. ¹⁵:²²For as in Adam all die, so also in Christ all will be made alive. ¹⁵:²³But each in his own order: Christ

the first fruits, then those who are Christ's, at his coming. [15:24]Then the end comes, when he will deliver up the Kingdom to God, even the Father; when he will have abolished all rule and all authority and power. [15:25]For he must reign until he has put all his enemies under his feet. [15:26]The last enemy that will be abolished is death. [15:27]For, "He put all things in subjection under his feet."[p] But when he says, "All things are put in subjection," it is evident that he is excepted who subjected all things to him. [15:28]When all things have been subjected to him, then the Son will also himself be subjected to him who subjected all things to him, that God may be all in all. [15:29]Or else what will they do who are baptized for the dead? If the dead aren't raised at all, why then are they baptized for the dead? [15:30]Why do we also stand in jeopardy every hour? [15:31]I affirm, by the boasting in you which I have in Christ Jesus our Lord, I die daily. [15:32]If I fought with animals at Ephesus for human purposes, what does it profit me? If the dead are not raised, then "let us eat and drink, for tomorrow we die."[q] [15:33]Don't be deceived! "Evil companionships corrupt good morals." [15:34]Wake up righteously, and don't sin, for some have no knowledge of God. I say this to your shame. [15:35]But someone will say, "How are the dead raised?" and, "With what kind of body do they come?" [15:36]You foolish one, that which you yourself sow is not made alive unless it dies. [15:37]That which you sow, you don't sow the body that will be, but a bare grain, maybe of wheat, or of some other kind. [15:38]But God gives it a body even as it pleased him, and to each seed a body of its own. [15:39]All flesh is not the same flesh, but there is one flesh of men, another flesh of animals, another of fish, and another of birds. [15:40]There are also celestial bodies, and terrestrial bodies; but the glory of the celestial differs from that of the terrestrial.

[15:41]There is one glory of the sun, another glory of the moon, and another glory of the stars; for one star differs from another star in glory. [15:42]So also is the resurrection of the dead. It is sown in corruption; it is raised in incorruption. [15:43]It is sown in dishonor; it is raised in glory. It is sown in weakness; it is raised in power. [15:44]It is sown a natural body; it is raised a spiritual body. There is a natural body and there is also a spiritual body.

[15:45]So also it is written, "The first man, Adam, became a living soul."[r] The last Adam became a life-giving spirit. [15:46]However that which is spiritual isn't first, but that which is natural, then that which is spiritual. [15:47]The first man is of the earth, made of dust. The second man is the Lord from heaven. [15:48]As is the one made of dust, such are those who are also made of dust; and as is the heavenly, such are they also that are heavenly. [15:49]As we have borne the image of those made of dust, let's[s] also bear the image of the heavenly. [15:50]Now I say this, brothers,[t] that flesh and blood can't inherit the Kingdom of God; neither does corruption inherit incorruption.

[15:51]Behold, I tell you a mystery. We will not all sleep, but we will all be changed, [15:52]in a moment, in the twinkling of an eye, at the last trumpet. For the trumpet will sound, and the dead will be raised incorruptible, and we will be changed. [15:53]For this corruptible must put on incorruption, and this mortal must put on immortality. [15:54]But when this corruptible will have put on incorruption, and this mortal will have put on immortality, then what is written will happen: "Death is swallowed up in victory."[u]

[15:55]"Death, where is your sting?

---

[p]15:27 Psalm 8:6
[q]15:32 Isaiah 22:13
[r]15:45 Genesis 2:7
[s]15:49 NU, TR read "we will" instead of "let's"
[t]15:50 The word for "brothers" here and where context allows may also be correctly translated "brothers and sisters" or "siblings."
[u]15:54 Isaiah 25:8

Hades[v], where is your victory?"[w] [15:56]The sting of death is sin, and the power of sin is the law. [15:57]But thanks be to God, who gives us the victory through our Lord Jesus Christ. [15:58]Therefore, my beloved brothers, be steadfast, immovable, always abounding in the Lord's work, because you know that your labor is not in vain in the Lord.

[16:1]Now concerning the collection for the saints, as I commanded the assemblies of Galatia, you do likewise. [16:2]On the first day of the week, let each one of you save, as he may prosper, that no collections be made when I come. [16:3]When I arrive, I will send whoever you approve with letters to carry your gracious gift to Jerusalem. [16:4]If it is appropriate for me to go also, they will go with me. [16:5]But I will come to you when I have passed through Macedonia, for I am passing through Macedonia. [16:6]But with you it may be that I will stay, or even winter, that you may send me on my journey wherever I go. [16:7]For I do not wish to see you now in passing, but I hope to stay a while with you, if the Lord permits. [16:8]But I will stay at Ephesus until Pentecost, [16:9]for a great and effective door has opened to me, and there are many adversaries. [16:10]Now if Timothy comes, see that he is with you without fear, for he does the work of the Lord, as I also do. [16:11]Therefore let no one despise him. But set him forward on his journey in peace, that he may come to me; for I expect him with the brothers.

[16:12]Now concerning Apollos, the brother, I strongly urged him to come to you with the brothers; and it was not at all his desire to come now; but he will come when he has an opportunity.

[16:13]Watch! Stand firm in the faith! Be courageous! Be strong! [16:14]Let all that you do be done in love.

[16:15]Now I beg you, brothers (you know the house of Stephanas, that it is the first fruits of Achaia, and that they have set themselves to serve the saints), [16:16]that you also be in subjection to such, and to everyone who helps in the work and labors. [16:17]I rejoice at the coming of Stephanas, Fortunatus, and Achaicus; for that which was lacking on your part, they supplied. [16:18]For they refreshed my spirit and yours. Therefore acknowledge those who are like that.

[16:19]The assemblies of Asia greet you. Aquila and Priscilla greet you much in the Lord, together with the assembly that is in their house. [16:20]All the brothers greet you. Greet one another with a holy kiss.

[16:21]This greeting is by me, Paul, with my own hand. [16:22]If any man doesn't love the Lord Jesus Christ, let him be accursed[x]. Come, Lord![y] [16:23]The grace of the Lord Jesus Christ be with you. [16:24]My love to all of you in Christ Jesus. Amen.

Paul's Second Letter to the Corinthians

[1:1]Paul, an apostle of Christ Jesus through the will of God, and Timothy our brother, to the assembly of God which is at Corinth, with all the saints who are in the whole of Achaia: [1:2]Grace to you and peace from God our Father and the Lord Jesus Christ.

[1:3]Blessed be the God and Father of our Lord Jesus Christ, the Father of mercies and God of all comfort; [1:4]who comforts us in all our affliction, that we may be able to comfort those who are in any affliction, through the comfort with which we ourselves are comforted by God. [1:5]For as the sufferings of Christ abound to us, even so our comfort also abounds through Christ. [1:6]But if we are afflicted, it is for your comfort and salvation. If we are comforted, it is for your comfort, which produces in you the patient enduring of the same sufferings which we also suffer. [1:7]Our hope for you is steadfast, knowing that, since you are partakers of the sufferings, so also are you of the comfort.

---

[v] 15:55 or, Hell
[w] 15:55 Hosea 13:14
[x] 16:22 Greek: anathema.
[y] 16:22 Aramaic: Maranatha!

[1:8]For we don't desire to have you uninformed, brothers,[a] concerning our affliction which happened to us in Asia, that we were weighed down exceedingly, beyond our power, so much that we despaired even of life. [1:9]Yes, we ourselves have had the sentence of death within ourselves, that we should not trust in ourselves, but in God who raises the dead, [1:10]who delivered us out of so great a death, and does deliver; on whom we have set our hope that he will also still deliver us; [1:11]you also helping together on our behalf by your supplication; that, for the gift bestowed on us by means of many, thanks may be given by many persons on your behalf. [1:12]For our boasting is this: the testimony of our conscience, that in holiness and sincerity of God, not in fleshly wisdom but in the grace of God we behaved ourselves in the world, and more abundantly toward you. [1:13]For we write no other things to you, than what you read or even acknowledge, and I hope you will acknowledge to the end; [1:14]as also you acknowledged us in part, that we are your boasting, even as you also are ours, in the day of our Lord Jesus. [1:15]In this confidence, I was determined to come first to you, that you might have a second benefit; [1:16]and by you to pass into Macedonia, and again from Macedonia to come to you, and to be sent forward by you on my journey to Judea. [1:17]When I therefore was thus determined, did I show fickleness? Or the things that I purpose, do I purpose according to the flesh, that with me there should be the "Yes, yes" and the "No, no?" [1:18]But as God is faithful, our word toward you was not "Yes and no." [1:19]For the Son of God, Jesus Christ, who was preached among you by us, by me, Silvanus, and Timothy, was not "Yes and no," but in him is "Yes." [1:20]For however many are the promises of God, in him is the "Yes." Therefore also through him is the "Amen," to the glory of God through us. [1:21]Now he who establishes us with you in Christ, and anointed us, is God; [1:22]who also sealed us, and gave us the down payment of the Spirit in our hearts. [1:23]But I call God for a witness to my soul, that I didn't come to Corinth to spare you. [1:24]Not that we have lordship over your faith, but are fellow workers with you for your joy. For you stand firm in faith.

[2:1]But I determined this for myself, that I would not come to you again in sorrow. [2:2]For if I make you sorry, then who will make me glad but he who is made sorry by me? [2:3]And I wrote this very thing to you, so that, when I came, I wouldn't have sorrow from them of whom I ought to rejoice; having confidence in you all, that my joy would be shared by all of you. [2:4]For out of much affliction and anguish of heart I wrote to you with many tears, not that you should be made sorry, but that you might know the love that I have so abundantly for you. [2:5]But if any has caused sorrow, he has caused sorrow, not to me, but in part (that I not press too heavily) to you all. [2:6]Sufficient to such a one is this punishment which was inflicted by the many; [2:7]so that on the contrary you should rather forgive him and comfort him, lest by any means such a one should be swallowed up with his excessive sorrow. [2:8]Therefore I beg you to confirm your love toward him. [2:9]For to this end I also wrote, that I might know the proof of you, whether you are obedient in all things. [2:10]Now I also forgive whomever you forgive anything. For if indeed I have forgiven anything, I have forgiven that one for your sakes in the presence of Christ, [2:11]that no advantage may be gained over us by Satan; for we are not ignorant of his schemes.

[2:12]Now when I came to Troas for the Good News of Christ, and when a door was opened to me in the Lord, [2:13]I had no relief for my spirit, because I didn't find Titus, my brother, but taking my leave of them, I went out into Macedonia. [2:14]Now thanks be to God, who always leads us in triumph in Christ, and reveals through us the sweet aroma of his knowledge in every place. [2:15]For we are a sweet aroma of Christ to God, in those who are saved, and in those who perish; [2:16]to the one a stench

---

[a]1:8 The word for "brothers" here and where context allows may also be correctly translated "brothers and sisters" or "siblings."

from death to death; to the other a sweet aroma from life to life. Who is sufficient for these things? [2:17]For we are not as so many, peddling the word of God. But as of sincerity, but as of God, in the sight of God, we speak in Christ.

[3:1]Are we beginning again to commend ourselves? Or do we need, as do some, letters of commendation to you or from you? [3:2]You are our letter, written in our hearts, known and read by all men; [3:3]being revealed that you are a letter of Christ, served by us, written not with ink, but with the Spirit of the living God; not in tablets of stone, but in tablets that are hearts of flesh. [3:4]Such confidence we have through Christ toward God; [3:5]not that we are sufficient of ourselves, to account anything as from ourselves; but our sufficiency is from God; [3:6]who also made us sufficient as servants of a new covenant; not of the letter, but of the Spirit. For the letter kills, but the Spirit gives life. [3:7]But if the service of death, written engraved on stones, came with glory, so that the children of Israel could not look steadfastly on the face of Moses for the glory of his face; which was passing away: [3:8]won't service of the Spirit be with much more glory? [3:9]For if the service of condemnation has glory, the service of righteousness exceeds much more in glory. [3:10]For most certainly that which has been made glorious has not been made glorious in this respect, by reason of the glory that surpasses. [3:11]For if that which passes away was with glory, much more that which remains is in glory.

[3:12]Having therefore such a hope, we use great boldness of speech, [3:13]and not as Moses, who put a veil on his face, that the children of Israel wouldn't look steadfastly on the end of that which was passing away. [3:14]But their minds were hardened, for until this very day at the reading of the old covenant the same veil remains, because in Christ it passes away. [3:15]But to this day, when Moses is read, a veil lies on their heart. [3:16]But whenever one turns to the Lord, the veil is taken away. [3:17]Now the Lord is the Spirit and where the Spirit of

the Lord is, there is liberty. [3:18]But we all, with unveiled face beholding as in a mirror the glory of the Lord, are transformed into the same image from glory to glory, even as from the Lord, the Spirit.

[4:1]Therefore seeing we have this ministry, even as we obtained mercy, we don't faint. [4:2]But we have renounced the hidden things of shame, not walking in craftiness, nor handling the word of God deceitfully; but by the manifestation of the truth commending ourselves to every man's conscience in the sight of God. [4:3]Even if our Good News is veiled, it is veiled in those who perish; [4:4]in whom the god of this world has blinded the minds of the unbelieving, that the light of the Good News of the glory of Christ, who is the image of God, should not dawn on them. [4:5]For we don't preach ourselves, but Christ Jesus as Lord, and ourselves as your servants for Jesus' sake; [4:6]seeing it is God who said, "Light will shine out of darkness,"[b] who has shone in our hearts, to give the light of the knowledge of the glory of God in the face of Jesus Christ.

[4:7]But we have this treasure in clay vessels, that the exceeding greatness of the power may be of God, and not from ourselves. [4:8]We are pressed on every side, yet not crushed; perplexed, yet not to despair; [4:9]pursued, yet not forsaken; struck down, yet not destroyed; [4:10]always carrying in the body the putting to death of the Lord Jesus, that the life of Jesus may also be revealed in our body. [4:11]For we who live are always delivered to death for Jesus' sake, that the life also of Jesus may be revealed in our mortal flesh. [4:12]So then death works in us, but life in you. [4:13]But having the same spirit of faith, according to that which is written, "I believed, and therefore I spoke."[c] We also believe, and therefore also we speak; [4:14]knowing that he who raised the Lord Jesus will raise us also with Jesus, and will present us with you. [4:15]For all things are for your sakes, that the grace, being multiplied through the many, may cause the thanksgiving to

---

[b]4:6 Genesis 1:3
[c]4:13 Psalm 116:10

abound to the glory of God. [4:16]Therefore we don't faint, but though our outward man is decaying, yet our inward man is renewed day by day. [4:17]For our light affliction, which is for the moment, works for us more and more exceedingly an eternal weight of glory; [4:18]while we don't look at the things which are seen, but at the things which are not seen. For the things which are seen are temporal, but the things which are not seen are eternal.

[5:1]For we know that if the earthly house of our tent is dissolved, we have a building from God, a house not made with hands, eternal, in the heavens. [5:2]For most certainly in this we groan, longing to be clothed with our habitation which is from heaven; [5:3]if so be that being clothed we will not be found naked. [5:4]For indeed we who are in this tent do groan, being burdened; not that we desire to be unclothed, but that we desire to be clothed, that what is mortal may be swallowed up by life. [5:5]Now he who made us for this very thing is God, who also gave to us the down payment of the Spirit.

[5:6]Therefore, we are always confident and know that while we are at home in the body, we are absent from the Lord; [5:7]for we walk by faith, not by sight. [5:8]We are of good courage, I say, and are willing rather to be absent from the body, and to be at home with the Lord. [5:9]Therefore also we make it our aim, whether at home or absent, to be well pleasing to him. [5:10]For we must all be revealed before the judgment seat of Christ; that each one may receive the things in the body, according to what he has done, whether good or bad. [5:11]Knowing therefore the fear of the Lord, we persuade men, but we are revealed to God; and I hope that we are revealed also in your consciences. [5:12]For we are not commending ourselves to you again, but speak as giving you occasion of boasting on our behalf, that you may have something to answer those who boast in appearance, and not in heart. [5:13]For if we are beside ourselves, it is for God. Or if we are of sober mind, it is for you. [5:14]For the love of Christ constrains us; because we judge thus, that one died

for all, therefore all died. [5:15]He died for all, that those who live should no longer live to themselves, but to him who for their sakes died and rose again. [5:16]Therefore we know no one after the flesh from now on. Even though we have known Christ after the flesh, yet now we know him so no more. [5:17]Therefore if anyone is in Christ, he is a new creation. The old things have passed away. Behold, all things have become new. [5:18]But all things are of God, who reconciled us to himself through Jesus Christ, and gave to us the ministry of reconciliation; [5:19]namely, that God was in Christ reconciling the world to himself, not reckoning to them their trespasses, and having committed to us the word of reconciliation. [5:20]We are therefore ambassadors on behalf of Christ, as though God were entreating by us. We beg you on behalf of Christ, be reconciled to God. [5:21]For him who knew no sin he made to be sin on our behalf; so that in him we might become the righteousness of God.

[6:1]Working together, we entreat also that you not receive the grace of God in vain, [6:2]for he says,

"At an acceptable time I listened to you,

in a day of salvation I helped you."[d]

Behold, now is the acceptable time. Behold, now is the day of salvation. [6:3]We give no occasion of stumbling in anything, that our service may not be blamed, [6:4]but in everything commending ourselves, as servants of God, in great endurance, in afflictions, in hardships, in distresses, [6:5]in beatings, in imprisonments, in riots, in labors, in watchings, in fastings; [6:6]in pureness, in knowledge, in patience, in kindness, in the Holy Spirit, in sincere love, [6:7]in the word of truth, in the power of God; by the armor of righteousness on the right hand and on the left, [6:8]by glory and dishonor, by evil report and good report; as deceivers, and yet true; [6:9]as unknown, and yet well known; as dying, and behold, we live; as punished, and not killed; [6:10]as sorrowful, yet always rejoicing; as poor, yet making many rich; as having nothing, and yet possessing all things.

---

[d]6:2 Isaiah 49:8

⁶:¹¹Our mouth is open to you, Corinthians. Our heart is enlarged. ⁶:¹²You are not restricted by us, but you are restricted by your own affections. ⁶:¹³Now in return, I speak as to my children, you also be open wide. ⁶:¹⁴Don't be unequally yoked with unbelievers, for what fellowship have righteousness and iniquity? Or what fellowship has light with darkness? ⁶:¹⁵What agreement has Christ with Belial? Or what portion has a believer with an unbeliever? ⁶:¹⁶What agreement has a temple of God with idols? For you are a temple of the living God. Even as God said, "I will dwell in them, and walk in them; and I will be their God, and they will be my people."ᵉ ⁶:¹⁷Therefore,

"'Come out from among them,
　　and be separate,' says the Lord.
'Touch no unclean thing.
　　I will receive you.ᶠ
⁶:¹⁸I will be to you a Father.
　　You will be to me sons and daughters,'
says the Lord Almighty."ᵍ

⁷:¹Having therefore these promises, beloved, let us cleanse ourselves from all defilement of flesh and spirit, perfecting holiness in the fear of God. ⁷:²Open your hearts to us. We wronged no one. We corrupted no one. We took advantage of no one. ⁷:³I say this not to condemn you, for I have said before, that you are in our hearts to die together and live together. ⁷:⁴Great is my boldness of speech toward you. Great is my boasting on your behalf. I am filled with comfort. I overflow with joy in all our affliction. ⁷:⁵For even when we had come into Macedonia, our flesh had no relief, but we were afflicted on every side. Fightings were outside. Fear was inside. ⁷:⁶Nevertheless, he who comforts the lowly, God, comforted us by the coming of Titus; ⁷:⁷and not by his coming only, but also by the comfort with which he was comforted in you, while he told us of your longing, your mourning, and your zeal for me; so that I rejoiced still more. ⁷:⁸For though I made you sorry with my letter, I do not regret it, though I did regret it. For I see that my letter made you sorry, though just for a while. ⁷:⁹I now rejoice, not that you were made sorry, but that you were made sorry to repentance. For you were made sorry in a godly way, that you might suffer loss by us in nothing. ⁷:¹⁰For godly sorrow works repentance to salvation, which brings no regret. But the sorrow of the world works death. ⁷:¹¹For behold, this same thing, that you were made sorry in a godly way, what earnest care it worked in you. Yes, what defense, indignation, fear, longing, zeal, and vengeance! In everything you demonstrated yourselves to be pure in the matter. ⁷:¹²So although I wrote to you, I wrote not for his cause that did the wrong, nor for his cause that suffered the wrong, but that your earnest care for us might be revealed in you in the sight of God. ⁷:¹³Therefore we have been comforted. In our comfort we rejoiced the more exceedingly for the joy of Titus, because his spirit has been refreshed by you all. ⁷:¹⁴For if in anything I have boasted to him on your behalf, I was not disappointed. But as we spoke all things to you in truth, so our glorying also which I made before Titus was found to be truth. ⁷:¹⁵His affection is more abundantly toward you, while he remembers all of your obedience, how with fear and trembling you received him. ⁷:¹⁶I rejoice that in everything I am of good courage concerning you.

⁸:¹Moreover, brothers, we make known to you the grace of God which has been given in the assemblies of Macedonia; ⁸:²how that in much proof of affliction the abundance of their joy and their deep poverty abounded to the riches of their liberality. ⁸:³For according to their power, I testify, yes and beyond their power, they gave of their own accord, ⁸:⁴begging us with much entreaty to receive this grace and the fellowship in the service to the saints. ⁸:⁵This was not as we had hoped, but first they gave their own selves to the Lord, and to us through the will of God.

ᵉ6:16 Leviticus 26:12; Jeremiah 32:38; Ezekiel 37:27
ᶠ6:17 Isaiah 52:11; Ezekiel 20:34,41
ᵍ6:18 2 Samuel 7:14; 7:8

[8:6]So we urged Titus, that as he made a beginning before, so he would also complete in you this grace. [8:7]But as you abound in everything, in faith, utterance, knowledge, all earnestness, and in your love to us, see that you also abound in this grace. [8:8]I speak not by way of commandment, but as proving through the earnestness of others the sincerity also of your love. [8:9]For you know the grace of our Lord Jesus Christ, that, though he was rich, yet for your sakes he became poor, that you through his poverty might become rich. [8:10]I give a judgment in this: for this is expedient for you, who were the first to start a year ago, not only to do, but also to be willing. [8:11]But now complete the doing also, that as there was the readiness to be willing, so there may be the completion also out of your ability. [8:12]For if the readiness is there, it is acceptable according to what you have, not according to what you don't have. [8:13]For this is not that others may be eased and you distressed, [8:14]but for equality. Your abundance at this present time supplies their lack, that their abundance also may become a supply for your lack; that there may be equality. [8:15]As it is written, "He who gathered much had nothing left over, and he who gathered little had no lack."[h]

[8:16]But thanks be to God, who puts the same earnest care for you into the heart of Titus. [8:17]For he indeed accepted our exhortation, but being himself very earnest, he went out to you of his own accord. [8:18]We have sent together with him the brother whose praise in the Good News is known through all the assemblies. [8:19]Not only so, but who was also appointed by the assemblies to travel with us in this grace, which is served by us to the glory of the Lord himself, and to show our readiness. [8:20]We are avoiding this, that any man should blame us concerning this abundance which is administered by us. [8:21]Having regard for honorable things, not only in the sight of the Lord, but also in the sight of men. [8:22]We have sent with them our brother, whom we have many times proved earnest in many things, but now

much more earnest, by reason of the great confidence which he has in you. [8:23]As for Titus, he is my partner and fellow worker for you. As for our brothers, they are the apostles of the assemblies, the glory of Christ. [8:24]Therefore show the proof of your love to them in front of the assemblies, and of our boasting on your behalf.

[9:1]It is indeed unnecessary for me to write to you concerning the service to the saints, [9:2]for I know your readiness, of which I boast on your behalf to them of Macedonia, that Achaia has been prepared for a year past. Your zeal has stirred up very many of them. [9:3]But I have sent the brothers that our boasting on your behalf may not be in vain in this respect, that, just as I said, you may be prepared, [9:4]so that I won't by any means, if there come with me any of Macedonia and find you unprepared, we (to say nothing of you) should be disappointed in this confident boasting. [9:5]I thought it necessary therefore to entreat the brothers that they would go before to you, and arrange ahead of time the generous gift that you promised before, that the same might be ready as a matter of generosity, and not of greediness. [9:6]Remember this: he who sows sparingly will also reap sparingly. He who sows bountifully will also reap bountifully. [9:7]Let each man give according as he has determined in his heart; not grudgingly, or under compulsion; for God loves a cheerful giver. [9:8]And God is able to make all grace abound to you, that you, always having all sufficiency in everything, may abound to every good work. [9:9]As it is written,

"He has scattered abroad, he has given to the poor.

His righteousness remains forever."[i]

[9:10]Now may he who supplies seed to the sower and bread for food, supply and multiply your seed for sowing, and increase the fruits of your righteousness; [9:11]you being enriched in everything to all liberality, which works through us thanksgiving to God. [9:12]For this service of giving that you perform not only makes up for lack

[h]8:15 Exodus 16:8
[i]9:9 Psalm 112:9

among the saints, but abounds also through many givings of thanks to God; [9:13]seeing that through the proof given by this service, they glorify God for the obedience of your confession to the Good News of Christ, and for the liberality of your contribution to them and to all; [9:14]while they themselves also, with supplication on your behalf, yearn for you by reason of the exceeding grace of God in you. [9:15]Now thanks be to God for his unspeakable gift!

[10:1]Now I Paul, myself, entreat you by the humility and gentleness of Christ; I who in your presence am lowly among you, but being absent am of good courage toward you. [10:2]Yes, I beg you that I may not, when present, show courage with the confidence with which I intend to be bold against some, who consider us to be walking according to the flesh. [10:3]For though we walk in the flesh, we don't wage war according to the flesh; [10:4]for the weapons of our warfare are not of the flesh, but mighty before God to the throwing down of strongholds, [10:5]throwing down imaginations and every high thing that is exalted against the knowledge of God, and bringing every thought into captivity to the obedience of Christ; [10:6]and being in readiness to avenge all disobedience, when your obedience will be made full. [10:7]Do you look at things only as they appear in front of your face? If anyone trusts in himself that he is Christ's, let him consider this again with himself, that, even as he is Christ's, so also we are Christ's. [10:8]For though I should boast somewhat abundantly concerning our authority, (which the Lord gave for building you up, and not for casting you down) I will not be disappointed, [10:9]that I may not seem as if I desire to terrify you by my letters. [10:10]For, "His letters," they say, "are weighty and strong, but his bodily presence is weak, and his speech is despised." [10:11]Let such a person consider this, that what we are in word by letters when we are absent, such are we also in deed when we are present. [10:12]For we are not bold to number or compare ourselves with some of those who commend themselves. But they themselves,

measuring themselves by themselves, and comparing themselves with themselves, are without understanding. [10:13]But we will not boast beyond proper limits, but within the boundaries with which God appointed to us, which reach even to you. [10:14]For we don't stretch ourselves too much, as though we didn't reach to you. For we came even as far as to you with the Good News of Christ, [10:15]not boasting beyond proper limits in other men's labors, but having hope that as your faith grows, we will be abundantly enlarged by you in our sphere of influence, [10:16]so as to preach the Good News even to the parts beyond you, not to boast in what someone else has already done. [10:17]But "he who boasts, let him boast in the Lord."[j] [10:18]For it isn't he who commends himself who is approved, but whom the Lord commends.

[11:1]I wish that you would bear with me in a little foolishness, but indeed you do bear with me. [11:2]For I am jealous over you with a godly jealousy. For I married you to one husband, that I might present you as a pure virgin to Christ. [11:3]But I am afraid that somehow, as the serpent deceived Eve in his craftiness, so your minds might be corrupted from the simplicity that is in Christ. [11:4]For if he who comes preaches another Jesus, whom we did not preach, or if you receive a different spirit, which you did not receive, or a different "good news", which you did not accept, you put up with that well enough. [11:5]For I reckon that I am not at all behind the very best apostles. [11:6]But though I am unskilled in speech, yet I am not unskilled in knowledge. No, in every way we have been revealed to you in all things. [11:7]Or did I commit a sin in humbling myself that you might be exalted, because I preached to you God's Good News free of charge? [11:8]I robbed other assemblies, taking wages from them that I might serve you. [11:9]When I was present with you and was in need, I wasn't a burden on anyone, for the brothers, when they came from Macedonia, supplied the measure of my need. In everything I kept myself from being burdensome to you,

---

[j]10:17 Jeremiah 9:24

and I will continue to do so. ^{11:10}As the truth of Christ is in me, no one will stop me from this boasting in the regions of Achaia. ^{11:11}Why? Because I don't love you? God knows. ^{11:12}But what I do, that I will do, that I may cut off occasion from them that desire an occasion, that in which they boast, they may be found even as we. ^{11:13}For such men are false apostles, deceitful workers, masquerading as Christ's apostles. ^{11:14}And no wonder, for even Satan masquerades as an angel of light. ^{11:15}It is no great thing therefore if his servants also masquerade as servants of righteousness, whose end will be according to their works.

^{11:16}I say again, let no one think me foolish. But if so, yet receive me as foolish, that I also may boast a little. ^{11:17}That which I speak, I don't speak according to the Lord, but as in foolishness, in this confidence of boasting. ^{11:18}Seeing that many boast after the flesh, I will also boast. ^{11:19}For you bear with the foolish gladly, being wise. ^{11:20}For you bear with a man, if he brings you into bondage, if he devours you, if he takes you captive, if he exalts himself, if he strikes you on the face. ^{11:21}I speak by way of disparagement, as though we had been weak. Yet however any is bold (I speak in foolishness), I am bold also. ^{11:22}Are they Hebrews? So am I. Are they Israelites? So am I. Are they the seed of Abraham? So am I. ^{11:23}Are they servants of Christ? (I speak as one beside himself) I am more so; in labors more abundantly, in prisons more abundantly, in stripes above measure, in deaths often. ^{11:24}Five times from the Jews I received forty stripes minus one. ^{11:25}Three times I was beaten with rods. Once I was stoned. Three times I suffered shipwreck. I have been a night and a day in the deep. ^{11:26}I have been in travels often, perils of rivers, perils of robbers, perils from my countrymen, perils from the Gentiles, perils in the city, perils in the wilderness, perils in the sea, perils among false brothers; ^{11:27}in labor and travail, in watchings often, in hunger and thirst, in fastings often, and in cold and nakedness.

^{11:28}Besides those things that are outside, there is that which presses on me daily,

anxiety for all the assemblies. ^{11:29}Who is weak, and I am not weak? Who is caused to stumble, and I don't burn with indignation? ^{11:30}If I must boast, I will boast of the things that concern my weakness. ^{11:31}The God and Father of the Lord Jesus Christ, he who is blessed forevermore, knows that I don't lie. ^{11:32}In Damascus the governor under Aretas the king guarded the city of the Damascenes desiring to arrest me. ^{11:33}Through a window I was let down in a basket by the wall, and escaped his hands.

^{12:1}It is doubtless not profitable for me to boast. For I will come to visions and revelations of the Lord. ^{12:2}I know a man in Christ, fourteen years ago (whether in the body, I don't know, or whether out of the body, I don't know; God knows), such a one caught up into the third heaven. ^{12:3}I know such a man (whether in the body, or outside of the body, I don't know; God knows), ^{12:4}how he was caught up into Paradise, and heard unspeakable words, which it is not lawful for a man to utter. ^{12:5}On behalf of such a one I will boast, but on my own behalf I will not boast, except in my weaknesses. ^{12:6}For if I would desire to boast, I will not be foolish; for I will speak the truth. But I refrain, so that no man may think more of me than that which he sees in me, or hears from me. ^{12:7}By reason of the exceeding greatness of the revelations, that I should not be exalted excessively, there was given to me a thorn in the flesh, a messenger of Satan to torment me, that I should not be exalted excessively. ^{12:8}Concerning this thing, I begged the Lord three times that it might depart from me. ^{12:9}He has said to me, **"My grace is sufficient for you, for my power is made perfect in weakness."** Most gladly therefore I will rather glory in my weaknesses, that the power of Christ may rest on me.

^{12:10}Therefore I take pleasure in weaknesses, in injuries, in necessities, in persecutions, in distresses, for Christ's sake. For when I am weak, then am I strong. ^{12:11}I have become foolish in boasting. You compelled me, for I ought to have been commended by you, for in nothing was I inferior to the very best apostles, though

I am nothing. [12:12]Truly the signs of an apostle were worked among you in all patience, in signs and wonders and mighty works. [12:13]For what is there in which you were made inferior to the rest of the assemblies, unless it is that I myself was not a burden to you? Forgive me this wrong.

[12:14]Behold, this is the third time I am ready to come to you, and I will not be a burden to you; for I seek not your possessions, but you. For the children ought not to save up for the parents, but the parents for the children. [12:15]I will most gladly spend and be spent for your souls. If I love you more abundantly, am I loved the less? [12:16]But be it so, I did not myself burden you. But, being crafty, I caught you with deception. [12:17]Did I take advantage of you by anyone of them whom I have sent to you? [12:18]I exhorted Titus, and I sent the brother with him. Did Titus take any advantage of you? Didn't we walk in the same spirit? Didn't we walk in the same steps? [12:19]Again, do you think that we are excusing ourselves to you? In the sight of God we speak in Christ. But all things, beloved, are for your edifying. [12:20]For I am afraid that by any means, when I come, I might find you not the way I want to, and that I might be found by you as you don't desire; that by any means there would be strife, jealousy, outbursts of anger, factions, slander, whisperings, proud thoughts, riots; [12:21]that again when I come my God would humble me before you, and I would mourn for many of those who have sinned before now, and not repented of the uncleanness and sexual immorality and lustfulness which they committed.

[13:1]This is the third time I am coming to you. "At the mouth of two or three witnesses shall every word be established."[k] [13:2]I have said beforehand, and I do say beforehand, as when I was present the second time, so now, being absent, I write to those who have sinned before now, and to all the rest, that, if I come again, I will not spare; [13:3]seeing that you seek a proof of Christ who speaks in me; who toward you is not weak, but is powerful in you. [13:4]For he was crucified through weakness, yet he lives through the power of God. For we also are weak in him, but we will live with him through the power of God toward you. [13:5]Test your own selves, whether you are in the faith. Test your own selves. Or don't you know as to your own selves, that Jesus Christ is in you?—unless indeed you are disqualified. [13:6]But I hope that you will know that we aren't disqualified.

[13:7]Now I pray to God that you do no evil; not that we may appear approved, but that you may do that which is honorable, though we are as reprobate. [13:8]For we can do nothing against the truth, but for the truth. [13:9]For we rejoice when we are weak and you are strong. And this we also pray for, even your perfecting. [13:10]For this cause I write these things while absent, that I may not deal sharply when present, according to the authority which the Lord gave me for building up, and not for tearing down.

[13:11]Finally, brothers, rejoice. Be perfected, be comforted, be of the same mind, live in peace, and the God of love and peace will be with you. [13:12]Greet one another with a holy kiss. [13:13]All the saints greet you. [13:14]The grace of the Lord Jesus Christ, the love of God, and the fellowship of the Holy Spirit, be with you all. Amen.

Paul's Letter to the Galatians

[1:1]Paul, an apostle (not from men, neither through man, but through Jesus Christ, and God the Father, who raised him from the dead), [1:2]and all the brothers[a] who are with me, to the assemblies of Galatia: [1:3]Grace to you and peace from God the Father, and our Lord Jesus Christ, [1:4]who gave himself for our sins, that he might deliver us out of this present evil age, according to the will

---

[k]13:1 Deuteronomy 19:15
[a]1:2 The word for "brothers" here and where context allows may also be correctly translated "brothers and sisters" or "siblings."

of our God and Father—[1:5]to whom be the glory forever and ever. Amen.

[1:6]I marvel that you are so quickly deserting him who called you in the grace of Christ to a different "good news"; [1:7]and there isn't another "good news." Only there are some who trouble you, and want to pervert the Good News of Christ. [1:8]But even though we, or an angel from heaven, should preach to you any "good news" other than that which we preached to you, let him be cursed. [1:9]As we have said before, so I now say again: if any man preaches to you any "good news" other than that which you received, let him be cursed. [1:10]For am I now seeking the favor of men, or of God? Or am I striving to please men? For if I were still pleasing men, I wouldn't be a servant of Christ. [1:11]But I make known to you, brothers, concerning the Good News which was preached by me, that it is not according to man. [1:12]For neither did I receive it from man, nor was I taught it, but it came to me through revelation of Jesus Christ. [1:13]For you have heard of my way of living in time past in the Jews' religion, how that beyond measure I persecuted the assembly of God, and ravaged it. [1:14]I advanced in the Jews' religion beyond many of my own age among my countrymen, being more exceedingly zealous for the traditions of my fathers. [1:15]But when it was the good pleasure of God, who separated me from my mother's womb, and called me through his grace, [1:16]to reveal his Son in me, that I might preach him among the Gentiles, I didn't immediately confer with flesh and blood, [1:17]nor did I go up to Jerusalem to those who were apostles before me, but I went away into Arabia. Then I returned to Damascus. [1:18]Then after three years I went up to Jerusalem to visit Peter, and stayed with him fifteen days. [1:19]But of the other apostles I saw no one, except James, the Lord's brother. [1:20]Now about the things which I write to you, behold, before God, I'm not lying. [1:21]Then I came to the regions of Syria and Cilicia. [1:22]I was still unknown by face to the assemblies of Judea which were in Christ, [1:23]but they only heard: "He who once persecuted us now preaches the

faith that he once tried to destroy." [1:24]And they glorified God in me.

[2:1]Then after a period of fourteen years I went up again to Jerusalem with Barnabas, taking Titus also with me. [2:2]I went up by revelation, and I laid before them the Good News which I preach among the Gentiles, but privately before those who were respected, for fear that I might be running, or had run, in vain. [2:3]But not even Titus, who was with me, being a Greek, was compelled to be circumcised. [2:4]This was because of the false brothers secretly brought in, who stole in to spy out our liberty which we have in Christ Jesus, that they might bring us into bondage; [2:5]to whom we gave no place in the way of subjection, not for an hour, that the truth of the Good News might continue with you. [2:6]But from those who were reputed to be important (whatever they were, it makes no difference to me; God doesn't show partiality to man)—they, I say, who were respected imparted nothing to me, [2:7]but to the contrary, when they saw that I had been entrusted with the Good News for the uncircumcision, even as Peter with the Good News for the circumcision [2:8](for he who appointed Peter to the apostleship of the circumcision appointed me also to the Gentiles); [2:9]and when they perceived the grace that was given to me, James and Cephas and John, they who were reputed to be pillars, gave to me and Barnabas the right hand of fellowship, that we should go to the Gentiles, and they to the circumcision. [2:10]They only asked us to remember the poor—which very thing I was also zealous to do.

[2:11]But when Peter came to Antioch, I resisted him to his face, because he stood condemned. [2:12]For before some people came from James, he ate with the Gentiles. But when they came, he drew back and separated himself, fearing those who were of the circumcision. [2:13]And the rest of the Jews joined him in his hypocrisy; so that even Barnabas was carried away with their hypocrisy. [2:14]But when I saw that they didn't walk uprightly according to the truth of the Good News, I said to Peter before them all, "If you, being a Jew, live as the Gentiles do, and not as the Jews do, why do you compel the Gentiles to live as the Jews do?

2:15 "We, being Jews by nature, and not Gentile sinners, 2:16 yet knowing that a man is not justified by the works of the law but through faith in Jesus Christ, even we believed in Christ Jesus, that we might be justified by faith in Christ, and not by the works of the law, because no flesh will be justified by the works of the law. 2:17 But if, while we sought to be justified in Christ, we ourselves also were found sinners, is Christ a servant of sin? Certainly not! 2:18 For if I build up again those things which I destroyed, I prove myself a law-breaker. 2:19 For I, through the law, died to the law, that I might live to God. 2:20 I have been crucified with Christ, and it is no longer I that live, but Christ living in me. That life which I now live in the flesh, I live by faith in the Son of God, who loved me, and gave himself up for me. 2:21 I don't make void the grace of God. For if righteousness is through the law, then Christ died for nothing!"

3:1 Foolish Galatians, who has bewitched you not to obey the truth, before whose eyes Jesus Christ was openly set forth among you as crucified? 3:2 I just want to learn this from you. Did you receive the Spirit by the works of the law, or by hearing of faith? 3:3 Are you so foolish? Having begun in the Spirit, are you now completed in the flesh? 3:4 Did you suffer so many things in vain, if it is indeed in vain? 3:5 He therefore who supplies the Spirit to you, and works miracles among you, does he do it by the works of the law, or by hearing of faith? 3:6 Even as Abraham "believed God, and it was counted to him for righteousness." 3:7 Know therefore that those who are of faith, the same are children of Abraham. 3:8 The Scripture, foreseeing that God would justify the Gentiles by faith, preached the Good News beforehand to Abraham, saying, "In you all the nations

will be blessed." [b] 3:9 So then, those who are of faith are blessed with the faithful Abraham. 3:10 For as many as are of the works of the law are under a curse. For it is written, "Cursed is everyone who doesn't continue in all things that are written in the book of the law, to do them." [c] 3:11 Now that no man is justified by the law before God is evident, for, "The righteous will live by faith." [d] 3:12 The law is not of faith, but, "The man who does them will live by them." [e]

3:13 Christ redeemed us from the curse of the law, having become a curse for us. For it is written, "Cursed is everyone who hangs on a tree," [f] 3:14 that the blessing of Abraham might come on the Gentiles through Christ Jesus; that we might receive the promise of the Spirit through faith. 3:15 Brothers, speaking of human terms, though it is only a man's covenant, yet when it has been confirmed, no one makes it void, or adds to it. 3:16 Now the promises were spoken to Abraham and to his seed. He doesn't say, "To seeds," as of many, but as of one, "To your seed," [g] which is Christ. 3:17 Now I say this. A covenant confirmed beforehand by God in Christ, the law, which came four hundred thirty years after, does not annul, so as to make the promise of no effect. 3:18 For if the inheritance is of the law, it is no more of promise; but God has granted it to Abraham by promise.

3:19 What then is the law? It was added because of transgressions, until the seed should come to whom the promise has been made. It was ordained through angels by the hand of a mediator. 3:20 Now a mediator is not between one, but God is one. 3:21 Is the law then against the promises of God? Certainly not! For if there had been a law given which could make alive, most certainly righteousness would have been of the law. 3:22 But the Scriptures imprisoned all things under sin, that the promise by faith in Jesus Christ might be given to those who believe. 3:23 But before faith

---

[b] 3:8 Genesis 12:3; 18:18; 22:18
[c] 3:10 Deuteronomy 27:26
[d] 3:11 Habakkuk 2:4
[e] 3:12 Leviticus 18:5
[f] 3:13 Deuteronomy 21:23
[g] 3:16 Genesis 12:7; 13:15; 24:7

came, we were kept in custody under the law, confined for the faith which should afterwards be revealed. ³:²⁴So that the law has become our tutor to bring us to Christ, that we might be justified by faith. ³:²⁵But now that faith has come, we are no longer under a tutor. ³:²⁶For you are all children of God, through faith in Christ Jesus. ³:²⁷For as many of you as were baptized into Christ have put on Christ. ³:²⁸There is neither Jew nor Greek, there is neither slave nor free man, there is neither male nor female; for you are all one in Christ Jesus. ³:²⁹If you are Christ's, then you are Abraham's seed and heirs according to promise.

⁴:¹But I say that so long as the heir is a child, he is no different from a bond-servant, though he is lord of all; ⁴:²but is under guardians and stewards until the day appointed by the father. ⁴:³So we also, when we were children, were held in bondage under the elemental principles of the world. ⁴:⁴But when the fullness of the time came, God sent out his Son, born to a woman, born under the law, ⁴:⁵that he might redeem those who were under the law, that we might receive the adoption of children. ⁴:⁶And because you are children, God sent out the Spirit of his Son into your hearts, crying, "Abba,ʰ Father!" ⁴:⁷So you are no longer a bondservant, but a son; and if a son, then an heir of God through Christ. ⁴:⁸However at that time, not knowing God, you were in bondage to those who by nature are not gods. ⁴:⁹But now that you have come to know God, or rather to be known by God, why do you turn back again to the weak and miserable elemental principles, to which you desire to be in bondage all over again? ⁴:¹⁰You observe days, months, seasons, and years. ⁴:¹¹I am afraid for you, that I might have wasted my labor for you. ⁴:¹²I beg you, brothers, become as I am, for I also have become as you are. You did me no wrong, ⁴:¹³but you know that because of weakness of the flesh I preached the Good News to you the first time. ⁴:¹⁴That which was a temptation to you in my flesh, you didn't despise nor reject; but you received me as an angel of God, even as Christ Jesus.

⁴:¹⁵What was the blessing you enjoyed? For I testify to you that, if possible, you would have plucked out your eyes and given them to me. ⁴:¹⁶So then, have I become your enemy by telling you the truth? ⁴:¹⁷They zealously seek you in no good way. No, they desire to alienate you, that you may seek them. ⁴:¹⁸But it is always good to be zealous in a good cause, and not only when I am present with you.

⁴:¹⁹My little children, of whom I am again in travail until Christ is formed in you— ⁴:²⁰but I could wish to be present with you now, and to change my tone, for I am perplexed about you. ⁴:²¹Tell me, you that desire to be under the law, don't you listen to the law? ⁴:²²For it is written that Abraham had two sons, one by the handmaid, and one by the free woman. ⁴:²³However, the son by the handmaid was born according to the flesh, but the son by the free woman was born through promise. ⁴:²⁴These things contain an allegory, for these are two covenants. One is from Mount Sinai, bearing children to bondage, which is Hagar. ⁴:²⁵For this Hagar is Mount Sinai in Arabia, and answers to the Jerusalem that exists now, for she is in bondage with her children. ⁴:²⁶But the Jerusalem that is above is free, which is the mother of us all. ⁴:²⁷For it is written,

"Rejoice, you barren who don't bear.

> Break forth and shout, you that don't travail.

> For more are the children of the desolate than of her who has a husband."ⁱ

⁴:²⁸Now we, brothers, as Isaac was, are children of promise. ⁴:²⁹But as then, he who was born according to the flesh persecuted him who was born according to the Spirit, so also it is now. ⁴:³⁰However what does the Scripture say? "Throw out the handmaid and her son, for the son of the handmaid will not inherit with the son of

---

ʰ4:6 Abba is a Greek spelling for the Aramaic word for "Father" or "Daddy" used in a familiar, respectful, and loving way.
ⁱ4:27 Isaiah 54:1

the free woman."[j] [4:31]So then, brothers, we are not children of a handmaid, but of the free woman.

[5:1]Stand firm therefore in the liberty by which Christ has made us free, and don't be entangled again with a yoke of bondage. [5:2]Behold, I, Paul, tell you that if you receive circumcision, Christ will profit you nothing. [5:3]Yes, I testify again to every man who receives circumcision, that he is a debtor to do the whole law. [5:4]You are alienated from Christ, you who desire to be justified by the law. You have fallen away from grace. [5:5]For we, through the Spirit, by faith wait for the hope of righteousness. [5:6]For in Christ Jesus neither circumcision amounts to anything, nor uncircumcision, but faith working through love. [5:7]You were running well! Who interfered with you that you should not obey the truth? [5:8]This persuasion is not from him who calls you. [5:9]A little yeast grows through the whole lump. [5:10]I have confidence toward you in the Lord that you will think no other way. But he who troubles you will bear his judgment, whoever he is.

[5:11]But I, brothers, if I still preach circumcision, why am I still persecuted? Then the stumbling block of the cross has been removed. [5:12]I wish that those who disturb you would cut themselves off. [5:13]For you, brothers, were called for freedom. Only don't use your freedom for gain to the flesh, but through love be servants to one another. [5:14]For the whole law is fulfilled in one word, in this: "You shall love your neighbor as yourself."[k] [5:15]But if you bite and devour one another, be careful that you don't consume one another. [5:16]But I say, walk by the Spirit, and you won't fulfill the lust of the flesh. [5:17]For the flesh lusts against the Spirit, and the Spirit against the flesh; and these are contrary to one another, that you may not do the things that you desire. [5:18]But if you are led by the Spirit, you are not under the law. [5:19]Now the works of the flesh are obvious, which are: adultery, sexual immorality, uncleanness, lustfulness, [5:20]idolatry, sorcery,

hatred, strife, jealousies, outbursts of anger, rivalries, divisions, heresies, [5:21]envyings, murders, drunkenness, orgies, and things like these; of which I forewarn you, even as I also forewarned you, that those who practice such things will not inherit the Kingdom of God.

[5:22]But the fruit of the Spirit is love, joy, peace, patience, kindness, goodness, faith,[l] [5:23]gentleness, and self-control. Against such things there is no law. [5:24]Those who belong to Christ have crucified the flesh with its passions and lusts. [5:25]If we live by the Spirit, let's also walk by the Spirit. [5:26]Let's not become conceited, provoking one another, and envying one another.

[6:1]Brothers, even if a man is caught in some fault, you who are spiritual must restore such a one in a spirit of gentleness; looking to yourself so that you also aren't tempted. [6:2]Bear one another's burdens, and so fulfill the law of Christ. [6:3]For if a man thinks himself to be something when he is nothing, he deceives himself. [6:4]But let each man test his own work, and then he will take pride in himself and not in his neighbor. [6:5]For each man will bear his own burden. [6:6]But let him who is taught in the word share all good things with him who teaches. [6:7]Don't be deceived. God is not mocked, for whatever a man sows, that he will also reap. [6:8]For he who sows to his own flesh will from the flesh reap corruption. But he who sows to the Spirit will from the Spirit reap eternal life. [6:9]Let us not be weary in doing good, for we will reap in due season, if we don't give up. [6:10]So then, as we have opportunity, let's do what is good toward all men, and especially toward those who are of the household of the faith.

[6:11]See with what large letters I write to you with my own hand. [6:12]As many as desire to look good in the flesh, they compel you to be circumcised; only that they may not be persecuted for the cross of Christ. [6:13]For even they who receive circumcision don't keep the law themselves, but they

[j]4:30 Genesis 21:10
[k]5:14 Leviticus 19:18
[l]5:22 or, faithfulness

desire to have you circumcised, that they may boast in your flesh. [6:14]But far be it from me to boast, except in the cross of our Lord Jesus Christ, through which the world has been crucified to me, and I to the world. [6:15]For in Christ Jesus neither is circumcision anything, nor uncircumcision, but a new creation. [6:16]As many as walk by this rule, peace and mercy be on them, and on God's Israel. [6:17]From now on, let no one cause me any trouble, for I bear the marks of the Lord Jesus branded on my body.

[6:18]The grace of our Lord Jesus Christ be with your spirit, brothers. Amen.

Paul's Letter to the Ephesians

[1:1]Paul, an apostle of Christ Jesus through the will of God,
to the saints who are at Ephesus, and the faithful in Christ Jesus: [1:2]Grace to you and peace from God our Father and the Lord Jesus Christ.

[1:3]Blessed be the God and Father of our Lord Jesus Christ, who has blessed us with every spiritual blessing in the heavenly places in Christ; [1:4]even as he chose us in him before the foundation of the world, that we would be holy and without blemish before him in love; [1:5]having predestined us for adoption as children through Jesus Christ to himself, according to the good pleasure of his desire, [1:6]to the praise of the glory of his grace, by which he freely bestowed favor on us in the Beloved, [1:7]in whom we have our redemption through his blood, the forgiveness of our trespasses, according to the riches of his grace, [1:8]which he made to abound toward us in all wisdom and prudence, [1:9]making known to us the mystery of his will, according to his good pleasure which he purposed in him [1:10]to an administration of the fullness of the times, to sum up all things in Christ, the things in the heavens, and the things on the earth, in him; [1:11]in whom also we were assigned an inheritance, having been

foreordained according to the purpose of him who works all things after the counsel of his will; [1:12]to the end that we should be to the praise of his glory, we who had before hoped in Christ: [1:13]in whom you also, having heard the word of the truth, the Good News of your salvation,—in whom, having also believed, you were sealed with the Holy Spirit of promise, [1:14]who is a pledge of our inheritance, to the redemption of God's own possession, to the praise of his glory. [1:15]For this cause I also, having heard of the faith in the Lord Jesus which is among you, and the love which you have toward all the saints, [1:16]don't cease to give thanks for you, making mention of you in my prayers, [1:17]that the God of our Lord Jesus Christ, the Father of glory, may give to you a spirit of wisdom and revelation in the knowledge of him; [1:18]having the eyes of your hearts[a] enlightened, that you may know what is the hope of his calling, and what are the riches of the glory of his inheritance in the saints, [1:19]and what is the exceeding greatness of his power toward us who believe, according to that working of the strength of his might [1:20]which he worked in Christ, when he raised him from the dead, and made him to sit at his right hand in the heavenly places, [1:21]far above all rule, and authority, and power, and dominion, and every name that is named, not only in this age, but also in that which is to come. [1:22]He put all things in subjection under his feet, and gave him to be head over all things for the assembly, [1:23]which is his body, the fullness of him who fills all in all.

[2:1]You were made alive when you were dead in transgressions and sins, [2:2]in which you once walked according to the course of this world, according to the prince of the powers of the air, the spirit who now works in the children of disobedience; [2:3]among whom we also all once lived in the lust of our flesh, doing the desires of the flesh and of the mind, and were by nature children of wrath, even as the rest. [2:4]But God, being rich in mercy, for his great love with which he loved us, [2:5]even when we were

---

[a]1:18 TR reads "understanding" instead of "hearts"

dead through our trespasses, made us alive together with Christ (by grace you have been saved), 2:6and raised us up with him, and made us to sit with him in the heavenly places in Christ Jesus, 2:7that in the ages to come he might show the exceeding riches of his grace in kindness toward us in Christ Jesus; 2:8for by grace you have been saved through faith, and that not of yourselves; it is the gift of God, 2:9not of works, that no one would boast. 2:10For we are his workmanship, created in Christ Jesus for good works, which God prepared before that we would walk in them.

2:11Therefore remember that once you, the Gentiles in the flesh, who are called "uncircumcision" by that which is called "circumcision," (in the flesh, made by hands); 2:12that you were at that time separate from Christ, alienated from the commonwealth of Israel, and strangers from the covenants of the promise, having no hope and without God in the world. 2:13But now in Christ Jesus you who once were far off are made near in the blood of Christ. 2:14For he is our peace, who made both one, and broke down the middle wall of partition, 2:15having abolished in the flesh the hostility, the law of commandments contained in ordinances, that he might create in himself one new man of the two, making peace; 2:16and might reconcile them both in one body to God through the cross, having killed the hostility thereby. 2:17He came and preached peace to you who were far off and to those who were near. 2:18For through him we both have our access in one Spirit to the Father. 2:19So then you are no longer strangers and foreigners, but you are fellow citizens with the saints, and of the household of God, 2:20being built on the foundation of the apostles and prophets, Christ Jesus himself being the chief cornerstone; 2:21in whom the whole building, fitted together, grows into a holy temple in the Lord; 2:22in whom you also are built together for a habitation of God in the Spirit.

3:1For this cause I, Paul, am the prisoner of Christ Jesus on behalf of you Gentiles, 3:2if it is so that you have heard of the administration of that grace of God which was given me toward you; 3:3how that by revelation the mystery was made known to me, as I wrote before in few words, 3:4by which, when you read, you can perceive my understanding in the mystery of Christ; 3:5which in other generations was not made known to the children of men, as it has now been revealed to his holy apostles and prophets in the Spirit; 3:6that the Gentiles are fellow heirs, and fellow members of the body, and fellow partakers of his promise in Christ Jesus through the Good News, 3:7of which I was made a servant, according to the gift of that grace of God which was given me according to the working of his power. 3:8To me, the very least of all saints, was this grace given, to preach to the Gentiles the unsearchable riches of Christ, 3:9and to make all men see what is the administrationᵇ of the mystery which for ages has been hidden in God, who created all things through Jesus Christ; 3:10to the intent that now through the assembly the manifold wisdom of God might be made known to the principalities and the powers in the heavenly places, 3:11according to the eternal purpose which he purposed in Christ Jesus our Lord; 3:12in whom we have boldness and access in confidence through our faith in him. 3:13Therefore I ask that you may not lose heart at my troubles for you, which are your glory.

3:14For this cause, I bow my knees to the Father of our Lord Jesus Christ, 3:15from whom every family in heaven and on earth is named, 3:16that he would grant you, according to the riches of his glory, that you may be strengthened with power through his Spirit in the inward man; 3:17that Christ may dwell in your hearts through faith; to the end that you, being rooted and grounded in love, 3:18may be strengthened to comprehend with all the saints what is the breadth and length and height and depth, 3:19and to know Christ's love which surpasses knowledge, that you may be filled with all the fullness of God. 3:20Now to him who is able to do exceedingly abundantly above all that we ask or think,

---

ᵇ3:9 TR reads "fellowship" instead of "administration"

according to the power that works in us, [3:21]to him be the glory in the assembly and in Christ Jesus to all generations forever and ever. Amen.

[4:1]I therefore, the prisoner in the Lord, beg you to walk worthily of the calling with which you were called, [4:2]with all lowliness and humility, with patience, bearing with one another in love; [4:3]being eager to keep the unity of the Spirit in the bond of peace. [4:4]There is one body, and one Spirit, even as you also were called in one hope of your calling; [4:5]one Lord, one faith, one baptism, [4:6]one God and Father of all, who is over all, and through all, and in us all. [4:7]But to each one of us was the grace given according to the measure of the gift of Christ. [4:8]Therefore he says, "When he ascended on high, he led captivity captive, and gave gifts to men."[c] [4:9]Now this, "He ascended," what is it but that he also first descended into the lower parts of the earth? [4:10]He who descended is the one who also ascended far above all the heavens, that he might fill all things.

[4:11]He gave some to be apostles; and some, prophets; and some, evangelists; and some, shepherds[d] and teachers; [4:12]for the perfecting of the saints, to the work of serving, to the building up of the body of Christ; [4:13]until we all attain to the unity of the faith, and of the knowledge of the Son of God, to a full grown man, to the measure of the stature of the fullness of Christ; [4:14]that we may no longer be children, tossed back and forth and carried about with every wind of doctrine, by the trickery of men, in craftiness, after the wiles of error; [4:15]but speaking truth in love, we may grow up in all things into him, who is the head, Christ; [4:16]from whom all the body, being fitted and knit together through that which every joint supplies, according to the working in measure of each individual part, makes the body increase to the building up of itself in love.

[4:17]This I say therefore, and testify in the Lord, that you no longer walk as the rest of the Gentiles also walk, in the futility of their mind, [4:18]being darkened in their understanding, alienated from the life of God, because of the ignorance that is in them, because of the hardening of their hearts; [4:19]who having become callous gave themselves up to lust, to work all uncleanness with greediness. [4:20]But you did not learn Christ that way; [4:21]if indeed you heard him, and were taught in him, even as truth is in Jesus: [4:22]that you put away, as concerning your former way of life, the old man, that grows corrupt after the lusts of deceit; [4:23]and that you be renewed in the spirit of your mind, [4:24]and put on the new man, who in the likeness of God has been created in righteousness and holiness of truth.

[4:25]Therefore, putting away falsehood, speak truth each one with his neighbor. For we are members of one another. [4:26]"Be angry, and don't sin."[e] Don't let the sun go down on your wrath, [4:27]neither give place to the devil. [4:28]Let him who stole steal no more; but rather let him labor, working with his hands the thing that is good, that he may have something to give to him who has need. [4:29]Let no corrupt speech proceed out of your mouth, but such as is good for building up as the need may be, that it may give grace to those who hear. [4:30]Don't grieve the Holy Spirit of God, in whom you were sealed for the day of redemption. [4:31]Let all bitterness, wrath, anger, outcry, and slander, be put away from you, with all malice. [4:32]And be kind to one another, tenderhearted, forgiving each other, just as God also in Christ forgave you.

[5:1]Be therefore imitators of God, as beloved children. [5:2]Walk in love, even as Christ also loved you, and gave himself up for us, an offering and a sacrifice to God for a sweet-smelling fragrance. [5:3]But sexual immorality, and all uncleanness, or covetousness, let it not even be mentioned among you, as becomes saints; [5:4]nor filthiness, nor foolish talking, nor jesting, which are not appropriate; but rather giving of thanks.

---

[c]4:8 Psalm 68:18

[d]4:11 or, pastors

[e]4:26 Psalm 4:4

^{5:5}Know this for sure, that no sexually immoral person, nor unclean person, nor covetous man, who is an idolater, has any inheritance in the Kingdom of Christ and God.

^{5:6}Let no one deceive you with empty words. For because of these things, the wrath of God comes on the children of disobedience. ^{5:7}Therefore don't be partakers with them. ^{5:8}For you were once darkness, but are now light in the Lord. Walk as children of light, ^{5:9}for the fruit of the Spirit is in all goodness and righteousness and truth, ^{5:10}proving what is well pleasing to the Lord. ^{5:11}Have no fellowship with the unfruitful works of darkness, but rather even reprove them. ^{5:12}For the things which are done by them in secret, it is a shame even to speak of. ^{5:13}But all things, when they are reproved, are revealed by the light, for everything that reveals is light. ^{5:14}Therefore he says, "Awake, you who sleep, and arise from the dead, and Christ will shine on you."

^{5:15}Therefore watch carefully how you walk, not as unwise, but as wise; ^{5:16}redeeming the time, because the days are evil. ^{5:17}Therefore don't be foolish, but understand what the will of the Lord is. ^{5:18}Don't be drunken with wine, in which is dissipation, but be filled with the Spirit, ^{5:19}speaking to one another in psalms, hymns, and spiritual songs; singing, and singing praises in your heart to the Lord; ^{5:20}giving thanks always concerning all things in the name of our Lord Jesus Christ, to God, even the Father; ^{5:21}subjecting yourselves one to another in the fear of Christ.

^{5:22}Wives, be subject to your own husbands, as to the Lord. ^{5:23}For the husband is the head of the wife, and Christ also is the head of the assembly, being himself the savior of the body. ^{5:24}But as the assembly is subject to Christ, so let the wives also be to their own husbands in everything.

^{5:25}Husbands, love your wives, even as Christ also loved the assembly, and gave himself up for it; ^{5:26}that he might sanctify it, having cleansed it by the washing of water with the word, ^{5:27}that he might present the assembly to himself gloriously, not having spot or wrinkle or any such thing; but that it should be holy and without blemish. ^{5:28}Even so husbands also ought to love their own wives as their own bodies. He who loves his own wife loves himself. ^{5:29}For no man ever hated his own flesh; but nourishes and cherishes it, even as the Lord also does the assembly; ^{5:30}because we are members of his body, of his flesh and bones. ^{5:31}"For this cause a man will leave his father and mother, and will be joined to his wife. The two will become one flesh."^f ^{5:32}This mystery is great, but I speak concerning Christ and of the assembly. ^{5:33}Nevertheless each of you must also love his own wife even as himself; and let the wife see that she respects her husband.

^{6:1}Children, obey your parents in the Lord, for this is right. ^{6:2}"Honor your father and mother," which is the first commandment with a promise: ^{6:3}"that it may be well with you, and you may live long on the earth."^g

^{6:4}You fathers, don't provoke your children to wrath, but nurture them in the discipline and instruction of the Lord.

^{6:5}Servants, be obedient to those who according to the flesh are your masters, with fear and trembling, in singleness of your heart, as to Christ; ^{6:6}not in the way of service only when eyes are on you, as men pleasers; but as servants of Christ, doing the will of God from the heart; ^{6:7}with good will doing service, as to the Lord, and not to men; ^{6:8}knowing that whatever good thing each one does, he will receive the same again from the Lord, whether he is bound or free.

^{6:9}You masters, do the same things to them, and give up threatening, knowing that he who is both their Master and yours is in heaven, and there is no partiality with him.

^{6:10}Finally, be strong in the Lord, and in the strength of his might. ^{6:11}Put on the whole armor of God, that you may be

---

^f5:31 Genesis 2:24
^g6:3 Deuteronomy 5:16

able to stand against the wiles of the devil. [6:12]For our wrestling is not against flesh and blood, but against the principalities, against the powers, against the world's rulers of the darkness of this age, and against the spiritual forces of wickedness in the heavenly places. [6:13]Therefore, put on the whole armor of God, that you may be able to withstand in the evil day, and, having done all, to stand. [6:14]Stand therefore, having the utility belt of truth buckled around your waist, and having put on the breastplate of righteousness, [6:15]and having fitted your feet with the preparation of the Good News of peace; [6:16]above all, taking up the shield of faith, with which you will be able to quench all the fiery darts of the evil one. [6:17]And take the helmet of salvation, and the sword of the Spirit, which is the spoken word of God; [6:18]with all prayer and requests, praying at all times in the Spirit, and being watchful to this end in all perseverance and requests for all the saints: [6:19]on my behalf, that utterance may be given to me in opening my mouth, to make known with boldness the mystery of the Good News, [6:20]for which I am an ambassador in chains; that in it I may speak boldly, as I ought to speak.

[6:21]But that you also may know my affairs, how I am doing, Tychicus, the beloved brother and faithful servant in the Lord, will make known to you all things; [6:22]whom I have sent to you for this very purpose, that you may know our state, and that he may comfort your hearts.

[6:23]Peace be to the brothers, and love with faith, from God the Father and the Lord Jesus Christ. [6:24]Grace be with all those who love our Lord Jesus Christ with incorruptible love. Amen.

Paul's Letter to the Philippians

[1:1]Paul and Timothy, servants of Jesus Christ;

To all the saints in Christ Jesus who are at Philippi, with the overseers[a] and servants[b]: [1:2]Grace to you, and peace from God, our Father, and the Lord Jesus Christ. [1:3]I thank my God whenever I remember you, [1:4]always in every request of mine on behalf of you all making my requests with joy, [1:5]for your partnership[c] in furtherance of the Good News from the first day until now; [1:6]being confident of this very thing, that he who began a good work in you will complete it until the day of Jesus Christ. [1:7]It is even right for me to think this way on behalf of all of you, because I have you in my heart, because, both in my bonds and in the defense and confirmation of the Good News, you all are partakers with me of grace. [1:8]For God is my witness, how I long after all of you in the tender mercies of Christ Jesus.

[1:9]This I pray, that your love may abound yet more and more in knowledge and all discernment; [1:10]so that you may approve the things that are excellent; that you may be sincere and without offense to the day of Christ; [1:11]being filled with the fruits of righteousness, which are through Jesus Christ, to the glory and praise of God.

[1:12]Now I desire to have you know, brothers,[d] that the things which happened to me have turned out rather to the progress of the Good News; [1:13]so that it became evident to the whole praetorian guard, and to all the rest, that my bonds are in Christ; [1:14]and that most of the brothers in the Lord, being confident through my bonds, are more abundantly bold to speak the word of God without fear. [1:15]Some indeed preach Christ even out of envy and strife, and some also out of good will. [1:16]The former insincerely preach Christ from selfish ambition, thinking that they add affliction to my chains; [1:17]but the latter out of love, knowing that I am appointed for the defense of the Good News.

[1:18]What does it matter? Only that in every way, whether in pretense or in truth, Christ is proclaimed. I rejoice in this, yes, and will rejoice. [1:19]For I know that this will turn out to my salvation, through your supplication and the supply of the Spirit of Jesus Christ, [1:20]according to my earnest expectation and hope, that I will in no way be disappointed, but with all boldness, as always, now also Christ will be magnified in my body, whether by life, or by death. [1:21]For to me to live is Christ, and to die is gain. [1:22]But if I live on in the flesh, this will bring fruit from my work; yet I don't make known what I will choose. [1:23]But I am in a dilemma between the two, having the desire to depart and be with Christ, which is far better. [1:24]Yet, to remain in the flesh is more needful for your sake. [1:25]Having this confidence, I know that I will remain, yes, and remain with you all, for your progress and joy in the faith, [1:26]that your rejoicing may abound in Christ Jesus in me through my presence with you again.

[1:27]Only let your manner of life be worthy of the Good News of Christ, that, whether I come and see you or am absent, I may hear of your state, that you stand firm in one spirit, with one soul striving for the faith of the Good News; [1:28]and in nothing frightened by the adversaries, which is for them a proof of destruction, but to you of salvation, and that from God. [1:29]Because it has been granted to you on behalf of Christ, not only to believe in him, but also to suffer on his behalf, [1:30]having the same conflict which you saw in me, and now hear is in me.

[2:1]If there is therefore any exhortation in Christ, if any consolation of love, if any fellowship of the Spirit, if any tender mercies and compassion, [2:2]make my joy full, by being like-minded, having the same love,

---

[a]1:1 or, superintendents, or bishops

[b]1:1 Or, deacons

[c]1:5 The word translated "partnership" (koinonia) also means "fellowship" and "sharing."

[d]1:12 The word for "brothers" here and where context allows may also be correctly translated "brothers and sisters" or "siblings."

being of one accord, of one mind; [2:3]doing nothing through rivalry or through conceit, but in humility, each counting others better than himself; [2:4]each of you not just looking to his own things, but each of you also to the things of others.

[2:5]Have this in your mind, which was also in Christ Jesus, [2:6]who, existing in the form of God, didn't consider equality with God a thing to be grasped, [2:7]but emptied himself, taking the form of a servant, being made in the likeness of men. [2:8]And being found in human form, he humbled himself, becoming obedient to death, yes, the death of the cross. [2:9]Therefore God also highly exalted him, and gave to him the name which is above every name; [2:10]that at the name of Jesus every knee should bow, of those in heaven, those on earth, and those under the earth, [2:11]and that every tongue should confess that Jesus Christ is Lord, to the glory of God the Father.

[2:12]So then, my beloved, even as you have always obeyed, not only in my presence, but now much more in my absence, work out your own salvation with fear and trembling. [2:13]For it is God who works in you both to will and to work, for his good pleasure. [2:14]Do all things without murmurings and disputes, [2:15]that you may become blameless and harmless, children of God without blemish in the midst of a crooked and perverse generation, among whom you are seen as lights in the world, [2:16]holding up the word of life; that I may have something to boast in the day of Christ, that I didn't run in vain nor labor in vain. [2:17]Yes, and if I am poured out on the sacrifice and service of your faith, I rejoice, and rejoice with you all. [2:18]In the same way, you also rejoice, and rejoice with me.

[2:19]But I hope in the Lord Jesus to send Timothy to you soon, that I also may be cheered up when I know how you are doing. [2:20]For I have no one else like-minded, who will truly care about you. [2:21]For they all seek their own, not the things of Jesus Christ. [2:22]But you know the proof of him, that, as a child serves a father, so he served with me in furtherance of the Good News. [2:23]Therefore I hope to send him at once, as soon as I see how it will go with me.

[2:24]But I trust in the Lord that I myself also will come shortly. [2:25]But I counted it necessary to send to you Epaphroditus, my brother, fellow worker, fellow soldier, and your apostle and servant of my need; [2:26]since he longed for you all, and was very troubled, because you had heard that he was sick. [2:27]For indeed he was sick, nearly to death, but God had mercy on him; and not on him only, but on me also, that I might not have sorrow on sorrow. [2:28]I have sent him therefore the more diligently, that, when you see him again, you may rejoice, and that I may be the less sorrowful. [2:29]Receive him therefore in the Lord with all joy, and hold such in honor, [2:30]because for the work of Christ he came near to death, risking his life to supply that which was lacking in your service toward me.

[3:1]Finally, my brothers, rejoice in the Lord. To write the same things to you, to me indeed is not tiresome, but for you it is safe. [3:2]Beware of the dogs, beware of the evil workers, beware of the false circumcision. [3:3]For we are the circumcision, who worship God in the Spirit, and rejoice in Christ Jesus, and have no confidence in the flesh; [3:4]though I myself might have confidence even in the flesh. If any other man thinks that he has confidence in the flesh, I yet more: [3:5]circumcised the eighth day, of the stock of Israel, of the tribe of Benjamin, a Hebrew of Hebrews; concerning the law, a Pharisee; [3:6]concerning zeal, persecuting the assembly; concerning the righteousness which is in the law, found blameless.

[3:7]However, what things were gain to me, these have I counted loss for Christ. [3:8]Yes most certainly, and I count all things to be loss for the excellency of the knowledge of Christ Jesus, my Lord, for whom I suffered the loss of all things, and count them nothing but refuse, that I may gain Christ [3:9]and be found in him, not having a righteousness of my own, that which is of the law, but that which is through faith in Christ, the righteousness which is from God by faith; [3:10]that I may know him, and the power of his resurrection, and the fellowship of his sufferings, becoming conformed to his death; [3:11]if by any means I may attain to the resurrection from the dead. [3:12]Not that I have already obtained, or am already made perfect; but I press on, if it is so that I may take hold of that for which also I was taken hold of by Christ Jesus.

3:13 Brothers, I don't regard myself as yet having taken hold, but one thing I do. Forgetting the things which are behind, and stretching forward to the things which are before, 3:14 I press on toward the goal for the prize of the high calling of God in Christ Jesus. 3:15 Let us therefore, as many as are perfect, think this way. If in anything you think otherwise, God will also reveal that to you. 3:16 Nevertheless, to the extent that we have already attained, let us walk by the same rule. Let us be of the same mind. 3:17 Brothers, be imitators together of me, and note those who walk this way, even as you have us for an example. 3:18 For many walk, of whom I told you often, and now tell you even weeping, as the enemies of the cross of Christ, 3:19 whose end is destruction, whose god is the belly, and whose glory is in their shame, who think about earthly things. 3:20 For our citizenship is in heaven, from where we also wait for a Savior, the Lord Jesus Christ; 3:21 who will change the body of our humiliation to be conformed to the body of his glory, according to the working by which he is able even to subject all things to himself.

4:1 Therefore, my brothers, beloved and longed for, my joy and crown, so stand firm in the Lord, my beloved. 4:2 I exhort Euodia, and I exhort Syntyche, to think the same way in the Lord. 4:3 Yes, I beg you also, true yokefellow, help these women, for they labored with me in the Good News, with Clement also, and the rest of my fellow workers, whose names are in the book of life. 4:4 Rejoice in the Lord always! Again I will say, Rejoice! 4:5 Let your gentleness be known to all men. The Lord is at hand. 4:6 In nothing be anxious, but in everything, by prayer and petition with thanksgiving, let your requests be made known to God. 4:7 And the peace of God, which surpasses all understanding, will guard your hearts and your thoughts in Christ Jesus.

4:8 Finally, brothers, whatever things are true, whatever things are honorable, whatever things are just, whatever things are pure, whatever things are lovely, whatever things are of good report; if there is any virtue, and if there is any praise, think about these things. 4:9 The things which you learned, received, heard, and saw in me: do these things, and the God of peace will be with you. 4:10 But I rejoice in the Lord greatly, that now at length you have revived your thought for me; in which you did indeed take thought, but you lacked opportunity. 4:11 Not that I speak in respect to lack, for I have learned in whatever state I am, to be content in it. 4:12 I know how to be humbled, and I know also how to abound. In everything and in all things I have learned the secret both to be filled and to be hungry, both to abound and to be in need. 4:13 I can do all things through Christ, who strengthens me. 4:14 However you did well that you shared in my affliction. 4:15 You yourselves also know, you Philippians, that in the beginning of the Good News, when I departed from Macedonia, no assembly shared with me in the matter of giving and receiving but you only. 4:16 For even in Thessalonica you sent once and again to my need. 4:17 Not that I seek for the gift, but I seek for the fruit that increases to your account. 4:18 But I have all things, and abound. I am filled, having received from Epaphroditus the things that came from you, a sweet-smelling fragrance, an acceptable and well-pleasing sacrifice to God. 4:19 My God will supply every need of yours according to his riches in glory in Christ Jesus. 4:20 Now to our God and Father be the glory forever and ever! Amen. 4:21 Greet every saint in Christ Jesus. The brothers who are with me greet you. 4:22 All the saints greet you, especially those who are of Caesar's household. 4:23 The grace of the Lord Jesus Christ be with you all. Amen.

Paul's Letter to the Colossians

[1:1] Paul, an apostle of Christ Jesus through the will of God, and Timothy our brother, [1:2] to the saints and faithful brothers[a] in Christ at Colossae: Grace to you and peace from God our Father, and the Lord Jesus Christ.

[1:3] We give thanks to God the Father of our Lord Jesus Christ, praying always for you, [1:4] having heard of your faith in Christ Jesus, and of the love which you have toward all the saints, [1:5] because of the hope which is laid up for you in the heavens, of which you heard before in the word of the truth of the Good News, [1:6] which has come to you; even as it is in all the world and is bearing fruit and growing, as it does in you also, since the day you heard and knew the grace of God in truth; [1:7] even as you learned of Epaphras our beloved fellow servant, who is a faithful servant of Christ on our behalf, [1:8] who also declared to us your love in the Spirit. [1:9] For this cause, we also, since the day we heard this, don't cease praying and making requests for you, that you may be filled with the knowledge of his will in all spiritual wisdom and understanding, [1:10] that you may walk worthily of the Lord, to please him in all respects, bearing fruit in every good work, and increasing in the knowledge of God; [1:11] strengthened with all power, according to the might of his glory, for all endurance and perseverance with joy; [1:12] giving thanks to the Father, who made us fit to be partakers of the inheritance of the saints in light; [1:13] who delivered us out of the power of darkness, and translated us into the Kingdom of the Son of his love; [1:14] in whom we have our redemption,[b] the forgiveness of our sins; [1:15] who is the image of the invisible God, the firstborn of all creation. [1:16] For by him all things were created, in the heavens and on the earth, things visible and things invisible, whether thrones or dominions or principalities or powers; all things have been created through him, and for him. [1:17] He is before all things, and in him all things are held together. [1:18] He is the head of the body, the assembly, who is the beginning, the firstborn from the dead; that in all things he might have the preeminence. [1:19] For all the fullness was pleased to dwell in him; [1:20] and through him to reconcile all things to himself, by him, whether things on the earth, or things in the heavens, having made peace through the blood of his cross.

[1:21] You, being in past times alienated and enemies in your mind in your evil works, [1:22] yet now he has reconciled in the body of his flesh through death, to present you holy and without blemish and blameless before him, [1:23] if it is so that you continue in the faith, grounded and steadfast, and not moved away from the hope of the Good News which you heard, which is being proclaimed in all creation under heaven; of which I, Paul, was made a servant.

[1:24] Now I rejoice in my sufferings for your sake, and fill up on my part that which is lacking of the afflictions of Christ in my flesh for his body's sake, which is the assembly; [1:25] of which I was made a servant, according to the stewardship of God which was given me toward you, to fulfill the word of God, [1:26] the mystery which has been hidden for ages and generations. But now it has been revealed to his saints, [1:27] to whom God was pleased to make known what are the riches of the glory of this mystery among the Gentiles, which is Christ in you, the hope of glory; [1:28] whom we proclaim, admonishing every man and teaching every man in all wisdom, that we may present every man perfect in Christ Jesus; [1:29] for which I also labor, striving according to his working, which works in me mightily.

[2:1] For I desire to have you know how greatly I struggle for you, and for those at Laodicea, and for as many as have not seen my face in the flesh; [2:2] that their hearts may be comforted, they being knit together in

---

[a] 1:2 The word for "brothers" here and where context allows may also be correctly translated "brothers and sisters" or "siblings."
[b] 1:14 TR adds "through his blood,"

love, and gaining all riches of the full assurance of understanding, that they may know the mystery of God, both of the Father and of Christ, [2:3]in whom are all the treasures of wisdom and knowledge hidden. [2:4]Now this I say that no one may delude you with persuasiveness of speech. [2:5]For though I am absent in the flesh, yet am I with you in the spirit, rejoicing and seeing your order, and the steadfastness of your faith in Christ. [2:6]As therefore you received Christ Jesus, the Lord, walk in him, [2:7]rooted and built up in him, and established in the faith, even as you were taught, abounding in it in thanksgiving. [2:8]Be careful that you don't let anyone rob you through his philosophy and vain deceit, after the tradition of men, after the elements of the world, and not after Christ. [2:9]For in him all the fullness of the Godhead dwells bodily, [2:10]and in him you are made full, who is the head of all principality and power; [2:11]in whom you were also circumcised with a circumcision not made with hands, in the putting off of the body of the sins of the flesh, in the circumcision of Christ; [2:12]having been buried with him in baptism, in which you were also raised with him through faith in the working of God, who raised him from the dead. [2:13]You were dead through your trespasses and the uncircumcision of your flesh. He made you alive together with him, having forgiven us all our trespasses, [2:14]wiping out the handwriting in ordinances which was against us; and he has taken it out of the way, nailing it to the cross; [2:15]having stripped the principalities and the powers, he made a show of them openly, triumphing over them in it.

[2:16]Let no man therefore judge you in eating, or in drinking, or with respect to a feast day or a new moon or a Sabbath day, [2:17]which are a shadow of the things to come; but the body is Christ's. [2:18]Let no one rob you of your prize by a voluntary humility and worshipping of the angels, dwelling in the things which he has not seen, vainly puffed up by his fleshly mind, [2:19]and not holding firmly to the Head, from whom all the body, being supplied and knit together through the joints and ligaments, grows with God's growth. [2:20]If

you died with Christ from the elements of the world, why, as though living in the world, do you subject yourselves to ordinances, [2:21]"Don't handle, nor taste, nor touch" [2:22](all of which perish with use), according to the precepts and doctrines of men? [2:23]Which things indeed appear like wisdom in self-imposed worship, and humility, and severity to the body; but aren't of any value against the indulgence of the flesh.

[3:1]If then you were raised together with Christ, seek the things that are above, where Christ is, seated on the right hand of God. [3:2]Set your mind on the things that are above, not on the things that are on the earth. [3:3]For you died, and your life is hidden with Christ in God. [3:4]When Christ, our life, is revealed, then you will also be revealed with him in glory. [3:5]Put to death therefore your members which are on the earth: sexual immorality, uncleanness, depraved passion, evil desire, and covetousness, which is idolatry; [3:6]for which things' sake the wrath of God comes on the children of disobedience. [3:7]You also once walked in those, when you lived in them; [3:8]but now you also put them all away: anger, wrath, malice, slander, and shameful speaking out of your mouth. [3:9]Don't lie to one another, seeing that you have put off the old man with his doings, [3:10]and have put on the new man, who is being renewed in knowledge after the image of his Creator, [3:11]where there can't be Greek and Jew, circumcision and uncircumcision, barbarian, Scythian, bondservant, freeman; but Christ is all, and in all.

[3:12]Put on therefore, as God's chosen ones, holy and beloved, a heart of compassion, kindness, lowliness, humility, and perseverance; [3:13]bearing with one another, and forgiving each other, if any man has a complaint against any; even as Christ forgave you, so you also do.

[3:14]Above all these things, walk in love, which is the bond of perfection. [3:15]And let the peace of God rule in your hearts, to which also you were called in one body; and be thankful. [3:16]Let the word of Christ dwell in you richly; in all wisdom teaching and admonishing one another with psalms, hymns, and spiritual songs, singing with grace in your heart to the Lord.

[3:17]Whatever you do, in word or in deed, do all in the name of the Lord Jesus, giving thanks to God the Father, through him.

[3:18]Wives, be in subjection to your husbands, as is fitting in the Lord.

[3:19]Husbands, love your wives, and don't be bitter against them.

[3:20]Children, obey your parents in all things, for this pleases the Lord.

[3:21]Fathers, don't provoke your children, so that they won't be discouraged.

[3:22]Servants, obey in all things those who are your masters according to the flesh, not just when they are looking, as men pleasers, but in singleness of heart, fearing God. [3:23]And whatever you do, work heartily, as for the Lord, and not for men, [3:24]knowing that from the Lord you will receive the reward of the inheritance; for you serve the Lord Christ. [3:25]But he who does wrong will receive again for the wrong that he has done, and there is no partiality.

[4:1]Masters, give to your servants that which is just and equal, knowing that you also have a Master in heaven.

[4:2]Continue steadfastly in prayer, watching therein with thanksgiving; [4:3]praying together for us also, that God may open to us a door for the word, to speak the mystery of Christ, for which I am also in bonds; [4:4]that I may reveal it as I ought to speak. [4:5]Walk in wisdom toward those who are outside, redeeming the time. [4:6]Let your speech always be with grace, seasoned with salt, that you may know how you ought to answer each one.

[4:7]All my affairs will be made known to you by Tychicus, the beloved brother, faithful servant, and fellow bondservant in the Lord. [4:8]I am sending him to you for this very purpose, that he may know your circumstances and comfort your hearts, [4:9]together with Onesimus, the faithful and beloved brother, who is one of you. They will make known to you everything that is going on here. [4:10]Aristarchus, my fellow prisoner greets you, and Mark, the cousin of Barnabas (concerning whom you received commandments, "if he comes to you, receive him"), [4:11]and Jesus who is called Justus, who are of the circumcision. These are my only fellow workers for the Kingdom of God, men who have been a comfort to me.

[4:12]Epaphras, who is one of you, a servant of Christ, salutes you, always striving for you in his prayers, that you may stand perfect and complete in all the will of God. [4:13]For I testify about him, that he has great zeal for you, and for those in Laodicea, and for those in Hierapolis. [4:14]Luke, the beloved physician, and Demas greet you. [4:15]Greet the brothers who are in Laodicea, and Nymphas, and the assembly that is in his house. [4:16]When this letter has been read among you, cause it to be read also in the assembly of the Laodiceans; and that you also read the letter from Laodicea. [4:17]Tell Archippus, "Take heed to the ministry which you have received in the Lord, that you fulfill it."

[4:18]The salutation of me, Paul, with my own hand: remember my bonds. Grace be with you. Amen.

Paul's First Letter to the Thessalonians

[1:1]Paul, Silvanus, and Timothy, to the assembly of the Thessalonians in God the Father and the Lord Jesus Christ: Grace to you and peace from God our Father and the Lord Jesus Christ.

[1:2]We always give thanks to God for all of you, mentioning you in our prayers, [1:3]remembering without ceasing your work of faith and labor of love and patience of hope in our Lord Jesus Christ, before our God and Father. [1:4]We know, brothers[a] loved by God, that you are chosen, [1:5]and that our Good News came to you not in word only, but also in power, and in the Holy Spirit, and with much assurance. You know what kind of men we showed

---

[a]1:4 The word for "brothers" here and where context allows may also be correctly translated "brothers and sisters" or "siblings."

ourselves to be among you for your sake. [1:6] You became imitators of us, and of the Lord, having received the word in much affliction, with joy of the Holy Spirit, [1:7] so that you became an example to all who believe in Macedonia and in Achaia. [1:8] For from you the word of the Lord has been declared, not only in Macedonia and Achaia, but also in every place your faith toward God has gone out; so that we need not to say anything. [1:9] For they themselves report concerning us what kind of a reception we had from you; and how you turned to God from idols, to serve a living and true God, [1:10] and to wait for his Son from heaven, whom he raised from the dead—Jesus, who delivers us from the wrath to come.

[2:1] For you yourselves know, brothers, our visit to you wasn't in vain, [2:2] but having suffered before and been shamefully treated, as you know, at Philippi, we grew bold in our God to tell you the Good News of God in much conflict. [2:3] For our exhortation is not of error, nor of uncleanness, nor in deception. [2:4] But even as we have been approved by God to be entrusted with the Good News, so we speak; not as pleasing men, but God, who tests our hearts. [2:5] For neither were we at any time found using words of flattery, as you know, nor a cloak of covetousness (God is witness), [2:6] nor seeking glory from men (neither from you nor from others), when we might have claimed authority as apostles of Christ. [2:7] But we were gentle among you, like a nursing mother cherishes her own children.

[2:8] Even so, affectionately longing for you, we were well pleased to impart to you, not the Good News of God only, but also our own souls, because you had become very dear to us. [2:9] For you remember, brothers, our labor and travail; for working night and day, that we might not burden any of you, we preached to you the Good News of God. [2:10] You are witnesses with God, how holy, righteously, and blamelessly we behaved ourselves toward you who believe. [2:11] As you know, we exhorted, comforted, and implored every one of you, as a father does his own children, [2:12] to the end that you should walk worthily of God, who calls you

into his own Kingdom and glory. [2:13] For this cause we also thank God without ceasing, that, when you received from us the word of the message of God, you accepted it not as the word of men, but, as it is in truth, the word of God, which also works in you who believe. [2:14] For you, brothers, became imitators of the assemblies of God which are in Judea in Christ Jesus; for you also suffered the same things from your own countrymen, even as they did from the Jews; [2:15] who killed both the Lord Jesus and their own prophets, and drove us out, and didn't please God, and are contrary to all men; [2:16] forbidding us to speak to the Gentiles that they may be saved; to fill up their sins always. But wrath has come on them to the uttermost.

[2:17] But we, brothers, being bereaved of you for a short season, in presence, not in heart, tried even harder to see your face with great desire, [2:18] because we wanted to come to you—indeed, I, Paul, once and again—but Satan hindered us. [2:19] For what is our hope, or joy, or crown of rejoicing? Isn't it even you, before our Lord Jesus[b] at his coming? [2:20] For you are our glory and our joy.

[3:1] Therefore, when we couldn't stand it any longer, we thought it good to be left behind at Athens alone, [3:2] and sent Timothy, our brother and God's servant in the Good News of Christ, to establish you, and to comfort you concerning your faith; [3:3] that no one be moved by these afflictions. For you know that we are appointed to this task. [3:4] For most certainly, when we were with you, we told you beforehand that we are to suffer affliction, even as it happened, and you know. [3:5] For this cause I also, when I couldn't stand it any longer, sent that I might know your faith, for fear that by any means the tempter had tempted you, and our labor would have been in vain. [3:6] But when Timothy came just now to us from you, and brought us glad news of your faith and love, and that you have good memories of us always, longing to see us, even as we also long to see you; [3:7] for this cause, brothers, we were comforted

---

[b]2:19 TR adds "Christ"

over you in all our distress and affliction through your faith. ³:⁸For now we live, if you stand fast in the Lord. ³:⁹For what thanksgiving can we render again to God for you, for all the joy with which we rejoice for your sakes before our God; ³:¹⁰night and day praying exceedingly that we may see your face, and may perfect that which is lacking in your faith? ³:¹¹Now may our God and Father himself, and our Lord Jesus Christ, direct our way to you; ³:¹²and the Lord make you to increase and abound in love one toward another, and toward all men, even as we also do toward you, ³:¹³to the end he may establish your hearts blameless in holiness before our God and Father, at the coming of our Lord Jesus with all his saints.

⁴:¹Finally then, brothers, we beg and exhort you in the Lord Jesus, that as you received from us how you ought to walk and to please God, that you abound more and more. ⁴:²For you know what instructions we gave you through the Lord Jesus. ⁴:³For this is the will of God: your sanctification, that you abstain from sexual immorality, ⁴:⁴that each one of you know how to possess himself of his own vessel in sanctification and honor, ⁴:⁵not in the passion of lust, even as the Gentiles who don't know God; ⁴:⁶that no one should take advantage of and wrong a brother or sister in this matter; because the Lord is an avenger in all these things, as also we forewarned you and testified. ⁴:⁷For God called us not for uncleanness, but in sanctification. ⁴:⁸Therefore he who rejects this doesn't reject man, but God, who has also given his Holy Spirit to you.

⁴:⁹But concerning brotherly love, you have no need that one write to you. For you yourselves are taught by God to love one another, ⁴:¹⁰for indeed you do it toward all the brothers who are in all Macedonia. But we exhort you, brothers, that you abound more and more; ⁴:¹¹and that you make it your ambition to lead a quiet life, and to do your own business, and to work with your own hands, even as we instructed you; ⁴:¹²that you may walk properly toward those who are outside, and may have need of nothing.

⁴:¹³But we don't want you to be ignorant, brothers, concerning those who have fallen asleep, so that you don't grieve like the rest, who have no hope. ⁴:¹⁴For if we believe that Jesus died and rose again, even so God will bring with him those who have fallen asleep in Jesus. ⁴:¹⁵For this we tell you by the word of the Lord, that we who are alive, who are left to the coming of the Lord, will in no way precede those who have fallen asleep. ⁴:¹⁶For the Lord himself will descend from heaven with a shout, with the voice of the archangel, and with God's trumpet. The dead in Christ will rise first, ⁴:¹⁷then we who are alive, who are left, will be caught up together with them in the clouds, to meet the Lord in the air. So we will be with the Lord forever. ⁴:¹⁸Therefore comfort one another with these words.

⁵:¹But concerning the times and the seasons, brothers, you have no need that anything be written to you. ⁵:²For you yourselves know well that the day of the Lord comes like a thief in the night. ⁵:³For when they are saying, "Peace and safety," then sudden destruction will come on them, like birth pains on a pregnant woman; and they will in no way escape. ⁵:⁴But you, brothers, aren't in darkness, that the day should overtake you like a thief. ⁵:⁵You are all children of light, and children of the day. We don't belong to the night, nor to darkness, ⁵:⁶so then let's not sleep, as the rest do, but let's watch and be sober. ⁵:⁷For those who sleep, sleep in the night, and those who are drunk are drunk in the night. ⁵:⁸But let us, since we belong to the day, be sober, putting on the breastplate of faith and love, and, for a helmet, the hope of salvation. ⁵:⁹For God didn't appoint us to wrath, but to the obtaining of salvation through our Lord Jesus Christ, ⁵:¹⁰who died for us, that, whether we wake or sleep, we should live together with him. ⁵:¹¹Therefore exhort one another, and build each other up, even as you also do. ⁵:¹²But we beg you, brothers, to know those who labor among you, and are over you in the Lord, and admonish you, ⁵:¹³and to respect and honor them in love for their work's sake.

Be at peace among yourselves. ⁵:¹⁴We

exhort you, brothers, admonish the disorderly, encourage the fainthearted, support the weak, be patient toward all. [5:15]See that no one returns evil for evil to anyone, but always follow after that which is good, for one another, and for all.

[5:16]Rejoice always. [5:17]Pray without ceasing. [5:18]In everything give thanks, for this is the will of God in Christ Jesus toward you. [5:19]Don't quench the Spirit. [5:20]Don't despise prophesies. [5:21]Test all things, and hold firmly that which is good. [5:22]Abstain from every form of evil.

[5:23]May the God of peace himself sanctify you completely. May your whole spirit, soul, and body be preserved blameless at the coming of our Lord Jesus Christ.

[5:24]He who calls you is faithful, who will also do it. [5:25]Brothers, pray for us. [5:26]Greet all the brothers with a holy kiss. [5:27]I solemnly command you by the Lord that this letter be read to all the holy brothers.

[5:28]The grace of our Lord Jesus Christ be with you. Amen.

Paul's Second Letter to the Thessalonians

[1:1]Paul, Silvanus, and Timothy, to the assembly of the Thessalonians in God our Father, and the Lord Jesus Christ: [1:2]Grace to you and peace from God our Father and the Lord Jesus Christ.

[1:3]We are bound to always give thanks to God for you, brothers,[a] even as it is appropriate, because your faith grows exceedingly, and the love of each and every one of you towards one another abounds; [1:4]so that we ourselves boast about you in the assemblies of God for your patience and faith in all your persecutions and in the afflictions which you endure. [1:5]This is an obvious sign of the righteous judgment of God, to the end that you may be counted worthy of the Kingdom of God, for which you also suffer. [1:6]Since it is a righteous

thing with God to repay affliction to those who afflict you, [1:7]and to give relief to you who are afflicted with us, when the Lord Jesus is revealed from heaven with his mighty angels in flaming fire, [1:8]giving vengeance to those who don't know God, and to those who don't obey the Good News of our Lord Jesus, [1:9]who will pay the penalty: eternal destruction from the face of the Lord and from the glory of his might, [1:10]when he comes to be glorified in his saints, and to be admired among all those who have believed (because our testimony to you was believed) in that day.

[1:11]To this end we also pray always for you, that our God may count you worthy of your calling, and fulfill every desire of goodness and work of faith, with power; [1:12]that the name of our Lord Jesus[b] may be glorified in you, and you in him, according to the grace of our God and the Lord Jesus Christ.

[2:1]Now, brothers, concerning the coming of our Lord Jesus Christ, and our gathering together to him, we ask you [2:2]not to be quickly shaken in your mind, nor yet be troubled, either by spirit, or by word, or by letter as from us, saying that the day of Christ had come. [2:3]Let no one deceive you in any way. For it will not be, unless the departure comes first, and the man of sin is revealed, the son of destruction, [2:4]he who opposes and exalts himself against all that is called God or that is worshiped; so that he sits as God in the temple of God, setting himself up as God. [2:5]Don't you remember that, when I was still with you, I told you these things? [2:6]Now you know what is restraining him, to the end that he may be revealed in his own season. [2:7]For the mystery of lawlessness already works. Only there is one who restrains now, until he is taken out of the way. [2:8]Then the lawless one will be revealed, whom the Lord will kill with the breath of his mouth, and destroy by the manifestation of his coming; [2:9]even he whose coming is according to the working of Satan with

---

[a]1:3 The word for "brothers" here and where context allows may also be correctly translated "brothers and sisters" or "siblings."

[b]1:12 TR adds "Christ"

all power and signs and lying wonders, [2:10] and with all deception of wickedness for those who are being lost, because they didn't receive the love of the truth, that they might be saved. [2:11] Because of this, God sends them a working of error, that they should believe a lie; [2:12] that they all might be judged who didn't believe the truth, but had pleasure in unrighteousness. [2:13] But we are bound to always give thanks to God for you, brothers loved by the Lord, because God chose you from the beginning for salvation through sanctification of the Spirit and belief in the truth; [2:14] to which he called you through our Good News, for the obtaining of the glory of our Lord Jesus Christ. [2:15] So then, brothers, stand firm, and hold the traditions which you were taught by us, whether by word, or by letter.

[2:16] Now our Lord Jesus Christ himself, and God our Father, who loved us and gave us eternal comfort and good hope through grace, [2:17] comfort your hearts and establish you in every good work and word.

[3:1] Finally, brothers, pray for us, that the word of the Lord may spread rapidly and be glorified, even as also with you; [3:2] and that we may be delivered from unreasonable and evil men; for not all have faith. [3:3] But the Lord is faithful, who will establish you, and guard you from the evil one. [3:4] We have confidence in the Lord concerning you, that you both do and will do the things we command. [3:5] May the Lord direct your hearts into the love of God, and into the patience of Christ.

[3:6] Now we command you, brothers, in the name of our Lord Jesus Christ, that you withdraw yourselves from every brother who walks in rebellion, and not after the tradition which they received from us. [3:7] For you know how you ought to imitate us. For we didn't behave ourselves rebelliously among you, [3:8] neither did we eat bread from anyone's hand without paying for it, but in labor and travail worked night and day, that we might not burden any of you; [3:9] not because we don't have the right, but to make ourselves an example to you, that you should imitate us. [3:10] For even when we were with you, we commanded you this: "If anyone will not work, neither

let him eat." [3:11] For we hear of some who walk among you in rebellion, who don't work at all, but are busybodies. [3:12] Now those who are that way, we command and exhort in the Lord Jesus Christ, that with quietness they work, and eat their own bread.

[3:13] But you, brothers, don't be weary in doing well. [3:14] If any man doesn't obey our word in this letter, note that man, that you have no company with him, to the end that he may be ashamed. [3:15] Don't count him as an enemy, but admonish him as a brother.

[3:16] Now may the Lord of peace himself give you peace at all times in all ways. The Lord be with you all.

[3:17] The greeting of me, Paul, with my own hand, which is the sign in every letter: this is how I write. [3:18] The grace of our Lord Jesus Christ be with you all. Amen.

Paul's First Letter to Timothy

[1:1] Paul, an apostle of Christ Jesus according to the commandment of God our Savior, and Christ Jesus our hope; [1:2] to Timothy, my true child in faith: Grace, mercy, and peace, from God our Father and Christ Jesus our Lord.

[1:3] As I urged you when I was going into Macedonia, stay at Ephesus that you might command certain men not to teach a different doctrine, [1:4] neither to pay attention to myths and endless genealogies, which cause disputes, rather than God's stewardship, which is in faith—[1:5] but the goal of this command is love, out of a pure heart and a good conscience and unfeigned faith; [1:6] from which things some, having missed the mark, have turned aside to vain talking; [1:7] desiring to be teachers of the law, though they understand neither what they say, nor about what they strongly affirm. [1:8] But we know that the law is good, if a man uses it lawfully, [1:9] as knowing this, that law is not made for a righteous man, but for the lawless and insubordinate, for the ungodly and sinners, for the unholy and profane, for murderers of fathers and murderers of mothers, for manslayers, [1:10]for the sexually immoral, for homosexuals, for slave-traders, for liars, for perjurers, and for any other thing contrary to the sound doctrine; [1:11]according to the Good News of the glory of the blessed God, which was committed to my trust. [1:12]And I thank him who enabled me, Christ Jesus our Lord, because he counted me faithful, appointing me to service; [1:13]although I was before a blasphemer, a persecutor, and insolent. However, I obtained mercy, because I did it ignorantly in unbelief. [1:14]The grace of our Lord abounded exceedingly with faith and love which is in Christ Jesus. [1:15]The saying is faithful and worthy of all acceptance, that Christ Jesus came into the world to save sinners; of whom I am chief. [1:16]However, for this cause I obtained mercy, that in me first, Jesus Christ might display all his patience, for an example of those who were going to believe in him for eternal life. [1:17]Now to the King eternal, immortal, invisible, to God who alone is wise, be honor and glory forever and ever. Amen.

[1:18]This instruction I commit to you, my child Timothy, according to the prophecies which led the way to you, that by them you may wage the good warfare; [1:19]holding faith and a good conscience; which some having thrust away made a shipwreck concerning the faith; [1:20]of whom is Hymenaeus and Alexander; whom I delivered to Satan, that they might be taught not to blaspheme.

[2:1]I exhort therefore, first of all, that petitions, prayers, intercessions, and givings of thanks, be made for all men: [2:2]for kings and all who are in high places; that we may lead a tranquil and quiet life in all godliness and reverence. [2:3]For this is good and acceptable in the sight of God our Savior; [2:4]who desires all people to be saved and come to full knowledge of the truth. [2:5]For there is one God, and one mediator between God and men, the man Christ Jesus, [2:6]who gave himself as a ransom for all; the

testimony in its own times; [2:7]to which I was appointed a preacher and an apostle (I am telling the truth in Christ, not lying), a teacher of the Gentiles in faith and truth.

[2:8]I desire therefore that the men in every place pray, lifting up holy hands without anger and doubting. [2:9]In the same way, that women also adorn themselves in decent clothing, with modesty and propriety; not just with braided hair, gold, pearls, or expensive clothing; [2:10]but (which becomes women professing godliness) with good works. [2:11]Let a woman learn in quietness with all subjection. [2:12]But I don't permit a woman to teach, nor to exercise authority over a man, but to be in quietness. [2:13]For Adam was first formed, then Eve. [2:14]Adam wasn't deceived, but the woman, being deceived, has fallen into disobedience; [2:15]but she will be saved through her childbearing, if they continue in faith, love, and sanctification with sobriety.

[3:1]This is a faithful saying: if a man seeks the office of an overseer[a], he desires a good work. [3:2]The overseer therefore must be without reproach, the husband of one wife, temperate, sensible, modest, hospitable, good at teaching; [3:3]not a drinker, not violent, not greedy for money, but gentle, not quarrelsome, not covetous; [3:4]one who rules his own house well, having children in subjection with all reverence; [3:5](but if a man doesn't know how to rule his own house, how will he take care of the assembly of God?) [3:6]not a new convert, lest being puffed up he fall into the same condemnation as the devil. [3:7]Moreover he must have good testimony from those who are outside, to avoid falling into reproach and the snare of the devil.

[3:8]Servants[b], in the same way, must be reverent, not double-tongued, not addicted to much wine, not greedy for money; [3:9]holding the mystery of the faith in a pure conscience. [3:10]Let them also first be tested; then let them serve[c] if they are blameless. [3:11]Their wives in the same way must be reverent, not slanderers, temperate, faithful

---

[a]3:1 or, superintendents, or bishops
[b]3:8 or, Deacons.
[c]3:10 or, serve as deacons

in all things. [3:12]Let servants[d] be husbands of one wife, ruling their children and their own houses well. [3:13]For those who have served well[e] gain for themselves a good standing, and great boldness in the faith which is in Christ Jesus.

[3:14]These things I write to you, hoping to come to you shortly; [3:15]but if I wait long, that you may know how men ought to behave themselves in the house of God, which is the assembly of the living God, the pillar and ground of the truth. [3:16]Without controversy, the mystery of godliness is great:

God was revealed in the flesh,
> justified in the spirit,
> seen by angels,
> preached among the nations,
> believed on in the world,
> and received up in glory.

[4:1]But the Spirit says expressly that in later times some will fall away from the faith, paying attention to seducing spirits and doctrines of demons, [4:2]through the hypocrisy of men who speak lies, branded in their own conscience as with a hot iron; [4:3]forbidding marriage and commanding to abstain from foods which God created to be received with thanksgiving by those who believe and know the truth. [4:4]For every creature of God is good, and nothing is to be rejected, if it is received with thanksgiving. [4:5]For it is sanctified through the word of God and prayer. [4:6]If you instruct the brothers of these things, you will be a good servant of Christ Jesus, nourished in the words of the faith, and of the good doctrine which you have followed. [4:7]But refuse profane and old wives' fables. Exercise yourself toward godliness. [4:8]For bodily exercise has some value, but godliness has value in all things, having the promise of the life which is now, and of that which is to come. [4:9]This saying is faithful and worthy of all acceptance. [4:10]For to this end we both labor and suffer reproach, because we have set our trust in the living God, who is the Savior of all men, especially of those who believe. [4:11]Command and teach these things.

[4:12]Let no man despise your youth; but be an example to those who believe, in word, in your way of life, in love, in spirit, in faith, and in purity. [4:13]Until I come, pay attention to reading, to exhortation, and to teaching. [4:14]Don't neglect the gift that is in you, which was given to you by prophecy, with the laying on of the hands of the elders. [4:15]Be diligent in these things. Give yourself wholly to them, that your progress may be revealed to all. [4:16]Pay attention to yourself, and to your teaching. Continue in these things, for in doing this you will save both yourself and those who hear you.

[5:1]Don't rebuke an older man, but exhort him as a father; the younger men as brothers; [5:2]the elder women as mothers; the younger as sisters, in all purity. [5:3]Honor widows who are widows indeed. [5:4]But if any widow has children or grandchildren, let them learn first to show piety towards their own family, and to repay their parents, for this is[f] acceptable in the sight of God. [5:5]Now she who is a widow indeed, and desolate, has her hope set on God, and continues in petitions and prayers night and day. [5:6]But she who gives herself to pleasure is dead while she lives. [5:7]Also command these things, that they may be without reproach. [5:8]But if anyone doesn't provide for his own, and especially his own household, he has denied the faith, and is worse than an unbeliever. [5:9]Let no one be enrolled as a widow under sixty years old, having been the wife of one man, [5:10]being approved by good works, if she has brought up children, if she has been hospitable to strangers, if she has washed the saints' feet, if she has relieved the afflicted, and if she has diligently followed every good work.

[5:11]But refuse younger widows, for when they have grown wanton against Christ, they desire to marry; [5:12]having condemnation, because they have rejected their first pledge. [5:13]Besides, they also learn to be idle, going about from house to house. Not

---

[d]3:12 or, deacons
[e]3:13 or, served well as deacons
[f]5:4 TR adds "good and"

only idle, but also gossips and busybodies, saying things which they ought not. [5:14]I desire therefore that the younger widows marry, bear children, rule the household, and give no occasion to the adversary for reviling. [5:15]For already some have turned aside after Satan. [5:16]If any man or woman who believes has widows, let them relieve them, and don't let the assembly be burdened; that it might relieve those who are widows indeed.

[5:17]Let the elders who rule well be counted worthy of double honor, especially those who labor in the word and in teaching. [5:18]For the Scripture says, "You shall not muzzle the ox when it treads out the grain."[g] And, "The laborer is worthy of his wages."[h]

[5:19]Don't receive an accusation against an elder, except at the word of two or three witnesses. [5:20]Those who sin, reprove in the sight of all, that the rest also may be in fear. [5:21]I command you in the sight of God, and Christ Jesus, and the chosen angels, that you observe these things without prejudice, doing nothing by partiality. [5:22]Lay hands hastily on no one, neither be a participant in other men's sins. Keep yourself pure. [5:23]Be no longer a drinker of water only, but use a little wine for your stomach's sake and your frequent infirmities.

[5:24]Some men's sins are evident, preceding them to judgment, and some also follow later. [5:25]In the same way also there are good works that are obvious, and those that are otherwise can't be hidden.

[6:1]Let as many as are bondservants under the yoke count their own masters worthy of all honor, that the name of God and the doctrine not be blasphemed. [6:2]Those who have believing masters, let them not despise them, because they are brothers, but rather let them serve them, because those who partake of the benefit are believing and beloved. Teach and exhort these things.

[6:3]If anyone teaches a different doctrine, and doesn't consent to sound words, the words of our Lord Jesus Christ, and to the doctrine which is according to godliness,

[6:4]he is conceited, knowing nothing, but obsessed with arguments, disputes, and word battles, from which come envy, strife, reviling, evil suspicions, [6:5]constant friction of people of corrupt minds and destitute of the truth, who suppose that godliness is a means of gain. Withdraw yourself from such.[i]

[6:6]But godliness with contentment is great gain. [6:7]For we brought nothing into the world, and we certainly can't carry anything out. [6:8]But having food and clothing, we will be content with that. [6:9]But those who are determined to be rich fall into a temptation and a snare and many foolish and harmful lusts, such as drown men in ruin and destruction. [6:10]For the love of money is a root of all kinds of evil. Some have been led astray from the faith in their greed, and have pierced themselves through with many sorrows.

[6:11]But you, man of God, flee these things, and follow after righteousness, godliness, faith, love, patience, and gentleness. [6:12]Fight the good fight of faith. Lay hold of the eternal life to which you were called, and you confessed the good confession in the sight of many witnesses. [6:13]I command you before God, who gives life to all things, and before Christ Jesus, who before Pontius Pilate testified the good confession, [6:14]that you keep the commandment without spot, blameless, until the appearing of our Lord Jesus Christ; [6:15]which in its own times he will show, who is the blessed and only Ruler, the King of kings, and Lord of lords; [6:16]who alone has immortality, dwelling in unapproachable light; whom no man has seen, nor can see: to whom be honor and eternal power. Amen.

[6:17]Charge those who are rich in this present world that they not be haughty, nor have their hope set on the uncertainty of riches, but on the living God, who richly provides us with everything to enjoy; [6:18]that they do good, that they be rich in good works, that they be ready to distribute, willing to communicate; [6:19]laying

g5:18 Deuteronomy 25:4
h5:18 Luke 10:7; Leviticus 19:13
i6:5 NU omits "Withdraw yourself from such."

up in store for themselves a good foundation against the time to come, that they may lay hold of eternal life.

6:20 Timothy, guard that which is committed to you, turning away from the empty chatter and oppositions of the knowledge which is falsely so called; 6:21 which some professing have erred concerning the faith. Grace be with you. Amen.

Paul's Second Letter to Timothy

1:1 Paul, an apostle of Jesus Christ through the will of God, according to the promise of the life which is in Christ Jesus, 1:2 to Timothy, my beloved child: Grace, mercy, and peace, from God the Father and Christ Jesus our Lord.

1:3 I thank God, whom I serve as my forefathers did, with a pure conscience. How unceasing is my memory of you in my petitions, night and day 1:4 longing to see you, remembering your tears, that I may be filled with joy; 1:5 having been reminded of the unfeigned faith that is in you; which lived first in your grandmother Lois, and your mother Eunice, and, I am persuaded, in you also.

1:6 For this cause, I remind you that you should stir up the gift of God which is in you through the laying on of my hands. 1:7 For God didn't give us a spirit of fear, but of power, love, and self-control. 1:8 Therefore don't be ashamed of the testimony of our Lord, nor of me his prisoner; but endure hardship for the Good News according to the power of God, 1:9 who saved us and called us with a holy calling, not according to our works, but according to his own purpose and grace, which was given to us in Christ Jesus before times eternal, 1:10 but has now been revealed by the appearing of our Savior, Christ Jesus, who abolished death, and brought life and immortality to light through the Good News. 1:11 For this, I was appointed as a preacher, an apostle, and a teacher of the Gentiles. 1:12 For this cause I also suffer these things.

Yet I am not ashamed, for I know him whom I have believed, and I am persuaded that he is able to guard that which I have committed to him against that day.

1:13 Hold the pattern of sound words which you have heard from me, in faith and love which is in Christ Jesus. 1:14 That good thing which was committed to you, guard through the Holy Spirit who dwells in us.

1:15 This you know, that all who are in Asia turned away from me; of whom are Phygelus and Hermogenes. 1:16 May the Lord grant mercy to the house of Onesiphorus, for he often refreshed me, and was not ashamed of my chain, 1:17 but when he was in Rome, he sought me diligently, and found me 1:18 (the Lord grant to him to find the Lord's mercy in that day); and in how many things he served at Ephesus, you know very well.

2:1 You therefore, my child, be strengthened in the grace that is in Christ Jesus. 2:2 The things which you have heard from me among many witnesses, commit the same to faithful men, who will be able to teach others also. 2:3 You therefore must endure hardship, as a good soldier of Christ Jesus. 2:4 No soldier on duty entangles himself in the affairs of life, that he may please him who enrolled him as a soldier. 2:5 Also, if anyone competes in athletics, he isn't crowned unless he has competed by the rules. 2:6 The farmers who labor must be the first to get a share of the crops. 2:7 Consider what I say, and may the Lord give you understanding in all things.

2:8 Remember Jesus Christ, risen from the dead, of the seed of David, according to my Good News, 2:9 in which I suffer hardship to the point of chains as a criminal. But God's word isn't chained. 2:10 Therefore I endure all things for the chosen ones' sake, that they also may obtain the salvation which is in Christ Jesus with eternal glory. 2:11 This saying is faithful:

"For if we died with him,
we will also live with him.
2:12 If we endure,
we will also reign with him.
If we deny him,
he also will deny us.

2:13 If we are faithless,

he remains faithful.

He can't deny himself."

2:14 Remind them of these things, charging them in the sight of the Lord, that they don't argue about words, to no profit, to the subverting of those who hear.

2:15 Give diligence to present yourself approved by God, a workman who doesn't need to be ashamed, properly handling the Word of Truth. 2:16 But shun empty chatter, for they will proceed further in ungodliness, 2:17 and their word will consume like gangrene, of whom is Hymenaeus and Philetus; 2:18 men who have erred concerning the truth, saying that the resurrection is already past, and overthrowing the faith of some. 2:19 However God's firm foundation stands, having this seal, "The Lord knows those who are his,"[a] and, "Let every one who names the name of the Lord[b] depart from unrighteousness." 2:20 Now in a large house there are not only vessels of gold and of silver, but also of wood and of clay. Some are for honor, and some for dishonor. 2:21 If anyone therefore purges himself from these, he will be a vessel for honor, sanctified, and suitable for the master's use, prepared for every good work.

2:22 Flee from youthful lusts; but pursue righteousness, faith, love, and peace with those who call on the Lord out of a pure heart. 2:23 But refuse foolish and ignorant questionings, knowing that they generate strife. 2:24 The Lord's servant must not quarrel, but be gentle towards all, able to teach, patient, 2:25 in gentleness correcting those who oppose him: perhaps God may give them repentance leading to a full knowledge of the truth, 2:26 and they may recover themselves out of the devil's snare, having been taken captive by him to his will.

3:1 But know this, that in the last days, grievous times will come. 3:2 For men will be lovers of self, lovers of money, boastful, arrogant, blasphemers, disobedient to parents, unthankful, unholy, 3:3 without natural affection, unforgiving, slanderers, without self-control, fierce, no lovers of good, 3:4 traitors, headstrong, conceited, lovers of pleasure rather than lovers of God; 3:5 holding a form of godliness, but having denied the power thereof. Turn away from these, also. 3:6 For of these are those who creep into houses, and take captive gullible women loaded down with sins, led away by various lusts, 3:7 always learning, and never able to come to the knowledge of the truth. 3:8 Even as Jannes and Jambres opposed Moses, so do these also oppose the truth; men corrupted in mind, reprobate concerning the faith. 3:9 But they will proceed no further. For their folly will be evident to all men, as theirs also came to be. 3:10 But you did follow my teaching, conduct, purpose, faith, patience, love, steadfastness, 3:11 persecutions, and sufferings: those things that happened to me at Antioch, Iconium, and Lystra. I endured those persecutions. Out of them all the Lord delivered me. 3:12 Yes, and all who desire to live godly in Christ Jesus will suffer persecution. 3:13 But evil men and impostors will grow worse and worse, deceiving and being deceived. 3:14 But you remain in the things which you have learned and have been assured of, knowing from whom you have learned them. 3:15 From infancy, you have known the sacred writings which are able to make you wise for salvation through faith, which is in Christ Jesus. 3:16 Every writing inspired by God[c] is profitable for teaching, for reproof, for correction, and for instruction which is in righteousness, 3:17 that the man of God may be complete, thoroughly equipped for every good work.

4:1 I command you therefore before God and the Lord Jesus Christ, who will judge the living and the dead at his appearing and his Kingdom: 4:2 preach the word; be urgent in season and out of season; reprove, rebuke, and exhort, with all patience and teaching. 4:3 For the time will come when they will not listen to the sound doctrine, but, having itching ears, will heap up for themselves teachers after their own lusts;

---

[a] 2:19 Numbers 16:5
[b] 2:19 TR reads "Christ" instead of "the Lord"
[c] 3:16 literally, God-breathed

⁴:⁴and will turn away their ears from the truth, and turn aside to fables. ⁴:⁵But you be sober in all things, suffer hardship, do the work of an evangelist, and fulfill your ministry.

⁴:⁶For I am already being offered, and the time of my departure has come. ⁴:⁷I have fought the good fight. I have finished the course. I have kept the faith. ⁴:⁸From now on, there is stored up for me the crown of righteousness, which the Lord, the righteous judge, will give to me on that day; and not to me only, but also to all those who have loved his appearing. ⁴:⁹Be diligent to come to me soon, ⁴:¹⁰for Demas left me, having loved this present world, and went to Thessalonica; Crescens to Galatia, and Titus to Dalmatia. ⁴:¹¹Only Luke is with me. Take Mark, and bring him with you, for he is useful to me for service. ⁴:¹²But I sent Tychicus to Ephesus. ⁴:¹³Bring the cloak that I left at Troas with Carpus when you come, and the books, especially the parchments. ⁴:¹⁴Alexander, the coppersmith, did much evil to me. The Lord will repay him according to his works, ⁴:¹⁵of whom you also must beware; for he greatly opposed our words.

⁴:¹⁶At my first defense, no one came to help me, but all left me. May it not be held against them. ⁴:¹⁷But the Lord stood by me, and strengthened me, that through me the message might be fully proclaimed, and that all the Gentiles might hear; and I was delivered out of the mouth of the lion. ⁴:¹⁸And the Lord will deliver me from every evil work, and will preserve me for his heavenly Kingdom; to whom be the glory forever and ever. Amen.

⁴:¹⁹Greet Prisca and Aquila, and the house of Onesiphorus. ⁴:²⁰Erastus remained at Corinth, but I left Trophimus at Miletus sick. ⁴:²¹Be diligent to come before winter. Eubulus salutes you, as do Pudens, Linus, Claudia, and all the brothers. ⁴:²²The Lord Jesus Christ be with your spirit. Grace be with you. Amen.

Paul's Letter to Titus

¹:¹Paul, a servant of God, and an apostle of Jesus Christ, according to the faith of God's chosen ones, and the knowledge of the truth which is according to godliness, ¹:²in hope of eternal life, which God, who can't lie, promised before time began; ¹:³but in his own time revealed his word in the message with which I was entrusted according to the commandment of God our Savior; ¹:⁴to Titus, my true child according to a common faith: Grace, mercy, and peace from God the Father and the Lord Jesus Christ our Savior.

¹:⁵I left you in Crete for this reason, that you would set in order the things that were lacking, and appoint elders in every city, as I directed you; ¹:⁶if anyone is blameless, the husband of one wife, having children who believe, who are not accused of loose or unruly behavior. ¹:⁷For the overseer must be blameless, as God's steward; not self-pleasing, not easily angered, not given to wine, not violent, not greedy for dishonest gain; ¹:⁸but given to hospitality, as a lover of good, sober minded, fair, holy, self-controlled; ¹:⁹holding to the faithful word which is according to the teaching, that he may be able to exhort in the sound doctrine, and to convict those who contradict him. ¹:¹⁰For there are also many unruly men, vain talkers and deceivers, especially those of the circumcision, ¹:¹¹whose mouths must be stopped; men who overthrow whole houses, teaching things which they ought not, for dishonest gain's sake. ¹:¹²One of them, a prophet of their own, said, "Cretans are always liars, evil beasts, and idle gluttons." ¹:¹³This testimony is true. For this cause, reprove them sharply, that they may be sound in the faith, ¹:¹⁴not paying attention to Jewish fables and commandments of men who turn away from the truth. ¹:¹⁵To the pure, all things are pure; but to those who are defiled and unbelieving, nothing is pure; but both their mind and their conscience are defiled. ¹:¹⁶They profess that they know God, but by their works they deny him, being abominable, disobedient, and unfit for any good work.

²:¹But say the things which fit sound doctrine, ²:²that older men should be temperate, sensible, sober minded, sound in

faith, in love, and in patience: ^{2:3}and that older women likewise be reverent in behavior, not slanderers nor enslaved to much wine, teachers of that which is good; ^{2:4}that they may train the young women to love their husbands, to love their children, ^{2:5}to be sober minded, chaste, workers at home, kind, being in subjection to their own husbands, that God's word may not be blasphemed. ^{2:6}Likewise, exhort the younger men to be sober minded; ^{2:7}in all things showing yourself an example of good works; in your teaching showing integrity, seriousness, incorruptibility, ^{2:8}and soundness of speech that can't be condemned; that he who opposes you may be ashamed, having no evil thing to say about us. ^{2:9}Exhort servants to be in subjection to their own masters, and to be well-pleasing in all things; not contradicting; ^{2:10}not stealing, but showing all good fidelity; that they may adorn the doctrine of God, our Savior, in all things. ^{2:11}For the grace of God has appeared, bringing salvation to all men, ^{2:12}instructing us to the intent that, denying ungodliness and worldly lusts, we would live soberly, righteously, and godly in this present world; ^{2:13}looking for the blessed hope and appearing of the glory of our great God and Savior, Jesus Christ; ^{2:14}who gave himself for us, that he might redeem us from all iniquity, and purify for himself a people for his own possession, zealous for good works. ^{2:15}Say these things and exhort and reprove with all authority. Let no man despise you.

^{3:1}Remind them to be in subjection to rulers and to authorities, to be obedient, to be ready for every good work, ^{3:2}to speak evil of no one, not to be contentious, to be gentle, showing all humility toward all men. ^{3:3}For we were also once foolish, disobedient, deceived, serving various lusts and pleasures, living in malice and envy, hateful, and hating one another. ^{3:4}But when the kindness of God our Savior and his love toward mankind appeared, ^{3:5}not by works of righteousness, which we did ourselves, but according to his mercy, he saved us, through the washing of regeneration and renewing by the Holy Spirit, ^{3:6}whom he poured out on us richly,

through Jesus Christ our Savior; ^{3:7}that, being justified by his grace, we might be made heirs according to the hope of eternal life. ^{3:8}This saying is faithful, and concerning these things I desire that you affirm confidently, so that those who have believed God may be careful to maintain good works. These things are good and profitable to men; ^{3:9}but shun foolish questionings, genealogies, strife, and disputes about the law; for they are unprofitable and vain. ^{3:10}Avoid a factious man after a first and second warning; ^{3:11}knowing that such a one is perverted, and sins, being self-condemned.

^{3:12}When I send Artemas to you, or Tychicus, be diligent to come to me to Nicopolis, for I have determined to winter there. ^{3:13}Send Zenas, the lawyer, and Apollos on their journey speedily, that nothing may be lacking for them. ^{3:14}Let our people also learn to maintain good works for necessary uses, that they may not be unfruitful.

^{3:15}All who are with me greet you. Greet those who love us in faith. Grace be with you all. Amen.

Paul's Letter to Philemon

^{1:1}Paul, a prisoner of Christ Jesus, and Timothy our brother, to Philemon, our beloved fellow worker, ^{1:2}to the beloved Apphia, to Archippus, our fellow soldier, and to the assembly in your house: ^{1:3}Grace to you and peace from God our Father and the Lord Jesus Christ.

^{1:4}I thank my God always, making mention of you in my prayers, ^{1:5}hearing of your love, and of the faith which you have toward the Lord Jesus, and toward all the saints; ^{1:6}that the fellowship of your faith may become effective, in the knowledge of every good thing which is in us in Christ Jesus. ^{1:7}For we have much joy and comfort in your love, because the hearts of the saints have been refreshed through you, brother.

^{1:8}Therefore, though I have all boldness in Christ to command you that which is appropriate, ^{1:9}yet for love's sake I rather

beg, being such a one as Paul, the aged, but also a prisoner of Jesus Christ. [1:10]I beg you for my child, whom I have become the father of in my chains, Onesimus,[a] [1:11]who once was useless to you, but now is useful to you and to me. [1:12]I am sending him back. Therefore receive him, that is, my own heart, [1:13]whom I desired to keep with me, that on your behalf he might serve me in my chains for the Good News. [1:14]But I was willing to do nothing without your consent, that your goodness would not be as of necessity, but of free will. [1:15]For perhaps he was therefore separated from you for a while, that you would have him forever, [1:16]no longer as a slave, but more than a slave, a beloved brother, especially to me, but how much rather to you, both in the flesh and in the Lord.

[1:17]If then you count me a partner, receive him as you would receive me. [1:18]But if he has wronged you at all, or owes you anything, put that to my account. [1:19]I, Paul, write this with my own hand: I will repay it (not to mention to you that you owe to me even your own self besides). [1:20]Yes, brother, let me have joy from you in the Lord. Refresh my heart in the Lord. [1:21]Having confidence in your obedience, I write to you, knowing that you will do even beyond what I say.

[1:22]Also, prepare a guest room for me, for I hope that through your prayers I will be restored to you.

[1:23]Epaphras, my fellow prisoner in Christ Jesus, greets you, [1:24]as do Mark, Aristarchus, Demas, and Luke, my fellow workers. [1:25]The grace of our Lord Jesus Christ be with your spirit. Amen.

The Letter to the Hebrews

[1:1]God, having in the past spoken to the fathers through the prophets at many times and in various ways, [1:2]has at the end of these days spoken to us by his Son, whom he appointed heir of all things, through whom also he made the worlds. [1:3]His Son is the radiance of his glory, the very image of his substance, and upholding all things by the word of his power, when he had by himself made purification for our sins, sat down on the right hand of the Majesty on high; [1:4]having become so much better than the angels, as he has inherited a more excellent name than they have. [1:5]For to which of the angels did he say at any time,
"You are my Son.

Today have I become your father?"[a]
and again,
"I will be to him a Father,
and he will be to me a Son?"[b]
[1:6]Again, when he brings in the firstborn into the world he says, "Let all the angels of God worship him." [1:7]Of the angels he says,
"Who makes his angels winds,
and his servants a flame of fire."[c]
[1:8]But of the Son he says,
"Your throne, O God, is forever and ever.
The scepter of uprightness is the scepter of your Kingdom.
[1:9]You have loved righteousness, and hated iniquity;
therefore God, your God, has anointed you with the oil of gladness above your fellows."[d]
[1:10]And,
"You, Lord, in the beginning, laid the foundation of the earth.
The heavens are the works of your hands.
[1:11]They will perish, but you continue.
They all will grow old like a garment does.
[1:12]As a mantle, you will roll them up, and they will be changed;
but you are the same.
Your years will not fail."[e]

---

[a]1:10 Onesimus means "useful."
[a]1:5 Psalm 2:7
[b]1:5 2 Samuel 7:14; 1 Chronicles 17:13
[c]1:7 Psalm 104:4
[d]1:9 Psalm 45:6-7
[e]1:12 Psalm 102:25-27

[1:13]But which of the angels has he told at any time,

"Sit at my right hand,

until I make your enemies the footstool of your feet?"[f]

[1:14]Aren't they all serving spirits, sent out to do service for the sake of those who will inherit salvation?

[2:1]Therefore we ought to pay greater attention to the things that were heard, lest perhaps we drift away. [2:2]For if the word spoken through angels proved steadfast, and every transgression and disobedience received a just recompense; [2:3]how will we escape if we neglect so great a salvation—which at the first having been spoken through the Lord, was confirmed to us by those who heard; [2:4]God also testifying with them, both by signs and wonders, by various works of power, and by gifts of the Holy Spirit, according to his own will? [2:5]For he didn't subject the world to come, of which we speak, to angels. [2:6]But one has somewhere testified, saying,

"What is man, that you think of him?

Or the son of man, that you care for him?

[2:7]You made him a little lower than the angels.

You crowned him with glory and honor.[g]

[2:8]You have put all things in subjection under his feet."[h]

For in that he subjected all things to him, he left nothing that is not subject to him. But now we don't see all things subjected to him, yet. [2:9]But we see him who has been made a little lower than the angels, Jesus, because of the suffering of death crowned with glory and honor, that by the grace of God he should taste of death for everyone. [2:10]For it became him, for whom are all things, and through whom are all things, in bringing many children to glory, to make the author of their salvation perfect through sufferings. [2:11]For both he who sanctifies and those who are sanctified are all from one, for which cause he is not ashamed to call them brothers[i], [2:12]saying,

"I will declare your name to my brothers.

In the midst of the congregation I will sing your praise."[j]

[2:13]Again, "I will put my trust in him."[k] Again, "Behold, here I am with the children whom God has given me."[l] [2:14]Since then the children have shared in flesh and blood, he also himself in like manner partook of the same, that through death he might bring to nothing him who had the power of death, that is, the devil, [2:15]and might deliver all of them who through fear of death were all their lifetime subject to bondage. [2:16]For most certainly, he doesn't give help to angels, but he gives help to the seed of Abraham. [2:17]Therefore he was obligated in all things to be made like his brothers, that he might become a merciful and faithful high priest in things pertaining to God, to make atonement for the sins of the people. [2:18]For in that he himself has suffered being tempted, he is able to help those who are tempted.

[3:1]Therefore, holy brothers, partakers of a heavenly calling, consider the Apostle and High Priest of our confession, Jesus; [3:2]who was faithful to him who appointed him, as also was Moses in all his house. [3:3]For he has been counted worthy of more glory than Moses, inasmuch as he who built the house has more honor than the house. [3:4]For every house is built by someone; but he who built all things is God. [3:5]Moses indeed was faithful in all his house as a servant, for a testimony of those things which were afterward to be spoken, [3:6]but Christ is faithful as a Son over his house; whose house we are, if we hold fast our confidence and the glorying of our hope

---

[f]1:13 Psalm 110:1

[g]2:7 TR adds "and set him over the works of your hands"

[h]2:8 Psalm 8:4-6

[i]2:11 The word for "brothers" here and where context allows may also be correctly translated "brothers and sisters" or "siblings."

[j]2:12 Psalm 22:22

[k]2:13 Isaiah 8:17

[l]2:13 Isaiah 8:18

firm to the end. [3:7]Therefore, even as the Holy Spirit says,

"Today if you will hear his voice,
[3:8]don't harden your hearts, as in the provocation,
  like as in the day of the trial in the wilderness,
[3:9]where your fathers tested me by proving me,
  and saw my works for forty years.
[3:10]Therefore I was displeased with that generation,
  and said, 'They always err in their heart,
  but they didn't know my ways;'
[3:11]as I swore in my wrath,
  'They will not enter into my rest.'"[m]

[3:12]Beware, brothers, lest perhaps there be in any one of you an evil heart of unbelief, in falling away from the living God; [3:13]but exhort one another day by day, so long as it is called "today;" lest any one of you be hardened by the deceitfulness of sin. [3:14]For we have become partakers of Christ, if we hold fast the beginning of our confidence firm to the end: [3:15]while it is said,

"Today if you will hear his voice,
  don't harden your hearts, as in the rebellion."[n]

[3:16]For who, when they heard, rebelled? No, didn't all those who came out of Egypt by Moses? [3:17]With whom was he displeased forty years? Wasn't it with those who sinned, whose bodies fell in the wilderness? [3:18]To whom did he swear that they wouldn't enter into his rest, but to those who were disobedient? [3:19]We see that they were not able to enter in because of unbelief.

[4:1]Let us fear therefore, lest perhaps anyone of you should seem to have come short of a promise of entering into his rest. [4:2]For indeed we have had good news preached to us, even as they also did, but the word they heard didn't profit them, because it wasn't mixed with faith by those who heard. [4:3]For we who have believed do enter into that rest, even as he has said, "As I swore in my wrath, they will not enter into my rest;"[o] although the works were finished from the foundation of the world. [4:4]For he has said this somewhere about the seventh day, "God rested on the seventh day from all his works;"[p] [4:5]and in this place again, "They will not enter into my rest."[q]

[4:6]Seeing therefore it remains that some should enter therein, and they to whom the good news was before preached failed to enter in because of disobedience, [4:7]he again defines a certain day, today, saying through David so long a time afterward (just as has been said),

"Today if you will hear his voice,
  don't harden your hearts."[r]

[4:8]For if Joshua had given them rest, he would not have spoken afterward of another day. [4:9]There remains therefore a Sabbath rest for the people of God. [4:10]For he who has entered into his rest has himself also rested from his works, as God did from his. [4:11]Let us therefore give diligence to enter into that rest, lest anyone fall after the same example of disobedience. [4:12]For the word of God is living, and active, and sharper than any two-edged sword, and piercing even to the dividing of soul and spirit, of both joints and marrow, and is able to discern the thoughts and intentions of the heart.

[4:13]There is no creature that is hidden from his sight, but all things are naked and laid open before the eyes of him with whom we have to do. [4:14]Having then a great high priest, who has passed through the heavens, Jesus, the Son of God, let us hold tightly to our confession. [4:15]For we don't have a high priest who can't be touched with the feeling of our infirmities, but one who has been in all points tempted like we are, yet without sin. [4:16]Let us therefore draw near with boldness to the throne of

---

[m]3:11 Psalm 95:7-11
[n]3:15 Psalm 95:7-8
[o]4:3 Psalm 95:11
[p]4:4 Genesis 2:2
[q]4:5 Psalm 95:11
[r]4:7 Psalm 95:7-8

grace, that we may receive mercy, and may find grace for help in time of need.

5:1 For every high priest, being taken from among men, is appointed for men in things pertaining to God, that he may offer both gifts and sacrifices for sins. 5:2 The high priest can deal gently with those who are ignorant and going astray, because he himself is also surrounded with weakness. 5:3 Because of this, he must offer sacrifices for sins for the people, as well as for himself. 5:4 Nobody takes this honor on himself, but he is called by God, just like Aaron was. 5:5 So also Christ didn't glorify himself to be made a high priest, but it was he who said to him,

"You are my Son.

Today I have become your father."[s]

5:6 As he says also in another place,

"You are a priest forever,

after the order of Melchizedek."[t]

5:7 He, in the days of his flesh, having offered up prayers and petitions with strong crying and tears to him who was able to save him from death, and having been heard for his godly fear, 5:8 though he was a Son, yet learned obedience by the things which he suffered. 5:9 Having been made perfect, he became to all of those who obey him the author of eternal salvation, 5:10 named by God a high priest after the order of Melchizedek. 5:11 About him we have many words to say, and hard to interpret, seeing you have become dull of hearing. 5:12 For when by reason of the time you ought to be teachers, you again need to have someone teach you the rudiments of the first principles of the oracles of God. You have come to need milk, and not solid food. 5:13 For everyone who lives on milk is not experienced in the word of righteousness, for he is a baby. 5:14 But solid food is for those who are full grown, who by reason of use have their senses exercised to discern good and evil.

6:1 Therefore leaving the doctrine of the first principles of Christ, let us press on to perfection—not laying again a foundation of repentance from dead works, of faith toward God, 6:2 of the teaching of baptisms, of laying on of hands, of resurrection of the dead, and of eternal judgment. 6:3 This will we do, if God permits. 6:4 For concerning those who were once enlightened and tasted of the heavenly gift, and were made partakers of the Holy Spirit, 6:5 and tasted the good word of God, and the powers of the age to come, 6:6 and then fell away, it is impossible to renew them again to repentance; seeing they crucify the Son of God for themselves again, and put him to open shame. 6:7 For the land which has drunk the rain that comes often on it, and brings forth a crop suitable for them for whose sake it is also tilled, receives blessing from God; 6:8 but if it bears thorns and thistles, it is rejected and near being cursed, whose end is to be burned.

6:9 But, beloved, we are persuaded of better things for you, and things that accompany salvation, even though we speak like this. 6:10 For God is not unrighteous, so as to forget your work and the labor of love which you showed toward his name, in that you served the saints, and still do serve them. 6:11 We desire that each one of you may show the same diligence to the fullness of hope even to the end, 6:12 that you won't be sluggish, but imitators of those who through faith and patience inherited the promises. 6:13 For when God made a promise to Abraham, since he could swear by none greater, he swore by himself, 6:14 saying, "Surely blessing I will bless you, and multiplying I will multiply you."[u] 6:15 Thus, having patiently endured, he obtained the promise. 6:16 For men indeed swear by a greater one, and in every dispute of theirs the oath is final for confirmation. 6:17 In this way God, being determined to show more abundantly to the heirs of the promise the immutability of his counsel, interposed with an oath; 6:18 that by two immutable things, in which it is impossible for God to lie, we may have a strong encouragement, who have fled for refuge to take hold of the hope set before

---

[s]5:5 Psalm 2:7

[t]5:6 Psalm 110:4

[u]6:14 Genesis 22:17

us. [6:19]This hope we have as an anchor of the soul, a hope both sure and steadfast and entering into that which is within the veil; [6:20]where as a forerunner Jesus entered for us, having become a high priest forever after the order of Melchizedek.

[7:1]For this Melchizedek, king of Salem, priest of God Most High, who met Abraham returning from the slaughter of the kings and blessed him, [7:2]to whom also Abraham divided a tenth part of all (being first, by interpretation, king of righteousness, and then also king of Salem, which is king of peace; [7:3]without father, without mother, without genealogy, having neither beginning of days nor end of life, but made like the Son of God), remains a priest continually. [7:4]Now consider how great this man was, to whom even Abraham, the patriarch, gave a tenth out of the best spoils. [7:5]They indeed of the sons of Levi who receive the priest's office have a commandment to take tithes of the people according to the law, that is, of their brothers, though these have come out of the body of Abraham, [7:6]but he whose genealogy is not counted from them has accepted tithes from Abraham, and has blessed him who has the promises. [7:7]But without any dispute the lesser is blessed by the greater. [7:8]Here people who die receive tithes, but there one receives tithes of whom it is testified that he lives. [7:9]We can say that through Abraham even Levi, who receives tithes, has paid tithes, [7:10]for he was yet in the body of his father when Melchizedek met him. [7:11]Now if there was perfection through the Levitical priesthood (for under it the people have received the law), what further need was there for another priest to arise after the order of Melchizedek, and not be called after the order of Aaron? [7:12]For the priesthood being changed, there is of necessity a change made also in the law. [7:13]For he of whom these things are said belongs to another tribe, from which no one has officiated at the altar. [7:14]For it is evident that our Lord has sprung out of Judah, about which tribe Moses spoke nothing concerning priesthood. [7:15]This is yet more abundantly evident, if after the likeness of Melchizedek there arises another priest, [7:16]who has been made, not after the law of a fleshly commandment, but after the power of an endless life: [7:17]for it is testified,

"You are a priest forever,
according to the order of Melchizedek."[v]

[7:18]For there is an annulling of a foregoing commandment because of its weakness and uselessness [7:19](for the law made nothing perfect), and a bringing in of a better hope, through which we draw near to God. [7:20]Inasmuch as he was not made priest without the taking of an oath [7:21](for they indeed have been made priests without an oath), but he with an oath by him that says of him,

"The Lord swore and will not change his mind,
'You are a priest forever,
according to the order of Melchizedek.'"[w]

[7:22]By so much, Jesus has become the collateral of a better covenant. [7:23]Many, indeed, have been made priests, because they are hindered from continuing by death. [7:24]But he, because he lives forever, has his priesthood unchangeable. [7:25]Therefore he is also able to save to the uttermost those who draw near to God through him, seeing that he lives forever to make intercession for them.

[7:26]For such a high priest was fitting for us: holy, guiltless, undefiled, separated from sinners, and made higher than the heavens; [7:27]who doesn't need, like those high priests, to offer up sacrifices daily, first for his own sins, and then for the sins of the people. For he did this once for all, when he offered up himself. [7:28]For the law appoints men as high priests who have weakness, but the word of the oath which came after the law appoints a Son forever who has been perfected.

[8:1]Now in the things which we are saying, the main point is this. We have such a high priest, who sat down on the right hand

---

v 7:17 Psalm 110:4
w 7:21 Psalm 110:4

of the throne of the Majesty in the heavens, [8:2]a servant of the sanctuary, and of the true tabernacle, which the Lord pitched, not man. [8:3]For every high priest is appointed to offer both gifts and sacrifices. Therefore it is necessary that this high priest also have something to offer. [8:4]For if he were on earth, he would not be a priest at all, seeing there are priests who offer the gifts according to the law; [8:5]who serve a copy and shadow of the heavenly things, even as Moses was warned by God when he was about to make the tabernacle, for he said, "See, you shall make everything according to the pattern that was shown to you on the mountain."[x] [8:6]But now he has obtained a more excellent ministry, by so much as he is also the mediator of a better covenant, which on better promises has been given as law. [8:7]For if that first covenant had been faultless, then no place would have been sought for a second. [8:8]For finding fault with them, he said,

"Behold, the days come," says the Lord,

that I will make a new covenant with the house of Israel and with the house of Judah;

[8:9]not according to the covenant that I made with their fathers,

in the day that I took them by the hand to lead them out of the land of Egypt;

for they didn't continue in my covenant,

and I disregarded them," says the Lord.

[8:10]"For this is the covenant that I will make with the house of Israel.

After those days," says the Lord;

"I will put my laws into their mind,

I will also write them on their heart.

I will be their God,

and they will be my people.

[8:11]They will not teach every man his fellow citizen,[y]

and every man his brother, saying, 'Know the Lord,'

for all will know me,

from the least of them to the greatest of them.

[8:12]For I will be merciful to their unrighteousness.

I will remember their sins and lawless deeds no more."[z]

[8:13]In that he says, "A new covenant," he has made the first old. But that which is becoming old and grows aged is near to vanishing away.

[9:1]Now indeed even the first[a] covenant had ordinances of divine service, and an earthly sanctuary. [9:2]For a tabernacle was prepared. In the first part were the lampstand, the table, and the show bread; which is called the Holy Place. [9:3]After the second veil was the tabernacle which is called the Holy of Holies, [9:4]having a golden altar of incense, and the ark of the covenant overlaid on all sides with gold, in which was a golden pot holding the manna, Aaron's rod that budded, and the tablets of the covenant; [9:5]and above it cherubim of glory overshadowing the mercy seat, of which things we can't speak now in detail. [9:6]Now these things having been thus prepared, the priests go in continually into the first tabernacle, accomplishing the services, [9:7]but into the second the high priest alone, once in the year, not without blood, which he offers for himself, and for the errors of the people. [9:8]The Holy Spirit is indicating this, that the way into the Holy Place wasn't yet revealed while the first tabernacle was still standing; [9:9]which is a symbol of the present age, where gifts and sacrifices are offered that are incapable, concerning the conscience, of making the worshipper perfect; [9:10]being only (with meats and drinks and various washings) fleshly ordinances, imposed until a time of reformation.

[9:11]But Christ having come as a high priest of the coming good things, through the greater and more perfect tabernacle, not made with hands, that is to say, not of this creation, [9:12]nor yet through the blood of goats and calves, but through his own blood, entered in once for all into the Holy Place, having obtained eternal redemption.

---

[x]8:5 Exodus 25:40
[y]8:11 TR reads "neighbor" instead of "fellow citizen"
[z]8:12 Jeremiah 31:31-34
[a]9:1 TR adds "tabernacle"

9:13 For if the blood of goats and bulls, and the ashes of a heifer sprinkling those who have been defiled, sanctify to the cleanness of the flesh: 9:14 how much more will the blood of Christ, who through the eternal Spirit offered himself without blemish to God, cleanse your conscience from dead works to serve the living God? 9:15 For this reason he is the mediator of a new covenant, since a death has occurred for the redemption of the transgressions that were under the first covenant, that those who have been called may receive the promise of the eternal inheritance. 9:16 For where a last will and testament is, there must of necessity be the death of him who made it. 9:17 For a will is in force where there has been death, for it is never in force while he who made it lives. 9:18 Therefore even the first covenant has not been dedicated without blood. 9:19 For when every commandment had been spoken by Moses to all the people according to the law, he took the blood of the calves and the goats, with water and scarlet wool and hyssop, and sprinkled both the book itself and all the people, 9:20 saying, "This is the blood of the covenant which God has commanded you."[b]

9:21 Moreover he sprinkled the tabernacle and all the vessels of the ministry in like manner with the blood. 9:22 According to the law, nearly everything is cleansed with blood, and apart from shedding of blood there is no remission. 9:23 It was necessary therefore that the copies of the things in the heavens should be cleansed with these; but the heavenly things themselves with better sacrifices than these. 9:24 For Christ hasn't entered into holy places made with hands, which are representations of the true, but into heaven itself, now to appear in the presence of God for us; 9:25 nor yet that he should offer himself often, as the high priest enters into the holy place year by year with blood not his own, 9:26 or else he must have suffered often since the foundation of the world. But now once at the end of the ages, he has been revealed to put away sin by the sacrifice of himself. 9:27 Inasmuch as it

is appointed for men to die once, and after this, judgment, 9:28 so Christ also, having been offered once to bear the sins of many, will appear a second time, without sin, to those who are eagerly waiting for him for salvation.

10:1 For the law, having a shadow of the good to come, not the very image of the things, can never with the same sacrifices year by year, which they offer continually, make perfect those who draw near. 10:2 Or else wouldn't they have ceased to be offered, because the worshippers, having been once cleansed, would have had no more consciousness of sins? 10:3 But in those sacrifices there is yearly reminder of sins. 10:4 For it is impossible that the blood of bulls and goats should take away sins. 10:5 Therefore when he comes into the world, he says,

"Sacrifice and offering you didn't desire,

but you prepared a body for me;

10:6 You had no pleasure in whole burnt offerings and sacrifices for sin.

10:7 Then I said, 'Behold, I have come (in the scroll of the book it is written of me)

to do your will, O God.'"[c]

10:8 Previously saying, "Sacrifices and offerings and whole burnt offerings and sacrifices for sin you didn't desire, neither had pleasure in them" (those which are offered according to the law), 10:9 then he has said, "Behold, I have come to do your will." He takes away the first, that he may establish the second, 10:10 by which will we have been sanctified through the offering of the body of Jesus Christ once for all. 10:11 Every priest indeed stands day by day serving and often offering the same sacrifices, which can never take away sins, 10:12 but he, when he had offered one sacrifice for sins forever, sat down on the right hand of God; 10:13 from that time waiting until his enemies are made the footstool of his feet. 10:14 For by one offering he has perfected forever those who are being sanctified. 10:15 The Holy Spirit also testifies to us, for after saying,

---

[b]9:20 Exodus 24:8
[c]10:7 Psalm 40:6-8

$^{10:16}$"This is the covenant that I will make with them:

'After those days,' says the Lord,
'I will put my laws on their heart,
I will also write them on their mind;'"^{d}
then he says,

$^{10:17}$"I will remember their sins and their iniquities no more."^{e}

$^{10:18}$Now where remission of these is, there is no more offering for sin. $^{10:19}$Having therefore, brothers, boldness to enter into the holy place by the blood of Jesus, $^{10:20}$by the way which he dedicated for us, a new and living way, through the veil, that is to say, his flesh; $^{10:21}$and having a great priest over the house of God, $^{10:22}$let's draw near with a true heart in fullness of faith, having our hearts sprinkled from an evil conscience, and having our body washed with pure water, $^{10:23}$let us hold fast the confession of our hope without wavering; for he who promised is faithful. $^{10:24}$Let us consider how to provoke one another to love and good works, $^{10:25}$not forsaking our own assembling together, as the custom of some is, but exhorting one another; and so much the more, as you see the Day approaching. $^{10:26}$For if we sin willfully after we have received the knowledge of the truth, there remains no more a sacrifice for sins, $^{10:27}$but a certain fearful expectation of judgment, and a fierceness of fire which will devour the adversaries. $^{10:28}$A man who disregards Moses' law dies without compassion on the word of two or three witnesses. $^{10:29}$How much worse punishment, do you think, will he be judged worthy of, who has trodden under foot the Son of God, and has counted the blood of the covenant with which he was sanctified an unholy thing, and has insulted the Spirit of grace? $^{10:30}$For we know him who said, "Vengeance belongs to me," says the Lord, "I will repay."^{f} Again, "The Lord will judge his people."^{g} $^{10:31}$It is a fearful thing to fall into the hands of the living God. $^{10:32}$But remember the former days, in which, after you were enlightened, you endured a great struggle with sufferings; $^{10:33}$partly, being exposed to both reproaches and oppressions; and partly, becoming partakers with those who were treated so. $^{10:34}$For you both had compassion on me in my chains, and joyfully accepted the plundering of your possessions, knowing that you have for yourselves a better possession and an enduring one in the heavens. $^{10:35}$Therefore don't throw away your boldness, which has a great reward. $^{10:36}$For you need endurance so that, having done the will of God, you may receive the promise.

$^{10:37}$"In a very little while,

he who comes will come, and will not wait.

$^{10:38}$But the righteous will live by faith.

If he shrinks back, my soul has no pleasure in him."^{h}

$^{10:39}$But we are not of those who shrink back to destruction, but of those who have faith to the saving of the soul.

$^{11:1}$Now faith is assurance of things hoped for, proof of things not seen. $^{11:2}$For by this, the elders obtained testimony. $^{11:3}$By faith, we understand that the universe has been framed by the word of God, so that what is seen has not been made out of things which are visible. $^{11:4}$By faith, Abel offered to God a more excellent sacrifice than Cain, through which he had testimony given to him that he was righteous, God testifying with respect to his gifts; and through it he, being dead, still speaks. $^{11:5}$By faith, Enoch was taken away, so that he wouldn't see death, and he was not found, because God translated him. For he has had testimony given to him that before his translation he had been well pleasing to God. $^{11:6}$Without faith it is impossible to be well pleasing to him, for he who comes to God must believe that he exists, and that he is a rewarder of those

^{d}10:16 Jeremiah 31:33
^{e}10:17 Jeremiah 31:34
^{f}10:30 Deuteronomy 32:35
^{g}10:30 Deuteronomy 32:36; Psalm 135:14
^{h}10:38 Habakkuk 2:3-4

who seek him. [11:7] By faith, Noah, being warned about things not yet seen, moved with godly fear, prepared a ship for the saving of his house, through which he condemned the world, and became heir of the righteousness which is according to faith. [11:8] By faith, Abraham, when he was called, obeyed to go out to the place which he was to receive for an inheritance. He went out, not knowing where he went. [11:9] By faith, he lived as an alien in the land of promise, as in a land not his own, dwelling in tents, with Isaac and Jacob, the heirs with him of the same promise. [11:10] For he looked for the city which has the foundations, whose builder and maker is God. [11:11] By faith, even Sarah herself received power to conceive, and she bore a child when she was past age, since she counted him faithful who had promised. [11:12] Therefore as many as the stars of the sky in multitude, and as innumerable as the sand which is by the sea shore, were fathered by one man, and him as good as dead. [11:13] These all died in faith, not having received the promises, but having seen[i] them and embraced them from afar, and having confessed that they were strangers and pilgrims on the earth. [11:14] For those who say such things make it clear that they are seeking a country of their own. [11:15] If indeed they had been thinking of that country from which they went out, they would have had enough time to return. [11:16] But now they desire a better country, that is, a heavenly one. Therefore God is not ashamed of them, to be called their God, for he has prepared a city for them.

[11:17] By faith, Abraham, being tested, offered up Isaac. Yes, he who had gladly received the promises was offering up his one and only son; [11:18] even he to whom it was said, "In Isaac will your seed be called;"[j] [11:19] concluding that God is able to raise up even from the dead. Figuratively speaking, he also did receive him back from the dead.

[11:20] By faith, Isaac blessed Jacob and Esau, even concerning things to come. [11:21] By faith, Jacob, when he was dying, blessed each of the sons of Joseph, and worshiped, leaning on the top of his staff. [11:22] By faith, Joseph, when his end was near, made mention of the departure of the children of Israel; and gave instructions concerning his bones. [11:23] By faith, Moses, when he was born, was hidden for three months by his parents, because they saw that he was a beautiful child, and they were not afraid of the king's commandment. [11:24] By faith, Moses, when he had grown up, refused to be called the son of Pharaoh's daughter, [11:25] choosing rather to share ill treatment with God's people, than to enjoy the pleasures of sin for a time; [11:26] accounting the reproach of Christ greater riches than the treasures of Egypt; for he looked to the reward. [11:27] By faith, he left Egypt, not fearing the wrath of the king; for he endured, as seeing him who is invisible. [11:28] By faith, he kept the Passover, and the sprinkling of the blood, that the destroyer of the firstborn should not touch them. [11:29] By faith, they passed through the Red Sea as on dry land. When the Egyptians tried to do so, they were swallowed up. [11:30] By faith, the walls of Jericho fell down, after they had been encircled for seven days. [11:31] By faith, Rahab the prostitute, didn't perish with those who were disobedient, having received the spies in peace. [11:32] What more shall I say? For the time would fail me if I told of Gideon, Barak, Samson, Jephthah, David, Samuel, and the prophets; [11:33] who, through faith subdued kingdoms, worked out righteousness, obtained promises, stopped the mouths of lions,[k] [11:34] quenched the power of fire,[l] escaped the edge of the sword,[m] from weakness were made strong, grew mighty in war, and caused foreign armies to flee. [11:35] Women received their dead by resurrection.[n] Others were tortured, not ac-

---

[i]11:13 TR adds "and being convinced of"
[j]11:18 Genesis 21:12
[k]11:33 Daniel 6:22-23
[l]11:34 Daniel 3:1-30
[m]11:34 1 Kings 19:1-3; 2 Kings 6:31-7:20
[n]11:35 1 Kings 19:1-3; 2 Kings 6:31-7:20

cepting their deliverance, that they might obtain a better resurrection. [11:36] Others were tried by mocking and scourging, yes, moreover by bonds and imprisonment. [11:37] They were stoned.[o] They were sawn apart. They were tempted. They were slain with the sword.[p] They went around in sheep skins and in goat skins; being destitute, afflicted, ill-treated [11:38] (of whom the world was not worthy), wandering in deserts, mountains, caves, and the holes of the earth. [11:39] These all, having had testimony given to them through their faith, didn't receive the promise, [11:40] God having provided some better thing concerning us, so that apart from us they should not be made perfect.

[12:1] Therefore let us also, seeing we are surrounded by so great a cloud of witnesses, lay aside every weight and the sin which so easily entangles us, and let us run with patience the race that is set before us, [12:2] looking to Jesus, the author and perfecter of faith, who for the joy that was set before him endured the cross, despising its shame, and has sat down at the right hand of the throne of God. [12:3] For consider him who has endured such contradiction of sinners against himself, that you don't grow weary, fainting in your souls. [12:4] You have not yet resisted to blood, striving against sin; [12:5] and you have forgotten the exhortation which reasons with you as with children,

"My son, don't take lightly the chastening
    of the Lord,
    nor faint when you are reproved by
        him;
[12:6] For whom the Lord loves, he chastens,
    and scourges every son whom he re-
        ceives."[q]

[12:7] It is for discipline that you endure. God deals with you as with children, for what son is there whom his father doesn't discipline? [12:8] But if you are without discipline, of which all have been made partakers, then are you illegitimate, and not children. [12:9] Furthermore, we had the fathers of our flesh to chasten us, and we paid them respect. Shall we not much rather be in subjection to the Father of spirits, and live? [12:10] For they indeed, for a few days, punished us as seemed good to them; but he for our profit, that we may be partakers of his holiness. [12:11] All chastening seems for the present to be not joyous but grievous; yet afterward it yields the peaceful fruit of righteousness to those who have been exercised thereby. [12:12] Therefore, lift up the hands that hang down and the feeble knees,[r] [12:13] and make straight paths for your feet,[s] so that which is lame may not be dislocated, but rather be healed. [12:14] Follow after peace with all men, and the sanctification without which no man will see the Lord, [12:15] looking carefully lest there be any man who falls short of the grace of God; lest any root of bitterness springing up trouble you, and many be defiled by it; [12:16] lest there be any sexually immoral person, or profane person, like Esau, who sold his birthright for one meal. [12:17] For you know that even when he afterward desired to inherit the blessing, he was rejected, for he found no place for a change of mind though he sought it diligently with tears. [12:18] For you have not come to a mountain that might be touched, and that burned with fire, and to blackness, darkness, storm, [12:19] the sound of a trumpet, and the voice of words; which those who heard it begged that not one more word should be spoken to them, [12:20] for they could not stand that which was commanded, "If even an animal touches the mountain, it shall be stoned[t];"[u] [12:21] and so fearful was the appearance, that Moses said, "I am terrified and trembling."[v]

---

[o] 11:37 2 Chronicles 24:20-21
[p] 11:37 Jeremiah 26:20-23; 1 Kings 19:10
[q] 12:6 Proverbs 3:11-12
[r] 12:12 Isaiah 35:3
[s] 12:13 Proverbs 4:26
[t] 12:20 TR adds "or shot with an arrow" [see Exodus 19:12-13]
[u] 12:20 Exodus 19:12-13
[v] 12:21 Deuteronomy 9:19

¹²:²²But you have come to Mount Zion, and to the city of the living God, the heavenly Jerusalem, and to innumerable multitudes of angels, ¹²:²³to the general assembly and assembly of the firstborn who are enrolled in heaven, to God the Judge of all, to the spirits of just men made perfect, ¹²:²⁴to Jesus, the mediator of a new covenant,ʷ and to the blood of sprinkling that speaks better than that of Abel.

¹²:²⁵See that you don't refuse him who speaks. For if they didn't escape when they refused him who warned on the Earth, how much more will we not escape who turn away from him who warns from heaven, ¹²:²⁶whose voice shook the earth then, but now he has promised, saying, "Yet once more I will shake not only the earth, but also the heavens."ˣ ¹²:²⁷This phrase, "Yet once more," signifies the removing of those things that are shaken, as of things that have been made, that those things which are not shaken may remain. ¹²:²⁸Therefore, receiving a Kingdom that can't be shaken, let us have grace, through which we serve God acceptably, with reverence and awe, ¹²:²⁹for our God is a consuming fire.ʸ

¹³:¹Let brotherly love continue. ¹³:²Don't forget to show hospitality to strangers, for in doing so, some have entertained angels without knowing it. ¹³:³Remember those who are in bonds, as bound with them; and those who are ill-treated, since you are also in the body. ¹³:⁴Let marriage be held in honor among all, and let the bed be undefiled: but God will judge the sexually immoral and adulterers.

¹³:⁵Be free from the love of money, content with such things as you have, for he has said, "I will in no way leave you, neither will I in any way forsake you."ᶻ ¹³:⁶So that with good courage we say,

"The Lord is my helper. I will not fear.

What can man do to me?"ᵃ

¹³:⁷Remember your leaders, men who spoke to you the word of God, and considering the results of their conduct, imitate their faith. ¹³:⁸Jesus Christ is the same yesterday, today, and forever. ¹³:⁹Don't be carried away by various and strange teachings, for it is good that the heart be established by grace, not by food, through which those who were so occupied were not benefited.

¹³:¹⁰We have an altar from which those who serve the holy tabernacle have no right to eat. ¹³:¹¹For the bodies of those animals, whose blood is brought into the holy place by the high priest as an offering for sin, are burned outside of the camp.ᵇ ¹³:¹²Therefore Jesus also, that he might sanctify the people through his own blood, suffered outside of the gate. ¹³:¹³Let us therefore go out to him outside of the camp, bearing his reproach. ¹³:¹⁴For we don't have here an enduring city, but we seek that which is to come. ¹³:¹⁵Through him, then, let us offer up a sacrifice of praise to Godᶜ continually, that is, the fruit of lips which proclaim allegiance to his name. ¹³:¹⁶But don't forget to be doing good and sharing, for with such sacrifices God is well pleased.

¹³:¹⁷Obey your leaders and submit to them, for they watch on behalf of your souls, as those who will give account, that they may do this with joy, and not with groaning, for that would be unprofitable for you.

¹³:¹⁸Pray for us, for we are persuaded that we have a good conscience, desiring to live honorably in all things. ¹³:¹⁹I strongly urge you to do this, that I may be restored to you sooner.

¹³:²⁰Now may the God of peace, who brought again from the dead the great shepherd of the sheep with the blood of an eternal covenant, our Lord Jesus, ¹³:²¹make you complete in every good work to do his will, working in you that which is well pleasing in his sight, through Jesus Christ,

---

ʷ12:24 Jeremiah 31:31
ˣ12:26 Haggai 2:6
ʸ12:29 Deuteronomy 4:24
ᶻ13:5 Deuteronomy 31:6
ᵃ13:6 Psalm 118:6-7
ᵇ13:11 Leviticus 16:27
ᶜ13:15 Psalm 50:23

to whom be the glory forever and ever. Amen.

[13:22]But I exhort you, brothers, endure the word of exhortation, for I have written to you in few words. [13:23]Know that our brother Timothy has been freed, with whom, if he comes shortly, I will see you. [13:24]Greet all of your leaders and all the saints. The Italians greet you. [13:25]Grace be with you all. Amen.

The Letter from James

[1:1]James, a servant of God and of the Lord Jesus Christ, to the twelve tribes which are in the Dispersion: Greetings. [1:2]Count it all joy, my brothers[a], when you fall into various temptations, [1:3]knowing that the testing of your faith produces endurance. [1:4]Let endurance have its perfect work, that you may be perfect and complete, lacking in nothing. [1:5]But if any of you lacks wisdom, let him ask of God, who gives to all liberally and without reproach; and it will be given to him. [1:6]But let him ask in faith, without any doubting, for he who doubts is like a wave of the sea, driven by the wind and tossed. [1:7]For let that man not think that he will receive anything from the Lord. [1:8]He is a double-minded man, unstable in all his ways.

[1:9]But let the brother in humble circumstances glory in his high position; [1:10]and the rich, in that he is made humble, because like the flower in the grass, he will pass away. [1:11]For the sun arises with the scorching wind, and withers the grass, and the flower in it falls, and the beauty of its appearance perishes. So also will the rich man fade away in his pursuits.

[1:12]Blessed is the man who endures temptation, for when he has been approved, he will receive the crown of life, which the Lord promised to those who love him. [1:13]Let no man say when he is tempted, "I am tempted by God," for God can't be tempted by evil, and he himself tempts no one. [1:14]But each one is tempted, when he is drawn away by his own lust, and enticed. [1:15]Then the lust, when it has conceived, bears sin; and the sin, when it is full grown, brings forth death. [1:16]Don't be deceived, my beloved brothers. [1:17]Every good gift and every perfect gift is from above, coming down from the Father of lights, with whom can be no variation, nor turning shadow. [1:18]Of his own will he brought us forth by the word of truth, that we should be a kind of first fruits of his creatures.

[1:19]So, then, my beloved brothers, let every man be swift to hear, slow to speak, and slow to anger; [1:20]for the anger of man doesn't produce the righteousness of God. [1:21]Therefore, putting away all filthiness and overflowing of wickedness, receive with humility the implanted word, which is able to save your souls[b]. [1:22]But be doers of the word, and not only hearers, deluding your own selves. [1:23]For if anyone is a hearer of the word and not a doer, he is like a man looking at his natural face in a mirror; [1:24]for he sees himself, and goes away, and immediately forgets what kind of man he was. [1:25]But he who looks into the perfect law of freedom, and continues, not being a hearer who forgets, but a doer of the work, this man will be blessed in what he does.

[1:26]If anyone among you thinks himself to be religious while he doesn't bridle his tongue, but deceives his heart, this man's religion is worthless. [1:27]Pure religion and undefiled before our God and Father is this: to visit the fatherless and widows in their affliction, and to keep oneself unstained by the world.

[2:1]My brothers, don't hold the faith of our Lord Jesus Christ of glory with partiality. [2:2]For if a man with a gold ring, in fine clothing, comes into your synagogue[c], and a poor man in filthy clothing also comes in; [2:3]and you pay special attention to him who wears the fine clothing, and say, "Sit here in a good place;" and you tell the poor man, "Stand there," or "Sit by my footstool;" [2:4]haven't you shown partiality among yourselves, and become judges with evil thoughts? [2:5]Listen, my beloved brothers. Didn't God choose those who are poor in this world to be rich in faith, and heirs of the Kingdom which he promised to those who love him? [2:6]But you have dishonored the poor man. Don't the rich oppress you, and personally drag

---

[a]1:2 The word for "brothers" here and where context allows may also be correctly translated "brothers and sisters" or "siblings."

[b]1:21 or, preserve your life.

[c]2:2 or, meeting

you before the courts? [2:7]Don't they blaspheme the honorable name by which you are called? [2:8]However, if you fulfill the royal law, according to the Scripture, "You shall love your neighbor as yourself,"[d] you do well. [2:9]But if you show partiality, you commit sin, being convicted by the law as transgressors. [2:10]For whoever keeps the whole law, and yet stumbles in one point, he has become guilty of all. [2:11]For he who said, "Do not commit adultery,"[e] also said, "Do not commit murder."[f] Now if you do not commit adultery, but murder, you have become a transgressor of the law. [2:12]So speak, and so do, as men who are to be judged by a law of freedom. [2:13]For judgment is without mercy to him who has shown no mercy. Mercy triumphs over judgment.

[2:14]What good is it, my brothers, if a man says he has faith, but has no works? Can faith save him? [2:15]And if a brother or sister is naked and in lack of daily food, [2:16]and one of you tells them, "Go in peace, be warmed and filled;" and yet you didn't give them the things the body needs, what good is it? [2:17]Even so faith, if it has no works, is dead in itself. [2:18]Yes, a man will say, "You have faith, and I have works." Show me your faith without works, and I by my works will show you my faith.

[2:19]You believe that God is one. You do well. The demons also believe, and shudder. [2:20]But do you want to know, vain man, that faith apart from works is dead? [2:21]Wasn't Abraham our father justified by works, in that he offered up Isaac his son on the altar? [2:22]You see that faith worked with his works, and by works faith was perfected; [2:23]and the Scripture was fulfilled which says, "Abraham believed God, and it was accounted to him as righteousness;"[g] and he was called the friend of God. [2:24]You see then that by works, a man is justified, and not only by faith. [2:25]In like manner wasn't Rahab the prostitute also justified by works, in that she received the messengers,

and sent them out another way? [2:26]For as the body apart from the spirit is dead, even so faith apart from works is dead.

[3:1]Let not many of you be teachers, my brothers, knowing that we will receive heavier judgment. [3:2]For in many things we all stumble. If anyone doesn't stumble in word, the same is a perfect man, able to bridle the whole body also. [3:3]Indeed, we put bits into the horses' mouths so that they may obey us, and we guide their whole body. [3:4]Behold, the ships also, though they are so big and are driven by fierce winds, are yet guided by a very small rudder, wherever the pilot desires. [3:5]So the tongue is also a little member, and boasts great things. See how a small fire can spread to a large forest! [3:6]And the tongue is a fire. The world of iniquity among our members is the tongue, which defiles the whole body, and sets on fire the course of nature, and is set on fire by Gehenna.[h] [3:7]For every kind of animal, bird, creeping thing, and thing in the sea, is tamed, and has been tamed by mankind. [3:8]But nobody can tame the tongue. It is a restless evil, full of deadly poison. [3:9]With it we bless our God and Father, and with it we curse men, who are made in the image of God. [3:10]Out of the same mouth comes forth blessing and cursing. My brothers, these things ought not to be so. [3:11]Does a spring send out from the same opening fresh and bitter water? [3:12]Can a fig tree, my brothers, yield olives, or a vine figs? Thus no spring yields both salt water and fresh water.

[3:13]Who is wise and understanding among you? Let him show by his good conduct that his deeds are done in gentleness of wisdom. [3:14]But if you have bitter jealousy and selfish ambition in your heart, don't boast and don't lie against the truth. [3:15]This wisdom is not that which comes down from above, but is earthly, sensual, and demonic. [3:16]For where jealousy and selfish ambition are, there is confusion and

---

[d]2:8 Leviticus 19:18
[e]2:11 Exodus 20:14; Deuteronomy 5:18
[f]2:11 Exodus 10:13; Deuteronomy 5:17
[g]2:23 Genesis 15:16
[h]3:6 or, Hell

every evil deed. ^{3:17}But the wisdom that is from above is first pure, then peaceful, gentle, reasonable, full of mercy and good fruits, without partiality, and without hypocrisy. ^{3:18}Now the fruit of righteousness is sown in peace by those who make peace.

^{4:1}Where do wars and fightings among you come from? Don't they come from your pleasures that war in your members? ^{4:2}You lust, and don't have. You kill, covet, and can't obtain. You fight and make war. You don't have, because you don't ask. ^{4:3}You ask, and don't receive, because you ask with wrong motives, so that you may spend it for your pleasures. ^{4:4}You adulterers and adulteresses, don't you know that friendship with the world is enmity with God? Whoever therefore wants to be a friend of the world makes himself an enemy of God. ^{4:5}Or do you think that the Scripture says in vain, "The Spirit who lives in us yearns jealously"? ^{4:6}But he gives more grace. Therefore it says, "God resists the proud, but gives grace to the humble."[i] ^{4:7}Be subject therefore to God. But resist the devil, and he will flee from you. ^{4:8}Draw near to God, and he will draw near to you. Cleanse your hands, you sinners; and purify your hearts, you double-minded. ^{4:9}Lament, mourn, and weep. Let your laughter be turned to mourning, and your joy to gloom. ^{4:10}Humble yourselves in the sight of the Lord, and he will exalt you.

^{4:11}Don't speak against one another, brothers. He who speaks against a brother and judges his brother, speaks against the law and judges the law. But if you judge the law, you are not a doer of the law, but a judge. ^{4:12}Only one is the lawgiver, who is able to save and to destroy. But who are you to judge another?

^{4:13}Come now, you who say, "Today or tomorrow let's go into this city, and spend a year there, trade, and make a profit." ^{4:14}Whereas you don't know what your life will be like tomorrow. For what is your life? For you are a vapor, that appears for a little time, and then vanishes away. ^{4:15}For you

ought to say, "If the Lord wills, we will both live, and do this or that." ^{4:16}But now you glory in your boasting. All such boasting is evil. ^{4:17}To him therefore who knows to do good, and doesn't do it, to him it is sin.

^{5:1}Come now, you rich, weep and howl for your miseries that are coming on you. ^{5:2}Your riches are corrupted and your garments are moth-eaten. ^{5:3}Your gold and your silver are corroded, and their corrosion will be for a testimony against you, and will eat your flesh like fire. You have laid up your treasure in the last days. ^{5:4}Behold, the wages of the laborers who mowed your fields, which you have kept back by fraud, cry out, and the cries of those who reaped have entered into the ears of the Lord of Armies[j]. ^{5:5}You have lived delicately on the earth, and taken your pleasure. You have nourished your hearts as in a day of slaughter. ^{5:6}You have condemned, you have murdered the righteous one. He doesn't resist you.

^{5:7}Be patient therefore, brothers, until the coming of the Lord. Behold, the farmer waits for the precious fruit of the earth, being patient over it, until it receives the early and late rain. ^{5:8}You also be patient. Establish your hearts, for the coming of the Lord is at hand.

^{5:9}Don't grumble, brothers, against one another, so that you won't be judged. Behold, the judge stands at the door. ^{5:10}Take, brothers, for an example of suffering and of patience, the prophets who spoke in the name of the Lord. ^{5:11}Behold, we call them blessed who endured. You have heard of the patience of Job, and have seen the Lord in the outcome, and how the Lord is full of compassion and mercy. ^{5:12}But above all things, my brothers, don't swear, neither by heaven, nor by the earth, nor by any other oath; but let your "yes" be "yes," and your "no," "no;" so that you don't fall into hypocrisy.[k]

^{5:13}Is any among you suffering? Let him pray. Is any cheerful? Let him sing praises. ^{5:14}Is any among you sick? Let him call

---

[i]4:6 Proverbs 3:34
[j]5:4 Greek: Sabaoth (for Hebrew: Tze'va'ot)
[k]5:12 TR reads "under judgment" instead of "into hypocrisy"

for the elders of the assembly, and let them pray over him, anointing him with oil in the name of the Lord, [5:15]and the prayer of faith will heal him who is sick, and the Lord will raise him up. If he has committed sins, he will be forgiven. [5:16]Confess your offenses to one another, and pray for one another, that you may be healed. The insistent prayer of a righteous person is powerfully effective. [5:17]Elijah was a man with a nature like ours, and he prayed earnestly that it might not rain, and it didn't rain on the earth for three years and six months. [5:18]He prayed again, and the sky gave rain, and the earth brought forth its fruit.

[5:19]Brothers, if any among you wanders from the truth, and someone turns him back, [5:20]let him know that he who turns a sinner from the error of his way will save a soul from death, and will cover a multitude of sins.

Peter's First Letter

[1:1]Peter, an apostle of Jesus Christ, to the chosen ones who are living as foreigners in the Dispersion in Pontus, Galatia, Cappadocia, Asia, and Bithynia, [1:2]according to the foreknowledge of God the Father, in sanctification of the Spirit, that you may obey Jesus Christ and be sprinkled with his blood: Grace to you and peace be multiplied. [1:3]Blessed be the God and Father of our Lord Jesus Christ, who according to his great mercy became our father again to a living hope through the resurrection of Jesus Christ from the dead, [1:4]to an incorruptible and undefiled inheritance that doesn't fade away, reserved in Heaven for you, [1:5]who by the power of God are guarded through faith for a salvation ready to be revealed in the last time. [1:6]Wherein you greatly rejoice, though now for a little while, if need be, you have been put to grief in various trials, [1:7]that the proof of your faith, which is more precious than gold that perishes even though it is tested by fire, may be found to result in praise, glory, and

honor at the revelation of Jesus Christ— [1:8]whom not having known you love; in whom, though now you don't see him, yet believing, you rejoice greatly with joy unspeakable and full of glory—[1:9]receiving the result of your faith, the salvation of your souls. [1:10]Concerning this salvation, the prophets sought and searched diligently, who prophesied of the grace that would come to you, [1:11]searching for who or what kind of time the Spirit of Christ, which was in them, pointed to, when he predicted the sufferings of Christ, and the glories that would follow them. [1:12]To them it was revealed, that not to themselves, but to you, they ministered these things, which now have been announced to you through those who preached the Good News to you by the Holy Spirit sent out from heaven; which things angels desire to look into.

[1:13]Therefore, prepare your minds for action,[a] be sober and set your hope fully on the grace that will be brought to you at the revelation of Jesus Christ—[1:14]as children of obedience, not conforming yourselves according to your former lusts as in your ignorance, [1:15]but just as he who called you is holy, you yourselves also be holy in all of your behavior; [1:16]because it is written, "You shall be holy; for I am holy."[b] [1:17]If you call on him as Father, who without respect of persons judges according to each man's work, pass the time of your living as foreigners here in reverent fear: [1:18]knowing that you were redeemed, not with corruptible things, with silver or gold, from the useless way of life handed down from your fathers, [1:19]but with precious blood, as of a faultless and pure lamb, the blood of Christ; [1:20]who was foreknown indeed before the foundation of the world, but was revealed at the end of times for your sake, [1:21]who through him are believers in God, who raised him from the dead, and gave him glory; so that your faith and hope might be in God.

[1:22]Seeing you have purified your souls in your obedience to the truth through the Spirit in sincere brotherly affection,

[a]1:13 literally, "gird up the waist of your mind"
[b]1:16 Leviticus 11:44-45

love one another from the heart fervently: [1:23]having been born again, not of corruptible seed, but of incorruptible, through the word of God, which lives and remains forever. [1:24]For,

"All flesh is like grass,
and all of man's glory like the flower in
　　the grass.
The grass withers, and its flower falls;
　　[1:25]but the Lord's word endures forever."[c]

This is the word of Good News which was preached to you.

[2:1]Putting away therefore all wickedness, all deceit, hypocrisies, envies, and all evil speaking, [2:2]as newborn babies, long for the pure milk of the Word, that you may grow thereby, [2:3]if indeed you have tasted that the Lord is gracious: [2:4]coming to him, a living stone, rejected indeed by men, but chosen by God, precious. [2:5]You also, as living stones, are built up as a spiritual house, to be a holy priesthood, to offer up spiritual sacrifices, acceptable to God through Jesus Christ. [2:6]Because it is contained in Scripture,

"Behold, I lay in Zion a chief cornerstone,
　　chosen, and precious:
　　He who believes in him will not be
　　disappointed."[d]

[2:7]For you who believe therefore is the honor, but for those who are disobedient,

"The stone which the builders rejected,
　　has become the chief cornerstone,"[e]

[2:8]and,

"a stone of stumbling, and a rock of offense."[f]

For they stumble at the word, being disobedient, to which also they were appointed. [2:9]But you are a chosen race, a royal priesthood, a holy nation, a people for God's own possession, that you may proclaim the excellence of him who called you out of darkness into his marvelous light: [2:10]who in time past were no people,

but now are God's people, who had not obtained mercy, but now have obtained mercy. [2:11]Beloved, I beg you as foreigners and pilgrims, to abstain from fleshly lusts, which war against the soul; [2:12]having good behavior among the nations, so in that of which they speak against you as evil-doers, they may by your good works, which they see, glorify God in the day of visitation. [2:13]Therefore subject yourselves to every ordinance of man for the Lord's sake: whether to the king, as supreme; [2:14]or to governors, as sent by him for vengeance on evil-doers and for praise to those who do well. [2:15]For this is the will of God, that by well-doing you should put to silence the ignorance of foolish men: [2:16]as free, and not using your freedom for a cloak of wickedness, but as bondservants of God.

[2:17]Honor all men. Love the brotherhood. Fear God. Honor the king. [2:18]Servants, be in subjection to your masters with all fear; not only to the good and gentle, but also to the wicked. [2:19]For it is commendable if someone endures pain, suffering unjustly, because of conscience toward God. [2:20]For what glory is it if, when you sin, you patiently endure beating? But if, when you do well, you patiently endure suffering, this is commendable with God. [2:21]For to this you were called, because Christ also suffered for us, leaving you[g] an example, that you should follow his steps, [2:22]who did not sin, "neither was deceit found in his mouth."[h] [2:23]Who, when he was cursed, didn't curse back. When he suffered, didn't threaten, but committed himself to him who judges righteously; [2:24]who his own self bore our sins in his body on the tree, that we, having died to sins, might live to righteousness; by whose stripes you were healed. [2:25]For you were going astray like sheep; but now have returned to the Shepherd and Overseer[i] of

---

[c]1:25 Isaiah 40:6-8
[d]2:6 Isaiah 28:16
[e]2:7 Psalm 118:22
[f]2:8 Isaiah 8:14
[g]2:21 TR reads "us" instead of "you"
[h]2:22 Isaiah 53:9
[i]2:25 "Overseer" is from the Greek episkopon, which can mean overseer, curator, guardian, or superintendent.

your souls.

[3:1] In like manner, wives, be in subjection to your own husbands; so that, even if any don't obey the Word, they may be won by the behavior of their wives without a word; [3:2] seeing your pure behavior in fear. [3:3] Let your beauty be not just the outward adorning of braiding the hair, and of wearing jewels of gold, or of putting on fine clothing; [3:4] but in the hidden person of the heart, in the incorruptible adornment of a gentle and quiet spirit, which is in the sight of God very precious. [3:5] For this is how the holy women before, who hoped in God also adorned themselves, being in subjection to their own husbands: [3:6] as Sarah obeyed Abraham, calling him lord, whose children you now are, if you do well, and are not put in fear by any terror.

[3:7] You husbands, in like manner, live with your wives according to knowledge, giving honor to the woman, as to the weaker vessel, as being also joint heirs of the grace of life; that your prayers may not be hindered.

[3:8] Finally, be all like-minded, compassionate, loving as brothers, tenderhearted, courteous, [3:9] not rendering evil for evil, or reviling for reviling; but instead blessing; knowing that to this were you called, that you may inherit a blessing. [3:10] For,
"He who would love life,
    and see good days,
let him keep his tongue from evil,
    and his lips from speaking deceit.
[3:11] Let him turn away from evil, and do
    good.
Let him seek peace, and pursue it.
[3:12] For the eyes of the Lord are on the
    righteous,
and his ears open to their prayer;
but the face of the Lord is against those
    who do evil."[j]
[3:13] Now who is he who will harm you, if you become imitators of that which is good? [3:14] But even if you should suffer for righteousness' sake, you are blessed. "Don't fear what they fear, neither be troubled."[k] [3:15] But sanctify the Lord God in your hearts; and always be ready to give an answer to everyone who asks you a reason concerning the hope that is in you, with humility and fear: [3:16] having a good conscience; that, while you are spoken against as evildoers, they may be disappointed who curse your good manner of life in Christ. [3:17] For it is better, if it is God's will, that you suffer for doing well than for doing evil. [3:18] Because Christ also suffered for sins once, the righteous for the unrighteous, that he might bring you to God; being put to death in the flesh, but made alive in the spirit; [3:19] in which he also went and preached to the spirits in prison, [3:20] who before were disobedient, when God waited patiently in the days of Noah, while the ship was being built. In it, few, that is, eight souls, were saved through water. [3:21] This is a symbol of baptism, which now saves you—not the putting away of the filth of the flesh, but the answer of a good conscience toward God, through the resurrection of Jesus Christ, [3:22] who is at the right hand of God, having gone into heaven, angels and authorities and powers being made subject to him.

[4:1] Forasmuch then as Christ suffered for us in the flesh, arm yourselves also with the same mind; for he who has suffered in the flesh has ceased from sin; [4:2] that you no longer should live the rest of your time in the flesh for the lusts of men, but for the will of God. [4:3] For we have spent enough of our past time doing the desire of the Gentiles, and having walked in lewdness, lusts, drunken binges, orgies, carousings, and abominable idolatries. [4:4] They think it is strange that you don't run with them into the same excess of riot, blaspheming: [4:5] who will give account to him who is ready to judge the living and the dead. [4:6] For to this end the Good News was preached even to the dead, that they might be judged indeed as men in the flesh, but live as to God in the spirit. [4:7] But the end of all things is near. Therefore be of sound mind, self-controlled, and sober in prayer. [4:8] And above all things be earnest in your love among yourselves, for love covers a

[j] 3:12 Psalm 34:12-16
[k] 3:14 Isaiah 8:12

multitude of sins. [4:9]Be hospitable to one another without grumbling. [4:10]As each has received a gift, employ it in serving one another, as good managers of the grace of God in its various forms. [4:11]If anyone speaks, let it be as it were the very words of God. If anyone serves, let it be as of the strength which God supplies, that in all things God may be glorified through Jesus Christ, to whom belong the glory and the dominion forever and ever. Amen.

[4:12]Beloved, don't be astonished at the fiery trial which has come upon you, to test you, as though a strange thing happened to you. [4:13]But because you are partakers of Christ's sufferings, rejoice; that at the revelation of his glory you also may rejoice with exceeding joy. [4:14]If you are insulted for the name of Christ, you are blessed; because the Spirit of glory and of God rests on you. On their part he is blasphemed, but on your part he is glorified. [4:15]For let none of you suffer as a murderer, or a thief, or an evil doer, or a meddler in other men's matters. [4:16]But if one of you suffers for being a Christian, let him not be ashamed; but let him glorify God in this matter. [4:17]For the time has come for judgment to begin with the household of God. If it begins first with us, what will happen to those who don't obey the Good News of God? [4:18]"If it is hard for the righteous to be saved, what will happen to the ungodly and the sinner?"[l] [4:19]Therefore let them also who suffer according to the will of God in doing good entrust their souls to him, as to a faithful Creator.

[5:1]I exhort the elders among you, as a fellow elder, and a witness of the sufferings of Christ, and who will also share in the glory that will be revealed. [5:2]Shepherd the flock of God which is among you, exercising the oversight, not under compulsion, but voluntarily, not for dishonest gain, but willingly; [5:3]neither as lording it over those entrusted to you, but making yourselves examples to the flock. [5:4]When the chief Shepherd is revealed, you will receive the crown of glory that doesn't fade away.

[5:5]Likewise, you younger ones, be sub-ject to the elder. Yes, all of you gird yourselves with humility, to subject yourselves to one another; for "God resists the proud, but gives grace to the humble."[m] [5:6]Humble yourselves therefore under the mighty hand of God, that he may exalt you in due time; [5:7]casting all your worries on him, because he cares for you.

[5:8]Be sober and self-controlled. Be watchful. Your adversary the devil, walks around like a roaring lion, seeking whom he may devour. [5:9]Withstand him steadfast in your faith, knowing that your brothers who are in the world are undergoing the same sufferings. [5:10]But may the God of all grace, who called you to his eternal glory by Christ Jesus, after you have suffered a little while, perfect, establish, strengthen, and settle you. [5:11]To him be the glory and the power forever and ever. Amen.

[5:12]Through Silvanus, our faithful brother, as I consider him, I have written to you briefly, exhorting, and testifying that this is the true grace of God in which you stand. [5:13]She who is in Babylon, chosen together with you, greets you; and so does Mark, my son. [5:14]Greet one another with a kiss of love. Peace be to you all who are in Christ Jesus. Amen.

Peter's Second Letter

[1:1]Simon Peter, a servant and apostle of Jesus Christ, to those who have obtained a like precious faith with us in the righteousness of our God and Savior, Jesus Christ: [1:2]Grace to you and peace be multiplied in the knowledge of God and of Jesus our Lord, [1:3]seeing that his divine power has granted to us all things that pertain to life and godliness, through the knowledge of him who called us by his own glory and virtue; [1:4]by which he has granted to us his precious and exceedingly great promises; that through these you may become partakers of the divine nature, having

---

[l]4:18 Proverbs 11:31
[m]5:5 Proverbs 3:34

escaped from the corruption that is in the world by lust. [1:5]Yes, and for this very cause adding on your part all diligence, in your faith supply moral excellence; and in moral excellence, knowledge; [1:6]and in knowledge, self-control; and in self-control patience; and in patience godliness; [1:7]and in godliness brotherly affection; and in brotherly affection, love. [1:8]For if these things are yours and abound, they make you to be not idle nor unfruitful to the knowledge of our Lord Jesus Christ. [1:9]For he who lacks these things is blind, seeing only what is near, having forgotten the cleansing from his old sins. [1:10]Therefore, brothers,[a] be more diligent to make your calling and election sure. For if you do these things, you will never stumble. [1:11]For thus you will be richly supplied with the entrance into the eternal Kingdom of our Lord and Savior, Jesus Christ.

[1:12]Therefore I will not be negligent to remind you of these things, though you know them, and are established in the present truth. [1:13]I think it right, as long as I am in this tent, to stir you up by reminding you; [1:14]knowing that the putting off of my tent comes swiftly, even as our Lord Jesus Christ made clear to me. [1:15]Yes, I will make every effort that you may always be able to remember these things even after my departure. [1:16]For we did not follow cunningly devised fables, when we made known to you the power and coming of our Lord Jesus Christ, but we were eyewitnesses of his majesty. [1:17]For he received from God the Father honor and glory, when the voice came to him from the Majestic Glory, "This is my beloved Son, in whom I am well pleased."[b] [1:18]We heard this voice come out of heaven when we were with him on the holy mountain.

[1:19]We have the more sure word of prophecy; and you do well that you heed it, as to a lamp shining in a dark place, until the day dawns, and the morning star arises in your hearts: [1:20]knowing this first, that no prophecy of Scripture is of private interpretation. [1:21]For no prophecy ever came by the will of man: but holy men of God spoke, being moved by the Holy Spirit.

[2:1]But false prophets also arose among the people, as false teachers will also be among you, who will secretly bring in destructive heresies, denying even the Master who bought them, bringing on themselves swift destruction. [2:2]Many will follow their immoral[c] ways, and as a result, the way of the truth will be maligned. [2:3]In covetousness they will exploit you with deceptive words: whose sentence now from of old doesn't linger, and their destruction will not slumber. [2:4]For if God didn't spare angels when they sinned, but cast them down to Tartarus[d], and committed them to pits of darkness, to be reserved for judgment; [2:5]and didn't spare the ancient world, but preserved Noah with seven others, a preacher of righteousness, when he brought a flood on the world of the ungodly; [2:6]and turning the cities of Sodom and Gomorrah into ashes, condemned them to destruction, having made them an example to those who would live ungodly; [2:7]and delivered righteous Lot, who was very distressed by the lustful life of the wicked [2:8](for that righteous man dwelling among them, was tormented in his righteous soul from day to day with seeing and hearing lawless deeds): [2:9]the Lord knows how to deliver the godly out of temptation and to keep the unrighteous under punishment for the day of judgment; [2:10]but chiefly those who walk after the flesh in the lust of defilement, and despise authority. Daring, self-willed, they are not afraid to speak evil of dignitaries; [2:11]whereas angels, though greater in might and power, don't bring a railing judgment against them before the Lord. [2:12]But these, as unreasoning creatures, born natural animals to be taken and destroyed, speaking evil in matters about which they are ignorant, will in their destroying surely be de-

---

[a]1:10 The word for "brothers" here and where context allows may also be correctly translated "brothers and sisters" or "siblings."

[b]1:17 Matthew 17:5; Mark 9:7; Luke 9:35

[c]2:2 TR reads "destructive" instead of "immoral"

[d]2:4 Tartarus is another name for Hell

stroyed, [2:13]receiving the wages of unrighteousness; people who count it pleasure to revel in the daytime, spots and blemishes, reveling in their deceit while they feast with you; [2:14]having eyes full of adultery, and who can't cease from sin; enticing unsettled souls; having a heart trained in greed; children of cursing; [2:15]forsaking the right way, they went astray, having followed the way of Balaam the son of Beor, who loved the wages of wrong-doing; [2:16]but he was rebuked for his own disobedience. A mute donkey spoke with a man's voice and stopped the madness of the prophet. [2:17]These are wells without water, clouds driven by a storm; for whom the blackness of darkness has been reserved forever. [2:18]For, uttering great swelling words of emptiness, they entice in the lusts of the flesh, by licentiousness, those who are indeed escaping from those who live in error; [2:19]promising them liberty, while they themselves are bondservants of corruption; for a man is brought into bondage by whoever overcomes him.

[2:20]For if, after they have escaped the defilement of the world through the knowledge of the Lord and Savior Jesus Christ, they are again entangled in it and overcome, the last state has become worse for them than the first. [2:21]For it would be better for them not to have known the way of righteousness, than, after knowing it, to turn back from the holy commandment delivered to them. [2:22]But it has happened to them according to the true proverb, "The dog turns to his own vomit again,"[e] and "the sow that has washed to wallowing in the mire."

[3:1]This is now, beloved, the second letter that I have written to you; and in both of them I stir up your sincere mind by reminding you; [3:2]that you should remember the words which were spoken before by the holy prophets, and the commandments of us, the apostles of the Lord and Savior: [3:3]knowing this first, that in the last days mockers will come, walking after their own lusts, [3:4]and saying, "Where is the promise of his coming? For, from the day that the fathers fell asleep, all things continue as they were from the beginning of the creation." [3:5]For this they willfully forget, that there were heavens from of old, and an earth formed out of water and amid water, by the word of God; [3:6]by which means the world that then was, being overflowed with water, perished. [3:7]But the heavens that now are, and the earth, by the same word have been stored up for fire, being reserved against the day of judgment and destruction of ungodly men. [3:8]But don't forget this one thing, beloved, that one day is with the Lord as a thousand years, and a thousand years as one day. [3:9]The Lord is not slow concerning his promise, as some count slowness; but is patient with us, not wishing that any should perish, but that all should come to repentance. [3:10]But the day of the Lord will come as a thief in the night; in which the heavens will pass away with a great noise, and the elements will be dissolved with fervent heat, and the earth and the works that are in it will be burned up. [3:11]Therefore since all these things will be destroyed like this, what kind of people ought you to be in holy living and godliness, [3:12]looking for and earnestly desiring the coming of the day of God, which will cause the burning heavens to be dissolved, and the elements will melt with fervent heat? [3:13]But, according to his promise, we look for new heavens and a new earth, in which righteousness dwells.

[3:14]Therefore, beloved, seeing that you look for these things, be diligent to be found in peace, without blemish and blameless in his sight. [3:15]Regard the patience of our Lord as salvation; even as our beloved brother Paul also, according to the wisdom given to him, wrote to you; [3:16]as also in all of his letters, speaking in them of these things. In those, there are some things that are hard to understand, which the ignorant and unsettled twist, as they also do to the other Scriptures, to their own destruction. [3:17]You therefore, beloved, knowing these things beforehand, beware, lest being carried away with the error of the wicked, you fall from your own steadfastness. [3:18]But grow in the grace and knowledge of our

---

[e]2:22 Proverbs 26:11

Lord and Savior Jesus Christ. To him be the glory both now and forever. Amen.

John's First Letter

[1:1]That which was from the beginning, that which we have heard, that which we have seen with our eyes, that which we saw, and our hands touched, concerning the Word of life [1:2](and the life was revealed, and we have seen, and testify, and declare to you the life, the eternal life, which was with the Father, and was revealed to us); [1:3]that which we have seen and heard we declare to you, that you also may have fellowship with us. Yes, and our fellowship is with the Father, and with his Son, Jesus Christ. [1:4]And we write these things to you, that our joy may be fulfilled.

[1:5]This is the message which we have heard from him and announce to you, that God is light, and in him is no darkness at all. [1:6]If we say that we have fellowship with him and walk in the darkness, we lie, and don't tell the truth. [1:7]But if we walk in the light, as he is in the light, we have fellowship with one another, and the blood of Jesus Christ, his Son, cleanses us from all sin. [1:8]If we say that we have no sin, we deceive ourselves, and the truth is not in us. [1:9]If we confess our sins, he is faithful and righteous to forgive us the sins, and to cleanse us from all unrighteousness. [1:10]If we say that we haven't sinned, we make him a liar, and his word is not in us.

[2:1]My little children, I write these things to you so that you may not sin. If anyone sins, we have a Counselor[a] with the Father, Jesus Christ, the righteous. [2:2]And he is the atoning sacrifice[b] for our sins, and not for ours only, but also for the whole world. [2:3]This is how we know that we know him: if we keep his commandments. [2:4]One who says, "I know him," and doesn't keep his commandments, is a liar, and the truth isn't in him. [2:5]But whoever keeps his word, God's love has most certainly been perfected in him. This is how we know that we are in him: [2:6]he who says he remains in him ought himself also to walk just like he walked.

[2:7]Brothers, I write no new commandment to you, but an old commandment which you had from the beginning. The old commandment is the word which you heard from the beginning. [2:8]Again, I write a new commandment to you, which is true in him and in you; because the darkness is passing away, and the true light already shines. [2:9]He who says he is in the light and hates his brother, is in the darkness even until now. [2:10]He who loves his brother remains in the light, and there is no occasion for stumbling in him. [2:11]But he who hates his brother is in the darkness, and walks in the darkness, and doesn't know where he is going, because the darkness has blinded his eyes.

[2:12]I write to you, little children, because your sins are forgiven you for his name's sake.

[2:13]I write to you, fathers, because you know him who is from the beginning.

I write to you, young men, because you have overcome the evil one.

I write to you, little children, because you know the Father.

[2:14]I have written to you, fathers, because you know him who is from the beginning.

I have written to you, young men, because you are strong, and the word of God remains in you, and you have overcome the evil one.

[2:15]Don't love the world, neither the things that are in the world. If anyone loves the world, the Father's love isn't in him. [2:16]For all that is in the world, the lust of the flesh, the lust of the eyes, and the pride of life, isn't the Father's, but is the world's. [2:17]The world is passing away with its lusts, but he who does God's will remains forever.

[2:18]Little children, these are the end times, and as you heard that the Antichrist is coming, even now many antichrists have arisen. By this we know that it is the final

---

[a]2:1 Greek Parakleton: Counselor, Helper, Intercessor, Advocate, and Comfortor.

[b]2:2 "atoning sacrifice" is from the Greek "hilasmos," an appeasing, propitiating, or the means of appeasement or propitiation—the sacrifice that turns away God's wrath because of our sin.

hour. [2:19]They went out from us, but they didn't belong to us; for if they had belonged to us, they would have continued with us. But they left, that they might be revealed that none of them belong to us. [2:20]You have an anointing from the Holy One, and you know the truth. [2:21]I have not written to you because you don't know the truth, but because you know it, and because no lie is of the truth. [2:22]Who is the liar but he who denies that Jesus is the Christ? This is the Antichrist, he who denies the Father and the Son. [2:23]Whoever denies the Son, the same doesn't have the Father. He who confesses the Son has the Father also.

[2:24]Therefore, as for you, let that remain in you which you heard from the beginning. If that which you heard from the beginning remains in you, you also will remain in the Son, and in the Father. [2:25]This is the promise which he promised us, the eternal life. [2:26]These things I have written to you concerning those who would lead you astray. [2:27]As for you, the anointing which you received from him remains in you, and you don't need for anyone to teach you. But as his anointing teaches you concerning all things, and is true, and is no lie, and even as it taught you, you will remain in him. [2:28]Now, little children, remain in him, that when he appears, we may have boldness, and not be ashamed before him at his coming. [2:29]If you know that he is righteous, you know that everyone who practices righteousness is born of him.

[3:1]Behold, how great a love the Father has bestowed on us, that we should be called children of God! For this cause the world doesn't know us, because it didn't know him. [3:2]Beloved, now we are children of God, and it is not yet revealed what we will be. But we know that, when he is revealed, we will be like him; for we will see him just as he is. [3:3]Everyone who has this hope set on him purifies himself, even as he is pure. [3:4]Everyone who sins also commits lawlessness. Sin is lawlessness. [3:5]You know that he was revealed to take away our sins, and in him is no sin. [3:6]Whoever remains in him doesn't sin. Whoever sins hasn't seen him, neither knows him.

[3:7]Little children, let no one lead you astray. He who does righteousness is righteous, even as he is righteous. [3:8]He who sins is of the devil, for the devil has been sinning from the beginning. To this end the Son of God was revealed, that he might destroy the works of the devil. [3:9]Whoever is born of God doesn't commit sin, because his seed remains in him; and he can't sin, because he is born of God. [3:10]In this the children of God are revealed, and the children of the devil. Whoever doesn't do righteousness is not of God, neither is he who doesn't love his brother. [3:11]For this is the message which you heard from the beginning, that we should love one another; [3:12]unlike Cain, who was of the evil one, and killed his brother. Why did he kill him? Because his works were evil, and his brother's righteous. [3:13]Don't be surprised, my brothers, if the world hates you. [3:14]We know that we have passed out of death into life, because we love the brothers. He who doesn't love his brother remains in death. [3:15]Whoever hates his brother is a murderer, and you know that no murderer has eternal life remaining in him.

[3:16]By this we know love, because he laid down his life for us. And we ought to lay down our lives for the brothers. [3:17]But whoever has the world's goods, and sees his brother in need, and closes his heart of compassion against him, how does the love of God remain in him? [3:18]My little children, let's not love in word only, neither with the tongue only, but in deed and truth. [3:19]And by this we know that we are of the truth, and persuade our hearts before him, [3:20]because if our heart condemns us, God is greater than our heart, and knows all things. [3:21]Beloved, if our hearts don't condemn us, we have boldness toward God; [3:22]and whatever we ask, we receive from him, because we keep his commandments and do the things that are pleasing in his sight. [3:23]This is his commandment, that we should believe in the name of his Son, Jesus Christ, and love one another, even as he commanded. [3:24]He who keeps his commandments remains in him, and he in him. By this we know that he remains in us, by the Spirit which he gave us.

⁴:¹Beloved, don't believe every spirit, but test the spirits, whether they are of God, because many false prophets have gone out into the world. ⁴:²By this you know the Spirit of God: every spirit who confesses that Jesus Christ has come in the flesh is of God, ⁴:³and every spirit who doesn't confess that Jesus Christ has come in the flesh is not of God, and this is the spirit of the antichrist, of whom you have heard that it comes. Now it is in the world already. ⁴:⁴You are of God, little children, and have overcome them; because greater is he who is in you than he who is in the world. ⁴:⁵They are of the world. Therefore they speak of the world, and the world hears them. ⁴:⁶We are of God. He who knows God listens to us. He who is not of God doesn't listen to us. By this we know the spirit of truth, and the spirit of error.

⁴:⁷Beloved, let us love one another, for love is of God; and everyone who loves is born of God, and knows God. ⁴:⁸He who doesn't love doesn't know God, for God is love. ⁴:⁹By this God's love was revealed in us, that God has sent his one and only Son into the world that we might live through him. ⁴:¹⁰In this is love, not that we loved God, but that he loved us, and sent his Son as the atoning sacrifice^c for our sins. ⁴:¹¹Beloved, if God loved us in this way, we also ought to love one another. ⁴:¹²No one has seen God at any time. If we love one another, God remains in us, and his love has been perfected in us.

⁴:¹³By this we know that we remain in him and he in us, because he has given us of his Spirit. ⁴:¹⁴We have seen and testify that the Father has sent the Son as the Savior of the world. ⁴:¹⁵Whoever confesses that Jesus is the Son of God, God remains in him, and he in God. ⁴:¹⁶We know and have believed the love which God has for us. God is love, and he who remains in love remains in God, and God remains in him. ⁴:¹⁷In this love has been made perfect among us, that we may have boldness in the day of judgment, because as he is, even so are we in this world. ⁴:¹⁸There is no fear in love; but perfect love casts out fear, because fear has punishment. He who fears is not made perfect in love. ⁴:¹⁹We love Him, because he first loved us. ⁴:²⁰If a man says, "I love God," and hates his brother, he is a liar; for he who doesn't love his brother whom he has seen, how can he love God whom he has not seen? ⁴:²¹This commandment we have from him, that he who loves God should also love his brother.

⁵:¹Whoever believes that Jesus is the Christ is born of God. Whoever loves the father also loves the child who is born of him. ⁵:²By this we know that we love the children of God, when we love God and keep his commandments. ⁵:³For this is the love of God, that we keep his commandments. His commandments are not grievous. ⁵:⁴For whatever is born of God overcomes the world. This is the victory that has overcome the world: your faith. ⁵:⁵Who is he who overcomes the world, but he who believes that Jesus is the Son of God? ⁵:⁶This is he who came by water and blood, Jesus Christ; not with the water only, but with the water and the blood. It is the Spirit who testifies, because the Spirit is the truth. ⁵:⁷For there are three who testify^d: ⁵:⁸the Spirit, the water, and the blood; and the three agree as one. ⁵:⁹If we receive the witness of men, the witness of God is greater; for this is God's testimony which he has testified concerning his Son. ⁵:¹⁰He who believes in the Son of God has the testimony in himself. He who doesn't believe God has made him a liar, because he has not believed in the testimony that God has given concerning his Son. ⁵:¹¹The testimony is this, that God gave to us eternal life, and this life is in his Son. ⁵:¹²He who has the Son has the life. He who doesn't have God's Son doesn't have the life. ⁵:¹³These things I have written to you who believe in the name of the Son of God, that you may know that you have

---

^{c}4:10 "atoning sacrifice" is from the Greek "hilasmos," an appeasing, propitiating, or the means of appeasement or propitiation—the sacrifice that turns away God's wrath because of our sin.

^{d}5:7 Only a few recent manuscripts add "in heaven: the Father, the Word, and the Holy Spirit; and these three are one. And there are three that testify on earth"

eternal life, and that you may continue to believe in the name of the Son of God. ^{5:14}This is the boldness which we have toward him, that, if we ask anything according to his will, he listens to us. ^{5:15}And if we know that he listens to us, whatever we ask, we know that we have the petitions which we have asked of him.

^{5:16}If anyone sees his brother sinning a sin not leading to death, he shall ask, and God will give him life for those who sin not leading to death. There is a sin leading to death. I don't say that he should make a request concerning this. ^{5:17}All unrighteousness is sin, and there is a sin not leading to death. ^{5:18}We know that whoever is born of God doesn't sin, but he who was born of God keeps himself, and the evil one doesn't touch him. ^{5:19}We know that we are of God, and the whole world lies in the power of the evil one. ^{5:20}We know that the Son of God has come, and has given us an understanding, that we know him who is true, and we are in him who is true, in his Son Jesus Christ. This is the true God, and eternal life. ^{5:21}Little children, keep yourselves from idols.

John's Second Letter

¹The elder, to the chosen lady and her children, whom I love in truth; and not I only, but also all those who know the truth; ²for the truth's sake, which remains in us, and it will be with us forever: ³Grace, mercy, and peace will be with us, from God the Father, and from the Lord Jesus Christ, the Son of the Father, in truth and love.

⁴I rejoice greatly that I have found some of your children walking in truth, even as we have been commanded by the Father. ⁵Now I beg you, dear lady, not as though I wrote to you a new commandment, but that which we had from the beginning, that we love one another. ⁶This is love, that we should walk according to his commandments. This is the commandment, even as you heard from the beginning,

that you should walk in it. ⁷For many deceivers have gone out into the world, those who don't confess that Jesus Christ came in the flesh. This is the deceiver and the Antichrist. ⁸Watch yourselves, that we don't lose the things which we have accomplished, but that we receive a full reward. ⁹Whoever transgresses and doesn't remain in the teaching of Christ, doesn't have God. He who remains in the teaching, the same has both the Father and the Son. ¹⁰If anyone comes to you, and doesn't bring this teaching, don't receive him into your house, and don't welcome him, ¹¹for he who welcomes him participates in his evil works.

¹²Having many things to write to you, I don't want to do so with paper and ink, but I hope to come to you, and to speak face to face, that our joy may be made full. ¹³The children of your chosen sister greet you. Amen.

John's Third Letter

¹The elder to Gaius the beloved, whom I love in truth.

²Beloved, I pray that you may prosper in all things and be healthy, even as your soul prospers. ³For I rejoiced greatly, when brothers came and testified about your truth, even as you walk in truth. ⁴I have no greater joy than this, to hear about my children walking in truth.

⁵Beloved, you do a faithful work in whatever you accomplish for those who are brothers and strangers. ⁶They have testified about your love before the assembly. You will do well to send them forward on their journey in a manner worthy of God, ⁷because for the sake of the Name they went out, taking nothing from the Gentiles. ⁸We therefore ought to receive such, that we may be fellow workers for the truth.

⁹I wrote to the assembly, but Diotrephes, who loves to be first among them, doesn't accept what we say. ¹⁰Therefore, if I come, I will call attention to his deeds which he does, unjustly accusing us with wicked

words. Not content with this, neither does he himself receive the brothers, and those who would, he forbids and throws out of the assembly. [11]Beloved, don't imitate that which is evil, but that which is good. He who does good is of God. He who does evil hasn't seen God. [12]Demetrius has the testimony of all, and of the truth itself; yes, we also testify, and you know that our testimony is true.

[13]I had many things to write to you, but I am unwilling to write to you with ink and pen; [14]but I hope to see you soon, and we will speak face to face. Peace be to you. The friends greet you. Greet the friends by name.

The Letter from Jude

[1]Jude,[a] a servant of Jesus Christ, and brother of James, to those who are called, sanctified by God the Father, and kept for Jesus Christ: [2]Mercy to you and peace and love be multiplied.

[3]Beloved, while I was very eager to write to you about our common salvation, I was constrained to write to you exhorting you to contend earnestly for the faith which was once for all delivered to the saints. [4]For there are certain men who crept in secretly, even those who were long ago written about for this condemnation: ungodly men, turning the grace of our God into lasciviousness, and denying our only Master, God, and Lord, Jesus Christ.

[5]Now I desire to remind you, though you already know this, that the Lord, having saved a people out of the land of Egypt, afterward destroyed those who didn't believe. [6]Angels who didn't keep their first domain, but deserted their own dwelling place, he has kept in everlasting bonds under darkness for the judgment of the great day. [7]Even as Sodom and Gomorrah, and the cities around them, having, in the same way as these, given themselves over to sexual immorality and gone after strange flesh, are set forth as an example, suffering the punishment of eternal fire. [8]Yet in like manner these also in their dreaming defile the flesh, despise authority, and slander celestial beings. [9]But Michael, the archangel, when contending with the devil and arguing about the body of Moses, dared not bring against him an abusive condemnation, but said, "May the Lord rebuke you!" [10]But these speak evil of whatever things they don't know. What they understand naturally, like the creatures without reason, they are destroyed in these things. [11]Woe to them! For they went in the way of Cain, and ran riotously in the error of Balaam for hire, and perished in Korah's rebellion. [12]These are hidden rocky reefs in your love feasts when they feast with you, shepherds who without fear feed themselves; clouds without water, carried along by winds; autumn leaves without fruit, twice dead, plucked up by the roots; [13]wild waves of the sea, foaming out their own shame; wandering stars, for whom the blackness of darkness has been reserved forever. [14]About these also Enoch, the seventh from Adam, prophesied, saying, "Behold, the Lord came with ten thousands of his holy ones, [15]to execute judgment on all, and to convict all the ungodly of all their works of ungodliness which they have done in an ungodly way, and of all the hard things which ungodly sinners have spoken against him." [16]These are murmurers and complainers, walking after their lusts (and their mouth speaks proud things), showing respect of persons to gain advantage.

[17]But you, beloved, remember the words which have been spoken before by the apostles of our Lord Jesus Christ. [18]They said to you that "In the last time there will be mockers, walking after their own ungodly lusts." [19]These are they who cause divisions, and are sensual, not having the Spirit. [20]But you, beloved, keep building up yourselves on your most holy faith, praying in the Holy Spirit. [21]Keep yourselves in the love of God, looking for the mercy of our Lord Jesus Christ to eternal life. [22]On some have compassion, making a distinction, [23]and some save, snatching

---

[a]1 or, Judah

them out of the fire with fear, hating even the clothing stained by the flesh.

[24] Now to him who is able to keep them[b] from stumbling, and to present you faultless before the presence of his glory in great joy, [25] to God our Savior, who alone is wise, be glory and majesty, dominion and power, both now and forever. Amen.

The Revelation to John

[1:1] This is the Revelation of Jesus Christ, which God gave him to show to his servants the things which must happen soon, which he sent and made known by his angel[a] to his servant, John, [1:2] who testified to God's word, and of the testimony of Jesus Christ, about everything that he saw.

[1:3] Blessed is he who reads and those who hear the words of the prophecy, and keep the things that are written in it, for the time is at hand.

[1:4] John, to the seven assemblies that are in Asia: Grace to you and peace, from God, who is and who was and who is to come; and from the seven Spirits who are before his throne; [1:5] and from Jesus Christ, the faithful witness, the firstborn of the dead, and the ruler of the kings of the earth. To him who loves us, and washed us from our sins by his blood; [1:6] and he made us to be a Kingdom, priests[b] to his God and Father; to him be the glory and the dominion forever and ever. Amen.

[1:7] Behold, he is coming with the clouds, and every eye will see him, including those who pierced him. All the tribes of the earth will mourn over him. Even so, Amen.

[1:8] **"I am the Alpha and the Omega,**[c]**"** says the Lord God,[d] **"who is and who was and who is to come, the Almighty."**

[1:9] I John, your brother and partner with you in oppression, Kingdom, and perseverance in Christ Jesus, was on the isle that is called Patmos because of God's Word and the testimony of Jesus Christ. [1:10] I was in the Spirit on the Lord's day, and I heard behind me a loud voice, like a trumpet [1:11] saying, **"**[e]**What you see, write in a book and send to the seven assemblies**[f]**: to Ephesus, Smyrna, Pergamum, Thyatira, Sardis, Philadelphia, and to Laodicea."**

[1:12] I turned to see the voice that spoke with me. Having turned, I saw seven golden lampstands. [1:13] And among the lampstands was one like a son of man,[g] clothed with a robe reaching down to his feet, and with a golden sash around his chest. [1:14] His head and his hair were white as white wool, like snow. His eyes were like a flame of fire. [1:15] His feet were like burnished brass, as if it had been refined in a furnace. His voice was like the voice of many waters. [1:16] He had seven stars in his right hand. Out of his mouth proceeded a sharp two-edged sword. His face was like the sun shining at its brightest. [1:17] When I saw him, I fell at his feet like a dead man.

He laid his right hand on me, saying, **"Don't be afraid. I am the first and the last,** [1:18] **and the Living one. I was dead, and behold, I am alive forevermore. Amen. I have the keys of Death and of Hades**[h]**.** [1:19] **Write therefore the things which you have seen, and the things which are, and the things which will happen hereafter;** [1:20] **the mystery of the seven stars which you saw in my right hand, and the seven golden lampstands. The seven stars are the angels**[i] **of the seven assemblies. The seven lampstands are seven assemblies.**

---

[b] 24 TR and NU read "you"
[a] 1:1 or, messenger (here and wherever angel is mentioned)
[b] 1:6 Exodus 19:6; Isaiah 61:6
[c] 1:8 TR adds "the Beginning and the End"
[d] 1:8 TR omits "God"
[e] 1:11 TR adds "I am the Alpha and the Omega, the First and the Last."
[f] 1:11 TR adds "which are in Asia"
[g] 1:13 Daniel 7:13
[h] 1:18 or, Hell
[i] 1:20 or, messengers (here and wherever angels are mentioned)

2:1"To the angel of the assembly in Ephesus write:

"He who holds the seven stars in his right hand, he who walks among the seven golden lampstands says these things:

2:2"I know your works, and your toil and perseverance, and that you can't tolerate evil men, and have tested those who call themselves apostles, and they are not, and found them false. 2:3You have perseverance and have endured for my name's sake, and have^j not grown weary. 2:4But I have this against you, that you left your first love. 2:5Remember therefore from where you have fallen, and repent and do the first works; or else I am coming to you swiftly, and will move your lampstand out of its place, unless you repent. 2:6But this you have, that you hate the works of the Nicolaitans, which I also hate. 2:7He who has an ear, let him hear what the Spirit says to the assemblies. To him who overcomes I will give to eat of the tree of life, which is in the Paradise of my God.

2:8"To the angel of the assembly in Smyrna write:

"The first and the last, who was dead, and has come to life says these things:

2:9"I know your works, oppression, and your poverty (but you are rich), and the blasphemy of those who say they are Jews, and they are not, but are a synagogue of Satan. 2:10Don't be afraid of the things which you are about to suffer. Behold, the devil is about to throw some of you into prison, that you may be tested; and you will have oppression for ten days. Be faithful to death, and I will give you the crown of life. 2:11He who has an ear, let him hear what the Spirit says to the assemblies. He who overcomes won't be harmed by the second death.

2:12"To the angel of the assembly in Pergamum write:

"He who has the sharp two-edged sword says these things:

2:13"I know your works and where you dwell, where Satan's throne is. You hold firmly to my name, and didn't deny my faith in the days of Antipas my witness, my faithful one, who was killed among you, where Satan dwells. 2:14But I have a few things against you, because you have there some who hold the teaching of Balaam, who taught Balak to throw a stumbling block before the children of Israel, to eat things sacrificed to idols, and to commit sexual immorality. 2:15So you also have some who hold to the teaching of the Nicolaitans likewise^k. 2:16Repent therefore, or else I am coming to you quickly, and I will make war against them with the sword of my mouth. 2:17He who has an ear, let him hear what the Spirit says to the assemblies. To him who overcomes, to him I will give of the hidden manna,^l and I will give him a white stone, and on the stone a new name written, which no one knows but he who receives it.

2:18"To the angel of the assembly in Thyatira write:

"The Son of God, who has his eyes like a flame of fire, and his feet are like burnished brass, says these things:

2:19"I know your works, your love, faith, service, patient endurance, and that your last works are more than the first. 2:20But I have this against you, that you tolerate your^m woman, Jezebel, who calls herself a prophetess. She teaches and seduces my servants to commit sexual immorality, and to eat things sacrificed to idols. 2:21I gave her time to repent, but she refuses to repent of her sexual immorality. 2:22Behold, I will throw her into a bed, and those who commit adultery with her into great oppression, unless they repent of her works. 2:23I will kill her children with Death, and all the assemblies will know that I am he who searches the minds and hearts. I will give to each one of you according to your deeds. 2:24But to you I say, to the rest who are in Thyatira, as many as don't

---

j2:3 TR adds "have labored and"

k2:15 TR reads "which I hate" instead of "likewise"

l2:17 Manna is supernatural food, named after the Hebrew for "What is it?". See Exodus 11:7-9.

m2:20 TR, NU read "that" instead of "your"

have this teaching, who don't know what some call 'the deep things of Satan,' to you I say, I am not putting any other burden on you. [2:25] Nevertheless, hold firmly that which you have, until I come. [2:26] He who overcomes, and he who keeps my works to the end, to him I will give authority over the nations. [2:27] He will rule them with a rod of iron, shattering them like clay pots;[n] as I also have received of my Father: [2:28] and I will give him the morning star. [2:29] He who has an ear, let him hear what the Spirit says to the assemblies.

[3:1] "And to the angel of the assembly in Sardis write:

"He who has the seven Spirits of God, and the seven stars says these things:

"I know your works, that you have a reputation of being alive, but you are dead. [3:2] Wake up, and keep the things that remain, which you were about to throw away, for I have found no works of yours perfected before my God. [3:3] Remember therefore how you have received and heard. Keep it, and repent. If therefore you won't watch, I will come as a thief, and you won't know what hour I will come upon you. [3:4] Nevertheless you have a few names in Sardis that did not defile their garments. They will walk with me in white, for they are worthy. [3:5] He who overcomes will be arrayed in white garments, and I will in no way blot his name out of the book of life, and I will confess his name before my Father, and before his angels. [3:6] He who has an ear, let him hear what the Spirit says to the assemblies.

[3:7] "To the angel of the assembly in Philadelphia write:

"He who is holy, he who is true, he who has the key of David, he who opens and no one can shut, and who shuts and no one opens, says these things:

[3:8] "I know your works (behold, I have set before you an open door, which no one can shut), that you have a little power, and kept my word, and didn't deny my name. [3:9] Behold, I give of the synagogue of Satan, of those who say they are Jews, and they are not, but lie. Behold, I will

make them to come and worship before your feet, and to know that I have loved you. [3:10] Because you kept my command to endure, I also will keep you from the hour of testing, which is to come on the whole world, to test those who dwell on the earth. [3:11] I am coming quickly! Hold firmly that which you have, so that no one takes your crown. [3:12] He who overcomes, I will make him a pillar in the temple of my God, and he will go out from there no more. I will write on him the name of my God, and the name of the city of my God, the new Jerusalem, which comes down out of heaven from my God, and my own new name. [3:13] He who has an ear, let him hear what the Spirit says to the assemblies.

[3:14] "To the angel of the assembly in Laodicea write:

"The Amen, the Faithful and True Witness, the Head of God's creation, says these things:

[3:15] "I know your works, that you are neither cold nor hot. I wish you were cold or hot. [3:16] So, because you are lukewarm, and neither hot nor cold, I will vomit you out of my mouth. [3:17] Because you say, 'I am rich, and have gotten riches, and have need of nothing;' and don't know that you are the wretched one, miserable, poor, blind, and naked; [3:18] I counsel you to buy from me gold refined by fire, that you may become rich; and white garments, that you may clothe yourself, and that the shame of your nakedness may not be revealed; and eye salve to anoint your eyes, that you may see. [3:19] As many as I love, I reprove and chasten. Be zealous therefore, and repent. [3:20] Behold, I stand at the door and knock. If anyone hears my voice and opens the door, then I will come in to him, and will dine with him, and he with me. [3:21] He who overcomes, I will give to him to sit down with me on my throne, as I also overcame, and sat down with my Father on his throne. [3:22] He who has an ear, let him hear what the Spirit says to the assemblies."

---

[n]2:27 Psalm 2:9

^{4:1}After these things I looked and saw a door opened in heaven, and the first voice that I heard, like a trumpet speaking with me, was one saying, "Come up here, and I will show you the things which must happen after this."

^{4:2}Immediately I was in the Spirit. Behold, there was a throne set in heaven, and one sitting on the throne ^{4:3}that looked like a jasper stone and a sardius. There was a rainbow around the throne, like an emerald to look at. ^{4:4}Around the throne were twenty-four thrones. On the thrones were twenty-four elders sitting, dressed in white garments, with crowns of gold on their heads. ^{4:5}Out of the throne proceed lightnings, sounds, and thunders. There were seven lamps of fire burning before his throne, which are the seven Spirits of God. ^{4:6}Before the throne was something like a sea of glass, similar to crystal. In the midst of the throne, and around the throne were four living creatures full of eyes before and behind. ^{4:7}The first creature was like a lion, and the second creature like a calf, and the third creature had a face like a man, and the fourth was like a flying eagle. ^{4:8}The four living creatures, each one of them having six wings, are full of eyes around and within. They have no rest day and night, saying, "Holy, holy, holy° is the Lord God, the Almighty, who was and who is and who is to come!"

^{4:9}When the living creatures give glory, honor, and thanks to him who sits on the throne, to him who lives forever and ever, ^{4:10}the twenty-four elders fall down before him who sits on the throne, and worship him who lives forever and ever, and throw their crowns before the throne, saying, ^{4:11}"Worthy are you, our Lord and God, the Holy One,^p to receive the glory, the honor, and the power, for you created all things, and because of your desire they existed, and were created!"

^{5:1}I saw, in the right hand of him who sat on the throne, a book written inside and outside, sealed shut with seven seals. ^{5:2}I saw a mighty angel proclaiming with a loud voice, "Who is worthy to open the book, and to break its seals?" ^{5:3}No one in heaven above, or on the earth, or under the earth, was able to open the book, or to look in it. ^{5:4}And I wept much, because no one was found worthy to open the book, or to look in it. ^{5:5}One of the elders said to me, "Don't weep. Behold, the Lion who is of the tribe of Judah, the Root of David, has overcome; he who opens the book and its seven seals." ^{5:6}I saw in the midst of the throne and of the four living creatures, and in the midst of the elders, a Lamb standing, as though it had been slain, having seven horns, and seven eyes, which are the seven Spirits of God, sent out into all the earth. ^{5:7}Then he came, and he took it out of the right hand of him who sat on the throne. ^{5:8}Now when he had taken the book, the four living creatures and the twenty-four elders fell down before the Lamb, each one having a harp, and golden bowls full of incense, which are the prayers of the saints. ^{5:9}They sang a new song, saying,

"You are worthy to take the book,
   and to open its seals:
for you were killed,
      and bought us for God with your blood,
      out of every tribe, language, people, and nation,
^{5:10}and made us kings and priests to our God,
      and we will reign on earth."

^{5:11}I saw, and I heard something like a voice of many angels around the throne, the living creatures, and the elders; and the number of them was ten thousands of ten thousands, and thousands of thousands; ^{5:12}saying with a loud voice, "Worthy is the Lamb who has been killed to receive the power, wealth, wisdom, strength, honor, glory, and blessing!"

^{5:13}I heard every created thing which is in heaven, on the earth, under the earth, on the sea, and everything in them, saying, "To him who sits on the throne, and to the Lamb be the blessing, the honor, the glory, and the

°4:8 Hodges/Farstad MT reads "holy" 9 times instead of 3.
P4:11 TR omits "and God, the Holy One,"

dominion, forever and ever! Amen!ᵠ"

⁵:¹⁴The four living creatures said, "Amen!" The ʳelders fell down and worshiped.ˢ

⁶:¹I saw that the Lamb opened one of the seven seals, and I heard one of the four living creatures saying, as with a voice of thunder, "Come and see!" ⁶:²And behold, a white horse, and he who sat on it had a bow. A crown was given to him, and he came forth conquering, and to conquer.

⁶:³When he opened the second seal, I heard the second living creature saying, "Come!" ⁶:⁴Another came forth, a red horse. To him who sat on it was given power to take peace from the earth, and that they should kill one another. There was given to him a great sword.

⁶:⁵When he opened the third seal, I heard the third living creature saying, "Come and see!" And behold, a black horse, and he who sat on it had a balance in his hand. ⁶:⁶I heard a voice in the midst of the four living creatures saying, "A choenixᵗ of wheat for a denarius, and three choenix of barley for a denarius! Don't damage the oil and the wine!"

⁶:⁷When he opened the fourth seal, I heard the fourth living creature saying, "Come and see!" ⁶:⁸And behold, a pale horse, and he who sat on it, his name was Death. Hadesᵘ followed with him. Authority over one fourth of the earth, to kill with the sword, with famine, with death, and by the wild animals of the earth was given to him.

⁶:⁹When he opened the fifth seal, I saw underneath the altar the souls of those who had been killed for the Word of God, and for the testimony of the Lamb which they had. ⁶:¹⁰They cried with a loud voice, saying, "How long, Master, the holy and true, until you judge and avenge our blood on those who dwell on the earth?" ⁶:¹¹A long white robe was given to each of them. They were told that they should rest yet for

a while, until their fellow servants and their brothers,ᵛ who would also be killed even as they were, should complete their course.

⁶:¹²I saw when he opened the sixth seal, and there was a great earthquake. The sun became black as sackcloth made of hair, and the whole moon became as blood. ⁶:¹³The stars of the sky fell to the earth, like a fig tree dropping its unripe figs when it is shaken by a great wind. ⁶:¹⁴The sky was removed like a scroll when it is rolled up. Every mountain and island were moved out of their places. ⁶:¹⁵The kings of the earth, the princes, the commanding officers, the rich, the strong, and every slave and free person, hid themselves in the caves and in the rocks of the mountains. ⁶:¹⁶They told the mountains and the rocks, "Fall on us, and hide us from the face of him who sits on the throne, and from the wrath of the Lamb, ⁶:¹⁷for the great day of his wrath has come; and who is able to stand?"

⁷:¹After this, I saw four angels standing at the four corners of the earth, holding the four winds of the earth, so that no wind would blow on the earth, or on the sea, or on any tree. ⁷:²I saw another angel ascend from the sunrise, having the seal of the living God. He cried with a loud voice to the four angels to whom it was given to harm the earth and the sea, ⁷:³saying, "Don't harm the earth, neither the sea, nor the trees, until we have sealed the bondservants of our God on their foreheads!" ⁷:⁴I heard the number of those who were sealed, one hundred forty-four thousand, sealed out of every tribe of the children of Israel:

⁷:⁵of the tribe of Judah were sealed twelve thousand,

of the tribe of Reuben twelve thousand,

of the tribe of Gad twelve thousand,

⁷:⁶of the tribe of Asher twelve thousand,

of the tribe of Naphtali twelve thousand,

ᵠ5:13 TR omits "Amen!"
ʳ5:14 TR adds "twenty-four"
ˢ5:14 TR adds "the one living forever and ever"
ᵗ6:6 A choenix is a dry volume measure that is a little more than a litre (a little more than a quart).
ᵘ6:8 or, Hell
ᵛ6:11 The word for "brothers" here and where context allows may also be correctly translated "brothers and sisters" or "siblings."

of the tribe of Manasseh twelve thousand, ^{7:7}of the tribe of Simeon twelve thousand, of the tribe of Levi twelve thousand, of the tribe of Issachar twelve thousand, ^{7:8}of the tribe of Zebulun twelve thousand, of the tribe of Joseph twelve thousand, of the tribe of Benjamin were sealed twelve thousand.

^{7:9}After these things I looked, and behold, a great multitude, which no man could number, out of every nation and of all tribes, peoples, and languages, standing before the throne and before the Lamb, dressed in white robes, with palm branches in their hands. ^{7:10}They cried with a loud voice, saying, "Salvation be to our God, who sits on the throne, and to the Lamb!" ^{7:11}All the angels were standing around the throne, the elders, and the four living creatures; and they fell on their faces before his throne, and worshiped God, ^{7:12}saying, "Amen! Blessing, glory, wisdom, thanksgiving, honor, power, and might, be to our God forever and ever! Amen." ^{7:13}One of the elders answered, saying to me, "These who are arrayed in white robes, who are they, and from where did they come?" ^{7:14}I told him, "My lord, you know."

He said to me, "These are those who came out of the great tribulation. They washed their robes, and made them white in the Lamb's blood. ^{7:15}Therefore they are before the throne of God, they serve him day and night in his temple. He who sits on the throne will spread his tent over them. ^{7:16}They will never be hungry, neither thirsty any more; neither will the sun beat on them, nor any heat; ^{7:17}for the Lamb who is in the midst of the throne shepherds them, and leads them to springs of waters of life. And God will wipe away every tear from their eyes."

^{8:1}When he opened the seventh seal, there was silence in heaven for about half an hour. ^{8:2}I saw the seven angels who stand before God, and seven trumpets were given to them. ^{8:3}Another angel came and stood over the altar, having a golden censer. Much incense was given to him, that he should add it to the prayers of all the saints on the golden altar which was before the throne. ^{8:4}The smoke of the incense, with the prayers of the saints, went up before God out of the angel's hand. ^{8:5}The angel took the censer, and he filled it with the fire of the altar, and threw it on the earth. There followed thunders, sounds, lightnings, and an earthquake.

^{8:6}The seven angels who had the seven trumpets prepared themselves to sound. ^{8:7}The first sounded, and there followed hail and fire, mixed with blood, and they were thrown to the earth. One third of the earth was burnt up,^w and one third of the trees were burnt up, and all green grass was burnt up.

^{8:8}The second angel sounded, and something like a great burning mountain was thrown into the sea. One third of the sea became blood, ^{8:9}and one third of the living creatures which were in the sea died. One third of the ships were destroyed.

^{8:10}The third angel sounded, and a great star fell from the sky, burning like a torch, and it fell on one third of the rivers, and on the springs of the waters. ^{8:11}The name of the star is called "Wormwood." One third of the waters became wormwood. Many people died from the waters, because they were made bitter.

^{8:12}The fourth angel sounded, and one third of the sun was struck, and one third of the moon, and one third of the stars; so that one third of them would be darkened, and the day wouldn't shine for one third of it, and the night in the same way. ^{8:13}I saw, and I heard an eagle,^x flying in mid heaven, saying with a loud voice, "Woe! Woe! Woe for those who dwell on the earth, because of the other voices of the trumpets of the three angels, who are yet to sound!"

^{9:1}The fifth angel sounded, and I saw a star from the sky which had fallen to the earth. The key to the pit of the abyss was given to him. ^{9:2}He opened the pit of the abyss, and smoke went up out of the pit,

---

^w8:7 TR omits "One third of the earth was burnt up"

^x8:13 TR reads "angel" instead of "eagle"

like the smoke from a[y] burning furnace. The sun and the air were darkened because of the smoke from the pit. [9:3]Then out of the smoke came forth locusts on the earth, and power was given to them, as the scorpions of the earth have power. [9:4]They were told that they should not hurt the grass of the earth, neither any green thing, neither any tree, but only those people who don't have God's seal on their foreheads. [9:5]They were given power not to kill them, but to torment them for five months. Their torment was like the torment of a scorpion, when it strikes a person. [9:6]In those days people will seek death, and will in no way find it. They will desire to die, and death will flee from them. [9:7]The shapes of the locusts were like horses prepared for war. On their heads were something like golden crowns, and their faces were like people's faces. [9:8]They had hair like women's hair, and their teeth were like those of lions. [9:9]They had breastplates, like breastplates of iron. The sound of their wings was like the sound of chariots, or of many horses rushing to war. [9:10]They have tails like those of scorpions, and stings. In their tails they have power to harm men for five months. [9:11]They have over them as king the angel of the abyss. His name in Hebrew is "Abaddon,"[z] but in Greek, he has the name "Apollyon."[a] [9:12]The first woe is past. Behold, there are still two woes coming after this.

[9:13]The sixth angel sounded. I heard a voice from the horns of the golden altar which is before God, [9:14]saying to the sixth angel who had one trumpet, "Free the four angels who are bound at the great river Euphrates!"

[9:15]The four angels were freed who had been prepared for that hour and day and month and year, so that they might kill one third of mankind. [9:16]The number of the armies of the horsemen was two hundred million[b]. I heard the number of them. [9:17]Thus I saw the horses in the vision, and those who sat on them, having breastplates of fiery red, hyacinth blue, and sulfur yellow; and the heads of lions. Out of their mouths proceed fire, smoke, and sulfur. [9:18]By these three plagues were one third of mankind killed: by the fire, the smoke, and the sulfur, which proceeded out of their mouths. [9:19]For the power of the horses is in their mouths, and in their tails. For their tails are like serpents, and have heads, and with them they harm. [9:20]The rest of mankind, who were not killed with these plagues, didn't repent of the works of their hands, that they wouldn't worship demons, and the idols of gold, and of silver, and of brass, and of stone, and of wood; which can neither see, nor hear, nor walk. [9:21]They didn't repent of their murders, nor of their sorceries,[c] nor of their sexual immorality, nor of their thefts.

[10:1]I saw a mighty angel coming down out of the sky, clothed with a cloud. A rainbow was on his head. His face was like the sun, and his feet like pillars of fire. [10:2]He had in his hand a little open book. He set his right foot on the sea, and his left on the land. [10:3]He cried with a loud voice, as a lion roars. When he cried, the seven thunders uttered their voices. [10:4]When the seven thunders sounded, I was about to write; but I heard a voice from the sky saying, "Seal up the things which the seven thunders said, and don't write them."

[10:5]The angel who I saw standing on the sea and on the land lifted up his right hand to the sky, [10:6]and swore by him who lives forever and ever, who created heaven and the things that are in it, the earth and the things that are in it, and the sea and the things that are in it, that there will no longer be delay, [10:7]but in the days of the voice of the seventh angel, when he is about to sound, then the mystery of God is finished, as he declared to his servants, the prophets. [10:8]The voice which I heard from heaven, again speaking with me, said, "Go, take the

[y]9:2 TR adds "great"
[z]9:11 "Abaddon" is a Hebrew word that means ruin, destruction, or the place of destruction
[a]9:11 "Apollyon" means "Destroyer."
[b]9:16 literally, "ten thousands of ten thousands"
[c]9:21 The word for "sorceries" (pharmakeia) also implies the use of potions, poisons, and drugs

book which is open in the hand of the angel who stands on the sea and on the land."

^{10:9}I went to the angel, telling him to give me the little book.

He said to me, "Take it, and eat it up. It will make your stomach bitter, but in your mouth it will be as sweet as honey."

^{10:10}I took the little book out of the angel's hand, and ate it up. It was as sweet as honey in my mouth. When I had eaten it, my stomach was made bitter. ^{10:11}They told me, "You must prophesy again over many peoples, nations, languages, and kings."

^{11:1}A reed like a rod was given to me. Someone said, "Rise, and measure God's temple, and the altar, and those who worship in it. ^{11:2}Leave out the court which is outside of the temple, and don't measure it, for it has been given to the nations. They will tread the holy city under foot for forty-two months. ^{11:3}I will give power to my two witnesses, and they will prophesy one thousand two hundred sixty days, clothed in sackcloth." ^{11:4}These are the two olive trees and the two lampstands, standing before the Lord of the earth. ^{11:5}If anyone desires to harm them, fire proceeds out of their mouth and devours their enemies. If anyone desires to harm them, he must be killed in this way. ^{11:6}These have the power to shut up the sky, that it may not rain during the days of their prophecy. They have power over the waters, to turn them into blood, and to strike the earth with every plague, as often as they desire. ^{11:7}When they have finished their testimony, the beast that comes up out of the abyss will make war with them, and overcome them, and kill them. ^{11:8}Their dead bodies will be in the street of the great city, which spiritually is called Sodom and Egypt, where also their Lord was crucified. ^{11:9}From among the peoples, tribes, languages, and nations people will look at their dead bodies for three and a half days, and will not allow their dead bodies to be laid in a tomb. ^{11:10}Those who dwell on the earth rejoice over them, and they will be glad. They will give gifts to one another, because these two prophets tormented those who dwell on the earth. ^{11:11}After the three and a half days,

the breath of life from God entered into them, and they stood on their feet. Great fear fell on those who saw them. ^{11:12}I heard a loud voice from heaven saying to them, "Come up here!" They went up into heaven in the cloud, and their enemies saw them. ^{11:13}In that day there was a great earthquake, and a tenth of the city fell. Seven thousand people were killed in the earthquake, and the rest were terrified, and gave glory to the God of heaven. ^{11:14}The second woe is past. Behold, the third woe comes quickly.

^{11:15}The seventh angel sounded, and great voices in heaven followed, saying, "The kingdom of the world has become the Kingdom of our Lord, and of his Christ. He will reign forever and ever!"

^{11:16}The twenty-four elders, who sit on their thrones before God's throne, fell on their faces and worshiped God, ^{11:17}saying: "We give you thanks, Lord God, the Almighty, the one who is and who was^d; because you have taken your great power, and reigned. ^{11:18}The nations were angry, and your wrath came, as did the time for the dead to be judged, and to give your bondservants the prophets, their reward, as well as to the saints, and those who fear your name, to the small and the great; and to destroy those who destroy the earth."

^{11:19}God's temple that is in heaven was opened, and the ark of the Lord's covenant was seen in his temple. Lightnings, sounds, thunders, an earthquake, and great hail followed.

^{12:1}A great sign was seen in heaven: a woman clothed with the sun, and the moon under her feet, and on her head a crown of twelve stars. ^{12:2}She was with child. She cried out in pain, laboring to give birth. ^{12:3}Another sign was seen in heaven. Behold, a great red dragon, having seven heads and ten horns, and on his heads seven crowns. ^{12:4}His tail drew one third of the stars of the sky, and threw them to the earth. The dragon stood before the woman who was about to give birth, so that when she gave birth he might devour her child. ^{12:5}She gave birth to a son, a male child,

---

^d11:17 TR adds "and who is coming"

who is to rule all the nations with a rod of iron. Her child was caught up to God, and to his throne. ^{12:6}The woman fled into the wilderness, where she has a place prepared by God, that there they may nourish her one thousand two hundred sixty days.

^{12:7}There was war in the sky. Michael and his angels made war on the dragon. The dragon and his angels made war. ^{12:8}They didn't prevail, neither was a place found for him any more in heaven. ^{12:9}The great dragon was thrown down, the old serpent, he who is called the devil and Satan, the deceiver of the whole world. He was thrown down to the earth, and his angels were thrown down with him. ^{12:10}I heard a loud voice in heaven, saying, "Now is come the salvation, the power, and the Kingdom of our God, and the authority of his Christ; for the accuser of our brothers has been thrown down, who accuses them before our God day and night. ^{12:11}They overcame him because of the Lamb's blood, and because of the word of their testimony. They didn't love their life, even to death. ^{12:12}Therefore rejoice, heavens, and you who dwell in them. Woe to the earth and to the sea, because the devil has gone down to you, having great wrath, knowing that he has but a short time."

^{12:13}When the dragon saw that he was thrown down to the earth, he persecuted the woman who gave birth to the male child. ^{12:14}Two wings of the great eagle were given to the woman, that she might fly into the wilderness to her place, so that she might be nourished for a time, and times, and half a time, from the face of the serpent. ^{12:15}The serpent spewed water out of his mouth after the woman like a river, that he might cause her to be carried away by the stream. ^{12:16}The earth helped the woman, and the earth opened its mouth and swallowed up the river which the dragon spewed out of his mouth. ^{12:17}The dragon grew angry with the woman, and went away to make war with the rest of her seed, who keep God's commandments and hold Jesus' testimony.

^{13:1}Then I stood on the sand of the sea. I saw a beast coming up out of the sea, having ten horns and seven heads. On his horns were ten crowns, and on his heads, blasphemous names. ^{13:2}The beast which I saw was like a leopard, and his feet were like those of a bear, and his mouth like the mouth of a lion. The dragon gave him his power, his throne, and great authority. ^{13:3}One of his heads looked like it had been wounded fatally. His fatal wound was healed, and the whole earth marveled at the beast. ^{13:4}They worshiped the dragon, because he gave his authority to the beast, and they worshiped the beast, saying, "Who is like the beast? Who is able to make war with him?" ^{13:5}A mouth speaking great things and blasphemy was given to him. Authority to make war for forty-two months was given to him. ^{13:6}He opened his mouth for blasphemy against God, to blaspheme his name, and his dwelling, those who dwell in heaven. ^{13:7}It was given to him to make war with the saints, and to overcome them. Authority over every tribe, people, language, and nation was given to him. ^{13:8}All who dwell on the earth will worship him, everyone whose name has not been written from the foundation of the world in the book of life of the Lamb who has been killed. ^{13:9}If anyone has an ear, let him hear. ^{13:10}If anyone has captivity, he will go. If anyone is with the sword, he must be killed.[e] Here is the endurance and the faith of the saints.

^{13:11}I saw another beast coming up out of the earth. He had two horns like a lamb, and he spoke like a dragon. ^{13:12}He exercises all the authority of the first beast in his presence. He makes the earth and those who dwell in it to worship the first beast, whose fatal wound was healed. ^{13:13}He performs great signs, even making fire come down out of the sky to the earth in the sight of people. ^{13:14}He deceives my own people who dwell on the earth because of the signs he was granted to do in front of the beast; saying to those who dwell on

---

[e]13:10 TR reads "If anyone leads into captivity, into captivity he goes. If anyone will kill with the sword, he must be killed with a sword." instead of "If anyone has captivity, he goes away. If anyone is with the sword, he must be killed."

the earth, that they should make an image to the beast who had the sword wound and lived. ^{13:15} It was given to him to give breath to it, to the image of the beast, that the image of the beast should both speak, and cause as many as wouldn't worship the image of the beast to be killed. ^{13:16} He causes all, the small and the great, the rich and the poor, and the free and the slave, to be given marks on their right hands, or on their foreheads; ^{13:17} and that no one would be able to buy or to sell, unless he has that mark, the name of the beast or the number of his name. ^{13:18} Here is wisdom. He who has understanding, let him calculate the number of the beast, for it is the number of a man. His number is six hundred sixty-six.

^{14:1} I saw, and behold, the Lamb standing on Mount Zion, and with him a number, one hundred forty-four thousand, having his name, and the name of his Father, written on their foreheads. ^{14:2} I heard a sound from heaven, like the sound of many waters, and like the sound of a great thunder. The sound which I heard was like that of harpists playing on their harps. ^{14:3} They sing a new song before the throne, and before the four living creatures and the elders. No one could learn the song except the one hundred forty-four thousand, those who had been redeemed out of the earth. ^{14:4} These are those who were not defiled with women, for they are virgins. These are those who follow the Lamb wherever he goes. These were redeemed by Jesus from among men, the first fruits to God and to the Lamb. ^{14:5} In their mouth was found no lie, for they are blameless.^f

^{14:6} I saw an angel flying in mid heaven, having an eternal Good News to proclaim to those who dwell on the earth, and to every nation, tribe, language, and people. ^{14:7} He said with a loud voice, "Fear the Lord, and give him glory; for the hour of his judgment has come. Worship him who made the heaven, the earth, the sea, and the springs of waters!"

^{14:8} Another, a second angel, followed, saying, "Babylon the great has fallen, which has made all the nations to drink of the wine of the wrath of her sexual immorality."

^{14:9} Another angel, a third, followed them, saying with a great voice, "If anyone worships the beast and his image, and receives a mark on his forehead, or on his hand, ^{14:10} he also will drink of the wine of the wrath of God, which is prepared unmixed in the cup of his anger. He will be tormented with fire and sulfur in the presence of the holy angels, and in the presence of the Lamb. ^{14:11} The smoke of their torment goes up forever and ever. They have no rest day and night, those who worship the beast and his image, and whoever receives the mark of his name. ^{14:12} Here is the patience of the saints, those who keep the commandments of God, and the faith of Jesus."

^{14:13} I heard the voice from heaven saying, "Write, 'Blessed are the dead who die in the Lord from now on.'"

"Yes," says the Spirit, "that they may rest from their labors; for their works follow with them."

^{14:14} I looked, and behold, a white cloud; and on the cloud one sitting like a son of man,^g having on his head a golden crown, and in his hand a sharp sickle. ^{14:15} Another angel came out from the temple, crying with a loud voice to him who sat on the cloud, "Send forth your sickle, and reap; for the hour to reap has come; for the harvest of the earth is ripe!" ^{14:16} He who sat on the cloud thrust his sickle on the earth, and the earth was reaped.

^{14:17} Another angel came out from the temple which is in heaven. He also had a sharp sickle. ^{14:18} Another angel came out from the altar, he who has power over fire, and he called with a great voice to him who had the sharp sickle, saying, "Send forth your sharp sickle, and gather the clusters of the vine of the earth, for the earth's grapes are fully ripe!" ^{14:19} The angel thrust his sickle into the earth, and gathered the vintage of the earth, and threw it into the great winepress of the wrath

---

^f14:5 TR adds "before the throne of God"
^g14:14 Daniel 7:13

of God. [14:20]The winepress was trodden outside of the city, and blood came out from the winepress, even to the bridles of the horses, as far as one thousand six hundred stadia.[h]

[15:1]I saw another great and marvelous sign in the sky: seven angels having the seven last plagues, for in them God's wrath is finished. [15:2]I saw something like a sea of glass mixed with fire, and those who overcame the beast, his image,[i] and the number of his name, standing on the sea of glass, having harps of God. [15:3]They sang the song of Moses, the servant of God, and the song of the Lamb, saying,

"Great and marvelous are your works, Lord
   God, the Almighty!
   Righteous and true are your ways, you
   King of the nations.
[15:4]Who wouldn't fear you, Lord,
   and glorify your name?
For you only are holy.
   For all the nations will come and wor-
   ship before you.
   For your righteous acts have been re-
   vealed."

[15:5]After these things I looked, and the temple of the tabernacle of the testimony in heaven was opened. [15:6]The seven angels who had the seven plagues came out, clothed with pure, bright linen, and wearing golden sashes around their breasts. [15:7]One of the four living creatures gave to the seven angels seven golden bowls full of the wrath of God, who lives forever and ever. [15:8]The temple was filled with smoke from the glory of God, and from his power. No one was able to enter into the temple, until the seven plagues of the seven angels would be finished.

[16:1]I heard a loud voice out of the temple, saying to the seven angels, "Go and pour out the seven bowls of the wrath of God on the earth!"

[16:2]The first went, and poured out his bowl into the earth, and it became a harmful and evil sore on the people who had the mark of the beast, and who worshiped his image.

[16:3]The second angel poured out his bowl into the sea, and it became blood as of a dead man. Every living thing in the sea died.

[16:4]The third poured out his bowl into the rivers and springs of water, and they became blood. [16:5]I heard the angel of the waters saying, "You are righteous, who are and who were, you Holy One, because you have judged these things. [16:6]For they poured out the blood of the saints and the prophets, and you have given them blood to drink. They deserve this." [16:7]I heard the altar saying, "Yes, Lord God, the Almighty, true and righteous are your judgments."

[16:8]The fourth poured out his bowl on the sun, and it was given to him to scorch men with fire. [16:9]People were scorched with great heat, and people blasphemed the name of God who has the power over these plagues. They didn't repent and give him glory.

[16:10]The fifth poured out his bowl on the throne of the beast, and his kingdom was darkened. They gnawed their tongues because of the pain, [16:11]and they blasphemed the God of heaven because of their pains and their sores. They didn't repent of their works.

[16:12]The sixth poured out his bowl on the great river, the Euphrates. Its water was dried up, that the way might be made ready for the kings that come from the sunrise. [16:13]I saw coming out of the mouth of the dragon, and out of the mouth of the beast, and out of the mouth of the false prophet, three unclean spirits, something like frogs; [16:14]for they are spirits of demons, performing signs; which go forth to the kings of the whole inhabited earth, to gather them together for the war of that great day of God, the Almighty.

[16:15]**"Behold, I come like a thief. Blessed is he who watches, and keeps his clothes, so that he doesn't walk naked, and they see his shame."** [16:16]He gathered them together into the place which is called in Hebrew, Megiddo.

[16:17]The seventh poured out his bowl into the air. A loud voice came forth out of the

---

[h]14:20 1600 stadia = 296 kilometers or 184 miles
[i]15:2 TR adds "his mark,"

temple of heaven, from the throne, saying, "It is done!" [16:18]There were lightnings, sounds, and thunders; and there was a great earthquake, such as was not since there were men on the earth, so great an earthquake, so mighty. [16:19]The great city was divided into three parts, and the cities of the nations fell. Babylon the great was remembered in the sight of God, to give to her the cup of the wine of the fierceness of his wrath. [16:20]Every island fled away, and the mountains were not found. [16:21]Great hailstones, about the weight of a talent,[j] came down out of the sky on people. People blasphemed God because of the plague of the hail, for this plague is exceedingly severe.

[17:1]One of the seven angels who had the seven bowls came and spoke with me, saying, "Come here. I will show you the judgment of the great prostitute who sits on many waters, [17:2]with whom the kings of the earth committed sexual immorality, and those who dwell in the earth were made drunken with the wine of her sexual immorality." [17:3]He carried me away in the Spirit into a wilderness. I saw a woman sitting on a scarlet-colored animal, full of blasphemous names, having seven heads and ten horns. [17:4]The woman was dressed in purple and scarlet, and decked with gold and precious stones and pearls, having in her hand a golden cup full of abominations and the impurities of the sexual immorality of the earth. [17:5]And on her forehead a name was written, "MYSTERY, BABYLON THE GREAT, THE MOTHER OF THE PROSTITUTES AND OF THE ABOMINATIONS OF THE EARTH." [17:6]I saw the woman drunken with the blood of the saints, and with the blood of the martyrs of Jesus. When I saw her, I wondered with great amazement. [17:7]The angel said to me, "Why do you wonder? I will tell you the mystery of the woman, and of the beast that carries her, which has the seven heads and the ten horns. [17:8]The beast that you saw was, and is not; and is about to come up out of the abyss and to go into destruction. Those who dwell on the earth and whose

names have not been written in the book of life from the foundation of the world will marvel when they see that the beast was, and is not, and shall be present.[k] [17:9]Here is the mind that has wisdom. The seven heads are seven mountains, on which the woman sits. [17:10]They are seven kings. Five have fallen, the one is, the other has not yet come. When he comes, he must continue a little while. [17:11]The beast that was, and is not, is himself also an eighth, and is of the seven; and he goes to destruction. [17:12]The ten horns that you saw are ten kings who have received no kingdom as yet, but they receive authority as kings, with the beast, for one hour. [17:13]These have one mind, and they give their power and authority to the beast. [17:14]These will war against the Lamb, and the Lamb will overcome them, for he is Lord of lords, and King of kings. They also will overcome who are with him, called and chosen and faithful." [17:15]He said to me, "The waters which you saw, where the prostitute sits, are peoples, multitudes, nations, and languages. [17:16]The ten horns which you saw, and the beast, these will hate the prostitute, and will make her desolate, and will make her naked, and will eat her flesh, and will burn her utterly with fire. [17:17]For God has put in their hearts to do what he has in mind, and to be of one mind, and to give their kingdom to the beast, until the words of God should be accomplished. [17:18]The woman whom you saw is the great city, which reigns over the kings of the earth."

[18:1]After these things, I saw another angel coming down out of the sky, having great authority. The earth was illuminated with his glory. [18:2]He cried with a mighty voice, saying, "Fallen, fallen is Babylon the great, and she has become a habitation of demons, a prison of every unclean spirit, and a prison of every unclean and hateful bird! [18:3]For all the nations have drunk of the wine of the wrath of her sexual immorality, the kings of the earth committed sexual immorality with her, and the merchants of the earth grew rich from the

---

[j]16:21 1 talent is about 34 kilograms or 75 pounds
[k]17:8 TR reads "yet is" instead of "shall be present"

abundance of her luxury."

18:4I heard another voice from heaven, saying, "Come out of her, my people, that you have no participation in her sins, and that you don't receive of her plagues, 18:5for her sins have reached to the sky, and God has remembered her iniquities. 18:6Return to her just as she returned, and repay her double as she did, and according to her works. In the cup which she mixed, mix to her double. 18:7However much she glorified herself, and grew wanton, so much give her of torment and mourning. For she says in her heart, 'I sit a queen, and am no widow, and will in no way see mourning.' 18:8Therefore in one day her plagues will come: death, mourning, and famine; and she will be utterly burned with fire; for the Lord God who has judged her is strong. 18:9The kings of the earth, who committed sexual immorality and lived wantonly with her, will weep and wail over her, when they look at the smoke of her burning, 18:10standing far away for the fear of her torment, saying, 'Woe, woe, the great city, Babylon, the strong city! For your judgment has come in one hour.' 18:11The merchants of the earth weep and mourn over her, for no one buys their merchandise any more; 18:12merchandise of gold, silver, precious stones, pearls, fine linen, purple, silk, scarlet, all expensive wood, every vessel of ivory, every vessel made of most precious wood, and of brass, and iron, and marble; 18:13and cinnamon, incense, perfume, frankincense, wine, olive oil, fine flour, wheat, sheep, horses, chariots, and people's bodies and souls. 18:14The fruits which your soul lusted after have been lost to you, and all things that were dainty and sumptuous have perished from you, and you will find them no more at all. 18:15The merchants of these things, who were made rich by her, will stand far away for the fear of her torment, weeping and mourning; 18:16saying, 'Woe, woe, the great city, she who was dressed in fine linen, purple, and scarlet, and decked with gold and precious stones and pearls! 18:17For in an hour such great riches are made desolate.' Every shipmaster, and everyone who sails anywhere, and mariners, and as many as

gain their living by sea, stood far away, 18:18and cried out as they looked at the smoke of her burning, saying, 'What is like the great city?' 18:19They cast dust on their heads, and cried, weeping and mourning, saying, 'Woe, woe, the great city, in which all who had their ships in the sea were made rich by reason of her great wealth!' For in one hour is she made desolate.

18:20"Rejoice over her, O heaven, you saints, apostles, and prophets; for God has judged your judgment on her." 18:21A mighty angel took up a stone like a great millstone and cast it into the sea, saying, "Thus with violence will Babylon, the great city, be thrown down, and will be found no more at all. 18:22The voice of harpists, minstrels, flute players, and trumpeters will be heard no more at all in you. No craftsman, of whatever craft, will be found any more at all in you. The sound of a mill will be heard no more at all in you. 18:23The light of a lamp will shine no more at all in you. The voice of the bridegroom and of the bride will be heard no more at all in you; for your merchants were the princes of the earth; for with your sorcery all the nations were deceived. 18:24In her was found the blood of prophets and of saints, and of all who have been slain on the earth."

19:1After these things I heard something like a loud voice of a great multitude in heaven, saying, "Hallelujah! Salvation, power, and glory belong to our God: 19:2for true and righteous are his judgments. For he has judged the great prostitute, who corrupted the earth with her sexual immorality, and he has avenged the blood of his servants at her hand."

19:3A second said, "Hallelujah! Her smoke goes up forever and ever." 19:4The twenty-four elders and the four living creatures fell down and worshiped God who sits on the throne, saying, "Amen! Hallelujah!"

19:5A voice came forth from the throne, saying, "Give praise to our God, all you his servants, you who fear him, the small and the great!"

19:6I heard something like the voice of a great multitude, and like the voice of many waters, and like the voice of mighty thunders, saying, "Hallelujah! For the Lord our God, the Almighty, reigns! ¹⁹:⁷Let us rejoice and be exceedingly glad, and let us give the glory to him. For the marriage of the Lamb has come, and his wife has made herself ready." ¹⁹:⁸It was given to her that she would array herself in bright, pure, fine linen: for the fine linen is the righteous acts of the saints.

¹⁹:⁹He said to me, "Write, 'Blessed are those who are invited to the marriage supper of the Lamb.'" He said to me, "These are true words of God."

¹⁹:¹⁰I fell down before his feet to worship him. He said to me, "Look! Don't do it! I am a fellow bondservant with you and with your brothers who hold the testimony of Jesus. Worship God, for the testimony of Jesus is the Spirit of Prophecy."

¹⁹:¹¹I saw the heaven opened, and behold, a white horse, and he who sat on it is called Faithful and True. In righteousness he judges and makes war. ¹⁹:¹²His eyes are a flame of fire, and on his head are many crowns. He has names written and a name written which no one knows but he himself. ¹⁹:¹³He is clothed in a garment sprinkled with blood. His name is called "The Word of God." ¹⁹:¹⁴The armies which are in heaven followed him on white horses, clothed in white, pure, fine linen. ¹⁹:¹⁵Out of his mouth proceeds a sharp, double-edged sword, that with it he should strike the nations. He will rule them with an iron rod.¹ He treads the winepress of the fierceness of the wrath of God, the Almighty. ¹⁹:¹⁶He has on his garment and on his thigh a name written, "KING OF KINGS, AND LORD OF LORDS."

¹⁹:¹⁷I saw an angel standing in the sun. He cried with a loud voice, saying to all the birds that fly in the sky, "Come! Be gathered together to the great supper of God,ᵐ ¹⁹:¹⁸that you may eat the flesh of kings, the flesh of captains, the flesh of mighty men, and the flesh of horses and of those who sit on them, and the flesh of all men, both free and slave, and small and great." ¹⁹:¹⁹I saw the beast, and the kings of the earth, and their armies, gathered

together to make war against him who sat on the horse, and against his army. ¹⁹:²⁰The beast was taken, and with him the false prophet who worked the signs in his sight, with which he deceived those who had received the mark of the beast and those who worshiped his image. These two were thrown alive into the lake of fire that burns with sulfur. ¹⁹:²¹The rest were killed with the sword of him who sat on the horse, the sword which came forth out of his mouth. All the birds were filled with their flesh.

²⁰:¹I saw an angel coming down out of heaven, having the key of the abyss and a great chain in his hand. ²⁰:²He seized the dragon, the old serpent, which is the devil and Satan, who deceives the whole inhabited earth, and bound him for a thousand years, ²⁰:³and cast him into the abyss, and shut it, and sealed it over him, that he should deceive the nations no more, until the thousand years were finished. After this, he must be freed for a short time. ²⁰:⁴I saw thrones, and they sat on them, and judgment was given to them. I saw the souls of those who had been beheaded for the testimony of Jesus, and for the word of God, and such as didn't worship the beast nor his image, and didn't receive the mark on their forehead and on their hand. They lived, and reigned with Christ for the thousand years. ²⁰:⁵The rest of the dead didn't live until the thousand years were finished. This is the first resurrection. ²⁰:⁶Blessed and holy is he who has part in the first resurrection. Over these, the second death has no power, but they will be priests of God and of Christ, and will reign with him one thousand years.

²⁰:⁷And after the thousand years, Satan will be released from his prison, ²⁰:⁸and he will come out to deceive the nations which are in the four corners of the earth, Gog and Magog, to gather them together to the war; the number of whom is as the sand of the sea. ²⁰:⁹They went up over the breadth of the earth, and surrounded the camp of the saints, and the beloved city. Fire came down out of heaven from God,

¹19:15 Psalm 2:9
ᵐ19:17 TR reads "supper of the great God" instead of "great supper of God"

and devoured them. [20:10]The devil who deceived them was thrown into the lake of fire and sulfur, where the beast and the false prophet are also. They will be tormented day and night forever and ever.

[20:11]I saw a great white throne, and him who sat on it, from whose face the earth and the heaven fled away. There was found no place for them. [20:12]I saw the dead, the great and the small, standing before the throne, and they opened books. Another book was opened, which is the book of life. The dead were judged out of the things which were written in the books, according to their works. [20:13]The sea gave up the dead who were in it. Death and Hades[n] gave up the dead who were in them. They were judged, each one according to his works. [20:14]Death and Hades[o] were thrown into the lake of fire. This is the second death, the lake of fire. [20:15]If anyone was not found written in the book of life, he was cast into the lake of fire.

[21:1]I saw a new heaven and a new earth: for the first heaven and the first earth have passed away, and the sea is no more. [21:2]I saw the holy city, New Jerusalem, coming down out of heaven from God, made ready like a bride adorned for her husband. [21:3]I heard a loud voice out of heaven saying, "Behold, God's dwelling is with people, and he will dwell with them, and they will be his people, and God himself will be with them as their God. [21:4]He will wipe away from them every tear from their eyes. Death will be no more; neither will there be mourning, nor crying, nor pain, any more. The first things have passed away."

[21:5]He who sits on the throne said, **"Behold, I am making all things new."** He said, **"Write, for these words of God are faithful and true."** [21:6]He said to me, **"It is done! I am the Alpha and the Omega, the Beginning and the End. I will give freely to him who is thirsty from the spring of the water of life.** [21:7]**He who overcomes,**

I will give him these things. I will be his God, and he will be my son. [21:8]**But for the cowardly, unbelieving, sinners, abominable, murderers, sexually immoral, sorcerers,[p] idolaters, and all liars, their part is in the lake that burns with fire and sulfur, which is the second death."**

[21:9]One of the seven angels who had the seven bowls, who were loaded with the seven last plagues came, and he spoke with me, saying, "Come here. I will show you the wife, the Lamb's bride." [21:10]He carried me away in the Spirit to a great and high mountain, and showed me the holy city, Jerusalem, coming down out of heaven from God, [21:11]having the glory of God. Her light was like a most precious stone, as if it was a jasper stone, clear as crystal; [21:12]having a great and high wall; having twelve gates, and at the gates twelve angels; and names written on them, which are the names of the twelve tribes of the children of Israel. [21:13]On the east were three gates; and on the north three gates; and on the south three gates; and on the west three gates. [21:14]The wall of the city had twelve foundations, and on them twelve names of the twelve Apostles of the Lamb. [21:15]He who spoke with me had for a measure, a golden reed, to measure the city, its gates, and its walls. [21:16]The city lies foursquare, and its length is as great as its breadth. He measured the city with the reed, Twelve thousand twelve stadia[q]. Its length, breadth, and height are equal. [21:17]Its wall is one hundred forty-four cubits,[r] by the measure of a man, that is, of an angel. [21:18]The construction of its wall was jasper. The city was pure gold, like pure glass. [21:19]The foundations of the city's wall were adorned with all kinds of precious stones. The first foundation was jasper; the second, sapphire[s]; the third, chalcedony; the fourth, emerald; [21:20]the

---

[n]20:13 or, Hell
[o]20:14 or, Hell
[p]21:8 The word for "sorcerers" here also includes users of potions and drugs.
[q]21:16 12,012 stadia = or 2,221 kilometers or 1,380 miles. TR reads 12,000 stadia instead of 12,012 stadia.
[r]21:17 144 cubits is about 65.8 meters or 216 feet
[s]21:19 or, lapis lazuli

fifth, sardonyx; the sixth, sardius; the seventh, chrysolite; the eighth, beryl; the ninth, topaz; the tenth, chrysoprasus; the eleventh, jacinth; and the twelfth, amethyst. 21:21 The twelve gates were twelve pearls. Each one of the gates was made of one pearl. The street of the city was pure gold, like transparent glass. 21:22 I saw no temple in it, for the Lord God, the Almighty, and the Lamb, are its temple. 21:23 The city has no need for the sun, neither of the moon, to shine, for the very glory of God illuminated it, and its lamp is the Lamb. 21:24 The nations will walk in its light. The kings of the earth bring the glory and honor of the nations into it. 21:25 Its gates will in no way be shut by day (for there will be no night there), 21:26 and they shall bring the glory and the honor of the nations into it so that they may enter. 21:27 There will in no way enter into it anything profane, or one who causes an abomination or a lie, but only those who are written in the Lamb's book of life.

22:1 He showed me a† river of water of life, clear as crystal, proceeding out of the throne of God and of the Lamb, 22:2 in the middle of its street. On this side of the river and on that was the tree of life, bearing twelve kinds of fruits, yielding its fruit every month. The leaves of the tree were for the healing of the nations. 22:3 There will be no curse any more. The throne of God and of the Lamb will be in it, and his servants serve him. 22:4 They will see his face, and his name will be on their foreheads. 22:5 There will be no night, and they need no lamp light; for the Lord God will illuminate them. They will reign forever and ever.

22:6 He said to me, "These words are faithful and true. The Lord God of the spirits of the prophets sent his angel to show to his bondservants the things which must happen soon."

22:7 **"Behold, I come quickly. Blessed is he who keeps the words of the prophecy of this book."**

22:8 Now I, John, am the one who heard and saw these things. When I heard and saw, I fell down to worship before the feet of the angel who had shown me these things. 22:9 He said to me, "See you don't do it! I am a fellow bondservant with you and with your brothers, the prophets, and with those who keep the words of this book. Worship God." 22:10 He said to me, "Don't seal up the words of the prophecy of this book, for the time is at hand. 22:11 He who acts unjustly, let him act unjustly still. He who is filthy, let him be filthy still. He who is righteous, let him do righteousness still. He who is holy, let him be holy still."

22:12 **"Behold, I come quickly. My reward is with me, to repay to each man according to his work. 22:13 I am the Alpha and the Omega, the First and the Last, the Beginning and the End. 22:14 Blessed are those who do his commandments, that they may have the right to the tree of life, and may enter in by the gates into the city. 22:15 Outside are the dogs, the sorcerers, the sexually immoral, the murderers, the idolaters, and everyone who loves and practices falsehood. 22:16 I, Jesus, have sent my angel to testify these things to you for the assemblies. I am the root and the offspring of David; the Bright and Morning Star."**

22:17 The Spirit and the bride say, "Come!" He who hears, let him say, "Come!" He who is thirsty, let him come. He who desires, let him take the water of life freely. 22:18 I testify to everyone who hears the words of the prophecy of this book, if anyone adds to them, may God add to him the plagues which are written in this book. 22:19 If anyone takes away from the words of the book of this prophecy, may God take away his part from the tree of life, and out of the holy city, which are written in this book. 22:20 He who testifies these things says, **"Yes, I come quickly."**

Amen! Yes, come, Lord Jesus.

22:21 The grace of the Lord Jesus Christ be with all the saints. Amen.

---

†22:1 TR adds "pure"

The Psalms

BOOK I

Psalm 1

[1] Blessed is the man who doesn't walk in the
  counsel of the wicked,
  nor stand in the way of sinners,
  nor sit in the seat of scoffers;
[2] but his delight is in Yahweh's law.
  On his law he meditates day and night.
[3] He will be like a tree planted by the
  streams of water,
  that brings forth its fruit in its season,
  whose leaf also does not wither.
  Whatever he does shall prosper.
[4] The wicked are not so,
  but are like the chaff which the wind
  drives away.
[5] Therefore the wicked shall not stand in the
  judgment,
  nor sinners in the congregation of the
  righteous.
[6] For Yahweh knows the way of the righteous,
  but the way of the wicked shall perish.

Psalm 2

[1] Why do the nations rage,
  and the peoples plot a vain thing?
[2] The kings of the earth take a stand,
  and the rulers take counsel together,
  against Yahweh, and against his
  Anointed,[a] saying,
[3] "Let's break their bonds apart,
  and cast their cords from us."
[4] He who sits in the heavens will laugh.
  The Lord will have them in derision.
[5] Then he will speak to them in his anger,
  and terrify them in his wrath:
[6] "Yet I have set my king on my holy hill of
  Zion."
[7] I will tell of the decree.
Yahweh said to me, "You are my son.
  Today I have become your father.
[8] Ask of me, and I will give the nations for
  your inheritance,

the uttermost parts of the earth for your
  possession.
[9] You shall break them with a rod of iron.
  You shall dash them in pieces like a
  potter's vessel."
[10] Now therefore be wise, you kings.
  Be instructed, you judges of the earth.
[11] Serve Yahweh with fear,
  and rejoice with trembling.
[12] Give sincere homage[b], lest he be angry,
  and you perish in the way,
  for his wrath will soon be kindled.
  Blessed are all those who take refuge in
  him.

Psalm 3

A Psalm by David, when he fled from
Absalom his son.

[1] Yahweh, how my adversaries have increased!
  Many are those who rise up against me.
[2] Many there are who say of my soul,
  "There is no help for him in God."
Selah.
[3] But you, Yahweh, are a shield around me,
  my glory, and the one who lifts up my
  head.
[4] I cry to Yahweh with my voice,
  and he answers me out of his holy hill.
Selah.
[5] I laid myself down and slept.
  I awakened; for Yahweh sustains me.
[6] I will not be afraid of tens of thousands of
  people
  who have set themselves against me on
  every side.
[7] Arise, Yahweh!
  Save me, my God!
For you have struck all of my enemies on
  the cheek bone.
  You have broken the teeth of the
  wicked.
[8] Salvation belongs to Yahweh.
  Your blessing be on your people.
Selah.

---

[a] 2:2 The word "Anointed" is the same as the word for "Messiah" or "Christ"
[b] 2:12 or, Kiss the son

Psalm 4

For the Chief Musician; on stringed instruments. A Psalm by David.

[1] Answer me when I call, God of my righteousness.

Give me relief from my distress.

Have mercy on me, and hear my prayer.

[2] You sons of men, how long shall my glory be turned into dishonor?

Will you love vanity, and seek after falsehood?

Selah.

[3] But know that Yahweh has set apart for himself him who is godly:

Yahweh will hear when I call to him.

[4] Stand in awe, and don't sin.

Search your own heart on your bed, and be still.

Selah.

[5] Offer the sacrifices of righteousness.

Put your trust in Yahweh.

[6] Many say, "Who will show us any good?"

Yahweh, let the light of your face shine on us.

[7] You have put gladness in my heart,

more than when their grain and their new wine are increased.

[8] In peace I will both lay myself down and sleep,

for you, Yahweh alone, make me live in safety.

Psalm 5

For the Chief Musician, with the flutes. A Psalm by David.

[1] Give ear to my words, Yahweh.

Consider my meditation.

[2] Listen to the voice of my cry, my King and my God;

for to you do I pray.

[3] Yahweh, in the morning you shall hear my voice.

In the morning I will lay my requests before you, and will watch expectantly.

[4] For you are not a God who has pleasure in wickedness.

Evil can't live with you.

[5] The arrogant shall not stand in your sight.

You hate all workers of iniquity.

[6] You will destroy those who speak lies.

Yahweh abhors the blood-thirsty and deceitful man.

[7] But as for me, in the abundance of your loving kindness I will come into your house.

I will bow toward your holy temple in reverence of you.

[8] Lead me, Yahweh, in your righteousness because of my enemies.

Make your way straight before my face.

[9] For there is no faithfulness in their mouth.

Their heart is destruction.

Their throat is an open tomb.

They flatter with their tongue.

[10] Hold them guilty, God.

Let them fall by their own counsels;

Thrust them out in the multitude of their transgressions,

for they have rebelled against you.

[11] But let all those who take refuge in you rejoice,

Let them always shout for joy, because you defend them.

Let them also who love your name be joyful in you.

[12] For you will bless the righteous.

Yahweh, you will surround him with favor as with a shield.

Psalm 6

For the Chief Musician; on stringed instruments, upon the eight-stringed lyre. A Psalm by David.

[1] Yahweh, don't rebuke me in your anger, neither discipline me in your wrath.

[2] Have mercy on me, Yahweh, for I am faint.

Yahweh, heal me, for my bones are troubled.

[3] My soul is also in great anguish.

But you, Yahweh—how long?

[4] Return, Yahweh. Deliver my soul,

and save me for your loving kindness' sake.

[5] For in death there is no memory of you.

In Sheol, who shall give you thanks?

[6]I am weary with my groaning.
> Every night I flood my bed.
> I drench my couch with my tears.

[7]My eye wastes away because of grief.
> It grows old because of all my adversaries.

[8]Depart from me, all you workers of iniquity,
> for Yahweh has heard the voice of my weeping.

[9]Yahweh has heard my supplication.
> Yahweh accepts my prayer.

[10]May all my enemies be ashamed and dismayed.
> They shall turn back, they shall be disgraced suddenly.

Psalm 7

A meditation by David, which he sang to Yahweh, concerning the words of Cush, the Benjamite.

[1]Yahweh, my God, I take refuge in you.
> Save me from all those who pursue me, and deliver me,

[2]lest they tear apart my soul like a lion,
> ripping it in pieces, while there is none to deliver.

[3]Yahweh, my God, if I have done this,
> if there is iniquity in my hands,

[4]if I have rewarded evil to him who was at peace with me
> (yes, if I have delivered him who without cause was my adversary),

[5]let the enemy pursue my soul, and overtake it;
yes, let him tread my life down to the earth,
> and lay my glory in the dust.

Selah.

[6]Arise, Yahweh, in your anger.
> Lift up yourself against the rage of my adversaries.

Awake for me. You have commanded judgment.
> [7]Let the congregation of the peoples surround you.
> Rule over them on high.

[8]Yahweh administers judgment to the peoples.
> Judge me, Yahweh, according to my righteousness,

and to my integrity that is in me.

[9]Oh let the wickedness of the wicked come to an end,
> but establish the righteous;
> their minds and hearts are searched by the righteous God.

[10]My shield is with God,
> who saves the upright in heart.

[11]God is a righteous judge,
> yes, a God who has indignation every day.

[12]If a man doesn't relent, he will sharpen his sword;
> he has bent and strung his bow.

[13]He has also prepared for himself the instruments of death.
> He makes ready his flaming arrows.

[14]Behold, he travails with iniquity.
> Yes, he has conceived mischief,
> and brought forth falsehood.

[15]He has dug a hole,
> and has fallen into the pit which he made.

[16]The trouble he causes shall return to his own head.
> His violence shall come down on the crown of his own head.

[17]I will give thanks to Yahweh according to his righteousness,
> and will sing praise to the name of Yahweh Most High.

Psalm 8

For the Chief Musician; on an instrument of Gath. A Psalm by David.

[1]Yahweh, our Lord, how majestic is your name in all the earth,
> who has set your glory above the heavens!

[2]From the lips of babes and infants you have established strength,
> because of your adversaries, that you might silence the enemy and the avenger.

[3]When I consider your heavens, the work of your fingers,
> the moon and the stars, which you have ordained;

[4]what is man, that you think of him?

What is the son of man, that you care
for him?
[5] For you have made him a little lower than
God,[c]
and crowned him with glory and
honor.
[6] You make him ruler over the works of
your hands.
You have put all things under his feet:
[7] All sheep and cattle,
yes, and the animals of the field,
[8] The birds of the sky, the fish of the sea,
and whatever passes through the paths
of the seas.
[9] Yahweh, our Lord,
how majestic is your name in all the
earth!

Psalm 9

For the Chief Musician. Set to "The
Death of the Son." A Psalm by David.

[1] I will give thanks to Yahweh with my
whole heart.
I will tell of all your marvelous works.
[2] I will be glad and rejoice in you.
I will sing praise to your name, O Most
High.
[3] When my enemies turn back,
they stumble and perish in your presence.
[4] For you have maintained my just cause.
You sit on the throne judging righteously.
[5] You have rebuked the nations.
You have destroyed the wicked.
You have blotted out their name forever and ever.
[6] The enemy is overtaken by endless ruin.
The very memory of the cities which
you have overthrown has perished.
[7] But Yahweh reigns forever.
He has prepared his throne for judgment.
[8] He will judge the world in righteousness.
He will administer judgment to the
peoples in uprightness.
[9] Yahweh will also be a high tower for the
oppressed;

a high tower in times of trouble.
[10] Those who know your name will put
their trust in you,
for you, Yahweh, have not forsaken
those who seek you.
[11] Sing praises to Yahweh, who dwells in
Zion,
and declare among the people what he
has done.
[12] For he who avenges blood remembers
them.
He doesn't forget the cry of the afflicted.
[13] Have mercy on me, Yahweh.
See my affliction by those who hate me,
and lift me up from the gates of death;
[14] that I may show forth all your praise.
In the gates of the daughter of Zion, I
will rejoice in your salvation.
[15] The nations have sunk down in the pit
that they made.
In the net which they hid, their own
foot is taken.
[16] Yahweh has made himself known.
He has executed judgment.
The wicked is snared by the work of his
own hands.
Meditation. Selah.
[17] The wicked shall be turned back to Sheol,
even all the nations that forget God.
[18] For the needy shall not always be forgotten,
nor the hope of the poor perish forever.
[19] Arise, Yahweh! Don't let man prevail.
Let the nations be judged in your sight.
[20] Put them in fear, Yahweh.
Let the nations know that they are only
men.
Selah.

Psalm 10

[1] Why do you stand far off, Yahweh?
Why do you hide yourself in times of
trouble?
[2] In arrogance, the wicked hunt down the
weak.
They are caught in the schemes that
they devise.

---

[c] 8:5 Hebrew: Elohim. The word Elohim, used here, usually means "God," but can also mean
"gods," "princes," or "angels."

³For the wicked boasts of his heart's crav-
ings.
   He blesses the greedy, and condemns
Yahweh.
⁴The wicked, in the pride of his face,
   has no room in his thoughts for God.
⁵His ways are prosperous at all times.
   He is haughty, and your laws are far
from his sight.
As for all his adversaries, he sneers at them.
   ⁶He says in his heart, "I shall not be
shaken.
   For generations I shall have no trouble."
⁷His mouth is full of cursing, deceit, and
oppression.
   Under his tongue is mischief and iniquity.
⁸He lies in wait near the villages.
   From ambushes, he murders the innocent.
His eyes are secretly set against the helpless.
⁹He lurks in secret as a lion in his ambush.
   He lies in wait to catch the helpless.
   He catches the helpless, when he draws
him in his net.
¹⁰The helpless are crushed.
   They collapse.
   They fall under his strength.
¹¹He says in his heart, "God has forgotten.
   He hides his face.
   He will never see it."
¹²Arise, Yahweh!
   God, lift up your hand!
   Don't forget the helpless.
¹³Why does the wicked person condemn
God,
   and say in his heart, "God won't call
me into account?"
¹⁴But you do see trouble and grief.
   You consider it to take it into your
hand.
   You help the victim and the fatherless.
¹⁵Break the arm of the wicked.
   As for the evil man, seek out his
wickedness until you find none.
¹⁶Yahweh is King forever and ever!
   The nations will perish out of his land.
¹⁷Yahweh, you have heard the desire of the
humble.
   You will prepare their heart.

You will cause your ear to hear,
   ¹⁸to judge the fatherless and the oppressed,
   that man who is of the earth may terrify
no more.

Psalm 11

For the Chief Musician. By David.

¹In Yahweh, I take refuge.
   How can you say to my soul, "Flee as a
bird to your mountain!"
²For, behold, the wicked bend their bows.
   They set their arrows on the strings,
   that they may shoot in darkness at the
upright in heart.
³If the foundations are destroyed,
   what can the righteous do?
⁴Yahweh is in his holy temple.
   Yahweh is on his throne in heaven.
His eyes observe.
   His eyes examine the children of men.
⁵Yahweh examines the righteous,
   but the wicked and him who loves
violence his soul hates.
⁶On the wicked he will rain blazing coals;
   fire, sulfur, and scorching wind shall be
the portion of their cup.
⁷For Yahweh is righteous.
   He loves righteousness.
   The upright shall see his face.

Psalm 12

For the Chief Musician; upon an eight-
stringed lyre. A Psalm of David.

¹Help, Yahweh; for the godly man ceases.
   For the faithful fail from among the
children of men.
²Everyone lies to his neighbor.
   They speak with flattering lips, and
with a double heart.
³May Yahweh cut off all flattering lips,
   and the tongue that boasts,
⁴who have said, "With our tongue we will
prevail.
   Our lips are our own.
   Who is lord over us?"

5 "Because of the oppression of the weak
and because of the groaning of the
needy,
I will now arise," says Yahweh;
"I will set him in safety from those who
malign him."
6 The words of Yahweh are flawless words,
as silver refined in a clay furnace, purified seven times.
7 You will keep them, Yahweh.
You will preserve them from this generation forever.
8 The wicked walk on every side,
when what is vile is exalted among the
sons of men.

Psalm 13

For the Chief Musician. A Psalm by
David.

1 How long, Yahweh?
Will you forget me forever?
How long will you hide your face from
me?
2 How long shall I take counsel in my soul,
having sorrow in my heart every day?
How long shall my enemy triumph
over me?
3 Behold, and answer me, Yahweh, my God.
Give light to my eyes, lest I sleep in
death;
4 Lest my enemy say, "I have prevailed
against him;"
Lest my adversaries rejoice when I fall.
5 But I trust in your loving kindness.
My heart rejoices in your salvation.
6 I will sing to Yahweh,
because he has been good to me.

Psalm 14

For the Chief Musician. By David.

1 The fool has said in his heart, "There is no
God."
They are corrupt.
They have done abominable works.
There is none who does good.
2 Yahweh looked down from heaven on the
children of men,
to see if there were any who did understand,
who did seek after God.
3 They have all gone aside.
They have together become corrupt.
There is none who does good, no, not
one.
4 Have all the workers of iniquity no knowledge,
who eat up my people as they eat
bread,
and don't call on Yahweh?
5 There they were in great fear,
for God is in the generation of the
righteous.
6 You frustrate the plan of the poor,
because Yahweh is his refuge.
7 Oh that the salvation of Israel would come
out of Zion!
When Yahweh restores the fortunes of
his people,
then Jacob shall rejoice, and Israel shall
be glad.

Psalm 15

A Psalm by David.

1 Yahweh, who shall dwell in your sanctuary?
Who shall live on your holy hill?
2 He who walks blamelessly does what is
right,
and speaks truth in his heart;
3 He who doesn't slander with his tongue,
nor does evil to his friend,
nor casts slurs against his fellow man;
4 In whose eyes a vile man is despised,
but who honors those who fear Yahweh;
he who keeps an oath even when it
hurts, and doesn't change;
5 he who doesn't lend out his money for
usury,
nor take a bribe against the innocent.
He who does these things shall never be
shaken.

Psalm 16

A Poem by David.

[1] Preserve me, God, for in you do I take refuge.

[2] My soul, you have said to Yahweh, "You are my Lord.

Apart from you I have no good thing."

[3] As for the saints who are in the earth,

they are the excellent ones in whom is all my delight.

[4] Their sorrows shall be multiplied who give gifts to another god.

Their drink offerings of blood I will not offer,

nor take their names on my lips.

[5] Yahweh assigned my portion and my cup.

You made my lot secure.

[6] The lines have fallen to me in pleasant places.

Yes, I have a good inheritance.

[7] I will bless Yahweh, who has given me counsel.

Yes, my heart instructs me in the night seasons.

[8] I have set Yahweh always before me.

Because he is at my right hand, I shall not be moved.

[9] Therefore my heart is glad, and my tongue rejoices.

My body shall also dwell in safety.

[10] For you will not leave my soul in Sheol,

neither will you allow your holy one to see corruption.

[11] You will show me the path of life.

In your presence is fullness of joy.

In your right hand there are pleasures forevermore.

Psalm 17

A Prayer by David.

[1] Hear, Yahweh, my righteous plea;

Give ear to my prayer, that doesn't go out of deceitful lips.

[2] Let my sentence come forth from your presence.

Let your eyes look on equity.

[3] You have proved my heart.

You have visited me in the night.

You have tried me, and found nothing.

I have resolved that my mouth shall not disobey.

[4] As for the works of men, by the word of your lips,

I have kept myself from the ways of the violent.

[5] My steps have held fast to your paths.

My feet have not slipped.

[6] I have called on you, for you will answer me, God.

Turn your ear to me.

Hear my speech.

[7] Show your marvelous loving kindness,

you who save those who take refuge by your right hand from their enemies.

[8] Keep me as the apple of your eye.

Hide me under the shadow of your wings,

[9] from the wicked who oppress me,

my deadly enemies, who surround me.

[10] They close up their callous hearts.

With their mouth they speak proudly.

[11] They have now surrounded us in our steps.

They set their eyes to cast us down to the earth.

[12] He is like a lion that is greedy of his prey,

as it were a young lion lurking in secret places.

[13] Arise, Yahweh, confront him.

Cast him down.

Deliver my soul from the wicked by your sword;

[14] from men by your hand, Yahweh,

from men of the world, whose portion is in this life.

You fill the belly of your cherished ones.

Your sons have plenty,

and they store up wealth for their children.

[15] As for me, I shall see your face in righteousness.

I shall be satisfied, when I awake, with seeing your form.

Psalm 18

For the Chief Musician. By David the servant of Yahweh, who spoke to Yahweh the words of this song in the day that Yahweh delivered him from the hand of all his enemies, and from the hand of Saul. He said,

[1] I love you, Yahweh, my strength.

²Yahweh is my rock, my fortress, and my
deliverer;
    my God, my rock, in whom I take
refuge;
    my shield, and the horn of my salva-
tion, my high tower.
³I call on Yahweh, who is worthy to be
praised;
    and I am saved from my enemies.
⁴The cords of death surrounded me.
    The floods of ungodliness made me
afraid.
⁵The cords of Sheol were around me.
    The snares of death came on me.
⁶In my distress I called on Yahweh,
    and cried to my God.
He heard my voice out of his temple.
    My cry before him came into his ears.
⁷Then the earth shook and trembled.
    The foundations also of the mountains
quaked and were shaken,
    because he was angry.
⁸Smoke went out of his nostrils.
    Consuming fire came out of his mouth.
    Coals were kindled by it.
⁹He bowed the heavens also, and came
down.
    Thick darkness was under his feet.
¹⁰He rode on a cherub, and flew.
    Yes, he soared on the wings of the
wind.
¹¹He made darkness his hiding place, his
pavilion around him,
    darkness of waters, thick clouds of the
skies.
¹²At the brightness before him his thick
clouds passed,
    hailstones and coals of fire.
¹³Yahweh also thundered in the sky.
    The Most High uttered his voice:
    hailstones and coals of fire.
¹⁴He sent out his arrows, and scattered
them;
    Yes, great lightning bolts, and routed
them.
¹⁵Then the channels of waters appeared.
    The foundations of the world were laid
bare at your rebuke, Yahweh,
    at the blast of the breath of your nos-
trils.
¹⁶He sent from on high.
    He took me.

He drew me out of many waters.
¹⁷He delivered me from my strong enemy,
    from those who hated me; for they
were too mighty for me.
¹⁸They came on me in the day of my
calamity,
    but Yahweh was my support.
¹⁹He brought me forth also into a large
place.
    He delivered me, because he delighted
in me.
²⁰Yahweh has rewarded me according to
my righteousness.
    According to the cleanness of my
hands has he recompensed me.
²¹For I have kept the ways of Yahweh,
    and have not wickedly departed from
my God.
²²For all his ordinances were before me.
    I didn't put away his statutes from me.
²³I was also blameless with him.
    I kept myself from my iniquity.
²⁴Therefore Yahweh has rewarded me according to my righteousness,
    according to the cleanness of my hands
in his eyesight.
²⁵With the merciful you will show yourself
merciful.
    With the perfect man, you will show
yourself perfect.
²⁶With the pure, you will show yourself
pure.
    With the crooked you will show your-
self shrewd.
²⁷For you will save the afflicted people,
    but the haughty eyes you will bring
down.
²⁸For you will light my lamp, Yahweh.
    My God will light up my darkness.
²⁹For by you, I advance through a troop.
    By my God, I leap over a wall.
³⁰As for God, his way is perfect.
    The word of Yahweh is tried.
    He is a shield to all those who take
refuge in him.
³¹For who is God, except Yahweh?
    Who is a rock, besides our God,
    ³²the God who arms me with strength,
    and makes my way perfect?
³³He makes my feet like deer's feet,
    and sets me on my high places.
³⁴He teaches my hands to war,

so that my arms bend a bow of bronze.

³⁵ You have also given me the shield of your salvation.

Your right hand sustains me.

Your gentleness has made me great.

³⁶ You have enlarged my steps under me,
My feet have not slipped.

³⁷ I will pursue my enemies, and overtake them.
Neither will I turn again until they are consumed.

³⁸ I will strike them through, so that they will not be able to rise.
They shall fall under my feet.

³⁹ For you have girded me with strength to the battle.
You have subdued under me those who rose up against me.

⁴⁰ You have also made my enemies turn their backs to me,
that I might cut off those who hate me.

⁴¹ They cried, but there was none to save;
even to Yahweh, but he didn't answer them.

⁴² Then I beat them small as the dust before the wind.
I cast them out as the mire of the streets.

⁴³ You have delivered me from the strivings of the people.
You have made me the head of the nations.
A people whom I have not known shall serve me.
⁴⁴ As soon as they hear of me they shall obey me.
The foreigners shall submit themselves to me.

⁴⁵ The foreigners shall fade away,
and shall come trembling out of their close places.

⁴⁶ Yahweh lives; and blessed be my rock.
Exalted be the God of my salvation,

⁴⁷ even the God who executes vengeance for me,
and subdues peoples under me.

⁴⁸ He rescues me from my enemies.
Yes, you lift me up above those who rise up against me.
You deliver me from the violent man.

⁴⁹ Therefore I will give thanks to you, Yahweh, among the nations,
and will sing praises to your name.

⁵⁰ He gives great deliverance to his king,
and shows loving kindness to his anointed,
to David and to his seed, forevermore.

Psalm 19

For the Chief Musician. A Psalm by David.

¹ The heavens declare the glory of God.
The expanse shows his handiwork.

² Day after day they pour forth speech,
and night after night they display knowledge.

³ There is no speech nor language,
where their voice is not heard.

⁴ Their voice has gone out through all the earth,
their words to the end of the world.
In them he has set a tent for the sun,

⁵ which is as a bridegroom coming out of his chamber,
like a strong man rejoicing to run his course.

⁶ His going forth is from the end of the heavens,
his circuit to its ends;
There is nothing hidden from its heat.

⁷ Yahweh's law is perfect, restoring the soul.
Yahweh's testimony is sure, making wise the simple.

⁸ Yahweh's precepts are right, rejoicing the heart.
Yahweh's commandment is pure, enlightening the eyes.

⁹ The fear of Yahweh is clean, enduring forever.
Yahweh's ordinances are true, and righteous altogether.

¹⁰ More to be desired are they than gold,
yes, than much fine gold;
sweeter also than honey and the extract of the honeycomb.

¹¹ Moreover by them is your servant warned.
In keeping them there is great reward.

¹² Who can discern his errors?
Forgive me from hidden errors.

¹³ Keep back your servant also from presumptuous sins.
Let them not have dominion over me.

Then I will be upright.

I will be blameless and innocent of great transgression.

[14] Let the words of my mouth and the meditation of my heart

be acceptable in your sight,

Yahweh, my rock, and my redeemer.

Psalm 20

For the Chief Musician. A Psalm by David.

[1] May Yahweh answer you in the day of trouble.

May the name of the God of Jacob set you up on high,

[2] send you help from the sanctuary,

grant you support from Zion,

[3] remember all your offerings,

and accept your burnt sacrifice.

Selah.

[4] May He grant you your heart's desire,

and fulfill all your counsel.

[5] We will triumph in your salvation.

In the name of our God, we will set up our banners.

May Yahweh grant all your requests.

[6] Now I know that Yahweh saves his anointed.

He will answer him from his holy heaven,

with the saving strength of his right hand.

[7] Some trust in chariots, and some in horses,

but we trust the name of Yahweh our God.

[8] They are bowed down and fallen,

but we rise up, and stand upright.

[9] Save, Yahweh!

Let the King answer us when we call!

Psalm 21

For the Chief Musician. A Psalm by David.

[1] The king rejoices in your strength, Yahweh!

How greatly he rejoices in your salvation!

[2] You have given him his heart's desire,

and have not withheld the request of his lips.

Selah.

[3] For you meet him with the blessings of goodness.

You set a crown of fine gold on his head.

[4] He asked life of you, you gave it to him,

even length of days forever and ever.

[5] His glory is great in your salvation.

You lay honor and majesty on him.

[6] For you make him most blessed forever.

You make him glad with joy in your presence.

[7] For the king trusts in Yahweh.

Through the loving kindness of the Most High, he shall not be moved.

[8] Your hand will find out all of your enemies.

Your right hand will find out those who hate you.

[9] You will make them as a fiery furnace in the time of your anger.

Yahweh will swallow them up in his wrath.

The fire shall devour them.

[10] You will destroy their descendants from the earth,

their posterity from among the children of men.

[11] For they intended evil against you.

They plotted evil against you which cannot succeed.

[12] For you will make them turn their back,

when you aim drawn bows at their face.

[13] Be exalted, Yahweh, in your strength,

so we will sing and praise your power.

Psalm 22

For the Chief Musician; set to "The Doe of the Morning." A Psalm by David.

[1] My God, my God, why have you forsaken me?

Why are you so far from helping me,

and from the words of my groaning?

[2] My God, I cry in the daytime, but you don't answer;

in the night season, and am not silent.

[3] But you are holy,

you who inhabit the praises of Israel.
⁴Our fathers trusted in you.
    They trusted, and you delivered them.
⁵They cried to you, and were delivered.
    They trusted in you, and were not
    disappointed.
⁶But I am a worm, and no man;
    a reproach of men, and despised by the
    people.
⁷All those who see me mock me.
    They insult me with their lips. They
    shake their heads, saying,
        ⁸"He trusts in Yahweh;
    let him deliver him.
    Let him rescue him, since he delights in
    him."
⁹But you brought me out of the womb.
    You made me trust at my mother's
    breasts.
¹⁰I was thrown on you from my mother's
    womb.
    You are my God since my mother bore
    me.
¹¹Don't be far from me, for trouble is near.
    For there is none to help.
¹²Many bulls have surrounded me.
    Strong bulls of Bashan have encircled
    me.
¹³They open their mouths wide against me,
    lions tearing prey and roaring.
¹⁴I am poured out like water.
    All my bones are out of joint.
My heart is like wax;
    it is melted within me.
¹⁵My strength is dried up like a potsherd.
    My tongue sticks to the roof of my
    mouth.
You have brought me into the dust of death.
¹⁶For dogs have surrounded me.
    A company of evil-doers have enclosed
    me.
    Like a lion, they pin my hands and
    feet.ᵈ
¹⁷I can count all of my bones.
They look and stare at me.
¹⁸They divide my garments among them.
    They cast lots for my clothing.
¹⁹But don't be far off, Yahweh.
    You are my help: hurry to help me.
²⁰Deliver my soul from the sword,

my precious life from the power of the
    dog.
²¹Save me from the lion's mouth!
    Yes, from the horns of the wild oxen,
    you have answered me.
²²I will declare your name to my brothers.
    In the midst of the assembly, I will
    praise you.
²³You who fear Yahweh, praise him!
    All you descendants of Jacob, glorify
    him!
    Stand in awe of him, all you descen-
    dants of Israel!
²⁴For he has not despised nor abhorred the
    affliction of the afflicted,
    Neither has he hidden his face from
    him;
    but when he cried to him, he heard.
²⁵Of you comes my praise in the great
    assembly.
    I will pay my vows before those who
    fear him.
²⁶The humble shall eat and be satisfied.
    They shall praise Yahweh who seek
    after him.
    Let your hearts live forever.
²⁷All the ends of the earth shall remember
    and turn to Yahweh.
    All the relatives of the nations shall
    worship before you.
²⁸For the kingdom is Yahweh's.
    He is the ruler over the nations.
²⁹All the rich ones of the earth shall eat and
    worship.
    All those who go down to the dust shall
    bow before him,
    even he who can't keep his soul alive.
³⁰Posterity shall serve him.
    Future generations shall be told about
    the Lord.
³¹They shall come and shall declare his
    righteousness to a people that shall
    be born,
    for he has done it.

Psalm 23

A Psalm by David.

¹Yahweh is my shepherd:
    I shall lack nothing.

ᵈ22:16 or, They have pierced my hands and feet. (DSS)

²He makes me lie down in green pastures.
  He leads me beside still waters.
³He restores my soul.
  He guides me in the paths of righteous-
    ness for his name's sake.
⁴Even though I walk through the valley of
    the shadow of death,
  I will fear no evil, for you are with me.
  Your rod and your staff, they comfort
    me.
⁵You prepare a table before me in the
    presence of my enemies.
You anoint my head with oil.
  My cup runs over.
⁶Surely goodness and loving kindness shall
    follow me all the days of my life,
  and I will dwell in Yahweh's house
    forever.

Psalm 24

A Psalm by David.

¹The earth is Yahweh's, with its fullness;
  the world, and those who dwell
    therein.
²For he has founded it on the seas,
  and established it on the floods.
³Who may ascend to Yahweh's hill?
  Who may stand in his holy place?
⁴He who has clean hands and a pure heart;
  who has not lifted up his soul to false-
    hood,
  and has not sworn deceitfully.
⁵He shall receive a blessing from Yahweh,
  righteousness from the God of his sal-
    vation.
⁶This is the generation of those who seek
    Him,
  who seek your face—even Jacob.
Selah.
⁷Lift up your heads, you gates!
  Be lifted up, you everlasting doors,
  and the King of glory will come in.
⁸Who is the King of glory?
  Yahweh strong and mighty,
  Yahweh mighty in battle.
⁹Lift up your heads, you gates;
  yes, lift them up, you everlasting doors,
  and the King of glory will come in.
¹⁰Who is this King of glory?
  Yahweh of Armies is the King of glory!

Selah.

Psalm 25

By David.

¹To you, Yahweh, do I lift up my soul.
²My God, I have trusted in you.
  Don't let me be shamed.
  Don't let my enemies triumph over me.
³Yes, no one who waits for you shall be
    shamed.
  They shall be shamed who deal treach-
    erously without cause.
⁴Show me your ways, Yahweh.
  Teach me your paths.
⁵Guide me in your truth, and teach me,
  For you are the God of my salvation,
  I wait for you all day long.
⁶Yahweh, remember your tender mercies
    and your loving kindness,
  for they are from old times.
⁷Don't remember the sins of my youth, nor
    my transgressions.
  Remember me according to your lov-
    ing kindness,
  for your goodness' sake, Yahweh.
⁸Good and upright is Yahweh,
  therefore he will instruct sinners in the
    way.
⁹He will guide the humble in justice.
  He will teach the humble his way.
¹⁰All the paths of Yahweh are loving kind-
    ness and truth
  to such as keep his covenant and his
    testimonies.
¹¹For your name's sake, Yahweh,
  pardon my iniquity, for it is great.
¹²What man is he who fears Yahweh?
  He shall instruct him in the way that he
    shall choose.
¹³His soul shall dwell at ease.
  His seed shall inherit the land.
¹⁴The friendship of Yahweh is with those
    who fear him.
  He will show them his covenant.
¹⁵My eyes are ever on Yahweh,
  for he will pluck my feet out of the net.
¹⁶Turn to me, and have mercy on me,
  for I am desolate and afflicted.
¹⁷The troubles of my heart are enlarged.
  Oh bring me out of my distresses.

[18]Consider my affliction and my travail.
> Forgive all my sins.

[19]Consider my enemies, for they are many.
> They hate me with cruel hatred.

[20]Oh keep my soul, and deliver me.
> Let me not be disappointed, for I take refuge in you.

[21]Let integrity and uprightness preserve me,
> for I wait for you.

[22]Redeem Israel, God,
> out all of his troubles.

Psalm 26

By David.

[1]Judge me, Yahweh, for I have walked in my integrity.
> I have trusted also in Yahweh without wavering.

[2]Examine me, Yahweh, and prove me.
> Try my heart and my mind.

[3]For your loving kindness is before my eyes.
> I have walked in your truth.

[4]I have not sat with deceitful men,
> neither will I go in with hypocrites.

[5]I hate the assembly of evil-doers,
> and will not sit with the wicked.

[6]I will wash my hands in innocence,
> so I will go about your altar, Yahweh;
> [7]that I may make the voice of thanksgiving to be heard,
> and tell of all your wondrous works.

[8]Yahweh, I love the habitation of your house,
> the place where your glory dwells.

[9]Don't gather my soul with sinners,
> nor my life with bloodthirsty men;
> [10]in whose hands is wickedness,
> their right hand is full of bribes.

[11]But as for me, I will walk in my integrity.
> Redeem me, and be merciful to me.

[12]My foot stands in an even place.
> In the congregations I will bless Yahweh.

Psalm 27

By David.

[1]Yahweh is my light and my salvation.
> Whom shall I fear?

Yahweh is the strength of my life.
> Of whom shall I be afraid?

[2]When evil-doers came at me to eat up my flesh,
> even my adversaries and my foes, they stumbled and fell.

[3]Though an army should encamp against me,
> my heart shall not fear.

Though war should rise against me,
> even then I will be confident.

[4]One thing I have asked of Yahweh, that I will seek after,
> that I may dwell in the house of Yahweh all the days of my life,
> to see Yahweh's beauty,
> and to inquire in his temple.

[5]For in the day of trouble he will keep me secretly in his pavilion.
> In the covert of his tent he will hide me.
> He will lift me up on a rock.

[6]Now my head will be lifted up above my enemies around me.

I will offer sacrifices of joy in his tent.
> I will sing, yes, I will sing praises to Yahweh.

[7]Hear, Yahweh, when I cry with my voice.
> Have mercy also on me, and answer me.

[8]When you said, "Seek my face,"
> my heart said to you, "I will seek your face, Yahweh."

[9]Don't hide your face from me.
> Don't put your servant away in anger.

You have been my help.
> Don't abandon me,
> neither forsake me, God of my salvation.

[10]When my father and my mother forsake me,
> then Yahweh will take me up.

[11]Teach me your way, Yahweh.
> Lead me in a straight path, because of my enemies.

[12]Don't deliver me over to the desire of my adversaries,
> for false witnesses have risen up against me,
> such as breathe out cruelty.

[13]I am still confident of this:

I will see the goodness of Yahweh in the
land of the living.
[14] Wait for Yahweh.
Be strong, and let your heart take
courage.
Yes, wait for Yahweh.

Psalm 28

By David.

[1] To you, Yahweh, I call.
My rock, don't be deaf to me;
lest, if you are silent to me,
I would become like those who go
down into the pit.
[2] Hear the voice of my petitions, when I cry
to you,
when I lift up my hands toward your
Most Holy Place.
[3] Don't draw me away with the wicked,
with the workers of iniquity who speak
peace with their neighbors,
but mischief is in their hearts.
[4] Give them according to their work, and
according to the wickedness of their
doings.
Give them according to the operation
of their hands.
Bring back on them what they deserve.
[5] Because they don't regard the works of
Yahweh,
nor the operation of his hands,
he will break them down and not build
them up.
[6] Blessed be Yahweh,
because he has heard the voice of my
petitions.
[7] Yahweh is my strength and my shield.
My heart has trusted in him, and I am
helped.
Therefore my heart greatly rejoices.
With my song I will thank him.
[8] Yahweh is their strength.
He is a stronghold of salvation to his
anointed.
[9] Save your people,
and bless your inheritance.
Be their shepherd also,
and bear them up forever.

Psalm 29

A Psalm by David.

[1] Ascribe to Yahweh, you sons of the
mighty,
ascribe to Yahweh glory and strength.
[2] Ascribe to Yahweh the glory due to his
name.
Worship Yahweh in holy array.
[3] Yahweh's voice is on the waters.
The God of glory thunders, even Yahweh on many waters.
[4] Yahweh's voice is powerful.
Yahweh's voice is full of majesty.
[5] The voice of Yahweh breaks the cedars.
Yes, Yahweh breaks in pieces the cedars
of Lebanon.
[6] He makes them also to skip like a calf;
Lebanon and Sirion like a young, wild
ox.
[7] Yahweh's voice strikes with flashes of
lightning.
[8] Yahweh's voice shakes the wilderness.
Yahweh shakes the wilderness of
Kadesh.
[9] Yahweh's voice makes the deer calve,
and strips the forests bare.
In his temple everything says, "Glory!"
[10] Yahweh sat enthroned at the Flood.
Yes, Yahweh sits as King forever.
[11] Yahweh will give strength to his people.
Yahweh will bless his people with
peace.

Psalm 30

A Psalm. A Song for the Dedication of
the Temple. By David.

[1] I will extol you, Yahweh, for you have
raised me up,
and have not made my foes to rejoice
over me.
[2] Yahweh my God, I cried to you,
and you have healed me.
[3] Yahweh, you have brought up my soul
from Sheol.
You have kept me alive, that I should
not go down to the pit.
[4] Sing praise to Yahweh, you saints of his.
Give thanks to his holy name.
[5] For his anger is but for a moment.

His favor is for a lifetime.
Weeping may stay for the night,
    but joy comes in the morning.
⁶As for me, I said in my prosperity,
    "I shall never be moved."
⁷You, Yahweh, when you favored me, made
    my mountain stand strong;
    but when you hid your face, I was
    troubled.
⁸I cried to you, Yahweh.
    To Yahweh I made supplication:
⁹"What profit is there in my destruction, if
    I go down to the pit?
    Shall the dust praise you?
    Shall it declare your truth?
¹⁰Hear, Yahweh, and have mercy on me.
    Yahweh, be my helper."
¹¹You have turned my mourning into danc-
    ing for me.
    You have removed my sackcloth, and
    clothed me with gladness,
    ¹²To the end that my heart may sing
    praise to you, and not be silent.
Yahweh my God, I will give thanks to you
    forever!

Psalm 31

For the Chief Musician. A Psalm by
David.

¹In you, Yahweh, I take refuge.
    Let me never be disappointed.
    Deliver me in your righteousness.
²Bow down your ear to me.
    Deliver me speedily.
Be to me a strong rock,
    a house of defense to save me.
³For you are my rock and my fortress,
    therefore for your name's sake lead me
    and guide me.
⁴Pluck me out of the net that they have laid
    secretly for me,
    for you are my stronghold.
⁵Into your hand I commend my spirit.
    You redeem me, Yahweh, God of truth.
⁶I hate those who regard lying vanities,
    but I trust in Yahweh.
⁷I will be glad and rejoice in your loving
    kindness,
    for you have seen my affliction.
    You have known my soul in adversi-
    ties.

⁸You have not shut me up into the hand of
    the enemy.
    You have set my feet in a large place.
⁹Have mercy on me, Yahweh, for I am in
    distress.
    My eye, my soul, and my body waste
    away with grief.
¹⁰For my life is spent with sorrow,
    my years with sighing.
My strength fails because of my iniquity.
    My bones are wasted away.
¹¹Because of all my adversaries I have
    become utterly contemptible to my
    neighbors,
    A fear to my acquaintances.
    Those who saw me on the street fled
    from me.
¹²I am forgotten from their hearts like a
    dead man.
    I am like broken pottery.
¹³For I have heard the slander of many,
    terror on every side,
    while they conspire together against
    me,
    they plot to take away my life.
¹⁴But I trust in you, Yahweh.
    I said, "You are my God."
¹⁵My times are in your hand.
    Deliver me from the hand of my ene-
    mies, and from those who persecute
    me.
¹⁶Make your face to shine on your servant.
    Save me in your loving kindness.
¹⁷Let me not be disappointed, Yahweh, for
    I have called on you.
    Let the wicked be disappointed.
    Let them be silent in Sheol.
¹⁸Let the lying lips be mute,
    which speak against the righteous inso-
    lently, with pride and contempt.
¹⁹Oh how great is your goodness,
    which you have laid up for those who
    fear you,
    which you have worked for those who
    take refuge in you,
    before the sons of men!
²⁰In the shelter of your presence you will
    hide them from the plotting of man.
    You will keep them secretly in a
    dwelling away from the strife of
    tongues.

²¹ Praise be to Yahweh,
for he has shown me his marvelous
loving kindness in a strong city.
²² As for me, I said in my haste, "I am cut off
from before your eyes."
Nevertheless you heard the voice of my
petitions when I cried to you.
²³ Oh love Yahweh, all you his saints!
Yahweh preserves the faithful,
and fully recompenses him who behaves
arrogantly.
²⁴ Be strong, and let your heart take
courage,
all you who hope in Yahweh.

Psalm 32

By David. A contemplative psalm.

¹ Blessed is he whose disobedience is forgiven,
whose sin is covered.
² Blessed is the man to whom Yahweh
doesn't impute iniquity,
in whose spirit there is no deceit.
³ When I kept silence, my bones wasted
away through my groaning all day
long.
⁴ For day and night your hand was heavy
on me.
My strength was sapped in the heat of
summer.
Selah.
⁵ I acknowledged my sin to you.
I didn't hide my iniquity.
I said, I will confess my transgressions to
Yahweh,
and you forgave the iniquity of my sin.
Selah.
⁶ For this, let everyone who is godly pray
to you in a time when you may be
found.
Surely when the great waters overflow,
they shall not reach to him.
⁷ You are my hiding place.
You will preserve me from trouble.
You will surround me with songs of
deliverance.
Selah.
⁸ I will instruct you and teach you in the
way which you shall go.
I will counsel you with my eye on you.

⁹ Don't be like the horse, or like the mule,
which have no understanding,
who are controlled by bit and bridle, or
else they will not come near to you.
¹⁰ Many sorrows come to the wicked,
but loving kindness shall surround him
who trusts in Yahweh.
¹¹ Be glad in Yahweh, and rejoice, you
righteous!
Shout for joy, all you who are upright
in heart!

Psalm 33

¹ Rejoice in Yahweh, you righteous!
Praise is fitting for the upright.
² Give thanks to Yahweh with the lyre.
Sing praises to him with the harp of ten
strings.
³ Sing to him a new song.
Play skillfully with a shout of joy!
⁴ For the word of Yahweh is right.
All his work is done in faithfulness.
⁵ He loves righteousness and justice.
The earth is full of the loving kindness
of Yahweh.
⁶ By Yahweh's word, the heavens were
made;
all their army by the breath of his
mouth.
⁷ He gathers the waters of the sea together
as a heap.
He lays up the deeps in storehouses.
⁸ Let all the earth fear Yahweh.
Let all the inhabitants of the world
stand in awe of him.
⁹ For he spoke, and it was done.
He commanded, and it stood firm.
¹⁰ Yahweh brings the counsel of the nations
to nothing.
He makes the thoughts of the peoples
to be of no effect.
¹¹ The counsel of Yahweh stands fast forever,
the thoughts of his heart to all generations.
¹² Blessed is the nation whose God is Yahweh,
the people whom he has chosen for his
own inheritance.
¹³ Yahweh looks from heaven.
He sees all the sons of men.

¹⁴From the place of his habitation he looks
out on all the inhabitants of the earth,
¹⁵he who fashions all of their hearts;
and he considers all of their works.
¹⁶There is no king saved by the multitude
of an army.
A mighty man is not delivered by great
strength.
¹⁷A horse is a vain thing for safety,
neither does he deliver any by his great
power.
¹⁸Behold, Yahweh's eye is on those who
fear him,
on those who hope in his loving kindness;
¹⁹to deliver their soul from death,
to keep them alive in famine.
²⁰Our soul has waited for Yahweh.
He is our help and our shield.
²¹For our heart rejoices in him,
because we have trusted in his holy
name.
²²Let your loving kindness be on us, Yah-
weh,
since we have hoped in you.

Psalm 34

By David; when he pretended to be
insane before Abimelech, who drove him
away, and he departed.^e

¹I will bless Yahweh at all times.
His praise will always be in my mouth.
²My soul shall boast in Yahweh.
The humble shall hear of it, and be
glad.
³Oh magnify Yahweh with me.
Let us exalt his name together.
⁴I sought Yahweh, and he answered me,
and delivered me from all my fears.
⁵They looked to him, and were radiant.
Their faces shall never be covered with
shame.
⁶This poor man cried, and Yahweh heard
him,
and saved him out of all his troubles.
⁷The angel of Yahweh encamps around
those who fear him,
and delivers them.

⁸Oh taste and see that Yahweh is good.
Blessed is the man who takes refuge in
him.
⁹Oh fear Yahweh, you his saints,
for there is no lack with those who fear
him.
¹⁰The young lions do lack, and suffer
hunger,
but those who seek Yahweh shall not
lack any good thing.
¹¹Come, you children, listen to me.
I will teach you the fear of Yahweh.
¹²Who is someone who desires life,
and loves many days, that he may see
good?
¹³Keep your tongue from evil,
and your lips from speaking lies.
¹⁴Depart from evil, and do good.
seek peace, and pursue it.
¹⁵Yahweh's eyes are toward the righteous.
His ears listen to their cry.
¹⁶Yahweh's face is against those who do
evil,
to cut off the memory of them from the
earth.
¹⁷The righteous cry, and Yahweh hears,
and delivers them out of all their troubles.
¹⁸Yahweh is near to those who have a
broken heart,
and saves those who have a crushed
spirit.
¹⁹Many are the afflictions of the righteous,
but Yahweh delivers him out of them
all.
²⁰He protects all of his bones.
Not one of them is broken.
²¹Evil shall kill the wicked.
Those who hate the righteous shall be
condemned.
²²Yahweh redeems the soul of his servants.
None of those who take refuge in him
shall be condemned.

Psalm 35

By David.

---

^e34:0 Psalm 34 is an acrostic poem, with each verse starting with a letter of the alphabet (ordered
from Alef to Tav).

¹Contend, Yahweh, with those who contend with me.

Fight against those who fight against me.

²Take hold of shield and buckler,
and stand up for my help.

³Brandish the spear and block those who pursue me.

Tell my soul, "I am your salvation."

⁴Let those who seek after my soul be disappointed and brought to dishonor.

Let those who plot my ruin be turned back and confounded.

⁵Let them be as chaff before the wind,
Yahweh's angel driving them on.

⁶Let their way be dark and slippery,
Yahweh's angel pursuing them.

⁷For without cause they have hidden their net in a pit for me.

Without cause they have dug a pit for my soul.

⁸Let destruction come on him unawares.

Let his net that he has hidden catch himself.

Let him fall into that destruction.

⁹My soul shall be joyful in Yahweh.

It shall rejoice in his salvation.

¹⁰All my bones shall say, "Yahweh, who is like you,

who delivers the poor from him who is too strong for him;

yes, the poor and the needy from him who robs him?"

¹¹Unrighteous witnesses rise up.

They ask me about things that I don't know about.

¹²They reward me evil for good,
to the bereaving of my soul.

¹³But as for me, when they were sick, my clothing was sackcloth.

I afflicted my soul with fasting.

My prayer returned into my own bosom.

¹⁴I behaved myself as though it had been my friend or my brother.

I bowed down mourning, as one who mourns his mother.

¹⁵But in my adversity, they rejoiced, and gathered themselves together.

The attackers gathered themselves together against me, and I didn't know it.

They tore at me, and didn't cease.

¹⁶Like the profane mockers in feasts,
they gnashed their teeth at me.

¹⁷Lord, how long will you look on?

Rescue my soul from their destruction,
my precious life from the lions.

¹⁸I will give you thanks in the great assembly.

I will praise you among many people.

¹⁹Don't let those who are my enemies wrongfully rejoice over me;

neither let those who hate me without a cause wink their eyes.

²⁰For they don't speak peace,

but they devise deceitful words against those who are quiet in the land.

²¹Yes, they opened their mouth wide against me.

They said, "Aha! Aha! Our eye has seen it!"

²²You have seen it, Yahweh. Don't keep silent.

Lord, don't be far from me.

²³Wake up! Rise up to defend me, my God!

My Lord, contend for me!

²⁴Vindicate me, Yahweh my God, according to your righteousness.

Don't let them gloat over me.

²⁵Don't let them say in their heart, "Aha! That's the way we want it!"

Don't let them say, "We have swallowed him up!"

²⁶Let them be disappointed and confounded together who rejoice at my calamity.

Let them be clothed with shame and dishonor who magnify themselves against me.

²⁷Let them shout for joy and be glad, who favor my righteous cause.

Yes, let them say continually, "Yahweh be magnified,

who has pleasure in the prosperity of his servant!"

²⁸My tongue shall talk about your righteousness and about your praise all day long.

Psalm 36

For the Chief Musician. By David, the servant of Yahweh.

[1] An oracle is within my heart about the disobedience of the wicked:
"There is no fear of God before his eyes."
[2] For he flatters himself in his own eyes,
too much to detect and hate his sin.
[3] The words of his mouth are iniquity and deceit.
He has ceased to be wise and to do good.
[4] He plots iniquity on his bed.
He sets himself in a way that is not good.
He doesn't abhor evil.
[5] Your loving kindness, Yahweh, is in the heavens.
Your faithfulness reaches to the skies.
[6] Your righteousness is like the mountains of God.
Your judgments are like a great deep.
Yahweh, you preserve man and animal.
[7] How precious is your loving kindness, God!
The children of men take refuge under the shadow of your wings.
[8] They shall be abundantly satisfied with the abundance of your house.
You will make them drink of the river of your pleasures.
[9] For with you is the spring of life.
In your light shall we see light.
[10] Oh continue your loving kindness to those who know you,
your righteousness to the upright in heart.
[11] Don't let the foot of pride come against me.
Don't let the hand of the wicked drive me away.
[12] There the workers of iniquity are fallen.
They are thrust down, and shall not be able to rise.

Psalm 37

By David.

[1] Don't fret because of evil-doers,
neither be envious against those who work unrighteousness.
[2] For they shall soon be cut down like the grass,
and wither like the green herb.
[3] Trust in Yahweh, and do good.
Dwell in the land, and enjoy safe pasture.
[4] Also delight yourself in Yahweh,
and he will give you the desires of your heart.
[5] Commit your way to Yahweh.
Trust also in him, and he will do this:
[6] he will make your righteousness go forth as the light,
and your justice as the noon day sun.
[7] Rest in Yahweh, and wait patiently for him.
Don't fret because of him who prospers in his way,
because of the man who makes wicked plots happen.
[8] Cease from anger, and forsake wrath.
Don't fret, it leads only to evildoing.
[9] For evildoers shall be cut off,
but those who wait for Yahweh shall inherit the land.
[10] For yet a little while, and the wicked will be no more.
Yes, though you look for his place, he isn't there.
[11] But the humble shall inherit the land,
and shall delight themselves in the abundance of peace.
[12] The wicked plots against the just,
and gnashes at him with his teeth.
[13] The Lord will laugh at him,
for he sees that his day is coming.
[14] The wicked have drawn out the sword,
and have bent their bow,
to cast down the poor and needy,
to kill those who are upright in the way.
[15] Their sword shall enter into their own heart.
Their bows shall be broken.
[16] Better is a little that the righteous has,
than the abundance of many wicked.
[17] For the arms of the wicked shall be broken,
but Yahweh upholds the righteous.

¹⁸Yahweh knows the days of the perfect.
Their inheritance shall be forever.
¹⁹They shall not be disappointed in the time
of evil.
In the days of famine they shall be
satisfied.
²⁰But the wicked shall perish.
The enemies of Yahweh shall be like the
beauty of the fields.
They will vanish—
vanish like smoke.
²¹The wicked borrow, and don't pay back,
but the righteous give generously.
²²For such as are blessed by him shall
inherit the land.
Those who are cursed by him shall be
cut off.
²³A man's goings are established by Yahweh.
He delights in his way.
²⁴Though he stumble, he shall not fall,
for Yahweh holds him up with his
hand.
²⁵I have been young, and now am old,
yet I have not seen the righteous forsaken,
nor his children begging for bread.
²⁶All day long he deals graciously, and
lends.
His seed is blessed.
²⁷Depart from evil, and do good.
Live securely forever.
²⁸For Yahweh loves justice,
and doesn't forsake his saints.
They are preserved forever,
but the children of the wicked shall be
cut off.
²⁹The righteous shall inherit the land,
and live in it forever.
³⁰The mouth of the righteous talks of wisdom.
His tongue speaks justice.
³¹The law of his God is in his heart.
None of his steps shall slide.
³²The wicked watches the righteous,
and seeks to kill him.
³³Yahweh will not leave him in his hand,
nor condemn him when he is judged.
³⁴Wait for Yahweh, and keep his way,
and he will exalt you to inherit the
land.

When the wicked are cut off, you shall
see it.
³⁵I have seen the wicked in great power,
spreading himself like a green tree in its
native soil.
³⁶But he passed away, and behold, he was
not.
Yes, I sought him, but he could not be
found.
³⁷Mark the perfect man, and see the upright,
for there is a future for the man of
peace.
³⁸As for transgressors, they shall be destroyed together.
The future of the wicked shall be cut
off.
³⁹But the salvation of the righteous is from
Yahweh.
He is their stronghold in the time of
trouble.
⁴⁰Yahweh helps them, and rescues them.
He rescues them from the wicked, and
saves them,
Because they have taken refuge in him.

Psalm 38

A Psalm by David, for a memorial.

¹Yahweh, don't rebuke me in your wrath,
neither chasten me in your hot displea-
sure.
²For your arrows have pierced me,
your hand presses hard on me.
³There is no soundness in my flesh because
of your indignation,
neither is there any health in my bones
because of my sin.
⁴For my iniquities have gone over my head.
As a heavy burden, they are too heavy
for me.
⁵My wounds are loathsome and corrupt,
because of my foolishness.
⁶I am pained and bowed down greatly.
I go mourning all day long.
⁷For my waist is filled with burning.
There is no soundness in my flesh.
⁸I am faint and severely bruised.
I have groaned by reason of the anguish of my heart.
⁹Lord, all my desire is before you.
My groaning is not hidden from you.

¹⁰My heart throbs.
> My strength fails me.
> As for the light of my eyes, it has also
> left me.

¹¹My lovers and my friends stand aloof
> from my plague.
> My kinsmen stand far away.

¹²They also who seek after my life lay
> snares.
> Those who seek my hurt speak mis-
> chievous things,
> and meditate deceits all day long.

¹³But I, as a deaf man, don't hear.
> I am as a mute man who doesn't open
> his mouth.

¹⁴Yes, I am as a man who doesn't hear,
> in whose mouth are no reproofs.

¹⁵For in you, Yahweh, do I hope.
> You will answer, Lord my God.

¹⁶For I said, "Don't let them gloat over me,
> or exalt themselves over me when my
> foot slips."

¹⁷For I am ready to fall.
> My pain is continually before me.

¹⁸For I will declare my iniquity.
> I will be sorry for my sin.

¹⁹But my enemies are vigorous and many.
> Those who hate me without reason are
> numerous.

²⁰They who also render evil for good are
> adversaries to me,
> because I follow what is good.

²¹Don't forsake me, Yahweh.
> My God, don't be far from me.

²²Hurry to help me,
> Lord, my salvation.

Psalm 39

For the Chief Musician. For Jeduthun.
A Psalm by David.

¹I said, "I will watch my ways, so that I
> don't sin with my tongue.
> I will keep my mouth with a bridle
> while the wicked is before me."

²I was mute with silence.
> I held my peace, even from good.
> My sorrow was stirred.

³My heart was hot within me.
> While I meditated, the fire burned:
I spoke with my tongue:

⁴"Yahweh, show me my end,
> what is the measure of my days.
> Let me know how frail I am.

⁵Behold, you have made my days hand-
> breadths.
> My lifetime is as nothing before you.
Surely every man stands as a breath."
Selah.

⁶"Surely every man walks like a shadow.
> Surely they busy themselves in vain.
> He heaps up, and doesn't know who
> shall gather.

⁷Now, Lord, what do I wait for?
> My hope is in you.

⁸Deliver me from all my transgressions.
> Don't make me the reproach of the
> foolish.

⁹I was mute.
> I didn't open my mouth,
> because you did it.

¹⁰Remove your scourge away from me.
> I am overcome by the blow of your
> hand.

¹¹When you rebuke and correct man for
> iniquity,
> You consume his wealth like a moth.
Surely every man is but a breath."
Selah.

¹²"Hear my prayer, Yahweh, and give ear
> to my cry.
> Don't be silent at my tears.
For I am a stranger with you,
> a foreigner, as all my fathers were.

¹³Oh spare me, that I may recover strength,
> before I go away, and exist no more."

Psalm 40

For the Chief Musician. A Psalm by
David.

¹I waited patiently for Yahweh.
> He turned to me, and heard my cry.

²He brought me up also out of a horrible
> pit,
> out of the miry clay.
He set my feet on a rock,
> and gave me a firm place to stand.

³He has put a new song in my mouth, even
> praise to our God.
> Many shall see it, and fear, and shall
> trust in Yahweh.

⁴Blessed is the man who makes Yahweh his
trust,
and doesn't respect the proud, nor such
as turn aside to lies.
⁵Many, Yahweh, my God, are the wonderful works which you have done,
and your thoughts which are toward
us.
They can't be declared back to you.
If I would declare and speak of them,
they are more than can be numbered.
⁶Sacrifice and offering you didn't desire.
You have opened my ears.
You have not required burnt offering
and sin offering.
⁷Then I said, "Behold, I have come.
It is written about me in the book in the
scroll.
⁸I delight to do your will, my God.
Yes, your law is within my heart."
⁹I have proclaimed glad news of righteousness in the great assembly.
Behold, I will not seal my lips, Yahweh,
you know.
¹⁰I have not hidden your righteousness
within my heart.
I have declared your faithfulness and
your salvation.
I have not concealed your loving kindness and your truth from the great
assembly.
¹¹Don't withhold your tender mercies from
me, Yahweh.
Let your loving kindness and your
truth continually preserve me.
¹²For innumerable evils have surrounded
me.
My iniquities have overtaken me, so
that I am not able to look up.
They are more than the hairs of my head.
My heart has failed me.
¹³Be pleased, Yahweh, to deliver me.
Hurry to help me, Yahweh.
¹⁴Let them be disappointed and confounded together who seek after my
soul to destroy it.
Let them be turned backward and
brought to dishonor who delight in
my hurt.
¹⁵Let them be desolate by reason of their
shame that tell me, "Aha! Aha!"

¹⁶Let all those who seek you rejoice and be
glad in you.
Let such as love your salvation say con-
tinually, "Let Yahweh be exalted!"
¹⁷But I am poor and needy.
May the Lord think about me.
You are my help and my deliverer.
Don't delay, my God.

Psalm 41

For the Chief Musician. A Psalm by
David.

¹Blessed is he who considers the poor.
Yahweh will deliver him in the day of
evil.
²Yahweh will preserve him, and keep him
alive.
He shall be blessed on the earth,
and he will not surrender him to the
will of his enemies.
³Yahweh will sustain him on his sickbed,
and restore him from his bed of illness.
⁴I said, "Yahweh, have mercy on me!
Heal me, for I have sinned against
you."
⁵My enemies speak evil against me:
"When will he die, and his name perish?"
⁶If he comes to see me, he speaks falsehood.
His heart gathers iniquity to itself.
When he goes abroad, he tells it.
⁷All who hate me whisper together against
me.
They imagine the worst for me.
⁸"An evil disease," they say, "has afflicted
him.
Now that he lies he shall rise up no
more."
⁹Yes, my own familiar friend, in whom I
trusted,
who ate bread with me,
has lifted up his heel against me.
¹⁰But you, Yahweh, have mercy on me, and
raise me up,
that I may repay them.
¹¹By this I know that you delight in me,
because my enemy doesn't triumph
over me.
¹²As for me, you uphold me in my integrity,
and set me in your presence forever.
¹³Blessed be Yahweh, the God of Israel,

from everlasting and to everlasting!
Amen and amen.

BOOK II

Psalm 42

For the Chief Musician. A contemplation by the sons of Korah.

[1] As the deer pants for the water brooks,
    so my soul pants after you, God.
[2] My soul thirsts for God, for the living God.
    When shall I come and appear before
        God?
[3] My tears have been my food day and
        night,
    while they continually ask me, "Where
        is your God?"
[4] These things I remember, and pour out my
        soul within me,
    how I used to go with the crowd, and
        led them to the house of God,
    with the voice of joy and praise, a
        multitude keeping a holy day.
[5] Why are you in despair, my soul?
    Why are you disturbed within me?
Hope in God!
    For I shall still praise him for the saving
        help of his presence.
[6] My God, my soul is in despair within me.
    Therefore I remember you from the
        land of the Jordan,
    the heights of Hermon, from the hill
        Mizar.
[7] Deep calls to deep at the noise of your
        waterfalls.
    All your waves and your billows have
        swept over me.
[8] Yahweh will command his loving kindness in the daytime.
    In the night his song shall be with me:
    a prayer to the God of my life.
[9] I will ask God, my rock, "Why have you
        forgotten me?
    Why do I go mourning because of the
        oppression of the enemy?"
[10] As with a sword in my bones, my adversaries reproach me,
    while they continually ask me, "Where
        is your God?"
[11] Why are you in despair, my soul?

Why are you disturbed within me?
Hope in God! For I shall still praise him,
    the saving help of my countenance,
    and my God.

Psalm 43

[1] Vindicate me, God, and plead my cause
    against an ungodly nation.
    Oh, deliver me from deceitful and
        wicked men.
[2] For you are the God of my strength. Why
        have you rejected me?
    Why do I go mourning because of the
        oppression of the enemy?
[3] Oh, send out your light and your truth.
    Let them lead me.
    Let them bring me to your holy hill,
    To your tents.
[4] Then I will go to the altar of God,
    to God, my exceeding joy.
I will praise you on the harp, God, my God.
[5] Why are you in despair, my soul?
    Why are you disturbed within me?
Hope in God!
    For I shall still praise him:
    my Savior, my helper, and my God.

Psalm 44

For the Chief Musician. By the sons of
Korah. A contemplative psalm.

[1] We have heard with our ears, God;
    our fathers have told us,
    what work you did in their days,
    in the days of old.
[2] You drove out the nations with your hand,
    but you planted them.
You afflicted the peoples,
    but you spread them abroad.
[3] For they didn't get the land in possession
        by their own sword,
    neither did their own arm save them;
but your right hand, and your arm, and the
        light of your face,
    because you were favorable to them.
[4] You are my King, God.
    Command victories for Jacob!
[5] Through you, will we push down our
        adversaries.

Through your name, will we tread
    them under who rise up against us.
[6] For I will not trust in my bow,
    neither shall my sword save me.
[7] But you have saved us from our adversaries,
    and have shamed those who hate us.
[8] In God we have made our boast all day
    long,
    we will give thanks to your name
    forever.
Selah.
[9] But now you rejected us, and brought us
    to dishonor,
    and don't go out with our armies.
[10] You make us turn back from the adversary.
    Those who hate us take spoil for themselves.
[11] You have made us like sheep for food,
    and have scattered us among the nations.
[12] You sell your people for nothing,
    and have gained nothing from their
    sale.
[13] You make us a reproach to our neighbors,
    a scoffing and a derision to those who
    are around us.
[14] You make us a byword among the nations,
    a shaking of the head among the peoples.
[15] All day long my dishonor is before me,
    and shame covers my face,
[16] At the taunt of one who reproaches
    and verbally abuses,
    because of the enemy and the avenger.
[17] All this has come on us,
    yet have we not forgotten you,
    Neither have we been false to your
    covenant.
[18] Our heart has not turned back,
    neither have our steps strayed from
    your path,
[19] Though you have crushed us in the
    haunt of jackals,
    and covered us with the shadow of
    death.
[20] If we have forgotten the name of our God,
    or spread forth our hands to a strange
    god;
[21] won't God search this out?

For he knows the secrets of the heart.
[22] Yes, for your sake we are killed all day
    long.
    We are regarded as sheep for the
    slaughter.
[23] Wake up!
    Why do you sleep, Lord?
Arise!
    Don't reject us forever.
[24] Why do you hide your face,
    and forget our affliction and our oppression?
[25] For our soul is bowed down to the dust.
    Our body cleaves to the earth.
[26] Rise up to help us.
    Redeem us for your loving kindness'
    sake.

Psalm 45

For the Chief Musician. Set to "The
Lilies." A contemplation by the sons of
Korah. A wedding song.

[1] My heart overflows with a noble theme.
    I recite my verses for the king.
    My tongue is like the pen of a skillful
    writer.
[2] You are the most excellent of the sons of
    men.
    Grace has anointed your lips,
    therefore God has blessed you forever.
[3] Gird your sword on your thigh, mighty
    one:
    your splendor and your majesty.
[4] In your majesty ride on victoriously on
    behalf of truth, humility, and righteousness.
    Let your right hand display awesome
    deeds.
[5] Your arrows are sharp.
    The nations fall under you, with arrows in the heart of the king's enemies.
[6] Your throne, God, is forever and ever.
    A scepter of equity is the scepter of
    your kingdom.
[7] You have loved righteousness, and hated
    wickedness.
    Therefore God, your God, has anointed
    you with the oil of gladness above
    your fellows.

[8] All your garments smell like myrrh, aloes, and cassia.

Out of ivory palaces stringed instruments have made you glad.
[9] Kings' daughters are among your honorable women.

At your right hand the queen stands in gold of Ophir.
[10] Listen, daughter, consider, and turn your ear.

Forget your own people, and also your father's house.
[11] So the king will desire your beauty, honor him, for he is your lord.
[12] The daughter of Tyre comes with a gift.

The rich among the people entreat your favor.
[13] The princess inside is all glorious.

Her clothing is interwoven with gold.
[14] She shall be led to the king in embroidered work.

The virgins, her companions who follow her, shall be brought to you.
[15] With gladness and rejoicing they shall be led.

They shall enter into the king's palace.
[16] Your sons will take the place of your fathers.

You shall make them princes in all the earth.
[17] I will make your name to be remembered in all generations.

Therefore the peoples shall give you thanks forever and ever.

Psalm 46

For the Chief Musician. By the sons of Korah. According to Alamoth.[f]

[1] God is our refuge and strength,
a very present help in trouble.
[2] Therefore we won't be afraid, though the earth changes,
though the mountains are shaken into the heart of the seas;
[3] though its waters roar and are troubled,
though the mountains tremble with their swelling.
Selah.

[4] There is a river, the streams of which make the city of God glad,
the holy place of the tents of the Most High.
[5] God is in her midst. She shall not be moved.

God will help her at dawn.
[6] The nations raged. The kingdoms were moved.

He lifted his voice, and the earth melted.
[7] Yahweh of Armies is with us.

The God of Jacob is our refuge.
Selah.
[8] Come, see Yahweh's works,
what desolations he has made in the earth.
[9] He makes wars cease to the end of the earth.

He breaks the bow, and shatters the spear.

He burns the chariots in the fire.
[10] "Be still, and know that I am God.

I will be exalted among the nations.

I will be exalted in the earth."
[11] Yahweh of Armies is with us.

The God of Jacob is our refuge.
Selah.

Psalm 47

For the Chief Musician. A Psalm by the sons of Korah.

[1] Oh clap your hands, all you nations.
Shout to God with the voice of triumph!
[2] For Yahweh Most High is awesome.

He is a great King over all the earth.
[3] He subdues nations under us,
and peoples under our feet.
[4] He chooses our inheritance for us,
the glory of Jacob whom he loved.
Selah.
[5] God has gone up with a shout,
Yahweh with the sound of a trumpet.
[6] Sing praise to God, sing praises.

Sing praises to our King, sing praises.
[7] For God is the King of all the earth.

Sing praises with understanding.

---

[f] 46:0 Alamoth is a musical term.

[8]God reigns over the nations.
> God sits on his holy throne.

[9]The princes of the peoples are gathered together,
> the people of the God of Abraham.
> For the shields of the earth belong to God.
> He is greatly exalted!

Psalm 48

A Song. A Psalm by the sons of Korah.

[1]Great is Yahweh, and greatly to be praised,
> in the city of our God, in his holy mountain.

[2]Beautiful in elevation, the joy of the whole earth,
> is Mount Zion, on the north sides,
> the city of the great King.

[3]God has shown himself in her citadels as a refuge.

[4]For, behold, the kings assembled themselves,
> they passed by together.

[5]They saw it, then they were amazed.
> They were dismayed.
> They hurried away.

[6]Trembling took hold of them there,
> pain, as of a woman in travail.

[7]With the east wind, you break the ships of Tarshish.

[8]As we have heard, so we have seen,
> in the city of Yahweh of Armies, in the city of our God.
God will establish it forever.
Selah.

[9]We have thought about your loving kindness, God,
> in the midst of your temple.

[10]As is your name, God,
> so is your praise to the ends of the earth.
> Your right hand is full of righteousness.

[11]Let Mount Zion be glad!
> Let the daughters of Judah rejoice,
> Because of your judgments.

[12]Walk about Zion, and go around her.
> Number its towers.

[13]Mark well her bulwarks.
> Consider her palaces,

that you may tell it to the next generation.

[14]For this God is our God forever and ever.
> He will be our guide even to death.

Psalm 49

For the Chief Musician. A Psalm by the sons of Korah.

[1]Hear this, all you peoples.
> Listen, all you inhabitants of the world,
> [2]both low and high,
> rich and poor together.

[3]My mouth will speak words of wisdom.
> My heart shall utter understanding.

[4]I will incline my ear to a proverb.
> I will open my riddle on the harp.

[5]Why should I fear in the days of evil,
> when iniquity at my heels surrounds me?

[6]Those who trust in their wealth,
> and boast in the multitude of their riches—
> [7]none of them can by any means redeem his brother,
> nor give God a ransom for him.

[8]For the redemption of their life is costly,
> no payment is ever enough,
> [9]That he should live on forever,
> that he should not see corruption.

[10]For he sees that wise men die;
> likewise the fool and the senseless perish,
> and leave their wealth to others.

[11]Their inward thought is that their houses will endure forever,
> and their dwelling places to all generations.
> They name their lands after themselves.

[12]But man, despite his riches, doesn't endure.
> He is like the animals that perish.

[13]This is the destiny of those who are foolish,
> and of those who approve their sayings.
Selah.

[14]They are appointed as a flock for Sheol.
> Death shall be their shepherd.
The upright shall have dominion over them in the morning.

Their beauty shall decay in Sheol,
far from their mansion.
[15]But God will redeem my soul from the
power of Sheol,
for he will receive me.
Selah.
[16]Don't be afraid when a man is made rich,
when the glory of his house is increased.
[17]For when he dies he shall carry nothing
away.
His glory shall not descend after him.
[18]Though while he lived he blessed his
soul—
and men praise you when you do well
for yourself—
[19]he shall go to the generation of his
fathers.
They shall never see the light.
[20]A man who has riches without understanding,
is like the animals that perish.

Psalm 50

A Psalm by Asaph.

[1]The Mighty One, God, Yahweh, speaks,
and calls the earth from sunrise to
sunset.
[2]Out of Zion, the perfection of beauty,
God shines forth.
[3]Our God comes, and does not keep silent.
A fire devours before him.
It is very stormy around him.
[4]He calls to the heavens above,
to the earth, that he may judge his
people:
[5]"Gather my saints together to me,
those who have made a covenant with
me by sacrifice."
[6]The heavens shall declare his righteousness,
for God himself is judge.
Selah.
[7]"Hear, my people, and I will speak;
Israel, and I will testify against you.
I am God, your God.
[8]I don't rebuke you for your sacrifices.
Your burnt offerings are continually
before me.
[9]I have no need for a bull from your stall,

nor male goats from your pens.
[10]For every animal of the forest is mine,
and the livestock on a thousand hills.
[11]I know all the birds of the mountains.
The wild animals of the field are mine.
[12]If I were hungry, I would not tell you,
for the world is mine, and all that is in
it.
[13]Will I eat the flesh of bulls,
or drink the blood of goats?
[14]Offer to God the sacrifice of thanksgiving.
Pay your vows to the Most High.
[15]Call on me in the day of trouble.
I will deliver you, and you will honor
me."
[16]But to the wicked God says,
"What right do you have to declare my
statutes,
that you have taken my covenant on
your lips,
[17]seeing you hate instruction,
and throw my words behind you?
[18]When you saw a thief, you consented
with him,
and have participated with adulterers.
[19]"You give your mouth to evil.
Your tongue frames deceit.
[20]You sit and speak against your brother.
You slander your own mother's son.
[21]You have done these things, and I kept
silent.
You thought that the I was just like you.
I will rebuke you, and accuse you in
front of your eyes.
[22]"Now consider this, you who forget God,
lest I tear you into pieces, and there be
none to deliver.
[23]Whoever offers the sacrifice of thanksgiving glorifies me,
and prepares his way so that I will
show God's salvation to him."

Psalm 51

For the Chief Musician. A Psalm by
David, when Nathan the prophet came to
him, after he had gone in to Bathsheba.

[1]Have mercy on me, God, according to
your loving kindness.

According to the multitude of your tender mercies, blot out my transgressions.

2 Wash me thoroughly from my iniquity.
    Cleanse me from my sin.
3 For I know my transgressions.
    My sin is constantly before me.
4 Against you, and you only, have I sinned,
    and done that which is evil in your sight;
that you may be proved right when you speak,
    and justified when you judge.
5 Behold, I was brought forth in iniquity.
    In sin my mother conceived me.
6 Behold, you desire truth in the inward parts.
    You teach me wisdom in the inmost place.
7 Purify me with hyssop, and I will be clean.
    Wash me, and I will be whiter than snow.
8 Let me hear joy and gladness,
    That the bones which you have broken may rejoice.
9 Hide your face from my sins,
    and blot out all of my iniquities.
10 Create in me a clean heart, O God.
    Renew a right spirit within me.
11 Don't throw me from your presence,
    and don't take your holy Spirit from me.
12 Restore to me the joy of your salvation.
    Uphold me with a willing spirit.
13 Then I will teach transgressors your ways.
    Sinners shall be converted to you.
14 Deliver me from bloodguiltiness, O God,
    the God of my salvation.
    My tongue shall sing aloud of your righteousness.
15 Lord, open my lips.
    My mouth shall declare your praise.
16 For you don't delight in sacrifice, or else I would give it.
    You have no pleasure in burnt offering.
17 The sacrifices of God are a broken spirit.
    A broken and contrite heart, O God, you will not despise.
18 Do well in your good pleasure to Zion.
    Build the walls of Jerusalem.

19 Then you will delight in the sacrifices of righteousness,
    in burnt offerings and in whole burnt offerings.
Then they will offer bulls on your altar.

Psalm 52

For the Chief Musician. A contemplation by David, when Doeg the Edomite came and told Saul, "David has come to Abimelech's house."

1 Why do you boast of mischief, mighty man?
    God's loving kindness endures continually.
2 Your tongue plots destruction,
    like a sharp razor, working deceitfully.
3 You love evil more than good,
    lying rather than speaking the truth.
Selah.
4 You love all devouring words,
    you deceitful tongue.
5 God will likewise destroy you forever.
    He will take you up, and pluck you out of your tent,
    and root you out of the land of the living.
Selah.
6 The righteous also will see it, and fear,
    and laugh at him, saying,
7 "Behold, this is the man who didn't make God his strength,
    but trusted in the abundance of his riches,
    and strengthened himself in his wickedness."
8 But as for me, I am like a green olive tree in God's house.
    I trust in God's loving kindness forever and ever.
9 I will give you thanks forever, because you have done it.
    I will hope in your name, for it is good, in the presence of your saints.

Psalm 53

For the Chief Musician. To the tune of "Mahalath." A contemplation by David.

[1]The fool has said in his heart, "There is no God."
> They are corrupt, and have done abominable iniquity.
> There is no one who does good.

[2]God looks down from heaven on the children of men,
> to see if there are any who understood,
> who seek after God.

[3]Every one of them has gone back.
> They have become filthy together.
> There is no one who does good, no, not one.

[4]Have the workers of iniquity no knowledge,
> who eat up my people as they eat bread,
> and don't call on God?

[5]There they were in great fear, where no fear was,
> for God has scattered the bones of him who encamps against you.

You have put them to shame,
> because God has rejected them.

[6]Oh that the salvation of Israel would come out of Zion!
> When God brings back his people from captivity,
> then Jacob shall rejoice,
> and Israel shall be glad.

Psalm 54

For the Chief Musician. On stringed instruments. A contemplation by David, when the Ziphites came and said to Saul, "Isn't David hiding himself among us?"

[1]Save me, God, by your name.
> Vindicate me in your might.

[2]Hear my prayer, God.
> Listen to the words of my mouth.

[3]For strangers have risen up against me.
> Violent men have sought after my soul.
> They haven't set God before them.

Selah.

[4]Behold, God is my helper.
> The Lord is the one who sustains my soul.

[5]He will repay the evil to my enemies.
> Destroy them in your truth.

[6]With a free will offering, I will sacrifice to you.
> I will give thanks to your name, Yahweh, for it is good.

[7]For he has delivered me out of all trouble.
> My eye has seen triumph over my enemies.

Psalm 55

For the Chief Musician. On stringed instruments. A contemplation by David.

[1]Listen to my prayer, God.
> Don't hide yourself from my supplication.

[2]Attend to me, and answer me.
> I am restless in my complaint, and moan,
> [3]Because of the voice of the enemy,
> Because of the oppression of the wicked.

For they bring suffering on me.
> In anger they hold a grudge against me.

[4]My heart is severely pained within me.
> The terrors of death have fallen on me.

[5]Fearfulness and trembling have come on me.
> Horror has overwhelmed me.

[6]I said, "Oh that I had wings like a dove!
> Then I would fly away, and be at rest.

[7]Behold, then I would wander far off.
> I would lodge in the wilderness."

Selah.

[8]"I would hurry to a shelter from the stormy wind and storm."

[9]Confuse them, Lord, and confound their language,
> for I have seen violence and strife in the city.

[10]Day and night they prowl around on its walls.
> Malice and abuse are also within her.

[11]Destructive forces are within her.
> Threats and lies don't depart from her streets.

[12]For it was not an enemy who insulted me,
> then I could have endured it.

Neither was it he who hated me who raised himself up against me,
> then I would have hid myself from him.

[13]But it was you, a man like me,

my companion, and my familiar friend.
¹⁴We took sweet fellowship together.
    We walked in God's house with company.
¹⁵Let death come suddenly on them.
    Let them go down alive into Sheol.
    For wickedness is in their dwelling, in the midst of them.
¹⁶As for me, I will call on God.
    Yahweh will save me.
¹⁷Evening, morning, and at noon, I will cry out in distress.
    He will hear my voice.
¹⁸He has redeemed my soul in peace from the battle that was against me,
    although there are many who oppose me.
¹⁹God, who is enthroned forever,
    will hear, and answer them.
Selah.
They never change,
    who don't fear God.
²⁰He raises his hands against his friends.
    He has violated his covenant.
²¹His mouth was smooth as butter,
    but his heart was war.
His words were softer than oil,
    yet they were drawn swords.
²²Cast your burden on Yahweh, and he will sustain you.
    He will never allow the righteous to be moved.
²³But you, God, will bring them down into the pit of destruction.
    Bloodthirsty and deceitful men shall not live out half their days,
    but I will trust in you.

Psalm 56

For the Chief Musician. To the tune of "Silent Dove in Distant Lands." A poem by David, when the Philistines seized him in Gath.

¹Be merciful to me, God, for man wants to swallow me up.
    All day long, he attacks and oppresses me.
²My enemies want to swallow me up all day long,

for they are many who fight proudly against me.
³When I am afraid,
    I will put my trust in you.
⁴In God, I praise his word.
    In God, I put my trust.
I will not be afraid.
    What can flesh do to me?
⁵All day long they twist my words.
    All their thoughts are against me for evil.
⁶They conspire and lurk,
    watching my steps, they are eager to take my life.
⁷Shall they escape by iniquity?
    In anger cast down the peoples, God.
⁸You number my wanderings.
    You put my tears into your bottle.
    Aren't they in your book?
⁹Then my enemies shall turn back in the day that I call.
    I know this, that God is for me.
¹⁰In God, I will praise his word.
    In Yahweh, I will praise his word.
¹¹I have put my trust in God.
    I will not be afraid.
    What can man do to me?
¹²Your vows are on me, God.
    I will give thank offerings to you.
¹³For you have delivered my soul from death,
    and prevented my feet from falling,
    that I may walk before God in the light of the living.

Psalm 57

For the Chief Musician. To the tune of "Do Not Destroy." A poem by David, when he fled from Saul, in the cave.

¹Be merciful to me, God, be merciful to me,
    for my soul takes refuge in you.
Yes, in the shadow of your wings, I will take refuge,
    until disaster has passed.
²I cry out to God Most High,
to God who accomplishes my requests for me.
³He will send from heaven, and save me,
    he rebukes the one who is pursuing me.
Selah.

God will send out his loving kindness and
his truth.

⁴My soul is among lions.

I lie among those who are set on fire,

even the sons of men, whose teeth are
spears and arrows,

and their tongue a sharp sword.

⁵Be exalted, God, above the heavens!

Let your glory be above all the earth!

⁶They have prepared a net for my steps.

My soul is bowed down.

They dig a pit before me.

They fall into its midst themselves.

Selah.

⁷My heart is steadfast, God, my heart is
steadfast.

I will sing, yes, I will sing praises.

⁸Wake up, my glory! Wake up, psaltery and
harp!

I will wake up the dawn.

⁹I will give thanks to you, Lord, among the
peoples.

I will sing praises to you among the
nations.

¹⁰For your great loving kindness reaches to
the heavens,

and your truth to the skies.

¹¹Be exalted, God, above the heavens.

Let your glory be over all the earth.

Psalm 58

For the Chief Musician. To the tune of
"Do Not Destroy." A poem by David.

¹Do you indeed speak righteousness, silent
ones?

Do you judge blamelessly, you sons of
men?

²No, in your heart you plot injustice.

You measure out the violence of your
hands in the earth.

³The wicked go astray from the womb.

They are wayward as soon as they are
born, speaking lies.

⁴Their poison is like the poison of a snake;

like a deaf cobra that stops its ear,

⁵which doesn't listen to the voice of
charmers,

no matter how skillful the charmer
may be.

⁶Break their teeth, God, in their mouth.

Break out the great teeth of the young
lions, Yahweh.

⁷Let them vanish as water that flows away.

When they draw the bow, let their
arrows be made blunt.

⁸Let them be like a snail which melts and
passes away,

like the stillborn child, who has not
seen the sun.

⁹Before your pots can feel the heat of the
thorns,

he will sweep away the green and the
burning alike.

¹⁰The righteous shall rejoice when he sees
the vengeance.

He shall wash his feet in the blood of
the wicked;

¹¹so that men shall say, "Most certainly
there is a reward for the righteous.

Most certainly there is a God who
judges the earth."

Psalm 59

For the Chief Musician. To the tune of
"Do Not Destroy." A poem by David, when
Saul sent, and they watched the house to
kill him.

¹Deliver me from my enemies, my God.

Set me on high from those who rise up
against me.

²Deliver me from the workers of iniquity.

Save me from the bloodthirsty men.

³For, behold, they lie in wait for my soul.

The mighty gather themselves together
against me,

not for my disobedience, nor for my
sin, Yahweh.

⁴I have done no wrong, yet they are ready
to attack me.

Rise up, behold, and help me!

⁵You, Yahweh God of Armies, the God of
Israel,

rouse yourself to punish the nations.

Show no mercy to the wicked traitors.

Selah.

⁶They return at evening, howling like dogs,

and prowl around the city.

⁷Behold, they spew with their mouth.

Swords are in their lips,

"For," they say, "who hears us?"

⁸But you, Yahweh, laugh at them.
    You scoff at all the nations.
⁹Oh, my Strength, I watch for you,
    for God is my high tower.
¹⁰My God will go before me with his loving
    kindness.
    God will let me look at my enemies in
    triumph.
¹¹Don't kill them, or my people may forget.
    Scatter them by your power, and bring
    them down, Lord our shield.
¹²For the sin of their mouth, and the words
    of their lips,
    let them be caught in their pride,
    for the curses and lies which they utter.
¹³Consume them in wrath.
    Consume them, and they will be no
    more.
Let them know that God rules in Jacob,
    to the ends of the earth.
Selah.
¹⁴At evening let them return.
    Let them howl like a dog, and go
    around the city.
¹⁵They shall wander up and down for food,
    and wait all night if they aren't satis-
    fied.
¹⁶But I will sing of your strength.
    Yes, I will sing aloud of your loving
    kindness in the morning.
For you have been my high tower,
    a refuge in the day of my distress.
¹⁷To you, my strength, I will sing praises.
    For God is my high tower, the God of
    my mercy.

Psalm 60

For the Chief Musician. To the tune of "The Lily of the Covenant." A teaching poem by David, when he fought with Aram Naharaim and with Aram Zobah, and Joab returned, and killed twelve thousand of Edom in the Valley of Salt.

¹God, you have rejected us.
    You have broken us down.
You have been angry.
    Restore us, again.
²You have made the land tremble.
    You have torn it.
Mend its fractures,
    for it quakes.
³You have shown your people hard things.
    You have made us drink the wine that
    makes us stagger.
⁴You have given a banner to those who fear
    you,
    that it may be displayed because of the
    truth.
Selah.
⁵So that your beloved may be delivered,
    save with your right hand, and answer
    us.
⁶God has spoken from his sanctuary:
    "I will triumph.
    I will divide Shechem,
    and measure out the valley of Succoth.
⁷Gilead is mine, and Manasseh is mine.
    Ephraim also is the defense of my head.
    Judah is my scepter.
⁸Moab is my wash basin.
    I will throw my shoe on Edom.
    I shout in triumph over Philistia."
⁹Who will bring me into the strong city?
    Who has led me to Edom?
¹⁰Haven't you, God, rejected us?
    You don't go out with our armies, God.
¹¹Give us help against the adversary,
    for the help of man is vain.
¹²Through God we shall do valiantly,
    for it is he who will tread down our
    adversaries.

Psalm 61

For the Chief Musician. For a stringed instrument. By David.

¹Hear my cry, God.
    Listen to my prayer.
²From the end of the earth, I will call to you,
    when my heart is overwhelmed.
    Lead me to the rock that is higher than
    I.
³For you have been a refuge for me,
    a strong tower from the enemy.
⁴I will dwell in your tent forever.
    I will take refuge in the shelter of your
    wings.
Selah.
⁵For you, God, have heard my vows.
    You have given me the heritage of
    those who fear your name.

⁶You will prolong the king's life;
  his years shall be for generations.
⁷He shall be enthroned in God's presence
    forever.
  Appoint your loving kindness and
    truth, that they may preserve him.
⁸So I will sing praise to your name forever,
  that I may fulfill my vows daily.

Psalm 62

For the Chief Musician. To Jeduthun. A
Psalm by David.

¹My soul rests in God alone.
  My salvation is from him.
²He alone is my rock and my salvation, my
    fortress—
  I will never be greatly shaken.
³How long will you assault a man,
  would all of you throw him down,
  Like a leaning wall, like a tottering
    fence?
⁴They fully intend to throw him down from
    his lofty place.
  They delight in lies.
  They bless with their mouth, but they
    curse inwardly.
Selah.
⁵My soul, wait in silence for God alone,
  for my expectation is from him.
⁶He alone is my rock and my salvation, my
    fortress.
  I will not be shaken.
⁷With God is my salvation and my honor.
  The rock of my strength, and my
    refuge, is in God.
⁸Trust in him at all times, you people.
  Pour out your heart before him.
  God is a refuge for us.
Selah.
⁹Surely men of low degree are just a breath,
  and men of high degree are a lie.
In the balances they will go up.
  They are together lighter than a breath.
¹⁰Don't trust in oppression.
  Don't become vain in robbery.
If riches increase,
  don't set your heart on them.
¹¹God has spoken once;
  twice I have heard this,
  that power belongs to God.

¹²Also to you, Lord, belongs loving kind-
    ness,
  for you reward every man according to
    his work.

Psalm 63

A Psalm by David, when he was in the
desert of Judah.

¹God, you are my God.
  I will earnestly seek you.
My soul thirsts for you.
  My flesh longs for you,
  in a dry and weary land, where there is
    no water.
²So I have seen you in the sanctuary,
  watching your power and your glory.
³Because your loving kindness is better
    than life,
  my lips shall praise you.
⁴So I will bless you while I live.
  I will lift up my hands in your name.
⁵My soul shall be satisfied as with the
    richest food.
  My mouth shall praise you with joyful
    lips,
  ⁶when I remember you on my bed,
  and think about you in the night
    watches.
⁷For you have been my help.
  I will rejoice in the shadow of your
    wings.
⁸My soul stays close to you.
  Your right hand holds me up.
⁹But those who seek my soul, to destroy it,
  shall go into the lower parts of the
    earth.
¹⁰They shall be given over to the power of
    the sword.
  They shall be jackal food.
¹¹But the king shall rejoice in God.
  Everyone who swears by him will
    praise him,
  for the mouth of those who speak lies
    shall be silenced.

Psalm 64

For the Chief Musician. A Psalm by
David.

[1]Hear my voice, God, in my complaint.
     Preserve my life from fear of the enemy.
[2]Hide me from the conspiracy of the
     wicked,
     from the noisy crowd of the ones doing
     evil;
[3]who sharpen their tongue like a sword,
     and aim their arrows, deadly words,
          [4]to shoot innocent men from am-
          bushes.
     They shoot at him suddenly and fear-
     lessly.
[5]They encourage themselves in evil plans.
     They talk about laying snares secretly.
     They say, "Who will see them?"
[6]They plot injustice, saying, "We have
     made a perfect plan!"
     Surely man's mind and heart are cun-
     ning.
[7]But God will shoot at them.
     They will be suddenly struck down
     with an arrow.
[8]Their own tongues shall ruin them.
     All who see them will shake their
     heads.
[9]All mankind shall be afraid.
     They shall declare the work of God,
     and shall wisely ponder what he has
     done.
[10]The righteous shall be glad in Yahweh,
     and shall take refuge in him.
     All the upright in heart shall praise
     him!

Psalm 65

For the Chief Musician. A Psalm by
David. A song.

[1]Praise waits for you, God, in Zion.
     To you shall vows be performed.
[2]You who hear prayer,
     to you all men will come.
[3]Sins overwhelmed me,
     but you atoned for our transgressions.
[4]Blessed is one whom you choose, and
     cause to come near,
     that he may live in your courts.
     We will be filled with the goodness of
     your house,
     your holy temple.
[5]By awesome deeds of righteousness, you
     answer us,

God of our salvation.
You who are the hope of all the ends of the
     earth,
     of those who are far away on the sea;
[6]Who by his power forms the mountains,
     having armed yourself with strength;
[7]who stills the roaring of the seas,
     the roaring of their waves,
     and the turmoil of the nations.
[8]They also who dwell in far-away places
     are afraid at your wonders.
     You call the morning's dawn and the
     evening with songs of joy.
[9]You visit the earth, and water it.
     You greatly enrich it.
The river of God is full of water.
     You provide them grain, for so you
     have ordained it.
[10]You drench its furrows.
     You level its ridges.
     You soften it with showers.
     You bless it with a crop.
[11]You crown the year with your bounty.
     Your carts overflow with abundance.
[12]The wilderness grasslands overflow.
     The hills are clothed with gladness.
[13]The pastures are covered with flocks.
     The valleys also are clothed with grain.
They shout for joy!
     They also sing.

Psalm 66

For the Chief Musician. A song. A
Psalm.

[1]Make a joyful shout to God, all the earth!
     [2]Sing to the glory of his name!
     Offer glory and praise!
[3]Tell God, "How awesome are your deeds!
     Through the greatness of your power,
     your enemies submit themselves to
     you.
[4]All the earth will worship you,
     and will sing to you;
     they will sing to your name."
Selah.
[5]Come, and see God's deeds—
     awesome work on behalf of the chil-
     dren of men.
[6]He turned the sea into dry land.

They went through the river on foot.
There, we rejoiced in him.
⁷He rules by his might forever.
His eyes watch the nations.
Don't let the rebellious rise up against him.
Selah.
⁸Praise our God, you peoples!
Make the sound of his praise heard,
⁹who preserves our life among the living,
and doesn't allow our feet to be moved.
¹⁰For you, God, have tested us.
You have refined us, as silver is refined.
¹¹You brought us into prison.
You laid a burden on our backs.
¹²You allowed men to ride over our heads.
We went through fire and through water,
but you brought us to the place of abundance.
¹³I will come into your temple with burnt offerings.
I will pay my vows to you, ¹⁴which my lips promised,
and my mouth spoke, when I was in distress.
¹⁵I will offer to you burnt offerings of fat animals,
with the offering of rams,
I will offer bulls with goats.
Selah.
¹⁶Come, and hear, all you who fear God.
I will declare what he has done for my soul.
¹⁷I cried to him with my mouth.
He was extolled with my tongue.
¹⁸If I cherished sin in my heart,
the Lord wouldn't have listened.
¹⁹But most certainly, God has listened.
He has heard the voice of my prayer.
²⁰Blessed be God, who has not turned away my prayer,
nor his loving kindness from me.

Psalm 67

For the Chief Musician. With stringed instruments. A Psalm. A song.

¹May God be merciful to us, bless us,
and cause his face to shine on us.
Selah.
²That your way may be known on earth,
and your salvation among all nations,
³let the peoples praise you, God.
Let all the peoples praise you.
⁴Oh let the nations be glad and sing for joy,
for you will judge the peoples with equity,
and govern the nations on earth.
Selah.
⁵Let the peoples praise you, God.
Let all the peoples praise you.
⁶The earth has yielded its increase.
God, even our own God, will bless us.
⁷God will bless us.
All the ends of the earth shall fear him.

Psalm 68

For the Chief Musician. A Psalm by David. A song.

¹Let God arise!
Let his enemies be scattered!
Let them who hate him also flee before him.
²As smoke is driven away,
so drive them away.
As wax melts before the fire,
so let the wicked perish at the presence of God.
³But let the righteous be glad.
Let them rejoice before God.
Yes, let them rejoice with gladness.
⁴Sing to God! Sing praises to his name!
Extol him who rides on the clouds:
to Yah, his name!
Rejoice before him!
⁵A father of the fatherless, and a defender of the widows,
is God in his holy habitation.
⁶God sets the lonely in families.
He brings out the prisoners with singing,
but the rebellious dwell in a sun-scorched land.
⁷God, when you went forth before your people,
when you marched through the wilderness...
Selah.
⁸The earth trembled.
The sky also poured down rain at the presence of the God of Sinai—

at the presence of God, the God of Israel.

⁹You, God, sent a plentiful rain.

You confirmed your inheritance, when it was weary.

¹⁰Your congregation lived therein.

You, God, prepared your goodness for the poor.

¹¹The Lord announced the word.

The ones who proclaim it are a great company.

¹²"Kings of armies flee! They flee!"

She who waits at home divides the spoil,

¹³while you sleep among the campfires,

the wings of a dove sheathed with silver,

her feathers with shining gold.

¹⁴When the Almighty scattered kings in her,

it snowed on Zalmon.

¹⁵The mountains of Bashan are majestic mountains.

The mountains of Bashan are rugged.

¹⁶Why do you look in envy, you rugged mountains,

at the mountain where God chooses to reign?

Yes, Yahweh will dwell there forever.

¹⁷The chariots of God are tens of thousands and thousands of thousands.

The Lord is among them, from Sinai, into the sanctuary.

¹⁸You have ascended on high.

You have led away captives.

You have received gifts among men,

yes, among the rebellious also, that Yah God might dwell there.

¹⁹Blessed be the Lord, who daily bears our burdens,

even the God who is our salvation.

Selah.

²⁰God is to us a God of deliverance.

To Yahweh, the Lord, belongs escape from death.

²¹But God will strike through the head of his enemies,

the hairy scalp of such a one as still continues in his guiltiness.

²²The Lord said, "I will bring you again from Bashan,

I will bring you again from the depths of the sea;

²³That you may crush them, dipping your foot in blood,

that the tongues of your dogs may have their portion from your enemies."

²⁴They have seen your processions, God,

even the processions of my God, my King, into the sanctuary.

²⁵The singers went before, the minstrels followed after,

in the midst of the ladies playing with tambourines,

²⁶"Bless God in the congregations,

even the Lord in the assembly of Israel!"

²⁷There is little Benjamin, their ruler,

the princes of Judah, their council,

the princes of Zebulun, and the princes of Naphtali.

²⁸Your God has commanded your strength.

Strengthen, God, that which you have done for us.

²⁹Because of your temple at Jerusalem,

kings shall bring presents to you.

³⁰Rebuke the wild animal of the reeds,

the multitude of the bulls, with the calves of the peoples.

Being humbled, may it bring bars of silver.

Scatter the nations that delight in war.

³¹Princes shall come out of Egypt.

Ethiopia shall hurry to stretch out her hands to God.

³²Sing to God, you kingdoms of the earth!

Sing praises to the Lord!

Selah.

³³To him who rides on the heaven of heavens, which are of old;

behold, he utters his voice, a mighty voice.

³⁴Ascribe strength to God!

His excellency is over Israel,

his strength is in the skies.

³⁵You are awesome, God, in your sanctuaries.

The God of Israel gives strength and power to his people.

Praise be to God!

Psalm 69

For the Chief Musician. To the tune of "Lilies." By David.

¹Save me, God,
    for the waters have come up to my neck!
²I sink in deep mire, where there is no foothold.
    I have come into deep waters, where the floods overflow me.
³I am weary with my crying.
    My throat is dry.
    My eyes fail, looking for my God.
⁴Those who hate me without a cause are more than the hairs of my head.
    Those who want to cut me off, being my enemies wrongfully, are mighty.
    I have to restore what I didn't take away.
⁵God, you know my foolishness.
    My sins aren't hidden from you.
⁶Don't let those who wait for you be shamed through me, Lord Yahweh of Armies.
    Don't let those who seek you be brought to dishonor through me, God of Israel.
⁷Because for your sake, I have borne reproach.
    Shame has covered my face.
⁸I have become a stranger to my brothers, an alien to my mother's children.
⁹For the zeal of your house consumes me.
    The reproaches of those who reproach you have fallen on me.
¹⁰When I wept and I fasted,
    that was to my reproach.
¹¹When I made sackcloth my clothing,
    I became a byword to them.
¹²Those who sit in the gate talk about me.
    I am the song of the drunkards.
¹³But as for me, my prayer is to you, Yahweh, in an acceptable time.
    God, in the abundance of your loving kindness, answer me in the truth of your salvation.
¹⁴Deliver me out of the mire, and don't let me sink.
    Let me be delivered from those who hate me, and out of the deep waters.

¹⁵Don't let the flood waters overwhelm me, neither let the deep swallow me up.
    Don't let the pit shut its mouth on me.
¹⁶Answer me, Yahweh, for your loving kindness is good.
    According to the multitude of your tender mercies, turn to me.
¹⁷Don't hide your face from your servant, for I am in distress.
    Answer me speedily!
¹⁸Draw near to my soul, and redeem it.
    Ransom me because of my enemies.
¹⁹You know my reproach, my shame, and my dishonor.
    My adversaries are all before you.
²⁰Reproach has broken my heart, and I am full of heaviness.
    I looked for some to take pity, but there was none;
    for comforters, but I found none.
²¹They also gave me gall for my food.
    In my thirst, they gave me vinegar to drink.
²²Let their table before them become a snare.
    May it become a retribution and a trap.
²³Let their eyes be darkened, so that they can't see.
    Let their backs be continually bent.
²⁴Pour out your indignation on them.
    Let the fierceness of your anger overtake them.
²⁵Let their habitation be desolate.
    Let no one dwell in their tents.
²⁶For they persecute him whom you have wounded.
    They tell of the sorrow of those whom you have hurt.
²⁷Charge them with crime upon crime.
    Don't let them come into your righteousness.
²⁸Let them be blotted out of the book of life, and not be written with the righteous.
²⁹But I am in pain and distress.
    Let your salvation, God, protect me.
³⁰I will praise the name of God with a song, and will magnify him with thanksgiving.
³¹It will please Yahweh better than an ox, or a bull that has horns and hoofs.
³²The humble have seen it, and are glad.

You who seek after God, let your heart live.

[33] For Yahweh hears the needy,
and doesn't despise his captive people.

[34] Let heaven and earth praise him;
the seas, and everything that moves therein!

[35] For God will save Zion, and build the cities of Judah.
They shall settle there, and own it.

[36] The children also of his servants shall inherit it.
Those who love his name shall dwell therein.

Psalm 70

For the Chief Musician. By David. A reminder.

[1] Hurry, God, to deliver me.
Come quickly to help me, Yahweh.

[2] Let them be disappointed and confounded who seek my soul.
Let those who desire my ruin be turned back in disgrace.

[3] Let them be turned because of their shame
Who say, "Aha! Aha!"

[4] Let all those who seek you rejoice and be glad in you.
Let those who love your salvation continually say,
"Let God be exalted!"

[5] But I am poor and needy.
Come to me quickly, God.
You are my help and my deliverer.
Yahweh, don't delay.

Psalm 71

[1] In you, Yahweh, I take refuge.
Never let me be disappointed.

[2] Deliver me in your righteousness, and rescue me.
Turn your ear to me, and save me.

[3] Be to me a rock of refuge to which I may always go.
Give the command to save me,
for you are my rock and my fortress.

[4] Rescue me, my God, from the hand of the wicked,
from the hand of the unrighteous and cruel man.

[5] For you are my hope, Lord Yahweh;
my confidence from my youth.

[6] I have relied on you from the womb.
You are he who took me out of my mother's womb.
I will always praise you.

[7] I am a marvel to many,
but you are my strong refuge.

[8] My mouth shall be filled with your praise,
with your honor all the day.

[9] Don't reject me in my old age.
Don't forsake me when my strength fails.

[10] For my enemies talk about me.
Those who watch for my soul conspire together,

[11] saying, "God has forsaken him.
Pursue and take him, for no one will rescue him."

[12] God, don't be far from me.
My God, hurry to help me.

[13] Let my accusers be disappointed and consumed.
Let them be covered with disgrace and scorn who want to harm me.

[14] But I will always hope,
and will add to all of your praise.

[15] My mouth will tell about your righteousness,
and of your salvation all day,
though I don't know its full measure.

[16] I will come with the mighty acts of the Lord Yahweh.
I will make mention of your righteousness, even of yours alone.

[17] God, you have taught me from my youth.
Until now, I have declared your wondrous works.

[18] Yes, even when I am old and gray-haired, God, don't forsake me,
until I have declared your strength to the next generation,
your might to everyone who is to come.

[19] Your righteousness also, God, reaches to the heavens;
you have done great things.
God, who is like you?

[20] You, who have shown us many and bitter troubles,
you will let me live.

You will bring us up again from the
depths of the earth.
²¹ Increase my honor,
and comfort me again.
²² I will also praise you with the harp for
your faithfulness, my God.
I sing praises to you with the lyre, Holy
One of Israel.
²³ My lips shall shout for joy!
My soul, which you have redeemed,
sings praises to you!
²⁴ My tongue will also talk about your
righteousness all day long,
for they are disappointed, and they are
confounded,
who want to harm me.

Psalm 72

By Solomon.

¹ God, give the king your justice;
your righteousness to the royal son.
² He will judge your people with righteousness,
and your poor with justice.
³ The mountains shall bring prosperity to
the people.
The hills bring the fruit of righteousness.
⁴ He will judge the poor of the people.
He will save the children of the needy,
and will break the oppressor in pieces.
⁵ They shall fear you while the sun endures;
and as long as the moon, throughout all
generations.
⁶ He will come down like rain on the mown
grass,
as showers that water the earth.
⁷ In his days, the righteous shall flourish,
and abundance of peace, until the
moon is no more.
⁸ He shall have dominion also from sea to
sea,
from the River to the ends of the earth.
⁹ Those who dwell in the wilderness shall
bow before him.
His enemies shall lick the dust.
¹⁰ The kings of Tarshish and of the islands
will bring tribute.
The kings of Sheba and Seba shall offer
gifts.

¹¹ Yes, all kings shall fall down before him.
All nations shall serve him.
¹² For he will deliver the needy when he
cries;
the poor, who has no helper.
¹³ He will have pity on the poor and needy.
He will save the souls of the needy.
¹⁴ He will redeem their soul from oppression and violence.
Their blood will be precious in his
sight.
¹⁵ They shall live, and to him shall be given
of the gold of Sheba.
Men shall pray for him continually.
They shall bless him all day long.
¹⁶ There shall be abundance of grain
throughout the land.
Its fruit sways like Lebanon.
Let it flourish, thriving like the grass of
the field.
¹⁷ His name endures forever.
His name continues as long as the sun.
Men shall be blessed by him.
All nations will call him blessed.
¹⁸ Praise be to Yahweh God, the God of
Israel,
who alone does marvelous deeds.
¹⁹ Blessed be his glorious name forever!
Let the whole earth be filled with his
glory!
Amen and amen.
²⁰ This ends the prayers by David, the son
of Jesse.

BOOK III

Psalm 73

A Psalm by Asaph.

¹ Surely God is good to Israel,
to those who are pure in heart.
² But as for me, my feet were almost gone.
My steps had nearly slipped.
³ For I was envious of the arrogant,
when I saw the prosperity of the
wicked.
⁴ For there are no struggles in their death,
but their strength is firm.
⁵ They are free from burdens of men,
neither are they plagued like other
men.

⁶Therefore pride is like a chain around their
 neck.
   Violence covers them like a garment.
⁷Their eyes bulge with fat.
   Their minds pass the limits of conceit.
⁸They scoff and speak with malice.
   In arrogance, they threaten oppression.
⁹They have set their mouth in the heavens.
   Their tongue walks through the earth.
¹⁰Therefore their people return to them,
   and they drink up waters of abundance.
¹¹They say, "How does God know?
   Is there knowledge in the Most High?"
¹²Behold, these are the wicked.
   Being always at ease, they increase in
   riches.
¹³Surely in vain I have cleansed my heart,
   and washed my hands in innocence,
¹⁴For all day long have I been plagued,
   and punished every morning.
¹⁵If I had said, "I will speak thus;"
   behold, I would have betrayed the
   generation of your children.
¹⁶When I tried to understand this,
   it was too painful for me;
¹⁷Until I entered God's sanctuary,
   and considered their latter end.
¹⁸Surely you set them in slippery places.
   You throw them down to destruction.
¹⁹How they are suddenly destroyed!
   They are completely swept away with
   terrors.
²⁰As a dream when one wakes up,
   so, Lord, when you awake, you will
   despise their fantasies.
²¹For my soul was grieved.
   I was embittered in my heart.
²²I was so senseless and ignorant.
   I was a brute beast before you.
²³Nevertheless, I am continually with you.
   You have held my right hand.
²⁴You will guide me with your counsel,
   and afterward receive me to glory.
²⁵Who do I have in heaven?
   There is no one on earth who I desire
   besides you.
²⁶My flesh and my heart fails,
   but God is the strength of my heart and
   my portion forever.
²⁷For, behold, those who are far from you
   shall perish.

You have destroyed all those who are
   unfaithful to you.
²⁸But it is good for me to come close to God.
   I have made the Lord Yahweh my
   refuge,
   that I may tell of all your works.

Psalm 74

A contemplation by Asaph.

¹God, why have you rejected us forever?
   Why does your anger smolder against
   the sheep of your pasture?
²Remember your congregation, which you
   purchased of old,
   which you have redeemed to be the
   tribe of your inheritance;
   Mount Zion, in which you have lived.
³Lift up your feet to the perpetual ruins,
   all the evil that the enemy has done in
   the sanctuary.
⁴Your adversaries have roared in the midst
   of your assembly.
   They have set up their standards as
   signs.
⁵They behaved like men wielding axes,
   cutting through a thicket of trees.
⁶Now they break all its carved work down
   with hatchet and hammers.
   ⁷They have burned your sanctuary to
   the ground.
   They have profaned the dwelling place
   of your Name.
⁸They said in their heart, "We will crush
   them completely."
   They have burned up all the places in
   the land where God was worshiped.
⁹We see no miraculous signs.
   There is no longer any prophet,
   neither is there among us anyone who
   knows how long.
¹⁰How long, God, shall the adversary reproach?
   Shall the enemy blaspheme your name
   forever?
¹¹Why do you draw back your hand, even
   your right hand?
   Take it out of your pocket and consume
   them!
¹²Yet God is my King of old,

working salvation in the midst of the earth.

[13] You divided the sea by your strength.

You broke the heads of the sea monsters in the waters.

[14] You broke the heads of Leviathan in pieces.

You gave him as food to people and desert creatures.

[15] You opened up spring and stream.

You dried up mighty rivers.

[16] The day is yours, the night is also yours.

You have prepared the light and the sun.

[17] You have set all the boundaries of the earth.

You have made summer and winter.

[18] Remember this, that the enemy has mocked you, Yahweh.

Foolish people have blasphemed your name.

[19] Don't deliver the soul of your dove to wild beasts.

Don't forget the life of your poor forever.

[20] Honor your covenant,

for haunts of violence fill the dark places of the earth.

[21] Don't let the oppressed return ashamed.

Let the poor and needy praise your name.

[22] Arise, God! Plead your own cause.

Remember how the foolish man mocks you all day.

[23] Don't forget the voice of your adversaries.

The tumult of those who rise up against you ascends continually.

Psalm 75

For the Chief Musician. To the tune of "Do Not Destroy." A Psalm by Asaph. A song.

[1] We give thanks to you, God.

We give thanks, for your Name is near.

Men tell about your wondrous works.

[2] When I choose the appointed time,

I will judge blamelessly.

[3] The earth and all its inhabitants quake.

I firmly hold its pillars.

Selah.

[4] I said to the arrogant, "Don't boast!"

I said to the wicked, "Don't lift up the horn.

[5] Don't lift up your horn on high.

Don't speak with a stiff neck."

[6] For neither from the east, nor from the west,

nor yet from the south, comes exaltation.

[7] But God is the judge.

He puts down one, and lifts up another.

[8] For in the hand of Yahweh there is a cup,

full of foaming wine mixed with spices.

He pours it out.

Indeed the wicked of the earth drink and drink it to its very dregs.

[9] But I will declare this forever:

I will sing praises to the God of Jacob.

[10] I will cut off all the horns of the wicked,

but the horns of the righteous shall be lifted up.

Psalm 76

For the Chief Musician. On stringed instruments. A Psalm by Asaph. A song.

[1] In Judah, God is known.

His name is great in Israel.

[2] His tent is also in Salem;

His dwelling place in Zion.

[3] There he broke the flaming arrows of the bow,

the shield, and the sword, and the weapons of war.

Selah.

[4] Glorious are you, and excellent,

more than mountains of game.

[5] Valiant men lie plundered,

they have slept their last sleep.

None of the men of war can lift their hands.

[6] At your rebuke, God of Jacob,

both chariot and horse are cast into a deep sleep.

[7] You, even you, are to be feared.

Who can stand in your sight when you are angry?

[8] You pronounced judgment from heaven.

The earth feared, and was silent,

[9] when God arose to judgment,

to save all the afflicted ones of the earth.

Selah.

¹⁰Surely the wrath of man praises you.
The survivors of your wrath are restrained.

¹¹Make vows to Yahweh your God, and fulfill them!
Let all of his neighbors bring presents to him who is to be feared.

¹²He will cut off the spirit of princes.
He is feared by the kings of the earth.

Psalm 77

For the Chief Musician. To Jeduthun. A Psalm by Asaph.

¹My cry goes to God!
Indeed, I cry to God for help,
and for him to listen to me.

²In the day of my trouble I sought the Lord.
My hand was stretched out in the night, and didn't get tired.
My soul refused to be comforted.

³I remember God, and I groan.
I complain, and my spirit is overwhelmed.

Selah.

⁴You hold my eyelids open.
I am so troubled that I can't speak.

⁵I have considered the days of old,
the years of ancient times.

⁶I remember my song in the night.
I consider in my own heart;
my spirit diligently inquires:

⁷"Will the Lord reject us forever?
Will he be favorable no more?

⁸Has his loving kindness vanished forever?
Does his promise fail for generations?

⁹Has God forgotten to be gracious?
Has he, in anger, withheld his compassion?"

Selah.

¹⁰Then I thought, "I will appeal to this:
the years of the right hand of the Most High."

¹¹I will remember Yah's deeds;
for I will remember your wonders of old.

¹²I will also meditate on all your work,
and consider your doings.

¹³Your way, God, is in the sanctuary.
What god is great like God?

¹⁴You are the God who does wonders.
You have made your strength known among the peoples.

¹⁵You have redeemed your people with your arm,
the sons of Jacob and Joseph.

Selah.

¹⁶The waters saw you, God.
The waters saw you, and they writhed.
The depths also convulsed.

¹⁷The clouds poured out water.
The skies resounded with thunder.
Your arrows also flashed around.

¹⁸The voice of your thunder was in the whirlwind.
The lightnings lit up the world.
The earth trembled and shook.

¹⁹Your way was through the sea;
your paths through the great waters.
Your footsteps were not known.

²⁰You led your people like a flock,
by the hand of Moses and Aaron.

Psalm 78

A contemplation by Asaph.

¹Hear my teaching, my people.
Turn your ears to the words of my mouth.

²I will open my mouth in a parable.
I will utter dark sayings of old,

³Which we have heard and known,
and our fathers have told us.

⁴We will not hide them from their children,
telling to the generation to come the praises of Yahweh,
his strength, and his wondrous works that he has done.

⁵For he established a testimony in Jacob,
and appointed a teaching in Israel,
which he commanded our fathers,
that they should make them known to their children;

⁶that the generation to come might know,
even the children who should be born;
who should arise and tell their children,

⁷that they might set their hope in God,

and not forget the works of God,
but keep his commandments,
⁸ and might not be as their fathers,
a stubborn and rebellious generation,
a generation that didn't make their
hearts loyal,
whose spirit was not steadfast with
God.
⁹ The children of Ephraim, being armed and
carrying bows,
turned back in the day of battle.
¹⁰ They didn't keep God's covenant,
and refused to walk in his law.
¹¹ They forgot his doings,
his wondrous works that he had shown
them.
¹² He did marvelous things in the sight of
their fathers,
in the land of Egypt, in the field of
Zoan.
¹³ He split the sea, and caused them to pass
through.
He made the waters stand as a heap.
¹⁴ In the daytime he also led them with a
cloud,
and all night with a light of fire.
¹⁵ He split rocks in the wilderness,
and gave them drink abundantly as out
of the depths.
¹⁶ He brought streams also out of the rock,
and caused waters to run down like
rivers.
¹⁷ Yet they still went on to sin against him,
to rebel against the Most High in the
desert.
¹⁸ They tempted God in their heart
by asking food according to their desire.
¹⁹ Yes, they spoke against God.
They said, "Can God prepare a table in
the wilderness?
²⁰ Behold, he struck the rock, so that waters
gushed out,
and streams overflowed.
Can he give bread also?
Will he provide flesh for his people?"
²¹ Therefore Yahweh heard, and was angry.
A fire was kindled against Jacob,
anger also went up against Israel,
²² because they didn't believe in God,
and didn't trust in his salvation.
²³ Yet he commanded the skies above,

and opened the doors of heaven.
²⁴ He rained down manna on them to eat,
and gave them food from the sky.
²⁵ Man ate the bread of angels.
He sent them food to the full.
²⁶ He caused the east wind to blow in the
sky.
By his power he guided the south
wind.
²⁷ He rained also flesh on them as the dust;
winged birds as the sand of the seas.
²⁸ He let them fall in the midst of their camp,
around their habitations.
²⁹ So they ate, and were well filled.
He gave them their own desire.
³⁰ They didn't turn from their cravings.
Their food was yet in their mouths,
³¹ when the anger of God went up
against them,
killed some of the fattest of them,
and struck down the young men of
Israel.
³² For all this they still sinned,
and didn't believe in his wondrous
works.
³³ Therefore he consumed their days in van-
ity,
and their years in terror.
³⁴ When he killed them, then they inquired
after him.
They returned and sought God
earnestly.
³⁵ They remembered that God was their
rock,
the Most High God, their redeemer.
³⁶ But they flattered him with their mouth,
and lied to him with their tongue.
³⁷ For their heart was not right with him,
neither were they faithful in his
covenant.
³⁸ But he, being merciful, forgave iniquity,
and didn't destroy them.
Yes, many times he turned his anger
away,
and didn't stir up all his wrath.
³⁹ He remembered that they were but flesh,
a wind that passes away, and doesn't
come again.
⁴⁰ How often they rebelled against him in
the wilderness,
and grieved him in the desert!
⁴¹ They turned again and tempted God,

and provoked the Holy One of Israel.

[42] They didn't remember his hand,
> nor the day when he redeemed them
> from the adversary;

[43] how he set his signs in Egypt,
> his wonders in the field of Zoan,

[44] he turned their rivers into blood,
> and their streams, so that they could
> not drink.

[45] He sent among them swarms of flies,
> which devoured them;
> and frogs, which destroyed them.

[46] He gave also their increase to the caterpillar,
> and their labor to the locust.

[47] He destroyed their vines with hail,
> their sycamore fig trees with frost.

[48] He gave over their livestock also to the hail,
> and their flocks to hot thunderbolts.

[49] He threw on them the fierceness of his anger,
> wrath, indignation, and trouble,
> and a band of angels of evil.

[50] He made a path for his anger.
> He didn't spare their soul from death,
> but gave their life over to the pestilence,

[51] and struck all the firstborn in Egypt,
> the chief of their strength in the tents of Ham.

[52] But he led forth his own people like sheep,
> and guided them in the wilderness like a flock.

[53] He led them safely, so that they weren't afraid,
> but the sea overwhelmed their enemies.

[54] He brought them to the border of his sanctuary,
> to this mountain, which his right hand had taken.

[55] He also drove out the nations before them,
> allotted them for an inheritance by line,
> and made the tribes of Israel to dwell in their tents.

[56] Yet they tempted and rebelled against the Most High God,
> and didn't keep his testimonies;

[57] but turned back, and dealt treacherously like their fathers.
> They were turned aside like a deceitful bow.

[58] For they provoked him to anger with their high places,
> and moved him to jealousy with their engraved images.

[59] When God heard this, he was angry,
> and greatly abhorred Israel;

[60] So that he forsook the tent of Shiloh,
> the tent which he placed among men;

[61] and delivered his strength into captivity,
> his glory into the adversary's hand.

[62] He also gave his people over to the sword,
> and was angry with his inheritance.

[63] Fire devoured their young men.
> Their virgins had no wedding song.

[64] Their priests fell by the sword,
> and their widows couldn't weep.

[65] Then the Lord awakened as one out of sleep,
> like a mighty man who shouts by reason of wine.

[66] He struck his adversaries backward.
> He put them to a perpetual reproach.

[67] Moreover he rejected the tent of Joseph,
> and didn't choose the tribe of Ephraim,

[68] But chose the tribe of Judah,
> Mount Zion which he loved.

[69] He built his sanctuary like the heights,
> like the earth which he has established forever.

[70] He also chose David his servant,
> and took him from the sheepfolds;

[71] from following the ewes that have their young,
> he brought him to be the shepherd of Jacob, his people,
> and Israel, his inheritance.

[72] So he was their shepherd according to the integrity of his heart,
> and guided them by the skillfulness of his hands.

Psalm 79

A Psalm by Asaph.

[1] God, the nations have come into your inheritance.
> They have defiled your holy temple.

They have laid Jerusalem in heaps.

[2] They have given the dead bodies of your servants to be food for the birds of the sky,

the flesh of your saints to the animals of the earth.

[3] Their blood they have shed like water around Jerusalem.

There was no one to bury them.

[4] We have become a reproach to our neighbors,

a scoffing and derision to those who are around us.

[5] How long, Yahweh?

Will you be angry forever?

Will your jealousy burn like fire?

[6] Pour out your wrath on the nations that don't know you;

on the kingdoms that don't call on your name;

[7] For they have devoured Jacob,

and destroyed his homeland.

[8] Don't hold the iniquities of our forefathers against us.

Let your tender mercies speedily meet us,

for we are in desperate need.

[9] Help us, God of our salvation, for the glory of your name.

Deliver us, and forgive our sins, for your name's sake.

[10] Why should the nations say, "Where is their God?"

Let it be known among the nations, before our eyes,

that vengeance for your servants' blood is being poured out.

[11] Let the sighing of the prisoner come before you.

According to the greatness of your power, preserve those who are sentenced to death.

[12] Pay back to our neighbors seven times into their bosom

their reproach with which they have reproached you, Lord.

[13] So we, your people and sheep of your pasture,

will give you thanks forever.

We will praise you forever, to all generations.

Psalm 80

For the Chief Musician. To the tune of "The Lilies of the Covenant." A Psalm by Asaph.

[1] Hear us, Shepherd of Israel,

you who lead Joseph like a flock,

you who sit above the cherubim, shine forth.

[2] Before Ephraim and Benjamin and Manasseh, stir up your might!

Come to save us!

[3] Turn us again, God.

Cause your face to shine,

and we will be saved.

[4] Yahweh God of Armies,

How long will you be angry against the prayer of your people?

[5] You have fed them with the bread of tears,

and given them tears to drink in large measure.

[6] You make us a source of contention to our neighbors.

Our enemies laugh among themselves.

[7] Turn us again, God of Armies.

Cause your face to shine,

and we will be saved.

[8] You brought a vine out of Egypt.

You drove out the nations, and planted it.

[9] You cleared the ground for it.

It took deep root, and filled the land.

[10] The mountains were covered with its shadow.

Its boughs were like God's cedars.

[11] It sent out its branches to the sea,

Its shoots to the River.

[12] Why have you broken down its walls,

so that all those who pass by the way pluck it?

[13] The boar out of the wood ravages it.

The wild animals of the field feed on it.

[14] Turn again, we beg you, God of Armies.

Look down from heaven, and see, and visit this vine,

[15] the stock which your right hand planted,

the branch that you made strong for yourself.

[16] It's burned with fire.

It's cut down.

They perish at your rebuke.

¹⁷Let your hand be on the man of your right
hand,
on the son of man whom you made
strong for yourself.
¹⁸So we will not turn away from you.
Revive us, and we will call on your
name.
¹⁹Turn us again, Yahweh God of Armies.
Cause your face to shine, and we will
be saved.

Psalm 81

For the Chief Musician. On an instrument of Gath. By Asaph.

¹Sing aloud to God, our strength!
Make a joyful shout to the God of
Jacob!
²Raise a song, and bring here the tambourine,
the pleasant lyre with the harp.
³Blow the trumpet at the New Moon,
at the full moon, on our feast day.
⁴For it is a statute for Israel,
an ordinance of the God of Jacob.
⁵He appointed it in Joseph for a testimony,
when he went out over the land of
Egypt,
I heard a language that I didn't know.
⁶"I removed his shoulder from the burden.
His hands were freed from the basket.
⁷You called in trouble, and I delivered you.
I answered you in the secret place of
thunder.
I tested you at the waters of Meribah."
Selah.
⁸"Hear, my people, and I will testify to you,
Israel, if you would listen to me!
⁹There shall be no strange god in you,
neither shall you worship any foreign
god.
¹⁰I am Yahweh, your God,
who brought you up out of the land of
Egypt.
Open your mouth wide, and I will fill
it.
¹¹But my people didn't listen to my voice.
Israel desired none of me.
¹²So I let them go after the stubbornness of
their hearts,
that they might walk in their own
counsels.

¹³Oh that my people would listen to me,
that Israel would walk in my ways!
¹⁴I would soon subdue their enemies,
and turn my hand against their adversaries.
¹⁵The haters of Yahweh would cringe before him,
and their punishment would last forever.
¹⁶But he would have also fed them with the
finest of the wheat.
I will satisfy you with honey out of the
rock."

Psalm 82

A Psalm by Asaph.

¹God presides in the great assembly.
He judges among the gods.
²"How long will you judge unjustly,
and show partiality to the wicked?"
Selah.
³"Defend the weak, the poor, and the fatherless.
Maintain the rights of the poor and
oppressed.
⁴Rescue the weak and needy.
Deliver them out of the hand of the
wicked."
⁵They don't know, neither do they understand.
They walk back and forth in darkness.
All the foundations of the earth are
shaken.
⁶I said, "You are gods,
all of you are sons of the Most High.
⁷Nevertheless you shall die like men,
and fall like one of the rulers."
⁸Arise, God, judge the earth,
for you inherit all of the nations.

Psalm 83

A song. A Psalm by Asaph.

¹God, don't keep silent.
Don't keep silent,
and don't be still, God.
²For, behold, your enemies are stirred up.

Those who hate you have lifted up
their heads.
[3]They conspire with cunning against your
people.
They plot against your cherished ones.
[4]"Come," they say, "and let's destroy them
as a nation,
that the name of Israel may be remembered no more."
[5]For they have conspired together with one
mind.
They form an alliance against you.
[6]The tents of Edom and the Ishmaelites;
Moab, and the Hagrites;
[7]Gebal, Ammon, and Amalek;
Philistia with the inhabitants of Tyre;
[8]Assyria also is joined with them.
They have helped the children of Lot.
Selah.
[9]Do to them as you did to Midian,
as to Sisera, as to Jabin, at the river
Kishon;
[10]who perished at Endor,
who became as dung for the earth.
[11]Make their nobles like Oreb and Zeeb;
yes, all their princes like Zebah and
Zalmunna;
[12]who said, "Let us take possession of
God's pasturelands."
[13]My God, make them like tumbleweed;
like chaff before the wind.
[14]As the fire that burns the forest,
as the flame that sets the mountains on
fire,
[15]so pursue them with your tempest,
and terrify them with your storm.
[16]Fill their faces with confusion,
that they may seek your name, Yahweh.
[17]Let them be disappointed and dismayed
forever.
Yes, let them be confounded and perish;
[18]that they may know that you alone,
whose name is Yahweh,
are the Most High over all the earth.

Psalm 84

For the Chief Musician. On an instrument of Gath. A Psalm by the sons of
Korah.

[1]How lovely are your dwellings,
Yahweh of Armies!
[2]My soul longs, and even faints for the
courts of Yahweh.
My heart and my flesh cry out for the
living God.
[3]Yes, the sparrow has found a home,
and the swallow a nest for herself,
where she may have her young,
near your altars, Yahweh of Armies,
my King, and my God.
[4]Blessed are those who dwell in your
house.
They are always praising you.
Selah.
[5]Blessed are those whose strength is in you;
who have set their hearts on a pilgrim-
age.
[6]Passing through the valley of Weeping,
they make it a place of springs.
Yes, the autumn rain covers it with
blessings.
[7]They go from strength to strength.
Everyone of them appears before God
in Zion.
[8]Yahweh, God of Armies, hear my prayer.
Listen, God of Jacob.
Selah.
[9]Behold, God our shield,
look at the face of your anointed.
[10]For a day in your courts is better than a
thousand.
I would rather be a doorkeeper in the
house of my God,
than to dwell in the tents of wickedness.
[11]For Yahweh God is a sun and a shield.
Yahweh will give grace and glory.
He withholds no good thing from those
who walk blamelessly.
[12]Yahweh of Armies,
blessed is the man who trusts in you.

Psalm 85

For the Chief Musician. A Psalm by the
sons of Korah.

[1]Yahweh, you have been favorable to your
land.
You have restored the fortunes of Jacob.

[2]You have forgiven the iniquity of your
people.
You have covered all their sin.
Selah.
[3]You have taken away all your wrath.
You have turned from the fierceness of
your anger.
[4]Turn us, God of our salvation,
and cause your indignation toward us
to cease.
[5]Will you be angry with us forever?
Will you draw out your anger to all
generations?
[6]Won't you revive us again,
that your people may rejoice in you?
[7]Show us your loving kindness, Yahweh.
Grant us your salvation.
[8]I will hear what God, Yahweh, will speak,
for he will speak peace to his people,
his saints;
but let them not turn again to folly.
[9]Surely his salvation is near those who fear
him,
that glory may dwell in our land.
[10]Mercy and truth meet together.
Righteousness and peace have kissed
each other.
[11]Truth springs out of the earth.
Righteousness has looked down from
heaven.
[12]Yes, Yahweh will give that which is good.
Our land will yield its increase.
[13]Righteousness goes before him,
And prepares the way for his steps.

Psalm 86

A Prayer by David.

[1]Hear, Yahweh, and answer me,
for I am poor and needy.
[2]Preserve my soul, for I am godly.
You, my God, save your servant who
trusts in you.
[3]Be merciful to me, Lord,
for I call to you all day long.
[4]Bring joy to the soul of your servant,
for to you, Lord, do I lift up my soul.
[5]For you, Lord, are good, and ready to
forgive;
abundant in loving kindness to all
those who call on you.

[6]Hear, Yahweh, my prayer.
Listen to the voice of my petitions.
[7]In the day of my trouble I will call on you,
for you will answer me.
[8]There is no one like you among the gods,
Lord,
nor any deeds like your deeds.
[9]All nations you have made will come and
worship before you, Lord.
They shall glorify your name.
[10]For you are great, and do wondrous
things.
You are God alone.
[11]Teach me your way, Yahweh.
I will walk in your truth.
Make my heart undivided to fear your
name.
[12]I will praise you, Lord my God, with my
whole heart.
I will glorify your name forevermore.
[13]For your loving kindness is great toward
me.
You have delivered my soul from the
lowest Sheol.
[14]God, the proud have risen up against me.
A company of violent men have sought
after my soul,
and they don't hold regard for you
before them.
[15]But you, Lord, are a merciful and gracious God,
slow to anger, and abundant in loving
kindness and truth.
[16]Turn to me, and have mercy on me!
Give your strength to your servant.
Save the son of your handmaid.
[17]Show me a sign of your goodness,
that those who hate me may see it, and
be shamed,
because you, Yahweh, have helped me,
and comforted me.

Psalm 87

A Psalm by the sons of Korah; a Song.

[1]His foundation is in the holy mountains.
[2]Yahweh loves the gates of Zion more
than all the dwellings of Jacob.
[3]Glorious things are spoken about you, city
of God.
Selah.

⁴I will record Rahab[g] and Babylon among
those who acknowledge me.
  Behold, Philistia, Tyre, and also
  Ethiopia:
  "This one was born there."
⁵Yes, of Zion it will be said, "This one and
that one was born in her;"
  the Most High himself will establish
  her.
⁶Yahweh will count, when he writes up the
peoples,
  "This one was born there."
Selah.
⁷Those who sing as well as those who
dance say,
  "All my springs are in you."

Psalm 88

A Song. A Psalm by the sons of Korah.
For the Chief Musician. To the tune of "The
Suffering of Affliction." A contemplation
by Heman, the Ezrahite.

¹Yahweh, the God of my salvation,
  I have cried day and night before you.
²Let my prayer enter into your presence.
  Turn your ear to my cry.
³For my soul is full of troubles.
  My life draws near to Sheol.
⁴I am counted among those who go down
into the pit.
  I am like a man who has no help,
  ⁵set apart among the dead,
  like the slain who lie in the grave,
  whom you remember no more.
  They are cut off from your hand.
⁶You have laid me in the lowest pit,
  in the darkest depths.
⁷Your wrath lies heavily on me.
  You have afflicted me with all your
  waves.
Selah.
⁸You have taken my friends from me.
  You have made me an abomination to
  them.
  I am confined, and I can't escape.
⁹My eyes are dim from grief.
  I have called on you daily, Yahweh.
  I have spread out my hands to you.
¹⁰Do you show wonders to the dead?

Do the dead rise up and praise you?
Selah.
¹¹Is your loving kindness declared in the
grave?
  Or your faithfulness in Destruction?
¹²Are your wonders made known in the
dark?
  Or your righteousness in the land of
  forgetfulness?
¹³But to you, Yahweh, I have cried.
  In the morning, my prayer comes before you.
¹⁴Yahweh, why do you reject my soul?
  Why do you hide your face from me?
¹⁵I am afflicted and ready to die from my
youth up.
  While I suffer your terrors, I am distracted.
¹⁶Your fierce wrath has gone over me.
  Your terrors have cut me off.
¹⁷They came around me like water all day
long.
  They completely engulfed me.
¹⁸You have put lover and friend far from
me,
  and my friends into darkness.

Psalm 89

A contemplation by Ethan, the Ezrahite.

¹I will sing of the loving kindness of Yahweh forever.
  With my mouth, I will make known
  your faithfulness to all generations.
²I indeed declare, "Love stands firm forever.
  You established the heavens.
  Your faithfulness is in them."
³"I have made a covenant with my chosen
one,
  I have sworn to David, my servant,
⁴'I will establish your seed forever,
  and build up your throne to all generations.'"
Selah.
⁵The heavens will praise your wonders,
Yahweh;
  your faithfulness also in the assembly
  of the holy ones.

---

[g]87:4 Rahab is a reference to Egypt.

⁶For who in the skies can be compared to Yahweh?

Who among the sons of the heavenly beings is like Yahweh,

⁷a very awesome God in the council of the holy ones,

to be feared above all those who are around him?

⁸Yahweh, God of Armies, who is a mighty one, like you?

Yah, your faithfulness is around you.

⁹You rule the pride of the sea.

When its waves rise up, you calm them.

¹⁰You have broken Rahab in pieces, like one of the slain.

You have scattered your enemies with your mighty arm.

¹¹The heavens are yours.

The earth also is yours;

the world and its fullness.

You have founded them.

¹²The north and the south, you have created them.

Tabor and Hermon rejoice in your name.

¹³You have a mighty arm.

Your hand is strong, and your right hand is exalted.

¹⁴Righteousness and justice are the foundation of your throne.

Loving kindness and truth go before your face.

¹⁵Blessed are the people who learn to acclaim you.

They walk in the light of your presence, Yahweh.

¹⁶In your name they rejoice all day.

In your righteousness, they are exalted.

¹⁷For you are the glory of their strength.

In your favor, our horn will be exalted.

¹⁸For our shield belongs to Yahweh;

our king to the Holy One of Israel.

¹⁹Then you spoke in vision to your saints, and said, "I have bestowed strength on the warrior.

I have exalted a young man from the people.

²⁰I have found David, my servant.

I have anointed him with my holy oil,

²¹with whom my hand shall be established.

My arm will also strengthen him.

²²No enemy will tax him.

No wicked man will oppress him.

²³I will beat down his adversaries before him,

and strike those who hate him.

²⁴But my faithfulness and my loving kindness will be with him.

In my name, his horn will be exalted.

²⁵I will set his hand also on the sea,

and his right hand on the rivers.

²⁶He will call to me, 'You are my Father,

my God, and the rock of my salvation!'

²⁷I will also appoint him my firstborn,

the highest of the kings of the earth.

²⁸I will keep my loving kindness for him forevermore.

My covenant will stand firm with him.

²⁹I will also make his seed endure forever,

and his throne as the days of heaven.

³⁰If his children forsake my law,

and don't walk in my ordinances;

³¹if they break my statutes,

and don't keep my commandments;

³²then I will punish their sin with the rod,

and their iniquity with stripes.

³³But I will not completely take my loving kindness from him,

nor allow my faithfulness to fail.

³⁴I will not break my covenant,

nor alter what my lips have uttered.

³⁵Once have I sworn by my holiness,

I will not lie to David.

³⁶His seed will endure forever,

his throne like the sun before me.

³⁷It will be established forever like the moon,

the faithful witness in the sky."

Selah.

³⁸But you have rejected and spurned.

You have been angry with your anointed.

³⁹You have renounced the covenant of your servant.

You have defiled his crown in the dust.

⁴⁰You have broken down all his hedges.

You have brought his strongholds to ruin.

⁴¹All who pass by the way rob him.

He has become a reproach to his neighbors.

⁴²You have exalted the right hand of his adversaries.

You have made all of his enemies rejoice.

43 Yes, you turn back the edge of his sword,
   and haven't supported him in battle.
44 You have ended his splendor,
   and thrown his throne down to the
   ground.
45 You have shortened the days of his youth.
   You have covered him with shame.
Selah.
46 How long, Yahweh?
   Will you hide yourself forever?
   Will your wrath burn like fire?
47 Remember how short my time is!
   For what vanity have you created all
   the children of men!
48 What man is he who shall live and not see
   death,
   who shall deliver his soul from the
   power of Sheol?
Selah.
49 Lord, where are your former loving kindnesses,
   which you swore to David in your
   faithfulness?
50 Remember, Lord, the reproach of your
   servants,
   how I bear in my heart the taunts of all
   the mighty peoples,
51 With which your enemies have mocked,
   Yahweh,
   with which they have mocked the footsteps of your anointed one.
52 Blessed be Yahweh forevermore.
Amen, and Amen.

BOOK IV

Psalm 90

A Prayer by Moses, the man of God.

1 Lord, you have been our dwelling place
   for all generations.
   2 Before the mountains were brought
   forth,
   before you had formed the earth and
   the world,
   even from everlasting to everlasting,
   you are God.
3 You turn man to destruction, saying,
   "Return, you children of men."
4 For a thousand years in your sight are just
   like yesterday when it is past,

like a watch in the night.
5 You sweep them away as they sleep.
   In the morning they sprout like new
   grass.
6 In the morning it sprouts and springs up.
   By evening, it is withered and dry.
7 For we are consumed in your anger.
   We are troubled in your wrath.
8 You have set our iniquities before you,
   our secret sins in the light of your
   presence.
9 For all our days have passed away in your
   wrath.
   We bring our years to an end as a sigh.
10 The days of our years are seventy,
   or even by reason of strength eighty
   years;
   yet their pride is but labor and sorrow,
   for it passes quickly, and we fly away.
11 Who knows the power of your anger,
   your wrath according to the fear that is
   due to you?
12 So teach us to number our days,
   that we may gain a heart of wisdom.
13 Relent, Yahweh!
   How long?
   Have compassion on your servants!
14 Satisfy us in the morning with your loving kindness,
   that we may rejoice and be glad all our
   days.
15 Make us glad for as many days as you
   have afflicted us,
   for as many years as we have seen evil.
16 Let your work appear to your servants;
   your glory to their children.
17 Let the favor of the Lord our God be on
   us;
   establish the work of our hands for us;
   yes, establish the work of our hands.

Psalm 91

1 He who dwells in the secret place of the
   Most High
   will rest in the shadow of the Almighty.
2 I will say of Yahweh, "He is my refuge and
   my fortress;
   my God, in whom I trust."
3 For he will deliver you from the snare of
   the fowler,

and from the deadly pestilence.
⁴He will cover you with his feathers.
Under his wings you will take refuge.
His faithfulness is your shield and rampart.
⁵You shall not be afraid of the terror by night,
nor of the arrow that flies by day;
⁶nor of the pestilence that walks in darkness,
nor of the destruction that wastes at noonday.
⁷A thousand may fall at your side,
and ten thousand at your right hand;
but it will not come near you.
⁸You will only look with your eyes,
and see the recompense of the wicked.
⁹Because you have made Yahweh your refuge,
and the Most High your dwelling place,
¹⁰no evil shall happen to you,
neither shall any plague come near your dwelling.
¹¹For he will put his angels in charge of you,
to guard you in all your ways.
¹²They will bear you up in their hands,
so that you won't dash your foot against a stone.
¹³You will tread on the lion and cobra.
You will trample the young lion and the serpent underfoot.
¹⁴"Because he has set his love on me, therefore I will deliver him.
I will set him on high, because he has known my name.
¹⁵He will call on me, and I will answer him.
I will be with him in trouble.
I will deliver him, and honor him.
¹⁶I will satisfy him with long life,
and show him my salvation."

Psalm 92

A Psalm. A song for the Sabbath day.

¹It is a good thing to give thanks to Yahweh,
to sing praises to your name, Most High;
²to proclaim your loving kindness in the morning,

and your faithfulness every night,
³with the ten-stringed lute, with the harp,
and with the melody of the lyre.
⁴For you, Yahweh, have made me glad through your work.
I will triumph in the works of your hands.
⁵How great are your works, Yahweh!
Your thoughts are very deep.
⁶A senseless man doesn't know,
neither does a fool understand this:
⁷though the wicked spring up as the grass,
and all the evil-doers flourish,
they will be destroyed forever.
⁸But you, Yahweh, are on high forevermore.
⁹For, behold, your enemies, Yahweh,
for, behold, your enemies shall perish.
All the evil-doers will be scattered.
¹⁰But you have exalted my horn like that of the wild ox.
I am anointed with fresh oil.
¹¹My eye has also seen my enemies.
My ears have heard of the wicked enemies who rise up against me.
¹²The righteous shall flourish like the palm tree.
He will grow like a cedar in Lebanon.
¹³They are planted in Yahweh's house.
They will flourish in our God's courts.
¹⁴They will still bring forth fruit in old age.
They will be full of sap and green,
¹⁵to show that Yahweh is upright.
He is my rock,
and there is no unrighteousness in him.

Psalm 93

¹Yahweh reigns!
He is clothed with majesty!
Yahweh is armed with strength.
The world also is established.
It can't be moved.
²Your throne is established from long ago.
You are from everlasting.
³The floods have lifted up, Yahweh,
the floods have lifted up their voice.
The floods lift up their waves.
⁴Above the voices of many waters,
the mighty breakers of the sea,
Yahweh on high is mighty.
⁵Your statutes stand firm.

Holiness adorns your house,
Yahweh, forevermore.

Psalm 94

¹Yahweh, you God to whom vengeance
belongs,
you God to whom vengeance belongs,
shine forth.
²Rise up, you judge of the earth.
Pay back the proud what they deserve.
³Yahweh, how long will the wicked,
how long will the wicked triumph?
⁴They pour out arrogant words.
All the evil-doers boast.
⁵They break your people in pieces, Yahweh,
and afflict your heritage.
⁶They kill the widow and the alien,
and murder the fatherless.
⁷They say, "Yah will not see,
neither will Jacob's God consider."
⁸Consider, you senseless among the people;
you fools, when will you be wise?
⁹He who implanted the ear, won't he hear?
He who formed the eye, won't he see?
¹⁰He who disciplines the nations, won't he
punish?
He who teaches man knows.
¹¹Yahweh knows the thoughts of man,
that they are futile.
¹²Blessed is the man whom you discipline,
Yah,
and teach out of your law;
¹³that you may give him rest from the days
of adversity,
until the pit is dug for the wicked.
¹⁴For Yahweh won't reject his people,
neither will he forsake his inheritance.
¹⁵For judgment will return to righteousness.
All the upright in heart shall follow it.
¹⁶Who will rise up for me against the
wicked?
Who will stand up for me against the
evil-doers?
¹⁷Unless Yahweh had been my help,
my soul would have soon lived in
silence.
¹⁸When I said, "My foot is slipping!"
Your loving kindness, Yahweh, held
me up.

¹⁹In the multitude of my thoughts within
me,
your comforts delight my soul.
²⁰Shall the throne of wickedness have fellowship with you,
which brings about mischief by
statute?
²¹They gather themselves together against
the soul of the righteous,
and condemn the innocent blood.
²²But Yahweh has been my high tower,
my God, the rock of my refuge.
²³He has brought on them their own iniquity,
and will cut them off in their own
wickedness.
Yahweh, our God, will cut them off.

Psalm 95

¹Oh come, let's sing to Yahweh.
Let's shout aloud to the rock of our
salvation!
²Let's come before his presence with
thanksgiving.
Let's extol him with songs!
³For Yahweh is a great God,
a great King above all gods.
⁴In his hand are the deep places of the earth.
The heights of the mountains are also
his.
⁵The sea is his, and he made it.
His hands formed the dry land.
⁶Oh come, let's worship and bow down.
Let's kneel before Yahweh, our Maker,
⁷for he is our God.
We are the people of his pasture,
and the sheep in his care.
Today, oh that you would hear his voice!
⁸Don't harden your heart, as at
Meribah,
as in the day of Massah in the wilderness,
⁹when your fathers tempted me,
tested me, and saw my work.
¹⁰Forty long years I was grieved with that
generation,
and said, "It is a people that errs in
their heart.
They have not known my ways."
¹¹Therefore I swore in my wrath,
"They won't enter into my rest."

Psalm 96

¹Sing to Yahweh a new song!
Sing to Yahweh, all the earth.
²Sing to Yahweh!
Bless his name!
Proclaim his salvation from day to day!
³Declare his glory among the nations,
his marvelous works among all the
peoples.
⁴For great is Yahweh, and greatly to be
praised!
He is to be feared above all gods.
⁵For all the gods of the peoples are idols,
but Yahweh made the heavens.
⁶Honor and majesty are before him.
Strength and beauty are in his sanctuary.
⁷Ascribe to Yahweh, you families of nations,
ascribe to Yahweh glory and strength.
⁸Ascribe to Yahweh the glory due to his
name.
Bring an offering, and come into his
courts.
⁹Worship Yahweh in holy array.
Tremble before him, all the earth.
¹⁰Say among the nations, "Yahweh reigns."
The world is also established.
It can't be moved.
He will judge the peoples with equity.
¹¹Let the heavens be glad, and let the earth
rejoice.
Let the sea roar, and its fullness!
¹²Let the field and all that is in it exult!
Then all the trees of the woods shall
sing for joy
¹³before Yahweh; for he comes,
for he comes to judge the earth.
He will judge the world with righteousness,
the peoples with his truth.

Psalm 97

¹Yahweh reigns!
Let the earth rejoice!
Let the multitude of islands be glad!
²Clouds and darkness are around him.
Righteousness and justice are the foundation of his throne.
³A fire goes before him,
and burns up his adversaries on every
side.

⁴His lightning lights up the world.
The earth sees, and trembles.
⁵The mountains melt like wax at the presence of Yahweh,
at the presence of the Lord of the whole
earth.
⁶The heavens declare his righteousness.
All the peoples have seen his glory.
⁷Let all them be shamed who serve engraved images,
who boast in their idols.
Worship him, all you gods!
⁸Zion heard and was glad.
The daughters of Judah rejoiced,
because of your judgments, Yahweh.
⁹For you, Yahweh, are most high above all
the earth.
You are exalted far above all gods.
¹⁰You who love Yahweh, hate evil.
He preserves the souls of his saints.
He delivers them out of the hand of the
wicked.
¹¹Light is sown for the righteous,
and gladness for the upright in heart.
¹²Be glad in Yahweh, you righteous people!
Give thanks to his holy Name.

Psalm 98

A Psalm.

¹Sing to Yahweh a new song,
for he has done marvelous things!
His right hand, and his holy arm, have
worked salvation for him.
²Yahweh has made known his salvation.
He has openly shown his righteousness
in the sight of the nations.
³He has remembered his loving kindness and his faithfulness toward the
house of Israel.
All the ends of the earth have seen the
salvation of our God.
⁴Make a joyful noise to Yahweh, all the
earth!
Burst out and sing for joy, yes, sing
praises!
⁵Sing praises to Yahweh with the harp,
with the harp and the voice of melody.
⁶With trumpets and sound of the ram's
horn,

make a joyful noise before the King,
Yahweh.
⁷Let the sea roar with its fullness;
the world, and those who dwell
therein.
⁸Let the rivers clap their hands.
Let the mountains sing for joy together.
⁹Let them sing before Yahweh,
for he comes to judge the earth.
He will judge the world with righteousness,
and the peoples with equity.

Psalm 99

¹Yahweh reigns! Let the peoples tremble.
He sits enthroned among the cherubim.
Let the earth be moved.
²Yahweh is great in Zion.
He is high above all the peoples.
³Let them praise your great and awesome
name.
He is Holy!
⁴The King's strength also loves justice.
You do establish equity.
You execute justice and righteousness
in Jacob.
⁵Exalt Yahweh our God.
Worship at his footstool.
He is Holy!
⁶Moses and Aaron were among his priests,
Samuel among those who call on his
name;
they called on Yahweh, and he answered them.
⁷He spoke to them in the pillar of cloud.
They kept his testimonies,
the statute that he gave them.
⁸You answered them, Yahweh our God.
You are a God who forgave them,
although you took vengeance for their
doings.
⁹Exalt Yahweh, our God.
Worship at his holy hill,
for Yahweh, our God, is holy!

Psalm 100

A Psalm of thanksgiving.

¹Shout for joy to Yahweh, all you lands!
²Serve Yahweh with gladness.
Come before his presence with singing.

³Know that Yahweh, he is God.
It is he who has made us, and we are
his.
We are his people, and the sheep of his
pasture.
⁴Enter into his gates with thanksgiving,
into his courts with praise.
Give thanks to him, and bless his name.
⁵For Yahweh is good.
His loving kindness endures forever,
his faithfulness to all generations.

Psalm 101

A Psalm by David.

¹I will sing of loving kindness and justice.
To you, Yahweh, I will sing praises.
²I will be careful to live a blameless life.
When will you come to me?
I will walk within my house with a
blameless heart.
³I will set no vile thing before my eyes.
I hate the deeds of faithless men.
They will not cling to me.
⁴A perverse heart will be far from me.
I will have nothing to do with evil.
⁵I will silence whoever secretly slanders his
neighbor.
I won't tolerate one who is haughty
and conceited.
⁶My eyes will be on the faithful of the land,
that they may dwell with me.
He who walks in a perfect way,
he will serve me.
⁷He who practices deceit won't dwell
within my house.
He who speaks falsehood won't be
established before my eyes.
⁸Morning by morning, I will destroy all the
wicked of the land;
to cut off all the workers of iniquity
from Yahweh's city.

Psalm 102

A Prayer of the afflicted, when he is
overwhelmed and pours out his complaint
before Yahweh.

¹Hear my prayer, Yahweh!
Let my cry come to you.

²Don't hide your face from me in the day of
my distress.
 Turn your ear to me.
 Answer me quickly in the day when I
call.
³For my days consume away like smoke.
 My bones are burned as a firebrand.
⁴My heart is blighted like grass, and with-
ered,
 for I forget to eat my bread.
⁵By reason of the voice of my groaning,
 my bones stick to my skin.
⁶I am like a pelican of the wilderness.
 I have become as an owl of the waste
places.
 ⁷I watch, and have become like a sparrow that is alone on the housetop.
⁸My enemies reproach me all day.
 Those who are mad at me use my name
as a curse.
⁹For I have eaten ashes like bread,
 and mixed my drink with tears,
¹⁰Because of your indignation and your
wrath,
 for you have taken me up, and thrown
me away.
¹¹My days are like a long shadow.
 I have withered like grass.
¹²But you, Yahweh, will abide forever;
 your renown endures to all genera-
tions.
¹³You will arise and have mercy on Zion;
 for it is time to have pity on her.
 Yes, the set time has come.
¹⁴For your servants take pleasure in her
stones,
 and have pity on her dust.
¹⁵So the nations will fear the name of
Yahweh;
 all the kings of the earth your glory.
¹⁶For Yahweh has built up Zion.
 He has appeared in his glory.
¹⁷He has responded to the prayer of the
destitute,
 and has not despised their prayer.
¹⁸This will be written for the generation to
come.
 A people which will be created will
praise Yah.
¹⁹For he has looked down from the height
of his sanctuary.
 From heaven, Yahweh saw the earth;

²⁰to hear the groans of the prisoner;
 to free those who are condemned to
death;
²¹that men may declare the name of Yah-
weh in Zion,
 and his praise in Jerusalem;
²²when the peoples are gathered together,
 the kingdoms, to serve Yahweh.
²³He weakened my strength along the
course.
 He shortened my days.
²⁴I said, "My God, don't take me away in
the midst of my days.
 Your years are throughout all generations.
²⁵Of old, you laid the foundation of the
earth.
 The heavens are the work of your
hands.
²⁶They will perish, but you will endure.
 Yes, all of them will wear out like a
garment.
 You will change them like a cloak, and
they will be changed.
²⁷But you are the same.
 Your years will have no end.
²⁸The children of your servants will con-
tinue.
 Their seed will be established before
you."

Psalm 103

By David.

¹Praise Yahweh, my soul!
 All that is within me, praise his holy
name!
²Praise Yahweh, my soul,
 and don't forget all his benefits;
³who forgives all your sins;
 who heals all your diseases;
⁴who redeems your life from destruction;
 who crowns you with loving kindness
and tender mercies;
⁵who satisfies your desire with good things,
 so that your youth is renewed like the
eagle's.
⁶Yahweh executes righteous acts,
 and justice for all who are oppressed.
⁷He made known his ways to Moses,
 his deeds to the children of Israel.

[8] Yahweh is merciful and gracious,
  slow to anger, and abundant in loving
    kindness.
[9] He will not always accuse;
  neither will he stay angry forever.
[10] He has not dealt with us according to our
    sins,
  nor repaid us for our iniquities.
[11] For as the heavens are high above the
    earth,
  so great is his loving kindness toward
    those who fear him.
[12] As far as the east is from the west,
  so far has he removed our transgres-
    sions from us.
[13] Like a father has compassion on his chil-
    dren,
  so Yahweh has compassion on those
    who fear him.
[14] For he knows how we are made.
  He remembers that we are dust.
[15] As for man, his days are like grass.
  As a flower of the field, so he flour-
    ishes.
[16] For the wind passes over it, and it is gone.
  Its place remembers it no more.
[17] But Yahweh's loving kindness is from
    everlasting to everlasting with those
    who fear him,
  his righteousness to children's chil-
    dren;
[18] to those who keep his covenant,
  to those who remember to obey his
    precepts.
[19] Yahweh has established his throne in the
    heavens.
  His kingdom rules over all.
[20] Praise Yahweh, you angels of his,
  who are mighty in strength, who fulfill
    his word,
  obeying the voice of his word.
[21] Praise Yahweh, all you armies of his,
  you servants of his, who do his plea-
    sure.
[22] Praise Yahweh, all you works of his,
  in all places of his dominion.
  Praise Yahweh, my soul!

Psalm 104

[1] Bless Yahweh, my soul.

Yahweh, my God, you are very great.
  You are clothed with honor and
    majesty.
[2] He covers himself with light as with a
    garment.
  He stretches out the heavens like a
    curtain.
[3] He lays the beams of his chambers in the
    waters.
  He makes the clouds his chariot.
  He walks on the wings of the wind.
[4] He makes his messengers[h] winds;
  his servants flames of fire.
[5] He laid the foundations of the earth,
  that it should not be moved forever.
[6] You covered it with the deep as with a
    cloak.
  The waters stood above the mountains.
[7] At your rebuke they fled.
  At the voice of your thunder they
    hurried away.
[8] The mountains rose,
  the valleys sank down,
  to the place which you had assigned to
    them.
[9] You have set a boundary that they may not
    pass over;
  that they don't turn again to cover the
    earth.
[10] He sends forth springs into the valleys.
  They run among the mountains.
[11] They give drink to every animal of the
    field.
  The wild donkeys quench their thirst.
[12] The birds of the sky nest by them.
  They sing among the branches.
[13] He waters the mountains from his cham-
    bers.
  The earth is filled with the fruit of your
    works.
[14] He causes the grass to grow for the
    livestock,
  and plants for man to cultivate,
  that he may bring forth food out of the
    earth:
[15] wine that makes glad the heart of man,
  oil to make his face to shine,
  and bread that strengthens man's
    heart.

---

[h] 104:4 or, angels

¹⁶Yahweh's trees are well watered,
the cedars of Lebanon, which he has
planted;
¹⁷where the birds make their nests.
The stork makes its home in the fir
trees.
¹⁸The high mountains are for the wild
goats.
The rocks are a refuge for the rock
badgers.
¹⁹He appointed the moon for seasons.
The sun knows when to set.
²⁰You make darkness, and it is night,
in which all the animals of the forest
prowl.
²¹The young lions roar after their prey,
and seek their food from God.
²²The sun rises, and they steal away,
and lay down in their dens.
²³Man goes forth to his work,
to his labor until the evening.
²⁴Yahweh, how many are your works!
In wisdom have you made them all.
The earth is full of your riches.
²⁵There is the sea, great and wide,
in which are innumerable living things,
both small and large animals.
²⁶There the ships go,
and leviathan, whom you formed to
play there.
²⁷These all wait for you,
that you may give them their food in
due season.
²⁸You give to them; they gather.
You open your hand; they are satisfied
with good.
²⁹You hide your face: they are troubled;
you take away their breath: they die,
and return to the dust.
³⁰You send forth your Spirit: they are
created.
You renew the face of the ground.
³¹Let the glory of Yahweh endure forever.
Let Yahweh rejoice in his works.
³²He looks at the earth, and it trembles.
He touches the mountains, and they
smoke.
³³I will sing to Yahweh as long as I live.
I will sing praise to my God while I
have any being.
³⁴Let your meditation be sweet to him.
I will rejoice in Yahweh.

³⁵Let sinners be consumed out of the earth.
Let the wicked be no more.
Bless Yahweh, my soul.
Praise Yah!

Psalm 105

¹Give thanks to Yahweh! Call on his name!
Make his doings known among the
peoples.
²Sing to him, sing praises to him!
Tell of all his marvelous works.
³Glory in his holy name.
Let the heart of those who seek Yahweh
rejoice.
⁴Seek Yahweh and his strength.
Seek his face forever more.
⁵Remember his marvelous works that he
has done;
his wonders, and the judgments of his
mouth,
⁶you seed of Abraham, his servant,
you children of Jacob, his chosen ones.
⁷He is Yahweh, our God.
His judgments are in all the earth.
⁸He has remembered his covenant forever,
the word which he commanded to a
thousand generations,
⁹the covenant which he made with Abra-
ham,
his oath to Isaac,
¹⁰and confirmed the same to Jacob for a
statute;
to Israel for an everlasting covenant,
¹¹saying, "To you I will give the land of
Canaan,
the lot of your inheritance;"
¹²when they were but a few men in number,
yes, very few, and foreigners in it.
¹³They went about from nation to nation,
from one kingdom to another people.
¹⁴He allowed no one to do them wrong.
Yes, he reproved kings for their sakes,
¹⁵"Don't touch my anointed ones!
Do my prophets no harm!"
¹⁶He called for a famine on the land.
He destroyed the food supplies.
¹⁷He sent a man before them.
Joseph was sold for a slave.
¹⁸They bruised his feet with shackles.
His neck was locked in irons,
¹⁹until the time that his word happened,

and Yahweh's word proved him true.
²⁰ The king sent and freed him;
    even the ruler of peoples, and let him
    go free.
²¹ He made him lord of his house,
    and ruler of all of his possessions;
²² to discipline his princes at his pleasure,
    and to teach his elders wisdom.
²³ Israel also came into Egypt.
    Jacob sojourned in the land of Ham.
²⁴ He increased his people greatly,
    and made them stronger than their
    adversaries.
²⁵ He turned their heart to hate his people,
    to conspire against his servants.
²⁶ He sent Moses, his servant,
    and Aaron, whom he had chosen.
²⁷ They performed miracles among them,
    and wonders in the land of Ham.
²⁸ He sent darkness, and made it dark.
    They didn't rebel against his words.
²⁹ He turned their waters into blood,
    and killed their fish.
³⁰ Their land swarmed with frogs,
    even in the chambers of their kings.
³¹ He spoke, and swarms of flies came,
    and lice in all their borders.
³² He gave them hail for rain,
    with lightning in their land.
³³ He struck their vines and also their fig
    trees,
    and shattered the trees of their country.
³⁴ He spoke, and the locusts came,
    and the grasshoppers, without number,
³⁵ ate up every plant in their land;
    and ate up the fruit of their ground.
³⁶ He struck also all the firstborn in their
    land,
    the first fruits of all their manhood.
³⁷ He brought them forth with silver and
    gold.
    There was not one feeble person among
    his tribes.
³⁸ Egypt was glad when they departed,
    for the fear of them had fallen on them.
³⁹ He spread a cloud for a covering,
    fire to give light in the night.
⁴⁰ They asked, and he brought quails,
    and satisfied them with the bread of the
    sky.

⁴¹ He opened the rock, and waters gushed
    out.
    They ran as a river in the dry places.
⁴² For he remembered his holy word,
    and Abraham, his servant.
⁴³ He brought forth his people with joy,
    his chosen with singing.
⁴⁴ He gave them the lands of the nations.
    They took the labor of the peoples in
    possession,
⁴⁵ that they might keep his statutes,
    and observe his laws.
    Praise Yah!

Psalm 106

¹ Praise Yahweh!
    Give thanks to Yahweh, for he is good,
    for his loving kindness endures forever.
² Who can utter the mighty acts of Yahweh,
    or fully declare all his praise?
³ Blessed are those who keep justice.
    Blessed is one who does what is right
    at all times.
⁴ Remember me, Yahweh, with the favor
    that you show to your people.
    Visit me with your salvation,
⁵ that I may see the prosperity of your
    chosen,
    that I may rejoice in the gladness of
    your nation,
    that I may glory with your inheritance.
⁶ We have sinned with our fathers.
    We have committed iniquity.
    We have done wickedly.
⁷ Our fathers didn't understand your won-
    ders in Egypt.
    They didn't remember the multitude of
    your loving kindnesses,
    but were rebellious at the sea, even at
    the Red Seaⁱ.
⁸ Nevertheless he saved them for his name's
    sake,
    that he might make his mighty power
    known.
⁹ He rebuked the Red Sea^j also, and it was
    dried up;
    so he led them through the depths, as
    through a desert.

ⁱ 106:7 or, Sea of Reeds
^j 106:9 or, Sea of Reeds

¹⁰He saved them from the hand of him who
hated them,
and redeemed them from the hand of
the enemy.
¹¹The waters covered their adversaries.
There was not one of them left.
¹²Then they believed his words.
They sang his praise.
¹³They soon forgot his works.
They didn't wait for his counsel,
¹⁴but gave in to craving in the desert,
and tested God in the wasteland.
¹⁵He gave them their request,
but sent leanness into their soul.
¹⁶They envied Moses also in the camp,
and Aaron, Yahweh's saint.
¹⁷The earth opened and swallowed up
Dathan,
and covered the company of Abiram.
¹⁸A fire was kindled in their company.
The flame burned up the wicked.
¹⁹They made a calf in Horeb,
and worshiped a molten image.
²⁰Thus they exchanged their glory
for an image of a bull that eats grass.
²¹They forgot God, their Savior,
who had done great things in Egypt,
²²Wondrous works in the land of Ham,
and awesome things by the Red Sea^k.
²³Therefore he said that he would destroy
them,
had Moses, his chosen, not stood before
him in the breach,
to turn away his wrath, so that he
wouldn't destroy them.
²⁴Yes, they despised the pleasant land.
They didn't believe his word,
²⁵but murmured in their tents,
and didn't listen to Yahweh's voice.
²⁶Therefore he swore to them
that he would overthrow them in the
wilderness,
²⁷that he would overthrow their seed
among the nations,
and scatter them in the lands.
²⁸They joined themselves also to Baal Peor,
and ate the sacrifices of the dead.
²⁹Thus they provoked him to anger with
their deeds.
The plague broke in on them.

³⁰Then Phinehas stood up, and executed
judgment,
so the plague was stopped.
³¹That was credited to him for righteousness,
for all generations to come.
³²They angered him also at the waters of
Meribah,
so that Moses was troubled for their
sakes;
³³because they were rebellious against his
spirit,
he spoke rashly with his lips.
³⁴They didn't destroy the peoples,
as Yahweh commanded them,
³⁵but mixed themselves with the nations,
and learned their works.
³⁶They served their idols,
which became a snare to them.
³⁷Yes, they sacrificed their sons and their
daughters to demons.
³⁸They shed innocent blood,
even the blood of their sons and of their
daughters,
whom they sacrificed to the idols of
Canaan.
The land was polluted with blood.
³⁹Thus were they defiled with their works,
and prostituted themselves in their
deeds.
⁴⁰Therefore Yahweh burned with anger
against his people.
He abhorred his inheritance.
⁴¹He gave them into the hand of the nations.
Those who hated them ruled over
them.
⁴²Their enemies also oppressed them.
They were brought into subjection under their hand.
⁴³Many times he delivered them,
but they were rebellious in their counsel,
and were brought low in their iniquity.
⁴⁴Nevertheless he regarded their distress,
when he heard their cry.
⁴⁵He remembered for them his covenant,
and repented according to the multitude of his loving kindnesses.

---

^k106:22 or, Sea of Reeds

⁴⁶He made them also to be pitied
  by all those who carried them captive.
⁴⁷Save us, Yahweh, our God,
  gather us from among the nations,
  to give thanks to your holy name,
  to triumph in your praise!
⁴⁸Blessed be Yahweh, the God of Israel,
  from everlasting even to everlasting!
Let all the people say, "Amen."
Praise Yah!

BOOK V

Psalm 107

¹Give thanks to Yahweh,
  for he is good,
for his loving kindness endures forever.
²Let the redeemed by Yahweh say so,
  whom he has redeemed from the hand
    of the adversary,
    ³And gathered out of the lands,
    from the east and from the west,
    from the north and from the south.
⁴They wandered in the wilderness in a
    desert way.
  They found no city to live in.
⁵Hungry and thirsty,
  their soul fainted in them.
⁶Then they cried to Yahweh in their trouble,
  and he delivered them out of their
    distresses,
⁷he led them also by a straight way,
  that they might go to a city to live in.
⁸Let them praise Yahweh for his loving
    kindness,
  for his wonderful works to the children
    of men!
⁹For he satisfies the longing soul.
  He fills the hungry soul with good.
¹⁰Some sat in darkness and in the shadow
    of death,
  being bound in affliction and iron,
    ¹¹because they rebelled against the
    words of God,
    and condemned the counsel of the
    Most High.
¹²Therefore he brought down their heart
    with labor.
  They fell down, and there was none to
    help.

¹³Then they cried to Yahweh in their trou-
    ble,
  and he saved them out of their dis-
    tresses.
¹⁴He brought them out of darkness and the
    shadow of death,
  and broke their bonds in sunder.
¹⁵Let them praise Yahweh for his loving
    kindness,
  for his wonderful works to the children
    of men!
¹⁶For he has broken the gates of brass,
  and cut through bars of iron.
¹⁷Fools are afflicted because of their disobe-
    dience,
  and because of their iniquities.
¹⁸Their soul abhors all kinds of food.
  They draw near to the gates of death.
¹⁹Then they cry to Yahweh in their trouble,
  he saves them out of their distresses.
²⁰He sends his word, and heals them,
  and delivers them from their graves.
²¹Let them praise Yahweh for his loving
    kindness,
  for his wonderful works to the children
    of men!
²²Let them offer the sacrifices of thanksgiv-
    ing,
  and declare his works with singing.
²³Those who go down to the sea in ships,
  who do business in great waters;
    ²⁴These see Yahweh's works,
    and his wonders in the deep.
²⁵For he commands, and raises the stormy
    wind,
  which lifts up its waves.
²⁶They mount up to the sky; they go down
    again to the depths.
  Their soul melts away because of trou-
    ble.
²⁷They reel back and forth, and stagger like
    a drunken man,
  and are at their wits' end.
²⁸Then they cry to Yahweh in their trouble,
  and he brings them out of their distress.
²⁹He makes the storm a calm,
  so that its waves are still.
³⁰Then they are glad because it is calm,
  so he brings them to their desired
    haven.
³¹Let them praise Yahweh for his loving
    kindness,

for his wonderful works for the children of men!

³²Let them exalt him also in the assembly of the people,
and praise him in the seat of the elders.

³³He turns rivers into a desert,
water springs into a thirsty ground,
³⁴and a fruitful land into a salt waste,
for the wickedness of those who dwell in it.

³⁵He turns a desert into a pool of water,
and a dry land into water springs.

³⁶There he makes the hungry live,
that they may prepare a city to live in,
³⁷sow fields, plant vineyards,
and reap the fruits of increase.

³⁸He blesses them also, so that they are multiplied greatly.
He doesn't allow their livestock to decrease.

³⁹Again, they are diminished and bowed down
through oppression, trouble, and sorrow.

⁴⁰He pours contempt on princes,
and causes them to wander in a trackless waste.

⁴¹Yet he lifts the needy out of their affliction,
and increases their families like a flock.

⁴²The upright will see it, and be glad.
All the wicked will shut their mouths.

⁴³Whoever is wise will pay attention to these things.
They will consider the loving kindnesses of Yahweh.

Psalm 108

A Song. A Psalm by David.

¹My heart is steadfast, God.
I will sing and I will make music with my soul.

²Wake up, harp and lyre!
I will wake up the dawn.

³I will give thanks to you, Yahweh, among the nations.
I will sing praises to you among the peoples.

⁴For your loving kindness is great above the heavens.

Your faithfulness reaches to the skies.

⁵Be exalted, God, above the heavens!
Let your glory be over all the earth.

⁶That your beloved may be delivered,
save with your right hand, and answer us.

⁷God has spoken from his sanctuary: "In triumph,
I will divide Shechem, and measure out the valley of Succoth.

⁸Gilead is mine. Manasseh is mine.
Ephraim also is my helmet.
Judah is my scepter.

⁹Moab is my wash pot.
I will toss my sandal on Edom.
I will shout over Philistia."

¹⁰Who will bring me into the fortified city?
Who has led me to Edom?

¹¹Haven't you rejected us, God?
You don't go forth, God, with our armies.

¹²Give us help against the enemy,
for the help of man is vain.

¹³Through God, we will do valiantly.
For it is he who will tread down our enemies.

Psalm 109

For the Chief Musician. A Psalm by David.

¹God of my praise, don't remain silent,
²for they have opened the mouth of the wicked and the mouth of deceit against me.
They have spoken to me with a lying tongue.

³They have also surrounded me with words of hatred,
and fought against me without a cause.

⁴In return for my love, they are my adversaries;
but I am in prayer.

⁵They have rewarded me evil for good,
and hatred for my love.

⁶Set a wicked man over him.
Let an adversary stand at his right hand.

⁷When he is judged, let him come forth guilty.
Let his prayer be turned into sin.

⁸Let his days be few.
> Let another take his office.

⁹Let his children be fatherless,
> and his wife a widow.

¹⁰Let his children be wandering beggars.
> Let them be sought from their ruins.

¹¹Let the creditor seize all that he has.
> Let strangers plunder the fruit of his labor.

¹²Let there be none to extend kindness to him,
> neither let there be any to have pity on his fatherless children.

¹³Let his posterity be cut off.
> In the generation following let their name be blotted out.

¹⁴Let the iniquity of his fathers be remembered by Yahweh.
> Don't let the sin of his mother be blotted out.

¹⁵Let them be before Yahweh continually,
> that he may cut off the memory of them from the earth;

¹⁶because he didn't remember to show kindness,
> but persecuted the poor and needy man,
> the broken in heart, to kill them.

¹⁷Yes, he loved cursing, and it came to him.
> He didn't delight in blessing, and it was far from him.

¹⁸He clothed himself also with cursing as with his garment.
> It came into his inward parts like water, like oil into his bones.

¹⁹Let it be to him as the clothing with which he covers himself,
> for the belt that is always around him.

²⁰This is the reward of my adversaries from Yahweh,
> of those who speak evil against my soul.

²¹But deal with me, Yahweh the Lord, for your name's sake,
> because your loving kindness is good, deliver me;

²²for I am poor and needy.
> My heart is wounded within me.

²³I fade away like an evening shadow.
> I am shaken off like a locust.

²⁴My knees are weak through fasting.
> My body is thin and lacks fat.

²⁵I have also become a reproach to them.
> When they see me, they shake their head.

²⁶Help me, Yahweh, my God.
> Save me according to your loving kindness;

²⁷that they may know that this is your hand;
> that you, Yahweh, have done it.

²⁸They may curse, but you bless.
> When they arise, they will be shamed, but your servant shall rejoice.

²⁹Let my adversaries be clothed with dishonor.
> Let them cover themselves with their own shame as with a robe.

³⁰I will give great thanks to Yahweh with my mouth.
> Yes, I will praise him among the multitude.

³¹For he will stand at the right hand of the needy,
> to save him from those who judge his soul.

Psalm 110

A Psalm by David.

¹Yahweh says to my Lord, "Sit at my right hand,
> until I make your enemies your footstool for your feet."

²Yahweh will send forth the rod of your strength out of Zion.
> Rule in the midst of your enemies.

³Your people offer themselves willingly in the day of your power, in holy array.
> Out of the womb of the morning, you have the dew of your youth.

⁴Yahweh has sworn, and will not change his mind:
> "You are a priest forever in the order of Melchizedek."

⁵The Lord is at your right hand.
> He will crush kings in the day of his wrath.

⁶He will judge among the nations.
> He will heap up dead bodies.
> He will crush the ruler of the whole earth.

⁷He will drink of the brook in the way;

therefore he will lift up his head.

Psalm 111

¹Praise Yah!^l
> I will give thanks to Yahweh with my
> whole heart,
> in the council of the upright, and in the
> congregation.
²Yahweh's works are great,
> pondered by all those who delight in
> them.
³His work is honor and majesty.
> His righteousness endures forever.
⁴He has caused his wonderful works to be
> remembered.
> Yahweh is gracious and merciful.
⁵He has given food to those who fear him.
> He always remembers his covenant.
⁶He has shown his people the power of his
> works,
> in giving them the heritage of the na-
> tions.
⁷The works of his hands are truth and
> justice.
> All his precepts are sure.
⁸They are established forever and ever.
> They are done in truth and upright-
> ness.
⁹He has sent redemption to his people.
> He has ordained his covenant forever.
> His name is holy and awesome!
¹⁰The fear of Yahweh is the beginning of
> wisdom.
> All those who do his work have a good
> understanding.
His praise endures forever!

Psalm 112

¹Praise Yah!^m
> Blessed is the man who fears Yahweh,
> who delights greatly in his command-
> ments.
²His seed will be mighty in the land.
> The generation of the upright will be
> blessed.
³Wealth and riches are in his house.

His righteousness endures forever.
⁴Light dawns in the darkness for the up-
> right,
> gracious, merciful, and righteous.
⁵It is well with the man who deals gra-
> ciously and lends.
> He will maintain his cause in judg-
> ment.
⁶For he will never be shaken.
> The righteous will be remembered for-
> ever.
⁷He will not be afraid of evil news.
> His heart is steadfast, trusting in Yah-
> weh.
⁸His heart is established.
> He will not be afraid in the end when
> he sees his adversaries.
⁹He has dispersed, he has given to the poor.
> His righteousness endures forever.
> His horn will be exalted with honor.
¹⁰The wicked will see it, and be grieved.
> He shall gnash with his teeth, and melt
> away.
> The desire of the wicked will perish.

Psalm 113

¹Praise Yah!
> Praise, you servants of Yahweh,
> praise the name of Yahweh.
²Blessed be the name of Yahweh,
> from this time forth and forevermore.
³From the rising of the sun to the going
> down of the same,
> Yahweh's name is to be praised.
⁴Yahweh is high above all nations,
> his glory above the heavens.
⁵Who is like Yahweh, our God,
> who has his seat on high,
> ⁶Who stoops down to see in heaven
> and in the earth?
⁷He raises up the poor out of the dust.
> Lifts up the needy from the ash heap;
⁸that he may set him with princes,
> even with the princes of his people.
⁹He settles the barren woman in her home,
> as a joyful mother of children.

---

^l111:1 Psalm 111 is an acrostic poem, with each verse after the initial "Praise Yah!" starting with a letter of the alphabet (ordered from Alef to Tav).

^m112:1 Psalm 112 is an acrostic poem, with each verse after the initial "Praise Yah!" starting with a letter of the alphabet (ordered from Alef to Tav).

Praise Yah!

Psalm 114

¹When Israel went forth out of Egypt,
  the house of Jacob from a people of
  foreign language;
²Judah became his sanctuary,
  Israel his dominion.
³The sea saw it, and fled.
  The Jordan was driven back.
⁴The mountains skipped like rams,
  the little hills like lambs.
⁵What was it, you sea, that you fled?
  You Jordan, that you turned back?
⁶You mountains, that you skipped like
  rams;
  you little hills, like lambs?
⁷Tremble, you earth, at the presence of the
  Lord,
  at the presence of the God of Jacob,
⁸who turned the rock into a pool of water,
  the flint into a spring of waters.

Psalm 115

¹Not to us, Yahweh, not to us,
  but to your name give glory,
  for your loving kindness, and for your
  truth's sake.
²Why should the nations say,
  "Where is their God, now?"
³But our God is in the heavens.
  He does whatever he pleases.
⁴Their idols are silver and gold,
  the work of men's hands.
⁵They have mouths, but they don't speak.
  They have eyes, but they don't see.
⁶They have ears, but they don't hear.
  They have noses, but they don't smell.
⁷They have hands, but they don't feel.
  They have feet, but they don't walk,
  neither do they speak through their
  throat.
⁸Those who make them will be like them;
  yes, everyone who trusts in them.
⁹Israel, trust in Yahweh!
  He is their help and their shield.
¹⁰House of Aaron, trust in Yahweh!
  He is their help and their shield.
¹¹You who fear Yahweh, trust in Yahweh!
  He is their help and their shield.

¹²Yahweh remembers us. He will bless us.
  He will bless the house of Israel.
  He will bless the house of Aaron.
¹³He will bless those who fear Yahweh,
  both small and great.
¹⁴May Yahweh increase you more and
  more,
  you and your children.
¹⁵Blessed are you by Yahweh,
  who made heaven and earth.
¹⁶The heavens are the heavens of Yahweh;
  but the earth has he given to the children of men.
¹⁷The dead don't praise Yah,
  neither any who go down into silence;
¹⁸But we will bless Yah,
  from this time forth and forevermore.
Praise Yah!

Psalm 116

¹I love Yahweh, because he listens to my
  voice,
  and my cries for mercy.
²Because he has turned his ear to me,
  therefore I will call on him as long as I
  live.
³The cords of death surrounded me,
  the pains of Sheol got a hold of me.
  I found trouble and sorrow.
⁴Then I called on the name of Yahweh:
  "Yahweh, I beg you, deliver my soul."
⁵Yahweh is Gracious and righteous.
  Yes, our God is merciful.
⁶Yahweh preserves the simple.
  I was brought low, and he saved me.
⁷Return to your rest, my soul,
  for Yahweh has dealt bountifully with
  you.
⁸For you have delivered my soul from
  death,
  my eyes from tears,
  and my feet from falling.
⁹I will walk before Yahweh in the land of
  the living.
¹⁰I believed, therefore I said,
  "I was greatly afflicted."
¹¹I said in my haste,
  "All men are liars."
¹²What will I give to Yahweh for all his
  benefits toward me?

¹³I will take the cup of salvation, and call on the name of Yahweh.
¹⁴I will pay my vows to Yahweh,
yes, in the presence of all his people.
¹⁵Precious in the sight of Yahweh is the death of his saints.
¹⁶Yahweh, truly I am your servant.
I am your servant, the son of your handmaid.
You have freed me from my chains.
¹⁷I will offer to you the sacrifice of thanksgiving,
and will call on the name of Yahweh.
¹⁸I will pay my vows to Yahweh,
yes, in the presence of all his people,
¹⁹in the courts of Yahweh's house,
in the midst of you, Jerusalem.
Praise Yah!

Psalm 117

¹Praise Yahweh, all you nations!
Extol him, all you peoples!
²For his loving kindness is great toward us.
Yahweh's faithfulness endures forever.
Praise Yah!

Psalm 118

¹Give thanks to Yahweh, for he is good,
for his loving kindness endures forever.
²Let Israel now say
that his loving kindness endures forever.
³Let the house of Aaron now say
that his loving kindness endures forever.
⁴Now let those who fear Yahweh say
that his loving kindness endures forever.
⁵Out of my distress, I called on Yah.
Yah answered me with freedom.
⁶Yahweh is on my side. I will not be afraid.
What can man do to me?
⁷Yahweh is on my side among those who help me.
Therefore I will look in triumph at those who hate me.
⁸It is better to take refuge in Yahweh,
than to put confidence in man.
⁹It is better to take refuge in Yahweh,
than to put confidence in princes.
¹⁰All the nations surrounded me,
but in the name of Yahweh, I cut them off.
¹¹They surrounded me, yes, they surrounded me.
In the name of Yahweh I indeed cut them off.
¹²They surrounded me like bees.
They are quenched like the burning thorns.
In the name of Yahweh I cut them off.
¹³You pushed me back hard, to make me fall,
but Yahweh helped me.
¹⁴Yah is my strength and song.
He has become my salvation.
¹⁵The voice of rejoicing and salvation is in the tents of the righteous.
"The right hand of Yahweh does valiantly.
¹⁶The right hand of Yahweh is exalted!
The right hand of Yahweh does valiantly!"
¹⁷I will not die, but live,
and declare Yah's works.
¹⁸Yah has punished me severely,
but he has not given me over to death.
¹⁹Open to me the gates of righteousness.
I will enter into them.
I will give thanks to Yah.
²⁰This is the gate of Yahweh;
the righteous will enter into it.
²¹I will give thanks to you, for you have answered me,
and have become my salvation.
²²The stone which the builders rejected has become the head of the corner.
²³This is Yahweh's doing.
It is marvelous in our eyes.
²⁴This is the day that Yahweh has made.
We will rejoice and be glad in it!
²⁵Save us now, we beg you, Yahweh!
Yahweh, we beg you, send prosperity now.
²⁶Blessed is he who comes in the name of Yahweh!
We have blessed you out of the house of Yahweh.
²⁷Yahweh is God, and he has given us light.
Bind the sacrifice with cords, even to the horns of the altar.

[28] You are my God, and I will give thanks to you.

You are my God, I will exalt you.

[29] Oh give thanks to Yahweh, for he is good,

for his loving kindness endures forever.

Psalm 119

ALEPH

[1] Blessed are those whose ways are blameless,

who walk according to Yahweh's law.

[2] Blessed are those who keep his statutes,

who seek him with their whole heart.

[3] Yes, they do nothing wrong.

They walk in his ways.

[4] You have commanded your precepts,

that we should fully obey them.

[5] Oh that my ways were steadfast

to obey your statutes!

[6] Then I wouldn't be disappointed,

when I consider all of your commandments.

[7] I will give thanks to you with uprightness of heart,

when I learn your righteous judgments.

[8] I will observe your statutes.

Don't utterly forsake me.

BET

[9] How can a young man keep his way pure?

By living according to your word.

[10] With my whole heart, I have sought you.

Don't let me wander from your commandments.

[11] I have hidden your word in my heart,

that I might not sin against you.

[12] Blessed are you, Yahweh.

Teach me your statutes.

[13] With my lips,

I have declared all the ordinances of your mouth.

[14] I have rejoiced in the way of your testimonies,

as much as in all riches.

[15] I will meditate on your precepts,

and consider your ways.

[16] I will delight myself in your statutes.

I will not forget your word.

GIMEL

[17] Do good to your servant.

I will live and I will obey your word.

[18] Open my eyes,

that I may see wondrous things out of your law.

[19] I am a stranger on the earth.

Don't hide your commandments from me.

[20] My soul is consumed with longing for your ordinances at all times.

[21] You have rebuked the proud who are cursed,

who wander from your commandments.

[22] Take reproach and contempt away from me,

for I have kept your statutes.

[23] Though princes sit and slander me,

your servant will meditate on your statutes.

[24] Indeed your statutes are my delight,

and my counselors.

DALED

[25] My soul is laid low in the dust.

Revive me according to your word!

[26] I declared my ways, and you answered me.

Teach me your statutes.

[27] Let me understand the teaching of your precepts!

Then I will meditate on your wondrous works.

[28] My soul is weary with sorrow:

strengthen me according to your word.

[29] Keep me from the way of deceit.

Grant me your law graciously!

[30] I have chosen the way of truth.

I have set your ordinances before me.

[31] I cling to your statutes, Yahweh.

Don't let me be disappointed.

[32] I run in the path of your commandments,

for you have set my heart free.

HEY

[33] Teach me, Yahweh, the way of your statutes.

I will keep them to the end.

³⁴Give me understanding, and I will keep
your law.
Yes, I will obey it with my whole heart.
³⁵Direct me in the path of your commandments,
for I delight in them.
³⁶Turn my heart toward your statutes,
not toward selfish gain.
³⁷Turn my eyes away from looking at
worthless things.
Revive me in your ways.
³⁸Fulfill your promise to your servant,
that you may be feared.
³⁹Take away my disgrace that I dread,
for your ordinances are good.
⁴⁰Behold, I long for your precepts!
Revive me in your righteousness.

WAW

⁴¹Let your loving kindness also come to me,
Yahweh,
your salvation, according to your
word.
⁴²So I will have an answer for him who
reproaches me,
for I trust in your word.
⁴³Don't snatch the word of truth out of my
mouth,
for I put my hope in your ordinances.
⁴⁴So I will obey your law continually,
forever and ever.
⁴⁵I will walk in liberty,
for I have sought your precepts.
⁴⁶I will also speak of your statutes before
kings,
and will not be disappointed.
⁴⁷I will delight myself in your commandments,
because I love them.
⁴⁸I reach out my hands for your commandments, which I love.
I will meditate on your statutes.

ZAYIN

⁴⁹Remember your word to your servant,
because you gave me hope.
⁵⁰This is my comfort in my affliction,
for your word has revived me.
⁵¹The arrogant mock me excessively,
but I don't swerve from your law.
⁵²I remember your ordinances of old, Yahweh,

and have comforted myself.
⁵³Indignation has taken hold on me,
because of the wicked who forsake
your law.
⁵⁴Your statutes have been my songs,
in the house where I live.
⁵⁵I have remembered your name, Yahweh,
in the night,
and I obey your law.
⁵⁶This is my way,
that I keep your precepts.

CHET

⁵⁷Yahweh is my portion.
I promised to obey your words.
⁵⁸I sought your favor with my whole heart.
Be merciful to me according to your
word.
⁵⁹I considered my ways,
and turned my steps to your statutes.
⁶⁰I will hurry, and not delay,
to obey your commandments.
⁶¹The ropes of the wicked bind me,
but I won't forget your law.
⁶²At midnight I will rise to give thanks to
you,
because of your righteous ordinances.
⁶³I am a friend of all those who fear you,
of those who observe your precepts.
⁶⁴The earth is full of your loving kindness,
Yahweh.
Teach me your statutes.

TET

⁶⁵Do good to your servant,
according to your word, Yahweh.
⁶⁶Teach me good judgment and knowledge,
for I believe in your commandments.
⁶⁷Before I was afflicted, I went astray;
but now I observe your word.
⁶⁸You are good, and do good.
Teach me your statutes.
⁶⁹The proud have smeared a lie upon me.
With my whole heart, I will keep your
precepts.
⁷⁰Their heart is as callous as the fat,
but I delight in your law.
⁷¹It is good for me that I have been afflicted,
that I may learn your statutes.

⁷²The law of your mouth is better to me than thousands of pieces of gold and silver.

YUD

⁷³Your hands have made me and formed me.
Give me understanding, that I may learn your commandments.
⁷⁴Those who fear you will see me and be glad,
because I have put my hope in your word.
⁷⁵Yahweh, I know that your judgments are righteous,
that in faithfulness you have afflicted me.
⁷⁶Please let your loving kindness be for my comfort,
according to your word to your servant.
⁷⁷Let your tender mercies come to me, that I may live;
for your law is my delight.
⁷⁸Let the proud be disappointed, for they have overthrown me wrongfully.
I will meditate on your precepts.
⁷⁹Let those who fear you turn to me.
They will know your statutes.
⁸⁰Let my heart be blameless toward your decrees,
that I may not be disappointed.

KAF

⁸¹My soul faints for your salvation.
I hope in your word.
⁸²My eyes fail for your word.
I say, "When will you comfort me?"
⁸³For I have become like a wineskin in the smoke.
I don't forget your statutes.
⁸⁴How many are the days of your servant?
When will you execute judgment on those who persecute me?
⁸⁵The proud have dug pits for me,
contrary to your law.
⁸⁶All of your commandments are faithful.
They persecute me wrongfully.
Help me!
⁸⁷They had almost wiped me from the earth,
but I didn't forsake your precepts.

⁸⁸Preserve my life according to your loving kindness,
so I will obey the statutes of your mouth.

LAMED

⁸⁹Yahweh, your word is settled in heaven forever.
⁹⁰Your faithfulness is to all generations.
You have established the earth, and it remains.
⁹¹Your laws remain to this day,
for all things serve you.
⁹²Unless your law had been my delight,
I would have perished in my affliction.
⁹³I will never forget your precepts,
for with them, you have revived me.
⁹⁴I am yours.
Save me, for I have sought your precepts.
⁹⁵The wicked have waited for me, to destroy me.
I will consider your statutes.
⁹⁶I have seen a limit to all perfection,
but your commands are boundless.

MEM

⁹⁷How I love your law!
It is my meditation all day.
⁹⁸Your commandments make me wiser than my enemies,
for your commandments are always with me.
⁹⁹I have more understanding than all my teachers,
for your testimonies are my meditation.
¹⁰⁰I understand more than the aged,
because I have kept your precepts.
¹⁰¹I have kept my feet from every evil way,
that I might observe your word.
¹⁰²I have not turned aside from your ordinances,
for you have taught me.
¹⁰³How sweet are your promises to my taste,
more than honey to my mouth!
¹⁰⁴Through your precepts, I get understanding;

therefore I hate every false way.

NUN

[105] Your word is a lamp to my feet,
and a light for my path.
[106] I have sworn, and have confirmed it,
that I will obey your righteous ordinances.
[107] I am afflicted very much.
Revive me, Yahweh, according to your
word.
[108] Accept, I beg you, the willing offerings
of my mouth.
Yahweh, teach me your ordinances.
[109] My soul is continually in my hand,
yet I won't forget your law.
[110] The wicked have laid a snare for me,
yet I haven't gone astray from your
precepts.
[111] I have taken your testimonies as a heritage forever,
for they are the joy of my heart.
[112] I have set my heart to perform your
statutes forever,
even to the end.

SAMEKH

[113] I hate double-minded men,
but I love your law.
[114] You are my hiding place and my shield.
I hope in your word.
[115] Depart from me, you evildoers,
that I may keep the commandments of
my God.
[116] Uphold me according to your word, that
I may live.
Let me not be ashamed of my hope.
[117] Hold me up, and I will be safe,
and will have respect for your statutes
continually.
[118] You reject all those who stray from your
statutes,
for their deceit is in vain.
[119] You put away all the wicked of the earth
like dross.
Therefore I love your testimonies.
[120] My flesh trembles for fear of you.
I am afraid of your judgments.

AYIN

[121] I have done what is just and righteous.
Don't leave me to my oppressors.

[122] Ensure your servant's well-being.
Don't let the proud oppress me.
[123] My eyes fail looking for your salvation,
for your righteous word.
[124] Deal with your servant according to
your loving kindness.
Teach me your statutes.
[125] I am your servant. Give me understanding,
that I may know your testimonies.
[126] It is time to act, Yahweh,
for they break your law.
[127] Therefore I love your commandments
more than gold,
yes, more than pure gold.
[128] Therefore I consider all of your precepts
to be right.
I hate every false way.

PEY

[129] Your testimonies are wonderful,
therefore my soul keeps them.
[130] The entrance of your words gives light.
It gives understanding to the simple.
[131] I opened my mouth wide and panted,
for I longed for your commandments.
[132] Turn to me, and have mercy on me,
as you always do to those who love
your name.
[133] Establish my footsteps in your word.
Don't let any iniquity have dominion
over me.
[134] Redeem me from the oppression of man,
so I will observe your precepts.
[135] Make your face shine on your servant.
Teach me your statutes.
[136] Streams of tears run down my eyes,
because they don't observe your law.

TZADI

[137] You are righteous, Yahweh.
Your judgments are upright.
[138] You have commanded your statutes in
righteousness.
They are fully trustworthy.
[139] My zeal wears me out,
because my enemies ignore your
words.
[140] Your promises have been thoroughly
tested,
and your servant loves them.
[141] I am small and despised.

I don't forget your precepts.
¹⁴²Your righteousness is an everlasting righteousness.
Your law is truth.
¹⁴³Trouble and anguish have taken hold of me.
Your commandments are my delight.
¹⁴⁴Your testimonies are righteous forever.
Give me understanding, that I may live.

KUF

¹⁴⁵I have called with my whole heart.
Answer me, Yahweh!
I will keep your statutes.
¹⁴⁶I have called to you. Save me!
I will obey your statutes.
¹⁴⁷I rise before dawn and cry for help.
I put my hope in your words.
¹⁴⁸My eyes stay open through the night watches,
that I might meditate on your word.
¹⁴⁹Hear my voice according to your loving kindness.
Revive me, Yahweh, according to your ordinances.
¹⁵⁰They draw near who follow after wickedness.
They are far from your law.
¹⁵¹You are near, Yahweh.
All your commandments are truth.
¹⁵²Of old I have known from your testimonies,
that you have founded them forever.

RESH

¹⁵³Consider my affliction, and deliver me,
for I don't forget your law.
¹⁵⁴Plead my cause, and redeem me!
Revive me according to your promise.
¹⁵⁵Salvation is far from the wicked,
for they don't seek your statutes.
¹⁵⁶Great are your tender mercies, Yahweh.
Revive me according to your ordinances.
¹⁵⁷Many are my persecutors and my adversaries.
I haven't swerved from your testimonies.
¹⁵⁸I look at the faithless with loathing,
because they don't observe your word.
¹⁵⁹Consider how I love your precepts.

Revive me, Yahweh, according to your loving kindness.
¹⁶⁰All of your words are truth.
Every one of your righteous ordinances endures forever.

SIN AND SHIN

¹⁶¹Princes have persecuted me without a cause,
but my heart stands in awe of your words.
¹⁶²I rejoice at your word,
as one who finds great spoil.
¹⁶³I hate and abhor falsehood.
I love your law.
¹⁶⁴Seven times a day, I praise you,
because of your righteous ordinances.
¹⁶⁵Those who love your law have great peace.
Nothing causes them to stumble.
¹⁶⁶I have hoped for your salvation, Yahweh.
I have done your commandments.
¹⁶⁷My soul has observed your testimonies.
I love them exceedingly.
¹⁶⁸I have obeyed your precepts and your testimonies,
for all my ways are before you.

TAV

¹⁶⁹Let my cry come before you, Yahweh.
Give me understanding according to your word.
¹⁷⁰Let my supplication come before you.
Deliver me according to your word.
¹⁷¹Let my lips utter praise,
for you teach me your statutes.
¹⁷²Let my tongue sing of your word,
for all your commandments are righteousness.
¹⁷³Let your hand be ready to help me,
for I have chosen your precepts.
¹⁷⁴I have longed for your salvation, Yahweh.
Your law is my delight.
¹⁷⁵Let my soul live, that I may praise you.
Let your ordinances help me.
¹⁷⁶I have gone astray like a lost sheep.
Seek your servant, for I don't forget your commandments.

Psalm 120

A Song of Ascents.

¹In my distress, I cried to Yahweh.
   He answered me.
²Deliver my soul, Yahweh, from lying lips,
   from a deceitful tongue.
³What will be given to you, and what will
      be done more to you,
   you deceitful tongue?
⁴Sharp arrows of the mighty,
   with coals of juniper.
⁵Woe is me, that I live in Meshech,
   that I dwell among the tents of Kedar!
⁶My soul has had her dwelling too long
   with him who hates peace.
⁷I am for peace,
   but when I speak, they are for war.

Psalm 121

A Song of Ascents.

¹I will lift up my eyes to the hills.
   Where does my help come from?
²My help comes from Yahweh,
   who made heaven and earth.
³He will not allow your foot to be moved.
   He who keeps you will not slumber.
⁴Behold, he who keeps Israel
   will neither slumber nor sleep.
⁵Yahweh is your keeper.
   Yahweh is your shade on your right
      hand.
⁶The sun will not harm you by day,
   nor the moon by night.
⁷Yahweh will keep you from all evil.
   He will keep your soul.
⁸Yahweh will keep your going out and your
      coming in,
   from this time forth, and forevermore.

Psalm 122

A Song of Ascents. By David.

¹I was glad when they said to me,
   "Let's go to Yahweh's house!"
²Our feet are standing within your gates,
   Jerusalem;
   ³Jerusalem, that is built as a city that is
      compact together;

⁴where the tribes go up, even Yah's tribes,
   according to an ordinance for Israel,
   to give thanks to the name of Yahweh.
⁵For there are set thrones for judgment,
   the thrones of David's house.
⁶Pray for the peace of Jerusalem.
   Those who love you will prosper.
⁷Peace be within your walls,
   and prosperity within your palaces.
⁸For my brothers' and companions' sakes,
   I will now say, "Peace be within you."
⁹For the sake of the house of Yahweh our
      God,
   I will seek your good.

Psalm 123

A Song of Ascents.

¹To you I do lift up my eyes,
   you who sit in the heavens.
²Behold, as the eyes of servants look to the
      hand of their master,
   as the eyes of a maid to the hand of her
      mistress;
   so our eyes look to Yahweh, our God,
   until he has mercy on us.
³Have mercy on us, Yahweh, have mercy
      on us,
   for we have endured much contempt.
⁴Our soul is exceedingly filled with the
      scoffing of those who are at ease,
   with the contempt of the proud.

Psalm 124

A Song of Ascents. By David.

¹If it had not been Yahweh who was on our
      side,
   let Israel now say,
²if it had not been Yahweh who was on our
      side,
   when men rose up against us;
³then they would have swallowed us up
      alive,
   when their wrath was kindled against
      us;
⁴then the waters would have overwhelmed
      us,

the stream would have gone over our
soul;
[5] then the proud waters would have gone
over our soul.
[6] Blessed be Yahweh,
who has not given us as a prey to their
teeth.
[7] Our soul has escaped like a bird out of the
fowler's snare.
The snare is broken, and we have
escaped.
[8] Our help is in the name of Yahweh,
who made heaven and earth.

Psalm 125

A Song of Ascents.

[1] Those who trust in Yahweh are as Mount
Zion,
which can't be moved, but remains
forever.
[2] As the mountains surround Jerusalem,
so Yahweh surrounds his people from
this time forth and forevermore.
[3] For the scepter of wickedness won't remain over the allotment of the righteous;
so that the righteous won't use their
hands to do evil.
[4] Do good, Yahweh, to those who are good,
to those who are upright in their hearts.
[5] But as for those who turn aside to their
crooked ways,
Yahweh will lead them away with the
workers of iniquity.
Peace be on Israel.

Psalm 126

A Song of Ascents.

[1] When Yahweh brought back those who
returned to Zion,
we were like those who dream.
[2] Then our mouth was filled with laughter,
and our tongue with singing.
Then they said among the nations,
"Yahweh has done great things for
them."
[3] Yahweh has done great things for us,
and we are glad.
[4] Restore our fortunes again, Yahweh,

like the streams in the Negev.
[5] Those who sow in tears will reap in joy.
[6] He who goes out weeping, carrying
seed for sowing,
will certainly come again with joy, carrying his sheaves.

Psalm 127

A Song of Ascents. By Solomon.

[1] Unless Yahweh builds the house,
they labor in vain who build it.
Unless Yahweh watches over the city,
the watchman guards it in vain.
[2] It is vain for you to rise up early,
to stay up late,
eating the bread of toil;
for he gives sleep to his loved ones.
[3] Behold, children are a heritage of Yahweh.
The fruit of the womb is his reward.
[4] As arrows in the hand of a mighty man,
so are the children of youth.
[5] Happy is the man who has his quiver full
of them.
They won't be disappointed when they
speak with their enemies in the gate.

Psalm 128

A Song of Ascents.

[1] Blessed is everyone who fears Yahweh,
who walks in his ways.
[2] For you will eat the labor of your hands.
You will be happy, and it will be well
with you.
[3] Your wife will be as a fruitful vine,
in the innermost parts of your house;
your children like olive plants,
around your table.
[4] Behold, thus is the man blessed who fears
Yahweh.
[5] May Yahweh bless you out of Zion,
and may you see the good of Jerusalem
all the days of your life.
[6] Yes, may you see your children's children.
Peace be upon Israel.

Psalm 129

A Song of Ascents.

[1]Many times they have afflicted me from
my youth up.
Let Israel now say,
[2]many times they have afflicted me from
my youth up,
yet they have not prevailed against me.
[3]The plowers plowed on my back.
They made their furrows long.
[4]Yahweh is righteous.
He has cut apart the cords of the
wicked.
[5]Let them be disappointed and turned
backward,
all those who hate Zion.
[6]Let them be as the grass on the housetops,
which withers before it grows up;
[7]with which the reaper doesn't fill his hand,
nor he who binds sheaves, his bosom.
[8]Neither do those who go by say,
"The blessing of Yahweh be on you.
We bless you in the name of Yahweh."

Psalm 130

A Song of Ascents.

[1]Out of the depths I have cried to you,
Yahweh.
[2]Lord, hear my voice.
Let your ears be attentive to the voice
of my petitions.
[3]If you, Yah, kept a record of sins,
Lord, who could stand?
[4]But there is forgiveness with you,
therefore you are feared.
[5]I wait for Yahweh.
My soul waits.
I hope in his word.
[6]My soul longs for the Lord more than
watchmen long for the morning;
more than watchmen for the morning.
[7]Israel, hope in Yahweh,
for with Yahweh there is loving kindness.
With him is abundant redemption.
[8]He will redeem Israel from all their sins.

Psalm 131

A Song of Ascents. By David.

[1]Yahweh, my heart isn't haughty, nor my
eyes lofty;
nor do I concern myself with great
matters,
or things too wonderful for me.
[2]Surely I have stilled and quieted my soul,
like a weaned child with his mother,
like a weaned child is my soul within
me.
[3]Israel, hope in Yahweh,
from this time forth and forevermore.

Psalm 132

A Song of Ascents.

[1]Yahweh, remember David and all his affliction,
[2]how he swore to Yahweh,
and vowed to the Mighty One of Jacob:
[3]"Surely I will not come into the structure
of my house,
nor go up into my bed;
[4]I will not give sleep to my eyes,
or slumber to my eyelids;
[5]until I find out a place for Yahweh,
a dwelling for the Mighty One of Jacob."
[6]Behold, we heard of it in Ephrathah.
We found it in the field of Jaar:
[7]"We will go into his dwelling place.
We will worship at his footstool.
[8]Arise, Yahweh, into your resting place;
you, and the ark of your strength.
[9]Let your priest be clothed with righteousness.
Let your saints shout for joy!"
[10]For your servant David's sake,
don't turn away the face of your
anointed one.
[11]Yahweh has sworn to David in truth.
He will not turn from it:
"I will set the fruit of your body on
your throne.
[12]If your children will keep my covenant,
my testimony that I will teach them,
their children also will sit on your
throne forevermore."
[13]For Yahweh has chosen Zion.

He has desired it for his habitation.
¹⁴"This is my resting place forever.
Here I will live, for I have desired it.
¹⁵I will abundantly bless her provision.
I will satisfy her poor with bread.
¹⁶Her priests I will also clothe with salvation.
Her saints will shout aloud for joy.
¹⁷There I will make the horn of David to bud.
I have ordained a lamp for my anointed.
¹⁸I will clothe his enemies with shame,
but on himself, his crown will be resplendent."

Psalm 133

A Song of Ascents. By David.

¹See how good and how pleasant it is
for brothers to live together in unity!
²It is like the precious oil on the head,
that ran down on the beard,
even Aaron's beard;
that came down on the edge of his robes;
³like the dew of Hermon,
that comes down on the hills of Zion:
for there Yahweh gives the blessing,
even life forevermore.

Psalm 134

A Song of Ascents.

¹Look! Praise Yahweh, all you servants of Yahweh,
who stand by night in Yahweh's house!
²Lift up your hands in the sanctuary.
Praise Yahweh!
³May Yahweh bless you from Zion;
even he who made heaven and earth.

Psalm 135

¹Praise Yah!
Praise the name of Yahweh!
Praise him, you servants of Yahweh,
²you who stand in the house of Yahweh,
in the courts of our God's house.
³Praise Yah, for Yahweh is good.

Sing praises to his name, for that is pleasant.
⁴For Yah has chosen Jacob for himself;
Israel for his own possession.
⁵For I know that Yahweh is great,
that our Lord is above all gods.
⁶Whatever Yahweh pleased, that he has done,
in heaven and in earth, in the seas and in all deeps;
⁷who causes the clouds to rise from the ends of the earth;
who makes lightnings with the rain;
who brings forth the wind out of his treasuries;
⁸Who struck the firstborn of Egypt,
both of man and animal;
⁹Who sent signs and wonders into the midst of you, Egypt,
on Pharaoh, and on all his servants;
¹⁰who struck many nations,
and killed mighty kings,
¹¹Sihon king of the Amorites,
Og king of Bashan,
and all the kingdoms of Canaan,
¹²and gave their land for a heritage,
a heritage to Israel, his people.
¹³Your name, Yahweh, endures forever;
your renown, Yahweh, throughout all generations.
¹⁴For Yahweh will judge his people,
and have compassion on his servants.
¹⁵The idols of the nations are silver and gold,
the work of men's hands.
¹⁶They have mouths, but they can't speak.
They have eyes, but they can't see.
¹⁷They have ears, but they can't hear;
neither is there any breath in their mouths.
¹⁸Those who make them will be like them;
yes, everyone who trusts in them.
¹⁹House of Israel, praise Yahweh!
House of Aaron, praise Yahweh!
²⁰House of Levi, praise Yahweh!
You who fear Yahweh, praise Yahweh!
²¹Blessed be Yahweh from Zion,
Who dwells at Jerusalem.
Praise Yah!

Psalm 136

[1]Give thanks to Yahweh, for he is good;
for his loving kindness endures forever.
[2]Give thanks to the God of gods;
for his loving kindness endures forever.
[3]Give thanks to the Lord of lords;
for his loving kindness endures forever:
[4]To him who alone does great wonders;
for his loving kindness endures forever:
[5]To him who by understanding made the heavens;
for his loving kindness endures forever:
[6]To him who spread out the earth above the waters;
for his loving kindness endures forever:
[7]To him who made the great lights;
for his loving kindness endures forever:
[8]The sun to rule by day;
for his loving kindness endures forever;
[9]The moon and stars to rule by night;
for his loving kindness endures forever:
[10]To him who struck down the Egyptian firstborn;
for his loving kindness endures forever;
[11]And brought out Israel from among them;
for his loving kindness endures forever;
[12]With a strong hand, and with an outstretched arm;
for his loving kindness endures forever:
[13]To him who divided the Red Sea[n] apart;
for his loving kindness endures forever;
[14]And made Israel to pass through its midst;
for his loving kindness endures forever;
[15]But overthrew Pharaoh and his army in the Red Sea[o];
for his loving kindness endures forever:

[16]To him who led his people through the wilderness;
for his loving kindness endures forever:
[17]To him who struck great kings;
for his loving kindness endures forever;
[18]And killed mighty kings;
for his loving kindness endures forever:
[19]Sihon king of the Amorites;
for his loving kindness endures forever;
[20]Og king of Bashan;
for his loving kindness endures forever;
[21]And gave their land as an inheritance;
for his loving kindness endures forever;
[22]Even a heritage to Israel his servant;
for his loving kindness endures forever:
[23]Who remembered us in our low estate;
for his loving kindness endures forever;
[24]And has delivered us from our adversaries;
for his loving kindness endures forever:
[25]Who gives food to every creature;
for his loving kindness endures forever.
[26]Oh give thanks to the God of heaven;
for his loving kindness endures forever.

Psalm 137

[1]By the rivers of Babylon, there we sat down.
Yes, we wept, when we remembered Zion.
[2]On the willows in its midst,
we hung up our harps.
[3]For there, those who led us captive asked us for songs.
Those who tormented us demanded songs of joy:
"Sing us one of the songs of Zion!"
[4]How can we sing Yahweh's song in a foreign land?

---

[n]136:13 or, Sea of Reeds
[o]136:15 or, Sea of Reeds

⁵If I forget you, Jerusalem,
  let my right hand forget its skill.
⁶Let my tongue stick to the roof of my
  mouth if I don't remember you;
  if I don't prefer Jerusalem above my
  chief joy.
⁷Remember, Yahweh, against the children
  of Edom,
  the day of Jerusalem;
  who said, "Raze it!
  Raze it even to its foundation!"
⁸Daughter of Babylon, doomed to destruction,
  he will be happy who rewards you,
  as you have served us.
⁹Happy shall he be,
  who takes and dashes your little ones
  against the rock.

Psalm 138

By David.

¹I will give you thanks with my whole
  heart.
  Before the gods^P, I will sing praises to
  you.
²I will bow down toward your holy temple,
  and give thanks to your Name for your
  loving kindness and for your truth;
  for you have exalted your Name and
  your Word above all.
³In the day that I called, you answered me.
  You encouraged me with strength in
  my soul.
⁴All the kings of the earth will give you
  thanks, Yahweh,
  for they have heard the words of your
  mouth.
⁵Yes, they will sing of the ways of Yahweh;
  for great is Yahweh's glory.
⁶For though Yahweh is high, yet he looks
  after the lowly;
  but the proud, he knows from afar.
⁷Though I walk in the midst of trouble, you
  will revive me.
  You will stretch forth your hand
  against the wrath of my enemies.
  Your right hand will save me.

⁸Yahweh will fulfill that which concerns
  me;
  your loving kindness, Yahweh, endures forever.
  Don't forsake the works of your own
  hands.

Psalm 139

For the Chief Musician. A Psalm by
David.

¹Yahweh, you have searched me,
  and you know me.
²You know my sitting down and my rising
  up.
  You perceive my thoughts from afar.
³You search out my path and my lying
  down,
  and are acquainted with all my ways.
⁴For there is not a word on my tongue,
  but, behold, Yahweh, you know it
  altogether.
⁵You hem me in behind and before.
  You laid your hand on me.
⁶This knowledge is beyond me.
  It's lofty.
  I can't attain it.
⁷Where could I go from your Spirit?
  Or where could I flee from your presence?
⁸If I ascend up into heaven, you are there.
  If I make my bed in Sheol, behold, you
  are there!
⁹If I take the wings of the dawn,
  and settle in the uttermost parts of the
  sea;
¹⁰Even there your hand will lead me,
  and your right hand will hold me.
¹¹If I say, "Surely the darkness will overwhelm me;
  the light around me will be night;"
¹²even the darkness doesn't hide from you,
  but the night shines as the day.
  The darkness is like light to you.
¹³For you formed my inmost being.
  You knit me together in my mother's
  womb.
¹⁴I will give thanks to you,

---

^P138:1 The word elohim, used here, usually means "God," but can also mean "gods," "princes,"
or "angels."

for I am fearfully and wonderfully
   made.
Your works are wonderful.
   My soul knows that very well.
¹⁵My frame wasn't hidden from you,
   when I was made in secret,
   woven together in the depths of the
   earth.
¹⁶Your eyes saw my body.
   In your book they were all written,
   the days that were ordained for me,
   when as yet there were none of them.
¹⁷How precious to me are your thoughts,
   God!
   How vast is the sum of them!
¹⁸If I would count them, they are more in
   number than the sand.
   When I wake up, I am still with you.
¹⁹If only you, God, would kill the wicked.
   Get away from me, you bloodthirsty
   men!
²⁰For they speak against you wickedly.
   Your enemies take your name in vain.
²¹Yahweh, don't I hate those who hate you?
   Am I not grieved with those who rise
   up against you?
²²I hate them with perfect hatred.
   They have become my enemies.
²³Search me, God, and know my heart.
   Try me, and know my thoughts.
²⁴See if there is any wicked way in me,
   and lead me in the everlasting way.

Psalm 140

For the Chief Musician.   A Psalm by
David.

¹Deliver me, Yahweh, from the evil man.
   Preserve me from the violent man;
²those who devise mischief in their hearts.
   They continually gather themselves to-
   gether for war.
³They have sharpened their tongues like a
   serpent.
   Viper's poison is under their lips.
Selah.
⁴Yahweh, keep me from the hands of the
   wicked.
   Preserve me from the violent men who
   have determined to trip my feet.
⁵The proud have hidden a snare for me,

they have spread the cords of a net by
   the path.
   They have set traps for me.
Selah.
⁶I said to Yahweh, "You are my God."
   Listen to the cry of my petitions, Yahweh.
⁷Yahweh, the Lord, the strength of my
   salvation,
   you have covered my head in the day
   of battle.
⁸Yahweh, don't grant the desires of the
   wicked.
   Don't let their evil plans succeed, or
   they will become proud.
Selah.
⁹As for the head of those who surround me,
   let the mischief of their own lips cover
   them.
¹⁰Let burning coals fall on them.
   Let them be thrown into the fire,
   into miry pits, from where they never
   rise.
¹¹An evil speaker won't be established in
   the earth.
   Evil will hunt the violent man to overthrow him.
¹²I know that Yahweh will maintain the
   cause of the afflicted,
   and justice for the needy.
¹³Surely the righteous will give thanks to
   your name.
   The upright will dwell in your presence.

Psalm 141

A Psalm by David.

¹Yahweh, I have called on you.
   Come to me quickly!
   Listen to my voice when I call to you.
²Let my prayer be set before you like
   incense;
   the lifting up of my hands like the
   evening sacrifice.
³Set a watch, Yahweh, before my mouth.
   Keep the door of my lips.
⁴Don't incline my heart to any evil thing,
   to practice deeds of wickedness with
   men who work iniquity.
   Don't let me eat of their delicacies.

⁵Let the righteous strike me, it is kindness;
    let him reprove me, it is like oil on the
        head;
    don't let my head refuse it;
    Yet my prayer is always against evil
        deeds.
⁶Their judges are thrown down by the sides
        of the rock.
    They will hear my words, for they are
        well spoken.
⁷"As when one plows and breaks up the
        earth,
    our bones are scattered at the mouth of
        Sheol."
⁸For my eyes are on you, Yahweh, the Lord.
    In you, I take refuge.
    Don't leave my soul destitute.
⁹Keep me from the snare which they have
        laid for me,
    from the traps of the workers of iniq-
        uity.
¹⁰Let the wicked fall together into their own
        nets,
    while I pass by.

Psalm 142

A contemplation by David, when he
was in the cave. A Prayer.

¹I cry with my voice to Yahweh.
    With my voice, I ask Yahweh for mercy.
²I pour out my complaint before him.
    I tell him my troubles.
³When my spirit was overwhelmed within
        me,
    you knew my path.
In the way in which I walk,
    they have hidden a snare for me.
⁴Look on my right, and see;
    for there is no one who is concerned for
        me.
    Refuge has fled from me.
    No one cares for my soul.
⁵I cried to you, Yahweh.
    I said, "You are my refuge,
    my portion in the land of the living."
⁶Listen to my cry,
    for I am in desperate need.
deliver me from my persecutors,
    For they are stronger than me.
⁷Bring my soul out of prison,

that I may give thanks to your name.
The righteous will surround me,
    for you will be good to me.

Psalm 143

A Psalm by David.

¹Hear my prayer, Yahweh.
    Listen to my petitions.
    In your faithfulness and righteousness,
        relieve me.
²Don't enter into judgment with your ser-
        vant,
    for in your sight no man living is
        righteous.
³For the enemy pursues my soul.
    He has struck my life down to the
        ground.
    He has made me live in dark places, as
        those who have been long dead.
⁴Therefore my spirit is overwhelmed
        within me.
    My heart within me is desolate.
⁵I remember the days of old.
    I meditate on all your doings.
    I contemplate the work of your hands.
⁶I spread forth my hands to you.
    My soul thirsts for you, like a parched
        land.
Selah.
⁷Hurry to answer me, Yahweh.
    My spirit fails.
Don't hide your face from me,
    so that I don't become like those who
        go down into the pit.
⁸Cause me to hear your loving kindness in
        the morning,
    for I trust in you.
Cause me to know the way in which I
        should walk,
    for I lift up my soul to you.
⁹Deliver me, Yahweh, from my enemies.
    I flee to you to hide me.
¹⁰Teach me to do your will,
    for you are my God.
Your Spirit is good.
    Lead me in the land of uprightness.
¹¹Revive me, Yahweh, for your name's
        sake.
    In your righteousness, bring my soul
        out of trouble.

[12] In your loving kindness, cut off my enemies,

and destroy all those who afflict my soul,

For I am your servant.

Psalm 144

By David.

[1] Blessed be Yahweh, my rock,

who teaches my hands to war,

and my fingers to battle:

[2] my loving kindness, my fortress,

my high tower, my deliverer,

my shield, and he in whom I take refuge;

who subdues my people under me.

[3] Yahweh, what is man, that you care for him?

Or the son of man, that you think of him?

[4] Man is like a breath.

His days are like a shadow that passes away.

[5] Part your heavens, Yahweh, and come down.

Touch the mountains, and they will smoke.

[6] Throw out lightning, and scatter them.

Send out your arrows, and rout them.

[7] Stretch out your hand from above,

rescue me, and deliver me out of great waters,

out of the hands of foreigners;

[8] whose mouths speak deceit,

Whose right hand is a right hand of falsehood.

[9] I will sing a new song to you, God.

On a ten-stringed lyre, I will sing praises to you.

[10] You are he who gives salvation to kings,

who rescues David, his servant, from the deadly sword.

[11] Rescue me, and deliver me out of the hands of foreigners,

whose mouths speak deceit,

whose right hand is a right hand of falsehood.

[12] Then our sons will be like well-nurtured plants,

our daughters like pillars carved to adorn a palace.

[13] Our barns are full, filled with all kinds of provision.

Our sheep bring forth thousands and ten thousands in our fields.

[14] Our oxen will pull heavy loads.

There is no breaking in, and no going away,

and no outcry in our streets.

[15] Happy are the people who are in such a situation.

Happy are the people whose God is Yahweh.

Psalm 145

A praise psalm by David.[q]

[1] I will exalt you, my God, the King.

I will praise your name forever and ever.

[2] Every day I will praise you.

I will extol your name forever and ever.

[3] Great is Yahweh, and greatly to be praised!

His greatness is unsearchable.

[4] One generation will commend your works to another,

and will declare your mighty acts.

[5] Of the glorious majesty of your honor,

of your wondrous works, I will meditate.

[6] Men will speak of the might of your awesome acts.

I will declare your greatness.

[7] They will utter the memory of your great goodness,

and will sing of your righteousness.

[8] Yahweh is gracious, merciful,

slow to anger, and of great loving kindness.

[9] Yahweh is good to all.

His tender mercies are over all his works.

[10] All your works will give thanks to you, Yahweh.

Your saints will extol you.

---

[q]145:0 This is an acrostic psalm, with every verse (including the second half of verse 13) starting with a consecutive letter of the Hebrew alphabet.

[11]They will speak of the glory of your kingdom,
and talk about your power;
[12]to make known to the sons of men his mighty acts,
the glory of the majesty of his kingdom.
[13]Your kingdom is an everlasting kingdom.
Your dominion endures throughout all generations.
Yahweh is faithful in all his words,
and loving in all his deeds.[r]
[14]Yahweh upholds all who fall,
and raises up all those who are bowed down.
[15]The eyes of all wait for you.
You give them their food in due season.
[16]You open your hand,
and satisfy the desire of every living thing.
[17]Yahweh is righteous in all his ways,
and gracious in all his works.
[18]Yahweh is near to all those who call on him,
to all who call on him in truth.
[19]He will fulfill the desire of those who fear him.
He also will hear their cry, and will save them.
[20]Yahweh preserves all those who love him,
but all the wicked he will destroy.
[21]My mouth will speak the praise of Yahweh.
Let all flesh bless his holy name forever and ever.

Psalm 146

[1]Praise Yah!
Praise Yahweh, my soul.
[2]While I live, I will praise Yahweh.
I will sing praises to my God as long as I exist.
[3]Don't put your trust in princes,
each a son of man in whom there is no help.
[4]His spirit departs, and he returns to the earth.
In that very day, his thoughts perish.
[5]Happy is he who has the God of Jacob for his help,
whose hope is in Yahweh, his God:

[6]who made heaven and earth,
the sea, and all that is in them;
who keeps truth forever;
[7]who executes justice for the oppressed;
who gives food to the hungry.
Yahweh frees the prisoners.
[8]Yahweh opens the eyes of the blind.
Yahweh raises up those who are bowed down.
Yahweh loves the righteous.
[9]Yahweh preserves the foreigners.
He upholds the fatherless and widow,
but the way of the wicked he turns upside down.
[10]Yahweh will reign forever;
your God, O Zion, to all generations.
Praise Yah!

Psalm 147

[1]Praise Yah,
for it is good to sing praises to our God;
for it is pleasant and fitting to praise him.
[2]Yahweh builds up Jerusalem.
He gathers together the outcasts of Israel.
[3]He heals the broken in heart,
and binds up their wounds.
[4]He counts the number of the stars.
He calls them all by their names.
[5]Great is our Lord, and mighty in power.
His understanding is infinite.
[6]Yahweh upholds the humble.
He brings the wicked down to the ground.
[7]Sing to Yahweh with thanksgiving.
Sing praises on the harp to our God,
[8]who covers the sky with clouds,
who prepares rain for the earth,
who makes grass grow on the mountains.
[9]He provides food for the livestock,
and for the young ravens when they call.
[10]He doesn't delight in the strength of the horse.
He takes no pleasure in the legs of a man.

---

[r]145:13 Some manuscripts omit these last two lines.

^{11}Yahweh takes pleasure in those who fear him,
　in those who hope in his loving kindness.
^{12}Praise Yahweh, Jerusalem!
　Praise your God, Zion!
^{13}For he has strengthened the bars of your gates.
　He has blessed your children within you.
^{14}He makes peace in your borders.
　He fills you with the finest of the wheat.
^{15}He sends out his commandment to the earth.
　His word runs very swiftly.
^{16}He gives snow like wool,
　and scatters frost like ashes.
^{17}He hurls down his hail like pebbles.
　Who can stand before his cold?
^{18}He sends out his word, and melts them.
　He causes his wind to blow, and the waters flow.
^{19}He shows his word to Jacob;
　his statutes and his ordinances to Israel.
^{20}He has not done this for just any nation.
　They don't know his ordinances.
Praise Yah!

Psalm 148

^{1}Praise Yah!
　Praise Yahweh from the heavens!
　Praise him in the heights!
^{2}Praise him, all his angels!
　Praise him, all his army!
^{3}Praise him, sun and moon!
　Praise him, all you shining stars!
^{4}Praise him, you heavens of heavens,
　You waters that are above the heavens.
^{5}Let them praise the name of Yahweh,
　For he commanded, and they were created.
^{6}He has also established them forever and ever.
　He has made a decree which will not pass away.
^{7}Praise Yahweh from the earth,
　you great sea creatures, and all depths!
^{8}Lightning and hail, snow and clouds;
　stormy wind, fulfilling his word;
^{9}mountains and all hills;
　fruit trees and all cedars;

^{10}wild animals and all livestock;
　small creatures and flying birds;
^{11}kings of the earth and all peoples;
　princes and all judges of the earth;
^{12}both young men and maidens;
　old men and children:
^{13}let them praise the name of Yahweh,
　for his name alone is exalted.
　His glory is above the earth and the heavens.
^{14}He has lifted up the horn of his people,
　the praise of all his saints;
　even of the children of Israel, a people near to him.
Praise Yah!

Psalm 149

^{1}Praise Yahweh!
　Sing to Yahweh a new song,
　his praise in the assembly of the saints.
^{2}Let Israel rejoice in him who made them.
　Let the children of Zion be joyful in their King.
^{3}Let them praise his name in the dance!
　Let them sing praises to him with tambourine and harp!
^{4}For Yahweh takes pleasure in his people.
　He crowns the humble with salvation.
^{5}Let the saints rejoice in honor.
　Let them sing for joy on their beds.
^{6}May the high praises of God be in their mouths,
　and a two-edged sword in their hand;
^{7}To execute vengeance on the nations,
　and punishments on the peoples;
^{8}To bind their kings with chains,
　and their nobles with fetters of iron;
^{9}to execute on them the written judgment.
　All his saints have this honor.
Praise Yah!

Psalm 150

^{1}Praise Yah!
　Praise God in his sanctuary!
　Praise him in his heavens for his acts of power!
^{2}Praise him for his mighty acts!
　Praise him according to his excellent greatness!
^{3}Praise him with the sounding of the trumpet!

Praise him with harp and lyre!
⁴Praise him with tambourine and dancing!
Praise him with stringed instruments
and flute!
⁵Praise him with loud cymbals!
Praise him with resounding cymbals!
⁶Let everything that has breath praise Yah!
Praise Yah!

Proverbs

1:1 The proverbs of Solomon, the son of David, king of Israel:

1:2 to know wisdom and instruction;
to discern the words of understanding;
1:3 to receive instruction in wise dealing,
in righteousness, justice, and equity;
1:4 to give prudence to the simple,
knowledge and discretion to the young man:
1:5 that the wise man may hear, and increase in learning;
that the man of understanding may attain to sound counsel:
1:6 to understand a proverb, and parables,
the words and riddles of the wise.
1:7 The fear of Yahweh is the beginning of knowledge;
but the foolish despise wisdom and instruction.
1:8 My son, listen to your father's instruction,
and don't forsake your mother's teaching:
1:9 for they will be a garland to grace your head,
and chains around your neck.
1:10 My son, if sinners entice you, don't consent.
1:11 If they say, "Come with us,
Let's lay in wait for blood;
let's lurk secretly for the innocent without cause;
1:12 let's swallow them up alive like Sheol,
and whole, like those who go down into the pit.
1:13 We'll find all valuable wealth.
We'll fill our houses with spoil.
1:14 You shall cast your lot among us.
We'll all have one purse."
1:15 My son, don't walk in the way with them.
Keep your foot from their path,
1:16 for their feet run to evil.
They hurry to shed blood.
1:17 For in vain is the net spread in the sight of any bird:
1:18 but these lay wait for their own blood.
They lurk secretly for their own lives.
1:19 So are the ways of everyone who is greedy for gain.

It takes away the life of its owners.
1:20 Wisdom calls aloud in the street.
She utters her voice in the public squares.
1:21 She calls at the head of noisy places.
At the entrance of the city gates, she utters her words:
1:22 "How long, you simple ones, will you love simplicity?
How long will mockers delight themselves in mockery,
and fools hate knowledge?
1:23 Turn at my reproof.
Behold, I will pour out my spirit on you.
I will make known my words to you.
1:24 Because I have called, and you have refused;
I have stretched out my hand, and no one has paid attention;
1:25 but you have ignored all my counsel,
and wanted none of my reproof;
1:26 I also will laugh at your disaster.
I will mock when calamity overtakes you;
1:27 when calamity overtakes you like a storm,
when your disaster comes on like a whirlwind;
when distress and anguish come on you.
1:28 Then will they call on me, but I will not answer.
They will seek me diligently, but they will not find me;
1:29 because they hated knowledge,
and didn't choose the fear of Yahweh.
1:30 They wanted none of my counsel.
They despised all my reproof.
1:31 Therefore they will eat of the fruit of their own way,
and be filled with their own schemes.
1:32 For the backsliding of the simple will kill them.
The careless ease of fools will destroy them.
1:33 But whoever listens to me will dwell securely,
and will be at ease, without fear of harm."
2:1 My son, if you will receive my words,

and store up my commandments within you;

2:2 So as to turn your ear to wisdom,
and apply your heart to understanding;

2:3 Yes, if you call out for discernment,
and lift up your voice for understanding;

2:4 If you seek her as silver,
and search for her as for hidden treasures:

2:5 then you will understand the fear of Yahweh,
and find the knowledge of God.

2:6 For Yahweh gives wisdom.
Out of his mouth comes knowledge and understanding.

2:7 He lays up sound wisdom for the upright.
He is a shield to those who walk in integrity;

2:8 that he may guard the paths of justice,
and preserve the way of his saints.

2:9 Then you will understand righteousness and justice,
equity and every good path.

2:10 For wisdom will enter into your heart.
Knowledge will be pleasant to your soul.

2:11 Discretion will watch over you.
Understanding will keep you,

2:12 to deliver you from the way of evil,
from the men who speak perverse things;

2:13 who forsake the paths of uprightness,
to walk in the ways of darkness;

2:14 who rejoice to do evil,
and delight in the perverseness of evil;

2:15 who are crooked in their ways,
and wayward in their paths:

2:16 To deliver you from the strange woman,
even from the foreigner who flatters with her words;

2:17 who forsakes the friend of her youth,
and forgets the covenant of her God:

2:18 for her house leads down to death,
her paths to the dead.

2:19 None who go to her return again,
neither do they attain to the paths of life:

2:20 that you may walk in the way of good men,

and keep the paths of the righteous.

2:21 For the upright will dwell in the land.
The perfect will remain in it.

2:22 But the wicked will be cut off from the land.
The treacherous will be rooted out of it.

3:1 My son, don't forget my teaching;
but let your heart keep my commandments:

3:2 for length of days, and years of life,
and peace, will they add to you.

3:3 Don't let kindness and truth forsake you.
Bind them around your neck.
Write them on the tablet of your heart.

3:4 So you will find favor,
and good understanding in the sight of God and man.

3:5 Trust in Yahweh with all your heart,
and don't lean on your own understanding.

3:6 In all your ways acknowledge him,
and he will make your paths straight.

3:7 Don't be wise in your own eyes.
Fear Yahweh, and depart from evil.

3:8 It will be health to your body,
and nourishment to your bones.

3:9 Honor Yahweh with your substance,
with the first fruits of all your increase:

3:10 so your barns will be filled with plenty,
and your vats will overflow with new wine.

3:11 My son, don't despise Yahweh's discipline,
neither be weary of his reproof:

3:12 for whom Yahweh loves, he reproves;
even as a father reproves the son in whom he delights.

3:13 Happy is the man who finds wisdom,
the man who gets understanding.

3:14 For her good profit is better than getting silver,
and her return is better than fine gold.

3:15 She is more precious than rubies.
None of the things you can desire are to be compared to her.

3:16 Length of days is in her right hand.
In her left hand are riches and honor.

3:17 Her ways are ways of pleasantness.
All her paths are peace.

3:18 She is a tree of life to those who lay hold of her.
Happy is everyone who retains her.

3:19 By wisdom Yahweh founded the earth.
By understanding, he established the heavens.

3:20 By his knowledge, the depths were broken up,
and the skies drop down the dew.

3:21 My son, let them not depart from your eyes.
Keep sound wisdom and discretion:

3:22 so they will be life to your soul,
and grace for your neck.

3:23 Then you shall walk in your way securely.
Your foot won't stumble.

3:24 When you lie down, you will not be afraid.
Yes, you will lie down, and your sleep will be sweet.

3:25 Don't be afraid of sudden fear,
neither of the desolation of the wicked, when it comes:

3:26 for Yahweh will be your confidence,
and will keep your foot from being taken.

3:27 Don't withhold good from those to whom it is due,
when it is in the power of your hand to do it.

3:28 Don't say to your neighbor, "Go, and come again;
tomorrow I will give it to you,"
when you have it by you.

3:29 Don't devise evil against your neighbor,
seeing he dwells securely by you.

3:30 Don't strive with a man without cause,
if he has done you no harm.

3:31 Don't envy the man of violence.
Choose none of his ways.

3:32 For the perverse is an abomination to Yahweh,
but his friendship is with the upright.

3:33 Yahweh's curse is in the house of the wicked,
but he blesses the habitation of the righteous.

3:34 Surely he mocks the mockers,
but he gives grace to the humble.

3:35 The wise will inherit glory,
but shame will be the promotion of fools.

4:1 Listen, sons, to a father's instruction.
Pay attention and know understanding;

4:2 for I give you sound learning.
Don't forsake my law.

4:3 For I was a son to my father,
tender and an only child in the sight of my mother.

4:4 He taught me, and said to me:
"Let your heart retain my words.
Keep my commandments, and live.

4:5 Get wisdom.
Get understanding.
Don't forget, neither swerve from the words of my mouth.

4:6 Don't forsake her, and she will preserve you.
Love her, and she will keep you.

4:7 Wisdom is supreme.
Get wisdom.
Yes, though it costs all your possessions, get understanding.

4:8 Esteem her, and she will exalt you.
She will bring you to honor, when you embrace her.

4:9 She will give to your head a garland of grace.
She will deliver a crown of splendor to you."

4:10 Listen, my son, and receive my sayings.
The years of your life will be many.

4:11 I have taught you in the way of wisdom.
I have led you in straight paths.

4:12 When you go, your steps will not be hampered.
When you run, you will not stumble.

4:13 Take firm hold of instruction.
Don't let her go.
Keep her, for she is your life.

4:14 Don't enter into the path of the wicked.
Don't walk in the way of evil men.

4:15 Avoid it, and don't pass by it.
Turn from it, and pass on.

4:16 For they don't sleep, unless they do evil.
Their sleep is taken away, unless they make someone fall.

4:17 For they eat the bread of wickedness,
and drink the wine of violence.

4:18 But the path of the righteous is like the dawning light,
that shines more and more until the perfect day.

4:19 The way of the wicked is like darkness.

They don't know what they stumble over.

^{4:20}My son, attend to my words.
Turn your ear to my sayings.
^{4:21}Let them not depart from your eyes.
Keep them in the midst of your heart.
^{4:22}For they are life to those who find them,
and health to their whole body.
^{4:23}Keep your heart with all diligence,
for out of it is the wellspring of life.
^{4:24}Put away from yourself a perverse mouth.
Put corrupt lips far from you.
^{4:25}Let your eyes look straight ahead.
Fix your gaze directly before you.
^{4:26}Make the path of your feet level.
Let all of your ways be established.
^{4:27}Don't turn to the right hand nor to the left.
Remove your foot from evil.
^{5:1}My son, pay attention to my wisdom.
Turn your ear to my understanding:
^{5:2}that you may maintain discretion,
that your lips may preserve knowledge.
^{5:3}For the lips of an adulteress drip honey.
Her mouth is smoother than oil,
^{5:4}But in the end she is as bitter as wormwood,
and as sharp as a two-edged sword.
^{5:5}Her feet go down to death.
Her steps lead straight to Sheol.
^{5:6}She gives no thought to the way of life.
Her ways are crooked, and she doesn't know it.
^{5:7}Now therefore, my sons, listen to me.
Don't depart from the words of my mouth.
^{5:8}Remove your way far from her.
Don't come near the door of her house,
^{5:9}lest you give your honor to others,
and your years to the cruel one;
^{5:10}lest strangers feast on your wealth,
and your labors enrich another man's house.
^{5:11}You will groan at your latter end,
when your flesh and your body are consumed,
^{5:12}and say, "How I have hated instruction,
and my heart despised reproof;
^{5:13}neither have I obeyed the voice of my teachers,

nor turned my ear to those who instructed me!
^{5:14}I have come to the brink of utter ruin,
in the midst of the gathered assembly."
^{5:15}Drink water out of your own cistern,
running water out of your own well.
^{5:16}Should your springs overflow in the streets,
streams of water in the public squares?
^{5:17}Let them be for yourself alone,
not for strangers with you.
^{5:18}Let your spring be blessed.
Rejoice in the wife of your youth.
^{5:19}A loving doe and a graceful deer—
let her breasts satisfy you at all times.
Be captivated always with her love.
^{5:20}For why should you, my son, be captivated with an adulteress?
Why embrace the bosom of another?
^{5:21}For the ways of man are before the eyes of Yahweh.
He examines all his paths.
^{5:22}The evil deeds of the wicked ensnare him.
The cords of his sin hold him firmly.
^{5:23}He will die for lack of instruction.
In the greatness of his folly, he will go astray.
^{6:1}My son, if you have become collateral for your neighbor,
if you have struck your hands in pledge for a stranger;
^{6:2}You are trapped by the words of your mouth.
You are ensnared with the words of your mouth.
^{6:3}Do this now, my son, and deliver yourself,
seeing you have come into the hand of your neighbor.
Go, humble yourself.
Press your plea with your neighbor.
^{6:4}Give no sleep to your eyes,
nor slumber to your eyelids.
^{6:5}Free yourself, like a gazelle from the hand of the hunter,
like a bird from the snare of the fowler.
^{6:6}Go to the ant, you sluggard.
Consider her ways, and be wise;
^{6:7}which having no chief, overseer, or ruler,
^{6:8}provides her bread in the summer,
and gathers her food in the harvest.

^{6:9}How long will you sleep, sluggard?
When will you arise out of your sleep?
^{6:10}A little sleep, a little slumber,
a little folding of the hands to sleep:
^{6:11}so your poverty will come as a robber,
and your scarcity as an armed man.
^{6:12}A worthless person, a man of iniquity,
is he who walks with a perverse mouth;
^{6:13}who winks with his eyes, who signals
with his feet,
who motions with his fingers;
^{6:14}in whose heart is perverseness,
who devises evil continually,
who always sows discord.
^{6:15}Therefore his calamity will come suddenly.
He will be broken suddenly, and that
without remedy.
^{6:16}There are six things which Yahweh
hates;
yes, seven which are an abomination to
him:
^{6:17}haughty eyes, a lying tongue,
hands that shed innocent blood;
^{6:18}a heart that devises wicked schemes,
feet that are swift in running to mischief,
^{6:19}a false witness who utters lies,
and he who sows discord among brothers.
^{6:20}My son, keep your father's commandment,
and don't forsake your mother's teaching.
^{6:21}Bind them continually on your heart.
Tie them around your neck.
^{6:22}When you walk, it will lead you.
When you sleep, it will watch over you.
When you awake, it will talk with you.
^{6:23}For the commandment is a lamp,
and the law is light.
Reproofs of instruction are the way of
life,
^{6:24}to keep you from the immoral woman,
from the flattery of the wayward wife's
tongue.
^{6:25}Don't lust after her beauty in your heart,
neither let her captivate you with her
eyelids.
^{6:26}For a prostitute reduces you to a piece
of bread.

The adulteress hunts for your precious
life.
^{6:27}Can a man scoop fire into his lap,
and his clothes not be burned?
^{6:28}Or can one walk on hot coals,
and his feet not be scorched?
^{6:29}So is he who goes in to his neighbor's
wife.
Whoever touches her will not be unpunished.
^{6:30}Men don't despise a thief,
if he steals to satisfy himself when he is
hungry:
^{6:31}but if he is found, he shall restore seven
times.
He shall give all the wealth of his
house.
^{6:32}He who commits adultery with a
woman is void of understanding.
He who does it destroys his own soul.
^{6:33}He will get wounds and dishonor.
His reproach will not be wiped away.
^{6:34}For jealousy arouses the fury of the
husband.
He won't spare in the day of
vengeance.
^{6:35}He won't regard any ransom,
neither will he rest content, though you
give many gifts.
^{7:1}My son, keep my words.
Lay up my commandments within
you.
^{7:2}Keep my commandments and live!
Guard my teaching as the apple of your
eye.
^{7:3}Bind them on your fingers.
Write them on the tablet of your heart.
^{7:4}Tell wisdom, "You are my sister."
Call understanding your relative,
^{7:5}that they may keep you from the strange
woman,
from the foreigner who flatters with her
words.
^{7:6}For at the window of my house,
I looked out through my lattice.
^{7:7}I saw among the simple ones.
I discerned among the youths a young
man void of understanding,
^{7:8}passing through the street near her corner,
he went the way to her house,
^{7:9}in the twilight, in the evening of the day,

in the middle of the night and in the darkness.

^{7:10}Behold, there a woman met him with the attire of a prostitute,
and with crafty intent.

^{7:11}She is loud and defiant.
Her feet don't stay in her house.

^{7:12}Now she is in the streets, now in the squares,
and lurking at every corner.

^{7:13}So she caught him, and kissed him.
With an impudent face she said to him:

^{7:14}"Sacrifices of peace offerings are with me.
This day I have paid my vows.

^{7:15}Therefore I came out to meet you,
to diligently seek your face,
and I have found you.

^{7:16}I have spread my couch with carpets of tapestry,
with striped cloths of the yarn of Egypt.

^{7:17}I have perfumed my bed with myrrh, aloes, and cinnamon.

^{7:18}Come, let's take our fill of loving until the morning.
Let's solace ourselves with loving.

^{7:19}For my husband isn't at home.
He has gone on a long journey.

^{7:20}He has taken a bag of money with him.
He will come home at the full moon."

^{7:21}With persuasive words, she led him astray.
With the flattering of her lips, she seduced him.

^{7:22}He followed her immediately,
as an ox goes to the slaughter,
as a fool stepping into a noose.

^{7:23}Until an arrow strikes through his liver,
as a bird hurries to the snare,
and doesn't know that it will cost his life.

^{7:24}Now therefore, sons, listen to me.
Pay attention to the words of my mouth.

^{7:25}Don't let your heart turn to her ways.
Don't go astray in her paths,

^{7:26}for she has thrown down many wounded.
Yes, all her slain are a mighty army.

^{7:27}Her house is the way to Sheol,
going down to the chambers of death.

^{8:1}Doesn't wisdom cry out?

Doesn't understanding raise her voice?

^{8:2}On the top of high places by the way,
where the paths meet, she stands.

^{8:3}Beside the gates, at the entry of the city,
at the entry doors, she cries aloud:

^{8:4}"To you men, I call!
I send my voice to the sons of mankind.

^{8:5}You simple, understand prudence.
You fools, be of an understanding heart.

^{8:6}Hear, for I will speak excellent things.
The opening of my lips is for right things.

^{8:7}For my mouth speaks truth.
Wickedness is an abomination to my lips.

^{8:8}All the words of my mouth are in righteousness.
There is nothing crooked or perverse in them.

^{8:9}They are all plain to him who understands,
right to those who find knowledge.

^{8:10}Receive my instruction rather than silver;
knowledge rather than choice gold.

^{8:11}For wisdom is better than rubies.
All the things that may be desired can't be compared to it.

^{8:12}"I, wisdom, have made prudence my dwelling.
Find out knowledge and discretion.

^{8:13}The fear of Yahweh is to hate evil.
I hate pride, arrogance, the evil way, and the perverse mouth.

^{8:14}Counsel and sound knowledge are mine.
I have understanding and power.

^{8:15}By me kings reign,
and princes decree justice.

^{8:16}By me princes rule;
nobles, and all the righteous rulers of the earth.

^{8:17}I love those who love me.
Those who seek me diligently will find me.

^{8:18}With me are riches, honor,
enduring wealth, and prosperity.

^{8:19}My fruit is better than gold, yes, than fine gold;
my yield than choice silver.

^{8:20}I walk in the way of righteousness,

in the midst of the paths of justice;

8:21 That I may give wealth to those who love me.

I fill their treasuries.

8:22 "Yahweh possessed me in the beginning of his work,

before his deeds of old.

8:23 I was set up from everlasting, from the beginning,

before the earth existed.

8:24 When there were no depths, I was brought forth,

when there were no springs abounding with water.

8:25 Before the mountains were settled in place,

before the hills, I was brought forth;

8:26 while as yet he had not made the earth, nor the fields,

nor the beginning of the dust of the world.

8:27 When he established the heavens, I was there;

when he set a circle on the surface of the deep,

8:28 when he established the clouds above,

when the springs of the deep became strong,

8:29 when he gave to the sea its boundary,

that the waters should not violate his commandment,

when he marked out the foundations of the earth;

8:30 then I was the craftsman by his side.

I was a delight day by day,

always rejoicing before him,

8:31 Rejoicing in his whole world.

My delight was with the sons of men.

8:32 "Now therefore, my sons, listen to me,

for blessed are those who keep my ways.

8:33 Hear instruction, and be wise.

Don't refuse it.

8:34 Blessed is the man who hears me,

watching daily at my gates,

waiting at my door posts.

8:35 For whoever finds me, finds life,

and will obtain favor from Yahweh.

8:36 But he who sins against me wrongs his own soul.

All those who hate me love death."

9:1 Wisdom has built her house.

She has carved out her seven pillars.

9:2 She has prepared her meat.

She has mixed her wine.

She has also set her table.

9:3 She has sent out her maidens.

She cries from the highest places of the city:

9:4 "Whoever is simple, let him turn in here!"

As for him who is void of understanding, she says to him,

9:5 "Come, eat some of my bread,

Drink some of the wine which I have mixed!

9:6 Leave your simple ways, and live.

Walk in the way of understanding."

9:7 He who corrects a mocker invites insult.

He who reproves a wicked man invites abuse.

9:8 Don't reprove a scoffer, lest he hate you.

Reprove a wise man, and he will love you.

9:9 Instruct a wise man, and he will be still wiser.

Teach a righteous man, and he will increase in learning.

9:10 The fear of Yahweh is the beginning of wisdom.

The knowledge of the Holy One is understanding.

9:11 For by me your days will be multiplied.

The years of your life will be increased

9:12 If you are wise, you are wise for yourself.

If you mock, you alone will bear it.

9:13 The foolish woman is loud,

Undisciplined, and knows nothing.

9:14 She sits at the door of her house,

on a seat in the high places of the city,

9:15 To call to those who pass by,

who go straight on their ways,

9:16 "Whoever is simple, let him turn in here."

as for him who is void of understanding, she says to him,

9:17 "Stolen water is sweet.

Food eaten in secret is pleasant."

9:18 But he doesn't know that the dead are there,

that her guests are in the depths of Sheol.

10:1 The proverbs of Solomon.

A wise son makes a glad father;
  but a foolish son brings grief to his
  mother.
10:2 Treasures of wickedness profit nothing,
  but righteousness delivers from death.
10:3 Yahweh will not allow the soul of the
  righteous to go hungry,
  but he thrusts away the desire of the
  wicked.
10:4 He becomes poor who works with a
  lazy hand,
  but the hand of the diligent brings
  wealth.
10:5 He who gathers in summer is a wise
  son,
  but he who sleeps during the harvest is
  a son who causes shame.
10:6 Blessings are on the head of the righteous,
  but violence covers the mouth of the
  wicked.
10:7 The memory of the righteous is blessed,
  but the name of the wicked will rot.
10:8 The wise in heart accept commandments,
  but a chattering fool will fall.
10:9 He who walks blamelessly walks surely,
  but he who perverts his ways will be
  found out.
10:10 One winking with the eye causes sorrow,
  but a chattering fool will fall.
10:11 The mouth of the righteous is a spring
  of life,
  but violence covers the mouth of the
  wicked.
10:12 Hatred stirs up strife,
  but love covers all wrongs.
10:13 Wisdom is found on the lips of him
  who has discernment,
  but a rod is for the back of him who is
  void of understanding.
10:14 Wise men lay up knowledge,
  but the mouth of the foolish is near
  ruin.
10:15 The rich man's wealth is his strong city.
  The destruction of the poor is their
  poverty.
10:16 The labor of the righteous leads to life.
  The increase of the wicked leads to sin.
10:17 He is in the way of life who heeds
  correction,

but he who forsakes reproof leads others astray.
10:18 He who hides hatred has lying lips.
  He who utters a slander is a fool.
10:19 In the multitude of words there is no
  lack of disobedience,
  but he who restrains his lips does
  wisely.
10:20 The tongue of the righteous is like
  choice silver.
  The heart of the wicked is of little
  worth.
10:21 The lips of the righteous feed many,
  but the foolish die for lack of understanding.
10:22 Yahweh's blessing brings wealth,
  and he adds no trouble to it.
10:23 It is a fool's pleasure to do wickedness,
  but wisdom is a man of understanding's pleasure.
10:24 What the wicked fear, will overtake
  them,
  but the desire of the righteous will be
  granted.
10:25 When the whirlwind passes, the
  wicked is no more;
  but the righteous stand firm forever.
10:26 As vinegar to the teeth, and as smoke
  to the eyes,
  so is the sluggard to those who send
  him.
10:27 The fear of Yahweh prolongs days,
  but the years of the wicked shall be
  shortened.
10:28 The prospect of the righteous is joy,
  but the hope of the wicked will perish.
10:29 The way of Yahweh is a stronghold to
  the upright,
  but it is a destruction to the workers of
  iniquity.
10:30 The righteous will never be removed,
  but the wicked will not dwell in the
  land.
10:31 The mouth of the righteous brings
  forth wisdom,
  but the perverse tongue will be cut off.
10:32 The lips of the righteous know what is
  acceptable,
  but the mouth of the wicked is perverse.
11:1 A false balance is an abomination to
  Yahweh,

but accurate weights are his delight.

^{11:2}When pride comes, then comes shame,

but with humility comes wisdom.

^{11:3}The integrity of the upright shall guide them,

but the perverseness of the treacherous shall destroy them.

^{11:4}Riches don't profit in the day of wrath,

but righteousness delivers from death.

^{11:5}The righteousness of the blameless will direct his way,

but the wicked shall fall by his own wickedness.

^{11:6}The righteousness of the upright shall deliver them,

but the unfaithful will be trapped by evil desires.

^{11:7}When a wicked man dies, hope perishes,

and expectation of power comes to nothing.

^{11:8}A righteous person is delivered out of trouble,

and the wicked takes his place.

^{11:9}With his mouth the godless man destroys his neighbor,

but the righteous will be delivered through knowledge.

^{11:10}When it goes well with the righteous, the city rejoices.

When the wicked perish, there is shouting.

^{11:11}By the blessing of the upright, the city is exalted,

but it is overthrown by the mouth of the wicked.

^{11:12}One who despises his neighbor is void of wisdom,

but a man of understanding holds his peace.

^{11:13}One who brings gossip betrays a confidence,

but one who is of a trustworthy spirit is one who keeps a secret.

^{11:14}Where there is no wise guidance, the nation falls,

but in the multitude of counselors there is victory.

^{11:15}He who is collateral for a stranger will suffer for it,

but he who refuses pledges of collateral is secure.

^{11:16}A gracious woman obtains honor,

but violent men obtain riches.

^{11:17}The merciful man does good to his own soul,

but he who is cruel troubles his own flesh.

^{11:18}Wicked people earn deceitful wages,

but one who sows righteousness reaps a sure reward.

^{11:19}He who is truly righteous gets life.

He who pursues evil gets death.

^{11:20}Those who are perverse in heart are an abomination to Yahweh,

but those whose ways are blameless are his delight.

^{11:21}Most certainly, the evil man will not be unpunished,

but the seed of the righteous will be delivered.

^{11:22}Like a gold ring in a pig's snout,

is a beautiful woman who lacks discretion.

^{11:23}The desire of the righteous is only good.

The expectation of the wicked is wrath.

^{11:24}There is one who scatters, and increases yet more.

There is one who withholds more than is appropriate, but gains poverty.

^{11:25}The liberal soul shall be made fat.

He who waters shall be watered also himself.

^{11:26}People curse someone who withholds grain,

but blessing will be on the head of him who sells it.

^{11:27}He who diligently seeks good seeks favor,

but he who searches after evil, it shall come to him.

^{11:28}He who trusts in his riches will fall,

but the righteous shall flourish as the green leaf.

^{11:29}He who troubles his own house shall inherit the wind.

The foolish shall be servant to the wise of heart.

^{11:30}The fruit of the righteous is a tree of life.

He who is wise wins souls.

^{11:31}Behold, the righteous shall be repaid in the earth;

how much more the wicked and the sinner!

12:1 Whoever loves correction loves knowledge,

but he who hates reproof is stupid.

12:2 A good man shall obtain favor from Yahweh,

but he will condemn a man of wicked devices.

12:3 A man shall not be established by wickedness,

but the root of the righteous shall not be moved.

12:4 A worthy woman is the crown of her husband,

but a disgraceful wife is as rottenness in his bones.

12:5 The thoughts of the righteous are just,

but the advice of the wicked is deceitful.

12:6 The words of the wicked are about lying in wait for blood,

but the speech of the upright rescues them.

12:7 The wicked are overthrown, and are no more,

but the house of the righteous shall stand.

12:8 A man shall be commended according to his wisdom,

but he who has a warped mind shall be despised.

12:9 Better is he who is lightly esteemed, and has a servant,

than he who honors himself, and lacks bread.

12:10 A righteous man regards the life of his animal,

but the tender mercies of the wicked are cruel.

12:11 He who tills his land shall have plenty of bread,

but he who chases fantasies is void of understanding.

12:12 The wicked desires the plunder of evil men,

but the root of the righteous flourishes.

12:13 An evil man is trapped by sinfulness of lips,

but the righteous shall come out of trouble.

12:14 A man shall be satisfied with good by the fruit of his mouth.

The work of a man's hands shall be rewarded to him.

12:15 The way of a fool is right in his own eyes,

but he who is wise listens to counsel.

12:16 A fool shows his annoyance the same day,

but one who overlooks an insult is prudent.

12:17 He who is truthful testifies honestly,

but a false witness lies.

12:18 There is one who speaks rashly like the piercing of a sword,

but the tongue of the wise heals.

12:19 Truth's lips will be established forever,

but a lying tongue is only momentary.

12:20 Deceit is in the heart of those who plot evil,

but joy comes to the promoters of peace.

12:21 No mischief shall happen to the righteous,

but the wicked shall be filled with evil.

12:22 Lying lips are an abomination to Yahweh,

but those who do the truth are his delight.

12:23 A prudent man keeps his knowledge,

but the hearts of fools proclaim foolishness.

12:24 The hands of the diligent ones shall rule,

but laziness ends in slave labor.

12:25 Anxiety in a man's heart weighs it down,

but a kind word makes it glad.

12:26 A righteous person is cautious in friendship,

but the way of the wicked leads them astray.

12:27 The slothful man doesn't roast his game,

but the possessions of diligent men are prized.

12:28 In the way of righteousness is life;

in its path there is no death.

13:1 A wise son listens to his father's instruction,

but a scoffer doesn't listen to rebuke.

13:2By the fruit of his lips, a man enjoys good things;
but the unfaithful crave violence.

13:3He who guards his mouth guards his soul.
One who opens wide his lips comes to ruin.

13:4The soul of the sluggard desires, and has nothing,
but the desire of the diligent shall be fully satisfied.

13:5A righteous man hates lies,
but a wicked man brings shame and disgrace.

13:6Righteousness guards the way of integrity,
but wickedness overthrows the sinner.

13:7There are some who pretend to be rich, yet have nothing.
There are some who pretend to be poor, yet have great wealth.

13:8The ransom of a man's life is his riches,
but the poor hear no threats.

13:9The light of the righteous shines brightly,
but the lamp of the wicked is snuffed out.

13:10Pride only breeds quarrels,
but with ones who take advice is wisdom.

13:11Wealth gained dishonestly dwindles away,
but he who gathers by hand makes it grow.

13:12Hope deferred makes the heart sick,
but when longing is fulfilled, it is a tree of life.

13:13Whoever despises instruction will pay for it,
but he who respects a command will be rewarded.

13:14The teaching of the wise is a spring of life,
to turn from the snares of death.

13:15Good understanding wins favor;
but the way of the unfaithful is hard.

13:16Every prudent man acts from knowledge,
but a fool exposes folly.

13:17A wicked messenger falls into trouble,
but a trustworthy envoy gains healing.

13:18Poverty and shame come to him who refuses discipline,
but he who heeds correction shall be honored.

13:19Longing fulfilled is sweet to the soul,
but fools detest turning from evil.

13:20One who walks with wise men grows wise,
but a companion of fools suffers harm.

13:21Misfortune pursues sinners,
but prosperity rewards the righteous.

13:22A good man leaves an inheritance to his children's children,
but the wealth of the sinner is stored for the righteous.

13:23An abundance of food is in poor people's fields,
but injustice sweeps it away.

13:24One who spares the rod hates his son,
but one who loves him is careful to discipline him.

13:25The righteous one eats to the satisfying of his soul,
but the belly of the wicked goes hungry.

14:1Every wise woman builds her house,
but the foolish one tears it down with her own hands.

14:2He who walks in his uprightness fears Yahweh,
but he who is perverse in his ways despises him.

14:3The fool's talk brings a rod to his back,
but the lips of the wise protect them.

14:4Where no oxen are, the crib is clean,
but much increase is by the strength of the ox.

14:5A truthful witness will not lie,
but a false witness pours out lies.

14:6A scoffer seeks wisdom, and doesn't find it,
but knowledge comes easily to a discerning person.

14:7Stay away from a foolish man,
for you won't find knowledge on his lips.

14:8The wisdom of the prudent is to think about his way,
but the folly of fools is deceit.

14:9Fools mock at making atonement for sins,

but among the upright there is good will.

14:10 The heart knows its own bitterness and joy;
he will not share these with a stranger.

14:11 The house of the wicked will be overthrown,
but the tent of the upright will flourish.

14:12 There is a way which seems right to a man,
but in the end it leads to death.

14:13 Even in laughter the heart may be sorrowful,
and mirth may end in heaviness.

14:14 The unfaithful will be repaid for his own ways;
likewise a good man will be rewarded for his ways.

14:15 A simple man believes everything,
but the prudent man carefully considers his ways.

14:16 A wise man fears, and shuns evil,
but the fool is hotheaded and reckless.

14:17 He who is quick to become angry will commit folly,
and a crafty man is hated.

14:18 The simple inherit folly,
but the prudent are crowned with knowledge.

14:19 The evil bow down before the good,
and the wicked at the gates of the righteous.

14:20 The poor person is shunned even by his own neighbor,
but the rich person has many friends.

14:21 He who despises his neighbor sins,
but blessed is he who has pity on the poor.

14:22 Don't they go astray who plot evil?
But love and faithfulness belong to those who plan good.

14:23 In all hard work there is profit,
but the talk of the lips leads only to poverty.

14:24 The crown of the wise is their riches,
but the folly of fools crowns them with folly.

14:25 A truthful witness saves souls,
but a false witness is deceitful.

14:26 In the fear of Yahweh is a secure fortress,
and he will be a refuge for his children.

14:27 The fear of Yahweh is a fountain of life,
turning people from the snares of death.

14:28 In the multitude of people is the king's glory,
but in the lack of people is the destruction of the prince.

14:29 He who is slow to anger has great understanding,
but he who has a quick temper displays folly.

14:30 The life of the body is a heart at peace,
but envy rots the bones.

14:31 He who oppresses the poor shows contempt for his Maker,
but he who is kind to the needy honors him.

14:32 The wicked is brought down in his calamity,
but in death, the righteous has a refuge.

14:33 Wisdom rests in the heart of one who has understanding,
and is even made known in the inward part of fools.

14:34 Righteousness exalts a nation,
but sin is a disgrace to any people.

14:35 The king's favor is toward a servant who deals wisely,
but his wrath is toward one who causes shame.

15:1 A gentle answer turns away wrath,
but a harsh word stirs up anger.

15:2 The tongue of the wise commends knowledge,
but the mouth of fools gush out folly.

15:3 Yahweh's eyes are everywhere,
keeping watch on the evil and the good.

15:4 A gentle tongue is a tree of life,
but deceit in it crushes the spirit.

15:5 A fool despises his father's correction,
but he who heeds reproof shows prudence.

15:6 In the house of the righteous is much treasure,
but the income of the wicked brings trouble.

15:7 The lips of the wise spread knowledge;
not so with the heart of fools.

15:8 The sacrifice made by the wicked is an abomination to Yahweh, but the prayer of the upright is his delight.

15:9 The way of the wicked is an abomination to Yahweh,

but he loves him who follows after righteousness.

15:10 There is stern discipline for one who forsakes the way:

whoever hates reproof shall die.

15:11 Sheol and Abaddon are before Yahweh—

how much more then the hearts of the children of men!

15:12 A scoffer doesn't love to be reproved; he will not go to the wise.

15:13 A glad heart makes a cheerful face; but an aching heart breaks the spirit.

15:14 The heart of one who has understanding seeks knowledge,

but the mouths of fools feed on folly.

15:15 All the days of the afflicted are wretched,

but one who has a cheerful heart enjoys a continual feast.

15:16 Better is little, with the fear of Yahweh, than great treasure with trouble.

15:17 Better is a dinner of herbs, where love is,

than a fattened calf with hatred.

15:18 A wrathful man stirs up contention, but one who is slow to anger appeases strife.

15:19 The way of the sluggard is like a thorn patch,

but the path of the upright is a highway.

15:20 A wise son makes a father glad, but a foolish man despises his mother.

15:21 Folly is joy to one who is void of wisdom,

but a man of understanding keeps his way straight.

15:22 Where there is no counsel, plans fail; but in a multitude of counselors they are established.

15:23 Joy comes to a man with the reply of his mouth.

How good is a word at the right time!

15:24 The path of life leads upward for the wise,

to keep him from going downward to Sheol.

15:25 Yahweh will uproot the house of the proud,

but he will keep the widow's borders intact.

15:26 Yahweh detests the thoughts of the wicked,

but the thoughts of the pure are pleasing.

15:27 He who is greedy for gain troubles his own house,

but he who hates bribes will live.

15:28 The heart of the righteous weighs answers,

but the mouth of the wicked gushes out evil.

15:29 Yahweh is far from the wicked, but he hears the prayer of the righteous.

15:30 The light of the eyes rejoices the heart. Good news gives health to the bones.

15:31 The ear that listens to reproof lives, and will be at home among the wise.

15:32 He who refuses correction despises his own soul,

but he who listens to reproof gets understanding.

15:33 The fear of Yahweh teaches wisdom. Before honor is humility.

16:1 The plans of the heart belong to man, but the answer of the tongue is from Yahweh.

16:2 All the ways of a man are clean in his own eyes;

but Yahweh weighs the motives.

16:3 Commit your deeds to Yahweh, and your plans shall succeed.

16:4 Yahweh has made everything for its own end—

yes, even the wicked for the day of evil.

16:5 Everyone who is proud in heart is an abomination to Yahweh:

they shall certainly not be unpunished.

16:6 By mercy and truth iniquity is atoned for.

By the fear of Yahweh men depart from evil.

16:7 When a man's ways please Yahweh, he makes even his enemies to be at peace with him.

16:8 Better is a little with righteousness, than great revenues with injustice.

16:9 A man's heart plans his course,

but Yahweh directs his steps.

16:10 Inspired judgments are on the lips of the king.

He shall not betray his mouth.

16:11 Honest balances and scales are Yahweh's;

all the weights in the bag are his work.

16:12 It is an abomination for kings to do wrong,

for the throne is established by righteousness.

16:13 Righteous lips are the delight of kings.

They value one who speaks the truth.

16:14 The king's wrath is a messenger of death,

but a wise man will pacify it.

16:15 In the light of the king's face is life.

His favor is like a cloud of the spring rain.

16:16 How much better it is to get wisdom than gold!

Yes, to get understanding is to be chosen rather than silver.

16:17 The highway of the upright is to depart from evil.

He who keeps his way preserves his soul.

16:18 Pride goes before destruction,

and a haughty spirit before a fall.

16:19 It is better to be of a lowly spirit with the poor,

than to divide the plunder with the proud.

16:20 He who heeds the Word finds prosperity.

Whoever trusts in Yahweh is blessed.

16:21 The wise in heart shall be called prudent.

Pleasantness of the lips promotes instruction.

16:22 Understanding is a fountain of life to one who has it,

but the punishment of fools is their folly.

16:23 The heart of the wise instructs his mouth,

and adds learning to his lips.

16:24 Pleasant words are a honeycomb,

sweet to the soul, and health to the bones.

16:25 There is a way which seems right to a man,

but in the end it leads to death.

16:26 The appetite of the laboring man labors for him;

for his mouth urges him on.

16:27 A worthless man devises mischief.

His speech is like a scorching fire.

16:28 A perverse man stirs up strife.

A whisperer separates close friends.

16:29 A man of violence entices his neighbor,

and leads him in a way that is not good.

16:30 One who winks his eyes to plot perversities,

one who compresses his lips, is bent on evil.

16:31 Gray hair is a crown of glory.

It is attained by a life of righteousness.

16:32 One who is slow to anger is better than the mighty;

one who rules his spirit, than he who takes a city.

16:33 The lot is cast into the lap,

but its every decision is from Yahweh.

17:1 Better is a dry morsel with quietness,

than a house full of feasting with strife.

17:2 A servant who deals wisely will rule over a son who causes shame,

and shall have a part in the inheritance among the brothers.

17:3 The refining pot is for silver, and the furnace for gold,

but Yahweh tests the hearts.

17:4 An evil-doer heeds wicked lips.

A liar gives ear to a mischievous tongue.

17:5 Whoever mocks the poor reproaches his Maker.

He who is glad at calamity shall not be unpunished.

17:6 Children's children are the crown of old men;

the glory of children are their parents.

17:7 Arrogant speech isn't fitting for a fool,

much less do lying lips fit a prince.

17:8 A bribe is a precious stone in the eyes of him who gives it;

wherever he turns, he prospers.

17:9 He who covers an offense promotes love;

but he who repeats a matter separates best friends.

17:10 A rebuke enters deeper into one who has understanding

than a hundred lashes into a fool.

17:11 An evil man seeks only rebellion;

therefore a cruel messenger shall be sent against him.

17:12 Let a bear robbed of her cubs meet a man,

rather than a fool in his folly.

17:13 Whoever rewards evil for good,

evil shall not depart from his house.

17:14 The beginning of strife is like breaching a dam,

therefore stop contention before quarreling breaks out.

17:15 He who justifies the wicked, and he who condemns the righteous,

both of them alike are an abomination to Yahweh.

17:16 Why is there money in the hand of a fool to buy wisdom,

seeing he has no understanding?

17:17 A friend loves at all times;

and a brother is born for adversity.

17:18 A man void of understanding strikes hands,

and becomes collateral in the presence of his neighbor.

17:19 He who loves disobedience loves strife.

One who builds a high gate seeks destruction.

17:20 One who has a perverse heart doesn't find prosperity,

and one who has a deceitful tongue falls into trouble.

17:21 He who becomes the father of a fool grieves.

The father of a fool has no joy.

17:22 A cheerful heart makes good medicine,

but a crushed spirit dries up the bones.

17:23 A wicked man receives a bribe in secret,

to pervert the ways of justice.

17:24 Wisdom is before the face of one who has understanding,

but the eyes of a fool wander to the ends of the earth.

17:25 A foolish son brings grief to his father,

and bitterness to her who bore him.

17:26 Also to punish the righteous is not good,

nor to flog officials for their integrity.

17:27 He who spares his words has knowledge.

He who is even tempered is a man of understanding.

17:28 Even a fool, when he keeps silent, is counted wise.

When he shuts his lips, he is thought to be discerning.

18:1 An unfriendly man pursues selfishness,

and defies all sound judgment.

18:2 A fool has no delight in understanding,

but only in revealing his own opinion.

18:3 When wickedness comes, contempt also comes,

and with shame comes disgrace.

18:4 The words of a man's mouth are like deep waters.

The fountain of wisdom is like a flowing brook.

18:5 To be partial to the faces of the wicked is not good,

nor to deprive the innocent of justice.

18:6 A fool's lips come into strife,

and his mouth invites beatings.

18:7 A fool's mouth is his destruction,

and his lips are a snare to his soul.

18:8 The words of a gossip are like dainty morsels:

they go down into a person's innermost parts.

18:9 One who is slack in his work

is brother to him who is a master of destruction.

18:10 The name of Yahweh is a strong tower:

the righteous run to him, and are safe.

18:11 The rich man's wealth is his strong city,

like an unscalable wall in his own imagination.

18:12 Before destruction the heart of man is proud,

but before honor is humility.

18:13 He who gives answer before he hears,

that is folly and shame to him.

18:14 A man's spirit will sustain him in sickness,

but a crushed spirit, who can bear?

18:15 The heart of the discerning gets knowledge.

The ear of the wise seeks knowledge.

18:16 A man's gift makes room for him,

and brings him before great men.

18:17 He who pleads his cause first seems right;

until another comes and questions him.

18:18 The lot settles disputes,
and keeps strong ones apart.

18:19 A brother offended is more difficult than a fortified city;
and disputes are like the bars of a castle.

18:20 A man's stomach is filled with the fruit of his mouth.
With the harvest of his lips he is satisfied.

18:21 Death and life are in the power of the tongue;
those who love it will eat its fruit.

18:22 Whoever finds a wife finds a good thing,
and obtains favor of Yahweh.

18:23 The poor plead for mercy,
but the rich answer harshly.

18:24 A man of many companions may be ruined,
but there is a friend who sticks closer than a brother.

19:1 Better is the poor who walks in his integrity
than he who is perverse in his lips and is a fool.

19:2 It isn't good to have zeal without knowledge;
nor being hasty with one's feet and missing the way.

19:3 The foolishness of man subverts his way;
his heart rages against Yahweh.

19:4 Wealth adds many friends,
but the poor is separated from his friend.

19:5 A false witness shall not be unpunished.
He who pours out lies shall not go free.

19:6 Many will entreat the favor of a ruler,
and everyone is a friend to a man who gives gifts.

19:7 All the relatives of the poor shun him:
how much more do his friends avoid him!
He pursues them with pleas, but they are gone.

19:8 He who gets wisdom loves his own soul.
He who keeps understanding shall find good.

19:9 A false witness shall not be unpunished.
He who utters lies shall perish.

19:10 Delicate living is not appropriate for a fool,
much less for a servant to have rule over princes.

19:11 The discretion of a man makes him slow to anger.
It is his glory to overlook an offense.

19:12 The king's wrath is like the roaring of a lion,
but his favor is like dew on the grass.

19:13 A foolish son is the calamity of his father.
A wife's quarrels are a continual dripping.

19:14 House and riches are an inheritance from fathers,
but a prudent wife is from Yahweh.

19:15 Slothfulness casts into a deep sleep.
The idle soul shall suffer hunger.

19:16 He who keeps the commandment keeps his soul,
but he who is contemptuous in his ways shall die.

19:17 He who has pity on the poor lends to Yahweh;
he will reward him.

19:18 Discipline your son, for there is hope;
don't be a willing party to his death.

19:19 A hot-tempered man must pay the penalty,
for if you rescue him, you must do it again.

19:20 Listen to counsel and receive instruction,
that you may be wise in your latter end.

19:21 There are many plans in a man's heart,
but Yahweh's counsel will prevail.

19:22 That which makes a man to be desired is his kindness.
A poor man is better than a liar.

19:23 The fear of Yahweh leads to life, then contentment;
he rests and will not be touched by trouble.

19:24 The sluggard buries his hand in the dish;
he will not so much as bring it to his mouth again.

19:25 Flog a scoffer, and the simple will learn prudence;
rebuke one who has understanding, and he will gain knowledge.

19:26 He who robs his father and drives away his mother,

is a son who causes shame and brings reproach.

19:27 If you stop listening to instruction, my son,

you will stray from the words of knowledge.

19:28 A corrupt witness mocks justice,

and the mouth of the wicked gulps down iniquity.

19:29 Penalties are prepared for scoffers,

and beatings for the backs of fools.

20:1 Wine is a mocker, and beer is a brawler.

Whoever is led astray by them is not wise.

20:2 The terror of a king is like the roaring of a lion.

He who provokes him to anger forfeits his own life.

20:3 It is an honor for a man to keep aloof from strife;

but every fool will be quarreling.

20:4 The sluggard will not plow by reason of the winter;

therefore he shall beg in harvest, and have nothing.

20:5 Counsel in the heart of man is like deep water;

but a man of understanding will draw it out.

20:6 Many men claim to be men of unfailing love,

but who can find a faithful man?

20:7 A righteous man walks in integrity.

Blessed are his children after him.

20:8 A king who sits on the throne of judgment

scatters away all evil with his eyes.

20:9 Who can say, "I have made my heart pure.

I am clean and without sin?"

20:10 Differing weights and differing measures,

both of them alike are an abomination to Yahweh.

20:11 Even a child makes himself known by his doings,

whether his work is pure, and whether it is right.

20:12 The hearing ear, and the seeing eye,

Yahweh has made even both of them.

20:13 Don't love sleep, lest you come to poverty.

Open your eyes, and you shall be satisfied with bread.

20:14 "It's no good, it's no good," says the buyer;

but when he is gone his way, then he boasts.

20:15 There is gold and abundance of rubies;

but the lips of knowledge are a rare jewel.

20:16 Take the garment of one who puts up collateral for a stranger;

and hold him in pledge for a wayward woman.

20:17 Fraudulent food is sweet to a man,

but afterwards his mouth is filled with gravel.

20:18 Plans are established by advice;

by wise guidance you wage war!

20:19 He who goes about as a tale-bearer reveals secrets;

therefore don't keep company with him who opens wide his lips.

20:20 Whoever curses his father or his mother,

his lamp shall be put out in blackness of darkness.

20:21 An inheritance quickly gained at the beginning,

won't be blessed in the end.

20:22 Don't say, "I will pay back evil."

Wait for Yahweh, and he will save you.

20:23 Yahweh detests differing weights,

and dishonest scales are not pleasing.

20:24 A man's steps are from Yahweh;

how then can man understand his way?

20:25 It is a snare to a man to make a rash dedication,

then later to consider his vows.

20:26 A wise king winnows out the wicked,

and drives the threshing wheel over them.

20:27 The spirit of man is Yahweh's lamp,

searching all his innermost parts.

20:28 Love and faithfulness keep the king safe.

His throne is sustained by love.

20:29 The glory of young men is their strength.

The splendor of old men is their gray hair.

20:30 Wounding blows cleanse away evil,
and beatings purge the innermost parts.

21:1 The king's heart is in Yahweh's hand like the watercourses.
He turns it wherever he desires.

21:2 Every way of a man is right in his own eyes,
but Yahweh weighs the hearts.

21:3 To do righteousness and justice
is more acceptable to Yahweh than sacrifice.

21:4 A high look, and a proud heart,
the lamp of the wicked, is sin.

21:5 The plans of the diligent surely lead to profit;
and everyone who is hasty surely rushes to poverty.

21:6 Getting treasures by a lying tongue
is a fleeting vapor for those who seek death.

21:7 The violence of the wicked will drive them away,
because they refuse to do what is right.

21:8 The way of the guilty is devious,
but the conduct of the innocent is upright.

21:9 It is better to dwell in the corner of the housetop,
than to share a house with a contentious woman.

21:10 The soul of the wicked desires evil;
his neighbor finds no mercy in his eyes.

21:11 When the mocker is punished, the simple gains wisdom.
When the wise is instructed, he receives knowledge.

21:12 The Righteous One considers the house of the wicked,
and brings the wicked to ruin.

21:13 Whoever stops his ears at the cry of the poor,
he will also cry out, but shall not be heard.

21:14 A gift in secret pacifies anger;
and a bribe in the cloak, strong wrath.

21:15 It is joy to the righteous to do justice;
but it is a destruction to the workers of iniquity.

21:16 The man who wanders out of the way of understanding
shall rest in the assembly of the dead.

21:17 He who loves pleasure shall be a poor man.
He who loves wine and oil shall not be rich.

21:18 The wicked is a ransom for the righteous;
the treacherous for the upright.

21:19 It is better to dwell in a desert land,
than with a contentious and fretful woman.

21:20 There is precious treasure and oil in the dwelling of the wise;
but a foolish man swallows it up.

21:21 He who follows after righteousness and kindness
finds life, righteousness, and honor.

21:22 A wise man scales the city of the mighty,
and brings down the strength of its confidence.

21:23 Whoever guards his mouth and his tongue
keeps his soul from troubles.

21:24 The proud and haughty man, "scoffer" is his name;
he works in the arrogance of pride.

21:25 The desire of the sluggard kills him,
for his hands refuse to labor.

21:26 There are those who covet greedily all day long;
but the righteous give and don't withhold.

21:27 The sacrifice of the wicked is an abomination:
how much more, when he brings it with a wicked mind!

21:28 A false witness will perish,
and a man who listens speaks to eternity.

21:29 A wicked man hardens his face;
but as for the upright, he establishes his ways.

21:30 There is no wisdom nor understanding nor counsel against Yahweh.

21:31 The horse is prepared for the day of battle;
but victory is with Yahweh.

22:1 A good name is more desirable than great riches,

and loving favor is better than silver and gold.

^{22:2}The rich and the poor have this in common:

Yahweh is the maker of them all.

^{22:3}A prudent man sees danger, and hides himself;

but the simple pass on, and suffer for it.

^{22:4}The result of humility and the fear of Yahweh

is wealth, honor, and life.

^{22:5}Thorns and snares are in the path of the wicked:

whoever guards his soul stays from them.

^{22:6}Train up a child in the way he should go,

and when he is old he will not depart from it.

^{22:7}The rich rule over the poor.

The borrower is servant to the lender.

^{22:8}He who sows wickedness reaps trouble,

and the rod of his fury will be destroyed.

^{22:9}He who has a generous eye will be blessed;

for he shares his food with the poor.

^{22:10}Drive out the mocker, and strife will go out;

yes, quarrels and insults will stop.

^{22:11}He who loves purity of heart and speaks gracefully

is the king's friend.

^{22:12}The eyes of Yahweh watch over knowledge;

but he frustrates the words of the unfaithful.

^{22:13}The sluggard says, "There is a lion outside!

I will be killed in the streets!"

^{22:14}The mouth of an adulteress is a deep pit:

he who is under Yahweh's wrath will fall into it.

^{22:15}Folly is bound up in the heart of a child:

the rod of discipline drives it far from him.

^{22:16}Whoever oppresses the poor for his own increase and whoever gives to the rich,

both come to poverty.

^{22:17}Turn your ear, and listen to the words of the wise.

Apply your heart to my teaching.

^{22:18}For it is a pleasant thing if you keep them within you,

if all of them are ready on your lips.

^{22:19}That your trust may be in Yahweh,

I teach you today, even you.

^{22:20}Haven't I written to you thirty excellent things

of counsel and knowledge,

^{22:21}To teach you truth, reliable words,

to give sound answers to the ones who sent you?

^{22:22}Don't exploit the poor, because he is poor;

and don't crush the needy in court;

^{22:23}for Yahweh will plead their case,

and plunder the life of those who plunder them.

^{22:24}Don't befriend a hot-tempered man,

and don't associate with one who harbors anger:

^{22:25}lest you learn his ways,

and ensnare your soul.

^{22:26}Don't you be one of those who strike hands,

of those who are collateral for debts.

^{22:27}If you don't have means to pay,

why should he take away your bed from under you?

^{22:28}Don't move the ancient boundary stone,

which your fathers have set up.

^{22:29}Do you see a man skilled in his work?

He will serve kings.

He won't serve obscure men.

^{23:1}When you sit to eat with a ruler,

consider diligently what is before you;

^{23:2}put a knife to your throat,

if you are a man given to appetite.

^{23:3}Don't be desirous of his dainties,

seeing they are deceitful food.

^{23:4}Don't weary yourself to be rich.

In your wisdom, show restraint.

^{23:5}Why do you set your eyes on that which is not?

For it certainly sprouts wings like an eagle and flies in the sky.

^{23:6}Don't eat the food of him who has a stingy eye,

and don't crave his delicacies:

^{23:7}for as he thinks about the cost, so he is.

"Eat and drink!" he says to you,
  but his heart is not with you.
23:8 The morsel which you have eaten you
    shall vomit up,
  and lose your good words.
23:9 Don't speak in the ears of a fool,
  for he will despise the wisdom of your
    words.
23:10 Don't move the ancient boundary
    stone.
  Don't encroach on the fields of the
    fatherless:
23:11 for their Defender is strong.
  He will plead their case against you.
23:12 Apply your heart to instruction,
  and your ears to the words of knowl-
    edge.
23:13 Don't withhold correction from a child.
  If you punish him with the rod, he will
    not die.
23:14 Punish him with the rod,
  and save his soul from Sheol.
23:15 My son, if your heart is wise,
  then my heart will be glad, even mine:
23:16 yes, my heart will rejoice,
  when your lips speak what is right.
23:17 Don't let your heart envy sinners;
  but rather fear Yahweh all the day long.
23:18 Indeed surely there is a future hope,
  and your hope will not be cut off.
23:19 Listen, my son, and be wise,
  and keep your heart on the right path!
23:20 Don't be among ones drinking too
    much wine,
  or those who gorge themselves on
    meat:
23:21 for the drunkard and the glutton shall
    become poor;
  and drowsiness clothes them in rags.
23:22 Listen to your father who gave you life,
  and don't despise your mother when
    she is old.
23:23 Buy the truth, and don't sell it.
  Get wisdom, discipline, and under-
    standing.
23:24 The father of the righteous has great
    joy.
  Whoever fathers a wise child delights
    in him.
23:25 Let your father and your mother be
    glad!
  Let her who bore you rejoice!

23:26 My son, give me your heart;
  and let your eyes keep in my ways.
23:27 For a prostitute is a deep pit;
  and a wayward wife is a narrow well.
23:28 Yes, she lies in wait like a robber,
  and increases the unfaithful among
    men.
23:29 Who has woe?
  Who has sorrow?
  Who has strife?
  Who has complaints?
  Who has needless bruises?
  Who has bloodshot eyes?
23:30 Those who stay long at the wine;
  those who go to seek out mixed wine.
23:31 Don't look at the wine when it is red,
  when it sparkles in the cup,
  when it goes down smoothly.
23:32 In the end, it bites like a snake,
  and poisons like a viper.
23:33 Your eyes will see strange things,
  and your mind will imagine confusing
    things.
23:34 Yes, you will be as he who lies down in
    the midst of the sea,
  or as he who lies on top of the rigging:
23:35 "They hit me, and I was not hurt!
  They beat me, and I don't feel it!
  When will I wake up? I can do it again.
  I can find another."
24:1 Don't be envious of evil men;
  neither desire to be with them:
24:2 for their hearts plot violence,
  and their lips talk about mischief.
24:3 Through wisdom a house is built;
  by understanding it is established;
24:4 by knowledge the rooms are filled
  with all rare and beautiful treasure.
24:5 A wise man has great power;
  and a knowledgeable man increases
    strength;
24:6 for by wise guidance you wage your
    war;
  and victory is in many advisors.
24:7 Wisdom is too high for a fool:
  he doesn't open his mouth in the gate.
24:8 One who plots to do evil
  will be called a schemer.
24:9 The schemes of folly are sin.
  The mocker is detested by men.
24:10 If you falter in the time of trouble,
  your strength is small.

24:11 Rescue those who are being led away to death!

Indeed, hold back those who are staggering to the slaughter!

24:12 If you say, "Behold, we didn't know this;"

doesn't he who weighs the hearts consider it?

He who keeps your soul, doesn't he know it?

Shall he not render to every man according to his work?

24:13 My son, eat honey, for it is good;

the droppings of the honeycomb, which are sweet to your taste:

24:14 so you shall know wisdom to be to your soul;

if you have found it, then there will be a reward,

your hope will not be cut off.

24:15 Don't lay in wait, wicked man, against the habitation of the righteous.

Don't destroy his resting place:

24:16 for a righteous man falls seven times, and rises up again;

but the wicked are overthrown by calamity.

24:17 Don't rejoice when your enemy falls.

Don't let your heart be glad when he is overthrown;

24:18 lest Yahweh see it, and it displease him, and he turn away his wrath from him.

24:19 Don't fret yourself because of evildoers;

neither be envious of the wicked:

24:20 for there will be no reward to the evil man;

and the lamp of the wicked shall be snuffed out.

24:21 My son, fear Yahweh and the king.

Don't join those who are rebellious:

24:22 for their calamity will rise suddenly;

the destruction from them both—who knows?

24:23 These also are sayings of the wise.

To show partiality in judgment is not good.

24:24 He who says to the wicked, "You are righteous;"

peoples shall curse him, and nations shall abhor him—

24:25 but it will go well with those who convict the guilty,

and a rich blessing will come on them.

24:26 An honest answer

is like a kiss on the lips.

24:27 Prepare your work outside,

and get your fields ready.

Afterwards, build your house.

24:28 Don't be a witness against your neighbor without cause.

Don't deceive with your lips.

24:29 Don't say, "I will do to him as he has done to me;

I will render to the man according to his work."

24:30 I went by the field of the sluggard,

by the vineyard of the man void of understanding;

24:31 Behold, it was all grown over with thorns.

Its surface was covered with nettles, and its stone wall was broken down.

24:32 Then I saw, and considered well.

I saw, and received instruction:

24:33 a little sleep, a little slumber,

a little folding of the hands to sleep;

24:34 so your poverty will come as a robber, and your want as an armed man.

25:1 These also are proverbs of Solomon, which the men of Hezekiah king of Judah copied out.

25:2 It is the glory of God to conceal a thing,

but the glory of kings is to search out a matter.

25:3 As the heavens for height, and the earth for depth,

so the hearts of kings are unsearchable.

25:4 Take away the dross from the silver,

and material comes out for the refiner;

25:5 Take away the wicked from the king's presence,

and his throne will be established in righteousness.

25:6 Don't exalt yourself in the presence of the king,

or claim a place among great men;

25:7 for it is better that it be said to you, "Come up here,"

than that you should be put lower in the presence of the prince,

whom your eyes have seen.

25:8 Don't be hasty in bringing charges to court.

What will you do in the end when your neighbor shames you?

^{25:9}Debate your case with your neighbor,

and don't betray the confidence of another;

^{25:10}lest one who hears it put you to shame,

and your bad reputation never depart.

^{25:11}A word fitly spoken

is like apples of gold in settings of silver.

^{25:12}As an earring of gold, and an ornament of fine gold,

so is a wise reprover to an obedient ear.

^{25:13}As the cold of snow in the time of harvest,

so is a faithful messenger to those who send him;

for he refreshes the soul of his masters.

^{25:14}As clouds and wind without rain,

so is he who boasts of gifts deceptively.

^{25:15}By patience a ruler is persuaded.

A soft tongue breaks the bone.

^{25:16}Have you found honey?

Eat as much as is sufficient for you,

lest you eat too much, and vomit it.

^{25:17}Let your foot be seldom in your neighbor's house,

lest he be weary of you, and hate you.

^{25:18}A man who gives false testimony against his neighbor

is like a club, a sword, or a sharp arrow.

^{25:19}Confidence in someone unfaithful in time of trouble

is like a bad tooth, or a lame foot.

^{25:20}As one who takes away a garment in cold weather,

or vinegar on soda,

so is one who sings songs to a heavy heart.

^{25:21}If your enemy is hungry, give him food to eat.

If he is thirsty, give him water to drink:

^{25:22}for you will heap coals of fire on his head,

and Yahweh will reward you.

^{25:23}The north wind brings forth rain:

so a backbiting tongue brings an angry face.

^{25:24}It is better to dwell in the corner of the housetop,

than to share a house with a contentious woman.

^{25:25}Like cold water to a thirsty soul,

so is good news from a far country.

^{25:26}Like a muddied spring, and a polluted well,

so is a righteous man who gives way before the wicked.

^{25:27}It is not good to eat much honey;

nor is it honorable to seek one's own honor.

^{25:28}Like a city that is broken down and without walls

is a man whose spirit is without restraint.

^{26:1}Like snow in summer, and as rain in harvest,

so honor is not fitting for a fool.

^{26:2}Like a fluttering sparrow,

like a darting swallow,

so the undeserved curse doesn't come to rest.

^{26:3}A whip is for the horse,

a bridle for the donkey,

and a rod for the back of fools!

^{26:4}Don't answer a fool according to his folly,

lest you also be like him.

^{26:5}Answer a fool according to his folly,

lest he be wise in his own eyes.

^{26:6}One who sends a message by the hand of a fool

is cutting off feet and drinking violence.

^{26:7}Like the legs of the lame that hang loose:

so is a parable in the mouth of fools.

^{26:8}As one who binds a stone in a sling,

so is he who gives honor to a fool.

^{26:9}Like a thornbush that goes into the hand of a drunkard,

so is a parable in the mouth of fools.

^{26:10}As an archer who wounds all,

so is he who hires a fool

or he who hires those who pass by.

^{26:11}As a dog that returns to his vomit,

so is a fool who repeats his folly.

^{26:12}Do you see a man wise in his own eyes?

There is more hope for a fool than for him.

^{26:13}The sluggard says, "There is a lion in the road!

A fierce lion roams the streets!"

26:14 As the door turns on its hinges,
so does the sluggard on his bed.

26:15 The sluggard buries his hand in the dish.
He is too lazy to bring it back to his mouth.

26:16 The sluggard is wiser in his own eyes
than seven men who answer with discretion.

26:17 Like one who grabs a dog's ears
is one who passes by and meddles in a quarrel not his own.

26:18 Like a madman who shoots firebrands, arrows, and death,
26:19 is the man who deceives his neighbor and says, "Am I not joking?"

26:20 For lack of wood a fire goes out.
Without gossip, a quarrel dies down.

26:21 As coals are to hot embers,
and wood to fire,
so is a contentious man to kindling strife.

26:22 The words of a whisperer are as dainty morsels,
they go down into the innermost parts.

26:23 Like silver dross on an earthen vessel
are the lips of a fervent one with an evil heart.

26:24 A malicious man disguises himself with his lips,
but he harbors evil in his heart.

26:25 When his speech is charming, don't believe him;
for there are seven abominations in his heart.

26:26 His malice may be concealed by deception,
but his wickedness will be exposed in the assembly.

26:27 Whoever digs a pit shall fall into it.
Whoever rolls a stone, it will come back on him.

26:28 A lying tongue hates those it hurts;
and a flattering mouth works ruin.

27:1 Don't boast about tomorrow;
for you don't know what a day may bring forth.

27:2 Let another man praise you,
and not your own mouth;
a stranger, and not your own lips.

27:3 A stone is heavy,
and sand is a burden;
but a fool's provocation is heavier than both.

27:4 Wrath is cruel,
and anger is overwhelming;
but who is able to stand before jealousy?

27:5 Better is open rebuke
than hidden love.

27:6 Faithful are the wounds of a friend;
although the kisses of an enemy are profuse.

27:7 A full soul loathes a honeycomb;
but to a hungry soul, every bitter thing is sweet.

27:8 As a bird that wanders from her nest,
so is a man who wanders from his home.

27:9 Perfume and incense bring joy to the heart;
so does earnest counsel from a man's friend.

27:10 Don't forsake your friend and your father's friend.
Don't go to your brother's house in the day of your disaster:
better is a neighbor who is near than a distant brother.

27:11 Be wise, my son,
and bring joy to my heart,
then I can answer my tormentor.

27:12 A prudent man sees danger and takes refuge;
but the simple pass on, and suffer for it.

27:13 Take his garment when he puts up collateral for a stranger.
Hold it for a wayward woman!

27:14 He who blesses his neighbor with a loud voice early in the morning,
it will be taken as a curse by him.

27:15 A continual dropping on a rainy day
and a contentious wife are alike:
27:16 restraining her is like restraining the wind,
or like grasping oil in his right hand.

27:17 Iron sharpens iron;
so a man sharpens his friend's countenance.

27:18 Whoever tends the fig tree shall eat its fruit.
He who looks after his master shall be honored.

27:19 As water reflects a face,

so a man's heart reflects the man.

27:20 Sheol and Abaddon are never satisfied;
and a man's eyes are never satisfied.

27:21 The crucible is for silver,
and the furnace for gold;
but man is refined by his praise.

27:22 Though you grind a fool in a mortar
with a pestle along with grain,
yet his foolishness will not be removed
from him.

27:23 Know well the state of your flocks,
and pay attention to your herds:

27:24 for riches are not forever,
nor does even the crown endure to all
generations.

27:25 The hay is removed, and the new
growth appears,
the grasses of the hills are gathered in.

27:26 The lambs are for your clothing,
and the goats are the price of a field.

27:27 There will be plenty of goats' milk for
your food,
for your family's food,
and for the nourishment of your servant girls.

28:1 The wicked flee when no one pursues;
but the righteous are as bold as a lion.

28:2 In rebellion, a land has many rulers,
but order is maintained by a man of
understanding and knowledge.

28:3 A needy man who oppresses the poor
is like a driving rain which leaves no
crops.

28:4 Those who forsake the law praise the
wicked;
but those who keep the law contend
with them.

28:5 Evil men don't understand justice;
but those who seek Yahweh understand it fully.

28:6 Better is the poor who walks in his
integrity,
than he who is perverse in his ways,
and he is rich.

28:7 Whoever keeps the law is a wise son;
but he who is a companion of gluttons
shames his father.

28:8 He who increases his wealth by excessive interest
gathers it for one who has pity on the
poor.

28:9 He who turns away his ear from hearing
the law,
even his prayer is an abomination.

28:10 Whoever causes the upright to go
astray in an evil way,
he will fall into his own trap;
but the blameless will inherit good.

28:11 The rich man is wise in his own eyes;
but the poor who has understanding
sees through him.

28:12 When the righteous triumph, there is
great glory;
but when the wicked rise, men hide
themselves.

28:13 He who conceals his sins doesn't prosper,
but whoever confesses and renounces
them finds mercy.

28:14 Blessed is the man who always fears;
but one who hardens his heart falls into
trouble.

28:15 As a roaring lion or a charging bear,
so is a wicked ruler over helpless people.

28:16 A tyrannical ruler lacks judgment.
One who hates ill-gotten gain will have
long days.

28:17 A man who is tormented by life blood
will be a fugitive until death;
no one will support him.

28:18 Whoever walks blamelessly is kept
safe;
but one with perverse ways will fall
suddenly.

28:19 One who works his land will have an
abundance of food;
but one who chases fantasies will have
his fill of poverty.

28:20 A faithful man is rich with blessings;
but one who is eager to be rich will not
go unpunished.

28:21 To show partiality is not good;
yet a man will do wrong for a piece of
bread.

28:22 A stingy man hurries after riches,
and doesn't know that poverty waits
for him.

28:23 One who rebukes a man will afterward
find more favor
than one who flatters with the tongue.

28:24 Whoever robs his father or his mother,
and says, "It's not wrong."

He is a partner with a destroyer.

^{28:25} One who is greedy stirs up strife;

but one who trusts in Yahweh will prosper.

^{28:26} One who trusts in himself is a fool;

but one who walks in wisdom is kept safe.

^{28:27} One who gives to the poor has no lack;

but one who closes his eyes will have many curses.

^{28:28} When the wicked rise, men hide themselves;

but when they perish, the righteous thrive.

^{29:1} He who is often rebuked and stiffens his neck

will be destroyed suddenly, with no remedy.

^{29:2} When the righteous thrive, the people rejoice;

but when the wicked rule, the people groan.

^{29:3} Whoever loves wisdom brings joy to his father;

but a companion of prostitutes squanders his wealth.

^{29:4} The king by justice makes the land stable,

but he who takes bribes tears it down.

^{29:5} A man who flatters his neighbor

spreads a net for his feet.

^{29:6} An evil man is snared by his sin,

but the righteous can sing and be glad.

^{29:7} The righteous care about justice for the poor.

The wicked aren't concerned about knowledge.

^{29:8} Mockers stir up a city,

but wise men turn away anger.

^{29:9} If a wise man goes to court with a foolish man,

the fool rages or scoffs, and there is no peace.

^{29:10} The bloodthirsty hate a man of integrity;

and they seek the life of the upright.

^{29:11} A fool vents all of his anger,

but a wise man brings himself under control.

^{29:12} If a ruler listens to lies,

all of his officials are wicked.

^{29:13} The poor man and the oppressor have this in common:

Yahweh gives sight to the eyes of both.

^{29:14} The king who fairly judges the poor,

his throne shall be established forever.

^{29:15} The rod of correction gives wisdom,

but a child left to himself causes shame to his mother.

^{29:16} When the wicked increase, sin increases;

but the righteous will see their downfall.

^{29:17} Correct your son, and he will give you peace;

yes, he will bring delight to your soul.

^{29:18} Where there is no revelation, the people cast off restraint;

but one who keeps the law is blessed.

^{29:19} A servant can't be corrected by words.

Though he understands, yet he will not respond.

^{29:20} Do you see a man who is hasty in his words?

There is more hope for a fool than for him.

^{29:21} He who pampers his servant from youth

will have him become a son in the end.

^{29:22} An angry man stirs up strife,

and a wrathful man abounds in sin.

^{29:23} A man's pride brings him low,

but one of lowly spirit gains honor.

^{29:24} Whoever is an accomplice of a thief is an enemy of his own soul.

He takes an oath, but dares not testify.

^{29:25} The fear of man proves to be a snare,

but whoever puts his trust in Yahweh is kept safe.

^{29:26} Many seek the ruler's favor,

but a man's justice comes from Yahweh.

^{29:27} A dishonest man detests the righteous,

and the upright in their ways detest the wicked.

^{30:1} The words of Agur the son of Jakeh, the oracle:

the man says to Ithiel,

to Ithiel and Ucal:

^{30:2} "Surely I am the most ignorant man,

and don't have a man's understanding.

^{30:3} I have not learned wisdom,

neither do I have the knowledge of the Holy One.

30:4 Who has ascended up into heaven, and descended?

Who has gathered the wind in his fists?

Who has bound the waters in his garment?

Who has established all the ends of the earth?

What is his name, and what is his son's name, if you know?

30:5 "Every word of God is flawless.

He is a shield to those who take refuge in him.

30:6 Don't you add to his words,

lest he reprove you, and you be found a liar.

30:7 "Two things I have asked of you;

don't deny me before I die:

30:8 Remove far from me falsehood and lies.

Give me neither poverty nor riches.

Feed me with the food that is needful for me;

30:9 lest I be full, deny you, and say, 'Who is Yahweh?'

or lest I be poor, and steal,

and so dishonor the name of my God.

30:10 "Don't slander a servant to his master,

lest he curse you, and you be held guilty.

30:11 There is a generation that curses their father,

and doesn't bless their mother.

30:12 There is a generation that is pure in their own eyes,

yet are not washed from their filthiness.

30:13 There is a generation, oh how lofty are their eyes!

Their eyelids are lifted up.

30:14 There is a generation whose teeth are like swords,

and their jaws like knives,

to devour the poor from the earth, and the needy from among men.

30:15 "The leach has two daughters:

'Give, give.'

"There are three things that are never satisfied;

four that don't say, 'Enough:'

30:16 Sheol,

the barren womb;

the earth that is not satisfied with water;

and the fire that doesn't say, 'Enough.'

30:17 "The eye that mocks at his father,

and scorns obedience to his mother:

the ravens of the valley shall pick it out,

the young eagles shall eat it.

30:18 "There are three things which are too amazing for me,

four which I don't understand:

30:19 The way of an eagle in the air;

the way of a serpent on a rock;

the way of a ship in the midst of the sea;

and the way of a man with a maiden.

30:20 "So is the way of an adulterous woman:

she eats and wipes her mouth,

and says, 'I have done nothing wrong.'

30:21 "For three things the earth tremble,

and under four, it can't bear up:

30:22 For a servant when he is king;

a fool when he is filled with food;

30:23 for an unloved woman when she is married;

and a handmaid who is heir to her mistress.

30:24 "There are four things which are little on the earth,

but they are exceedingly wise:

30:25 the ants are not a strong people,

yet they provide their food in the summer.

30:26 The conies are but a feeble folk,

yet make they their houses in the rocks.

30:27 The locusts have no king,

yet they advance in ranks.

30:28 You can catch a lizard with your hands,

yet it is in kings' palaces.

30:29 "There are three things which are stately in their march,

four which are stately in going:

30:30 The lion, which is mightiest among animals,

and doesn't turn away for any;

30:31 the greyhound,

the male goat also;

and the king against whom there is no rising up.

30:32 "If you have done foolishly in lifting up yourself,

or if you have thought evil,

put your hand over your mouth.

^{30:33}For as the churning of milk brings
forth butter,
and the wringing of the nose brings
forth blood;
so the forcing of wrath brings forth
strife."

^{31:1}The words of king Lemuel; the oracle
which his mother taught him.
^{31:2}"Oh, my son!
Oh, son of my womb!
Oh, son of my vows!
^{31:3}Don't give your strength to women,
nor your ways to that which destroys
kings.
^{31:4}It is not for kings, Lemuel;
it is not for kings to drink wine;
nor for princes to say, 'Where is strong
drink?'
^{31:5}lest they drink, and forget the law,
and pervert the justice due to anyone
who is afflicted.
^{31:6}Give strong drink to him who is ready
to perish;
and wine to the bitter in soul:
^{31:7}Let him drink, and forget his poverty,
and remember his misery no more.
^{31:8}Open your mouth for the mute,
in the cause of all who are left desolate.
^{31:9}Open your mouth, judge righteously,
and serve justice to the poor and
needy."
^{31:10a}Who can find a worthy woman?
For her price is far above rubies.
^{31:11}The heart of her husband trusts in her.
He shall have no lack of gain.
^{31:12}She does him good, and not harm,
all the days of her life.
^{31:13}She seeks wool and flax,
and works eagerly with her hands.
^{31:14}She is like the merchant ships.
She brings her bread from afar.
^{31:15}She rises also while it is yet night,
gives food to her household,
and portions for her servant girls.
^{31:16}She considers a field, and buys it.
With the fruit of her hands, she plants
a vineyard.
^{31:17}She girds her waist with strength,
and makes her arms strong.

^{31:18}She perceives that her merchandise is
profitable.
Her lamp doesn't go out by night.
^{31:19}She lays her hands to the distaff,
and her hands hold the spindle.
^{31:20}She opens her arms to the poor;
yes, she extends her hands to the needy.
^{31:21}She is not afraid of the snow for her
household;
for all her household are clothed with
scarlet.
^{31:22}She makes for herself carpets of
tapestry.
Her clothing is fine linen and purple.
^{31:23}Her husband is respected in the gates,
when he sits among the elders of the
land.
^{31:24}She makes linen garments and sells
them,
and delivers sashes to the merchant.
^{31:25}Strength and dignity are her clothing.
She laughs at the time to come.
^{31:26}She opens her mouth with wisdom.
Faithful instruction is on her tongue.
^{31:27}She looks well to the ways of her
household,
and doesn't eat the bread of idleness.
^{31:28}Her children rise up and call her
blessed.
Her husband also praises her:
^{31:29}"Many women do noble things,
but you excel them all."
^{31:30}Charm is deceitful, and beauty is vain;
but a woman who fears Yahweh, she
shall be praised.
^{31:31}Give her of the fruit of her hands!
Let her works praise her in the gates!

---

[a] 31:10 Proverbs 31:10-31 form an acrostic, with each verse starting with each letter of the Hebrew
alphabet, in order.

Glossary

Abaddon: Abaddon is Hebrew for destruction.

Abba: Abba is a Chaldee word for father, used in a respectful, affectionate, and familiar way, like papa, dad, or daddy. Often used in prayer to refer to our Father in Heaven.

adultery: Adultery is having sexual intercourse with someone besides your own husband or wife. In the Bible, the only legitimate sexual intercourse is between a man and a woman who are married to each other.

alpha: Alpha is the first letter of the Greek alphabet. It is sometimes used to mean the beginning or the first.

amen: Amen means "so be it" or "it is certainly so."

angel: "Angel" literally means "messenger" or "envoy," and is usually used to refer to spiritual beings who normally are invisible to us, but can also appear as exceedingly strong creatures or as humans.

Apollyon: Apollyon is Greek for destroyer.

apostle: "Apostle" means a delegate, messenger, or one sent forth with orders. This term is applied in the New Testament in both a general sense connected with a ministry of establishing and strengthening church fellowships, as well as in a specific sense to "The 12 Apostles of the Lamb" (Revelation 21:14). The former category applies to a specific ministry that continues in the Church (Ephesians 4:11-13) and which includes many more than 12 people, while the latter refers to the apostles named in Matthew 10:2-4, except with Judas Iscariot replaced by Matthias (Acts 1:26).

Armageddon: See Har-magedon.

assarion: An assarion is a small Roman copper coin worth one tenth of a drachma, or about an hour's wages for an agricultural laborer.

aureus: An aureus is a Roman gold coin, worth 25 silver denarii. An aureus weighed from 115 to 126.3 grains (7.45 to 8.18 grams).

baptize: Baptize means to immerse in, or wash with something, usually water. Baptism in the Holy Spirit, fire, the Body of Christ, and suffering are also mentioned in the New Testament, along with baptism in water. Baptism is not just to cleanse the body, but as an outward sign of an inward spiritual cleansing and commitment. Baptism is a sign of repentance, as practiced by John the Baptizer, and of faith in Jesus Christ, as practiced by Jesus' disciples.

bath: A bath is a liquid measure of about 22 liters, 5.8 U. S. gallons, or 4.8 imperial gallons.

batos: A batos is a liquid measure of about 39.5 liters, 10.4 U. S. gallons, or 8.7 imperial gallons.

Beersheba: Beersheba is Hebrew for "well of the oath" or "well of the seven." A city in Israel.

behold: Look! See! Wow! Notice this! Lo!

cherub: A cherub is a kind of angel with wings and hands that is associated with the throne room of God and guardian duty. See Ezekiel 10.

cherubim: Cherubim means more than one cherub or a mighty cherub.

choenix: A choenix is a dry volume measure that is a little more than a liter (which is a little more than a quart). A choenix was the daily ration of grain for a soldier in some armies.

concubine: a woman who is united to a man for the purpose of providing him with sexual pleasure and children, but not being honored as a full partner in marriage; a second-class wife. In Old Testament times (and in some places now), it was the custom of middle-eastern kings, chiefs, and wealthy men to mary multiple wives and concubines, but God commanded the Kings of Israel not to do so (Deuteronomy 17:17) and Jesus encouraged people to either remain single or marry as God originally intended: one man married to one woman (Matthew 19:3-12; 1 Corinthians 7:1-13).

cor: A cor is a dry measure of about 391 liters, 103 U. S. gallons, or 86 imperial gallons.

corban: Corban is a Hebrew word for an offering devoted to God.

crucify: Crucify means to execute someone by nailing them to a cross with metal spikes. Their hands are stretched out on the crossbeam with spikes driven through their wrists or hands. Their feet or ankles are attached to a cross with a metal spike. The weight of the victim's body tends to force the air out of his lungs. To raise up to breathe, the victim has to put weight on the wounds, and use a lot of strength. The victim is nailed to the cross while the cross is on the ground, then the cross is raised up and dropped into a hole, thus jarring the wounds. Before crucifiction, the victim was usually whipped with a Roman cat of nine tails, which had bits of glass and metal tied to its ends. This caused chunks of flesh to be removed and open wounds to be placed against the raw wood of the cross. The victim was made to carry the heavy crossbeam of his cross from the place of judgment to the place of crucifixion, but often was physically unable after the scourging, so another person would be pressed into involuntary service to carry the cross for him. Roman crucifixion was generally done totally naked to maximize both shame and discomfort. Eventually, the pain, weakness, dehydration, and exhaustion of the muscles needed to breathe make breathing impossible, and the victim suffocates.

cubit: A cubit is a unit of linear measure, from the elbow to the tip of the longest finger of a man. This unit is commonly converted to 0.46 meters or 18 inches, although that varies with height of the man doing the measurement. There is also a "long" cubit that is longer than a regular cubit by a handbreadth. (Ezekiel 43:13)

cummin: Cummin is an aromatic seed from Cuminum cyminum, resembling caraway in flavor and appearance. It is used as a spice.

darnel: Darnel is a weed grass (probably bearded darnel or Lolium temulentum) that looks very much like wheat until it is mature, when the seeds reveal a great difference. Darnel seeds aren't good for much except as chicken feed or to burn to prevent the spread of this weed.

denarii: denarii: plural form of denarius, a silver Roman coin worth about a days wages for a laborer.

denarius: A denarius is a silver Roman coin worth about a day's wages for an agricultural laborer. A denarius was worth 1/25th of a Roman aureus.

devil: The word "devil" comes from the Greek "diabolos," which means "one prone to slander; a liar." "Devil" is used to refer to a fallen angel, also called "Satan," who works to steal, kill, destroy, and do evil. The devil's doom is certain, and it is only a matter of time before he is thrown into the Lake of Fire, never to escape.

didrachma: A didrachma is a Greek silver coin worth 2 drachmas, about as much as 2 Roman denarii, or about 2 days wages. It was commonly used to pay the half-shekel temple tax.

distaff: part of a spinning wheel used for twisting threads.

drachma: A drachma is a Greek silver coin worth about one Roman denarius, or about a day's wages for an agricultural laborer.

El-Elohe-Israel: El-Elohe-Israel means "God, the God of Israel" or "The God of Israel is mighty."

ephah: An ephah is a measure of volume of about 22 liters, 5.8 U. S. gallons, 4.8 imperial gallons, or a bit more than half a bushel.

Gehenna: Gehenna is one word used for Hell. It comes from the Hebrew Gey-Hinnom, literally "valley of Hinnom." This word originated as the name for a place south of the old city of Jerusalem where the city's rubbish was burned. At one time, live babies were thrown crying into the fire under the arms of the idol, Moloch, to die there. This place was so despised by the people after the righteous King Josiah abolished this hideous practice that it was made into a garbage heap. Bodies of diseased animals and executed criminals were thrown there and burned.

gittith: Gittith is a musical term possibly meaning "an instrument of Gath."

goad: a sharp, pointed prodding device used to motivate reluctant animals (such as oxen and mules) to move in the right direction.

gospel: Gospel means "good news" or "glad tidings," specifically the Good News of Jesus' life, death, and resurrection for our salvation, healing, and provision; and the hope of eternal life that Jesus made available to us by God's grace.

Hades: Hades: The nether realm of the disembodied spirits.

Har-magedon: Har-magedon, also called Armegeddon, is most likely a reference to hill ("har") of Megiddo, near the Carmel Range in Israel. This area has a large valley plain with plenty of room for armies to maneuver.

hin: A hin was about 6.5 liters or 1.7 gallons.

homer: One homer is about 220 liters, 6.2 U. S. bushels, 6.1 imperial bushels, 58 U. S. gallons, or 48.4 imperial gallons.

hypocrite: a stage actor; someone who pretends to be someone other than who they really are; a pretender; a dissembler

Ishmael: Ishmael is the son of Abraham and Hagar. Ishmael literally means, "God hears."

Jehovah: See "Yahweh."

Jesus: Jesus is Greek for the Hebrew name Yeshua, which is a short version of Yehoshua, which comes from Yoshia, which means He will save.

kodrantes: A kodrantes is a small coin worth one half of an Attic chalcus or two lepta. It is worth less than 2% of a day's wages for an agricultural laborer.

lepta: Lepta are very small, brass, Jewish coins worth half a Roman quadrans each, which is worth a quarter of the copper assarion. Lepta are worth less than 1% of an agricultural worker's daily wages.

Leviathan: Leviathan is a poetic name for a large aquatic creature, posssibly a crocodile or a dinosaur.

Mahalath: Mahalath is the name of a tune or a musical term.

manna: Name for the food that God miraculously provided to the Israelites while they were wandering in the wilderness between Egypt and the promised land. From Hebrew man-hu (What is that?) or manan (to allot). See Exodus 16:14-35.

Maschil: Maschil is a musical and literary term for "contemplation" or "meditative psalm."

michtam: A michtam is a poem.

mina: A mina is a Greek coin worth 100 Greek drachmas (or 100 Roman denarii), or about 100 day's wages for an agricultural laborer.

myrrh: Myrrh is the fragrant substance that oozes out of the stems and branches of the low, shrubby tree commiphora myrrha or comiphora kataf native to the Arabian deserts and parts of Africa. The fragrant gum drops to the ground and hardens into an oily yellowish-brown resin. Myrrh was highly valued as a perfume, and as an ingredient in medicinal and ceremonial ointments.

Nicolaitans: Nicolaitans were most likely Gnostics who taught the detestable lie that the material and physical realms were entirely separate and that immorality in the physical realm wouldn't harm your spiritual health.

omega: Omega is the last letter of the Greek alphabet. It is sometimes used to mean the last or the end.

Peniel: Peniel is Hebrew for "face of God."

phylactery: a leather container for holding a small scroll containing important Scripture passages that is worn on the arm or forehead in prayer. These phylacteries (tefillin in Hebrew) are still used by orthodox Jewish men. See Deuteronomy 6:8.

Praetorium: Praetorium: the Roman governor's residence and office building, and those who work there.

quadrans: A quadrans is a Roman coin worth about 1/64 of a denarius. A denarius is about one day's wages for an agricultural laborer.

rabbi: Rabbi is a transliteration of the Hebrew word for "my teacher," used as a title of respect for Jewish teachers.

Rahab: Rahab is either (1) The prostitute who hid Joshua's 2 spies in Jericho (Joshua 2,6) and later became an ancestor of Jesus (Matthew 1:5) and an example of faith (Hebrews 11:31; James 2:25). (2) Literally, "pride" or "arrogance" – possibly a reference to a large aquatic creature (Job 9:13; 26:12; Isaiah 51:9) or symbolically referring to Egypt (Psalm 87:4; 89:10; Isaiah 30:7).

Rhabboni: Rhabboni: a transliteration of the Hebrew word for "great teacher."

Sabbath: The seventh day of the week, set aside by God for man to rest.

saints: The Greek word for "saints" literally means "holy ones." Saints are people set apart for service to God as holy and separate, living in righteousness. Used in the Bible to refer to all Christians and to all of those who worship Yahweh in Old Testament times.

Samaritan: A Samaritan is a resident of Samaria. The Samaritans and the Jews generally detested each other during the time that Jesus walked the Earth.

sata: A sata is: a dry measure of capacity approximately equal to 13 liters or 1.5 pecks.

Satan: Satan means "accuser." This is one name for the devil, an enemy of God and God's people.

scribe: A scribe is one who copies God's law. They were often respected as teachers and authorities on God's law.

selah: Selah is a musical term indicating a pause or instrumental interlude for reflection.

sexual immorality: The term "sexual immorality" in the New Testament comes from the Greek "porneia," which refers to any sexual activity besides that between a husband and his wife. In other words, prostitution (male or female), bestiality, homosexual activity, any sexual intercourse outside of marriage, and the production and consumption of pornography all are included in this term.

shekel: A measure of weight, and when referring to that weight in gold, silver, or brass, of money. A shekel is approximately

16 grams, about a half an ounce, or 20 gerahs (Ezekiel 45:12).

Sheol: Sheol is the place of the dead.

Shibah: Shibah is Hebrew for "oath" or "seven." See Beersheba.

shigionoth: Victorious music.

soul: "Soul" refers to the emotions and intellect of a living person, as well as that person's very life. It is distinguished in the Bible from a person's spirit and body. (1 Thessalonians 5:23, Hebrews 4:12)

span: The length from the tip of the thumb to the tip of the little finger when the hand is stretched out (about 9 inches or 22.8 cm.).

spirit: Spirit, breath, and wind all derive from the same Hebrew and Greek words. A person's spirit is the very essence of that person's life, which comes from God, who is a Spirit being (John 4:24, Genesis 1:2; 2:7). The Bible distinguishes between a person's spirit, soul, and body (1 Thessalonians 5:23, Hebrews 4:12). Some beings may exist as spirits without necessarily having a visible body, such as angels and demons (Luke 9:39, 1 John 4:1-3).

stadia: stadia: plural for "stadion," a linear measure of about 184.9 meters or 606.6 feet (the length of the race course at Olympia).

stater: A stater is a Greek silver coin equivalent to four Attic or two Alexandrian drachmas, or a Jewish shekel: just exactly enough to cover the half-shekel Temple Tax for two people.

talent: A measure of weight or mass of 3000 shekels.

Tartarus: Tartarus is the Greek name for an underworld for the wicked dead; another name for Gehenna or Hell.

teraphim: Teraphim are household idols that may have been associated with inheritance rights to the household property.

Yah: "Yah" is a shortened form of "Yahweh," which is God's proper name. This form is used occasionally in the Old Testament, mostly in the Psalms. See "Yahweh."

Yahweh: "Yahweh" is God's proper name. In Hebrew, the four consonants roughly equivalent to YHWH were considered too holy to pronounce, so the Hebrew word for "Lord" (Adonai) was substituted when reading it aloud. When vowel points were added to the Hebrew Old Testament, the vowel points for "Adonai" were mixed with the consonants for "Yahweh," which if you pronounced it literally as written, would be pronounced "Yehovah" or "Jehovah." When the Old Testament was translated to Greek, the tradition of substituting "Lord" for God's proper name continued in the translation of God's name to "Lord" (Kurios). Some English Bibles translate God's proper name to "LORD" or "GOD" (usually with small capital letters), based on that same tradition. This can get really confusing, since two other words ("Adonai" and "Elohim") translate to "Lord" and "God," and they are sometimes used together. The ASV of 1901 (and some other translations) render YHWH as "Jehovah." The most probable pronunciation of God's proper name is "Yahweh." In Hebrew, the name "Yahweh" is related to the active declaration "I AM." See Exodus 3:13-14. Since Hebrew has no tenses, the declaration "I AM" also implies "I WAS" and "I WILL BE." Compare Revelation 1:8.

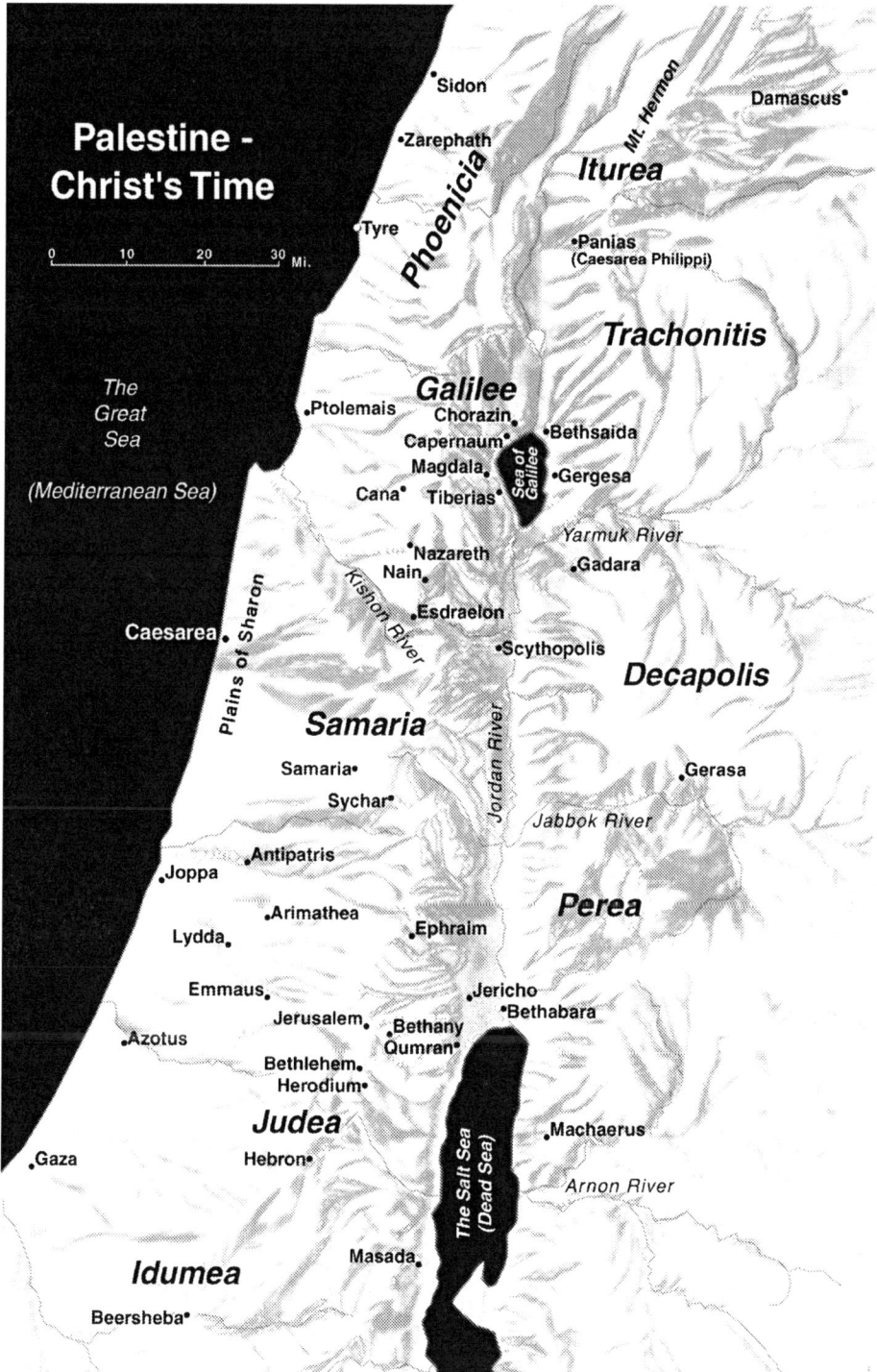

Palestine - Christ's Time

0 10 20 30 Mi.

The Great Sea
(Mediterranean Sea)

Sidon
Zarephath
Tyre
Phoenicia
Mt. Hermon
Damascus
Iturea
Panias (Caesarea Philippi)
Trachonitis

Ptolemais
Galilee
Chorazin
Capernaum
Bethsaida
Magdala
Gergesa
Cana
Tiberias
Sea of Galilee
Yarmuk River
Nazareth
Nain
Gadara
Esdraelon
Scythopolis
Decapolis

Caesarea
Plains of Sharon
Kishon River
Samaria
Samaria
Sychar
Jordan River
Gerasa
Jabbok River

Antipatris
Joppa
Arimathea
Ephraim
Perea
Lydda
Emmaus
Jericho
Bethabara
Jerusalem
Bethany
Qumran
Azotus
Bethlehem
Herodium

Judea
Gaza
Hebron
Machaerus
The Salt Sea (Dead Sea)
Arnon River

Idumea
Masada
Beersheba

Lightning Source UK Ltd.
Milton Keynes UK
18 June 2010

155802UK00001B/257/A